VISUAL QUICKSTART GUIDE

FrontPage 98

FOR WINDOWS

Phyllis Davis and Deborah Craig

Peachpit Press

Visual QuickStart Guide
FrontPage 98 for Windows
Phyllis Davis and Deborah Craig

Peachpit Press
1249 Eighth Street
Berkeley, CA 94710
510-524-2178
800-283-9444
510-524-2347 (fax)

Find us on the World Wide Web at:
http://www.peachpit.com

Peachpit Press is a division of Addison Wesley Longman

Cover design: The Visual Group
Interior design and production: Phyllis Davis and Melanie Haage

ISBN 0-201-69694-0

9 8 7 6 5 4 3 2 1

Printed and bound in the United States of America

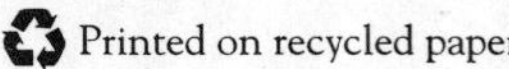

This book is dedicated to my mother, Barbara Owens Hopper.
P.D.

Once more for Lisa.
D.C.

Heartfelt thanks to

♡ Nancy Davis, the nicest and best editor a writer could ever hope to have.

and

♡ Matt Wagner for his trust in us. Without him, this book would have never happened.

and

♡ Kate Reber for her wise suggestions about layout and production.

Table of Contents

1 The Basics

Welcome to FrontPage 98! If you want to design and create your own Web site, you've come to the right place. FrontPage 98 is an innovative Web site creation program that helps you build Web sites using templates or from the ground up. *And*, you don't need to know one bit of HTML programming to use FrontPage 98. FrontPage takes care of the nitty gritty business that goes on behind the scenes, leaving you free to easily add the content you want to your Web pages.

Our purpose in writing this book is to show just how easy it is to create a professional Web site using the tools that FrontPage offers. In keeping with the *Visual QuickStart Guide* format, our aim is to present easy, step-by-step directions with illustrations to take the mystery out of designing and creating Web sites.

FrontPage 98 offers a complete set of tools for building any kind of Web site you can image, from a sweet home page and personal Web site to a classically styled corporate Web presence complete with press releases, newsletters, and a table of contents. This program has incredible power and loads of features, all incorporated into a user interface that will be familiar to those who've used word processing programs. As sophisticated as it is, it's also easy to use. You can run with it as far as you please. With FrontPage 98 and your imagination, the sky's the limit.

Have a great time building your Web site!

How does FrontPage work?

FrontPage 98 is made up of two programs, FrontPage Explorer and FrontPage Editor. FrontPage Explorer, or just Explorer, is used to create and maintain Web sites. FrontPage Editor, or the Editor for short, is used to work with the individual Web pages that make up the sites.

With FrontPage Explorer, you can create many kinds of Web sites using predesigned templates and Wizards, then modify these sites to suit your taste, or you can build a Web site from the ground up. Using Explorer commands, you can create new sites, open existing ones, and delete sites. You can view a Web site in any one of seven views, including Folders, All Files, Navigation, Hyperlinks, Hyperlinks Status, Themes, and Tasks views. (More about these in a moment.) FrontPage 98 now lets you quickly add new Web pages in Folders, All Files, or Navigation view. You can also check spelling throughout an entire Web site, and verify and recalculate *hyperlinks*. In addition, if you are an administrator working with a team, you can use Explorer to set up *permissions*, setting the type of access rights each team member has.

With FrontPage Editor, you can add many types of new pages to a Web site using page templates and Wizards, then modify them as you please, or add a blank Web page and design it yourself. Using Editor commands, you can create new pages, open existing ones, and add great content, such as images, sounds, and videos, as well as hyperlinks to other pages in your site or to other sites on the World Wide Web.

The Editor comes with six special toolbars that help you get the job done quickly. With the toolbars you can change text formatting, create interactive forms, add *hotspots* to images, draw and edit tables, and insert FrontPage components.

FrontPage components are programs that perform various tasks for you such as creating a table of contents for a site, adding a timestamp, including the same information on several Web pages, scheduling text or images that will appear during a specific time period, or setting up a "hit counter" that indicates how many people have visited your site.

When you've finished creating a Web page, the Editor makes it easy to view it in Preview view, in a browser of your choice, and at different *screen resolutions*. You can also view a page in print preview mode and print it.

The FrontPage Tasks view helps you keep track of tasks that need to be completed and lets you assign a priority for each task. In Tasks view, you can add tasks, modify existing ones, remove tasks, and mark them as finished.

When you finish your Web site and thoroughly test all its pages and hyperlinks, it's time to take it "live." Using the Explorer you can quickly *publish* the site to a *Web server* that supports the *FrontPage Server Extensions* or to an intranet—a private Web.

SOME FRONTPAGE AND WEB TERMINOLOGY

cell The smallest part of a table. In a table, each row or column contains one or more cells.

content All items placed on or associated with a Web page, such as text, images, sounds, hyperlinks, forms, and tables.

external hyperlink A hyperlink to a file, Web page, or Web site located outside of the Web site that is currently open.

form A set of form fields on a Web page whose information is processed by a Web server. The information on a form is sent to a server when the user submits the form by clicking a button or image.

form field Any of the controls in a form that the user enters information into, such as text boxes, radio buttons, check boxes, drop-down menus, and push buttons.

HTML *(Hypertext Markup Language)* A computer language used for describing the contents of Web pages. FrontPage Editor reads and writes HTML files, taking care of the coding for you. You don't need to know HTML to use FrontPage.

hotspot A specially defined area on an image that contains a clickable hyperlink.

hyperlink An image or text that the user can click to jump to another Web page in the same Web site or to another Web site.

ISP *(Internet Service Provider)* A business that provides the service of connecting users to the Internet, usually through telephone dial-up access.

protocol An agreement about how to communicate. Some examples of protocols are TCP/IP (Transfer Control Protocol/Internet Protocol), HTTP (Hypertext Transfer Protocol), and FTP (File Transfer Protocol).

table One or more columns and/or rows of cells on a Web page that are used to organize data or line up images and other page content.

URL *(Uniform Resource Locator)* An address of a Web site or other resource on the World Wide Web combined with a protocol. Some examples of typical URLs are:

- http://www.yahoo.com
- http://www.microsoft.com

The FrontPage Explorer Screen in Hyperlinks View

As you just learned, there are many different ways of looking at Web sites in the Explorer. Here are descriptions of the elements of Hyperlinks view **(Figure 1)**, which graphically illustrates the links in your Web site.

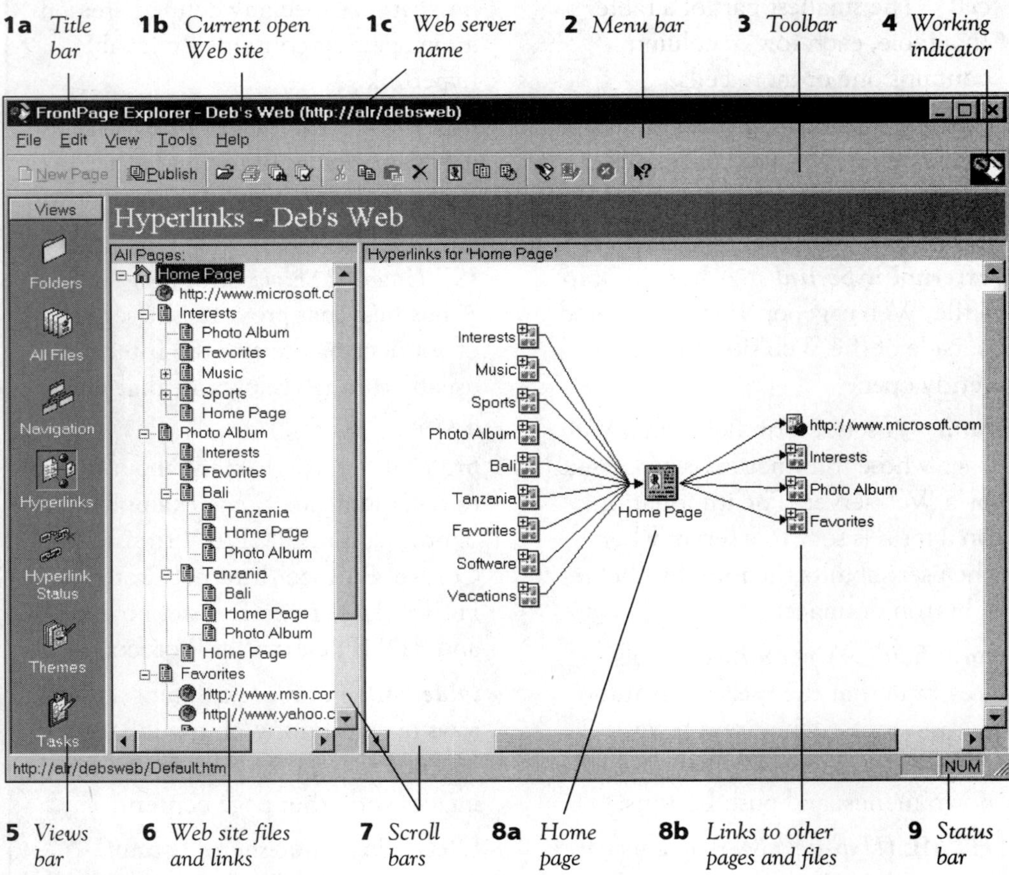

Figure 1. *The FrontPage Explorer screen in Hyperlinks view.*

Key to the Explorer Screen

1a, b, c *Title bar*

Displays the program name, current open Web site, and location of the site—whether it's saved on a Web server or regular computer folder.

2 *Menu bar*

Click any menu title to access commands, fly-outs, dialog boxes, special tools, and other programs such as the FrontPage Editor.

3 *Toolbar*

Gives you quick access to such commands as creating a new Web page, publishing a Web site, opening an existing Web site, and showing the FrontPage Editor.

4 *Working indicator*

When a command makes the Web server work, this icon rotates, showing you the server is busy.

5 *Views bar*

The Views bar is the quickest way to switch between views. Just click on a button to move to that view.

6 *All Pages pane*

The left side of the Explorer window in Hyperlinks view shows the hierarchical structure of your entire Web site. The home page is at the top, pages linked to the home page are shown one level down in the hierarchy and so on. (For example, in Figure 1, the Tanzania page contains links to the Bali, Home Page, and Photo Album pages. The selected item—Home Page —is shown graphically in the Hyperlinks pane on the right.) The All Pages pane shows all the files contained in the Web site, including Web pages, image and multimedia files, other associated files such as Microsoft Word documents and Excel spreadsheets, and hyperlinks to World Wide Web pages and e-mail. You can click a plus sign to reveal that page's links, or click a minus sign to hide them.

7 *Scroll bars*

Used to navigate around the Explorer panes. If you click the down arrow on a vertical scroll bar, the Explorer pane will move up. If you click the right arrow on a horizontal scroll bar, the page will move left.

8a, b *Hyperlinks pane*

The right side of the Explorer window in Hyperlinks view graphically shows Web pages with their links. Links to a page come in from the left, whereas links to other pages and files go to the right. Double-click on any Web page icon to open it in the Editor.

9 *Status bar*

Displays information about the currently selected command or an operation in progress.

The FrontPage Explorer Screen in Navigation View

Below is the Explorer in Navigation view, FrontPage's exciting new graphical view (**Figure 2**). You can use this view to plan your site's navigational structure. You can also add new pages and move pages here.

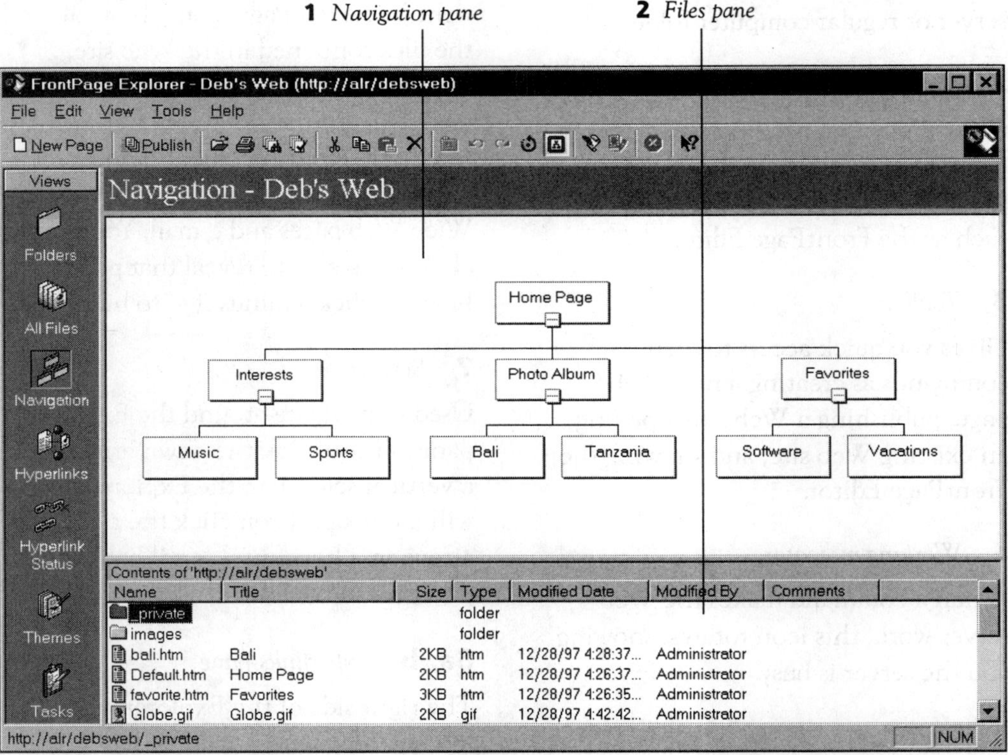

Figure 2. *The FrontPage Explorer screen in Navigation view.*

Key to Navigation View

1 *Navigation pane*

This pane shows the navigational structure of your Web site. Each box stands for a page in the Web site and the diagram represents the hierarchy of pages in your Web site.

2 *Files pane*

This pane shows all the files and folders in an open Web site. To see the files contained in a folder, double click on it. To close the folder, click the Up One Level button on the Toolbar (**Figure 3**).

THE FRONTPAGE EXPLORER TOOLBAR IS INTERACTIVE

When you're in Folders view, the Explorer toolbar looks like the one shown in Figure 3. The toolbar changes a bit, depending on what view you're in—for example, in Navigation view there are buttons for rotating the display and for undoing changes—but most of these buttons are available in all views.

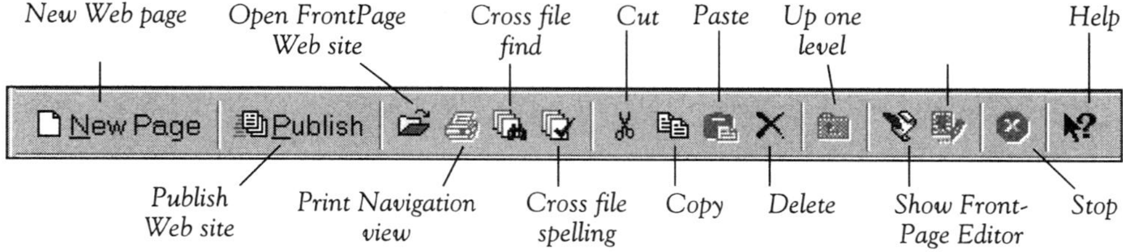

Figure 3. *This is how the FrontPage Explorer toolbar looks when Folders view is selected.*

DIFFERENT WAYS TO VIEW YOUR WEB SITES

FrontPage 97 only provided two views: Hyperlink view and Folder view. FrontPage 98 gives you many more ways of looking at your site. Besides Hyperlinks and Navigation views, which you just saw, you can use Folders view to look at your Web's file and folder structure, All Files view to review each file in your site, and Hyperlink Status view to check the links in your Web. Themes view lets you select a theme—or ready-made Web site design. Tasks view helps you keep track of changes and additions you need to make to your Web site.

The Explorer Toolbar; Conventions

FRONTPAGE CONVENTIONS

As you use FrontPage and access its help file, you will notice that certain terms are used in a way that is unique to FrontPage. These terms include:

- *FrontPage Web*—FrontPage uses the word "Web" to denote a Web site.
- *Radio button*—Those of you up on your Windows terms may know these buttons as option buttons.

Direction
Up
Down

- *Drop-down menu*—Many of you may know this control as a drop-down list box.

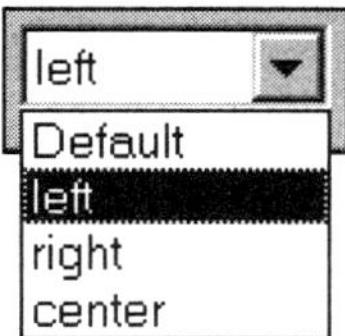

The FrontPage Editor Screen

You can view the Editor in a few different ways—by clicking the tabs at the bottom of the screen, clicking the Show FrontPage Editor button on the Explorer toolbar (**Figure 3**) or by double clicking on a .htm file in the Explorer window. By default, you'll see the Normal view (**Figure 4**), which shows the Web page you're working on pretty much as it will appear when published. HTML view lets you see the underlying HTML code for your page. If you're feeling adventurous, you can even use HTML view to add and edit HTML code (see the next chapter for the scoop on HTML). Preview view lets you preview your page in a browser (see Chapter 8 for the lowdown on previewing Web pages).

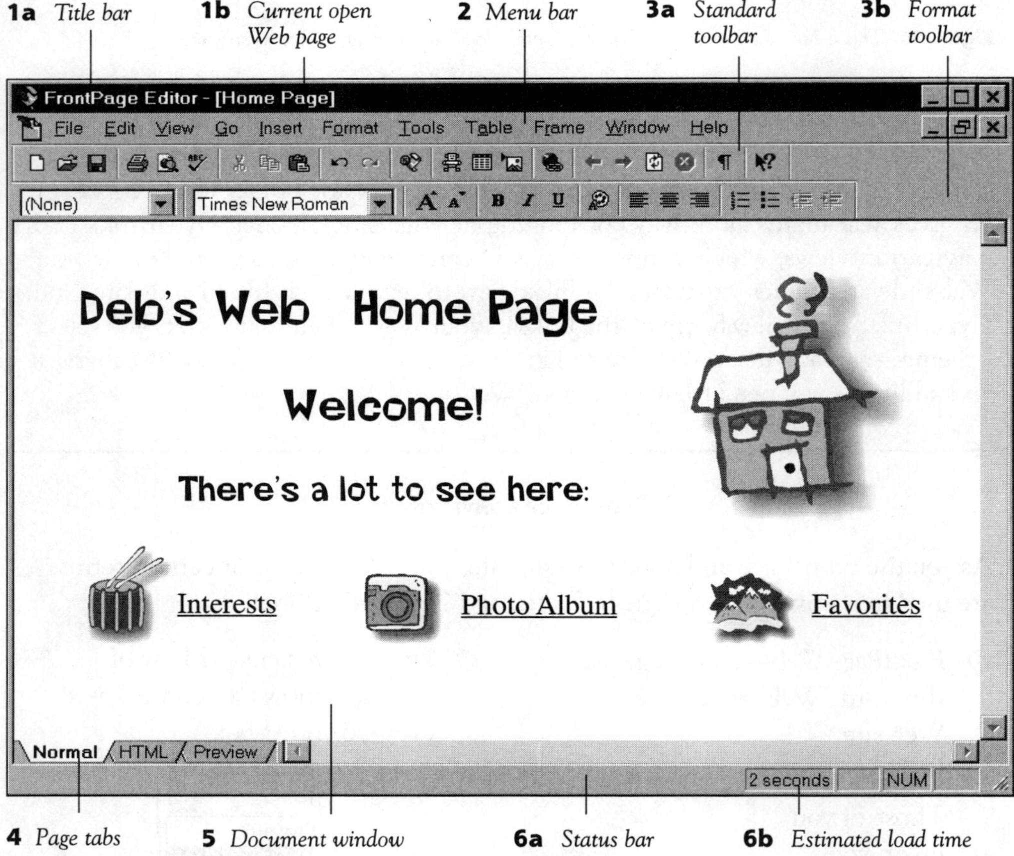

Figure 4. *The FrontPage Editor screen in Normal view.*

Key to the Editor Screen

1a, b *Title bar*

Displays the program name and the page title of the currently open Web page in square brackets.

2 *Menu bar*

Click any of the eleven menu titles to access commands, fly-outs, dialog boxes, and special tools.

3a, b *Toolbars*

FrontPage Editor comes equipped with six toolbars that give you quick access to almost everything you need to create Web pages. The Standard toolbar gives access to basic commands such as creating a new Web page, opening an existing Web page, saving, printing, inserting a FrontPage Component, and creating a hyperlink. The Format toolbar lets you quickly format text with predefined text styles, change text size, alignment, and color. The Image toolbar appears when an image is selected in the document window. It lets you add hotspots to images, make a GIF image *transparent*, add text to an image, crop images, change the contrast or brightness of images, apply a a *washout* or bevel effect, restore images to their original form, and more. The Forms toolbar has everything you need to create interactive forms. The Advanced toolbar lets you insert ActiveX controls, scripts, plug-ins, and Java applets. The Table toolbar provides a whole bevy of tools for creating and editing tables.

4 *Page tabs*

You can use these tabs to switch between three Editor views: Normal view, HTML view, and Preview view. When you work with frames, you'll see two extra tabs, the No Frames tab and the Frames Page HTML tab. To find out about frames, turn to Chapter 15.

5 *Document window*

This is where you design and add content to Web pages. Since the Editor is WYSIWYG (What You See Is What You Get), the Web page you see in the Editor window appears almost as it will in a browser. This is a great development for those Web veterans who had to constantly switch between the HTML code and a browser to see what effect new code had on page layout.

6a, b *Status bar*

Displays information about the currently selected commands, hyperlinks, operations in progress, and the estimated amount of time it will take for the Web page to load on a computer equipped with a 28.8kb modem.

THE FRONTPAGE EDITOR TOOLBARS

FrontPage Editor comes with six toolbars used for adding content to Web pages. To access any of these toolbars, open the View menu and choose the toolbar of your choice (**Figure 5**). A check mark next to a toolbar item on the View menu indicates that the toolbar is already open. The number/letter combinations to the right of the View menu in Figure 5 indicate the corresponding toolbar figures on pages 10 and 11.

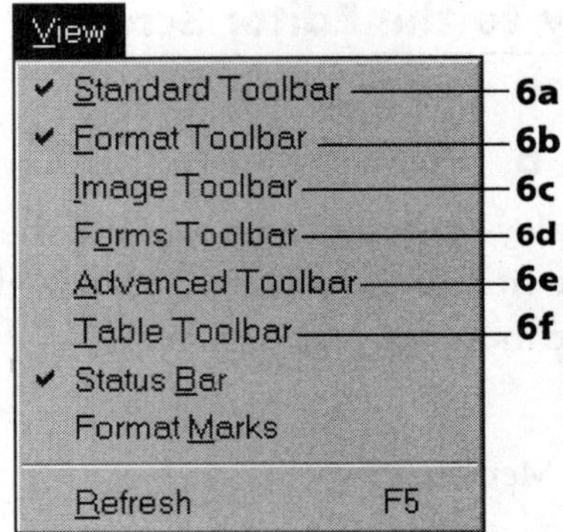

Figure 5. *To view a toolbar, choose the toolbar item you want to see.*

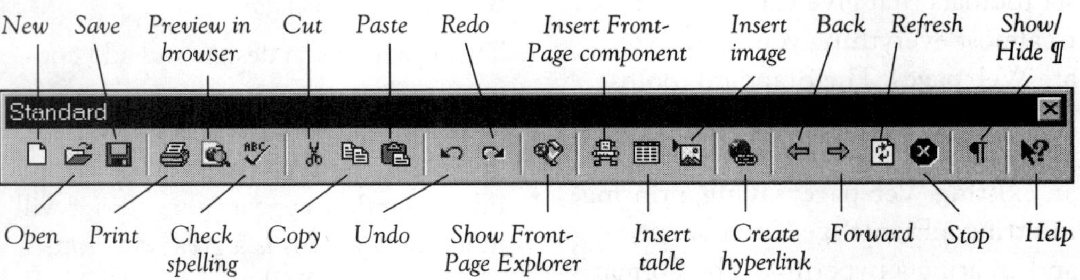

Figure 6a. *The Standard toolbar.*

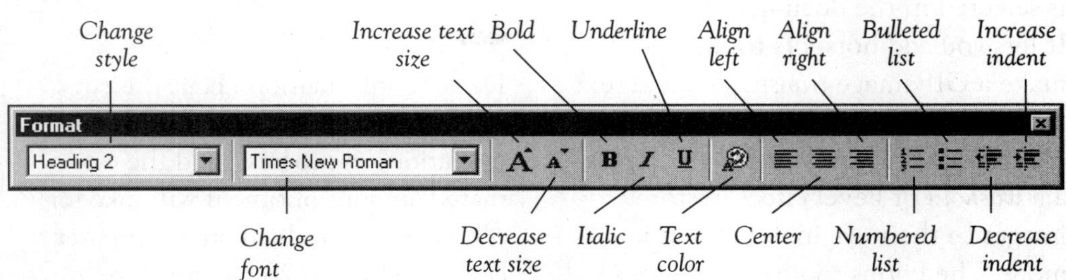

Figure 6b. *The Format toolbar.*

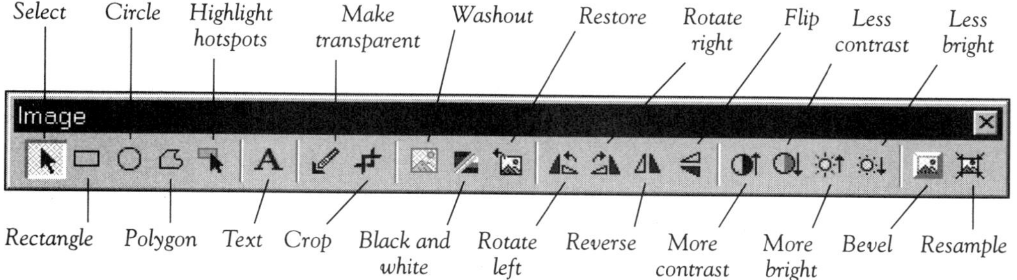

Figure 6c. *The Image toolbar.*

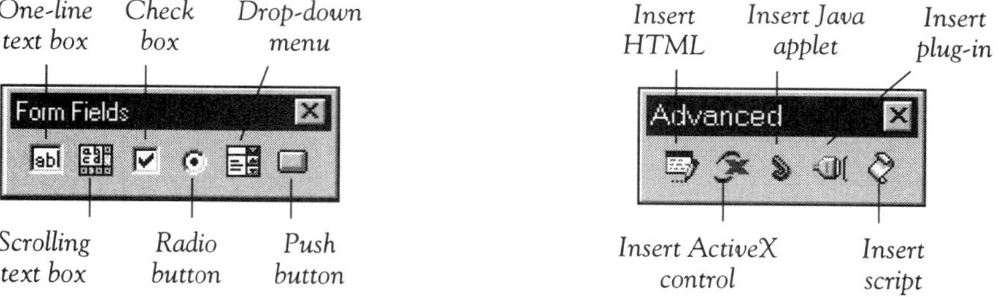

Figure 6d. *The Forms toolbar.*

Figure 6e. *The Advanced toolbar.*

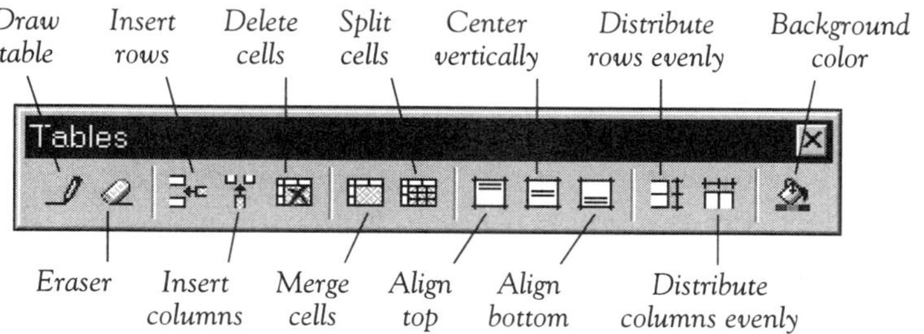

Figure 6f. *The Table toolbar.*

The FrontPage Editor Toolbars

MORE ABOUT TOOLBARS

Do some of your toolbar buttons look washed out? This just means that they are "disabled" and won't work in the current context. For example, if you haven't selected any images or text, the Cut and Copy buttons will look grayed out because there's nothing for FrontPage to cut or copy.

Have you noticed how some toolbars show up in the middle of your document window and some fasten themselves to the edges? The ones on the edges are called *docked toolbars*, and the ones in the middle of the screen are called *floating toolbars*. If a floating toolbar is in your way, you can drag its title bar to move it; dragging it to the edge of the screen will dock it there. (You can also double-click a toolbar's title bar to dock it.) If you want to "undock" a toolbar, you can drag it by its edges to make it float.

Large Menus and Dialog Boxes

FrontPage menus and dialog boxes contain many commands and items to select. Consequently, some of them are quite large. Several of the figures in this *Visual QuickStart Guide* are too big to display in their entirety or become very small when sized to fit the page. In order to fit these large items, some menus have been shortened using a jagged edge (**Figure 7**). The menu item being selected is shown, but lower or middle menu items are removed to conserve space. In a large dialog box, a circle has been drawn around the area under discussion (**Figure 8**).

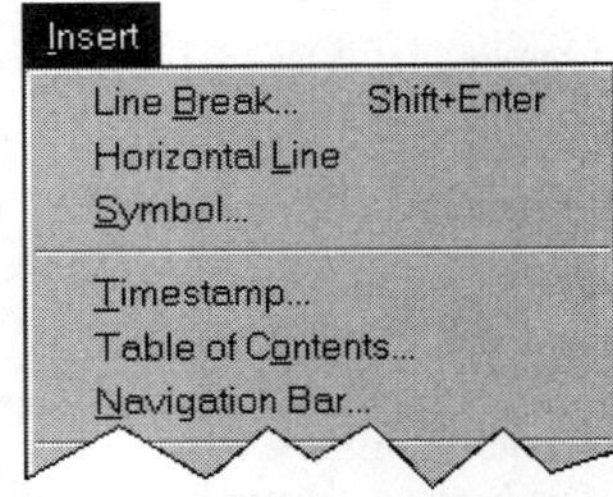

Figure 7. *Menus in some figures have been cropped using a jagged edge.*

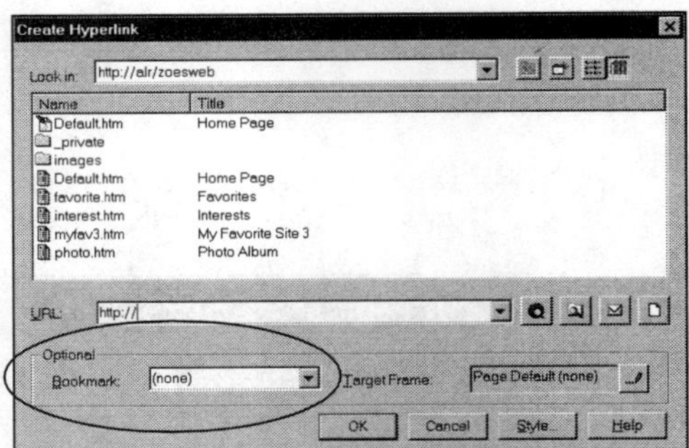

Figure 8. *A circle appears around the area under discussion in a large dialog box.*

Getting Help

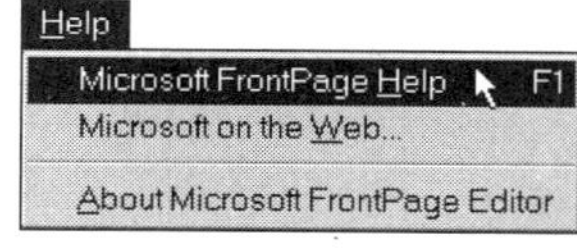

Figure 9. *Choose Microsoft FrontPage Help from the Help menu.*

At times you won't be able to figure out how to do something even if you consult this book or click on every button or menu option in sight. When this happens, FrontPage's online help system can quickly lead you to the information you need. Better yet, if you've used the help system in any other Windows program, this one will seem pleasantly familiar.

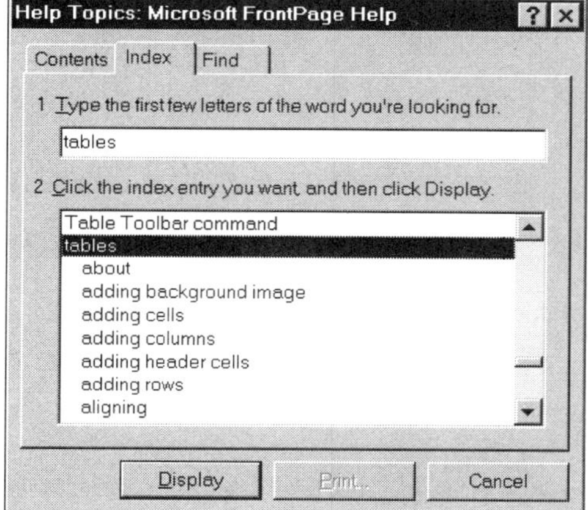

Figure 10. *The Help Topics dialog box is one of the main ways to get help with FrontPage.*

Getting help is easy, no matter where you are. From either Explorer or the Editor, just press F1 or choose Microsoft FrontPage Help from the Help menu (**Figure 9**). The Help Topics dialog box will open. Click the Index tab if necessary, and then start typing the topic you need help with. You should see a list of relevant topics (**Figure 10**), and from here you can double-click a topic (or click once and choose the Display button) to display a help screen of information about it (**Figure 11**). Use the scroll bars to keep reading, click underlined terms to see their definitions (click again to hide the definitions), and click the Help Topics button if you want to return to the Help Topics dialog box. When you're done, close the help system by clicking the Close button (the X) in the upper-right corner of the window.

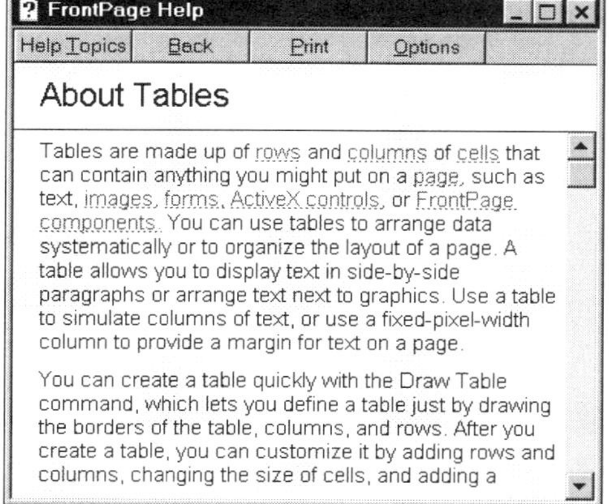

Figure 11. *Double-clicking help topics leads to screens of useful information about them.*

OTHER WAYS TO GET HELP

There are a bunch of other ways to get help. You can use the Contents tab of the Help Topics dialog box to search through a series of topics (double-click the book icons to reveal a list of related subtopics; double-click the question mark icons to reveal a help screen of information). Or you can experiment with the Find tab, which lets you look for words or phrases that occur within help topics. Finally, you can click the Help button on the toolbar (in either Explorer or the Editor) and then click items such as toolbar buttons or menu options to get "context-sensitive" help about them. Which method is best? A good approach is to try them all and use the one that feels most comfortable to you.

HARDWARE CONSIDERATIONS

Microsoft recommends the following as the minimum system requirements for running FrontPage 98:

- A computer with a 486 or higher processor and a 28 KBPS or higher modem.
- 16 MB RAM if running Windows 95 or 32 MB RAM if running Windows NT and/or the Microsoft Personal Web Server. You should also have a minimum of 36 MB free hard disk space for a full installation.
- A VGA or higher graphics card.

This book was created using a 100 MHz Pentium with 32 MB RAM and an SVGA graphics card with 4 MB RAM. When testing FrontPage 98 and working with large Web sites, this hardware was fine.

SUMMARY

In this chapter you learned about:

- The way FrontPage works
- FrontPage and Web terms
- The Explorer screen and views
- The Explorer toolbar
- The Editor screen and views
- The six Editor toolbars
- Getting help
- System requirements

2 Web Concepts

The Internet was started in the 1960s as a way for scientists at universities to communicate and by the military for national defense purposes). Mostly, the early Internet was used to send e-mail (electronic mail) back and forth. Things didn't really start to get exciting until the concepts underlying the World Wide Web—the Web, or WWW, for short—were introduced a few years ago.

The Web introduced a visual, easy-to-understand interface that anyone with a computer and modem can use to connect to the Internet. It also provides a way for all of us to create Web page *content* that can be placed on the Internet for others to view and use—this is what FrontPage 98 is all about.

The great joy of FrontPage 98 is that when you use it to create world class Web pages and sites, you don't need to know anything about underlying Web concepts and mechanisms. The FrontPage interface is intuitive and straightforward. If you've already used any one of the Microsoft Office applications, particularly Microsoft Word, you shouldn't have too much trouble with it. But sometimes, a little bit of insight about what is going on under the hood helps clarify things. This chapter explains the basic mechanisms of the Web. If you don't want to be bothered with this stuff, you can just skip it for now and come back later if you need a concept clarified.

Protocols

A *protocol*, in computer networking lingo, is an agreement about how to communicate. For instance, Paul Revere established a very simple protocol when he agreed to communicate if the Redcoats were coming by placing lanterns on a church steeple ("One if by land, and two if by sea!").

TCP/IP—short for *Transfer Control Protocol/Internet Protocol*—is the protocol used by all computers on the Internet to send and receive data. Actually, TCP/IP is a whole bunch of protocols stuck together that handle all the nitty-gritty details of breaking up out-going TCP/IP communications into *packets* and pasting them back together at the other end. You don't have to know too much about TCP/IP to create great Web pages, but you probably will want to know something about the protocols that are "pasted" on top of TCP/IP because you may wish to include some of them in your FrontPage Web pages.

Addresses on the Web

An address, used to find a resource such as a site or a page on the Internet, is referred to as a *URL—or Uniform Resource Locator—* and pronounced "you are ell."

The first part of a URL, ending with ://, is always the protocol used. The URL for World Wide Web sites always starts *http://*. Usually—but not always—*www* follows as the next part of the URL. For example: *http://www.netscape.com*.

In the latest versions of Netscape Navigator and Microsoft Internet Explorer, you don't have to enter the protocol. *www.netscape.com* gets you to the same place (opens the same Web page) as *http://www.netscape.com*.

HTTP—meaning *Hypertext Transfer Protocol*—is the most important protocol for World Wide Web users. When a browser is told to open a Web address—or URL—that begins with http://, it knows that the connection is to a Web site, and that the requested page on the site should be displayed. For example, http://www.bearhome.com displays the indicated page in a browser (**Figure 1**).

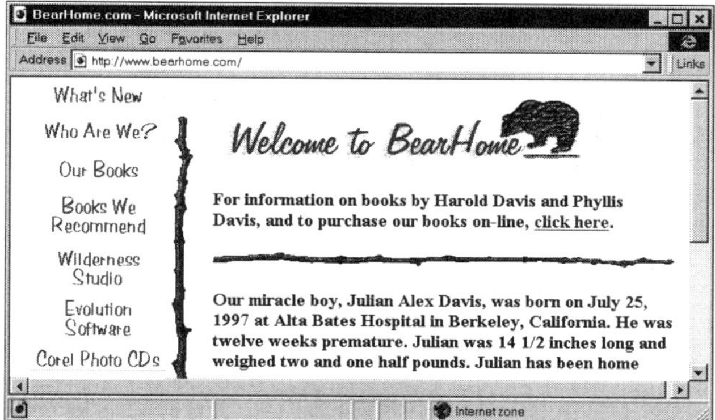

Figure 1. *When you enter a URL in a browser, the corresponding Web page is displayed.*

FTP—*File Transfer Protocol*—is used to send and receive files from other computers on the Internet. Archives holding files on the Internet that you can download are called *FTP sites*. A URL that starts with ftp:// will either download a specific file to your system or open an FTP site that you can select a file from. For example, you can connect to the Tucows FTP site—one of the largest software archives of all categories available for download on the Internet—by entering ftp://tucows.com.

> You can access a vast collection of software available for Windows from the Tucows collection using your browser by visiting the Tucows site at *http://www.tucows.com*.

File—file:/// is used at the beginning of a URL to indicate a file on a local disk, such as a hard drive, should be opened. For example, *file:///c:\program files\test\test.htm* opens the file *test.htm* in the *c:\program files\test* folder.

Mailto:—If a URL begins mailto: it means that the rest of the URL is an e-mail address. When a browser hits a hyperlink containing a mailto URL—for example, mailto:phyllis@bearhome.com—the e-mail program on your computer will launch, ready to send mail to that address.

HTML

When a browser requests a Web page across the Internet from a Web server using the HTTP protocol, for instance http://www.bearhome.com/julian6.htm, the Web server expects to deliver (and the Web browser expects to receive) a page written in a particular language, *HTML*. HTML—*Hypertext Markup Language*—is **the** language of the Web.

When you surf the Web, the browser you use knows how to convert the HTML pages it receives from Web servers into recognizable Web pages.

The name of HTML tells one a lot about the kind of language it is. "Hypertext" means that it can be used to create *hyperlinks*, or *jumps*, from one page to another. Hyperlinks are activated by clicking on underlined text or on a graphical hotspot in an HTML page.

> You may not realize that when you ask your browser to open a Web site, such as *http://www.bearhome.com/*, *http://www.microsoft.com/*, or *http://www.netscape.com*, you are actually opening a specific page on the site. Exactly which page depends on the settings in the Web server software, but it is usually something like *default.htm* or *index.html*.

Actually, the process of surfing the Web means choosing one hyperlink after another in your browser. Depending on the URL of the hyperlink, the Web server you access uses the TCP/IP and HTTP protocols to send the specified HTML page back to your browser. (This process, the reverse of surfing, is called serving. Think of it this way: some folks serve so others can surf.)

VIEWING HTML SOURCE CODE

When you use FrontPage 98 to create Web pages, you don't ever have to look at HTML codes, unless you want to.

Should you decide at some point that you have a burning to desire to see what's really going on behind that beautiful FrontPage exterior, you can view the HTML source code for any Web page open in the FrontPage Editor by clicking the HTML page tab in the Editor (**Figure 2**).

Most browsers will also allow you to look at the HTML source code for World Wide Web pages open in a browser. Looking at professional Web page code can be very educational. For instance, to view a document's HTML source in Microsoft Internet Explorer, choose Source from the View menu. To view HTML source code in Netscape Navigator, choose Page Source from the View menu.

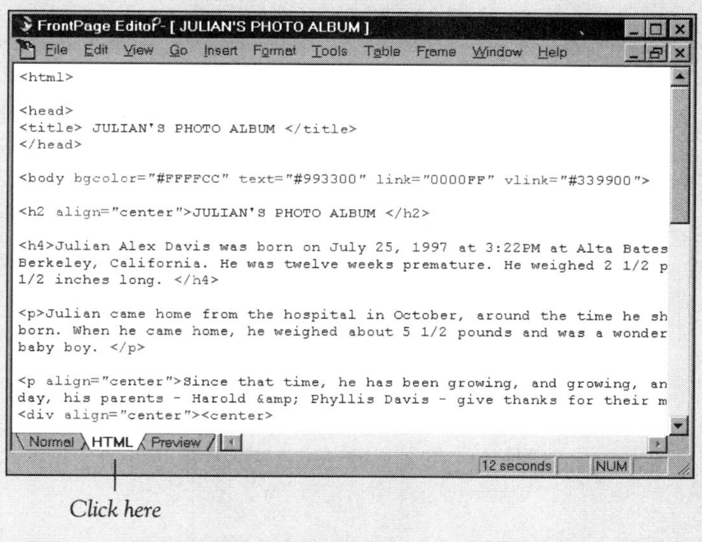

Figure 2. *Click the HTML page tab in the Editor to view the HTML code for your Web page.*

"Markup" means that the language is marked up, in much the same way that an editor marks up a manuscript. In the case of HTML, *tags* are codes used to mark up the HTML page. These tags are used to tell the browser what the related text is supposed to be. The browser uses this information to decide how to actually present the content.

HTML tags are always enclosed in angle brackets (<>). For example, <a> is the tag that means anchor. Most tags come in pairs with a beginning tag and an end tag. The end tag is indicated with a slash (/) and comes at the end of the text that the tags mark up. For example, <a>I'm anchored!</a>.

Many tags have *attributes*, sometimes called *parameters*. Attributes are used to give more information to the browser about what the tag does. For example, the attribute *href* can be used with the <a> (anchor) tag, to embed a hyperlink in the anchor, <a href="http://www.bearhome.com">
I am anchored!</a>.

You can use any simple text editor to create HTML files, for instance, Notepad (**Figure 3**). In fact, you can even add HTML using the HTML tab page of the Editor if you like. But the Normal tab page of the FrontPage Editor does an excellent job of visual HTML page creation. After you've used it, it's unlikely that you'd want to deal with hand coding HTML.

Figure 3 shows a very simple HTML file that you can save as a text file and open in your browser as shown in Figure 4. (It's probably as complex as you'd want to get doing it by hand!)

Like the animals in Noah's ark, you can see from this HTML page that most tags come in pairs. Think of them as parentheses: one to open an HTML phrase, the other to close it.

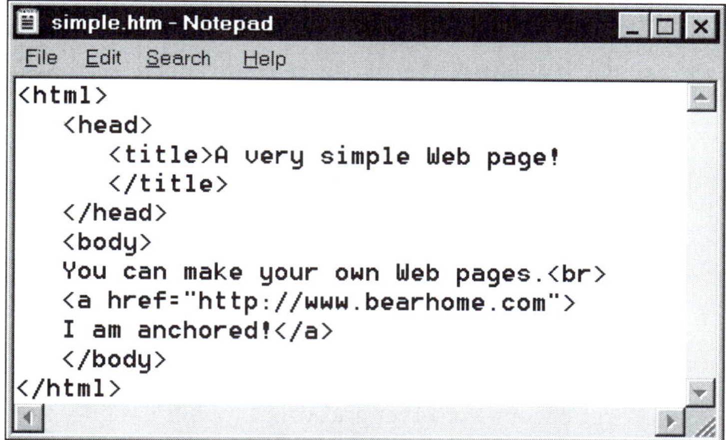

Figure 3. *You can use a simple text editor such as Notepad to create a Web page.*

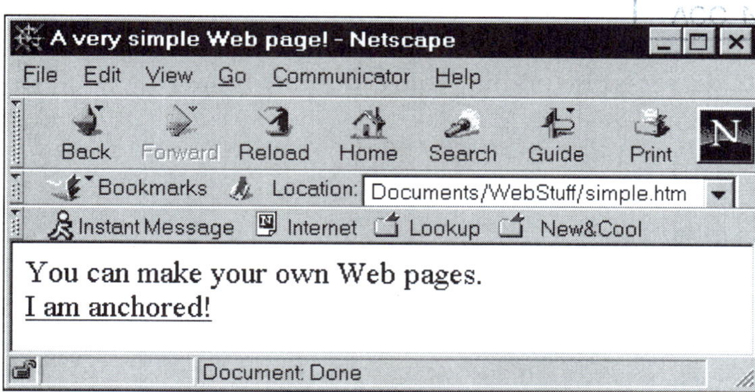

Figure 4. *The same simple Web page created in Notepad, viewed in a browser.*

In case you want to know, you'll find information about the hypertext tags used to create effects throughout *FrontPage 98 for Windows: Visual QuickStart Guide* in the "What's My Tag?" sidebars.

Clients and Servers on the Web

You may have worked at an office that is networked. This might mean that desktop PCs are connected to each other, to peripheral devices such as scanners and printers, and maybe even to databases on a larger computer (**Figure 5**). In this kind of network, the larger computer is called a *server* and the desktop computers are called *clients*.

When your computer is connected to the Internet, a computer on the World Wide Web using the HTTP protocol becomes a server and your browser is a client, similar to the set up of an office network (**Figure 6**). When you have loaded an HTML page in your browser (the client), the HTTP server has different contributions to make to the appearance of the Web page. You can think of it this way: during the conversation between a browser and a Web server, the browser is pulling things off the server—but the server is also pushing things into the browser.

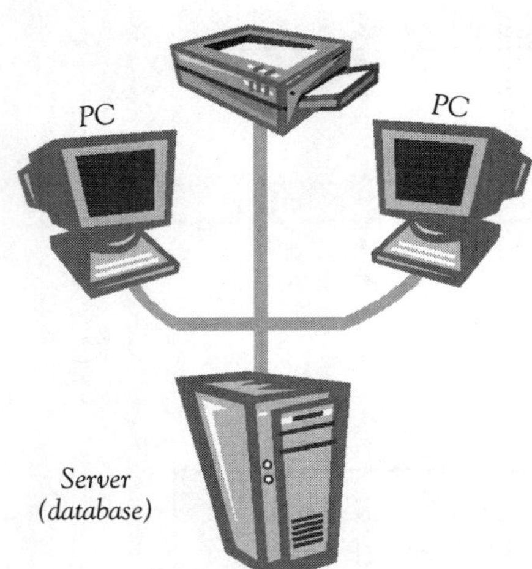

Figure 5. *A network can contain PCs and peripheral devices connected to a server.*

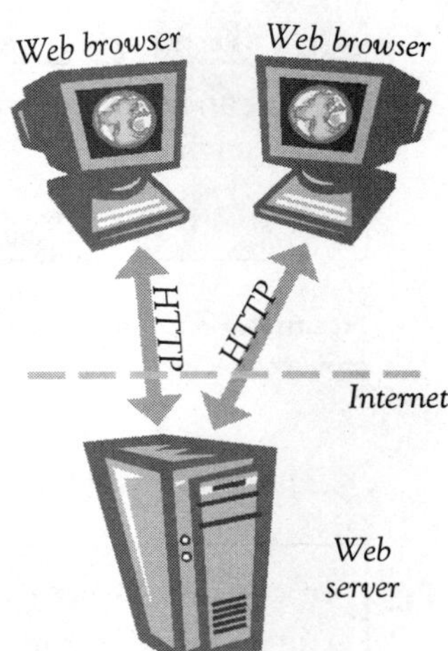

Figure 6. *Web browsers connected to the Internet are clients connected to a Web server.*

The browser handles client-side duties, including translating HTML codes and *scripts*. Scripts are instructions telling the browser to do something and are written in *JavaScript* or *VBScript*.

The Web server delivers programs that do things within the browser, programs such as FrontPage Components, *Java Applets*, and *ActiveX controls*. The server is also responsible for answering requests made by the browser, such as starting a *CGI* program.

Downloading Current Web Browsers

It's important that you view your Web pages in a number of different browsers. HTML tags only describe a Web page's content—they do not tell the browser how to display it. This means that there can be considerable difference between the appearance of a page in different browsers.

The two most popular browsers are Microsoft Internet Explorer and Netscape Navigator. Version 3.02 of Internet Explorer ships with FrontPage 98. You can install the browser using the FrontPage CD-ROM. The most recent updates to Internet Explorer, including Explorer 4 can be downloaded from http://www.microsoft.com/ie/.

You can download current versions of Netscape Navigator from Netscape's World Wide Web home page, http://www.netscape.com.

Among the many varieties of browser animals out there is Lynx—a text-only browser that runs primarily on Unix platforms. Lynx makes a compelling case for providing text alternatives to any graphics on a Web page: otherwise you risk producing pages that not all browsers can read. As for why anyone would want to use a text-only browser, have a look at the cute and silly Ode to Lynx page, http://www.batch.com/ode-to-lynx.

Build It and They Will Come

The question, on the Web, is, how will they find you? This is not only a question of publicity, promotion, and advertising—those things come later. The first question is, when someone connected to the Internet enters your URL in their browser, how does the browser know to load your Web page from your Web site? Because the first part of the URL is http://, the browser knows it's supposed to be using Hypertext Transfer Protocol to load an HTML page from the *domain* in the URL.

But, how does the browser find your domain? This depends on how your Web page—and site—is connected to the Internet.

Every Web server connected to the Internet is assigned an *Internet Protocol* (or *IP*) address. An IP address is an unwieldy quadruplet of numbers separated by periods, for example, 207.71.18.55 (sometimes called a *dotted quad*). These numbers represent a *node* on the Internet. You could open a Web site in a browser using its IP address, but

GETTING YOUR OWN DOMAIN NAME

A company named InterNIC is currently charged with handling domain name registrations. InterNIC can be found on the Web at *http://www.internic.net*. You can browse their site to find out if the name you want is already taken or to start the registration process. (Most likely, if an ISP or other organization is hosting your Web site, they will handle this for you.)

InterNIC currently handles United States domain name requests ending in .com, .edu, .gov, .net, and .org. (International domain names tend to use the country of origin; for example, .ca means Canada and .uk means United Kingdom.)

Proposals are in discussion to help alleviate domain name crowding by adding seven new domain names: .arts, .info, .firm, .nom, .rec, .store, and .web.

domain names are usually used instead since they are easier for human beings—as opposed to computers—to understand.

An *Internet Service Provider* (or *ISP*) is a business that provides the service of connecting users to the Internet, usually through telephone dial-up access.

Most Internet dial-up access accounts do not assign you a fixed IP number (called a *static* IP). Instead, you are given a new IP (called a *dynamic* IP) each time you call into your ISP.

A dynamic IP, by itself, doesn't provide a means for other browsers to find your Web page because the location of your server on the Internet will be different each time you log on. One answer is to arrange to have an ISP assign you a static IP.

You can obtain your own domain name which can be used to access your Web site and pages. Domain names are translated into IP addresses using a utility known as *Domain Name System* (or *DNS*). Each ISP maintains a DNS server that translates registered domain names into IP addresses.

How to Find an ISP

With all this talk about ISPs you may be wondering how to find one of your own. There are a number of ways to go about it. Several mega-corporations, such as Pacific Bell and Microsoft, act as ISPs and charge reasonable fees. If small is more your style, you should be able to find a local service provider. Try asking friends if they have an ISP they like, flip through local computer magazines, or even check the yellow pages. If you can get online before acquiring your own ISP, check sites such as *http://www.thelist.com*, a list of service providers that you can search by area code or by country. This site tells you what services each ISP provides and what their fees are.

Hosting a Web Site

It's a fact of life that you will probably not want to connect a Web server directly to the Internet. These days, this is something that only hard-core propeller-heads, and/or large, well-funded organizations with high-speed Internet connections, should attempt.

But, don't worry! If you're using FrontPage 98 in an environment that is not already connected to the Web, you can easily arrange for an ISP or other organization to *host* your Web pages and site for you. (A Web site host is also sometimes called a *Web Presence Provider*.) This usually can be done quite inexpensively and is far and away the easiest way to put a site up on the Web.

You should know that there is a special requirement for Web Presence Providers who host Web sites created using FrontPage 98: they must have the *FrontPage Server Extensions* installed. The FrontPage Server Extensions are special programs that allow you to take full advantage of FrontPage's capabilities when you create your Web (to learn more about the Server Extensions, see page 46).

You'll find an extensive list of registered Web Presence Providers who specialize in hosting sites created with FrontPage on Microsoft's site, http://microsoft.saltmine.com/frontpage/wpp/list/ (**Figure 7**). (A quick way to travel to this site is to click the Publish button on the Explorer toolbar,

What is a FrontPage Web?

When you import a World Wide Web site into FrontPage or start a new Web site in FrontPage, behind-the-scenes scaffolding is added to the Web site to support FrontPage's special features. A Web site that has had this scaffolding added to it is referred to as a *FrontPage Web*.

then click the Connect to Microsoft FrontPage Web site button at the left of the Publish FrontPage Web dialog box to go to the Microsoft FrontPage site.) As you'd expect, these Web Presence Providers all have the FrontPage Server Extensions installed.

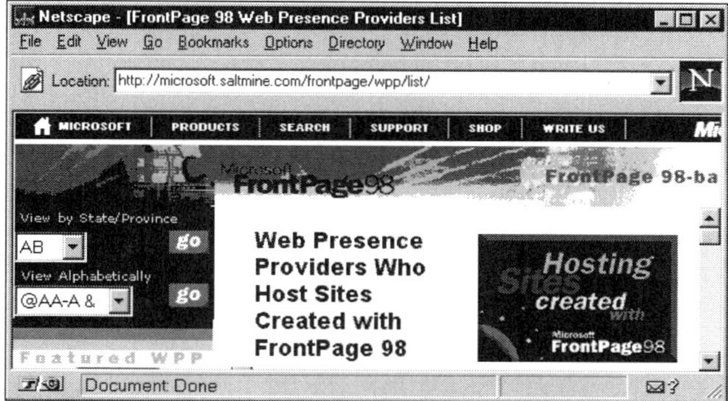

Figure 7. *You can find Web Presence Providers who host FrontPage 98 Web sites at http://microsoft.saltmine.com/frontpage/wpp/list/.*

Channels and Push Technology

Up until now, the standard way to use the Web has been to actively go to sites and track down information. This setup is known as *pull technology* since you have to use your browser to pull in the information you need. One of the latest Web innovations is *push technology*, where content providers "push" information to users, so they don't have to go to the trouble of actually grabbing it themselves. (This arrangement is especially appropriate for Web sites that change fairly often—the updated information can be pushed to users as needed—but makes little sense for sites that tend to be static.) A Web site that pushes information to users is called a *channel*, and you need to subscribe to the channel to have the information pushed to you automatically. The current generation of Web browsers—such as

Microsoft's Internet Explorer 4.0—allow users to easily "subscribe" to channels in essentially the same way that they would browse a Web page (**Figure 8**).

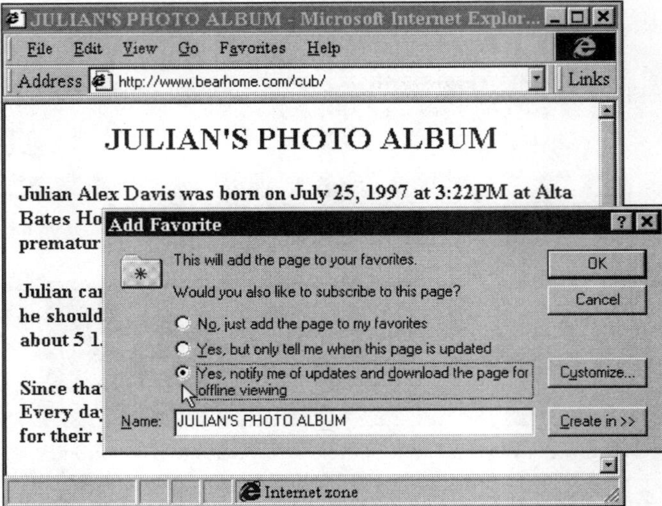

Figure 8. *You can subscribe to a channel in Microsoft Explorer 4 using the Add Favorite dialog box found on the Favorites menu.*

SUMMARY

In this chapter you learned about:

- Protocols
- Addresses on the Web and URLs
- HTML code and tags
- Downloading current browsers
- Obtaining domain names
- Channels and push technology

3 Principles of Good Web Design

Web sites—and Web pages—can be designed well or poorly. FrontPage 98 makes it easy to throw many different kinds of elements into a Web page; the results can often be a confusing hodge-podge (**Figure 1**). In Web page design, as in design in general, less is often more.

It's important to maintain a consistent look and feel across an entire Web site. Maintaining visual standards for all the pages in a site gives a Web site cohesion (**Figure 2**), and differentiates it from the World Wide Web at large.

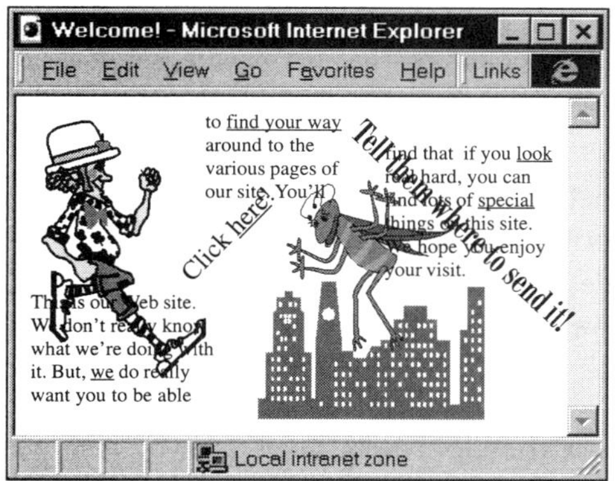

Figure 1. *A jumble of elements can make a Web page confusing and difficult to read.*

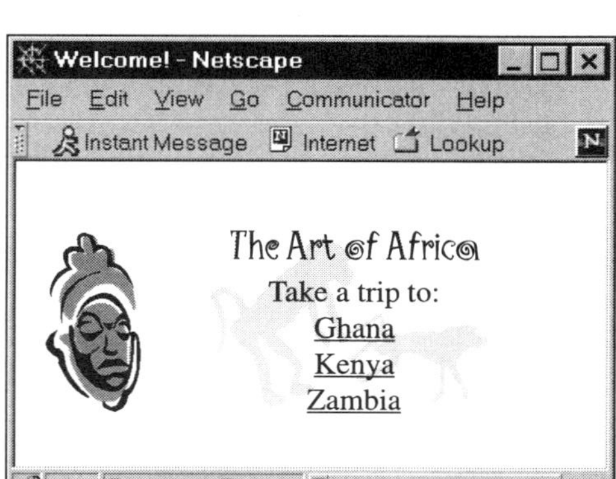

Figure 2. *A well-designed Web page is easy to understand and looks good.*

Of course, it is essential that Web pages and sites should present information in an easy-to-comprehend fashion. Sites should be navigable without confusion, and users should be able to easily find what they are looking for on a site. And, in the best of all possible worlds, Web page design uses the architectural principle that form should follow function. In other words, there should be a relationship between a Web site's visual appearance and what it is supposed to do.

This chapter explains how you can use FrontPage 98 to implement principles of good Web design. With FrontPage it's easy to create a consistent, sophisticated, professional-looking Web site.

Naming Web Pages

After you've created a Web page, you'll need to save it. (Turn to Chapter 6 to find out about saving Web pages.) When you save a Web page, you'll have to name the file that makes it up. FrontPage 98 will let you name files pretty much anything you'd like. If you wanted, you could save a Web page as "This is my Pretty little Web page.htm." Saving a Web page with a name like this is not a very good idea. The fact is, you'll avoid trouble by sticking to these simple file-naming rules for all your FrontPage Web pages:

- Use only lowercase letters of the alphabet.
- Do not include punctuation marks or spaces.
- Name the file extension .htm.
- Stick to a short filename, followed by a period and the three-character file extension.

Here are some examples of "good" Web page file names: julian.htm, denali.htm, and concord.htm.

TITLING A WEB PAGE

Besides the file name it is saved with, every Web page should also have a title. When you save a Web page in FrontPage, you are given a chance to enter the page's title (**Figure 3**).

When the Web page is viewed in a browser, its title is displayed in the title bar of the browser (**Figure 4**). Because it is given such prominent attention, Web page titles are important. They are used to navigate your site, and search engines use them to determine the contents of your site. Therefore, you should think carefully about the titles of your Web pages. Try to give them titles that are related to what they contain.

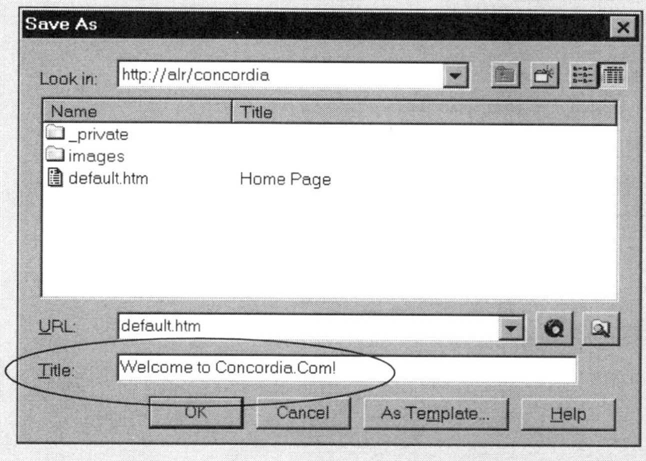

Figure 3. *When you save a new Web page, you can give it an informative page title.*

Page title

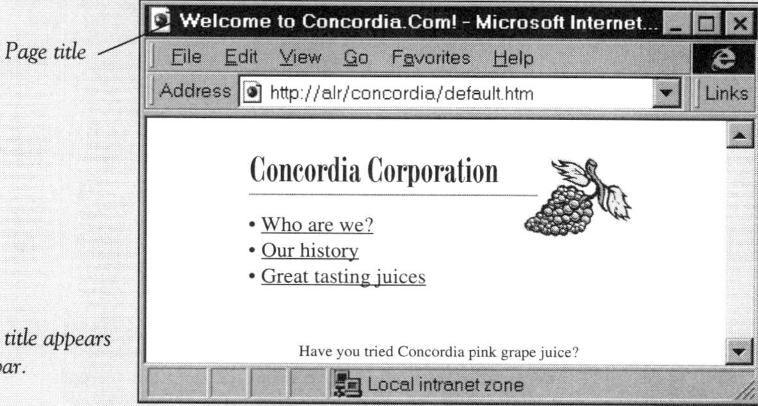

Figure 4. *The page title appears in the browser's title bar.*

Planning Web Site Flow

If you want to complete a complex task, good planning helps. You'll find that this is very true when it comes to designing Web site flow.

Web site flow is the way users will move around your site. Often, this involves navigation through hierarchical information. For example, if part of your site were used to display photographs from around the world, there might be a link to the photo page from your site's main page.

> Your Web site's main page is usually—but not always—the page that your Web server opens first when a browser accesses your site. Sometimes the main page is called a *home* page. FrontPage 98 automatically saves the home page as default.htm.

The main photo page might contain a link to an Italy photo page. The Italy photo page might contain links to pages of Italian cities, such as Rome, Florence, and so on (**Figure 5**).

Figure 5. *A Web site's pages should be interconnected with links.*

If there are parallel branches to this hierarchical structure—for example, a France photo page with links to the Paris and Chartres pages, and a China photo page that is reached from the main photo page—this can get pretty complicated very fast.

It's a great idea to plan this hierarchical structure in advance. When you do, be sure to keep in mind how users will navigate your site.

One way to plan a Web site is to create a diagram similar to a flow chart showing the connections between all the pages (**Figure 6**). (You can do this using pencil and paper or a flow-charting program.)

> Explorer's Hyperlinks view shows the links between the pages in your Web site. Navigation view also shows a flow chart-like view of a Web site's structure. You can use these views to understand the hierarchical relationships in your Web site better.

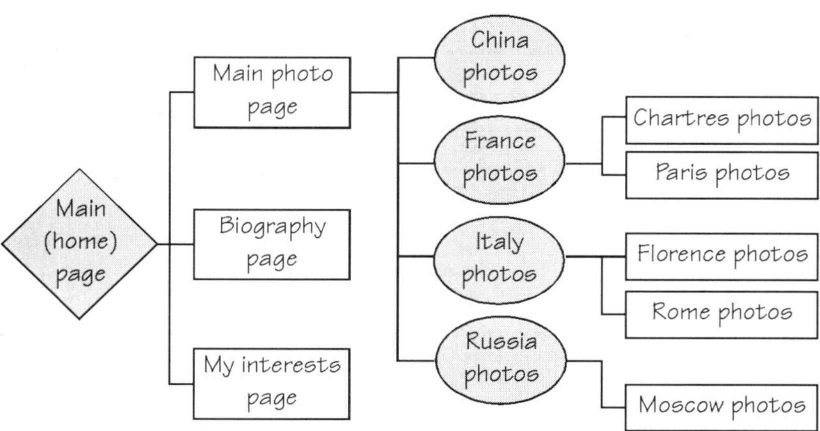

Figure 6. *You can use a pencil and paper or a flow-charting program to create a diagram of your Web site.*

Some Web designers prefer to create a hierarchical outline so they can understand the relationship between the pages in their Web site before the pages are created. You can use Microsoft Word in Outline View for this purpose (**Figure 7**).

It's important to provide a consistent way to move through your site, using, for example, a navigation bar or hyperlinks repeated on every page. The user should be able to easily reach all important pages from any page (and, certainly, the main page should be accessible).

For example, a user might reach the Paris photo page, and decide she really wants to see photos of Africa. It would be great if there were a navigation link over to the Africa photo page so the user didn't have to navigate back through the France photo page and the main photo page to reach the hyperlink for the Africa photo page.

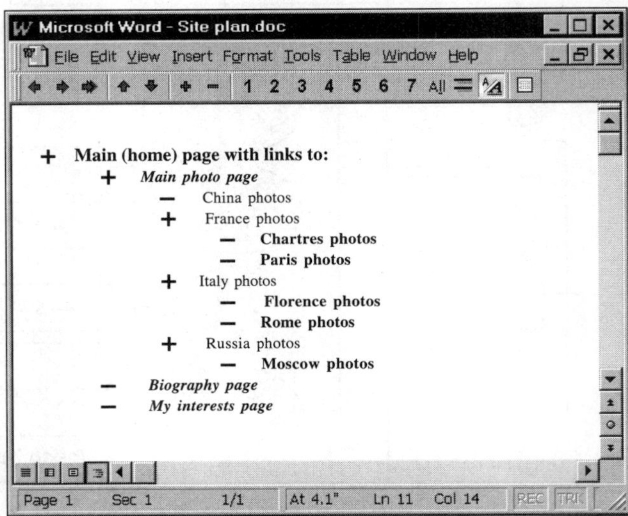

Figure 7. *You can use Microsoft Word in Outline View to create a plan for your Web site.*

With FrontPage 98, you can generate *navigation* bars automatically, saving an enormous amount of time in the process. Navigation bars usually appear on every page in a Web site and include hyperlinks to other relevant pages in the site. If the structure of the site changes, the navigation bars are updated automatically, so you don't have to redo all those links manually. Turn to Chapter 14 for the scoop on how to create navigation bars.

Not only is it courteous to provide consistent links to other parts of your site, it also helps establish one overall look and feel for your entire site.

Consistent links within a site can be provided as a navigation bar or as a graphic *image map*, perhaps looking like the subject (**Figure 8**).

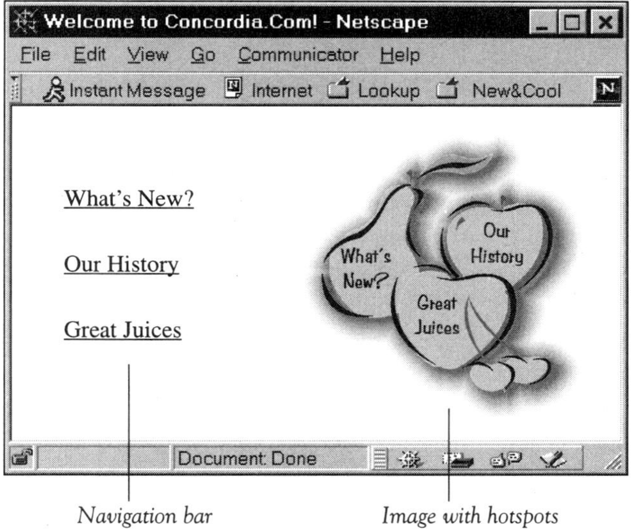

Figure 8. *To organize links throughout a Web site, you can use a navigation bar or an image with hotspots.*

Through the Generations with Web Sites

Some observers of the World Wide Web have said that Web sites can be categorized as first generation, second generation, or third generation. Here's what they mean:

- First-generation Web sites are text only. These are just-plain-vanilla Web sites, primarily designed to distribute information.
- Second-generation Web sites provide fancy graphics and interactive features. Users decide how to navigate through these sites. Web sites created using FrontPage 98 are normally second-generation sites.
- Third-generation Web sites guide users through the site with a gentle, but firm invisible hand. FrontPage can be used to create third-generation sites.

Third-generation sites are more like a fun house than a place to dig for information. There is an expected flow to what is presented on the site, just like in a movie.

When a third-generation site is planned, it usually includes an ante-room with only one way into the site (**Figure 9**). From this entrance room, the user is gently (but firmly) guided through a progression of pages. Finally, an Exit page is reached. This will often give the user the chance to exit to related sites, or start at the beginning again.

FrontPage 98 can certainly be used to create third-generation Web sites. If this kind of site conceptually suits the logic of your Web project, by all means go for it! You should understand, however, that controlling the user requires more work than simply providing a clear menu of choices.

Being Visually Consistent

Visual consistency within a Web site is very important. If you are creating a personal Web site, you can choose images and colors that suit your personality, but aren't necessarily consistent from page to page. Sites created in a business context give the wrong impression if they are not internally consistent. A Web site is an extension of the business it represents. It is inappropriate to create business sites that do not maintain a consistent look and feel, even if the look and feel is one of zany wackiness.

In order to maintain visual consistency between Web pages in a site, you should establish standardized fonts, colors, graphic styles used, and site navigation tools.

The easiest way to maintain consistency in a FrontPage 98 Web site is to use a theme—a professionally created Web page design. FrontPage 98 ships with more than 50 themes. Applying a theme to your site gives each page the same background pattern and

Figure 9. *A third-generation site uses an ante-room to welcome you to the Web site.*

color, bullet styles, font and font color, navigation bars, hyperlink colors, and more. (You can also apply a different theme, or no theme at all, to individual pages in the site if you like.) One of the best things about a theme is that if you modify one, or choose a different one, FrontPage will automatically change every page in your site. You don't need to change each page individually. Themes are simple to apply, and just as easy to modify, as you'll discover in Chapter 10.

UNDERSTANDING CASCADING STYLE SHEETS

Like themes, cascading style sheets are a new and exciting way to ensure consistency in your Web sites. (In fact, themes are essentially prefab style sheets.) Unlike themes, however, style sheets give *you* control over the look of your pages—you define the fonts, alignment, foreground and background colors, and much more. If you've used a word processing program, you might already know that a style is a collection of formatting characteristics. Styles provide a swift way to apply a lot of formatting all at once. Even better, they make it easy to change the formatting—if you change a style in the style sheet—for all elements affected by that style since they are updated automatically.

In theory this sounds wonderful: You just set up a style sheet establishing how you want your Web pages formatted, and then apply it to all the pages in your Web. But in practice it's a much stickier process. FrontPage 98 provides three approaches to style sheets: *External* style sheets are style sheets in separate files that can affect all pages in your Web; *Embedded* style sheets are embedded within a particular page and can affect only that page; and *Inline* styles apply only to particular elements on specific pages. (Note that you shouldn't use embedded style sheets or inline styles with themes.) Setting up these style sheets can get fairly technical. What's more, cascading style sheets are not supported by all browsers. In short, cascading style sheets are a cool and powerful new feature that you may want to research on your own, but they're beyond the scope of this book.

There are several ways besides theme to ensure consistency in your Web site. The FrontPage wizards make it very easy to create consistent Web sites. For example, the Corporate Presence Wizard, available in FrontPage Explorer, gives you a very good start on a corporate Web site. To find out how to start a site using a Wizard, take a look at page 60.

Page Wizards, available in the FrontPage Editor, allow you to create Web pages that start with consistent elements every time. For details on how to start a page with a Page Wizard, see page 84.

In addition, you can save any Web page as a template. New Web pages based on your custom template start with exactly the same visual elements. To find out how to create a page template, see page 88.

Another way to keep pages consistent is to use one Web page as the basis for colors on other pages. FrontPage makes it easy to set a Web page's colors using another Web page. For details on how to do this, see page 146.

Using Clip Art

The Web is a very visual medium. It's important to add art to your pages. Don't hesitate to be creative!

Included on the FrontPage 98 CD-ROM you'll find a sophisticated, yet easy to use drawing and image creation program, Microsoft Image Composer 1.5. You can use this program to create your own art for the Web as well as modify existing art. The details of how to use Image Composer are beyond the scope of this book. However, the program is pretty straightforward and has a tutorial you can run through to get your bearings.

Image Composer contains an extensive clip art library arranged in category collections, such as retro, techno, and western. If you find a particular category that pleases you, that category collection will provide you with all the necessary graphics, such as backgrounds, buttons, panels, and bullets. To access the clip art collection that comes with Image Composer, launch Image Composer, then choose From File from the Insert menu. In the Inserts an Image File dialog box that opens, move to the hard drive where Image Composer was installed, then open Multimedia Files\Graphics\Web\Microsoft Image Composer Themes.

FrontPage 98 also includes a nice collection of clip art you can use in your Web pages. (The amount of available clip art will depend on how you installed the program.) This clip art consists of many things you'll need when creating a Web page such as backgrounds, banners, dividers, and buttons. For details on how to add FrontPage clip art to your Web pages, take a look at page 153.

If you need additional styles of clip art, you should be able to find commercially released clip art collections on the Web or in software catalogs.

Whether you create your own art, or use existing clip art, it's important to use only one style of art in a Web site. For example, if your site uses high-tech space ships and deep space stations as illustrations, you probably should not also include pen and ink drawings styled after Disney cartoons.

It's important in Web page design to place art precisely, rather than just plopping it anywhere. The easiest way to precisely place art is to put it in a table. Take a look at Chapter 12 for more about tables.

Background Patterns and Colors

Background patterns and colors offer a thorny path for you to follow.

On the one hand, as Spike Lee sort of said, you gotta have 'em. Web pages with a gray background are just not acceptable any more.

On the other hand, nothing does more damage to a Web page than an inappropriate background choice. A page that is hard to read because the text and the background blend together is one that will most likely remain unread.

The golden rule here is that if it looks even slightly difficult for you to read, it's much too hard for anyone else. (After all, you know what it is supposed to say before you try reading it.)

You should also try to avoid garish color combinations. Text in shocking pink and a background in fluorescent green can be rather jarring as well as eye straining. The watch words for color combinations in your Web pages should be mellow, complementary, low key, and supportive of the page's content. Anything else, and you risk having your page look like a house whose colors were chosen because the paint was on sale.

Understanding Spatial Relationships

Designing Web pages should be regarded as a two-dimensional design exercise. As such, there are some standard principles that apply.

You need to understand the spatial relationships between the objects on your page. The size of the objects—and how they are positioned—should, in some way, reflect their relationships.

In order to understand the spatial relationships between objects, it helps to evaluate the *white space* (sometimes called *negative space*) on a page. White space is the area not taken up by objects **(Figure 10)**. (It's called "white space" even if the background is yellow or another color.) You will see how objects spatially relate to one another more clearly if you look at the white space rather than the objects themselves.

One common—and sound—principle for organizing spatial relationships is to divide your page into groups of related objects. The folks who browse your page should be able to quickly grasp the organization of the page. Grouping related objects together helps accomplish this.

Pages should be clean, and never cluttered. A cluttered Web page is like a messy room: no one wants to visit. Make sure to leave plenty of white space, so that the eye "has room to breathe."

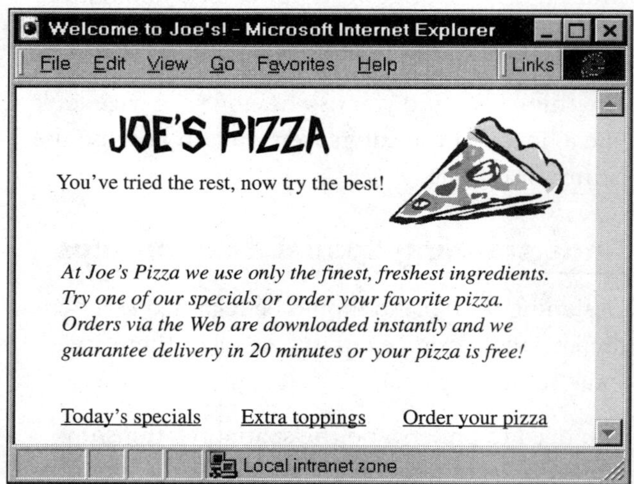

Figure 10. *White space gives a Web page and the user's eyes room to breathe.*

Neatness and white space, while a good start, are not quite enough. Your pages should also use contrast to make the page more visually interesting and to highlight important elements.

Visual contrast can be generated in many ways, such as by manipulating spatial relationships, using placement and weight of fonts, and much more.

The Importance of Narrative

Have you ever noticed how important the story is to a novel or movie? If you have a good story, sometimes the writing can be terrible or the film-making bad but you still want to stay to the end.

It's the same way with a well-designed Web site: it should tell a story. Some Web sites—for example, some third-generation sites—are explicitly designed to tell a story with a beginning, middle, and end. For these sites, the narrative is quite clear.

But even sites that don't have an obvious story are narrating something. If visitors to your Web site get the impression that there is no direction to the site, that your site is made up of random collections of pages, they will probably become confused and leave quickly.

When you first start to plan your Web site, try to determine what story you are trying to tell or what you want your readers to know when they leave your site. This may be quite obvious. For example, "Paul's Deli: we sell Pastrami mail-order and were the first Kosher Deli over 12,000 feet in the Rockies" has a story from the start. Other times, the story you are telling may not be so clear.

If you can figure out the narrative thread behind your Web site, use this information. It is precious!

Each page should, in some way, further the thrust of your narrative. Perhaps the page helps to set the stage for the rest of your Web site. Perhaps the page serves to answer a question a viewer might have. But every page, in some way or other, should play a narrative role.

INTERESTING WEB DESIGN BOOKS

There are many wonderful books available about designing exciting, visually consistent Web pages and sites. Here's a brief list that by no means includes all the interesting books on the topic:

- *Creating Killer Web Sites: The Art of Third-Generation Site Design* by David S. Siegel (Hayden Books)
- *<designing web graphics 2>* by Lynda Weinman (New Riders)
- *Elements of Web Design* by Darcy DiNucci, Maria Giudice, and Lynne Stiles (Peachpit Press)
- *The Non-Designer's Web Book* by Robin Williams and John Tollett (Peachpit Press)

SUMMARY

In this chapter you learned about:

- Naming and titling Web pages
- Planning Web site flow
- Third-generation Web sites
- Visual consistency
- Themes
- Cascading style sheets
- Using clip art
- Background patterns and colors
- Spatial relationships and your Web page
- Web site narrative

Installing FrontPage 98

This chapter explains how to install FrontPage 98 on your computer. Most likely you'll be able to get by with a Typical installation—the plain-vanilla installation option—which installs FrontPage 98, proofing tools and converters, and additional FrontPage themes. The other option is to go with a Custom installation, which gives you more control over what FrontPage 98 places on your computer—allowing you to add additional clip art, for example. If you're upgrading from a previous version of FrontPage, we'll show you the different road signs along the way, and help you avoid a few pitfalls.

When you install FrontPage 98, it recommends that you also install the Microsoft Personal Web Server, a program that turns your PC into a Web server and lets you set up and test your FrontPage Web sites on your local computer. To confuse matters, FrontPage supplies another Web server, FrontPage Personal Web Server. At this point, FrontPage Personal Web Server is included for the sake of backward compatibility. Unless you have a good reason not to, it's best to stick with Microsoft Personal Web Server, which is by far the more powerful of the two Web servers.

When you perform a Typical installation, FrontPage also takes care of installing the FrontPage Server Extensions on your machine. If you're going to have an ISP host your Web site, you will need to make sure that they also have the server extensions installed.

WHAT ARE THE FRONTPAGE SERVER EXTENSIONS?

The FrontPage Server Extensions are programs that let Web servers, such as the Microsoft Personal Web Server, talk to FrontPage Web sites. In order for a server to talk to FrontPage and vice versa, the server must be set up to use a specific *port* on your computer. You can think of a port as the "telephone line" that the server and FrontPage use to talk to each other. The default port is 80.

If an ISP will be hosting your FrontPage Web site, the ISP *must* have the FrontPage Server Extensions installed. For information about where to find an ISP that can host FrontPage Web sites, see the sidebar on page 25 and pages 26–27.

YOU CAN ALWAYS GO BACK WHEN INSTALLING FRONTPAGE

When you install FrontPage 98 on your computer, an installation wizard will guide you through the process. As with any other wizard, you will click Next to move forward from panel to panel. If you decide that you want to change something on a previous panel, just click the Back button to move back to that panel. From there, you can change what you want, then click the Next button to return to the panel from which you came.

WEB SITE ADMINISTRATION AND FRONTPAGE 98

Once you have installed FrontPage 98, you're ready to start creating Web sites and designing Web pages!

If, however, you find that you need to change the way FrontPage is set up, for instance changing server extensions, altering passwords, or setting who can have access to your Web site (this is known as *permissions*), you can do so. To learn more about these features, check out Chapter 16, *Web Site Administration*.

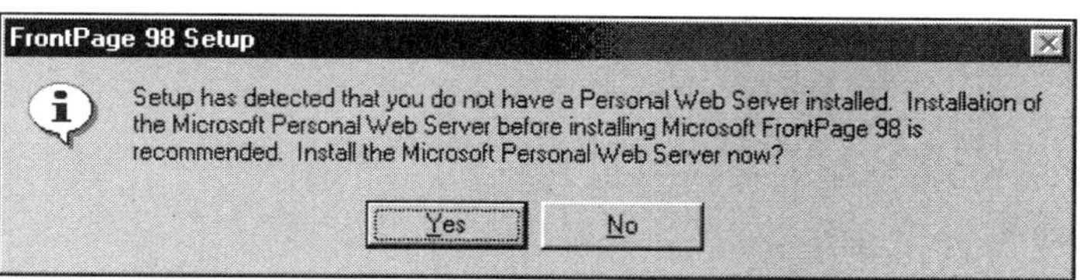

Figure 1. *The installation routine will ask whether you want to install the Microsoft Personal Web Server.*

The steps for installing FrontPage may seem complicated at first, but if you follow them along, you'll find that the installation is not hard at all. After you have installed FrontPage, you'll discover just how easy it is to create your own Web sites!

To install FrontPage 98:

1. Close any applications you might have open on your computer.
2. Insert the FrontPage 98 CD-ROM into your computer's CD-ROM drive.
3. If no server is installed on your computer, a FrontPage Setup dialog box will appear, asking whether you want to install the Microsoft Personal Web Server (**Figure 1**).
4. Click Yes. A License Agreement dialog box will appear on the screen (**Figure 2**). After reading the license agreement, if you accept the agreement, click the I Agree button. The Microsoft Personal Web Server will be installed on your computer. When installation is complete, a Personal Web Server dialog box will appear, telling you that you must restart your computer (**Figure 3**).

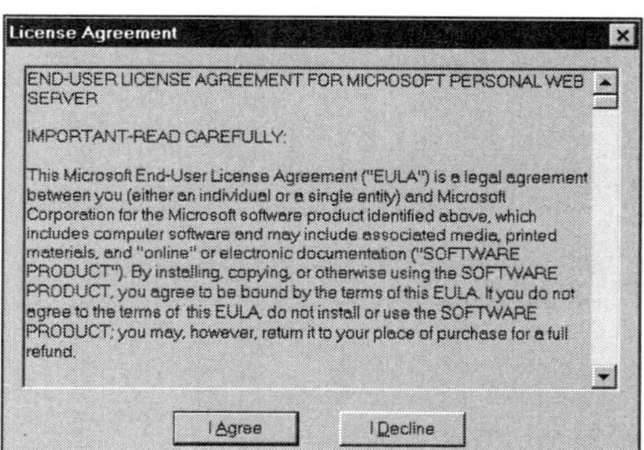

Figure 2. *The License Agreement for the Microsoft Personal Web Server.*

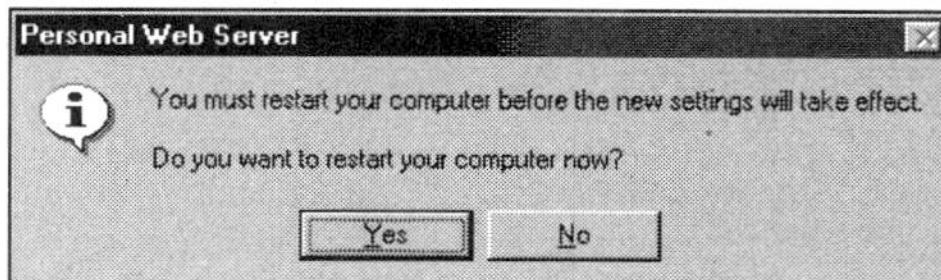

Figure 3. *Click Yes to restart your computer.*

5. Click Yes. Your computer will reboot. After a moment, the Microsoft FrontPage 98 installation window will open (**Figure 4**).

   or

   If this window does not appear, double-click the My Computer icon. The My Computer dialog box will open (**Figure 5**). Find the icon for your CD-ROM drive and double-click it. The Microsoft FrontPage 98 installation window will appear (**Figure 4**).

   Using this window you can choose to install:

   - Microsoft FrontPage 98.
   - Microsoft Image Composer, an easy-to-use program for creating graphics for your Web site.
   - Microsoft Internet Explorer, a Web browser.

Figure 4. *The Microsoft FrontPage 98 installation window.*

CD-ROM icon

Figure 5. *Double-click the CD-ROM icon to open the Microsoft FrontPage 98 installation window.*

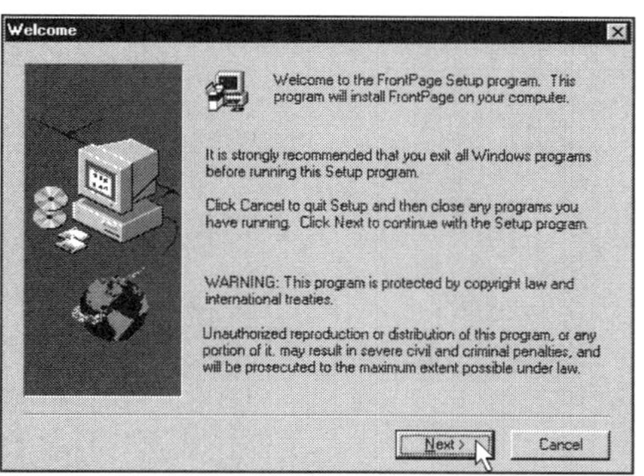

Figure 6. *The Welcome panel of the installation wizard.*

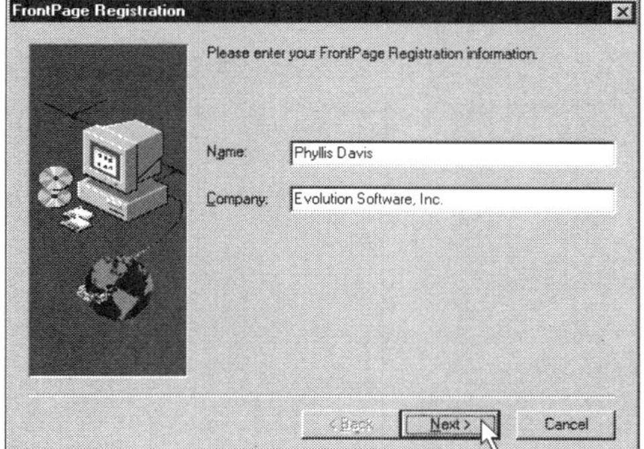

Figure 7. *Enter your name and company in the text boxes on the FrontPage Registration panel.*

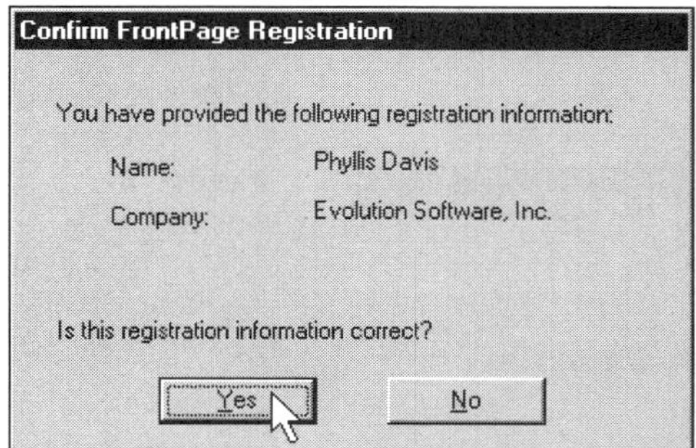

Figure 8. *The Confirm FrontPage Registration dialog box.*

6. Click the Install FrontPage 98 button. Setup for the installation will begin.
7. The Welcome panel of the installation wizard will appear (**Figure 6**).
8. Click Next to move to the FrontPage Registration panel (**Figure 7**).
9. Type your name and company name in the appropriate text boxes.
10. Click Next to move on to the Confirm FrontPage Registration dialog box (**Figure 8**).
11. If the information in the dialog box is correct, click Yes. The Microsoft FrontPage 98 CD Key dialog box will appear (**Figure 9**). If the information in the Confirm FrontPage Registration dialog box is not correct, click No. The FrontPage Registration panel will reappear so you can try again (**Figure 7**).

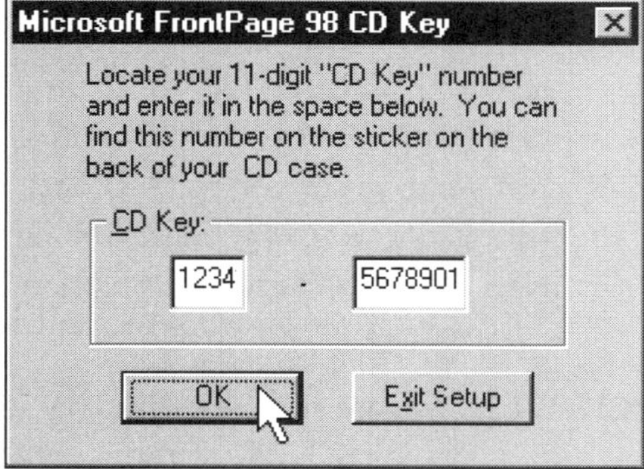

Figure 9. *Enter the CD Key from the back of the CD case.*

12. In the Microsoft FrontPage 98 CD Key dialog box, type in the 11-digit CD Key number in the text boxes from the sticker on the back of your CD case (**Figure 9**).

13. Click OK. The Setup Type panel of the installation wizard will appear (**Figure 10**). With this panel, you can choose either a Typical installation or a Custom installation.

14. A Typical installation should be sufficient, so click Next. The Choose Microsoft FrontPage Personal Web Server Directory panel of the installation wizard will appear (**Figure 11**). This panel is used to set where the Microsoft Personal Web Server program will be installed on your hard drive. The default location is C:\FrontPage Webs. If you want to put the program in a different location, such as on another hard drive, click the Browse button and select a new location from the Choose Directory dialog box (**Figure 12**). (A Custom installation gives you more control over what pieces of FrontPage are installed on your computer. You'll learn how do a Custom installation on page 55.)

15. When you are finished with the dialog box, click OK to return to the wizard panel.

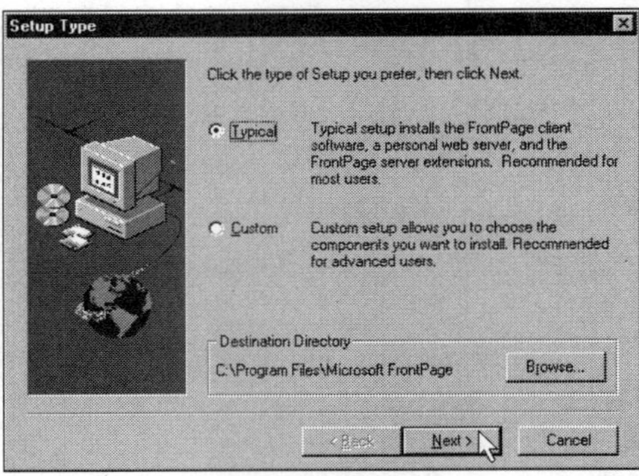

Figure 10. *The Typical installation should meet most folks' needs.*

Figure 11. *If you would like the Microsoft Personal Web Server installed in another location, click Browse.*

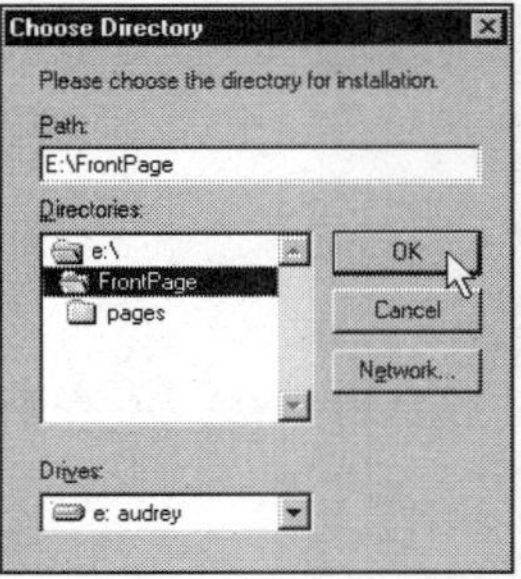

Figure 12. *Use the Choose Directory dialog box to select a different location for the files.*

Figure 13. *The files you selected are installed onto your computer.*

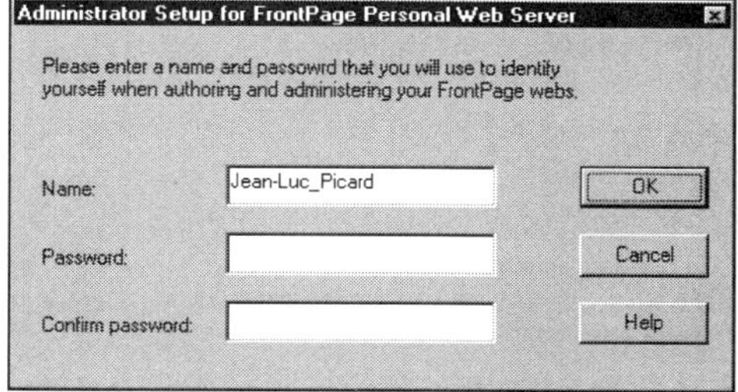

Figure 14. *Enter your name and a password in the Administrator Setup dialog box.*

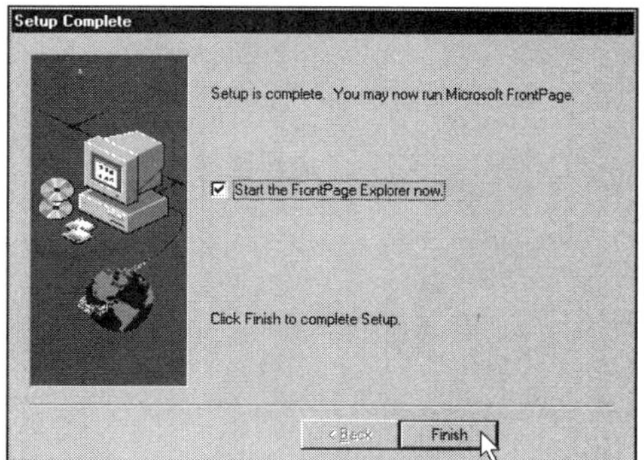

Figure 15. *The Setup Complete panel appears when installation is finished.*

16. Click Next. The setup program will install the items you selected (**Figure 13**). When it is almost finished the following *might* appear:

- An Administrator Setup for FrontPage Personal Web Server dialog box might appear (**Figure 14**). Enter your name with no spaces (you can use an underscore to connect a first and last name) in the name text box, a password in the Password text box, and the password again in the Confirm password text box. The password is *case sensitive*. This means that FrontPage sees *Pasha* and *pasha* as two different passwords. When you are finished, click OK.
- A dialog box recommending that you restart Windows to finish the installation. Click Yes.

17. If you don't need to restart your computer, the Setup Complete panel of the installation wizard will appear (**Figure 15**).

18. If you want to launch FrontPage 98 right away, click Finish. Otherwise, remove the check mark from the Start the FrontPage Explorer now check box, then click Finish. *Congratulations!* The installation is complete.

If you're already running FrontPage 97, you may have bought the upgrade version of FrontPage 98. You should know that it's much easier to install the upgrade version of FrontPage if you actually have FrontPage 97 installed on your machine. If you don't, you'll have to jump through a few hoops.

Microsoft FrontPage 98 - Upgrade Check

This product is an upgrade to Microsoft FrontPage 98. To use it, you must own one of the qualifying products listed on the Microsoft FrontPage 98 box.

Setup will examine your system to confirm that you are eligible for this upgrade. If you have de-installed the prior product, you will be prompted to insert the setup diskette that came with the product.

Continue | Exit Setup

Figure 16. *The Microsoft FrontPage 98 - Upgrade Check dialog box appears if FrontPage determines that you are installing an upgrade version of the program.*

To upgrade to FrontPage 98 when FrontPage 97 is installed on your computer:

1. Follow the installation instructions starting on page 47 through step 12. After you enter the CD Key in step 12, you'll see an Upgrade Check dialog box (**Figure 16**).
2. Click Continue to let FrontPage determine whether you're eligible for the upgrade. If you have FrontPage 97 installed, you should be fine. A license agreement dialog box will open.

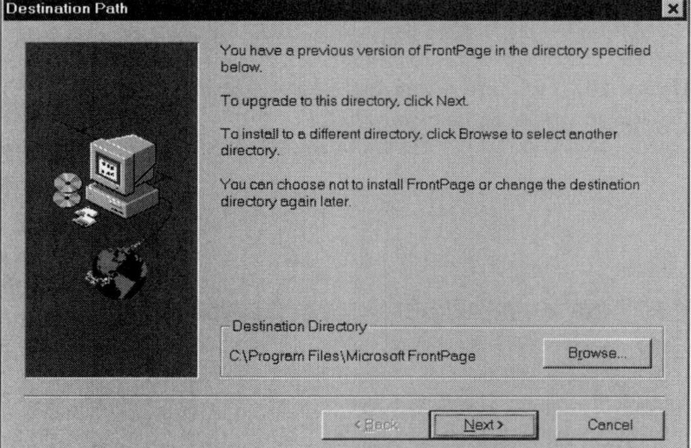

Figure 17. *Using the Destination Path dialog box, you can install FrontPage 98 over FrontPage 97 or put it in a different folder.*

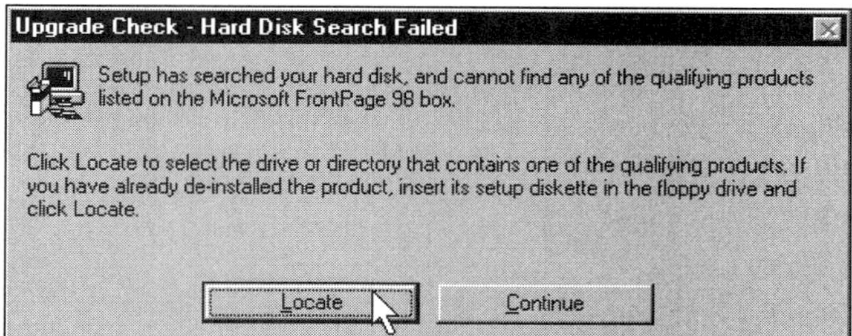

Figure 18. *The Upgrade Check - Hard Disk Search Failed dialog box appears if you don't have FrontPage 97 installed.*

3. If you agree with the licensing terms, click Yes to continue. A Destination Path dialog box will appear (**Figure 17**). This dialog box allows you to over-write the previous version of the program or put the new version in a different directory.

4. Click Next to install FrontPage 98 over FrontPage 97, or click Browse to choose a different directory. Finally, you'll reach the Setup Type screen (see step 13 on page 50), where you can choose a Typical or Custom installation and proceed with the installation normally.

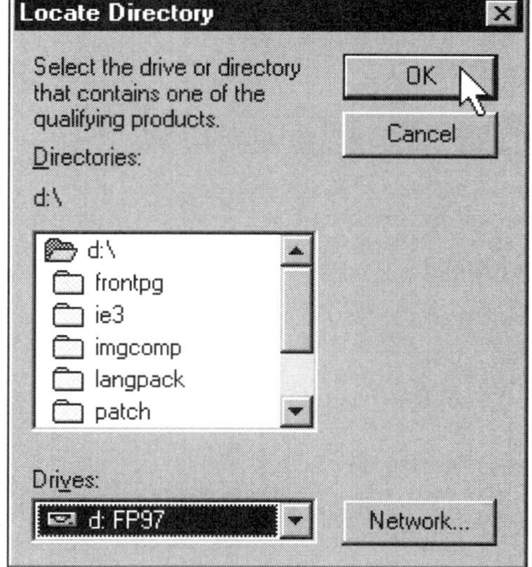

Figure 19. *Use the Locate Directory dialog box to tell FrontPage where to look for the previous version of the program.*

To upgrade to FrontPage 98 when FrontPage 97 is not installed on your computer:

1. Follow the installation instructions starting on page 47 through step 12. After you enter the CD Key in step 12, the Upgrade Check dialog box will appear (**Figure 16**).
2. Click Continue. The Upgrade Check - Hard Disk Search Failed dialog box will appear (**Figure 18**).
3. Click the Locate button. The Locate Directory dialog box will open (**Figure 19**). (The process from here on out is more than mildly counterintuitive!)

4. Insert the FrontPage 97 disk in your CD-ROM drive.
5. When you see the FrontPage 97 installation window, close it by clicking the Close button in the upper-right corner (**Figure 20**). You do not want to reinstall FrontPage 97!
6. In the Locate Directory dialog box, use the Drives drop-down list to choose your CD-ROM drive (**Figure 21**).
7. Click OK. The Locate Directory dialog box will close. The Setup Type screen described earlier in step 13 on page 50 will appear (**Figure 10**).
8. *Before you continue*, put the FrontPage 98 CD back in the drive. You can now proceed with the installation from step 14 on page 50. If the FrontPage 98 install window opens again, click the Close box in the upper-right corner to close it.

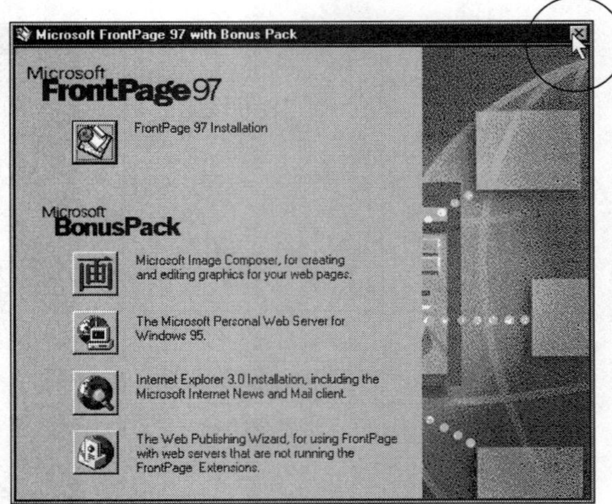

Figure 20. *Click the Close button in the upper-right corner of the Microsoft FrontPage 97 with Bonus Pack window.*

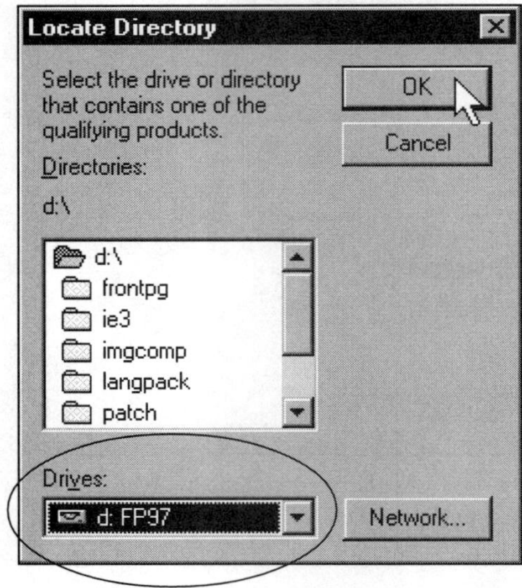

Figure 21. *Use the Drives drop-down list to choose your CD-ROM drive.*

UPGRADING TO FRONTPAGE 98

You must have the FrontPage 97 disk handy when upgrading to FrontPage 98; otherwise, you won't be able to complete the upgrade.

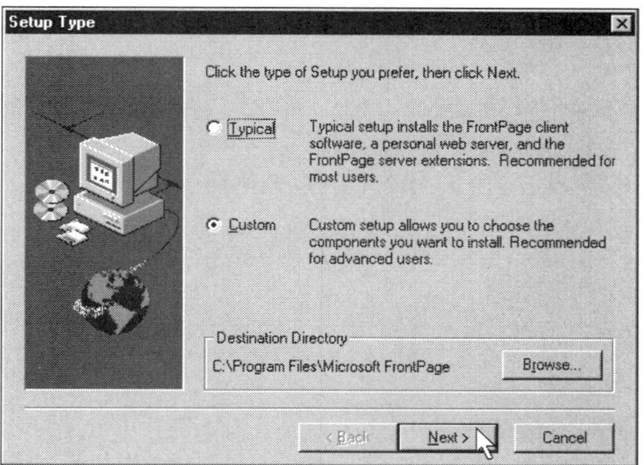

Figure 22. *In the Setup Type dialog box, choose the Custom option button if you want more control over how FrontPage is installed.*

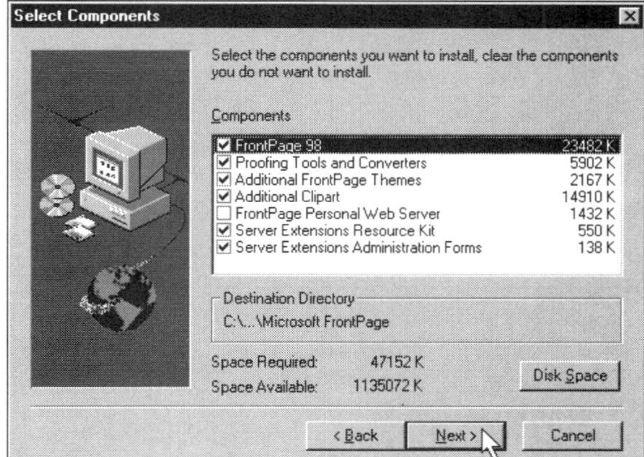

Figure 23. *Put check marks in the check boxes next to the components you want to install in the Select Components dialog box.*

A Typical FrontPage installation should be adequate for most users, but if you want or need more control over the installation process, you can perform a Custom installation. You might do this, for example, if you want to install more clip art or to use FrontPage Personal Web Server instead of, or in addition to, Microsoft Personal Web Server.

To perform a custom installation:

1. Follow the normal installation procedure up until step 13 on page 50.
2. Choose Custom in the Setup Type dialog box and click Next (**Figure 22**). The Select Components dialog box will open (**Figure 23**).
3. Put check marks in the check boxes next to the components you want to install.
4. Click Next. You can now proceed with the installation from step 14 on page 50.

Custom Installation Components

When you select a Custom installation as described on page 55, there are several components you can select when you reach the Select Components panel (**Figure 23**). Here's a brief description of what each item is:

- The FrontPage 98 option installs the essential components of the FrontPage 98 program—the Explorer, the Editor, plus various other items including a handful of themes.
- The Proofing Tools and Converters option installs the spell checker, the thesaurus, and converters that allow FrontPage to interpret the file formats of other programs.
- The Additional FrontPage Themes option installs more than 50 themes that you can apply to your Web site to give it consistency and a professional appearance.
- The Additional Clipart option installs extra clip art.
- The FrontPage Personal Web Server option installs the FrontPage Personal Web Server, a more rudimentary Web server than the Microsoft Web server.
- The Server Extensions Resource Kit option installs an HTML document that supplies material about working with FrontPage server extensions.
- The Server Extensions Administration Forms option will give you the capability to manage form returns by e-mail at the server level.

Summary

In this chapter you learned:

- How to install FrontPage 98
- How to install the upgrade version of FrontPage 98 if a previous version is or is not installed on your computer
- How to perform a custom installation
- About the components you can choose during a custom installation

Getting Started with Explorer

5

Designing a Web site may seem like a complex task at first, but FrontPage 98 makes it simple with FrontPage Explorer, FrontPage Editor, and Tasks view.

This chapter gets you started on the road to creating professional Web sites with FrontPage Explorer. Explorer is used to create a Web site and organize the different files that make up a Web site, as well as manage links, and perform operations across an entire site.

In this chapter you will launch FrontPage Explorer, create a new site, and open an existing one. After a brief discussion of the templates and wizards that come with FrontPage, you'll find out how to use the Explorer, and look at a Web site in *Navigation*, *Hyperlinks* and *Folders* views. From there, you'll learn how to import and export a Web site, close and delete a Web site, and exit Explorer.

Microsoft Likes to Go Exploring

You may have already noticed that several "Explorers" are being used in this book: FrontPage 98 Explorer, Windows Explorer, and Microsoft Internet Explorer. As explained above, FrontPage 98 Explorer is used to view a Web site's files. You use Windows Explorer to view a computer's hard drives and files. Internet Explorer is a browser, used to view Web pages on the World Wide Web.

To keep confusion at bay, FrontPage 98 Explorer will just be called "Explorer," and the others "Windows Explorer" and "Internet Explorer."

To launch FrontPage 98:

1. On the Windows desktop, click the Start button on the Task Bar.
2. Move the mouse up to Programs to open that fly-out.
3. Click the Microsoft FrontPage icon on the Programs fly-out (**Figure 1**).

To put a shortcut to FrontPage on the Windows desktop:

1. Right mouse click on the Start button and select Explore from the pop-up menu (**Figure 2**). This will open the Windows Explorer with the Start Menu folder near the bottom of the left pane (**Figure 3**).
2. Click the word "Programs." The folders and shortcuts available in this folder will display in the right Windows Explorer pane.
3. Position the mouse over the Microsoft FrontPage shortcut in the right pane. Press the right mouse button and drag the shortcut from Windows Explorer to the Windows desktop.
4. Release the mouse button. A pop-up menu will appear on the desktop (**Figure 4**).
5. Click Create Shortcut(s) Here. The Microsoft FrontPage shortcut will appear on the desktop (**Figure 5**). Now you can launch FrontPage just by double-clicking on this shortcut.

Figure 1. *Launching FrontPage 98.*

Figure 2. *Right click on the Start button, then choose Explore from the pop-up menu.*

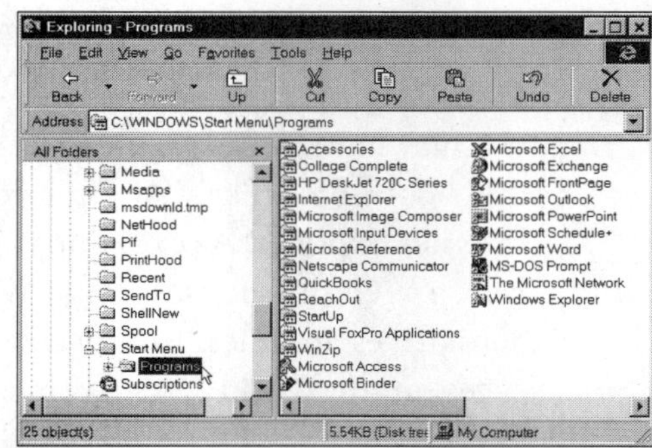

Figure 3. *Click the word "Programs." Several folders and shortcuts will appear in the right pane.*

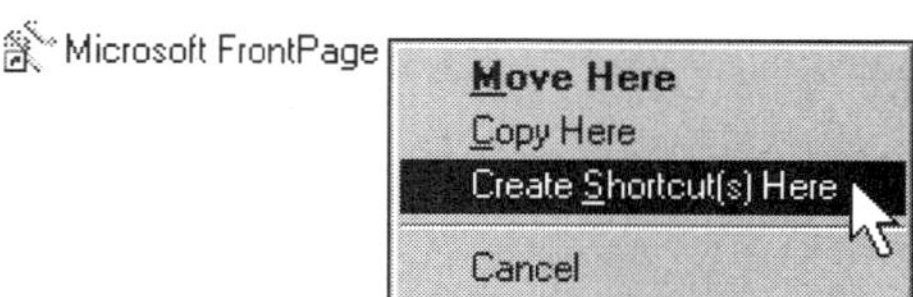

Figure 4. *Click Create Shortcut(s) Here on the pop-up menu.*

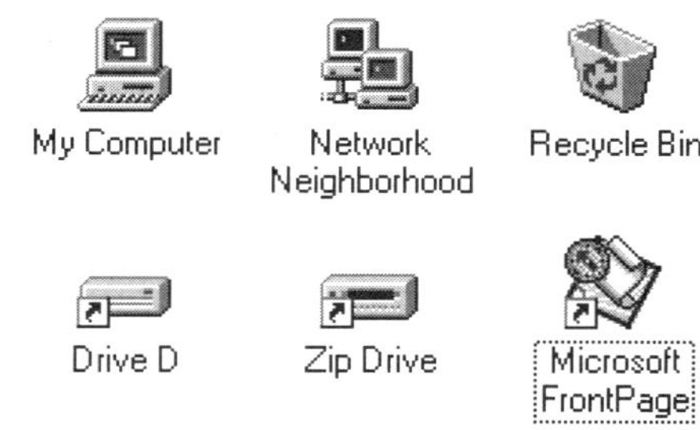

Figure 5. *The Microsoft FrontPage shortcut appears on the Windows desktop.*

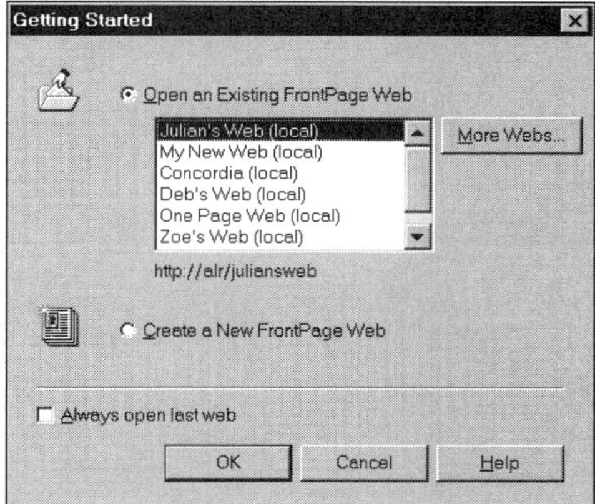

Figure 6. *The Getting Started dialog box appears when you launch FrontPage.*

When you launch FrontPage 98 for the first time, you will see the Getting Started dialog box (**Figure 6**). This window displays two options from which to select:

- Open an existing FrontPage Web site
- Create a new Web site using FrontPage

To choose one of these options, select the radio button next to the desired item, then click OK.

If you always want to open the last Web site you worked on, put a check in the Always open last web check box. This will bypass the Getting Started dialog box.

If you click the Cancel button on the Getting Started dialog box, FrontPage Explorer will open without loading a Web site.

Tips:

- You can always return to the Getting Started dialog box by choosing Open FrontPage Web from the File menu in Explorer.
- If you don't want to see the Getting Started dialog box every time you launch FrontPage, choose Options from the Tools menu, click the General tab to move to that tab page, then uncheck the check box next to Show Getting Started dialog.

The easiest way to go about creating your own Web site is to use one of the templates or wizards that come with FrontPage 98.

To start a new Web site:

1. Launch FrontPage 98. The Getting Started dialog box will appear (**Figure 6**).
2. Select the Create a New FrontPage Web radio button.
3. Click OK. The New FrontPage Web dialog box will open (**Figure 7**).
4. Select the From Wizard or Template radio button.
5. Choose a wizard or template from the list box. (See the next page for a description of the wizards and templates.)
6. In the text box below Choose a title for your FrontPage web, type in a name for your Web site. This title will appear in the Explorer title bar when the Web site is open.

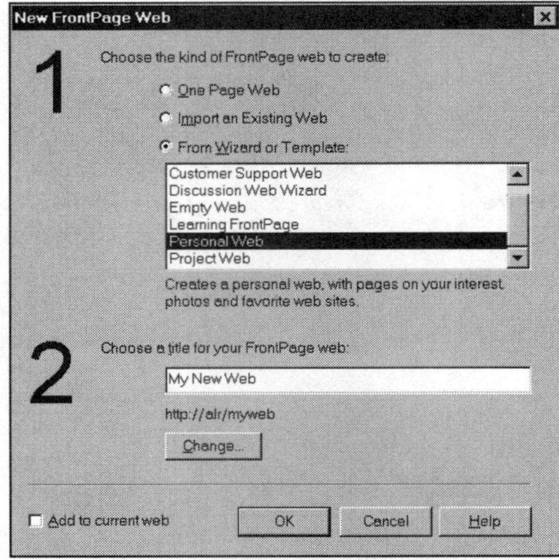

Figure 7. *Use the New FrontPage Web dialog box to select a wizard or template.*

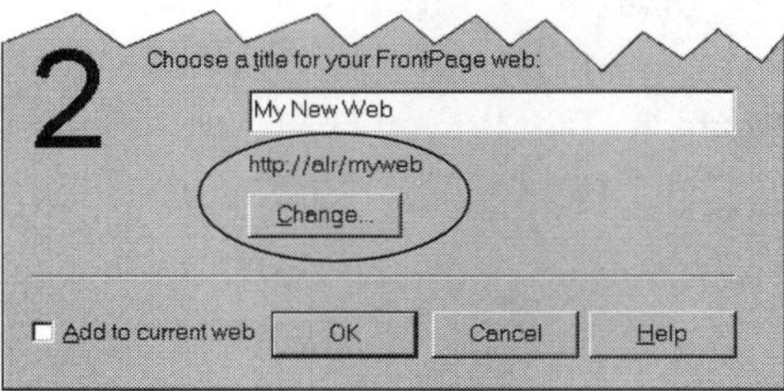

Figure 8. *Click the Change button to place the new Web site in a different location.*

Create a New Web Site

STARTING A NEW SITE IN EXPLORER

If you are already working on a Web site in Explorer or if you removed the Getting Started dialog box as described on the previous page and you want to create a new site, choose FrontPage Web from the New fly-out on the File menu (**Figure 9**). The New FrontPage Web dialog box will appear (**Figure 7**).

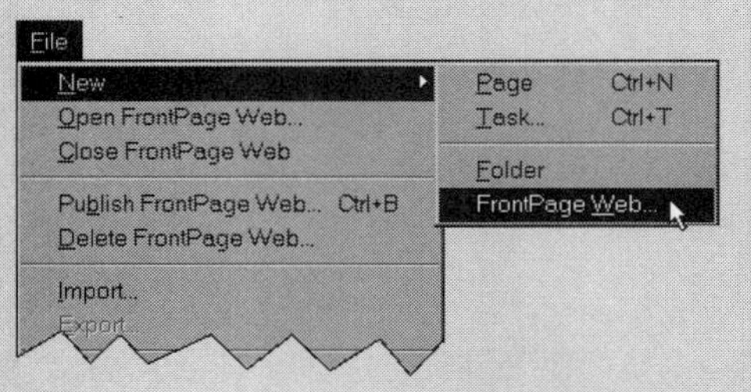

Figure 9. *Choose FrontPage Web from the New fly-out on the File menu.*

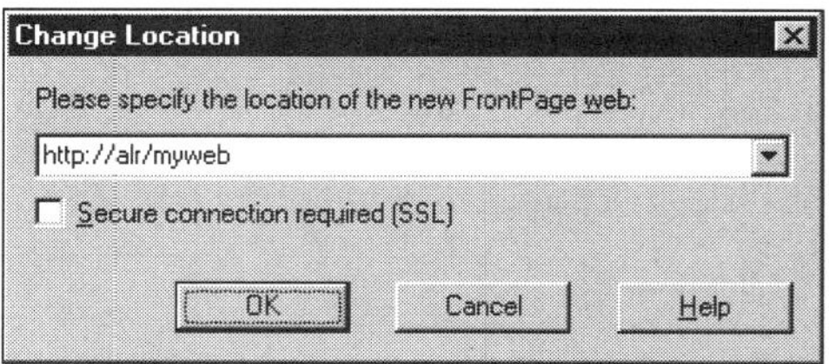

Figure 10. *Use the Change Location dialog box to set where the new Web site will be located.*

7. The location where the new Web site will be placed is listed above the Change button (**Figure 8**). If you want to change this location, click the Change button. The Change Location dialog box will open (**Figure 10**).

FrontPage Web Site Wizards and Templates

The New FrontPage Web dialog box offers several templates and wizards from which to choose. They are as follows:

- ***Corporate Presence Wizard*** This wizard gets you started with creating a business Web site.
- ***Customer Support Web*** This template quickly creates a business site for customer support.
- ***Discussion Web Wizard*** This wizard makes a Web site for discussions that includes a table of contents and text searching.
- ***Empty Web*** This template creates a new site with no Web pages.
- ***Learning FrontPage*** This template is for use with the FrontPage tutorial available in the *Getting Started with Microsoft FrontPage* 98 manual.
- ***Personal Web*** This template gets you started on a personal Web site that you can fill with such information as who you are, what interests you, and what you do.
- ***Project Web*** This template creates a Web site that helps you manage projects, including scheduling, who is involved, and more.

You can use any of these templates and wizards to quickly create a professional Web site that suits your needs.

8. In the drop-down list below "Please specify the location of the new FrontPage web," use the drop-down list to select a location, or type in a directory path, if you want to place the site on a hard drive. In Figure 10, the "alr" Web server has been specified. If you enter a path name that does not exist, FrontPage will create it for you.

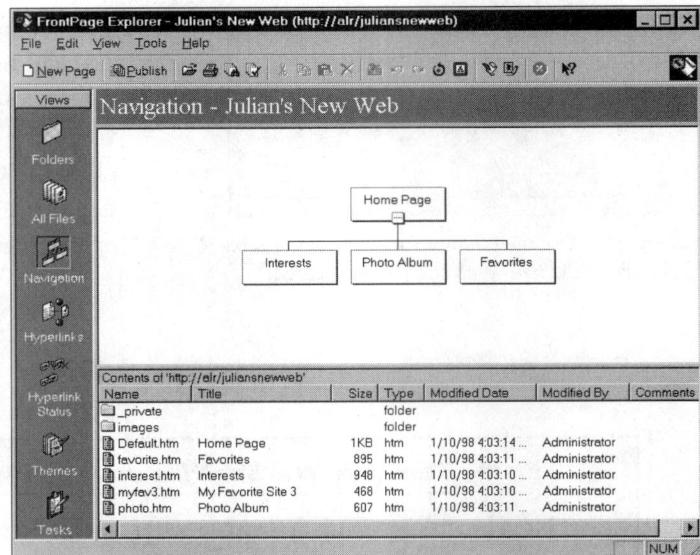

Figure 11. *After you click OK, FrontPage creates the Web site and displays it in Navigation view.*

9. Click OK to close the Change Location dialog box and return to the New FrontPage Web dialog box.

10. Click OK. If prompted, enter your name and password. FrontPage will create your new Web site, adding all the files you will need. The new Web site will appear in Navigation view in Explorer (**Figure 11**). If you selected a wizard, FrontPage will ask you various questions first, so it can customize your site before generating it.

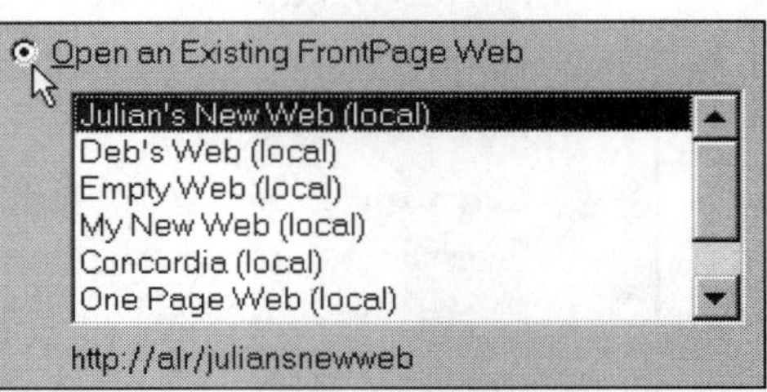

Figure 12. *Select the Open an Existing FrontPage Web radio button, select a Web site from the list box, then click OK.*

Tip:

- Depending on the speed of your computer, it may take a few minutes for FrontPage to create your Web site.

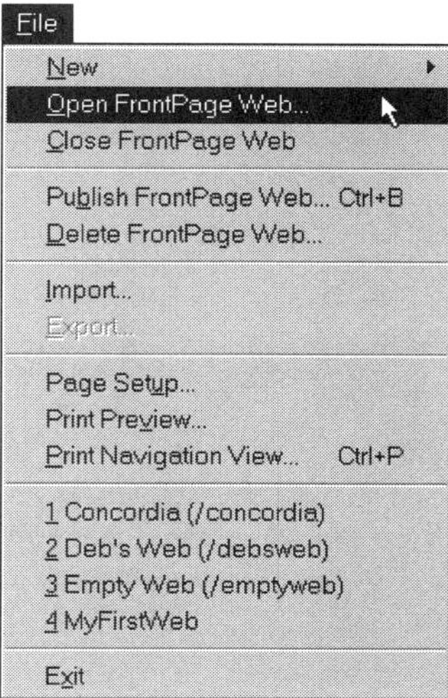

Figure 13. *Choose Open FrontPage Web from the File menu to open the Getting Started dialog box.*

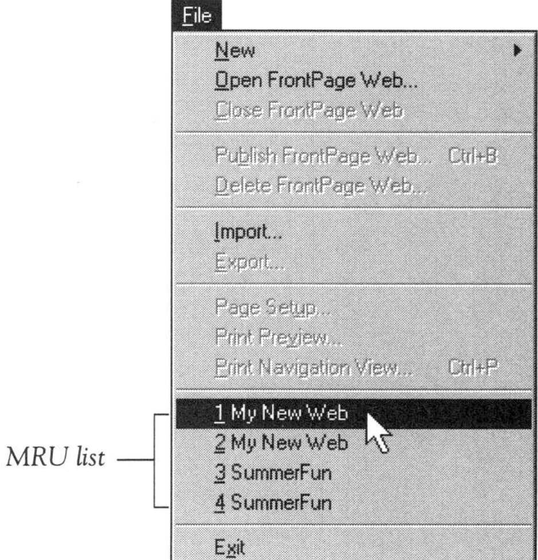

Figure 14. *You can quickly open a Web site that's been recently opened by selecting it from the MRU list.*

To open an existing FrontPage Web site:

1. Launch FrontPage. The Getting Started dialog box will open (**Figure 6**).
2. Select the Open an Existing FrontPage Web radio button (**Figure 12**).
3. Use the list box to select a Web site, then click OK. If prompted, enter your name and password. The site you selected will open in FrontPage 98 Explorer.

Tips:

- If you are already working in Explorer, click the Open FrontPage Web button on the toolbar or choose Open FrontPage Web from the File menu (**Figure 13**). The Getting Started dialog box will appear (**Figure 6**). Continue from step 2 above.
- To quickly open a Web site you have recently used, choose its name from the MRU—*most recently used*—list at the bottom of the File menu (**Figure 14**).

Now that you've created a Web site and opened an existing one, it's time to see how the Explorer works. As you saw in Chapter 1, there are several ways to view a Web site in FrontPage Explorer—three of the views you'll be using are Hyperlinks, Folders, and Navigation view. The way you want to view your Web sites is up to you. Each view gives you a different perspective of your site.

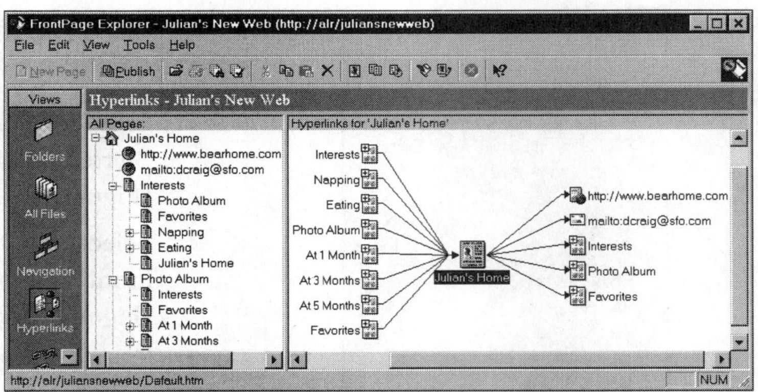

Figure 15. *A Web site displayed in Hyperlinks view.*

Hyperlinks view (**Figure 15**) displays a Web site graphically. The left pane shows an outline of the link structure of your entire Web site and the right pane displays individual pages as icons, linked together with arrows.

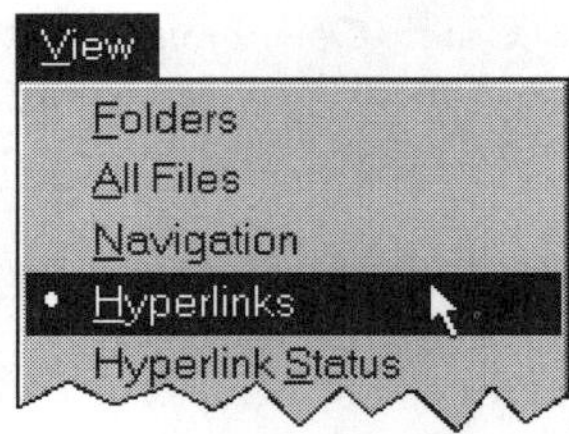

Figure 16. *Choose Hyperlinks from the View menu.*

To show a Web site in Hyperlinks view:

1. Open or create a Web site in Explorer.
2. Choose Hyperlinks from the View menu (**Figure 16**) or click the Hyperlinks button on the Views bar (**Figure 17**).

Figure 17. *Click the Hyperlinks button on the Views bar at the left of the Explorer screen.*

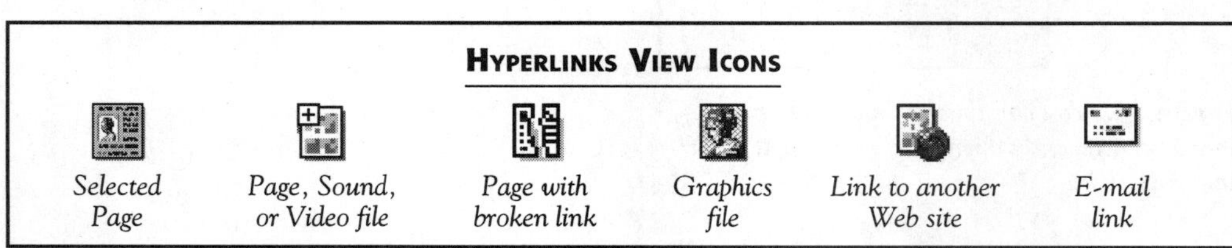

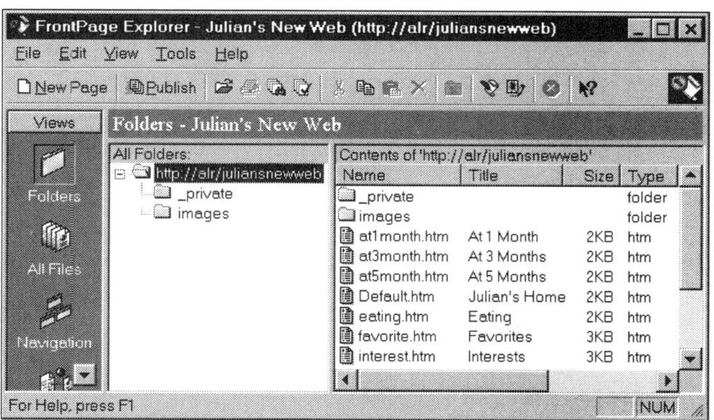

Figure 18. *A Web site displayed in Folders View.*

Folders view is very similar to Windows Explorer (**Figure 18**). The All Folders pane on the left shows the folder structure for the Web site. FrontPage automatically creates this folder structure when you use a wizard or template to create a Web site. The Contents pane on the right displays the contents of the folder that is selected in the left pane. Just like the Details view in Windows Explorer, the right pane shows a file's or folder's name, size, type, and other information.

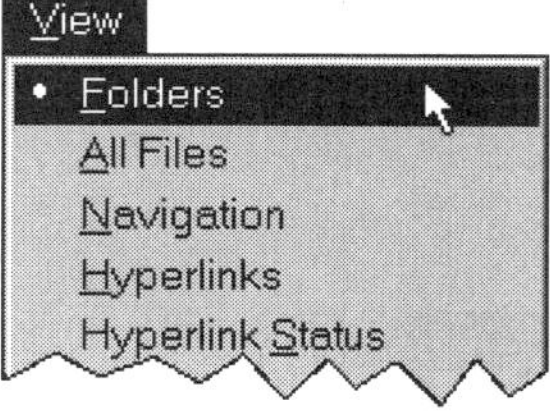

Figure 19. *Choose Folders from the View menu.*

To display a Web site in Folders view:

1. Open or create a Web site in Explorer.
2. Choose Folders from the View menu (**Figure 19**) or click the Folders button on the Views bar (**Figure 20**).

Figure 20. *Click the Folders button on the Views bar at the left of the Explorer screen.*

Navigation view (**Figure 21**) shows a graphical view of your Web site's structure, with the home page on top, pages linked to the home page directly beneath it, and folders and files in the Files pane at the bottom. For example, in this version of Julian's Web, the home page (Julian's Home) has links that lead directly to the page's Interests, Photo Album, and Favorites. (These are called *child* pages, and the home page is their *parent*. Pages at the same level in the hierarchy are called *peer* pages.) The Photo Album page, in turn, has links that lead directly to the pages At 1 Month, At 3 Months, and At 5 Months.

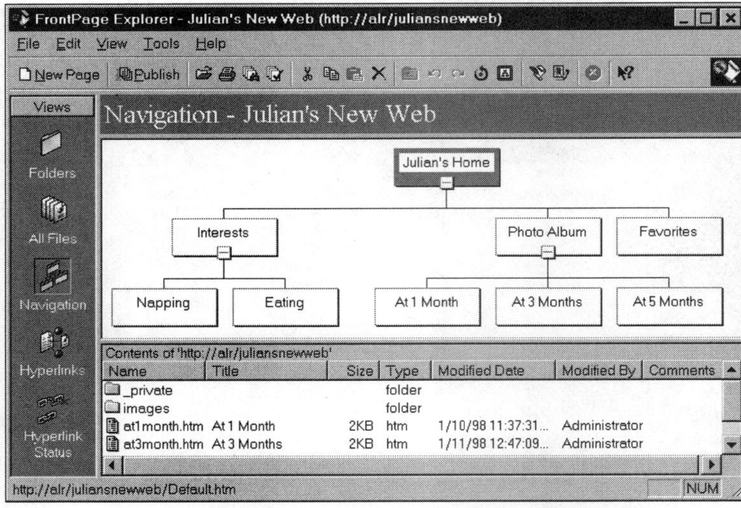

Figure 21. *Navigation view displays the structure of your Web site.*

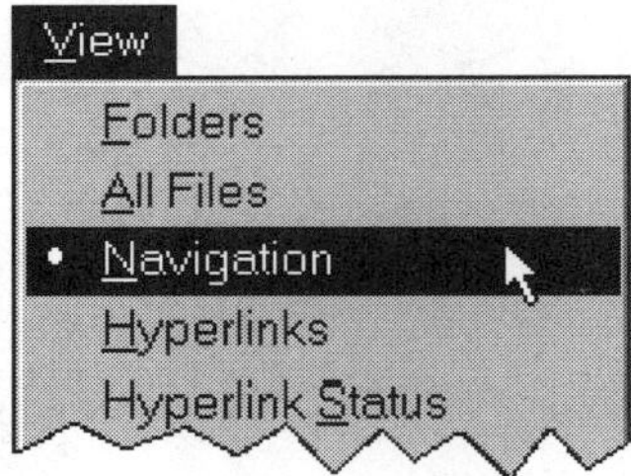

Figure 22. *Choose Navigation from the View menu.*

To show a Web site in Navigation view:

1. Open or create a Web site in Explorer.
2. If Navigation view isn't already displayed, choose Navigation from the View menu (**Figure 22**) or click Navigation on the Views bar (**Figure 23**).

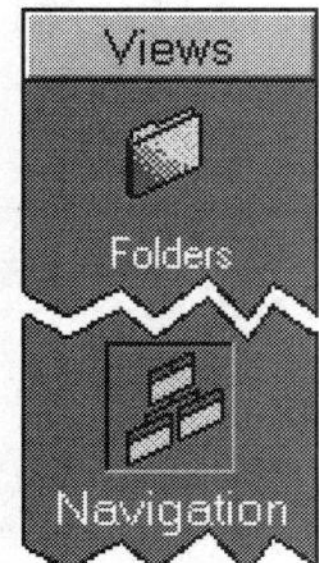

Figure 23. *Click the Navigation button on the Views bar at the left of the Explorer screen.*

Tips about Folders, Hyperlinks, and Navigation Views

Hyperlinks view (page 64):

- In the right pane in Figure 15, links from the selected page that point to other pages are shown as arrows pointing away from the page. Any links that connect to the selected page are shown with arrows pointing to the page.

Folders view (page 65):

- In Figure 18, the files in the Contents pane can be sorted by name, title, size, and so forth just by clicking the appropriate column heading. To reverse the order, click the column heading again.
- Are you befuddled about where the folders shown in Folders view are actually located? After all, there isn't a place on your hard drive called something such as http://alr/juliansnewweb. (This is the protocol http://, followed by the host name of the machine, followed by the name of the Web site.) Because Microsoft Personal Web Server is installed on your computer, your machine is acting like a Web server. Using your browser, you can view a Web site created on your computer by specifying the URL. If you are curious to know where these files are really located on your hard drive, try looking in c:\webshare\wwwroot. (If you don't have FrontPage installed on drive C, look on the drive where it's installed.) You should see a folder that uses the name of the Web site, as well as the subfolders and files that make up the site.

Navigation view (page 66):

- Besides simply being able to view your Web site in Navigation view, you can also modify its structure. To do this, just drag one of the boxes to a different location. For example, in Figure 21 if you decided that you want the Napping and Eating pages to be linked to Favorites rather than Interests, just drag the boxes to the right until they're connected to Favorites.
- You can also view as much of a Web site's structure in Navigation view as you want to see. To collapse the view and hide any child pages, click any minus sign; to show all child pages, click any plus sign.
- Navigation view lets you automatically generate navigation bars that make it easy for users to travel around your site. For the scoop on how navigation bars work, turn to Chapter 14.

You'll probably use Navigation, Hyperlinks, and Folders view most often as you create and tinker with Web sites. But FrontPage provides several other views that can come in quite handy. All Files view (**Figure 24**) lists all files in your Web, indicating their name, title, location, size, and more. This view is convenient for getting a bird's eye view of all the files in your site.

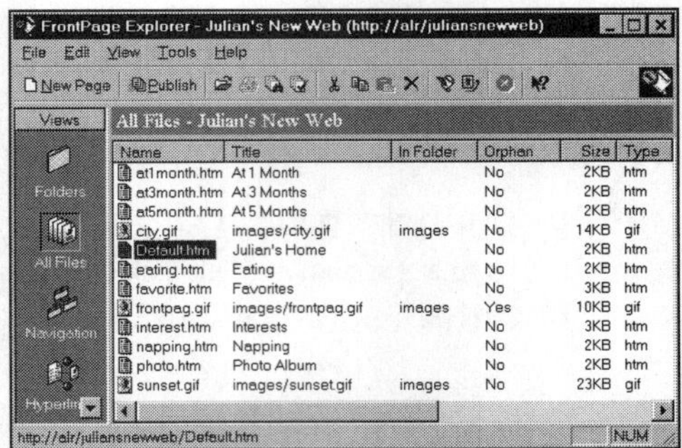

Figure 24. *A Web site displayed in All Files view.*

To display a Web site in All Files view:

1. Open or create a Web site in Explorer.
2. Choose All Files from the View menu (**Figure 25**) or click the All Files button on the Views bar.

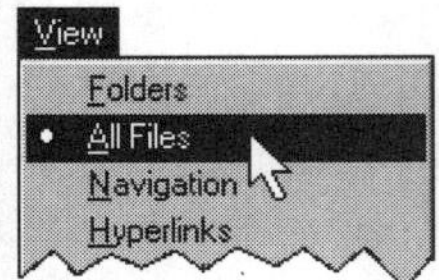

Figure 25. *Choose All Files from the View menu.*

Hyperlink Status view (**Figure 26**) lets you check all the hyperlinks in your site. Links marked as Broken are not working, links marked as OK are fine, and links marked as Unknown haven't been checked out yet. See Chapter 19 for more information about testing the links in your site.

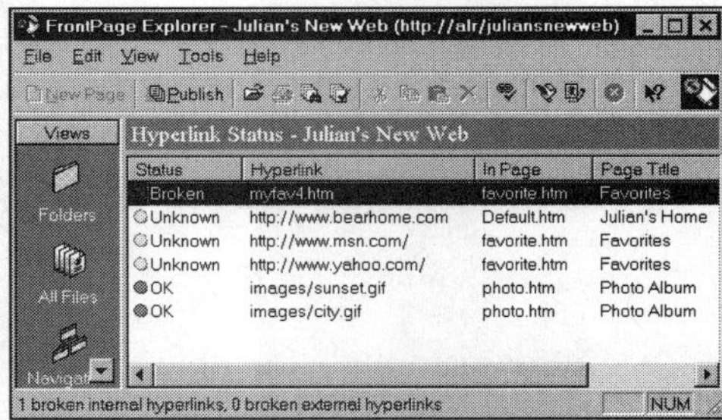

Figure 26. *A Web site displayed in Hyperlink Status view.*

To display a Web site in Hyperlink Status view:

1. Open or create a Web site in Explorer.
2. Choose Hyperlink Status from the View menu (**Figure 27**) or click the Hyperlink Status button on the Views bar.

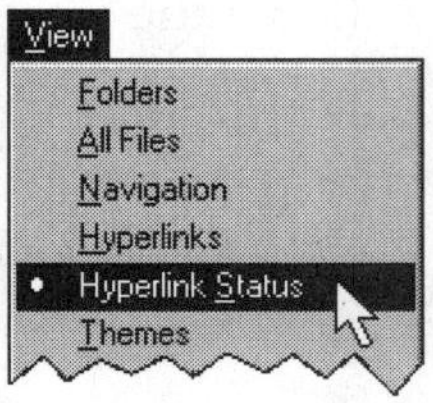

Figure 27. *Choose Hyperlink Status from the View menu.*

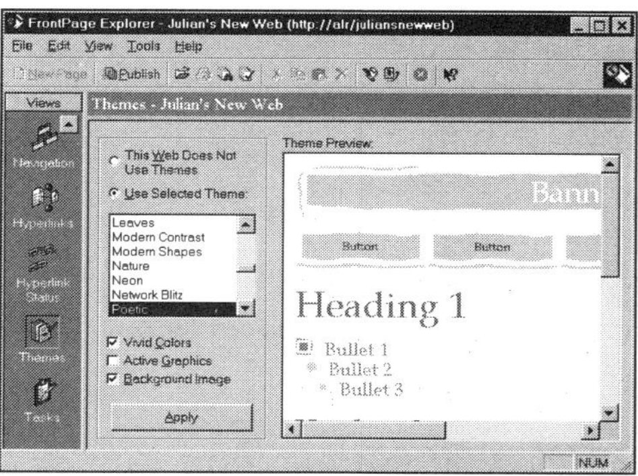

Figure 28. *A Web site displayed in Themes view.*

As you learned in Chapter 3, FrontPage ships with over 50 professionally designed themes that you can apply to your Web sites to give them a consistent appearance. Themes view (**Figure 28**) is where you preview and apply themes. With the Use Selected Theme radio button selected, choose a theme from the list displayed in the preview on the right. To learn more about themes, turn to Chapter 10.

To see a Web site in Themes view:

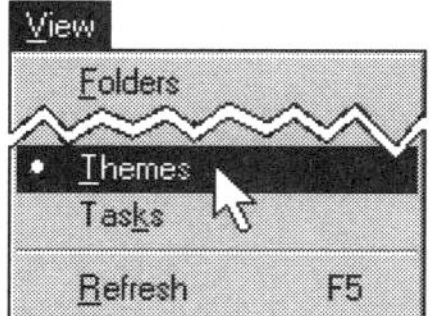

Figure 29. *Choose Themes from the View menu.*

1. Open or create a Web site in Explorer.
2. Choose Themes from the View menu (**Figure 29**) or click the Themes button on the Views bar.

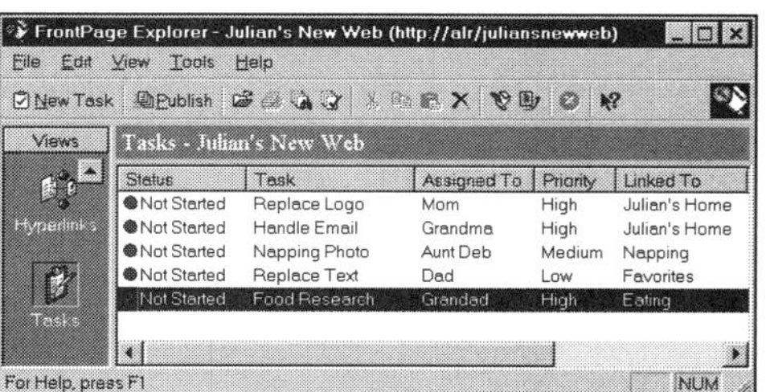

Figure 30. *Tasks view shows what jobs need to be done, who will do them, and what their priority is.*

Tasks view (**Figure 30**) displays a list of tasks associated with an open Web site. (This view used to be called the To Do List.) To learn about Task view, check out Chapter 13.

To look at a Web site in Tasks view:

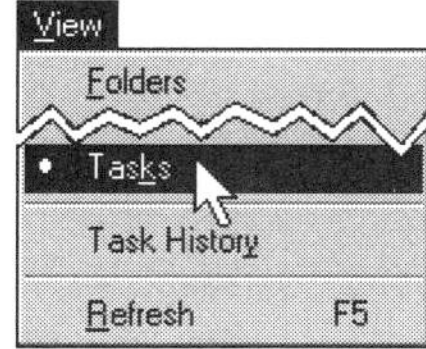

Figure 31. *Choose Tasks from the View menu.*

1. Open or create a Web site in Explorer.
2. Choose Tasks from the View menu (**Figure 31**) or click the Tasks button on the Views bar.

If you created Web sites before you started using FrontPage, you can turn them into FrontPage Web sites using the Import Web Wizard. You can also import older FrontPage Web sites, built with previous versions of FrontPage.

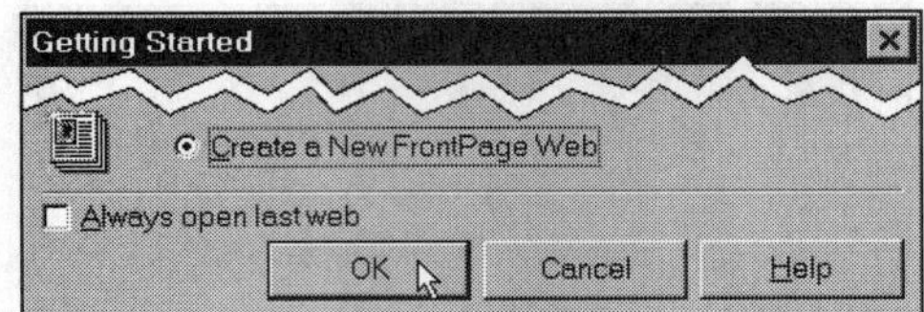

Figure 32. *Select the Create a New FrontPage Web radio button, then click OK.*

To import a Web site:

1. Launch FrontPage. The Getting Started dialog box will open (**Figure 32**).
2. Select the Create a New FrontPage Web radio button, then click OK. The New FrontPage Web dialog box will appear (**Figure 33**).
3. Select the Import an Existing Web radio button.
4. Type a name for the Web site in the Choose a title for your FrontPage web text box.
5. Click OK. The Import Web Wizard – Choose Source panel will appear with the top radio button—From a source directory of files on a local computer or network—selected (**Figure 34**). Leave this radio button selected.
6. Click the Browse button to locate the folder where the Web site you want to import currently resides. If there are subfolders under the folder you've selected that you want to import, put a check in the Include subfolders check box.

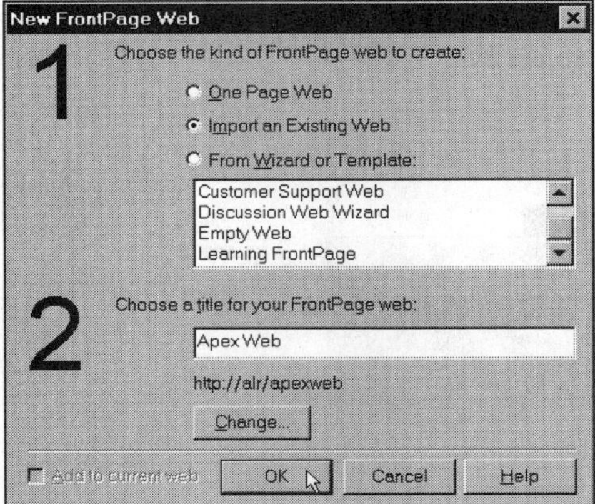

Figure 33. *Select the Import an Existing Web radio button, then enter a name for the Web site in the Choose a title for your FrontPage web text box.*

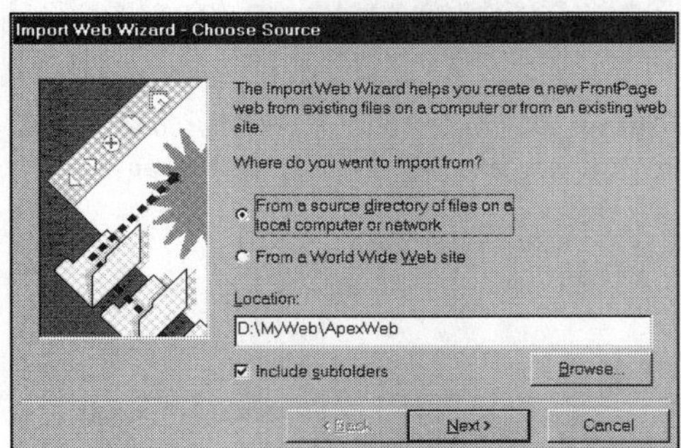

Figure 34. *On the Choose Source panel, click the Browse button to locate the folder where the Web site resides.*

Import a Web Site

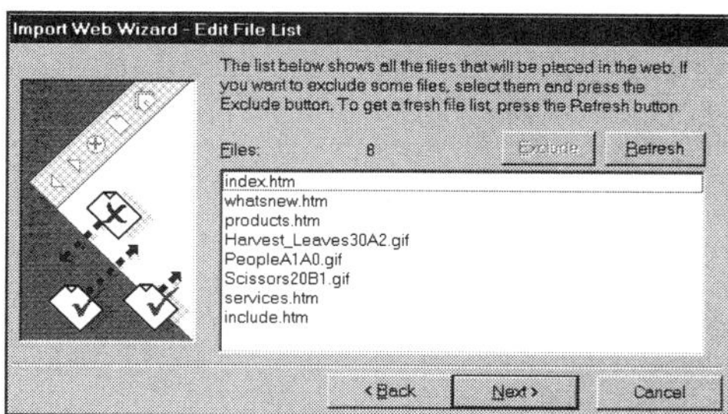

Figure 35. *Use the Edit File List panel to select files that will be imported.*

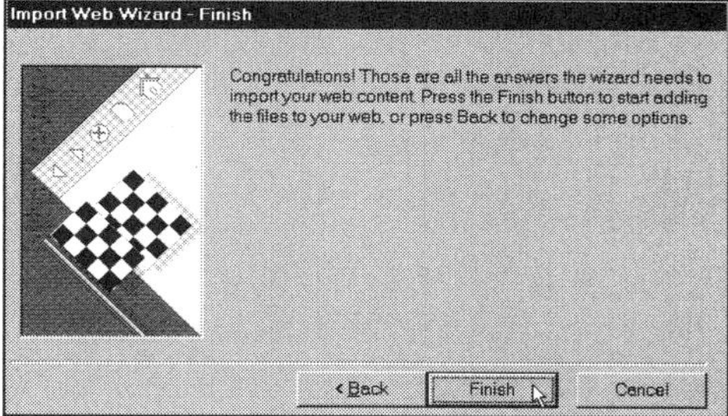

Figure 36. *Click Finish to import the files you selected.*

Importing a Site from the Web

To import a Web site from the World Wide Web, select the From a World Wide Web site radio button on the Choose Source panel (**Figure 34**). When you click the Next button, the Import Web Wizard - Choose Download Amount panel will appear. Use this panel to decide how many pages and kilobytes of information will be downloaded.

7. Click Next. The wizard will move to the next panel, Import Web Wizard – Edit File List (**Figure 35**). This panel contains a list of all the files contained in the folder (and subfolders) that you selected. It is used to select the specific files you want to import.

8. To exclude a file from being imported, select it with the mouse, then click the Exclude button. If you remove some files, but realize you don't want to exclude them, click Refresh. The original list will appear again.

9. When you have finished excluding files, click Next. The Import Web Wizard – Finish panel will appear (**Figure 36**).

10. Click Finish. The Web site will be imported.

Tips:

- If you want to change some information on a wizard panel after you've moved to another panel, just click Back to move to that panel.
- If you are already working in FrontPage and want to import a Web site, choose New from the File menu, then choose FrontPage Web from the fly-out. Continue from step 3.

To import a file into a Web site:

1. Launch Explorer and open the site to which you want to add the file.
2. Change to Folders View.
3. Click the folder to which you want to add the file.
4. Choose Import from the File menu (**Figure 37**). The Import File to FrontPage Web dialog box will open (**Figure 38**).

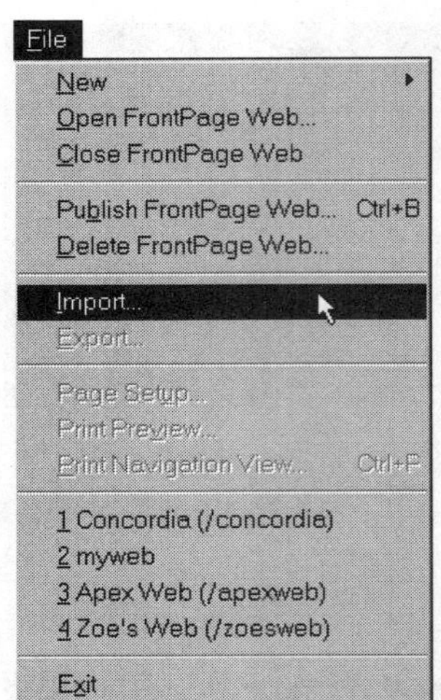

Figure 37. *Choose Import from the File menu.*

WHAT'S SSL?

If you choose to import a Web site from the World Wide Web, you'll see (for example, see Figures 10 and 43), there's a check box option "Secure connection required (SSL)." SSL stands for Secure Socket Layer. SSL is a security protocol that encrypts the data passing between a client computer and a server computer. Most Web servers need to be specially configured to use SSL.

Generally, SSL should be used on Web sites that involve data transmission that requires protection, such as credit card numbers or private financial information.

Not all browsers support SSL. However, the current versions of Microsoft Internet Explorer and Netscape Navigator do.

If you need to work with an SSL server and

- You are using a corporate server, talk to your Webmaster or Web site administrator to see if your server has been configured for SSL.
- You will be posting your Web site to an Internet Service Provider (ISP) host equipped with the FrontPage Server Extensions, follow the instructions provided by the ISP to enable SSL.
- You are maintaining your own Web server connected directly to the Internet, follow the steps outlined in the server software documentation to enable SSL.

Figure 38. *The Import File to FrontPage Web dialog box.*

5. Click the Add File button. The Add File to Import List dialog box will appear (**Figure 39**).

6. Use the Files of type drop-down list near the bottom of the dialog box to select the type of file you want to import. If you don't know what kind of file it is, select All Files (*.*).

7. Move to the folder where the file is stored and select the file.

8. Click Open. The Add File to Import List dialog box will close and the file you selected will appear in the Import File to FrontPage Web dialog box (**Figure 40**).

9. If you want to add files from other folder locations, repeat steps 3 through 8.

10. Click OK. The file(s) will be added to your Web site.

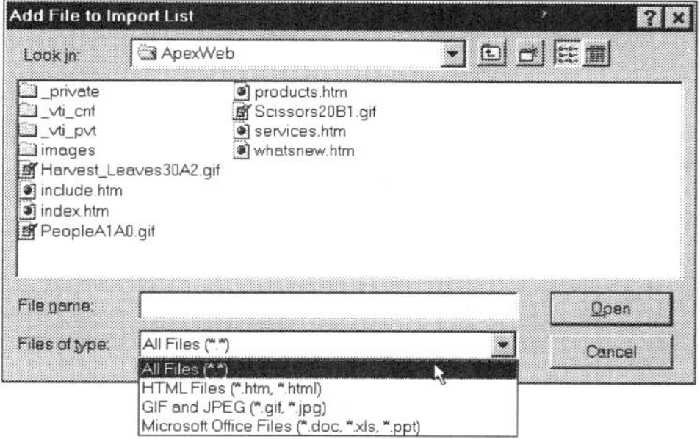

Figure 39. *Use the Add File to Import List dialog box to select files.*

Tips:

- Files can also be imported using All Files, Hyperlinks, or Navigation views in FrontPage Explorer.
- After you click OK in the Import File to FrontPage Web dialog box, the OK button changes to a Stop button. So if you need to, you can click Stop to halt the files being imported.

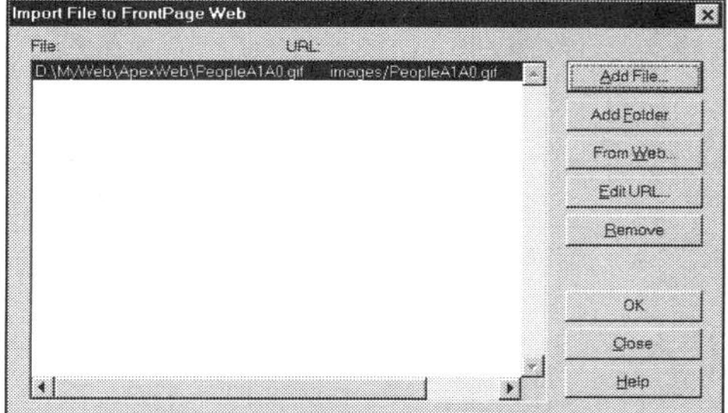

Figure 40. *Once you've selected the files you want to import, click OK.*

To export a Web site:

1. Open the Web site you want to move in Explorer.
2. Choose Publish FrontPage Web from the File menu (**Figure 41**), press Ctrl+B on the keyboard or click the Publish button on the Toolbar (**Figure 42**). The Publish FrontPage Web dialog box will open (**Figure 43**).
3. In the drop-down list, select a server or directory path where you want to place the exported Web site, or type in the name of a server or directory path.
4. Click OK. FrontPage will copy the Web site. The left side of the Status Bar will display how far along FrontPage is while it is copying the site, then let you know when the process is complete.

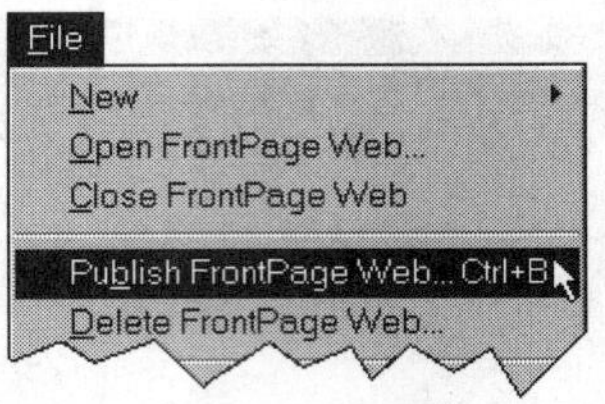

Figure 41. *Choose Publish FrontPage Web from the File menu.*

Figure 42. *Click the Publish button on the Toolbar.*

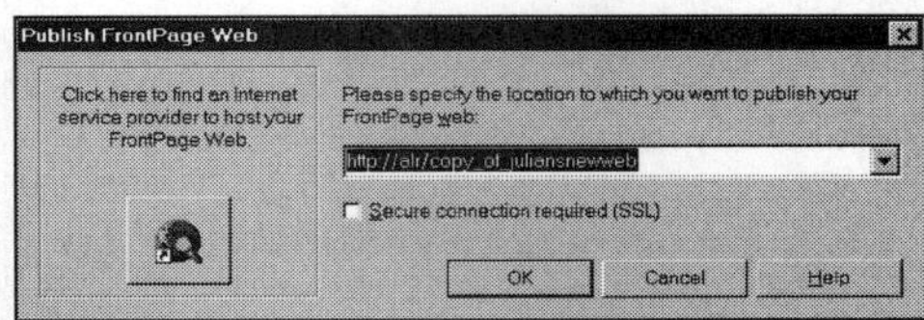

Figure 43. *Use the Publish FrontPage Web dialog box to select an export location and locate a service provider if necessary.*

Tip:

- If you don't have an Internet Service Provider (ISP) lined up to host your Web site, click the "Click here to find an Internet service provider to host your FrontPage Web" button in the Publish FrontPage Web dialog box (**Figure 43**). This will take you to a page on Microsoft's Web site that lists ISPs who support FrontPage Web sites.

Why Export a Web Site?

- To move your site to another Web server to go "live."
- To save a copy of a site for safe keeping as a backup.

FrontPage also refers to exporting as *publishing*. Take a look at Chapter 19 for details on publishing and testing a Web site.

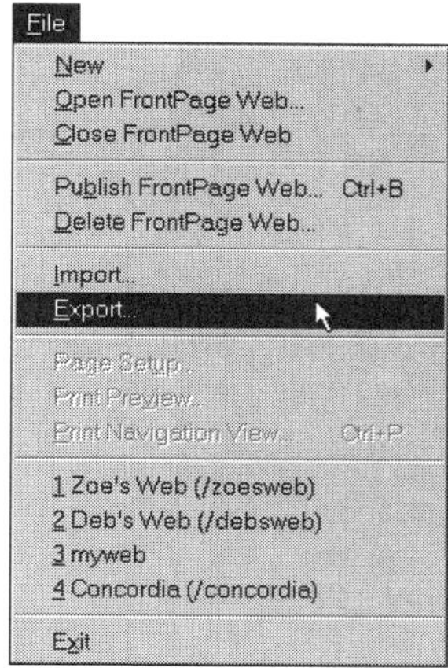

Figure 44. *Choose Export from the File menu.*

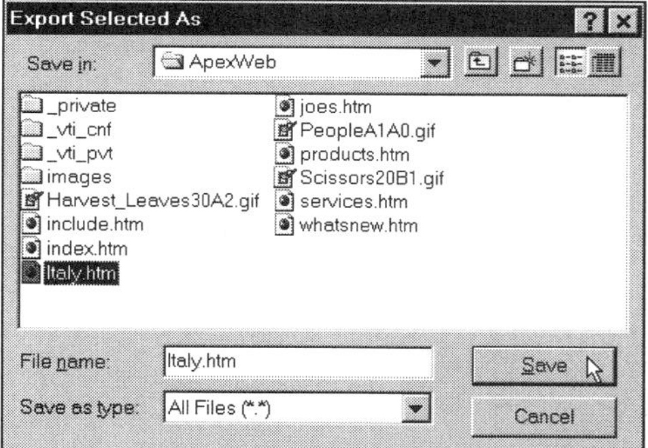

Figure 45. *Use the Export Selected As dialog box to select the location where the exported files will reside.*

Figure 46. *A FrontPage Explorer dialog box appears, telling you the file has been successfully exported.*

To export a file from a Web site:

1. Using Explorer, open the site that contains the file you want to export.
2. Select the file you want to export by clicking on it.
3. Choose Export from the File menu (**Figure 44**). The Export Selected As dialog box will open (**Figure 45**).
4. Move to the folder where you want to place the file.
5. If you want to rename the file, type a new name in the File name text box.
6. Click Save. A FrontPage Explorer dialog box will appear, telling you that the file has been successfully exported (**Figure 46**).
7. Click OK.

Tips:

- To export a file, you must view the site in either Folders, All Files, Navigation, or Hyperlinks views.
- When you export a file, it is not actually removed from the Web site. Instead, a copy of the file is exported. To completely remove a file from a site, you have to delete it (see page 77).

To close a Web site:

Choose Close FrontPage Web from the File menu (**Figure 47**).

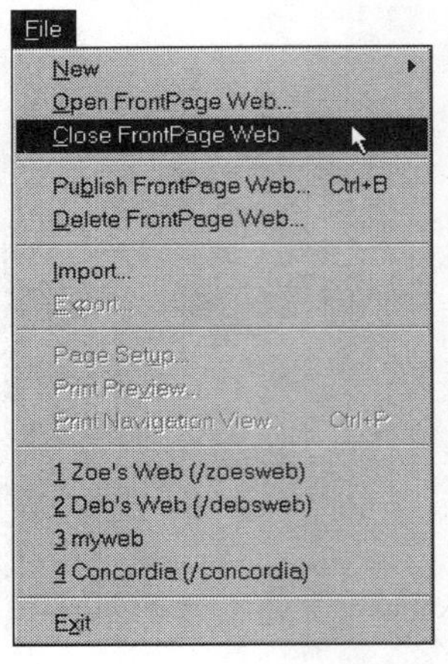

Figure 47. *Choose Close FrontPage Web from the File menu.*

Tip:

- FrontPage can only display one Web site at a time, so if you create a new site or open an existing one, FrontPage will automatically close the current site.

To delete a Web site:

1. Open the site you want to delete in Explorer.
2. Choose Delete FrontPage Web from the File menu (**Figure 48**). A Confirm Delete dialog box will appear on the screen (**Figure 49**).
3. Click Yes to delete the Web site.

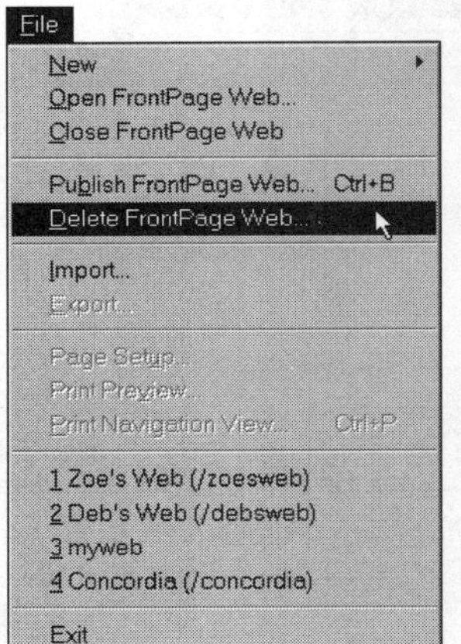

Figure 48. *Choose Delete FrontPage Web from the File menu.*

Tips:

- If you want to delete a Web site from a server, you must have administrative access. For more about user permissions and Web site administration, see Chapter 16.
- Once you've deleted a site using the steps above, *it's gone*. You won't find it in the Windows Recycle Bin, so look before you leap!

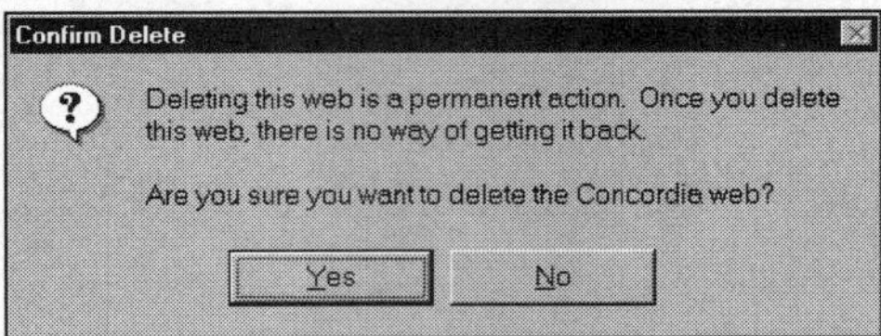

Figure 49. *The Confirm Delete dialog box lets you make sure you really want to delete the Web site.*

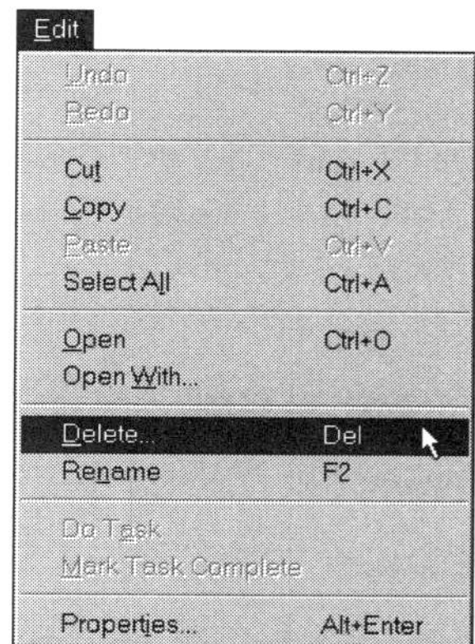

Figure 50. *Choose Delete from the Edit menu.*

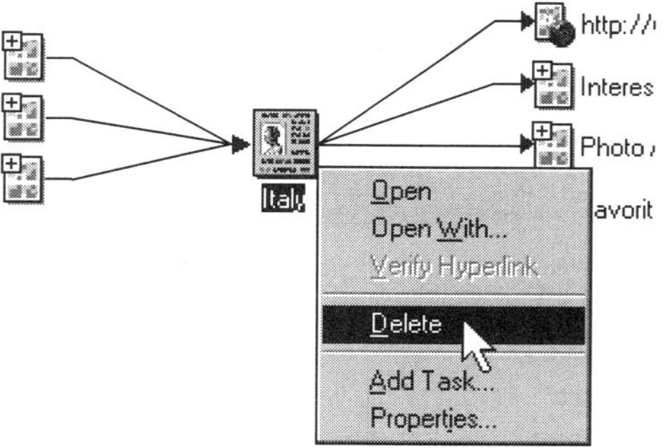

Figure 51. *Right mouse click on the file, then select Delete from the pop-up menu.*

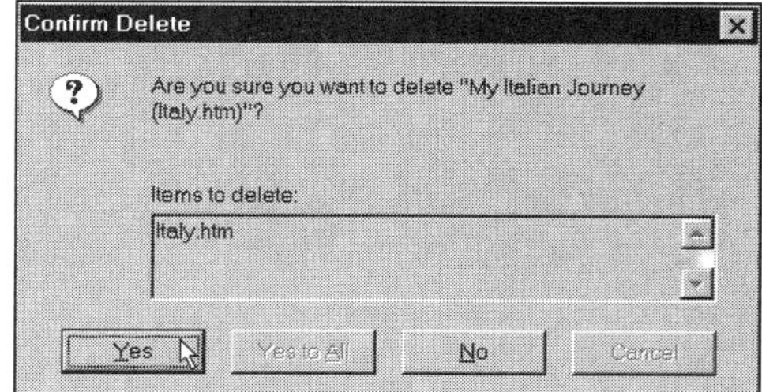

Figure 52. *The Confirm Delete dialog box lets you reconsider your course of action.*

To delete a file from a Web site:

1. Open the Web site in Explorer.
2. Select the file with the mouse.
3. Choose Delete from the Edit menu (**Figure 50**).

   or

   Press the Delete key on the keyboard.

   or

   Right mouse click on the file and select Delete from the pop-up menu (**Figure 51**).
4. Click Yes in the Confirm Delete dialog box that appears (**Figure 52**).

Tips:

- To delete a file, you must view the site in either Folders, All Files, Navigation, or Hyperlinks views.
- You can select several files to delete at one time by holding down the Shift key while clicking the mouse.
- When you delete a file from a Web site, it's gone forever. You won't find it in the Windows Recycle Bin.

To exit FrontPage 98 Explorer:

Choose Exit from the File menu (**Figure 53**).

or

Press Alt+F4 on the keyboard.

or

Click the Close button in the extreme upper-right corner of the screen (**Figure 54**).

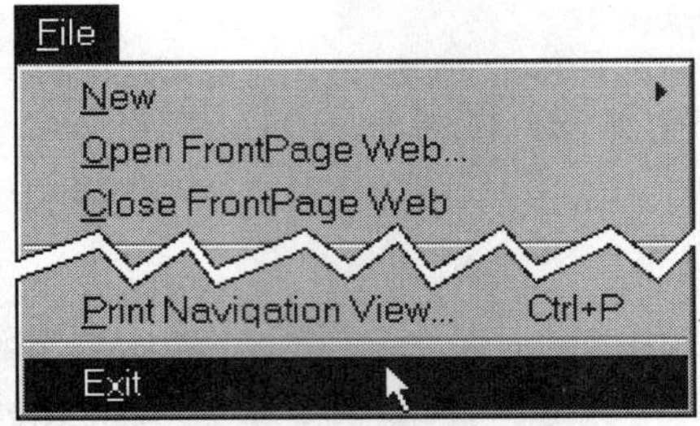

Figure 53. *Choose Exit from the File menu.*

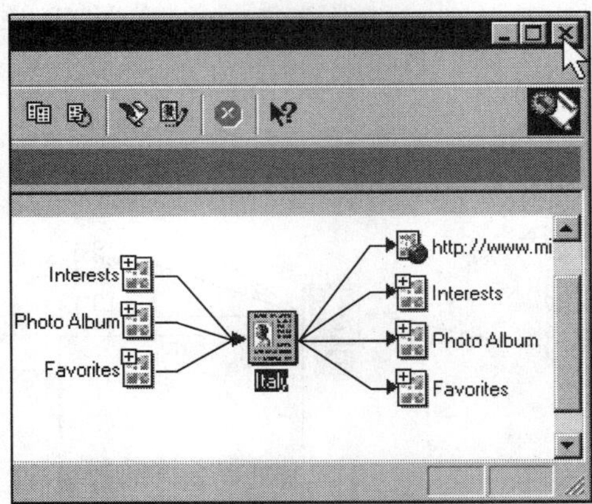

Figure 54. *Click the Close button at the upper-right corner of the screen.*

SUMMARY

In this chapter you learned how to:

- Launch FrontPage 98
- Create a new Web site
- Open an existing Web site
- Show a Web site in Folders, All Files, Hyperlinks, Tasks, Navigation, Hyperlink Status, and Themes views
- Move Web pages in Navigation view
- Import a Web site or file
- Export a site or file
- Close a Web site
- Delete a site or file
- Exit Explorer

Using FrontPage Editor

6

Chapter 5 showed you how to create Web sites with FrontPage 98 Explorer. Now it's time to take a look at those pages with FrontPage 98 Editor.

FrontPage Editor is used to open Web pages and add new pages to a site. It is also used to add to and edit the content of Web pages. The Editor is easy to use because it displays the page you are designing almost as it will appear on the Web. FrontPage Editor uses a WYSIWYG interface, meaning What You See Is What You Get. You won't have to switch back and forth between FrontPage and a browser to see what you've done.

In this chapter, you will open a FrontPage Web page in the Editor, then discover how to open other types of files, such as WordPerfect and Word documents, and pages on the Web itself. Next, you'll add a Web page to a site and save your work. Finally, you will discover how to create a custom Web page template, use Print Preview, print a Web page, and close the Editor.

With both FrontPage Explorer and Editor, you can open many types of files, including FrontPage Web pages, other document files, such as a Word document or Excel spreadsheet, and even Web site pages on an intranet or the World Wide Web.

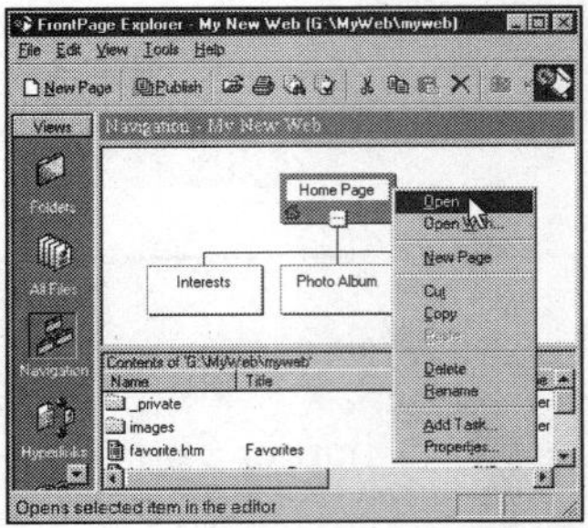

Figure 1. *Select Open from the pop-up menu.*

To open a FrontPage Web page:

1. Launch FrontPage Explorer.
2. Create a new Web site or open an existing one.
3. Double-click on a Web page icon or right mouse click on a Web page icon and select Open from the pop-up menu (**Figure 1**). FrontPage Editor will launch and open the Web page that you clicked (**Figure 2**). (You can do this in Folders, Navigation, All Files, or Hyperlinks views.)

or

1. If you are already working in Editor, choose Open from the File menu (**Figure 3**), or press Ctrl+O on the keyboard, or click the Open button on the toolbar (**Figure 4**). The Open dialog box will appear (**Figure 5**).
2. If you see the name of the page you want to open, click it to select it, and then click OK. The Web page you selected will open in the Editor.

Figure 2. *The Web page open in FrontPage Editor.*

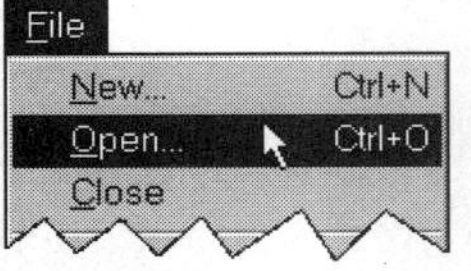

Figure 3. *Choose Open from the File menu.*

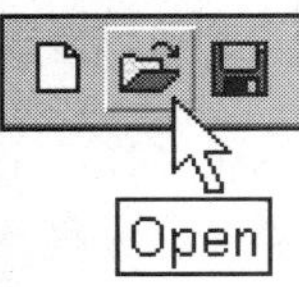

Figure 4. *Click the Open button on the Editor toolbar.*

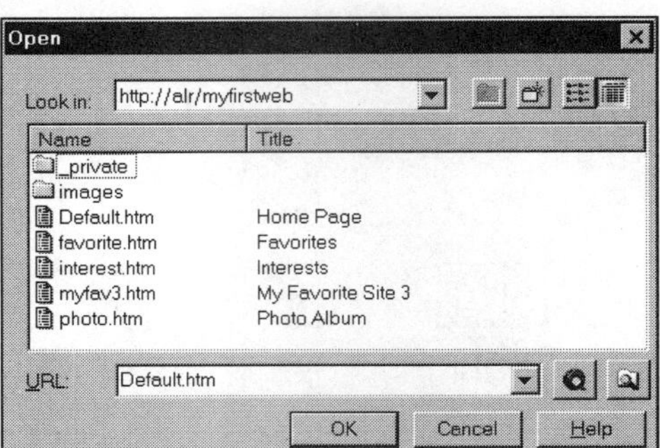

Figure 5. *The Open dialog box.*

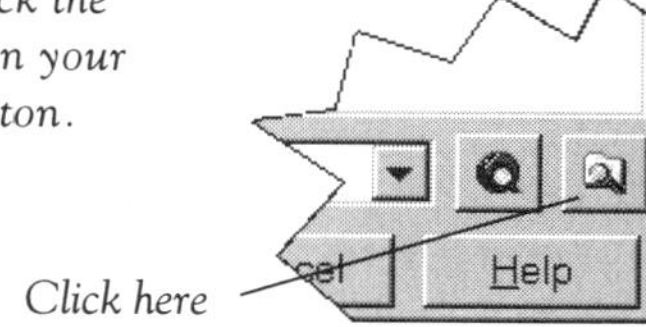

Figure 6. *Click the "Select a file on your computer" button.*

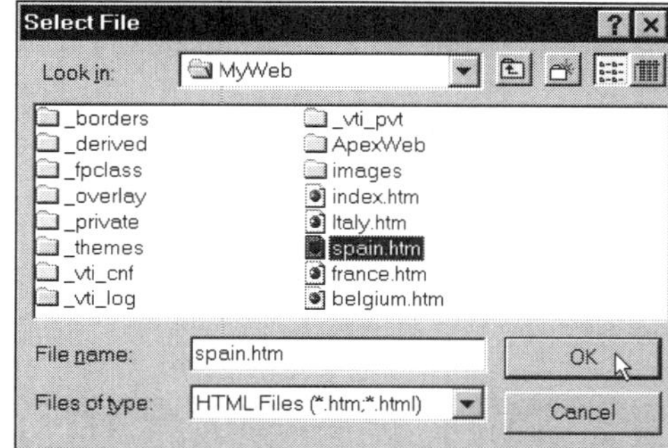

Figure 7. *Use the Select File dialog box to select a file to open.*

Figure 8. *Choose Show FrontPage Editor from the Tools menu.*

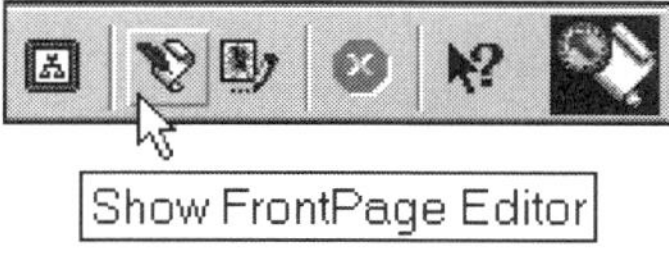

Figure 9. *Click the Show FrontPage Editor button on the Explorer toolbar.*

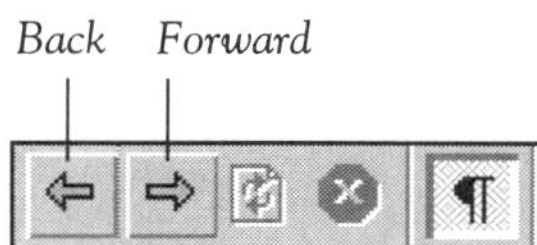

Figure 10. *Use the Back and Forward buttons to move between pages.*

3. If you don't see the name of the page you want to open:
   a. Click the "Select a file on your computer" button at the lower right of the Open dialog box (**Figure 6**). The Select File dialog box will open (**Figure 7**).
   b. Use the dialog box to select the file, then click OK to return to the Open dialog box.
   c. Click OK again. The Web page you selected will open.

Tips:

- You can also open the Editor from Explorer by choosing Show FrontPage Editor from the Tools menu (**Figure 8**) or clicking the Show FrontPage Editor button on the toolbar (**Figure 9**).
- You can open several Web pages in the Editor at the same time. To quickly move between these pages, click the Forward and Back buttons on the toolbar (**Figure 10**) or select the page from the Window menu (**Figure 11**).

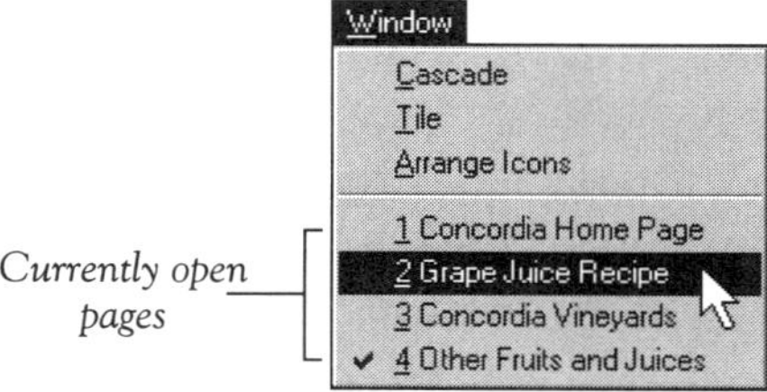

Figure 11. *Use the Window menu to move from open page to open page.*

To open another type of document:

1. In the Editor, choose Open from the File menu (**Figure 3**) or click the Open button on the toolbar (**Figure 4**). The Open dialog box will appear (**Figure 5**).
2. Click the "Select a file on your computer" button at the lower right of the Open dialog box (**Figure 6**). The Select File dialog box will open (**Figure 12**).
3. Locate the file you want to open. If you don't know the extension of your file, select All Files (*.*) from the Files of type drop-down list. When you find the file, select it, then click OK.
4. The Open File As dialog box will appear (**Figure 13**). Use this dialog box to choose how the file will be opened. FrontPage will automatically select the best choice, so click OK.
5. FrontPage will translate the file and open it in the Editor (**Figure 14**). You can now work with it like any other FrontPage file.

Tip:

- You can open many types of files in the Editor, including Word and WordPerfect documents (.doc and .wpd), Excel worksheets (.xls and .xlw), and HTML files (.htm and .html) not created in FrontPage.

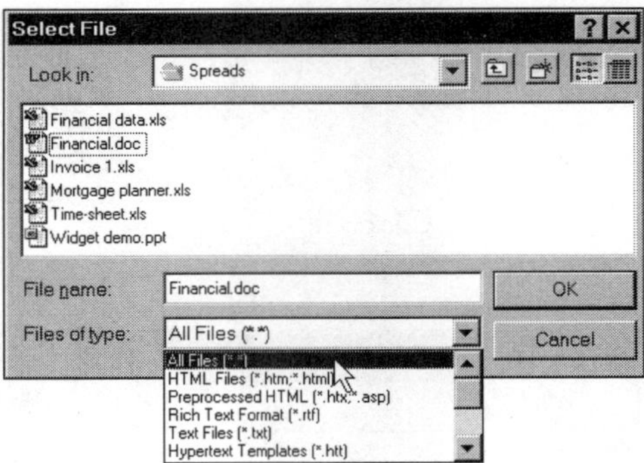

Figure 12. *Use the Select File dialog box to select a file to open in the Editor.*

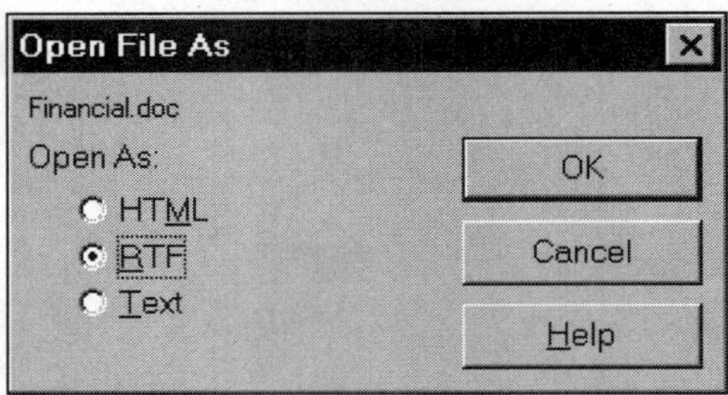

Figure 13. *Use the radio buttons to select the format with which a file will be opened, then click OK.*

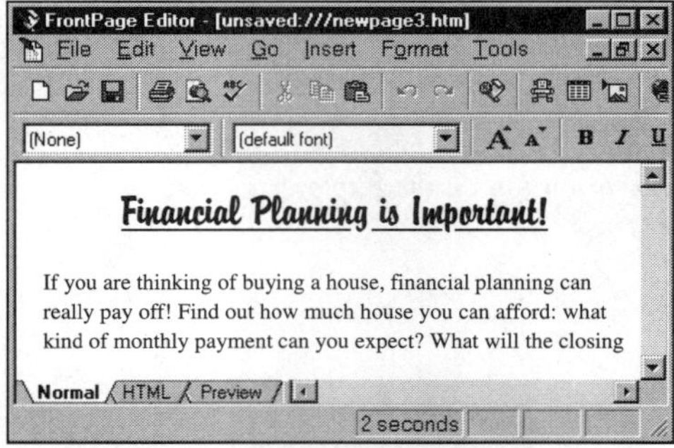

Figure 14. *FrontPage translates the document and loads it into the Editor.*

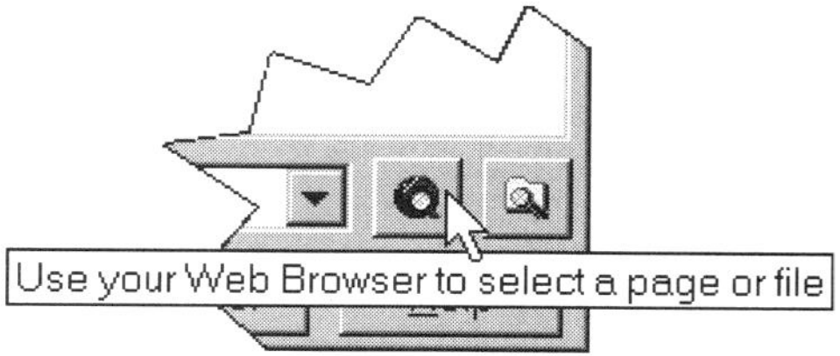

Figure 15. *Click the button near the bottom right of the Open dialog box to select a page from the World Wide Web.*

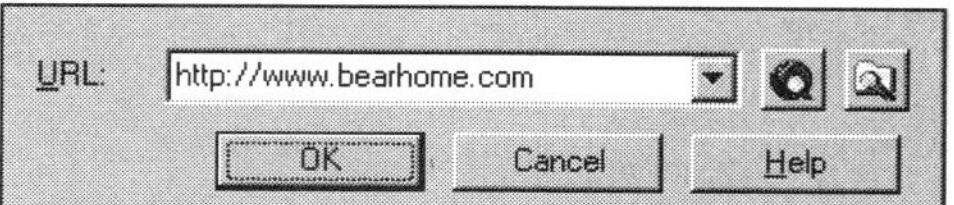

Figure 16. *When you minimize your browser, the address of the Web page appears in the URL drop-down list.*

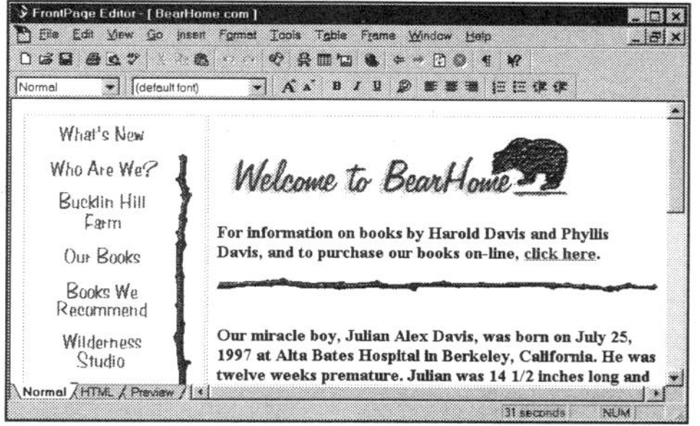

Figure 17. *A page on the Web opened in the Editor.*

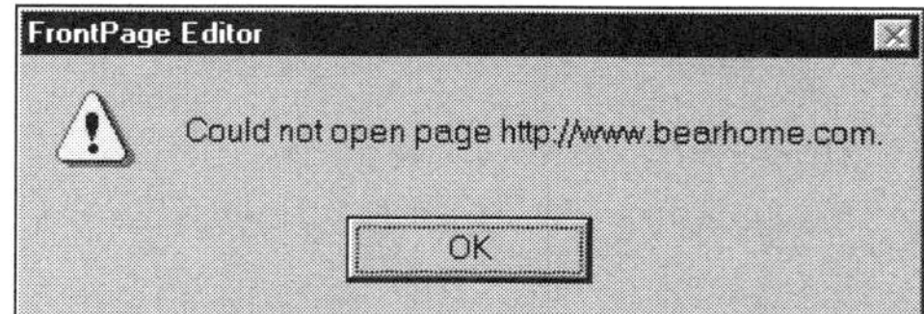

Figure 18. *This error message tells you FrontPage cannot open the Web page.*

To open a Web page that's on an intranet or the Web:

1. In the Editor, choose Open from the File menu (**Figure 3**) or click the Open button on the toolbar (**Figure 4**). The Open dialog box will appear (**Figure 5**).
2. Click the "Use your Web Browser to select a page or file" button at the lower right of the dialog box (**Figure 15**). Your default browser will open. If you aren't already connected to the Web, you will be prompted to do so.
3. Use your browser to move to the page you want to open.
4. Minimize your browser (don't close it) and don't disconnect. The address of the Web page will appear in the URL drop-down list at the bottom of the Open dialog box (**Figure 16**).
5. Click OK. The page will load into the Editor (**Figure 17**).

Tip:

- If you are trying to open a page on the Web and you get an error message (**Figure 18**), check to see if your connection to the Web is still live. Then, make sure the connection is working by viewing the page you want to open with a browser.

To add a new Web page to a site:

1. Open the Web site in Explorer, then move to the Editor by double-clicking on a page file or clicking the Show FrontPage Editor button on the toolbar.
2. In the Editor, choose New from the File menu (**Figure 19**), or press Ctrl+N on the keyboard. The New dialog box will appear (**Figure 20**), displaying an extensive list of types of Web pages (see the next page for a brief description of many of the templates and wizards).
3. Select a template or wizard from the list box.
4. Click OK. The new page will open in the Editor. If you selected a wizard, FrontPage will ask you various questions first, so it can customize your new page before creating it.

Tip:

- When you add a new page to a site, it is not automatically saved with the site. To make sure you don't lose any work, save your changes frequently! See page 86 for details on saving a Web page.

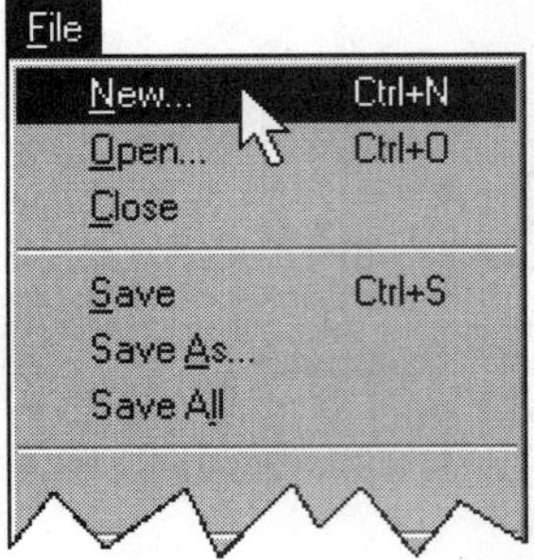

Figure 19. *Choose New from the File menu.*

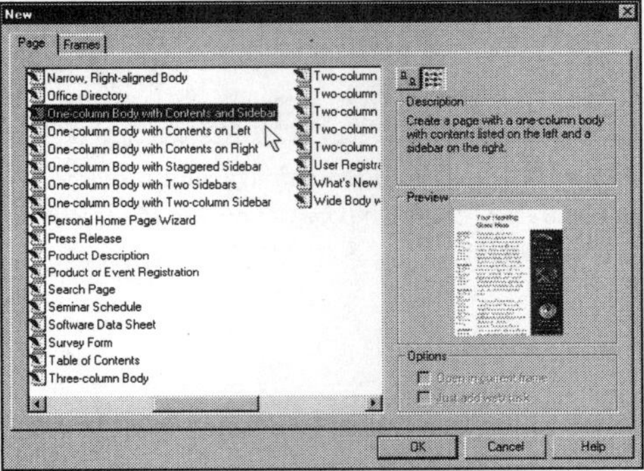

Figure 20. *The New dialog box offers many templates and wizards from which to choose.*

WHAT HAPPENS IF I CLICK THE NEW BUTTON ON THE TOOLBAR?

Clicking the New button is not the same as choosing New from the File menu or pressing Ctrl+N on the keyboard. If you click the New button, the New dialog box won't appear. Instead, a new, blank Web page will be created. If the open Web site uses a theme, that theme will be applied to the new page.

Add a New Page to a Web Site

FRONTPAGE WEB PAGE WIZARDS AND TEMPLATES

The New dialog box offers many templates and wizards from which to choose. These wizards and templates are used to create specific kinds of Web pages, based on your input. You'll probably understand what each wizard and template is supposed to do just by looking at its title. Here's a sampling of what's available:

- ***Normal Page*** This template creates a blank page. If the open Web site uses a theme, that theme will be applied to the new page.
- ***Bibliography*** If you need to create a bibliography page for your site, this template will get you started with some examples.
- ***Confirmation Form*** If your Web site will be collecting data from users, this template will create a page that displays the information entered by the users.
- ***Frequently Asked Questions*** Also known as a FAQ sheet or page, this template creates a page where users can get answers to questions.
- ***Guest Book*** This template helps you generate a page that visitors can use to comment on your Web site.
- ***Office Directory*** This template is used to create a complete directory of a company's employees and their locations.
- ***Search Page*** If you want users of your site to be able to search for keywords throughout the entire site, this template is for you.
- ***Table of Conents*** This template automatically builds a Web page listing all the pages in your site, showing them in outline form.
- ***What's New*** This template gets you started on creating a page that lists changes to your site by date.

FrontPage 98 ships with over forty Web page templates and wizards. To see the complete list and a description of each one, check out the list box in the New dialog box (select New from the File menu to open it). When you select a template or wizard from the list, its description appears in the Description area.

If you don't see a template or wizard on the list that fits your needs or if you will be creating several pages with the same look, you can create a custom template. For directions on how to do this, see page 88.

To save your work:

In the Editor, choose Save from the File menu (**Figure 21**) or press Ctrl+S on the keyboard or click the Save button on the toolbar (**Figure 22**).

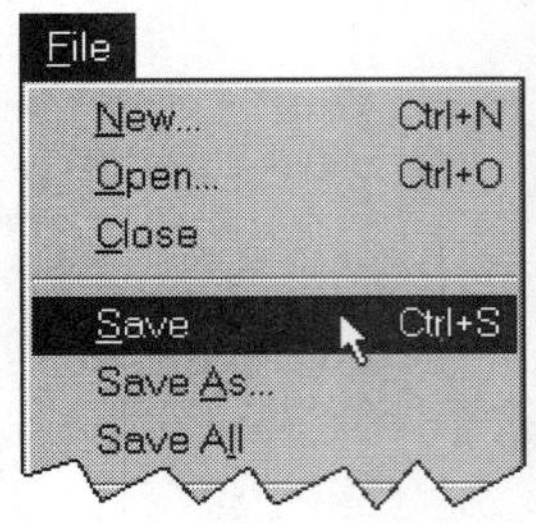

Figure 21. *Choose Save from the File menu.*

Tips:

- If you have added a new page to your site, the Save As dialog box will open (**Figure 23**). This dialog box is used to give the page a name and title and set the location where it's saved. For a complete description of how to use this dialog box, see "To save a copy of a page" on the next page.
- If you have added a graphic or multimedia file to your site, special Save As dialog boxes will open. For a description of these dialog boxes, see Chapter 10.

Figure 22. *Click the Save button on the toolbar.*

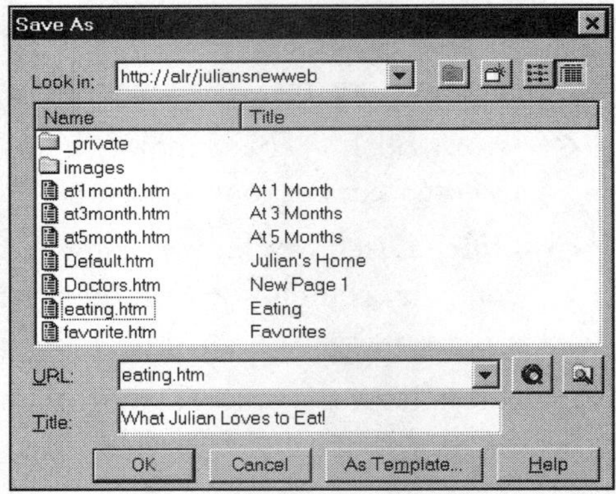

Figure 23. *The Save As dialog box.*

To save changes to all open pages:

Choose Save All from the File menu (**Figure 24**).

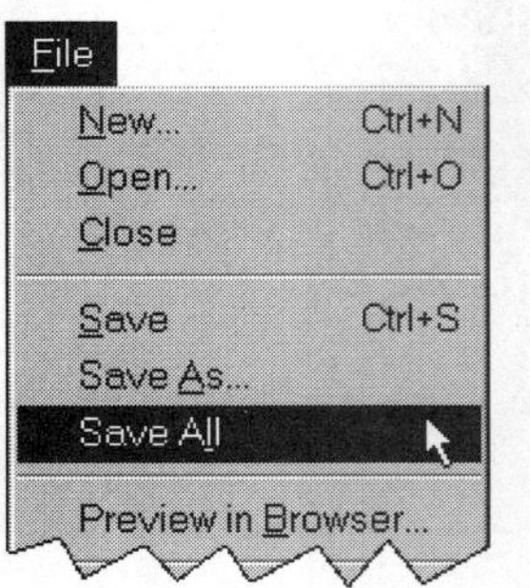

Figure 24. *Choose Save All from the File menu.*

Save Your Work; Save All Open Pages

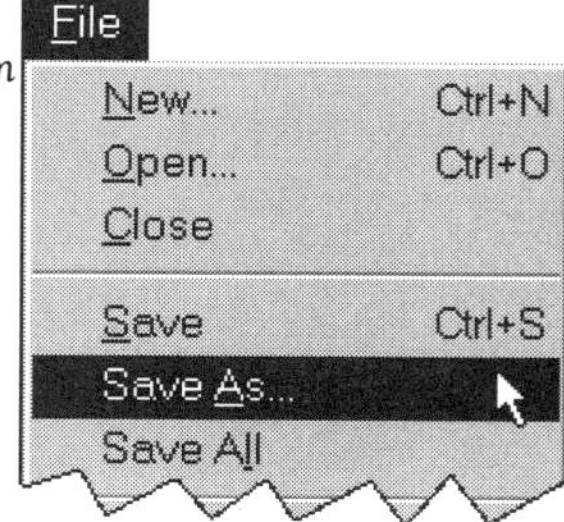

Figure 25. *Choose Save As from the File menu.*

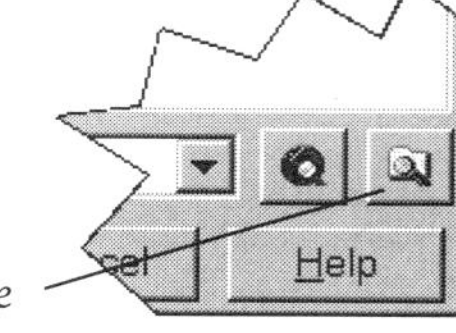

Figure 26. *Click the "Select a file on your computer" button.*

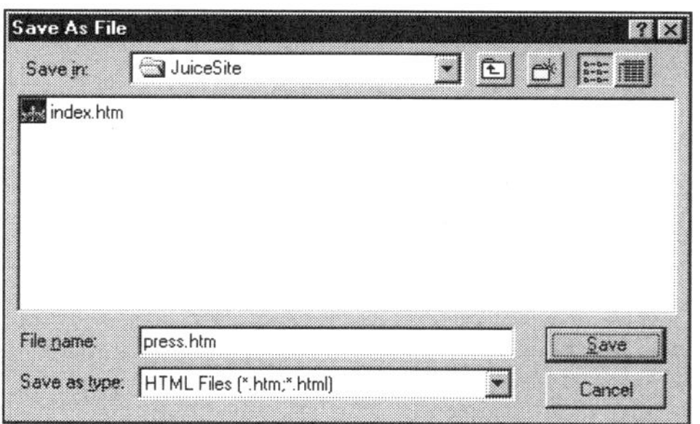

Figure 27. *The Save As File dialog box lets you save a Web page on a hard drive.*

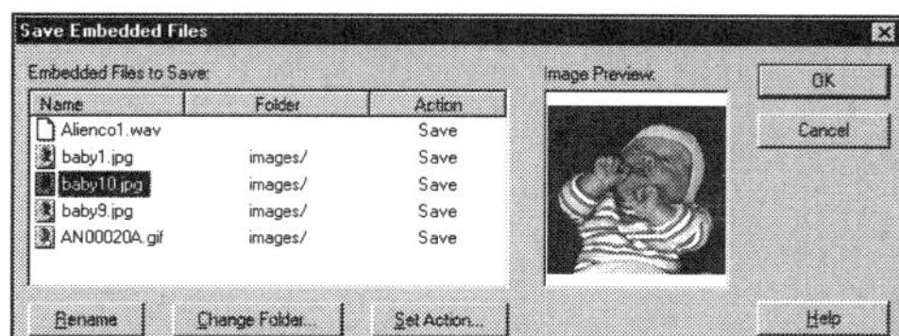

Figure 28. *The Save Embedded Files dialog box lets you set where sound, graphic, and video files are saved.*

To save a copy of a page:

1. Open the page in the Editor.
2. Choose Save As from the File menu (**Figure 25**). The Save As dialog box will open (**Figure 23**).
3. Type a Web address for the page in the URL text box, then enter a title in the Title text box.
4. You can save the page in two ways:
   - If you have a Web site open that is loaded on a server, the page will automatically be saved with that Web site. Click OK to save the Web page.
   - If you want to save the Web page on a hard drive instead of a server, click the "Select a file on your computer" button (**Figure 26**). Use the Save As File dialog box that opens (**Figure 27**) to move to a location for the file, enter a name in the File name text box, then click Save.
5. If your Web page contains any sounds, images, or other elements, the Save Embedded Files dialog box will open (**Figure 28**). Use this dialog box to set the files' names and the location where they are stored. Click OK when you are done.

Part of the beauty of FrontPage is being able to quickly create Web pages. If you don't see a Web page template that contains what you need, you can create your own custom template. For instance, if you are part of a team designing a Web site and all of you need to create pages with the same background color, fonts, and company logos, then a template will minimize the work and help create a consistent look.

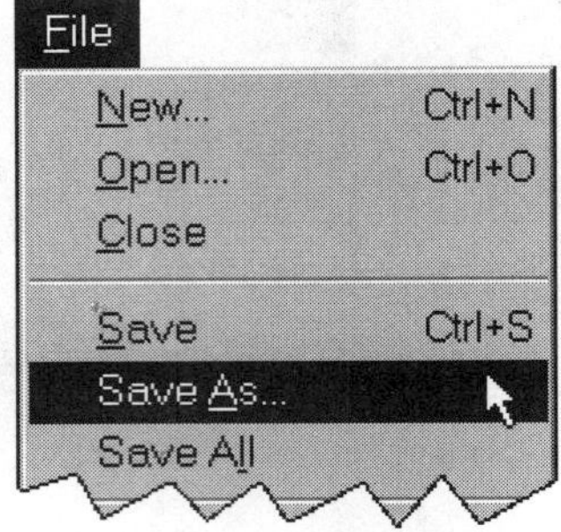

Figure 29. *Choose Save As from the File menu.*

To create a Web page template:

1. In the Editor, create a new Web page using the template that is closest to the template you want to create.
2. Customize the Web page with the content, such as logos, custom navigation buttons, disclaimer text, etc., that you want to appear when a Web page is created with your template.
3. Choose Save As from the File menu (**Figure 29**). The Save As dialog box will open (**Figure 30**).
4. Click the As Template button. The Save As Template dialog box will open (**Figure 31**).
5. Type in a Title, Name, and Description for the custom template.

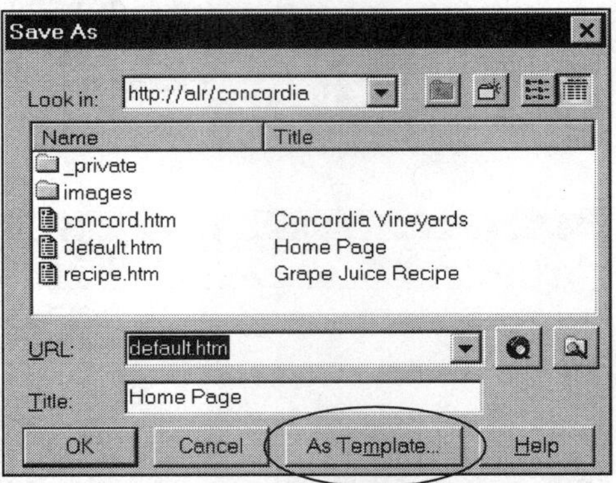

Figure 30. *Don't enter a title or path in the Save As dialog box, just click the As Template button.*

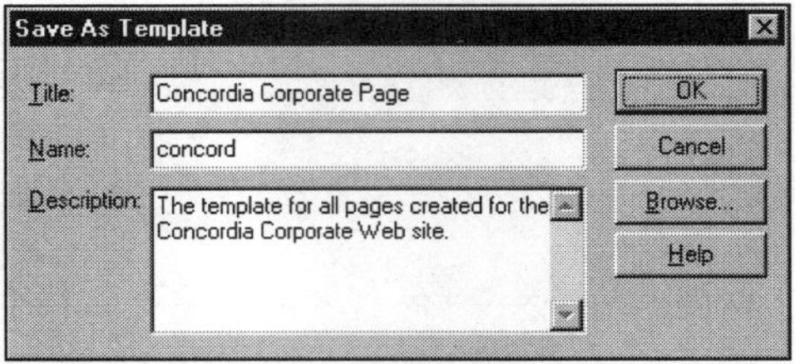

Figure 31. *Enter a title, name and description for your custom template.*

Create a Web Page Template

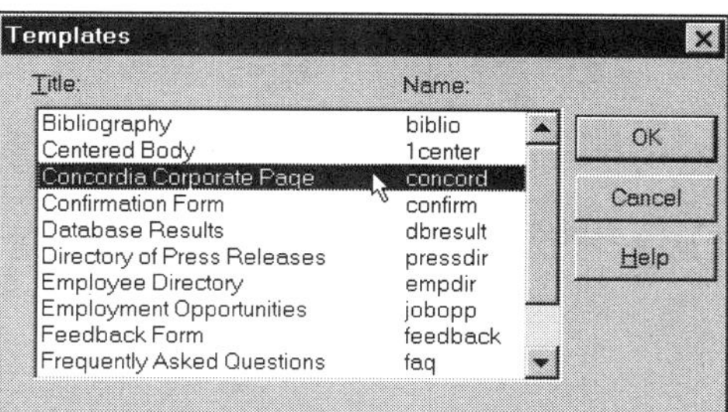

Figure 32. *Choose a template in the Templates dialog box that you want to replace.*

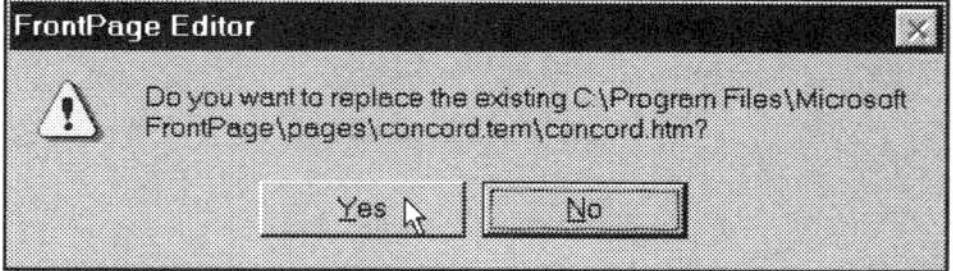

Figure 33. *Click Yes to replace an existing template.*

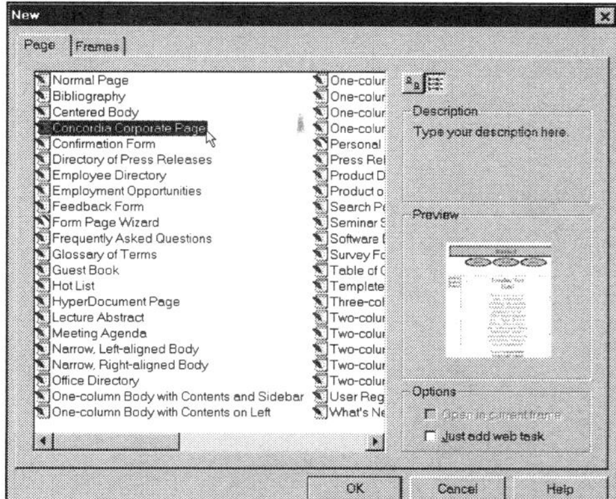

Figure 34. *The next time you create a new page, your custom template will be available in the New dialog box.*

6. To save the template in place of another template, click the Browse button. The Templates dialog box will open (**Figure 32**).
7. Select the template you want to replace, then click OK to close the Templates dialog box.
8. Click OK to close the Save As Template dialog box. If you selected a template for replacement in the Templates dialog box, FrontPage will ask you if are sure about that change (**Figure 33**). Click Yes.
9. If your template includes graphics, sounds, or videos, the Save Embedded Files dialog box will open (**Figure 28**). Use this dialog box to set where these files will be saved, and then click OK. FrontPage will save the Web page as a template. The next time you create a new Web page, you will see your custom template in the New dialog box (**Figure 34**).

Tip:

- If none of the existing templates use the elements you need for your custom template, start with a Normal Page template. This will create a blank Web page that you can modify to suit your needs.

Looking at a hard copy of a Web page can be helpful. Many times you will see things differently on a hard copy than you will on a computer monitor. Also, there are always folks who print Web pages for later reading. So, if you print copies of your Web pages, you can see what they will look like to others.

To see what a Web page will look like before you print it, use the Editor's Print Preview command.

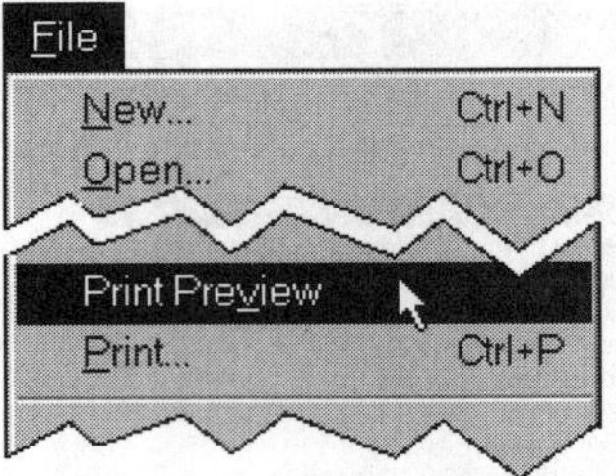

Figure 35. *Choose Print Preview from the File menu.*

To view a Web page in Print Preview:

1. Open the page you want to preview in the Editor.
2. Choose Print Preview from the File menu (**Figure 35**). The Web page will appear in a Print Preview window (**Figure 36**).
3. To print the page from this window, click Print. To close the window and make adjustments to the Web page, click Close.

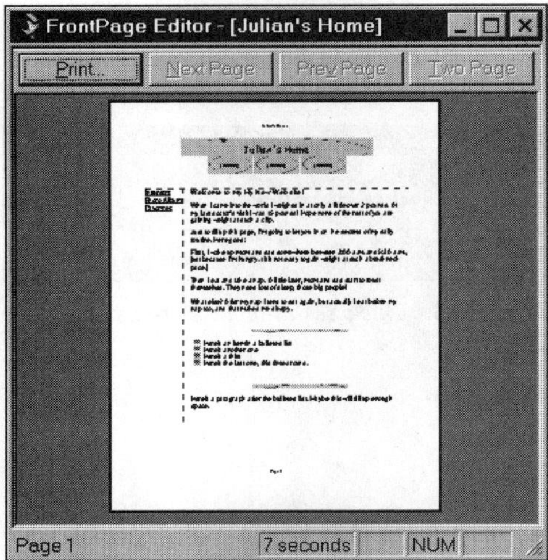

Figure 36. *A Web page displayed in the Print Preview window.*

Tip:

- What you see in Print Preview is not what the user will see in a browser. Check out page 123 for information about viewing your Web pages in the browser(s) you have installed on your computer.

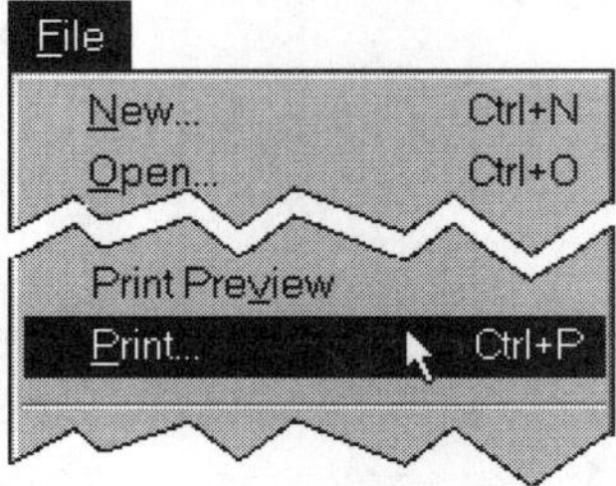

Figure 37. *Choose Print from the File menu.*

View a Web Page in Print Preview

Figure 38. *Click Print on the toolbar.*

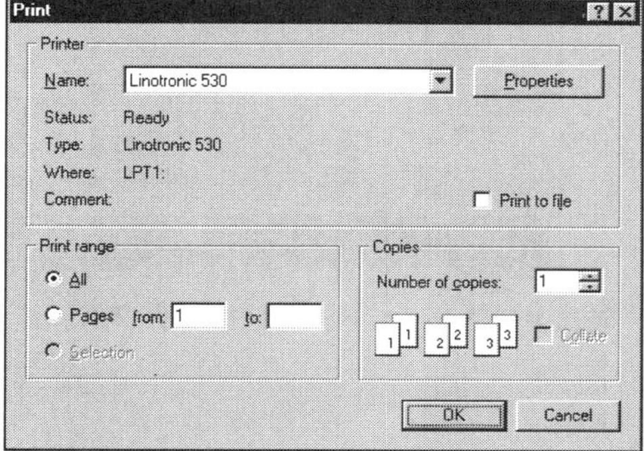

Figure 39. *The standard Windows Print dialog box lets you change settings for your printer. To print the Web page, click OK.*

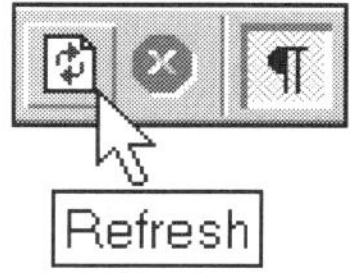

Figure 40. *Click Refresh on the toolbar.*

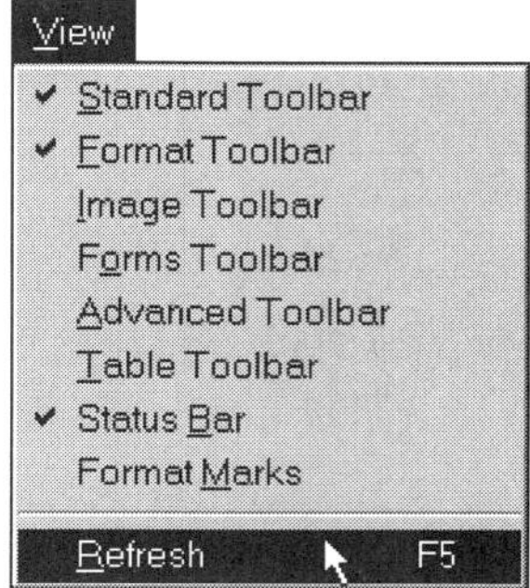

Figure 41. *Choose Refresh from the View menu.*

To print a Web page:

1. Open the Web page you want to print in the Editor.
2. Choose Print from the File menu (**Figure 37**), or press Ctrl+P on the keyboard, or click the Print button on the toolbar (**Figure 38**). The standard Windows Print dialog box will open (**Figure 39**).
3. Click OK. The Web page will print.

Tips:

- If you need to change the settings for your printer (for instance, you want to print the page in a landscape orientation), click the Properties button in the Print dialog box.
- If your Web page is longer than the paper you are printing on, FrontPage Editor will split the Web page onto multiple printed pages.

Refreshing Your Pages

If you are working on a page and want to revert to the last saved version of that page, click the Refresh button on the toolbar (**Figure 40**) or choose Refresh from the View menu (**Figure 41**). Refreshing a page is also handy for displaying changes made to a page by another person.

To exit FrontPage Editor:

Choose Exit from the File menu (**Figure 42**).

or

Press Alt+F4 on the keyboard.

or

Click the Close button at the extreme upper-right corner of the Editor window (**Figure 43**).

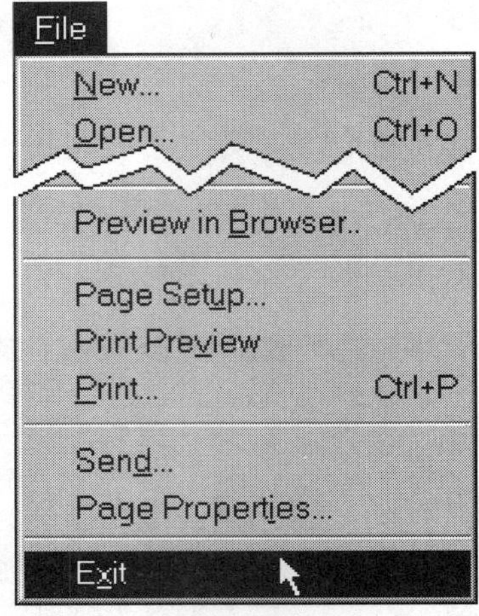

Figure 42. *Choose Exit from the File menu.*

Tip:

- If you exit FrontPage Editor with open Web pages that haven't been saved, FrontPage will ask whether you want to save the changes before closing.

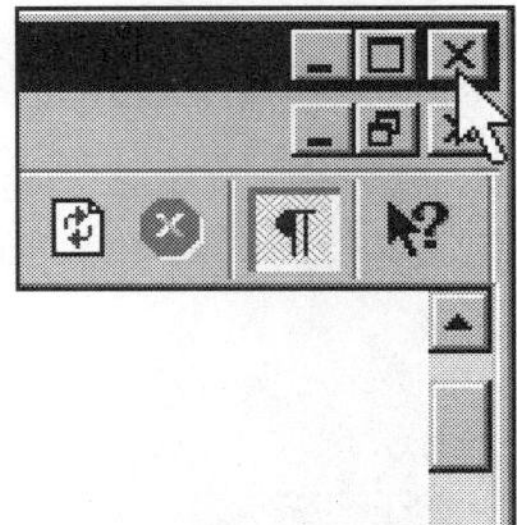

Figure 43. *Click the Close button in the extreme upper-right corner of the Editor window.*

SUMMARY

In this chapter you learned how to:

- Launch FrontPage Editor
- Open a Web page
- Open other documents
- Create a new Web page
- Save your work
- Create a custom template
- Preview and print a Web page
- Exit the Editor

7 Working with Text

Now that you know how to create Web sites with Explorer and Web pages with the Editor, it's time to start adding content to your Web pages.

If you are familiar with Microsoft Word, you have probably already noticed that FrontPage Editor resembles Word. In fact, it works in a very similar fashion and uses Word's most popular keyboard shortcuts and toolbars. FrontPage Editor works just like a word processing program, using menus, toolbar buttons, and a work space where you add content to and design your Web pages.

This chapter shows you how to add text, comments, and special characters to a Web page. Then, you'll find out how to select a portion of text and select everything on a page. Next you'll discover how to delete, move, and copy text, find and replace words, and check the spelling on a Web page. Finally, you will move back to the FrontPage Explorer and learn how easy it is to find and replace words and spell check an entire Web site.

To enter text on a Web page:

1. Click on the place where you want the text to start (**Figure 1**). A vertical, blinking line will appear where you clicked. This is called the *insertion marker.*
2. Type your text. As you type, corresponding characters will appear on the screen (**Figure 2**).

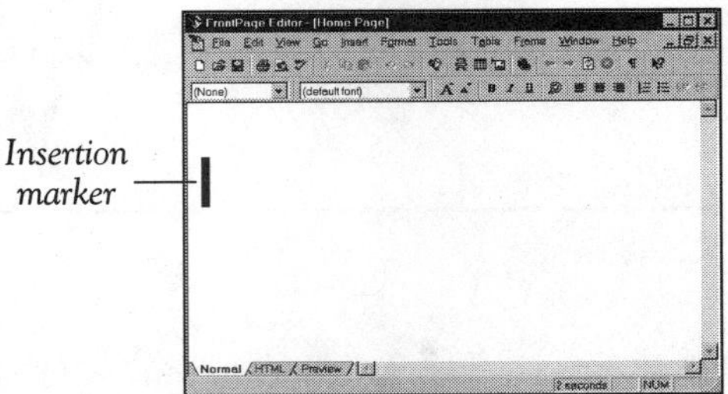

Figure 1. *Click where you want the text to start.*

Tip:

- Since the Editor works like a word processor, the text will automatically wrap when you reach the end of a line.

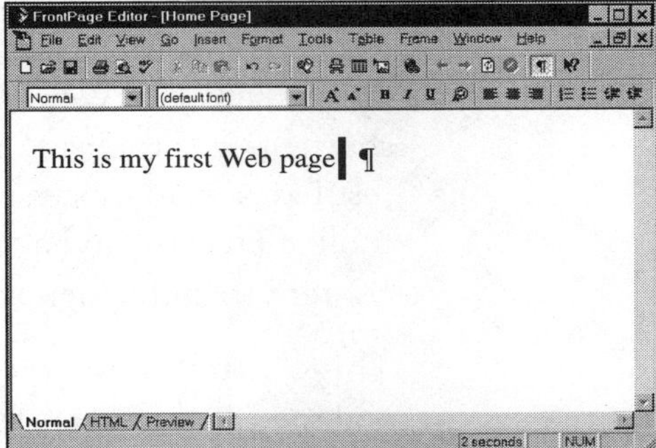

Figure 2. *As you type, the characters appear in the Editor.*

There are two ways to add breaks between lines of text. Creating a new paragraph adds a blank line between paragraphs. A *line break* starts a new line without adding any blank lines in between.

To start a new paragraph:

1. Move the insertion marker to the place where you want to end a paragraph.
2. Press the Enter key on the keyboard. The insertion marker will move down two lines (**Figure 3**).

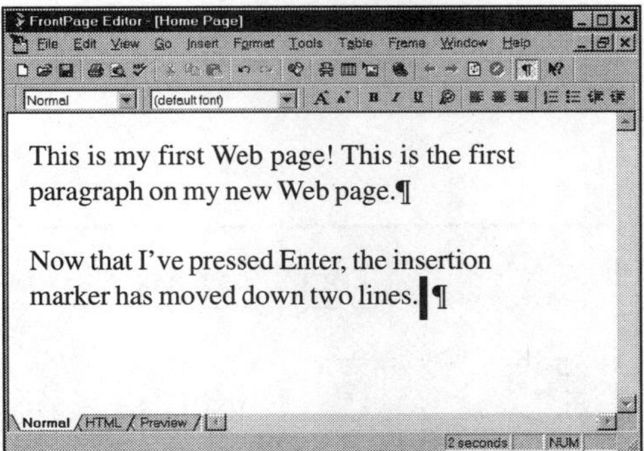

Figure 3. *When you press the Enter key, the insertion marker moves down two lines.*

Enter Text; Start a New Paragraph

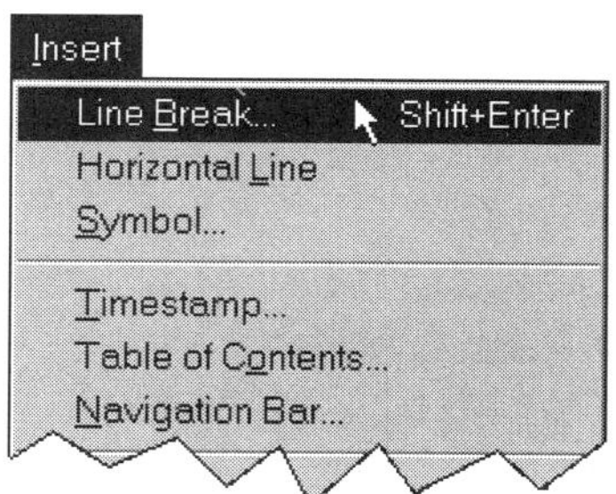

Figure 4. *Choose Line Break from the Insert menu.*

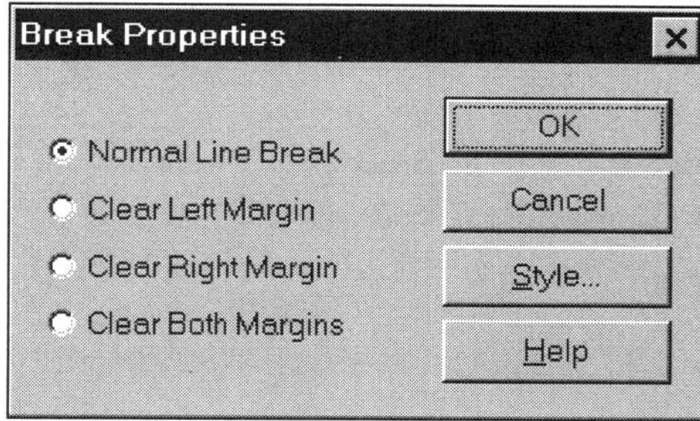

Figure 5. *Select the Normal Line Break radio button in the Break Properties dialog box, then click OK.*

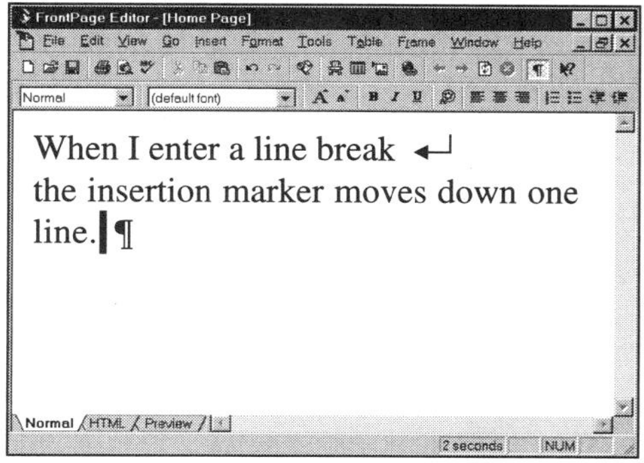

Figure 6. *A line break moves the insertion marker to the next line down.*

To add a line break:

1. Move the insertion marker to the place where you want to add the line break.
2. Choose Line Break from the Insert menu (**Figure 4**). The Break Properties dialog box will open (**Figure 5**).
3. Select the Normal Line Break radio button.
4. Click OK. A left pointing arrow will appear at the end of the line to mark the line break and the insertion marker will move down one line. As you type more text, you will see that there's no extra space between the lines (**Figure 6**).

Tip:

- You can also press Shift+Enter on the keyboard to insert a line break.

What's my tag?

The HTML tag for a paragraph is <p>. The tag for a line break is <br>. They are used like this:

<p>I am a paragraph.</p>

I am a sentence that
uses a line break.

Add a Line Break

Comments are the electronic version of "sticky notes." You can add comments to your Web pages using the Editor as a reminder to yourself or for someone else working on the Web page. You will be able to see them in the Editor window, but they will be invisible to folks browsing your pages on the Web.

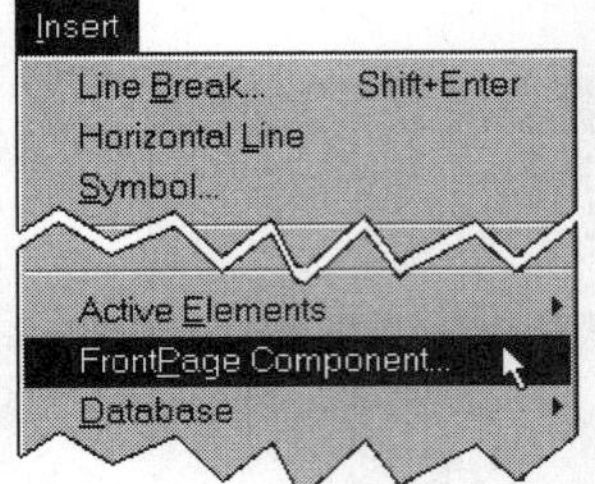

Figure 7. *Choose FrontPage Component from the Insert menu.*

To add a comment:

1. Move the insertion marker to the place where you want to add a comment.
2. Choose FrontPage Component from the Insert menu. The Insert FrontPage Component dialog box will appear (**Figure 8**).
3. Choose Comment from the Select a component list box.
4. Click OK. The Comment dialog box will appear (**Figure 9**).
5. Type your comment in the large text box.
6. Click OK. Your comment will be added to the Web page (**Figure 10**).

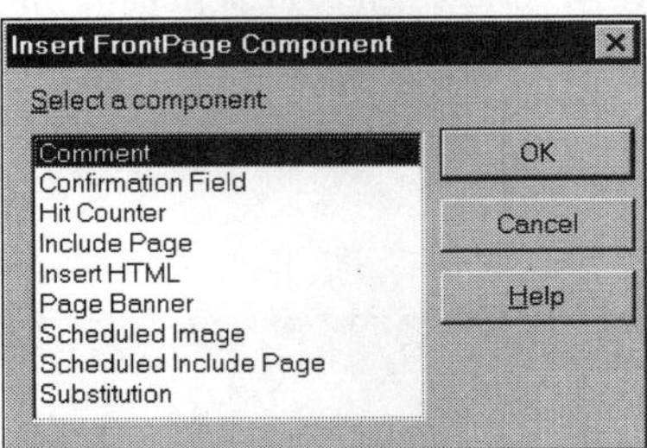

Figure 8. *Use the Select a component list box to choose Comment, then click OK.*

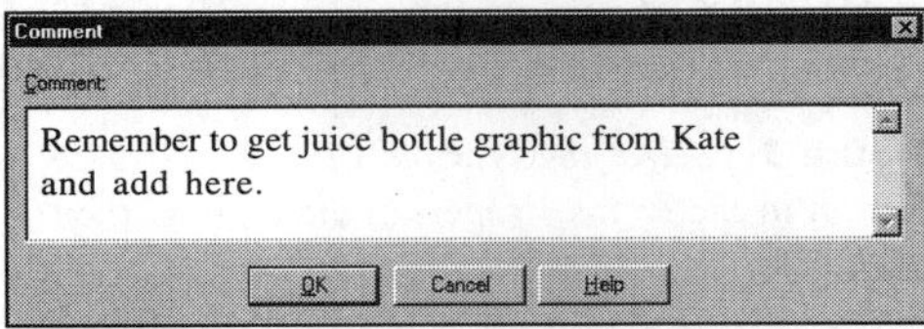

Figure 9. *Enter your comment in the dialog box, then click OK.*

Tip:

- If you want to change a comment's text, double-click on the comment or right click on the comment and select Comment Properties from the pop-up menu (**Figure 11**). The Comment dialog box will open. Change the comment, then click OK.

Figure 10. *The comment will appear on the Editor Web page.*

Add a Comment

Figure 11. *Select Comment Properties from the pop-up menu.*

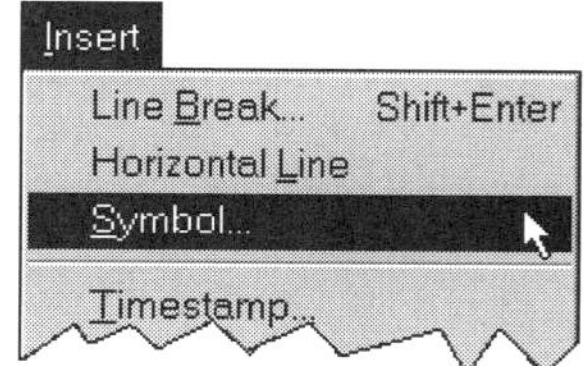

Figure 12. *Choose Symbol from the Insert menu.*

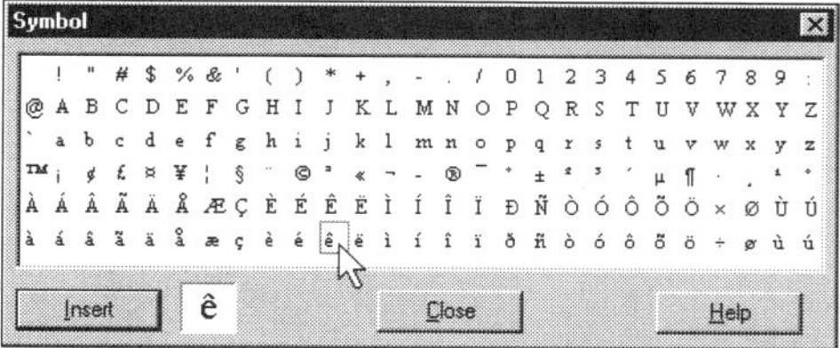

Figure 13. *Select the character you want to add, then click Insert.*

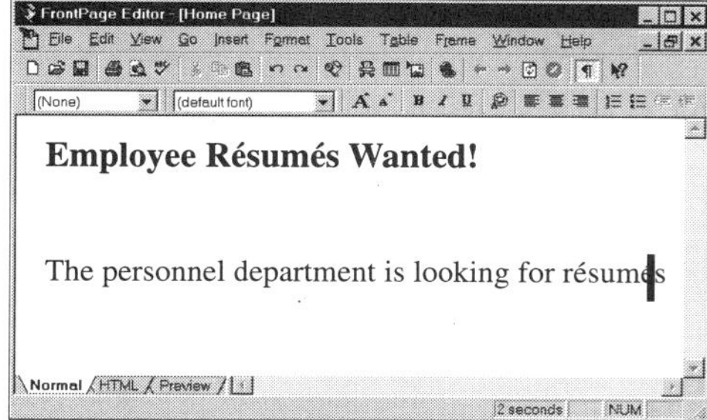

Figure 14. *When you click Insert, the symbol is added to your Web page.*

Many Web sites contain foreign words and measurements that use *special characters*. Special characters are those symbols—such as ©, é, and ™—that do not appear on a standard keyboard.

To insert a special character:

1. Move the insertion marker to the place where you want to insert a special character.
2. Choose Symbol from the Insert menu (**Figure 12**). The Symbol dialog box will open (**Figure 13**).
3. In the list box, click the symbol you want to insert. It will appear in the small window to the right of the Insert button.
4. Click Insert. The character will be added to your Web page (**Figure 14**). If you want to add another symbol, repeat steps 2 through 4.
5. Click Close. The dialog box will close and you can continue working on your Web page.

What's my tag?

The HTML tag for a comment is <!-- -->. It's used like this:

<!--This is a comment-->

To select text:

1. Position the mouse pointer where you want to start selecting text.
2. Press the left mouse button and drag across the text you want to select. The text will become highlighted as it is selected (**Figure 15**).

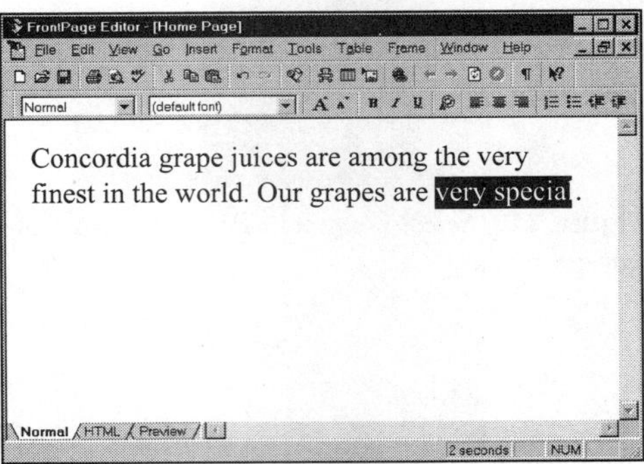

Figure 15. *Select text by dragging the mouse.*

Tips:

- To select an entire paragraph, hold down the Alt key, then click once.
- To select any amount of text, position the insertion marker at the beginning of the text you want to select, hold down the Shift key, and then click at the end of the text.

To deselect text:

Click the mouse anywhere in the Editor window.

To select everything on a page:

Choose Select All from the Edit Menu (**Figure 16**) or press Ctrl+A on the keyboard.

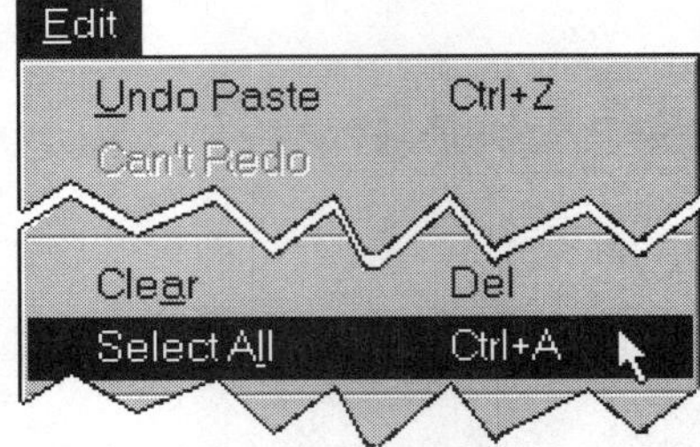

Figure 16. *Choose Select All from the Edit menu.*

To delete text:

1. Select the text you want to delete.
2. Choose Clear from the Edit menu (**Figure 17**) or press the Delete key or the Backspace key on the keyboard.

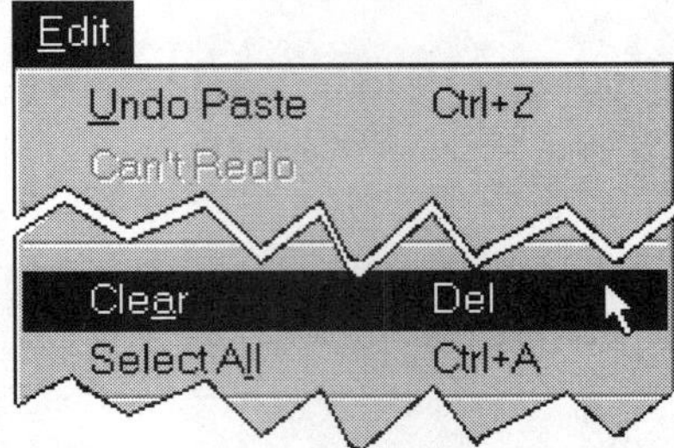

Figure 17. *Choose Clear from the Edit menu.*

Select Text; Select All; Delete Text

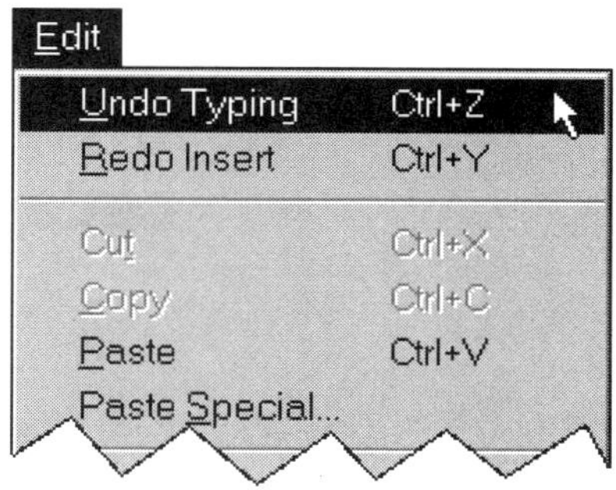

Figure 18. *Choose Undo from the Edit menu.*

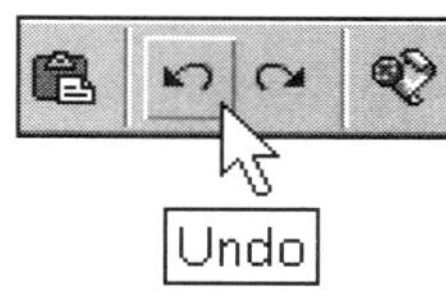

Figure 19. *Click the Undo button on the toolbar.*

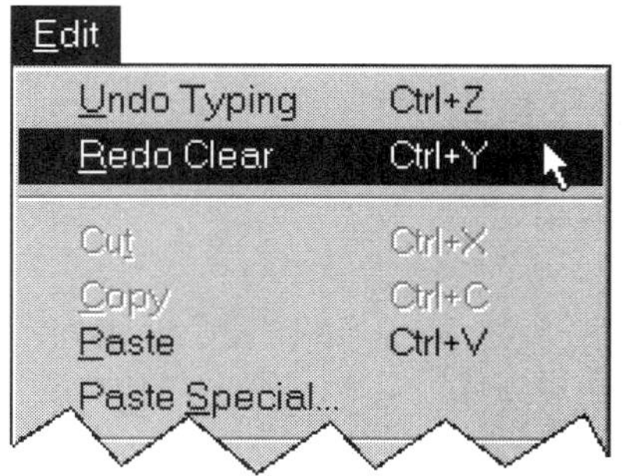

Figure 20. *Choose Redo from the Edit menu.*

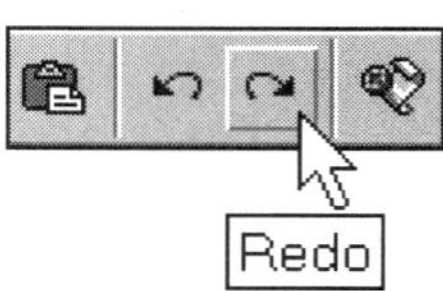

Figure 21. *Click the Redo button on the toolbar.*

Undo is a favorite command of many users. If you happen to delete or move something you don't mean to, don't panic! You can always undo.

To undo an action:

Choose Undo from the Edit menu (**Figure 18**) or press Ctrl+Z on the keyboard or click the Undo button on the toolbar (**Figure 19**).

Tips:

- In FrontPage Editor, you can undo up to the last 30 actions!
- The Undo command item on the Edit menu is dynamic, meaning that it changes depending on your previous action. For instance, if you just typed some text, it will read "Undo Typing;" if you just added a picture, it will read "Undo Insert."

To redo an action:

Choose Redo from the Edit menu (**Figure 20**) or press Ctrl+Y on the keyboard or click the Redo button on the toolbar (**Figure 21**).

Tip:

- You can redo up to the last 30 Undo commands.

To move text:

1. Select the text you want to move (**Figure 22**).
2. Position the mouse pointer over the selected text.
3. Press the left mouse button and drag the mouse to the new location. As you drag, the pointer will change to an arrow with a gray rectangle attached to it and the insertion marker will change to a gray line.
4. Release the mouse button. The selected text will spring to its new location (**Figure 23**).

or

1. Select the text you want to move.
2. Choose Cut from the Edit menu (**Figure 24**) or press Ctrl+X on the keyboard or click the Cut button on the toolbar (**Figure 25**).

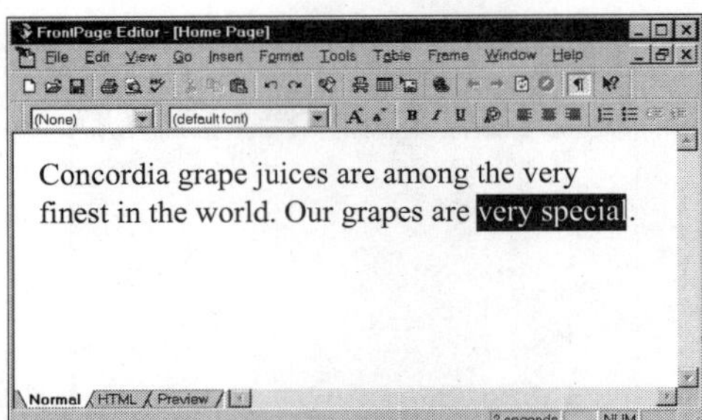

Figure 22. *Select the text you want to move.*

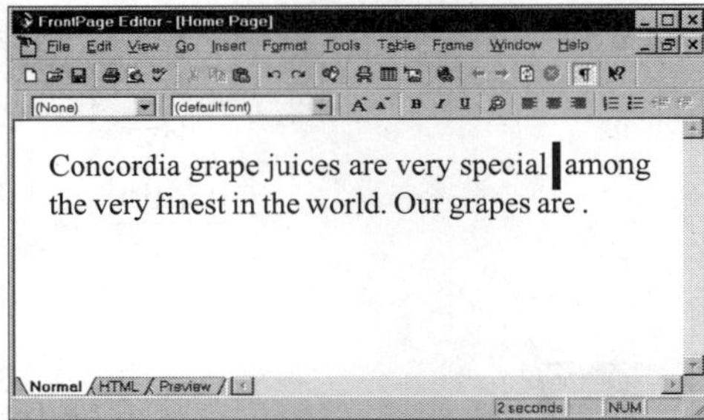

Figure 23. *When you release the mouse, the text moves to its new position.*

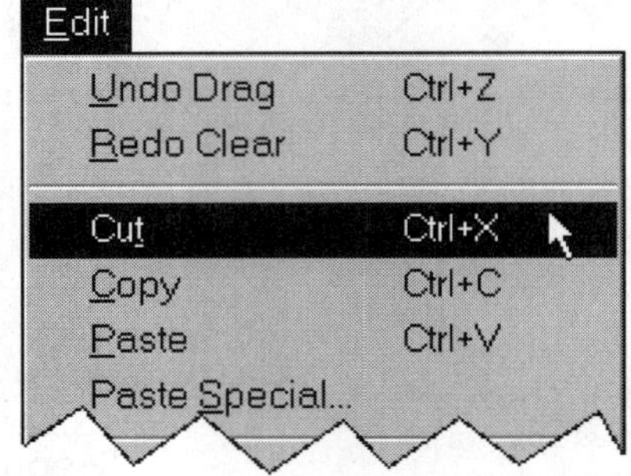

Figure 24. *Choose Cut from the Edit menu.*

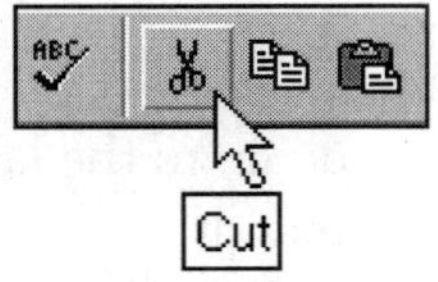

Figure 25. *Click the Cut button on the toolbar.*

Move Text

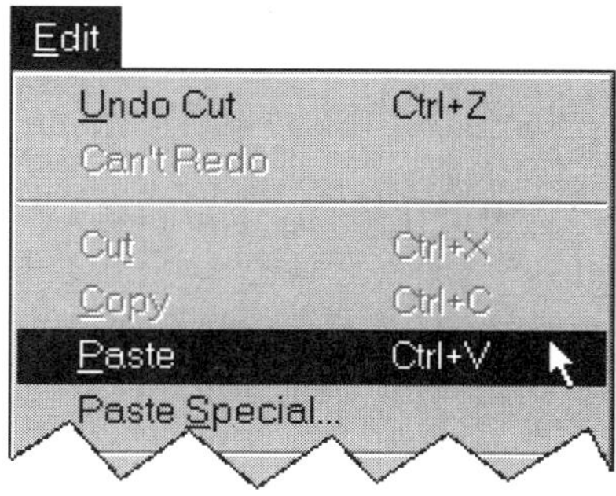

Figure 26. *Choose Paste from the Edit menu.*

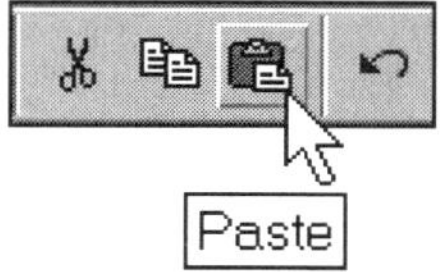

Figure 27. *Click the Paste button on the toolbar.*

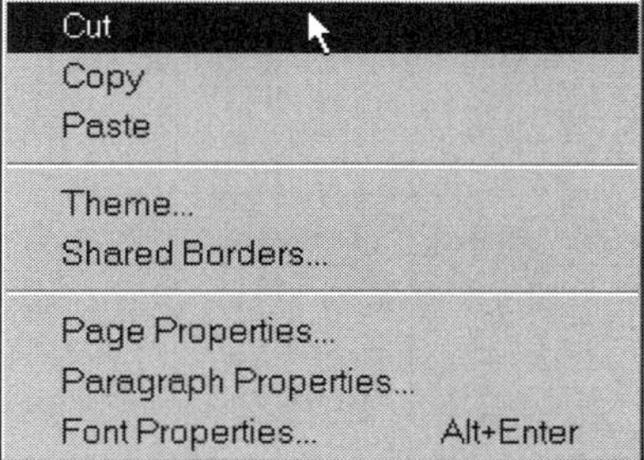

Figure 28. *Choose Cut from the pop-up menu.*

3. Position the insertion marker at the place where you want to move the text.
4. Choose Paste from the Edit menu (**Figure 26**) or press Ctrl+V on the keyboard or press the Paste button on the toolbar (**Figure 27**).

Tip:

- You can also right click on the selected text and choose Cut from the pop-up menu (**Figure 28**), then move the insertion point to where you want to place the text, right click, and choose Paste from the pop-up menu.

Hiding Format Marks

When you add a line break, a special line break format mark, ↵ , is added at the end of the line. Paragraph marks, ¶, also show up at the end of every paragraph. If you don't want to see these marks, just click the Show/Hide Paragraph button on the toolbar or choose Format Marks from the View menu. To show the marks again, just click the button or reselect the menu item.

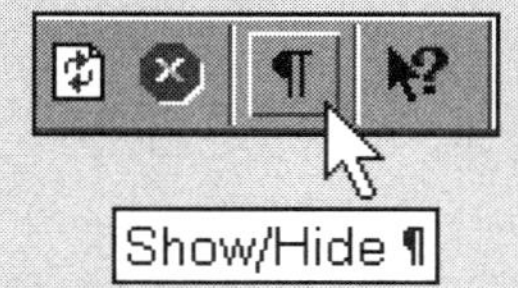

To copy text:

1. Select the text you want to copy (**Figure 29**).
2. Position the mouse pointer over the selected text.
3. Press the Ctrl key and the left mouse button. The mouse pointer will change to an arrow with a little plus sign attached to it.
4. Move the mouse to the new location for the copied text (**Figure 30**).
5. Release the mouse button and *then* the Ctrl key. (If you release the Ctrl key *before* the mouse button, the text will be moved instead of copied.) The copied text will appear in the new location.

or

1. Select the text you want to copy.
2. Click the Copy button on the toolbar (**Figure 31**) or press Ctrl+C on the keyboard or choose Copy from the Edit menu (**Figure 32**).

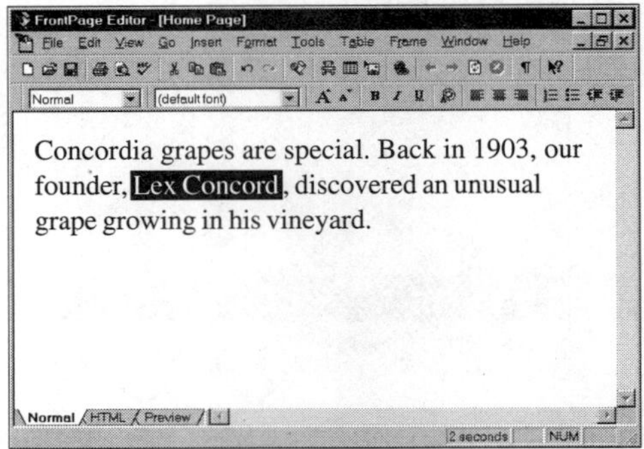

Figure 29. *Select the text you want to copy.*

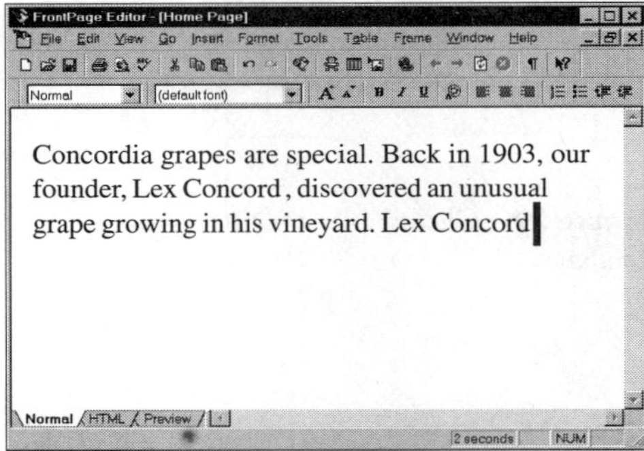

Figure 30. *When you release first the mouse button and then the Ctrl key, the copied text is added to the new position.*

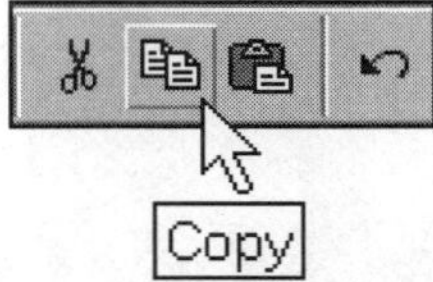

Figure 31. *Click the Copy button on the toolbar.*

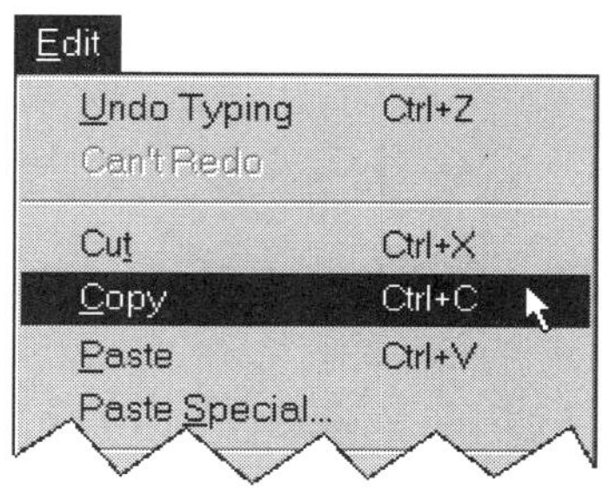

Figure 32. *Choose Copy from the Edit menu.*

Figure 33. *Click the Paste button on the toolbar.*

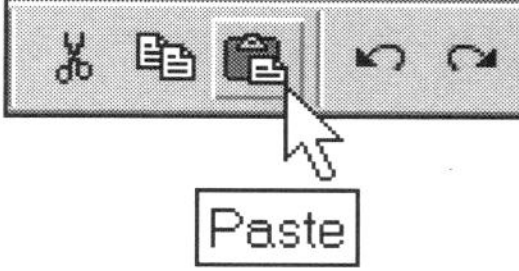

Figure 34. *Choose Copy from the pop-up menu.*

3. Position the insertion marker where you want to place the text.

4. Choose Paste from the Edit menu (**Figure 26**) or press Ctrl+V on the keyboard or click the Paste button on the toolbar (**Figure 33**). The copied text will appear in the new location.

Tip:

- You can also right click on the selected text and choose Copy from the pop-up menu (**Figure 34**), then move the insertion point to where you want to place the text, right click, and choose Paste from the pop-up menu.

Copy and Paste Text

THE WINDOWS CLIPBOARD

When you copy or cut text, it is held in the Windows Clipboard. The text will remain in the Clipboard until you cut or copy other text. This means you can paste in the same text any number of times if it suits your needs.

You can cut or paste text between two FrontPage Web pages by opening both pages in the Editor and toggling between them—cutting or copying text from one page and pasting it to another.

In addition, you can copy or cut text from other types of documents, such as a Word or WordPerfect document, then paste it into a FrontPage Web page.

FrontPage 98 makes it easy to find and/or replace any kind of text on your Web page.

To find text on a Web page:

1. In the Editor, choose Find from the Edit menu (**Figure 35**) or press Ctrl+F on the keyboard. The Find dialog box will open (**Figure 36**).
2. In the Find what text box type in the text you want to search for.
3. Using the radio buttons, select a direction for your search, up or down through the text.
4. Click Find Next. When FrontPage finds an instance of the text, it will highlight it (**Figure 37**). To find the next occurrence of the word, click Find Next again.
5. When you have finished searching the text, click Cancel or the Close button to close the dialog box.

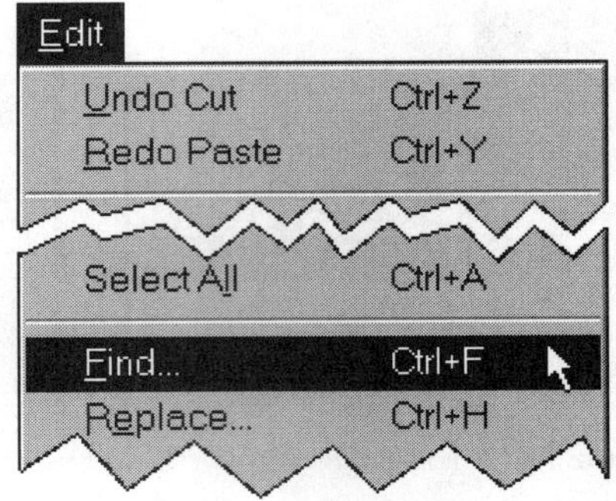

Figure 35. *Choose Find from the Edit menu.*

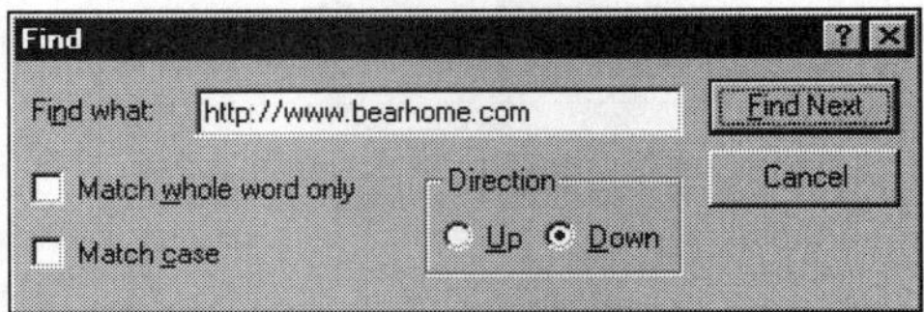

Figure 36. *Type the text you want to find in the Find what text box, then click Find Next.*

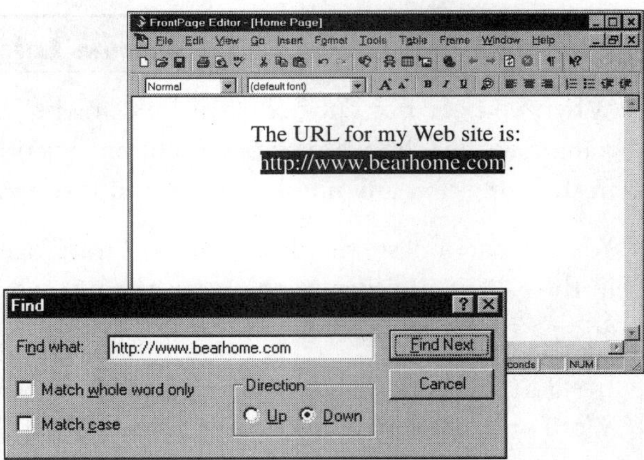

Figure 37. *When FrontPage finds a match, it highlights the text. To find the next match, click Find Next.*

Find Text on a Web Page

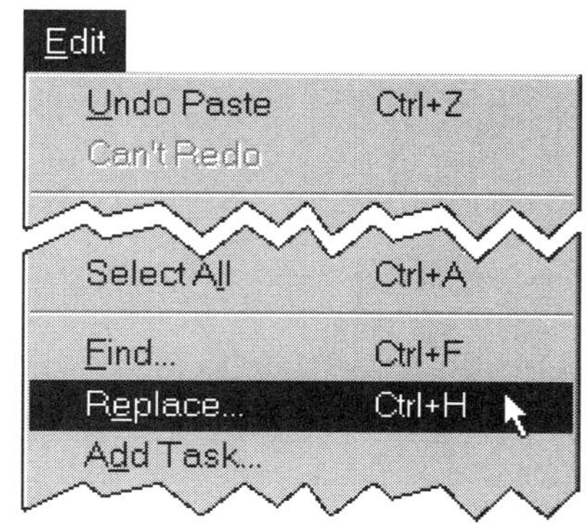

Figure 38. *Choose Replace from the Edit menu.*

Figure 39. *Enter the text you want to replace in the Find what text box. Next, enter the replacement text in the Replace with text box.*

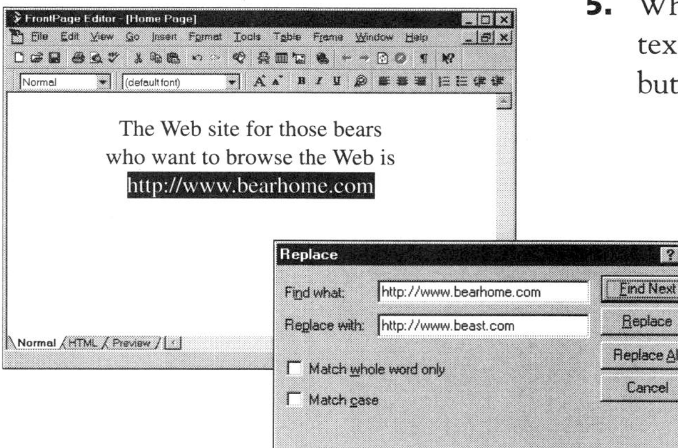

Figure 40. *When FrontPage finds a match, it highlights the text. To replace the text, click Replace. To move on to the next match, click Find Next.*

To replace text on a Web page:

1. In the Editor, choose Replace from the Edit menu (**Figure 38**)

   or

   press Ctrl+H on the keyboard. The Replace dialog box will appear (**Figure 39**).
2. In the Find what text box, type the text you want to replace.
3. In the Replace with text box, type in the text with which you want to replace the found text.
4. To replace all occurrences of the text on a page, click Replace All, or to locate the first matching occurrence, click Find Next. When the Editor finds the text, it will highlight it (**Figure 40**). You can then click Replace to change the text or click Find Next to move on to the next instance without changing the current one.
5. When you have finished replacing text, click Cancel or the Close button to close the dialog box.

Spelling is very important. How many times have you browsed a Web site and seen spelling errors? To avoid typos, let the Editor spell check your Web pages.

To spell check a Web page:

1. Open the page you want to check in the Editor.
2. Choose Spelling from the Tools menu (**Figure 41**), or press F7 on the keyboard, or click the Check Spelling button on the toolbar (**Figure 42**). The Spelling dialog box will open (**Figure 43**) and FrontPage will start spell checking.
3. If FrontPage finds a misspelling, the word will appear in the Not in Dictionary text box and offer a suggestion in the Change To text box. You can click:
   - Ignore: to ignore the current word
   - Ignore All: to ignore all instances of the word on the Web page
   - Change: to change the current word
   - Change All: to change all instances of the word on the Web page
   - Add: to add the word to the dictionary
   - Suggest: for a list of suggested words

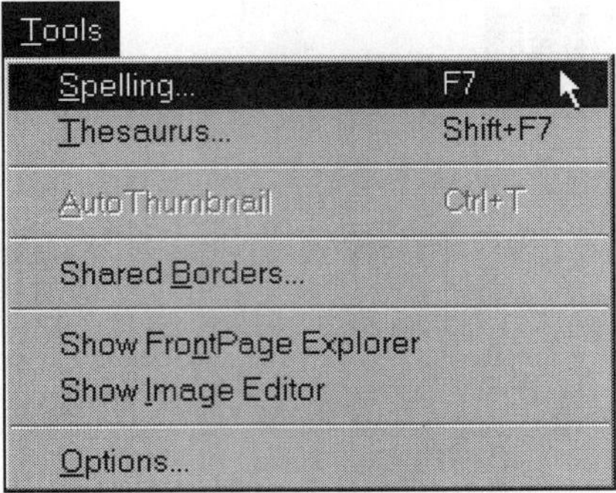

Figure 41. *Choose Spelling from the Tools menu.*

Figure 42. *Click the Check Spelling button on the toolbar.*

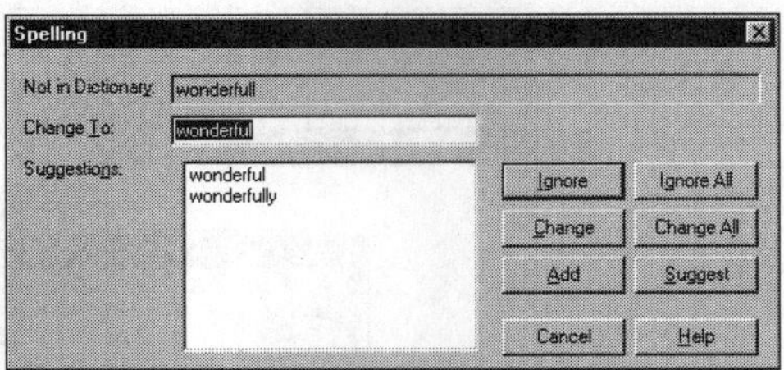

Figure 43. *Use the Spelling dialog box to change misspellings or add specialized words to the FrontPage dictionary.*

Spell Check a Web Page

Figure 44. *When FrontPage is finished checking a Web page, it will tell you so.*

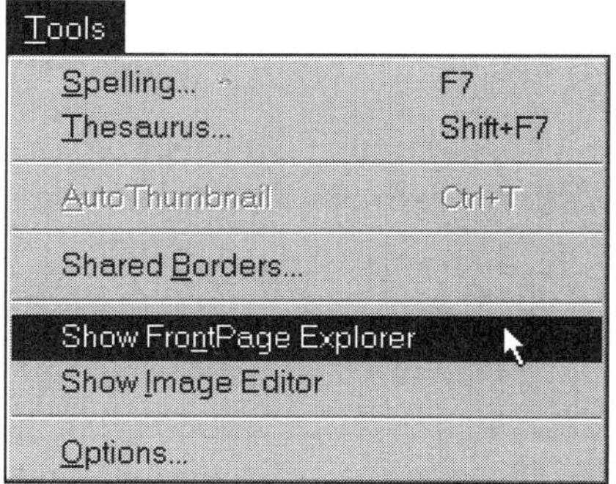

Figure 45. *Choose Show FrontPage Explorer from the Tools menu.*

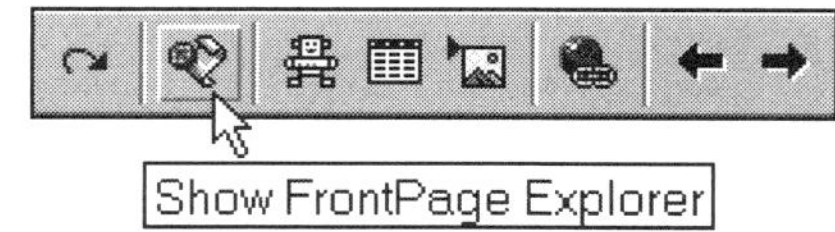

Figure 46. *Click the Show FrontPage Explorer button on the toolbar.*

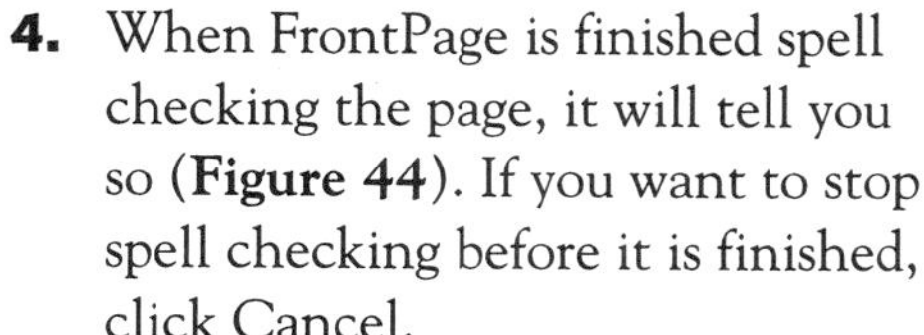

4. When FrontPage is finished spell checking the page, it will tell you so (**Figure 44**). If you want to stop spell checking before it is finished, click Cancel.

Tip:

- If you want to spell check a few words or a paragraph, select the text, then choose Spelling from the Tools menu.

To move from Editor back to Explorer:

Choose Show FrontPage Explorer from the Tools menu (**Figure 45**) or click the Show FrontPage Explorer button on the toolbar (**Figure 46**).

Tip:

- If you minimized FrontPage Explorer when you opened the Editor, you can restore the Explorer by clicking the FrontPage Explorer button on the Windows task bar.

Quickly finding and replacing text and spell checking throughout an entire Web site uses very similar dialog boxes as finding and replacing text on a Web page. The only difference is that Explorer performs the tasks over a Web site, whereas the Editor performs the tasks on a single Web page.

To find text throughout an entire Web site:

1. Open the Web site you want to search in Explorer.
2. Choose Find from the Tools menu (**Figure 47**) or press Ctrl+F on the keyboard or click the Cross File Find button on the toolbar (**Figure 48**). The Find in FrontPage Web dialog box will appear (**Figure 49**).
3. In the Find what text box, type the text you want to find.
4. In the Find in area, select either the All pages radio button or the Selected pages radio button. If you choose Selected pages, the finder will only search the pages that are selected in Explorer.
5. Click OK. FrontPage will perform the search. When it has finished, a Find occurrences dialog box will appear (**Figure 50**). If instances of the text have been found, you will see how many times on how many pages at the bottom left of the Find occurrences dialog box. The

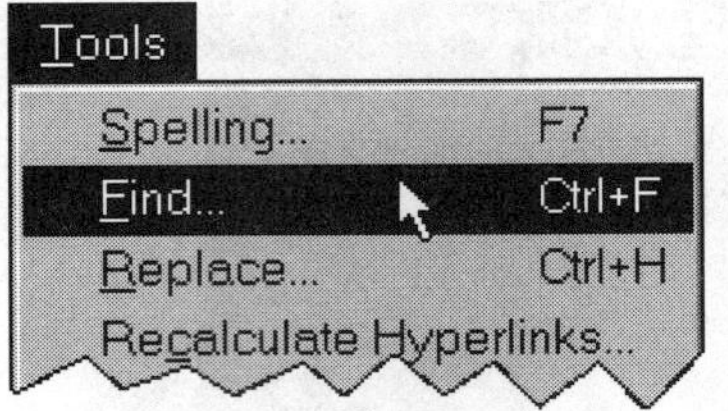

Figure 47. *Choose Find from the Explorer's Tools menu.*

Figure 48. *Click the Cross File Find button on the Explorer's toolbar.*

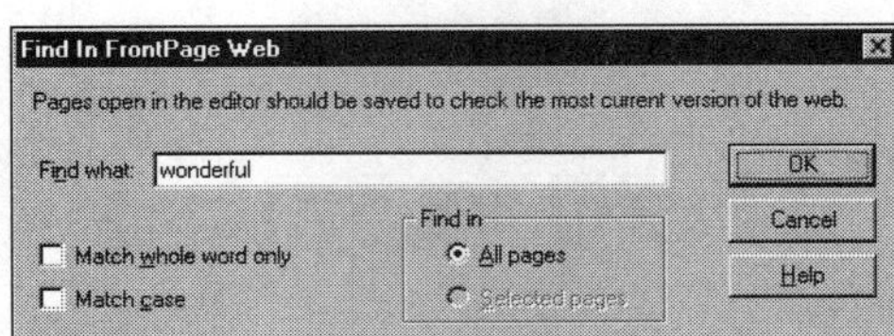

Figure 49. *Type the text you want to find in the Find what text box, then click OK.*

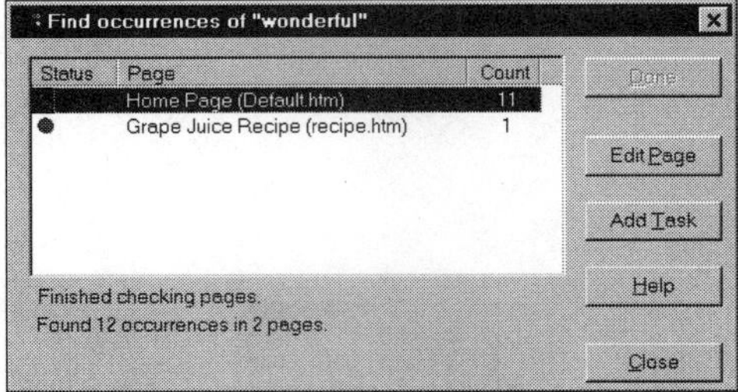

Figure 50. *When FrontPage has found the text, the Find occurrences dialog box lists how many occurrences and on what pages.*

Find Text Throughout a Web Site

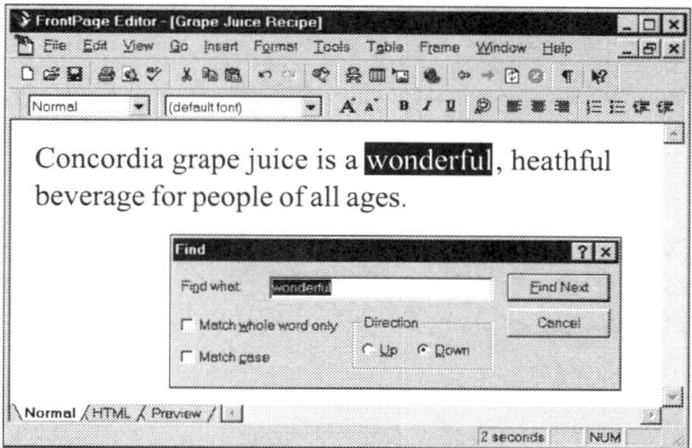

Figure 51. *When FrontPage finds a match, it highlights the text.*

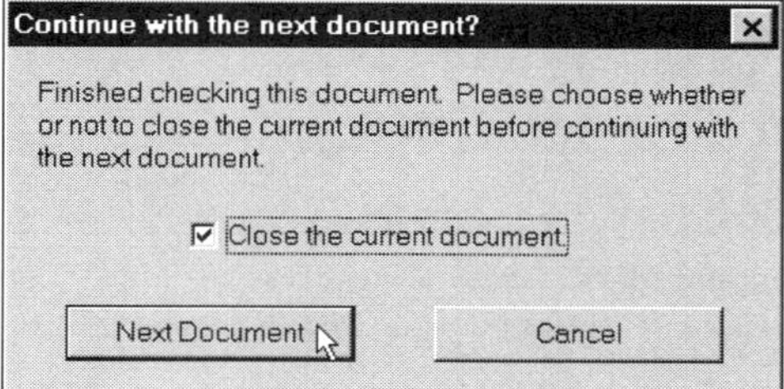

Figure 52. *Click Next Document to continue finding text.*

Figure 53. *Click OK to close the current Web page.*

pages where the text was found will be shown in the list box.

6. To edit the Web pages in the Editor, click Edit Page. The first page listed in the Find occurrences dialog box will open in the Editor. In addition, the Find dialog box will open and the first matched text will be highlighted (**Figure 51**). Edit the page as you choose.

7. Click Find Next to move to the next match.

8. If more than one page was listed in the Find occurrences dialog box and FrontPage has finished searching the first page in the Editor, the Continue with the next document dialog box will open (**Figure 52**). Click Next Document to continue finding text on the next page or click Cancel to return to the Find occurrences dialog box.

9. When FrontPage has finished finding word matches on all the Web pages listed in the Find occurrences dialog box, the Finished checking documents dialog box will open (**Figure 53**).

10. Click OK to save and close the current page, then switch to Explorer to return to the Find occurrences dialog box.

11. Click OK to close the Find occurrences dialog box.

To replace text throughout an entire Web site:

1. Open the Web site in Explorer.
2. Choose Replace from the Tools menu (**Figure 54**) or press Ctrl+H on the keyboard. The Replace in FrontPage Web dialog box will open (**Figure 55**).
3. Type the text you want to replace in the Find what text box.
4. In the Replace with text box, enter the text with which you want to replace the found text.
5. Select either the All pages radio button or the Selected pages radio button in the Find in area. If you choose Selected pages, only those pages selected in Explorer will be searched.
6. Click OK. FrontPage will perform the search for the text and the Find occurrences dialog box will open (**Figure 56**). If instances of the text have been found, you will see how many occurrences on how many pages at the bottom left of the Find occurrences dialog box. The pages where the text was found will be shown in the list box.

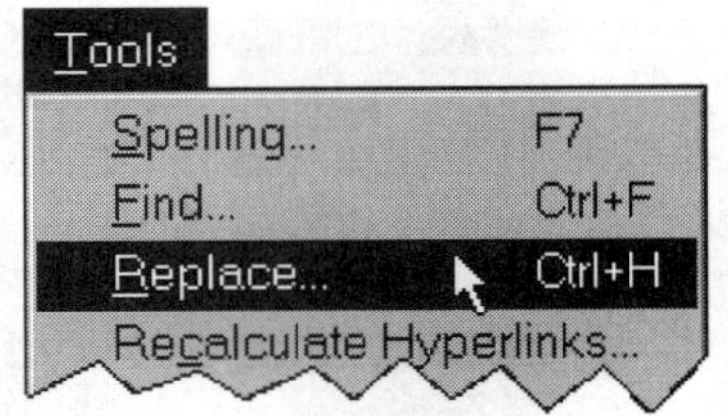

Figure 54. *Choose Replace from the Explorer's Tools menu.*

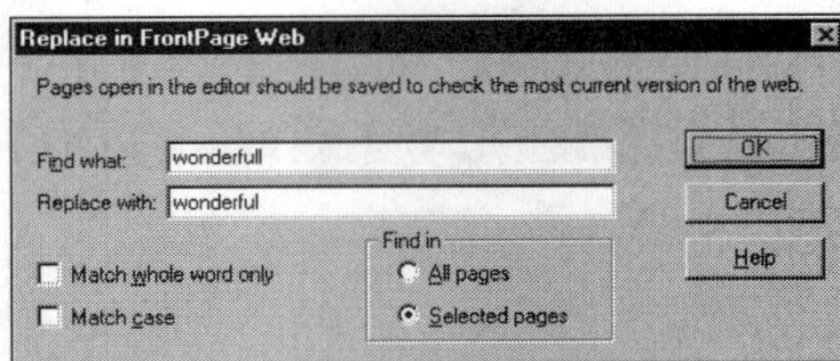

Figure 55. *After entering text in the Find what and Replace with text boxes, click OK.*

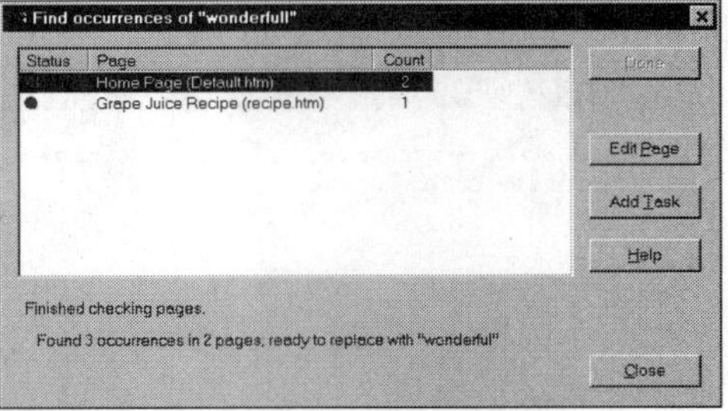

Figure 56. *When FrontPage has found the text, the Find occurrences dialog box lists how many occurrences and on what pages.*

Replace Text Throughout a Web Site

Figure 57. *When FrontPage finds a match, it highlights the text.*

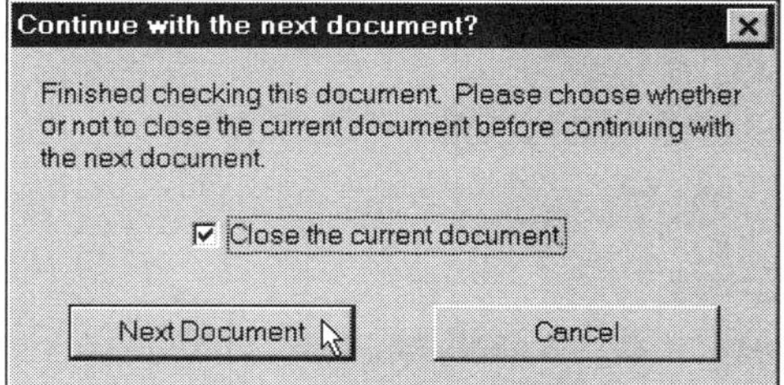

Figure 58. *Click Next Document to continue replacing text.*

Figure 59. *Click OK to save the changes made to the current Web page and close it.*

7. To edit the Web pages in the Editor, click Edit Page. The first page listed in the Find occurrences dialog box will open in the Editor. In addition, the Replace dialog box will open and the first matched text will be highlighted (**Figure 57**). Edit the page as you choose.

8. Click Find Next to move to the next match.

9. If more than one page was listed in the Find occurrences dialog box and FrontPage has finished searching the first page in the Editor, the Continue with the next document dialog box will open (**Figure 58**). Click Next Document to continue replacing words on the next page or click Cancel to return to the Find occurrences dialog box.

10. When FrontPage has finished finding word matches on all the Web pages listed in the Find occurrences dialog box, the Finished checking documents dialog box will open (**Figure 59**).

11. Click OK to save and close the current page, then switch to the Explorer to return to the Find occurrences dialog box.

12. Click OK to close the Find occurrences dialog box.

To spell check an entire Web site:

1. Open the Web site in Explorer.
2. Choose Spelling from the Tools menu (**Figure 60**), or press F7 on the keyboard, or click the Cross File Spelling button on the toolbar (**Figure 61**). The Spelling dialog box will open (**Figure 62**).
3. In the Check spelling of area, select whether you want to spell check the entire Web site or just pages you have selected in Explorer.
4. Click Start. FrontPage will start the check and open a Spelling dialog box (**Figure 63**). You can use this dialog box to select a specific page and edit it by clicking Edit Page, or save the task for later and put it in Tasks view by clicking Add Task (to find out more about Tasks view, take a look at Chapter 13).
5. When you are finished editing pages, click Close to return to Explorer.

Figure 60. *Choose Spelling from the Explorer's Tools menu.*

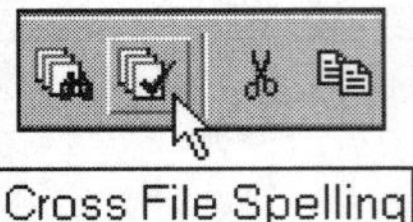

Figure 61. *Click the Cross File Spelling button on the Explorer's toolbar.*

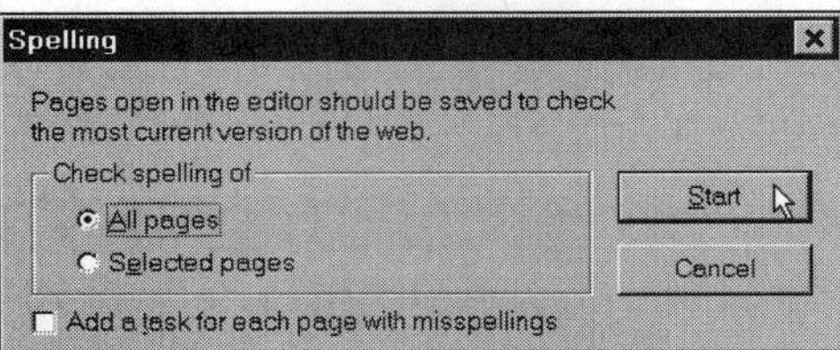

Figure 62. *Select the pages you want to search, then click Start.*

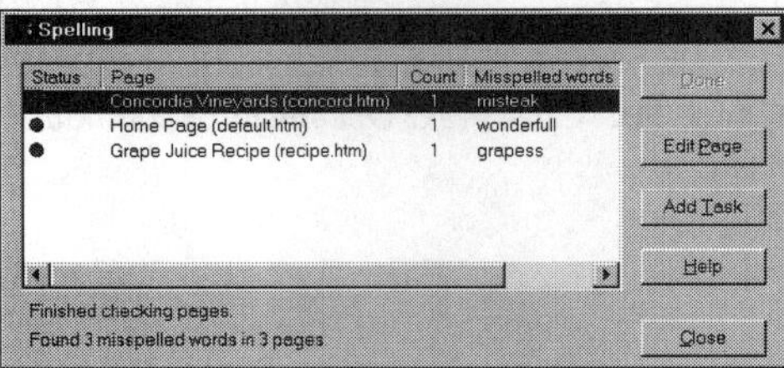

Figure 63. *The Check Spelling dialog box tells you where the mistakes are.*

SUMMARY

In this chapter you learned how to:

- Add text, line breaks, and comments
- Select and delete text
- Move and copy text
- Spell check a Web page and an entire site

Spell Check a Web Site

Fun with Text 8

A large part of the content of many Web pages is text. Text doesn't have to be boring! Now that you know how to add text in the FrontPage Editor, it's time to jazz it up using styles, different fonts, and colors.

The size of text on Web pages is measured in increments from 1 to 7. These sizes move from smallest to largest. Size 1 is text that is a bit less than 1/8" high. Size 7 is text that is 1/2" high.

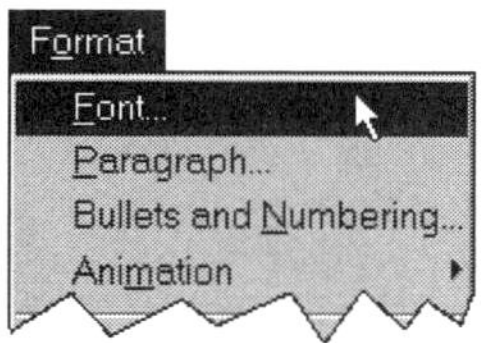

Figure 1. *Choose Font from the Format menu.*

To change text size:

1. Select the text you want to change.
2. Choose Font from the Format menu (**Figure 1**). The Font dialog box will open (**Figure 2**). Use the Size list box to select a new size, then click OK.

   or

   Click the Increase Text Size button or Decrease Text Size button on the Format toolbar (**Figure 3**).

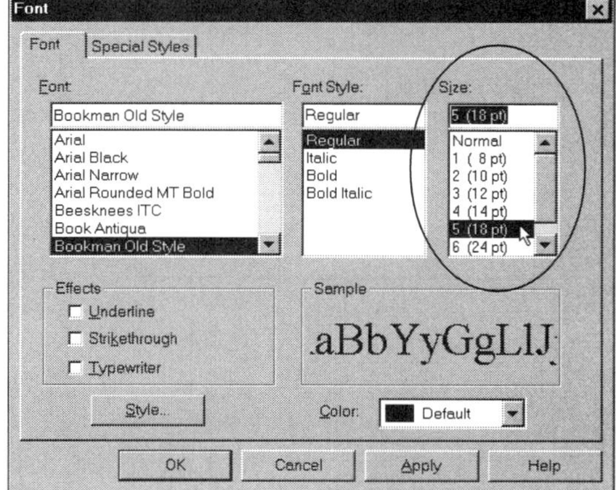

Figure 2. *Use the Size list box in the Font dialog box to select a new font size.*

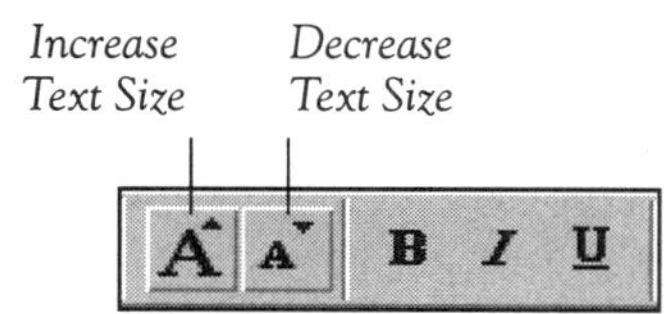

Figure 3. *Click the Decrease Text Size or Increase Text Size buttons.*

You can easily add more emphasis to text by changing its formatting and making it bold, italic, or underlined.

To change text formatting:

1. Select the text you want to change.
2. Click the Bold, Italic, or Underline buttons on the Format toolbar (**Figure 4**).

   or

   Choose Font from the Format menu (**Figure 1**). The Font dialog box will open (**Figure 5**). Use the Font Style list box to select Bold, Italic, or Bold Italic, or use the Effects area to put a check mark next to Underline, Strikethrough, or Typewriter. Click OK.

   The selected text will be reformatted (**Figure 6**).

Tips:

- You can select more than one formatting option at a time. For instance, you could make some selected text bold and italic.
- When formatting text, don't use too many styles and effects at the same time because the text can become hard to read.
- The Typewriter effect makes the selected text into a monotype font—all characters are the same width.

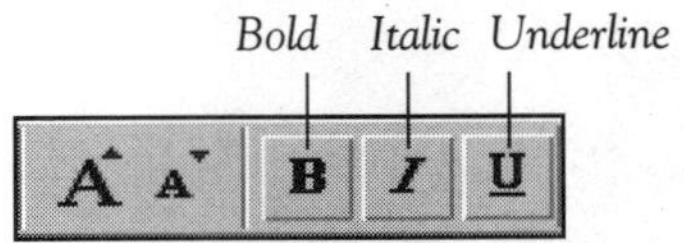

Figure 4. *Click the Bold, Italic, or Underline buttons on the Format toolbar.*

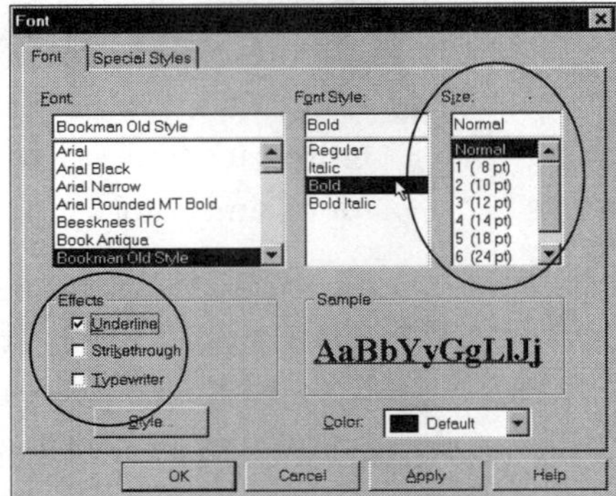

Figure 5. *Use the Font Style list box and the Effects area to select the formatting you want to use.*

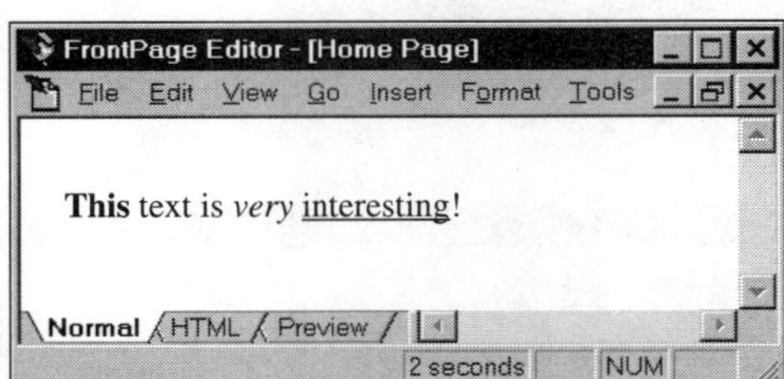

Figure 6. *When you format text, the Editor window shows the effects.*

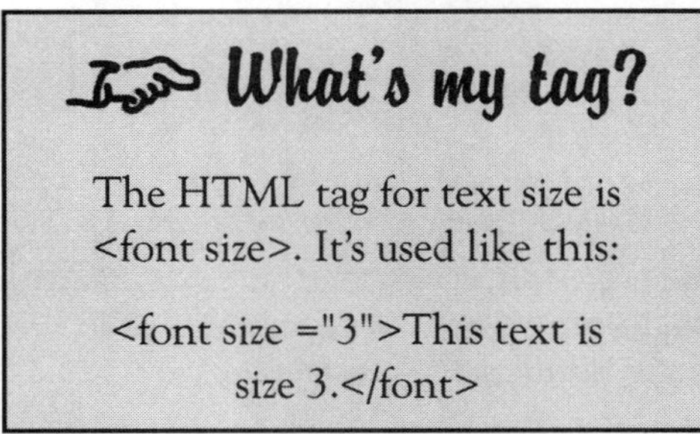

What's my tag?

The HTML tag for text size is <font size>. It's used like this:

<font size ="3">This text is size 3.</font>

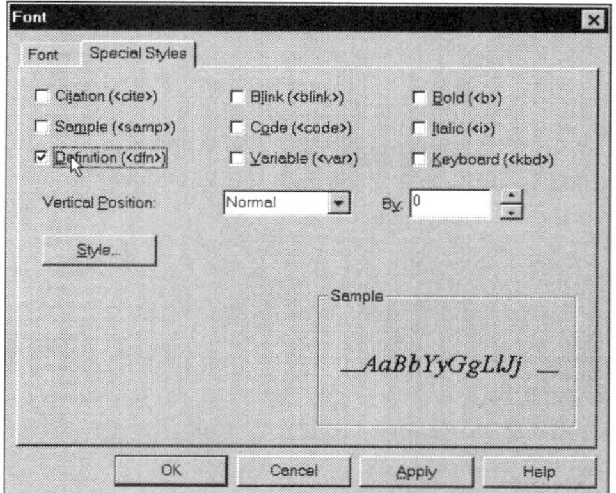

Figure 7. *Use the Special Styles tab of the Font dialog box to pick special effects such as blinking text.*

What's my tag?

There are two HTML tags for bold, <b> and <strong>. They are used like this:

<b>Bold text</b> is very <strong>distinct</strong>.

There are two tags for italic, <i> and <em>. They are used like this:

I <i>am</i> very <em>emphasized</em>!

The tag for underline is <u>. It's used like this: <u>Please</u> be careful!

In addition to standard text formatting, such as bold or italic, there are *special styles*. These styles include Citation, an italic that can be used for the name of a book, Keyboard, a typewriter-like font that can be used to indicate text the user should type, and Blink, which makes text blink. Not all browsers support these special styles. For instance, blinking text is only supported by Netscape Navigator.

To use a special style:

1. Select the text you want to change.
2. Choose Font from the Format menu (**Figure 1**). The Font dialog box will appear (**Figure 5**).
3. Click the Special Styles tab to bring that tab page forward (**Figure 7**).
4. Select the style you want to use by clicking the appropriate text box.
5. Click OK. The text you selected will change to that style in the Editor.

Tips:

- Blinking text is a novelty and draws attention to something, but it can quickly become annoying. Use blinking text *sparingly*.
- The HTML tag for each special style is listed next to the style on the Special Styles tab in the Font dialog box.

Back in the old days of the Web (not *that* long ago!), the only typefaces or *fonts* that most browsers would display were Times and `Courier`.

These days, you can use any font that you have to design your Web pages. *However*, if you use a special font, the folks browsing your Web page must also have that font loaded on their computers. Otherwise, the text will appear in their browser's default font, most likely Times.

For instance, if you created a Web page using the Caveman font, it would look something like **Figure 8** on your computer. But, when folks browse your Web site using computers that do not have the Caveman font installed on them, your page would look something like **Figure 9**.

With that in mind, use special fonts carefully. Don't hesitate to use them for special emphasis, but design your pages so they will look good with either the special font or a default font such as Times.

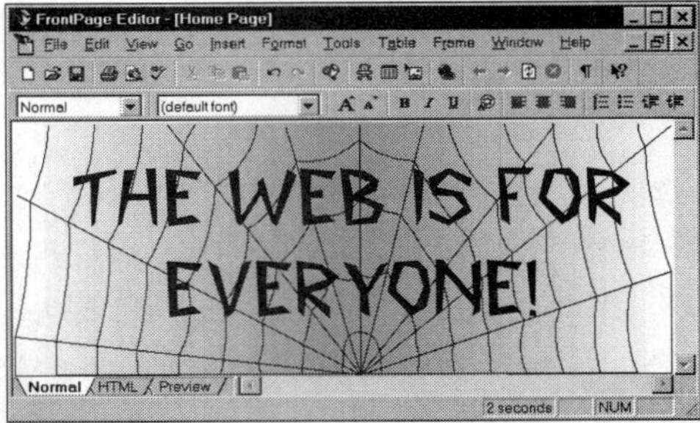

Figure 8. *A Web page shown in FrontPage Editor that uses the Caveman font.*

Figure 9. *The same Web page viewed in a browser on a computer that does not have the Caveman font installed on it.*

DEFAULT FONTS AND BROWSERS

Some browsers let users set their own default fonts. For instance, default fonts can be set in Netscape Navigator by selecting Preferences from the Edit menu, clicking Fonts under Category in the Preferences dialog box that opens, and then making your font selections.

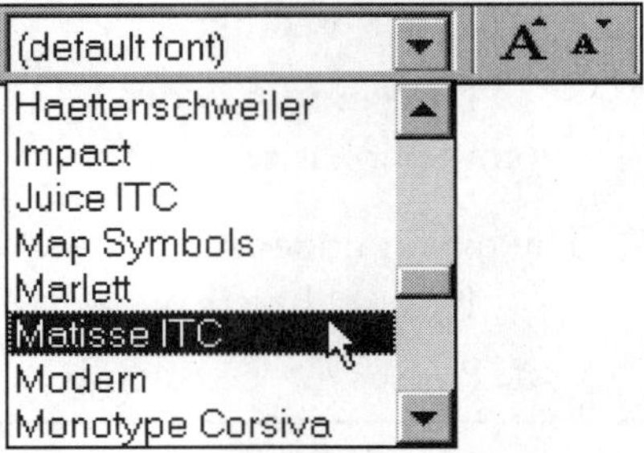

Figure 10. *Use the Change Font drop-down list to select a new font.*

Special Fonts and Your Web Pages

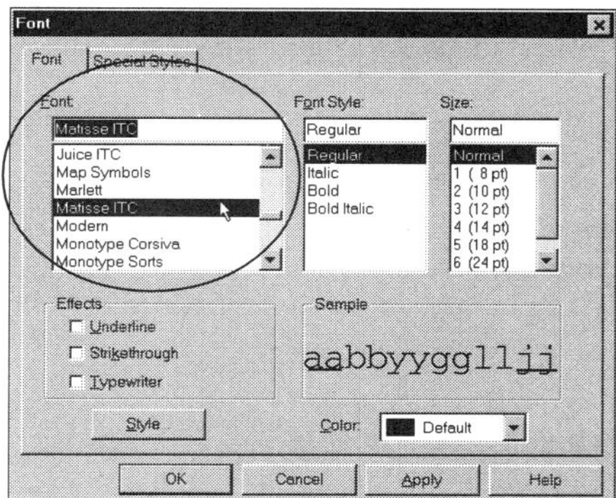

Figure 11. *Select a new font from the Font list box in the Font dialog box, then click OK.*

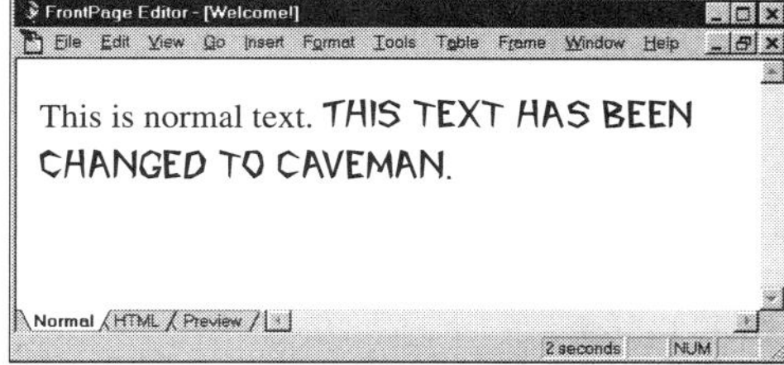

Figure 12. *In the Editor window, the text changes to the font you selected.*

Figure 13. *Choose Font Properties from the pop-up menu to open the Font dialog box.*

To change fonts:

1. Select the text you want to change or position the insertion marker at the place where you would like the new font to begin.
2. Use the Change Font drop-down list on the Format toolbar to select a new font (**Figure 10**).

   or

   Choose Font from the Format menu (**Figure 1**). The Font dialog box will open (**Figure 11**). Use the Font list box to select a new font, then click OK.

   The text will change to the font you selected (**Figure 12**).

Tips:

- You can see a preview of the font you've selected in the Sample area in the Font dialog box.
- If you need to use a special font and want to make sure it shows up correctly in any browser, convert the text to a graphic using a graphics program such as Photoshop or the Image Composer program included on the FrontPage 98 CD-ROM.

More Ways to Open the Font Dialog Box

With the text selected, press Alt+Enter on the keyboard or right mouse click and choose Font Properties from the pop-up menu (**Figure 13**).

Another way to emphasize text is to change its color. You can change the color of a selected bit of text or set the default text color for an entire Web page.

Figure 14. *Click the Text Color button on the Format toolbar.*

To change selected text's color:

1. Select the text you want to change.
2. Click the Text Color button on the Format toolbar (**Figure 14**). The Color dialog box will open (**Figure 15**).
3. Click one of the *color wells* to select a color.
4. Click OK. The selected text will change to the color you chose. Deselect the text to get a better view of its new color.

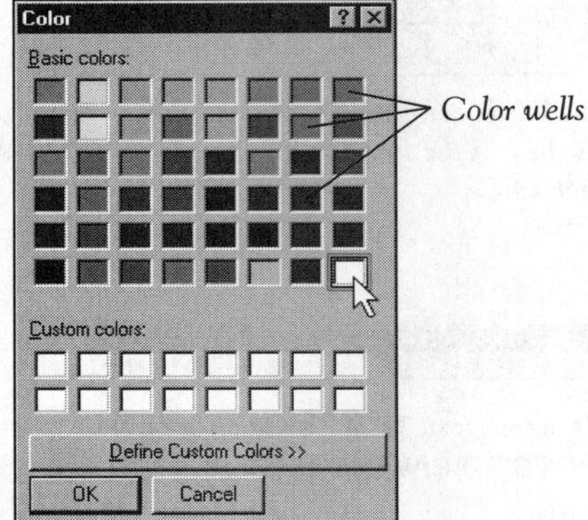

Figure 15. *Select a color by clicking on one of the color wells, then click OK.*

or

1. Choose Font from the Format menu (**Figure 1**). The Font dialog box will open (**Figure 16**).
2. Use the Color drop-down list to select a color.
3. Click OK. The selected text will change color in the Editor window.

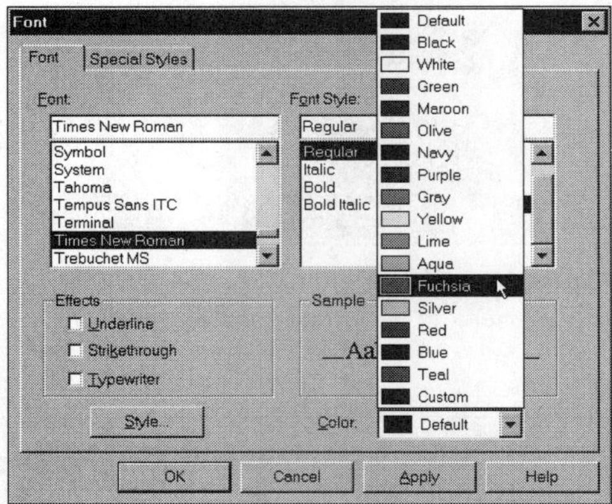

Figure 16. *In the Font dialog box, use the Color drop-down list to select a new color.*

Tip:

- Like text styles, text colors are most effective when used in moderation.

Change Selected Text's Color

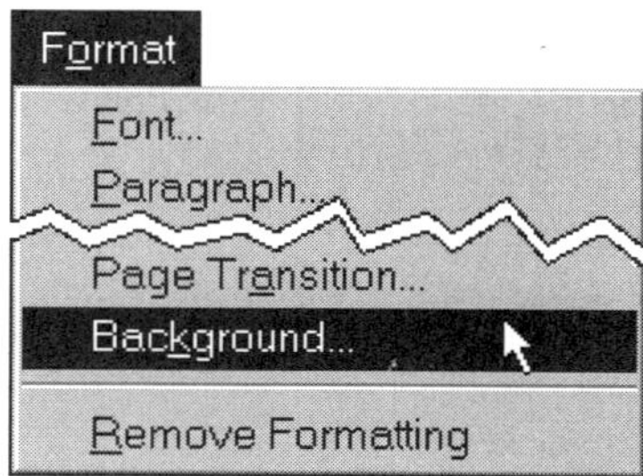

Figure 17. *Choose Background from the Format menu.*

Figure 18. *Choose Page Properties from the pop-up menu.*

To set the default text color:

1. Open the Page Properties dialog box by choosing Background from the Format menu (**Figure 17**) or right clicking anywhere on the Editor page and choosing Page Properties from the pop-up menu (**Figure 18**).
2. If necessary, click the Background tab to bring that tab page to the front (**Figure 19**).
3. Make sure the Specify Background and Colors radio button is selected.
4. Use the Text drop-down list to select a color (**Figure 20**).
5. Click OK. Type some text. It will appear in the color you just selected.

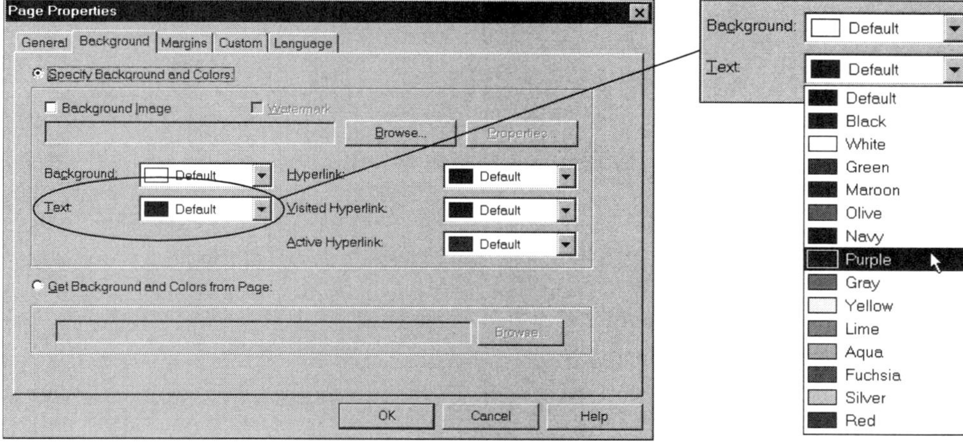

Figure 19. *If necessary, click the Background tab to move to that tab page.*

Figure 20. *Select a text color from the Text drop-down list.*

M*arquees* are lines of text that scroll or slide across a page. Using a marquee is a great way to get someone browsing your Web site to notice an important message. FrontPage makes its easy to create marquees. You should know, however, that only advanced browsers support marquees. Any other browser will display it just like regular text.

To create a marquee:

1. Position the insertion marker where you want to insert the marquee.
2. Choose Marquee from the Active Elements fly-out found on the Insert menu (**Figure 21**). The Marquee Properties dialog box will open (**Figure 22**).
3. Type the text for the marquee in the Text box at the top of the dialog box.
4. In the Direction area, select whether you want the marquee to move toward the left or toward the right.
5. In the Movement Speed area set the Delay (the length in milliseconds between each movement of the marquee) and the Amount (the number of pixels between each movement of the marquee). The default values for these items are good settings.

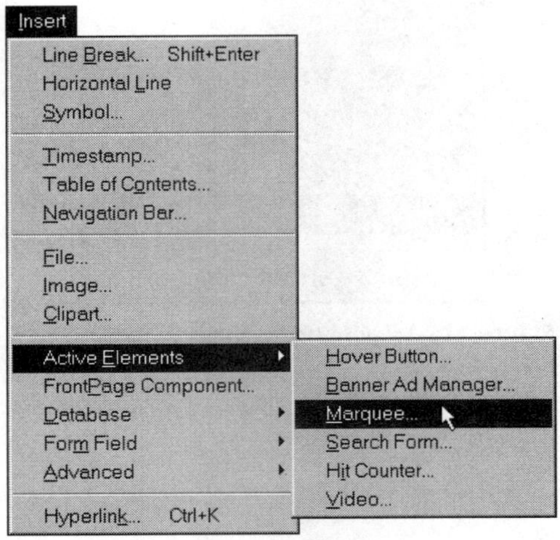

Figure 21. *Choose Marquee from the Active Elements fly-out found on the Insert menu.*

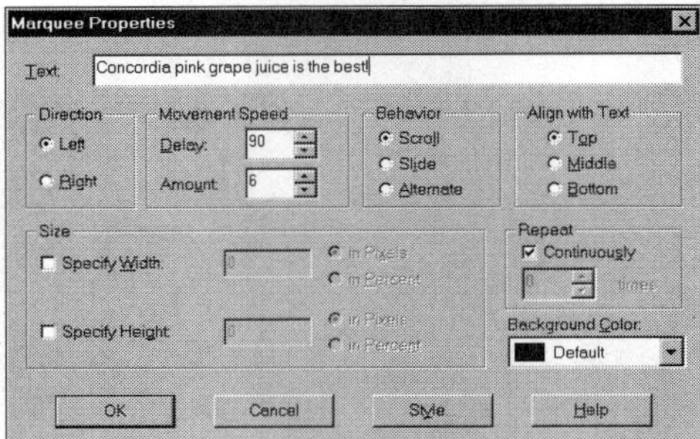

Figure 22. *The Marquee Properties dialog box is used to set up the direction and how fast the marquee will move.*

Marquee

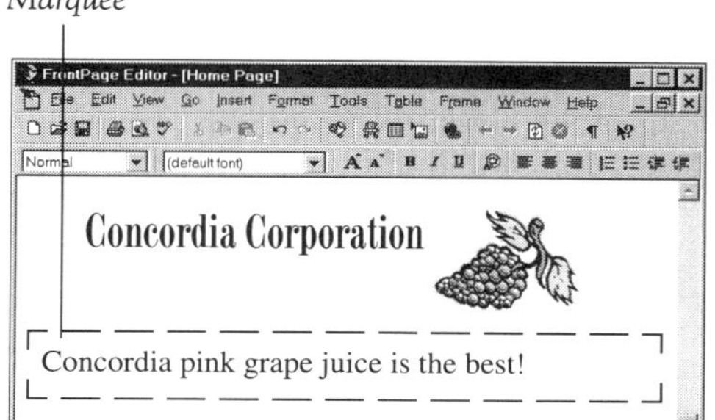

Figure 23. *To see the marquee move, you will have to view it in an advanced browser.*

Figure 24. *Choose Marquee Properties from the pop-up menu.*

> **Changing Marquee Settings**
>
> To change any setting in a marquee, select the marquee, then press Alt+Enter on the keyboard or right mouse click on the marquee and choose Marquee Properties from the pop-up menu (**Figure 24**). The Marquee Properties dialog box will appear.

6. In the Behavior area, select one of the following:
   - Scroll: the text will appear at one end of the marquee and disappear at the other end.
   - Slide: the text will appear at one end of the marquee and stop when it reaches the other end.
   - Alternate: the text moves back and forth across the screen, never disappearing.
7. In the Align with Text area, select whether the marquee text will be aligned to the top, middle, or bottom of the marquee area.
8. Use the Repeat area to set whether the marquee will continuously repeat or repeat only a specified number of times.
9. Select a color in the Background Color area, if you want the marquee text to move against a colored background.
10. Click OK. The marquee will appear on the Editor page but will not move (**Figure 23**). To see it function, you will have to view the Web page using a Microsoft Explorer browser. (To find out how to preview pages in a browser, turn to page 123.)

Create a Marquee

Web page titles are important. They appear in the title bar of the Editor. In addition, a page title is displayed in the title bar of a browser, giving the user basic information as to what the Web page is about. In the Editor, you can easily change a Web page's title.

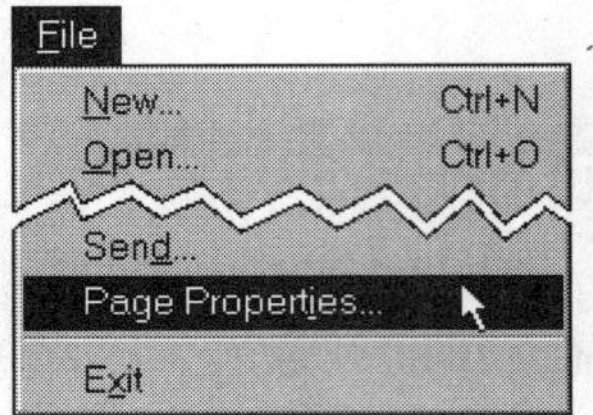

Figure 25. *Choose Page Properties from the File menu.*

To change the page title:

1. Open the Page Properties dialog box by choosing Page Properties from the File menu (**Figure 25**) or right clicking anywhere on the Editor page and choosing Page Properties from the pop-up menu (**Figure 18**).
2. Click the General tab to bring that tab page to the front (**Figure 26**).
3. Enter a new page title in the Title text box (**Figure 27**).
4. Click OK to close the dialog box. The page title is shown in the title bar of a browser (**Figure 28**).

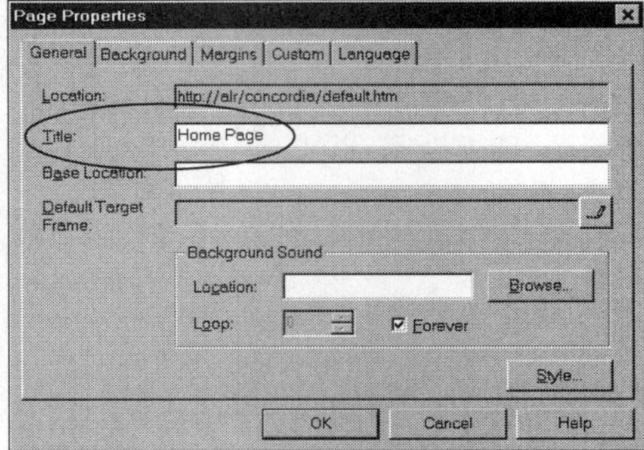

Figure 26. *Use the General tab page of the Page Properties dialog box to set a new page title.*

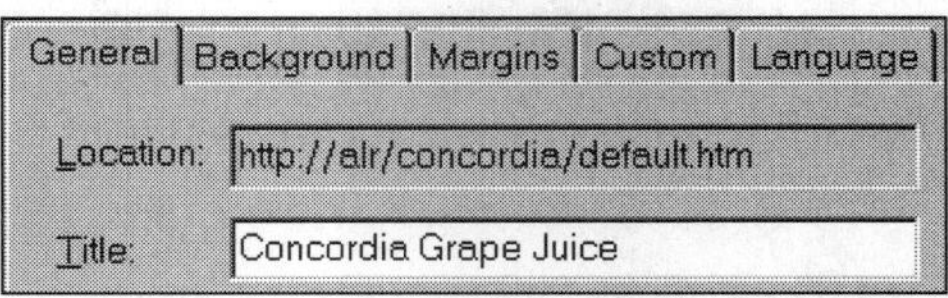

Figure 27. *Enter the new page title in the Title text box, then click OK.*

Tips:

- For more about the Editor's title bar, take a look at page 9.
- See the next page for directions about viewing your Web pages in a browser.

Page title

Figure 28. *The page title appears in a browser's title bar.*

Change the Page Title

Figure 29. *Click the Preview tab to view your Web page in Preview view.*

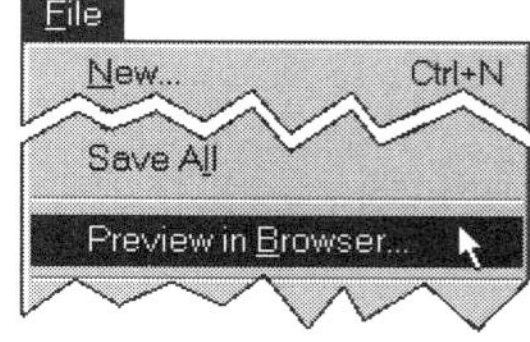

Figure 30. *Choose Preview in Browser from the File menu.*

Figure 31. *Click the Preview in Browser button on the Standard toolbar.*

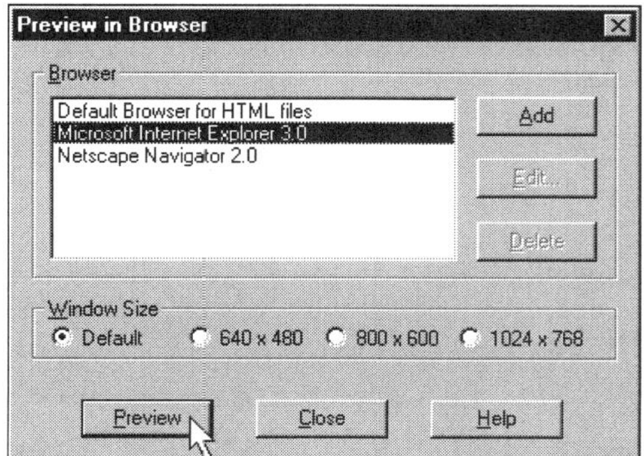

Figure 32. *Select the browser you want to use from the Browser list box or click Add to include another browser on the list.*

Now that you've created some stunning effects with text, it's time to see what you've done by viewing it in a browser. FrontPage makes this easy with the Preview tab and the Preview in Browser command.

To preview your Web page in Preview view:

Click the Preview tab at the bottom of the Editor window. Your Web page will appear in Preview view (**Figure 29**).

To preview your Web page in a browser:

1. Choose Preview in Browser from the File menu (**Figure 30**) or click the Preview in Browser button on the Standard toolbar (**Figure 31**). The Preview in Browser dialog box will open (**Figure 32**).
2. Select the browser you want to use from the list box in the Browser area. If you don't see the browser you want to use and you know it's installed on your computer, click Add. The Add Browser dialog box will appear (**Figure 33**). Type in a name for the browser and click the Browse button to find the program file (.exe) for the browser. Click OK to return to the Preview in Browser dialog box.

3. Use the Window Size area to see what the browser window will look like to folks using other screen resolutions. In order for the different window sizes to work, your monitor must be set at the same or higher screen resolution than the one you select.

4. Click Preview. If the Web page you want to view is located on a remote server, the Connect To dialog box will appear (**Figure 34**). Click Connect. The Web page will appear in the browser you selected (**Figure 35**).

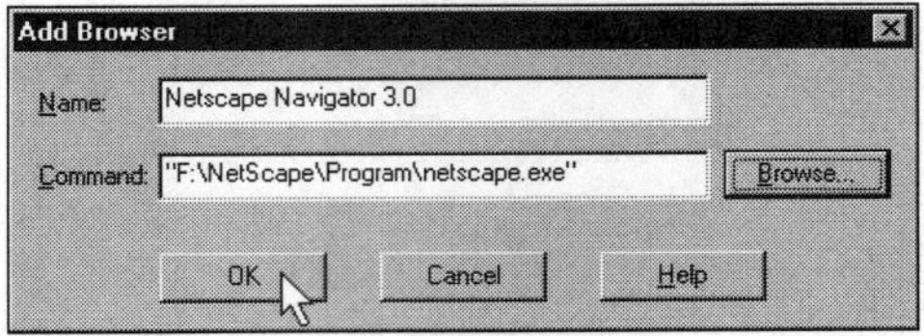

Figure 33. *Use the Add Browser dialog box to find a new browser's program file.*

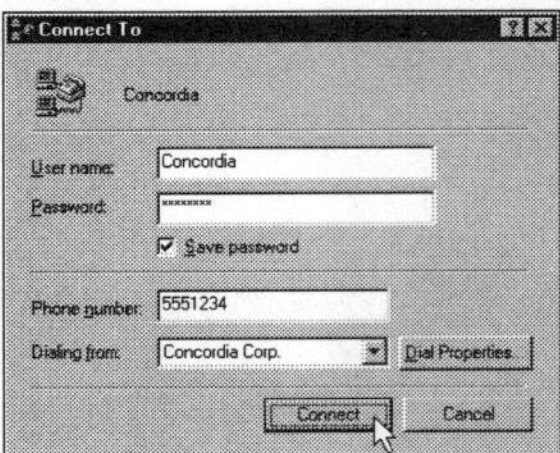

Figure 34. *If the Web site is loaded on a remote server, you'll need to connect to it via modem.*

Tips:

- It's a good idea to have several of the most popular browsers installed on your computer. That way, you can test to see what your Web site will look like in the different browsers.
- If you connected to the Web site via modem, don't forget to disconnect once you're finished.

Figure 35. *The Web page viewed in a browser.*

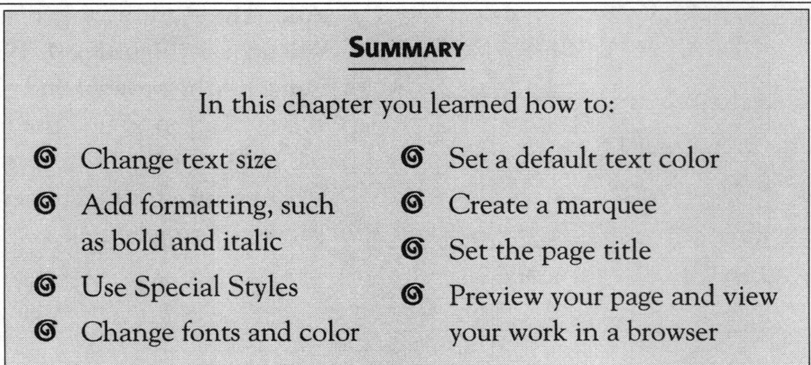

SUMMARY

In this chapter you learned how to:

- Change text size
- Add formatting, such as bold and italic
- Use Special Styles
- Change fonts and color
- Set a default text color
- Create a marquee
- Set the page title
- Preview your page and view your work in a browser

9 Formatting Paragraphs

Chapter 8 showed you how to format individual characters and words by selecting them. It dealt with character-level formatting. This chapter will tell you all about paragraph-level formatting, such as alignment, paragraph styles, and numbered and bulleted lists.

Paragraph alignment specifies how text is positioned between the left and right sides of the browser window.

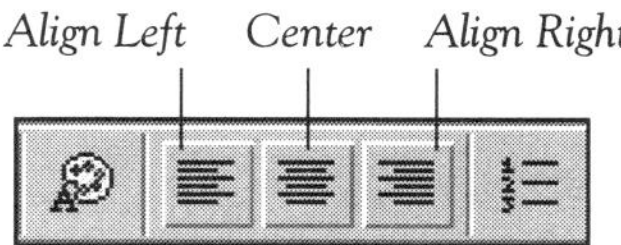

Figure 1. *Click the Align Left, Center, or Align Right buttons on the Format toolbar.*

To set paragraph alignment:

1. Place the insertion marker inside the paragraph you want to change.
2. Click the Align Left, Center, or Align Right buttons on the Format toolbar (**Figure 1**).

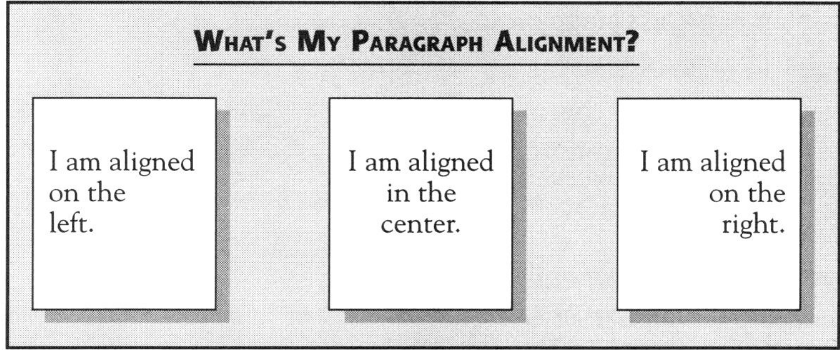

When you just type along in FrontPage Editor without adding any fancy formatting, the default style that the Editor places your text in is *Normal.* This Normal style is left aligned, Times text.

Formatted style creates paragraphs with a *monospaced* font, meaning that each character takes up the same amount of room. Formatted style also preserves any tabs or spaces that you create with the spacebar on the keyboard. `Courier` is generally used as a browser's default monospaced font. So, if you want to create columns using spaces or tabs, you can do so and be sure that the columns will look the same in every browser. They would line up correctly, as in **Figure 2**. (A more elegant way to create columns is to use tables, which are discussed in Chapter 12.)

To use the Formatted style:

1. Position the insertion marker where you would like the paragraph to begin or place the insertion marker in an existing paragraph to change it to Formatted style.
2. Choose Formatted from the Change Style drop-down list on the Format toolbar (**Figure 3**). Type your text.
3. When you are finished, choose Normal from the Change Style drop-down list.

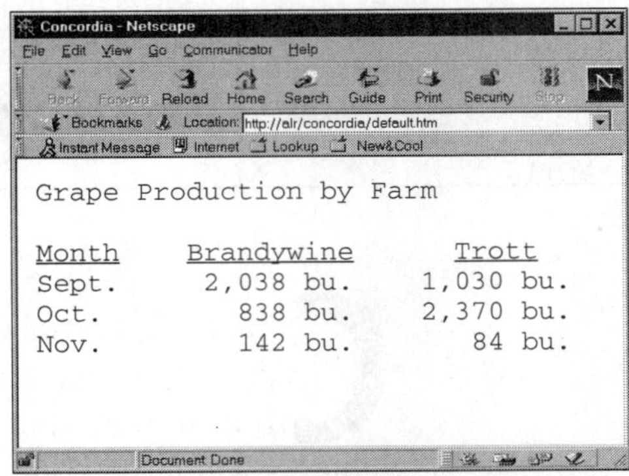

Figure 2. *The Formatted style uses a monospaced font, so every character and space lines up evenly.*

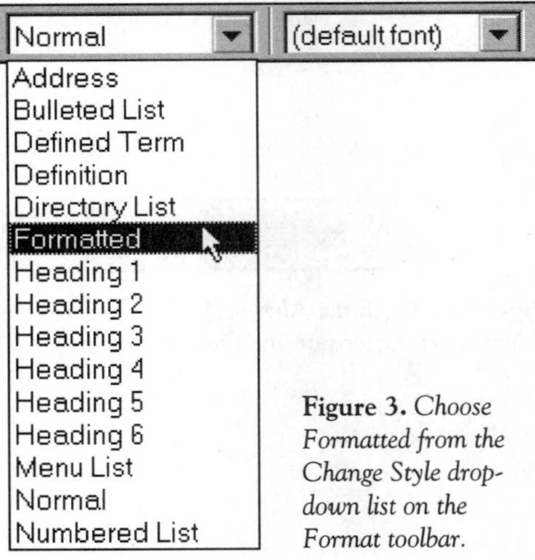

Figure 3. *Choose Formatted from the Change Style drop-down list on the Format toolbar.*

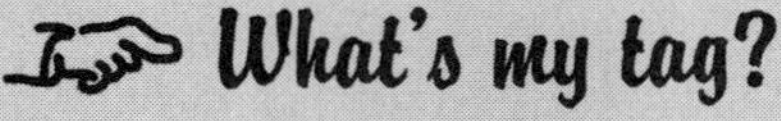

The HTML tag for Formatted style is <pre>. It's used like this:

```
<pre>If you add s p a c e s,
they will be preserved!</pre>
```

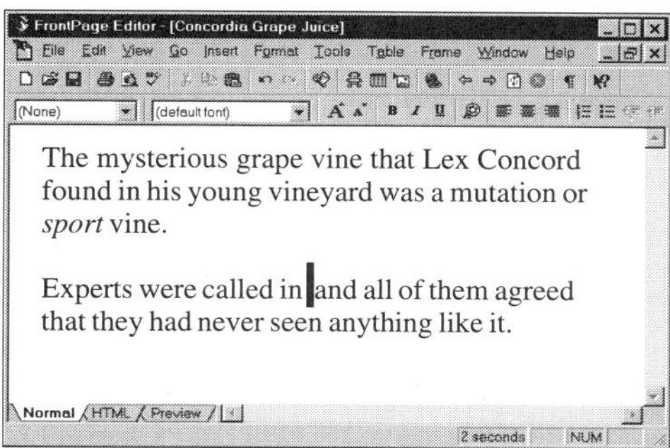

Figure 4. *Place the insertion marker inside a paragraph.*

Figure 5. *Click the Increase Indent button on the Format toolbar.*

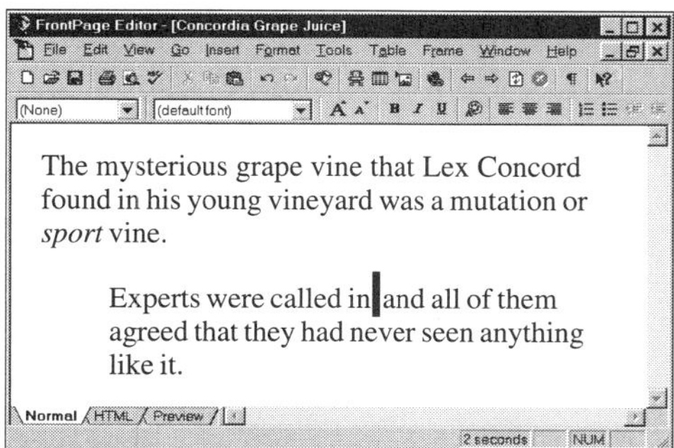

Figure 6. *When the Increase Indent button is clicked, the paragraph becomes indented.*

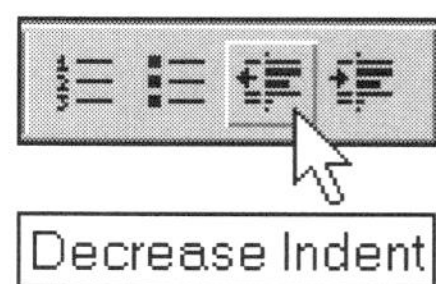

Figure 7. *Click the Decrease Indent button on the Format toolbar.*

Using the FrontPage Editor, you can indent entire paragraphs with just the click of a button.

To indent a paragraph:

1. Place the insertion marker anywhere in the paragraph (**Figure 4**).
2. Click the Increase Indent button on the Format toolbar (**Figure 5**). The paragraph will become indented (**Figure 6**).

Tips:

- To indent several paragraphs at once, select the paragraphs before clicking the Increase Indent button.
- To remove the indent from a paragraph, place the insertion marker in the paragraph, then click the Decrease Indent button on the Format toolbar (**Figure 7**).
- You can click the Increase Indent or Decrease Indent buttons more than once to add or reduce the amount of indentation.
- Increasing and decreasing indents doesn't work on centered paragraphs.

Headings are an important part of any Web page. Typically, a large heading will be found near the top of a page to tell the user what the page is about. Smaller headings will be used throughout the page to separate it into manageable sections. As you learned in Chapter 8, text sizes are measured in increments from 1 to 7, with 1 being the smallest and 7 the largest. Heading increments work in the opposite fashion. Headings are measured in increments from 1 to 6, but 1 is the largest size and 6 is the smallest. **Figure 8** shows the relative sizes of the six heading formats.

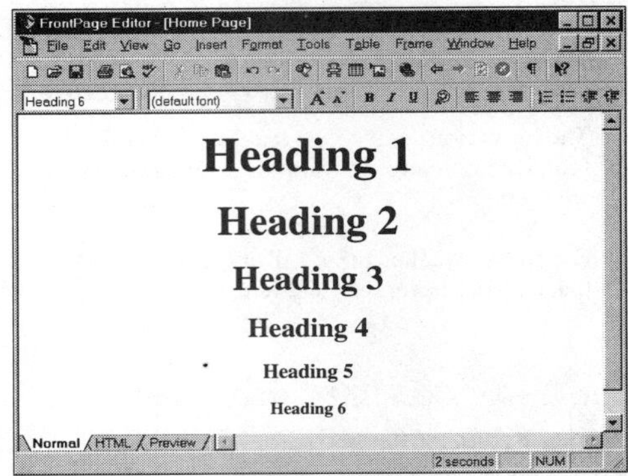

Figure 8. *The six different Heading styles.*

PARAGRAPHS VS. LINE BREAKS

Every time you press the Enter key on the keyboard, FrontPage starts a new paragraph. As the insertion marker moves down to begin the new paragraph, it adds extra space between the previous line and the new line.

To move the insertion marker down to the next line without creating a new paragraph and adding that extra space, press Shift+Enter on the keyboard. This inserts a line break.

For more information about paragraphs and line breaks, turn to pages 94 and 95 in Chapter 7.

What's my tag?

The HTML tag for paragraph alignment is <p align>.
It's used like this:

```
<p align="left">I am on the left!</p>
<p align="center">I am centered!</p>
<p align="right">I am on the right!</p>
```

The tag for the Heading styles is <h>.
It's used like this:

```
<h1>I am Heading 1 style</h1>
<h2>I am Heading 2 style</h2>
<h3>I am Heading 3 style</h3>
<h4>I am Heading 4 style</h4>
<h5>I am Heading 5 style</h5>
<h6>I am Heading 6 style</h6>
```

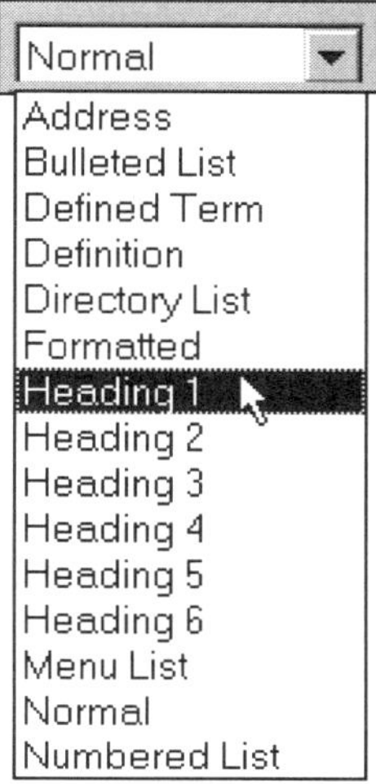

Figure 9. *Choose a Heading style from the Change Style drop-down list on the Format toolbar.*

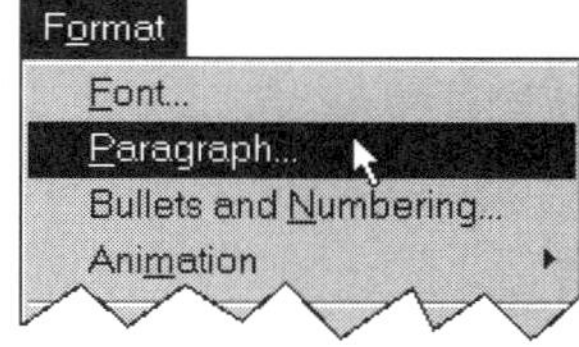

Figure 10. *Choose Paragraph from the Format menu.*

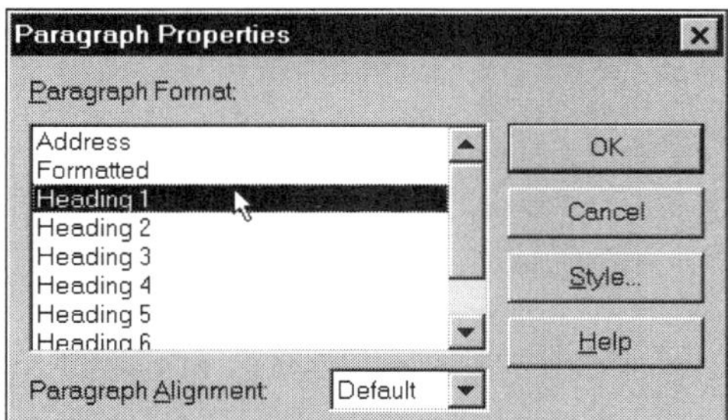

Figure 11. *Use the Paragraph Properties dialog box to select a Heading style.*

Figure 12. *Choose Paragraph Properties from the pop-up menu.*

To apply a Heading style:

1. Select the paragraph(s) you want to change.
2. Use the Change Style drop-down list on the Format toolbar to select a heading style (**Figure 9**). The text you selected will change to that heading style.

   or

   Choose Paragraph from the Format menu (**Figure 10**). The Paragraph Properties dialog box will open (**Figure 11**). Select the heading style you would like, then click OK. The text you selected will change to that heading style.

Tips:

- Another way to open the Paragraph Properties dialog box is to right click on the selected paragraph, then select Paragraph Properties from the pop-up menu (**Figure 12**).
- You can apply several types of paragraph formatting to a paragraph. For instance, you could change a paragraph to Heading 1 style, then center align it.

Apply Heading Styles

Organized lists are a great way to show information in an easy-to-read format. You can use the Editor to create bulleted and numbered lists, as well as nested lists and definition lists.

Figure 13. *Click the Bulleted List button on the Format toolbar.*

To create a bulleted list using plain bullets:

1. Position the insertion marker where you want the bulleted list to begin. If you place the insertion marker on a line that contains text, that line will become the first item of the list.
2. Click the Bulleted List button on the Format toolbar (**Figure 13**).

   or

   Choose Bulleted List from the Change Style drop-down list on the Format toolbar (**Figure 14**).

   or

   Choose Bullets and Numbering from the Format menu (**Figure 15**). The Bullets and Numbering dialog box will open. Click the Plain Bullets tab to bring it to the front (**Figure 16**). Select a bullet style by clicking on a sample, then click OK.

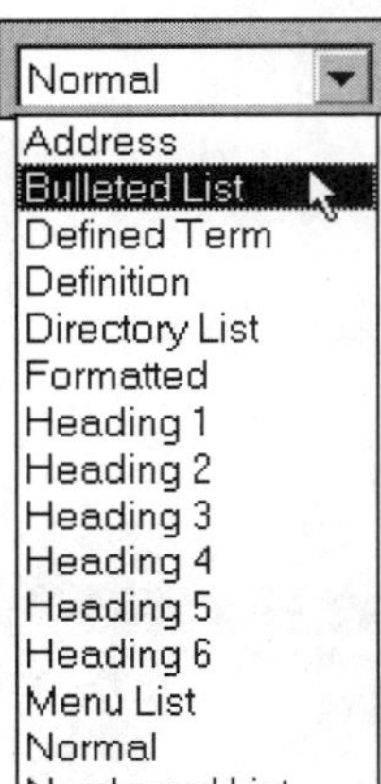

Figure 14. *Choose Bulleted List from the Change Style drop-down list on the Format toolbar.*

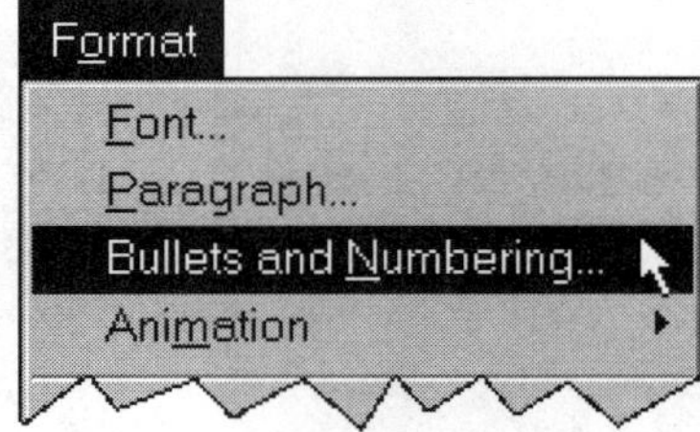

Figure 15. *Choose Bullets and Numbering from the Format menu.*

BROWSERS AND SPECIAL BULLET SHAPES

Only the Netscape Navigator browser supports bullet shapes other than a dot. If you use another bullet style on a Web page, such as a square, and the person browsing the page is not using Navigator, the bullets will appear as dots.

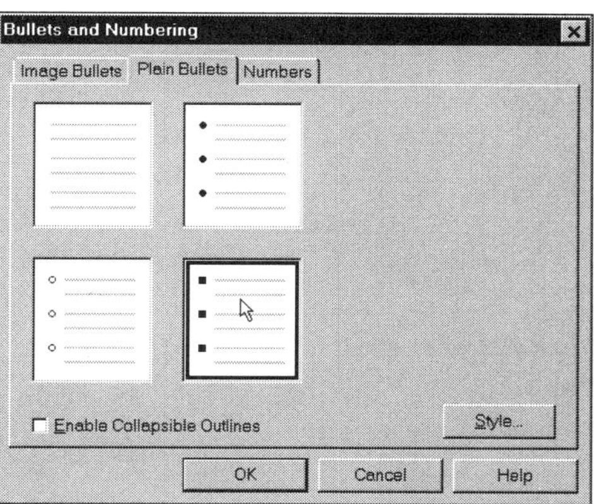

Figure 16. *Use the Plain Bullets tab page of the List Properties dialog box to select a bullet style, then click OK.*

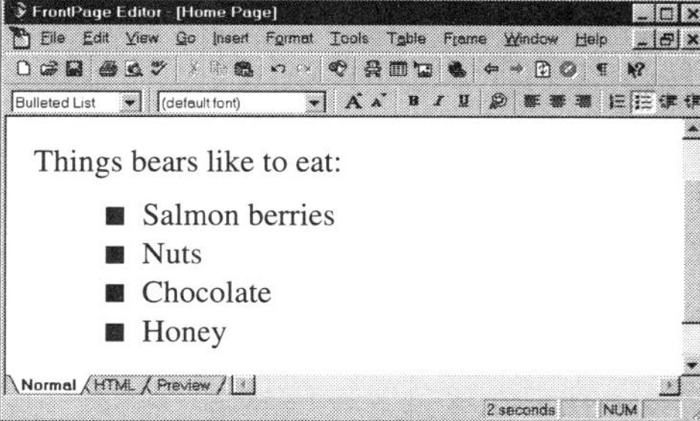

Figure 17. *As you type and press Enter, the bulleted list takes shape.*

3. Where the bullet appears on the page, type in your first list item.
4. When you are finished with the first item, press Enter on the keyboard to create another bullet. Continue typing and pressing Enter until your list is complete (**Figure 17**).
5. When you are finished adding the last bulleted item, press Ctrl+Enter or press Enter twice to change back to the Normal style.

Tips:

- You can also turn existing paragraphs into a bulleted list by selecting the paragraphs, then proceeding from step 2.
- If you're using a theme, the Plain Bullets tab in the Bullets and Numbering dialog box will not be available.
- The name of the Bullets and Numbering dialog box changes to List Properties if you are editing a list that already exists.

What's my tag?

There are two HTML tags for a bulleted list. <ul> lets the browser know a bulleted list is coming and <li> denotes a bulleted list item.

These tags are used like this:

```
<ul>
    <li>I am the first item!
    <li>I am the second item!
</ul>
```

A new feature of FrontPage 98 is the ability to use graphics as bullets. So instead of using the dots and squares that are typically part of a list, you can give your lists a great look with just a few clicks of the mouse!

To create a bulleted list using graphical bullets:

1. Position the insertion marker where you want the bulleted list to begin.
2. Choose Bullets and Numbering from the Format menu (**Figure 15**). The Bullets and Numbering dialog box will open.
3. If necessary, click the Image Bullets tab to bring it to the front (**Figure 18**).
4. To use a bullet graphic that is included in a theme in use, select the Use images from current theme radio button (**Figure 19**). A preview of the bullets used will appear in the preview area on the left side of the dialog box. If you want to use a different image, select the Specify image radio button and follow the directions in steps 5–7 below. Otherwise, click OK and move on to step 8.
5. If you select the Specify image radio button, type the image location and name in the text box below the Specify image radio button (**Figure 20**).

   or

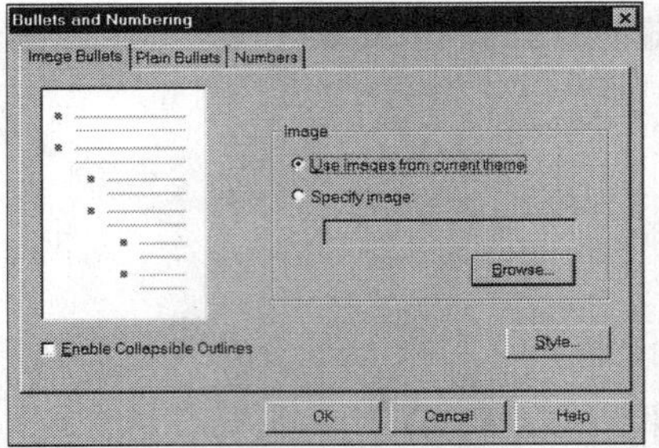

Figure 18. *Click the Image Bullets tab to bring that tab page to the front.*

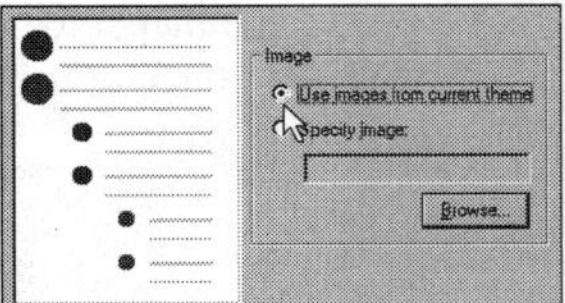

Figure 19. *Select the Use images from current theme radio button.*

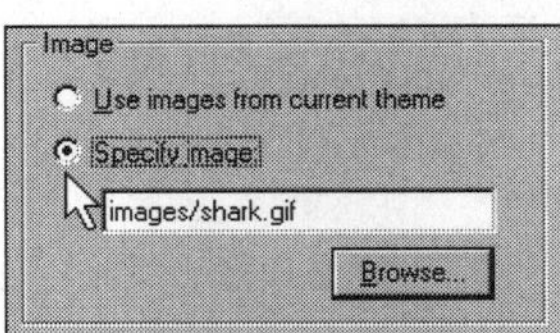

Figure 20. *Click the Specify image radio button, then enter the location of the graphic. If you want to go find the image on the Web or your computer, click Browse.*

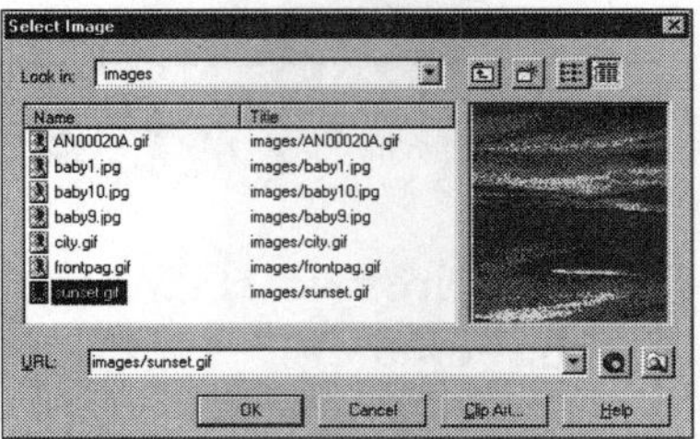

Figure 21. *Use the Select Image dialog box to find an image saved with the open Web site, on the Web, or located elsewhere on your omputer.*

Click to find an image on your computer

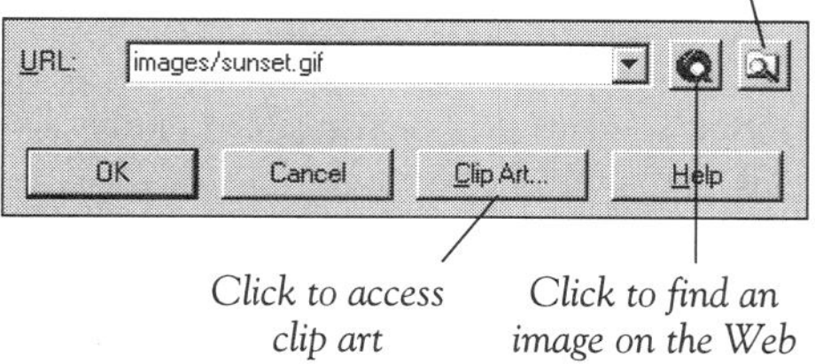

Click to access clip art

Click to find an image on the Web

Figure 22. *Click the appropriate button to find an image on the Web, on your computer, or in the clip art gallery that ships with FrontPage 98.*

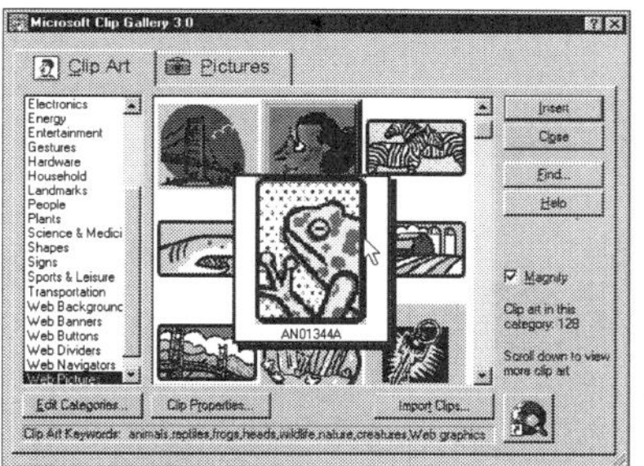

Figure 23. *The Microsoft Clip Gallery 3.0 dialog box displays many images that you can select for use as bullets.*

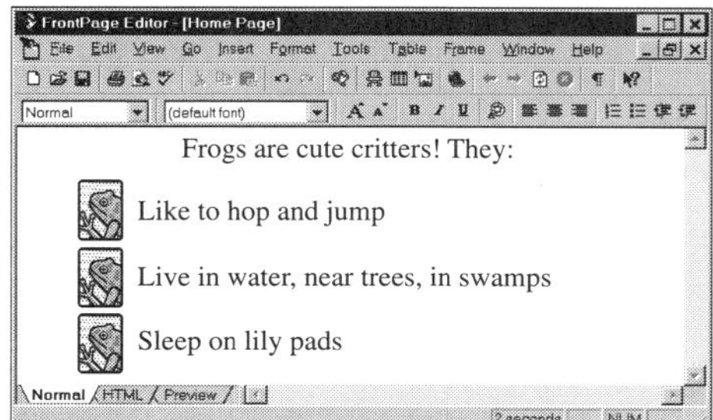

Figure 24. *Press Enter to add bullets and complete your list.*

Click the Browse button to use an image from the Web or one that is saved on your computer. The Select Image dialog box will open (**Figure 21**). There are three places you can get an image (**Figure 22**):

- To find an image on the Web, click the "Use your Browser to select a page or file" button.
- To use an image saved on your computer, click the "Select a file on your computer" button.
- To use the clip art provided with FrontPage, click the Clip Art button. The Microsoft Clip Gallery 3.0 dialog box will open (**Figure 23**). Select an image from the preview pane, then click Insert. (To find out more about using clip art and this dialog box, turn to Chapter 10.)

6. Once you've found the graphic you want to use, click OK to close the Select Image dialog box and return to the Bullets and Numbering dialog box.

7. Click OK to close the Bullets and Numbering dialog box.

8. Where the bullet appears on the page, type your first list item.

9. Press Enter to create another bullet, and type in your text. Continue typing text and pressing Enter until you finish with your list (**Figure 24**).

10. When you're done, press Ctrl+Enter to end the bulleted list and switch back to Normal style.

To create a numbered list:

1. Position the insertion marker where you would like the numbered list to begin. If you place the insertion marker on a line that contains text, that line will become the first item of the list.
2. Click the Numbered List button on the Format toolbar (**Figure 25**).

   or

   Choose Numbered List from the Change Style drop-down list on the Format toolbar (**Figure 26**).

   or

   a. Choose Bullets and Numbering from the Format menu (**Figure 27**). The Bullets and Numbering dialog box will open.

   b. Click the Numbers tab to bring that tab page forward (**Figure 28**).

   c. Select a number style by clicking on a sample.

   d. Click OK.

Figure 25. *Click the Numbered List button on the Format toolbar.*

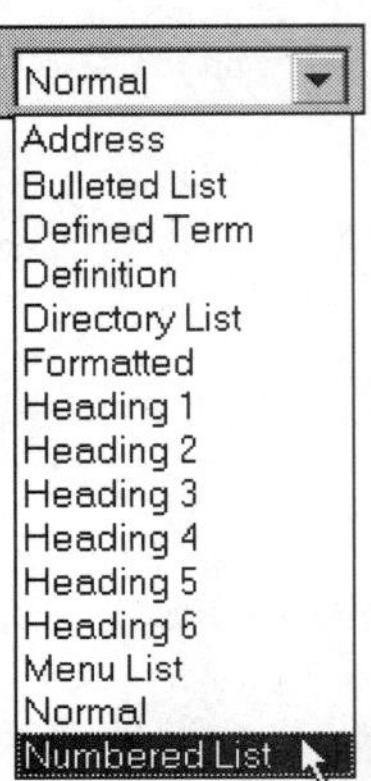

Figure 26. *Choose Numbered List from the Change Style drop-down list on the Format toolbar.*

Figure 27. *Choose Bullets and Numbering from the Format menu.*

Browsers and Numbered Lists

When you create a numbered list using the Bullets and Numbering dialog box shown in Figure 28, you can select special numbering styles such as Roman numerals and letters. Only Netscape Navigator and Microsoft Internet Explorer will display these special numbers. Other browsers will ignore them and just display Arabic numerals which are the default.

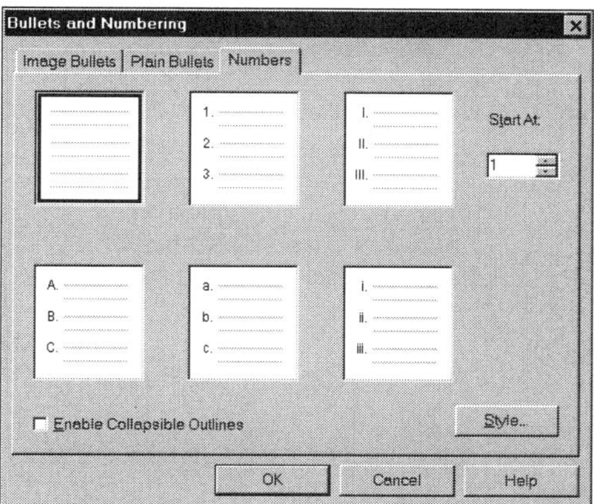

Figure 28. *Use the Numbers tab in the Bullets and Numbering dialog box to select a numbered list style, then click OK.*

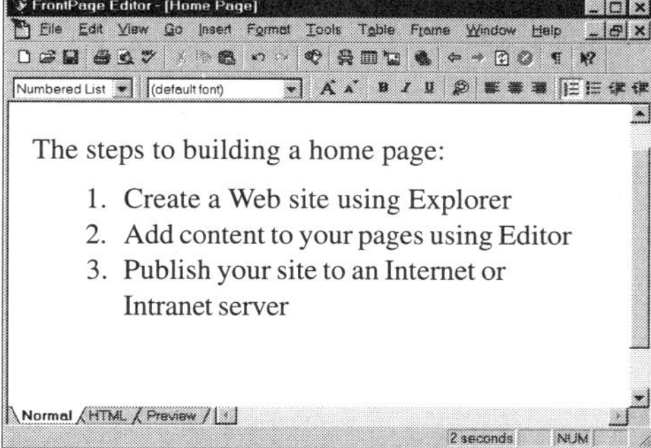

Figure 29. *As you type and press Enter, your numbered list takes shape.*

3. Where the number appears on the page, type in your first list item.
4. When you are finished with the first item, press Enter on the keyboard to create the next number. Continue typing and pressing Enter until your list is complete (**Figure 29**).
5. When you are finished adding the last numbered item, press Ctrl+Enter or press Enter twice to change back to the Normal style.

Tips:

- If you use the Bullets and Numbering dialog box to create your numbered list, you can choose from different numbering styles including Roman numerals and letters.
- To start a numbered list at a number other than 1, enter the number in the Start At text box on the right of the Numbers tab page in the Bullets and Numbering dialog box.

What's my tag?

There are two HTML tags for numbered lists. <ol> tells the browser a numbered list is coming and <li> denotes a numbered item.

These tags are used like this:

```
<ol>
    <li>I am the first item!
    <li>I am the second item!
</ol>
```

You can also create nested bulleted and numbered lists. Some folks call this "a list in a list." FrontPage makes creating multilevel lists easy.

To create a nested list:

1. Create a bulleted or numbered list containing the top-level items (**Figure 30**).
2. Move the insertion marker to the end of the line above where you want to add a second-level (nested) list.
3. Press Enter on the keyboard, then click the Increase Indent button on the Format toolbar twice. FrontPage 98 will create a nested list of the same type as the original list (**Figure 31**).
4. Type the secondary list, pressing Enter each time you want to add a new secondary item.

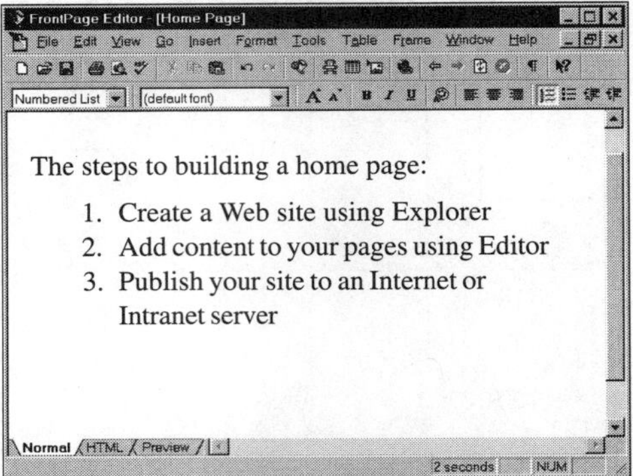

Figure 30. *Use the Editor to create a bulleted or numbered list of top-level items.*

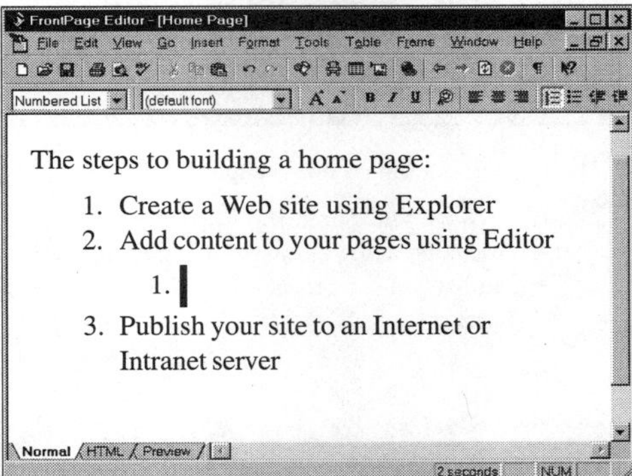

Figure 31. *Click the Increase Indent button twice to create a secondary list.*

LISTS AND HYPERLINKS

Lists are great for presenting information in an organized way. You can use them to create a table of contents Web page with hyperlinks to related topics. For more about hyperlinks, see Chapter 14.

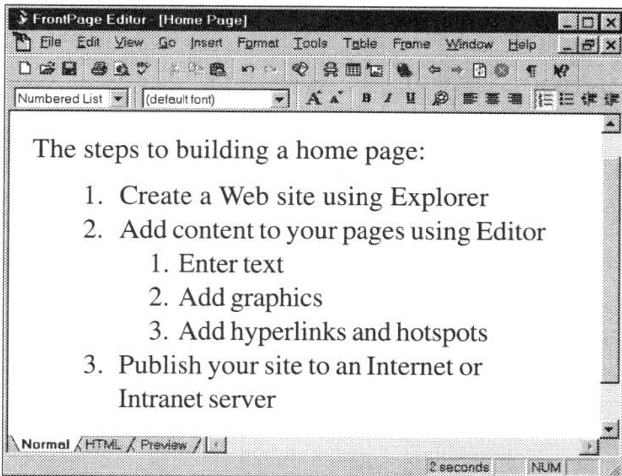

Figure 32. *The secondary list appears as you type and press Enter.*

5. When you are finished typing the secondary list, click anywhere on the page outside of the list (**Figure 32**).
6. To add another secondary list to another main list item, repeat steps 2 through 5.

Tips:

- If you want to change the bullet type (round or square) or number type (Roman numerals or letters) of a secondary list, type in your secondary list as described above. Select the secondary list and choose Bullets and Numbering from the Format menu. Use the List Properties dialog box to select the bullet or number type you would like to use.
- To move a secondary list item up to a main list item, select the secondary item, then click the Decrease Indent button twice.
- To move a main list item down to the secondary list below it, select the main item, then click the Increase Indent button twice.
- You can create nested lists within nested lists if you like. But be careful not to nest lists too deeply or they may become confusing.

The Bullets and Numbering Dialog Box has Changed Names!

When you create a new list and open the Bullets and Numbering dialog box for the first time, the name you see in the dialog box's title bar will be just that—Bullets and Numbering. If you go to edit an existing list by selecting it and opening the dialog box again, the name in the dialog box's title bar will be List Properties. This may be confusing at first, but don't worry, it's the same dialog box!

A definition list presents information in a dictionary-type format. The term being defined is on the first line and the definition is indented on the next line. When you create a definition list, FrontPage automatically alternates between two styles, Defined Term and Definition.

Figure 33. *Choose Defined Term from the Change Style drop-down list on the Format toolbar.*

To create a definition list:

1. Position the insertion marker where you want the list to begin.
2. Choose Defined Term from the Change Style drop-down list on the Format toolbar (**Figure 33**).
3. Type the term that you want to define (**Figure 34**).
4. Press Enter. The insertion marker will move down and the style will automatically change to Definition.

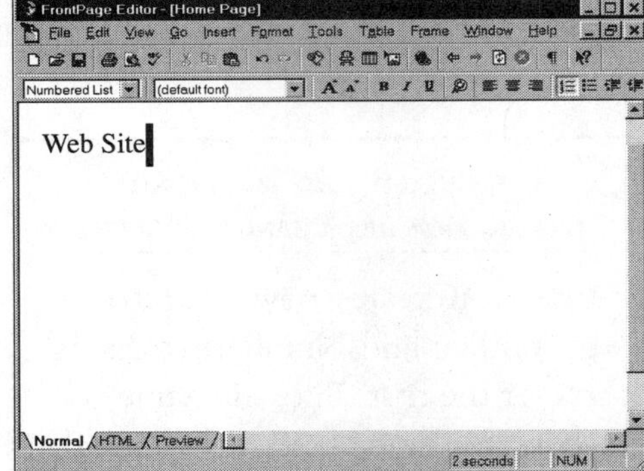

Figure 34. *Type the term you want to define, then press Enter.*

Other List Styles

You may have noticed that there are two other list styles available on the Change Style drop-down list on the Format toolbar. These two styles are called Directory List and Menu List. These styles are very similar to the Bulleted List style and work in exactly the same way. A few browsers, including the latest versions of Netscape Navigator and Microsoft Internet Explorer, recognize these styles and apply a special bulleted formatting to them, but many browsers will display these styles exactly the same as the Bulleted List style.

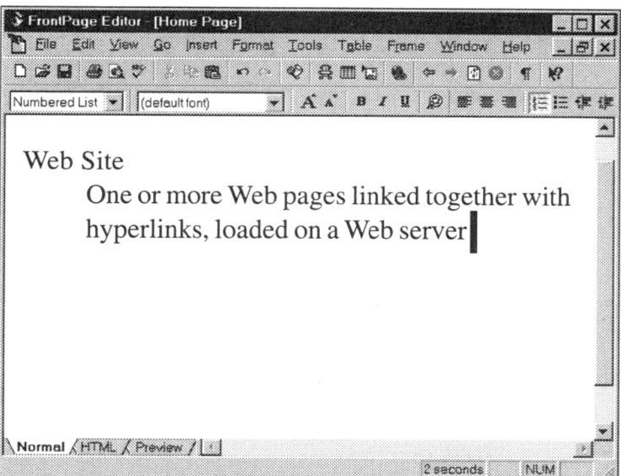

Figure 35. *Type the definition for the term, then press Enter.*

5. Type in the definition for the term (**Figure 35**).
6. Press Enter. The insertion marker will move down and the style will automatically change back to Defined Term.
7. Repeat steps 3 through 6 for every term you want to define (**Figure 36**).
8. When you are finished, either press Ctrl+Enter or press Enter twice to return to the Normal style.

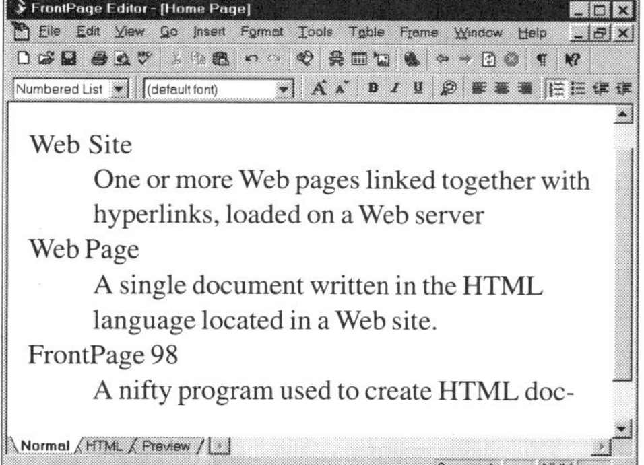

Figure 36. *As you type terms and definitions and press Enter, the definition list takes shape.*

What's my tag?

There are three HTML tags used to create a definition list. <dl> tells the browser a definition list is coming, <dt> denotes a defined term and <dd> denotes a definition.

These tags are used like this:

```
<dl>
<dt>This is a term
    <dd>This is the definition
<dt>This is a second term
    <dd>This is the definition
</dl>
```

FrontPage 98 lets you create bulleted or numbered lists that users can collapse and expand to see less and more information. This cool new feature lets you fit a large amount of material in a relatively small space. (The collapsed list—just showing the major topics—might fit easily within one screen, even if the fully expanded list takes up many pages.) The only catch is that visitors to your site have to be running Explorer 4.0 or another DHTML-capable browser for collapsible lists to work.

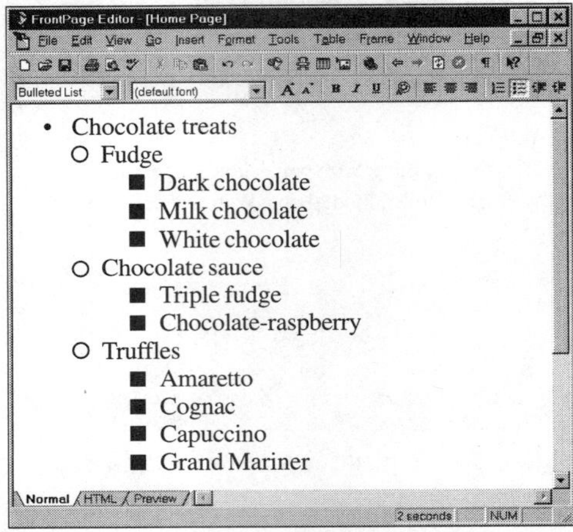

Figure 37. *A list like this one shown in the Editor can be collapsed and expanded if viewed in Microsoft Internet Explorer 4.*

To create a collapsible outline:

1. Create a bulleted or numbered list that contains one or more levels of nesting (**Figure 37**).
2. Place the insertion marker in any item in the top-level list.
3. Choose Bullets and Numbering from the Format menu (**Figure 27**). The List Properties dialog box will open (**Figure 38**).
4. Put a check mark in the Enable Collapsible Outlines check box (**Figure 39**).
5. Click OK to close the dialog box.
6. Choose Preview in Browser from the File menu. The Preview in Browser dialog box will open (**Figure 40**). (See pages 123–124 for complete directions on how to view your Web pages in a browser.)

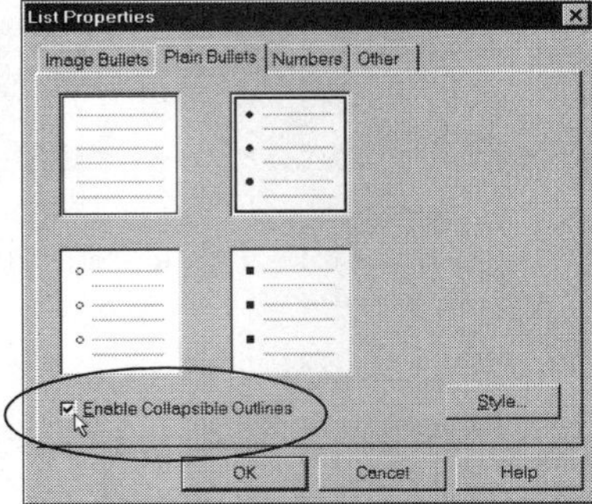

Figure 38. *The List Properties dialog box is used to create collapsible lists.*

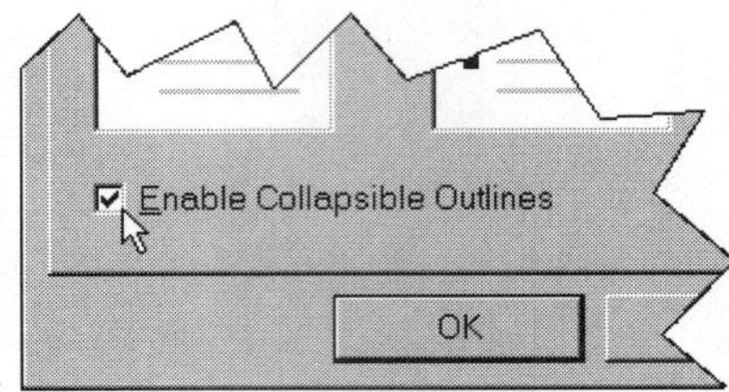

Figure 39. *Put a check mark in the Enable Collapsible Outlines check box.*

Create a Collapsible Outline

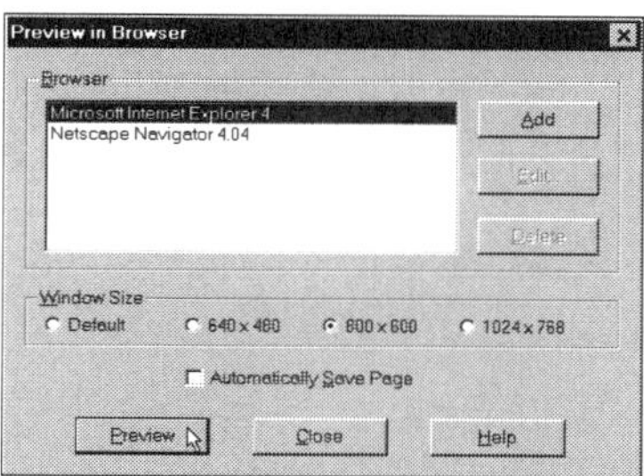

Figure 40. *Select Microsoft Internet Explorer 4 from the list, then click Preview.*

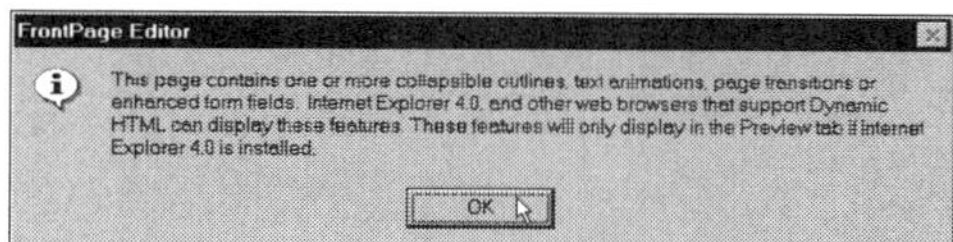

Figure 41. *Click OK to close the FrontPage Editor dialog box.*

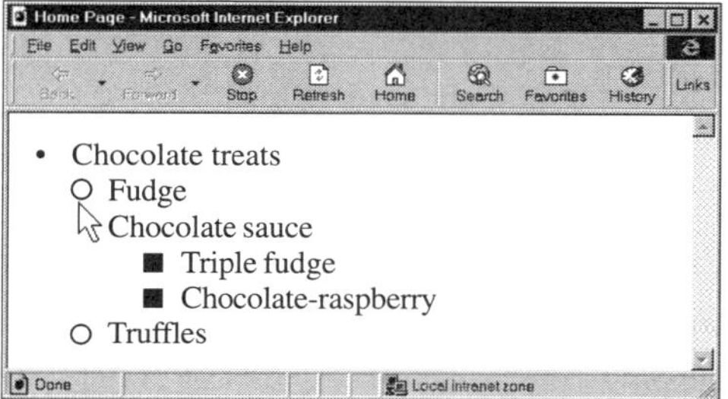

Figure 42. *A click of the mouse contracts a portion of the nested list.*

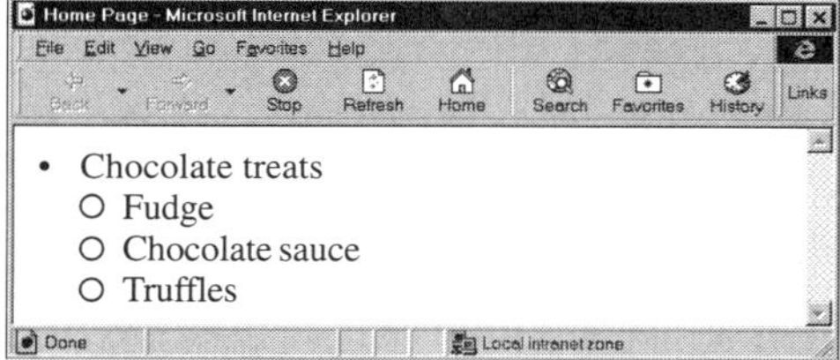

Figure 43. *The list in its collapsed version viewed in Microsoft Internet Explorer 4.*

7. Choose Microsoft Internet Explorer 4 from the list of browsers.

8. Click Preview. A Front Page Editor dialog box warning that this feature will only work with Internet Explorer 4.0 may open (**Figure 41**). Click OK to close the dialog box. Your list will appear in the Microsoft Internet Explorer 4 browser (**Figure 42**).

9. In the browser, click a bulleted or numbered item that has a nested list or lists underneath it. The nested list(s) will collapse, disappearing from view (**Figure 43**). You can do the same for any other nested portions of the list you want to conceal.

10. Click the same item a second time to bring the hidden items backinto view.

Tips:

- If you view your page in Netscape Navigator or another browser that doesn't support DHTML, you'll see the entire list and won't be able to collapse it.
- You can also view and test out collapsible lists in the Editor's Preview tab, as long as you are running Internet Explorer 4.0.

With FrontPage Editor, you can remove any extra formatting that you have applied to words or paragraphs using the Remove Formatting command. When you use Remove Formatting, the words or paragraphs are returned to the default setting for the style that the text is using.

Figure 44. *Select the paragraphs or characters you want to change back.*

To return a style to its default look:

1. Select the characters or paragraph(s) that you want to return to the format's default style (**Figure 44**).
2. Choose Remove Formatting from the Format menu (**Figure 45**). The characters or paragraph(s) will revert to the style's default settings (**Figure 46**).

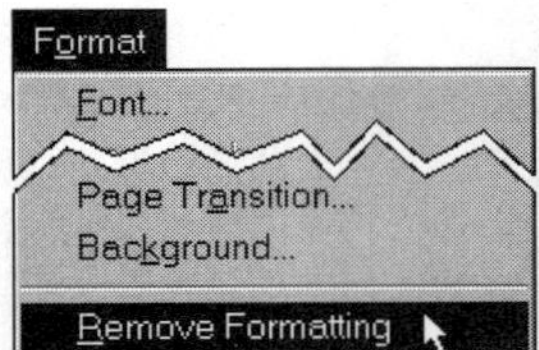

Figure 45. *Choose Remove Formatting from the Format menu.*

Figure 46. *The text reverts to the default formatting.*

Tip:

- This removes character formatting only. Any changes you have made to the paragraph, such as alignment, will remain the same.

SUMMARY

In this chapter you learned how to:

- Align paragraphs
- Apply the Formatted style
- Indent a paragraph
- Use the Heading styles
- Create nested lists
- Create bulleted, graphical bulleted, and numbered lists
- Create a definition list
- Create a collapsible outline

Return a Style to its Default Look

Fun with Graphics

10

One of the great features of the World Wide Web is the support of graphics, sounds, and videos. These multimedia elements make Web browsing fun while communicating a message to users. Adding multimedia elements to your Web pages is just a click away with FrontPage Editor.

The simplest graphical element you can add to a Web page is a horizontal line. Horizontal lines are great for separating topics and large blocks of text.

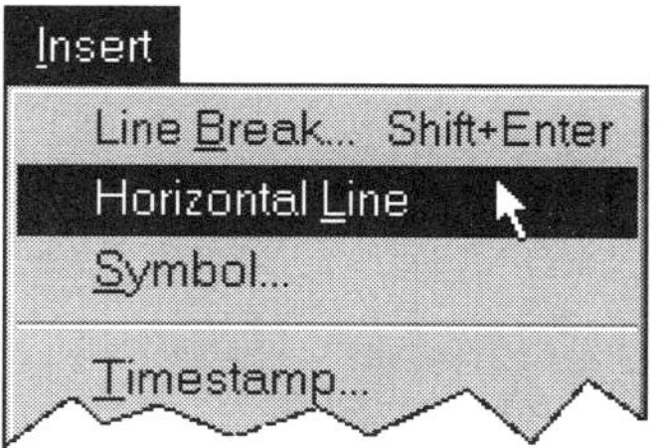

Figure 1. *Choose Horizontal Line from the Insert menu.*

To insert a horizontal line:

1. Position the insertion marker where you want the line to appear.
2. Choose Horizontal Line from the Insert menu (**Figure 1**). The line will appear on your Web page (**Figure 2**).

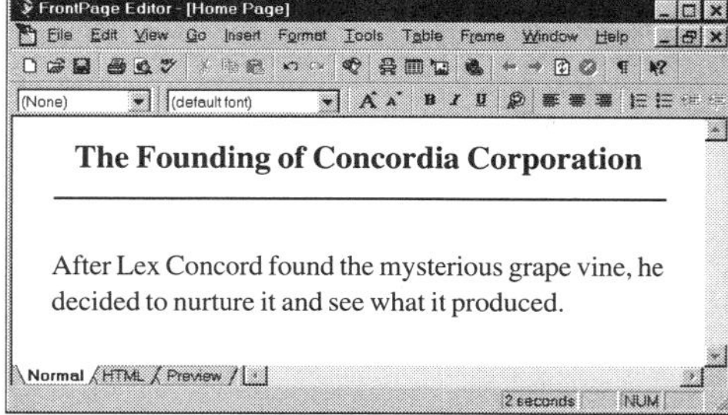

Figure 2. *The horizontal line appears on the Web page.*

What's my tag?

The HTML tag for a horizontal line is <hr>. It is used like this:

```
<p>I am a paragraph.</p>
<hr>
<p>I am below the line.</p>
```

You can change the way a horizontal line looks and customize it for your needs.

To format a horizontal line:

1. Right mouse click on the horizontal line. A pop-up menu will appear (**Figure 3**).
2. Choose Horizontal Line Properties from the pop-up menu. The Horizontal Line Properties dialog box will open (**Figure 4**).
3. Use the Width area to specify the length of the line as a percentage of the browser window width or as a specific length in pixels.
4. Use the Height area to specify how tall the line will be in pixels.
5. In the Alignment area, select how the line will be aligned in the browser window.
6. Use the Color drop-down list to choose a color for the line.
7. If you want the line to be all one color, instead of shaded, put a check mark in the Solid line (no shading) check box.
8. Click OK. Your custom line will appear on the Web page (**Figure 5**).

Tip:

- To delete a horizontal rule, select it, then press Delete or Backspace on the keyboard.

Figure 3. *Choose Horizontal Line Properties from the pop-up menu.*

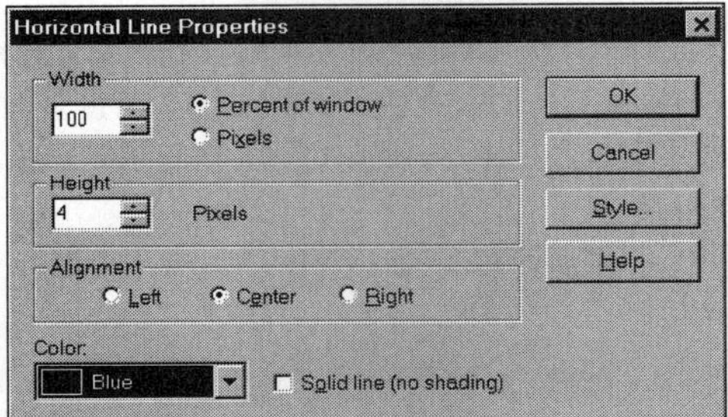

Figure 4. *Use the Horizontal Line Properties dialog box to set the width, height, alignment, and color of a horizontal line.*

Figure 5. *The horizontal line takes on the custom qualities you selected.*

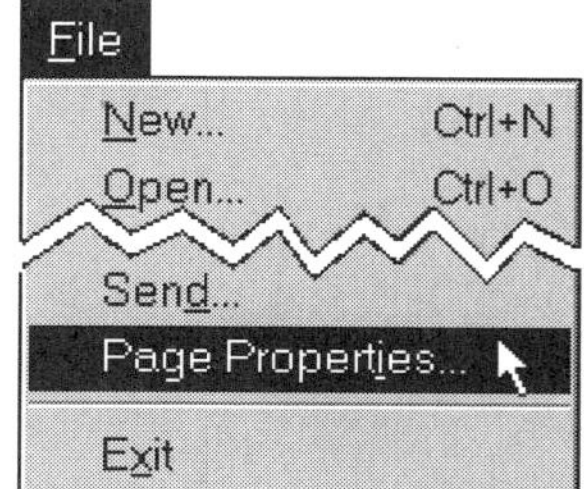

Figure 6. *Choose Page Properties from the File menu.*

Figure 7. *Choose Page Properties from the pop-up menu.*

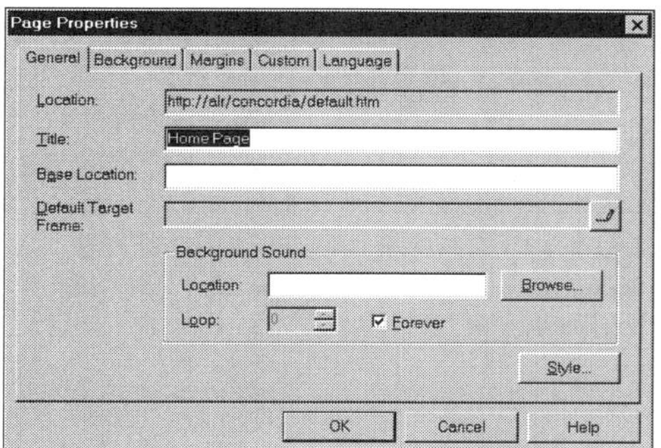

Figure 8. *The Page Properties dialog box.*

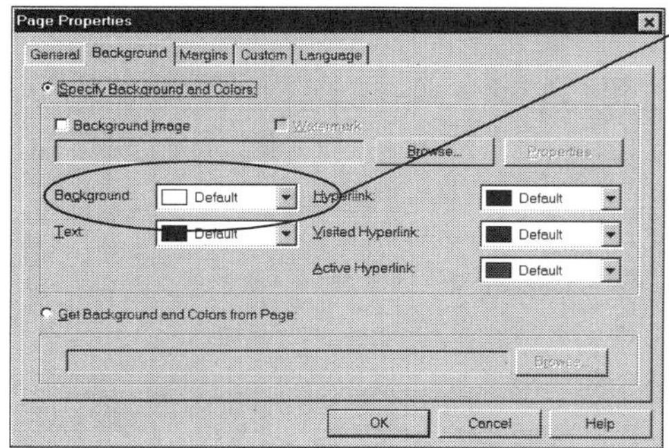

Figure 9. *The Background tab page.*

The next page element that you may want to change is the background color of your page. Whatever color you decide on, make sure the page's text is still easy to read.

To change a page's background color:

1. Open the Web page in the Editor.
2. Choose Page Properties from the File menu (**Figure 6**) or right click on the page area and select Page Properties from the pop-up menu (**Figure 7**). The Page Properties dialog box will open with the General tab page in front (**Figure 8**).
3. Click the Background tab to move to that tab page (**Figure 9**).
4. Use the Background drop-down list to choose a color (**Figure 10**).
5. Click OK. The dialog box will close and the page will redraw with the background color you selected.

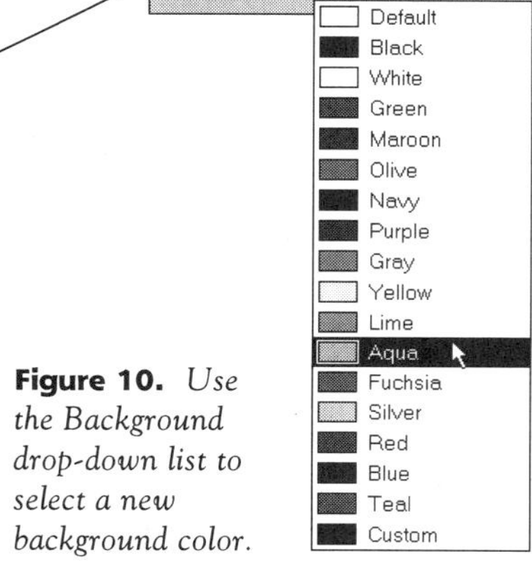

Figure 10. *Use the Background drop-down list to select a new background color.*

Change a Page's Background Color

FrontPage makes it easy to create Web pages with the same background, text, and hyperlink text colors. (Hyperlinks are discussed in Chapter 14.) All you have to do is set up one page, then use that page as the color basis for any other pages you create.

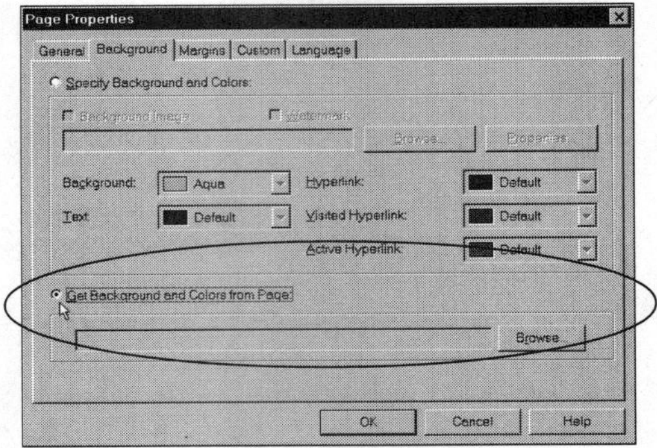

Figure 11. *The Background tab page of the Page Properties dialog box.*

To set up page colors using another Web page:

1. Use the Editor to open the page whose colors you want to change.
2. Open the Page Properties dialog box by selecting Page Properties from the File menu (**Figure 6**) or right clicking on the page area and selecting Page Properties from the pop-up menu (**Figure 7**).
3. Click the Background tab to move to that tab page (**Figure 11**).
4. Select the Get Background and Colors from Page radio button near the bottom of the Background tab page in the Page Properties dialog box (**Figure 12**).
5. Click the Browse button. The Current Web dialog box will open (**Figure 13**).
6. Choose the Web page whose colors you want to copy, then click OK.
7. Click OK to close the Page Properties dialog box. Your Web page will assume the colors specified by the Web page you selected.

Figure 12. *Select the Get Background and Colors from Page radio button, then click the Browse button.*

Figure 13. *Select a Web page from the list box in the Current Web dialog box, then click OK.*

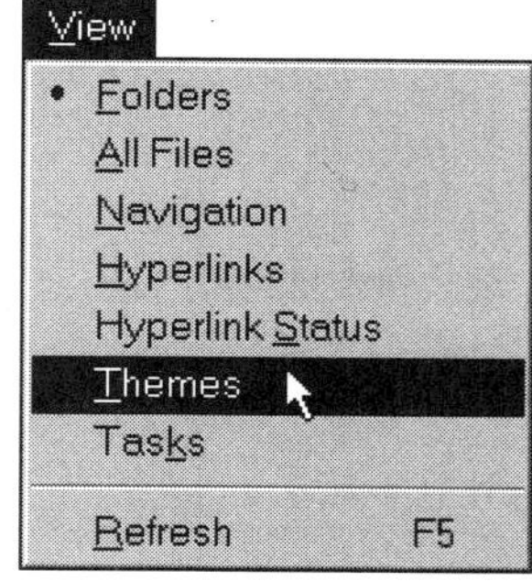

Figure 14. *Choose Themes from the View menu.*

Another way to set background colors automatically (and other Web page elements, such as fonts, text color, bullet styles, etc.) is to use a FrontPage theme. Themes are Web page designs that make it easy to quickly build consistent and sophisticated looking sites. Normally, a theme is applied to an entire site, but you can also apply themes to individual pages if that suits your needs.

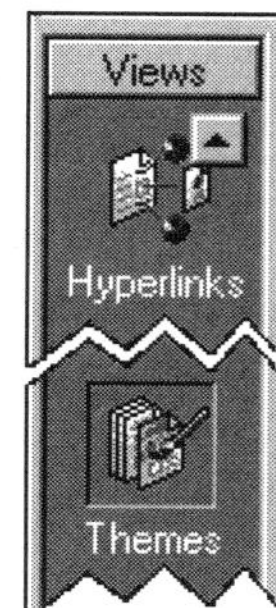

Figure 15. *Click the Themes button on the Views bar.*

To apply a theme to an entire Web site:

1. Create a new Web site or open an existing one in Explorer. If you're in the Editor and the Web site you want to change is already open, switch to Explorer by choosing Show FrontPage Explorer from the Tools menu or clicking the Show FrontPage Explorer toolbar button.

Figure 16. *The Themes view in FrontPage 98 Explorer.*

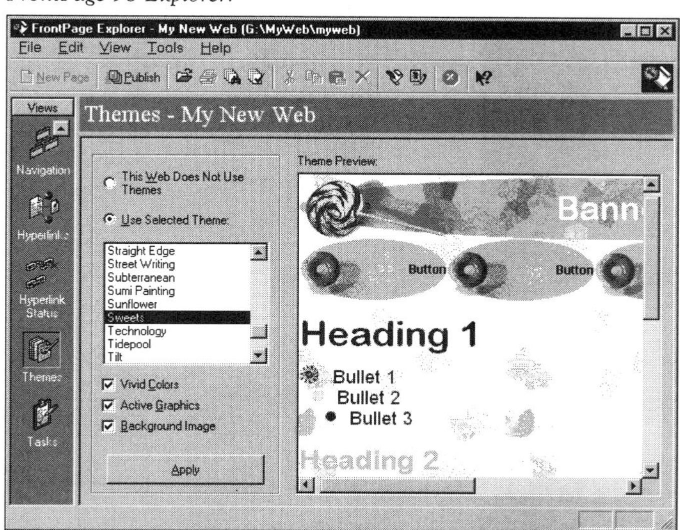

2. Choose Themes from the View menu (**Figure 14**) or click the Themes button on the Views bar (**Figure 15**). The Themes view will appear in the Explorer window (**Figure 16**). If your Web site doesn't have a theme applied to it, the This Web Does Not Use Themes radio button will be selected.

3. Select the radio button Use Selected Theme (**Figure 17**).
4. Select a theme using the list box below the Use Selected Theme radio button. A preview of the theme you have chosen will appear on the right side of the screen in the Theme Preview pane (**Figure 18**).
5. When you find the theme you want to use, click the Apply button. The theme will be applied to all the pages in the open Web site (**Figure 19**).

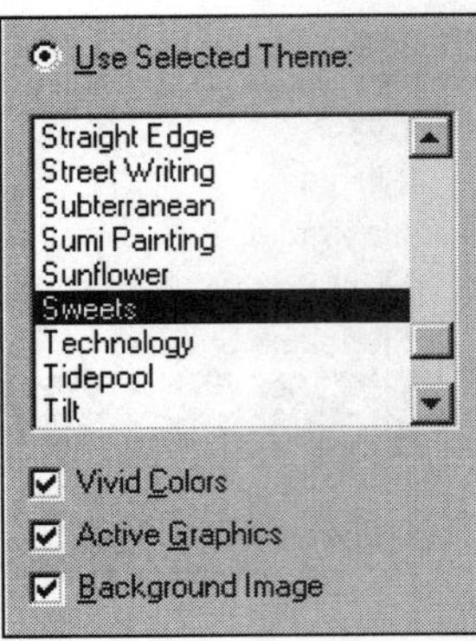

Figure 17. *Select the Use Selected Theme radio button, then choose a theme from the list box.*

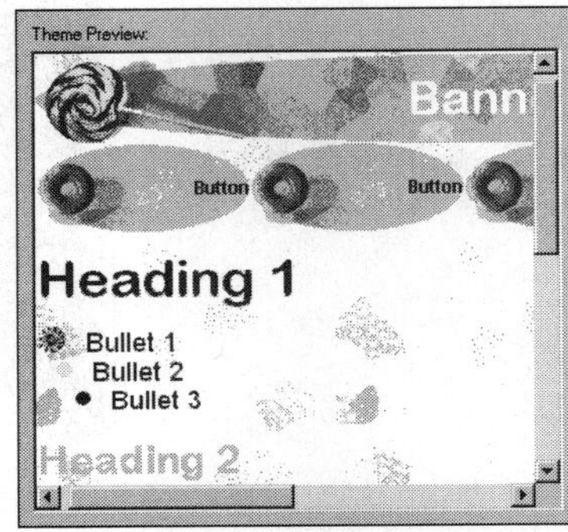

Figure 18. *A preview of the theme you've selected appears in the Theme Preview pane.*

Tips:

- To remove a theme from a Web site, select the This Web Does Not Use Themes radio button.
- If you apply a theme to an individual page, as described on page 149, that page won't be affected when you change the theme for the entire site.
- To use brighter colors in a theme, put a check mark in the Vivid Colors check box (**Figure 17**).

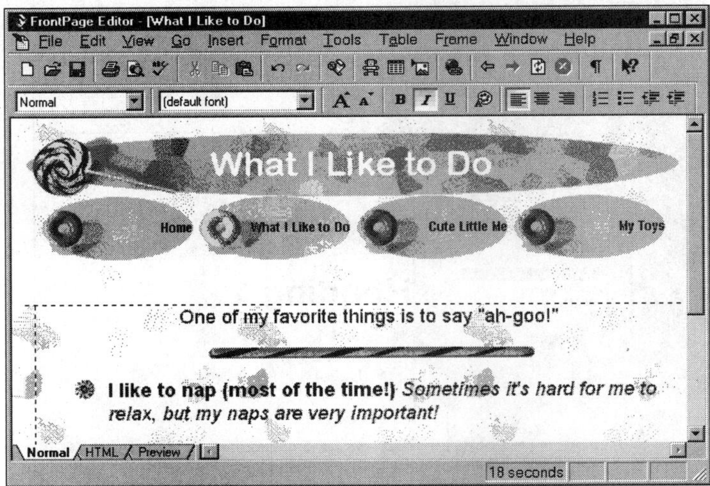

Figure 19. *The selected theme applied to the open Web site.*

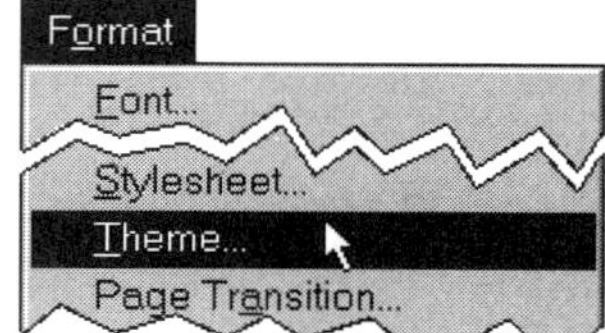

Figure 20. *Choose Theme from the Format menu.*

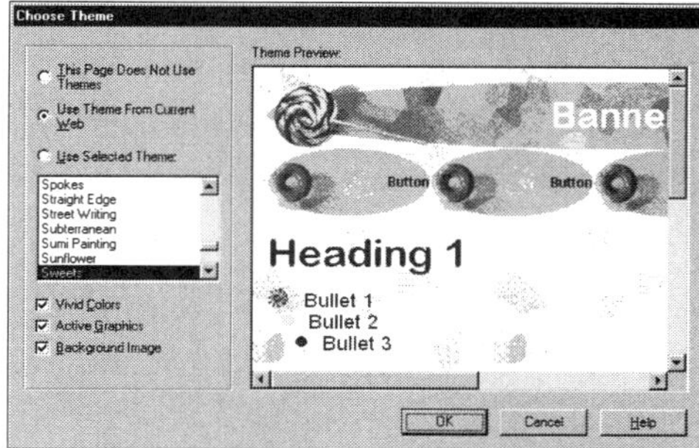

Figure 21. *The Choose Theme dialog box is used to select a theme for a Web page.*

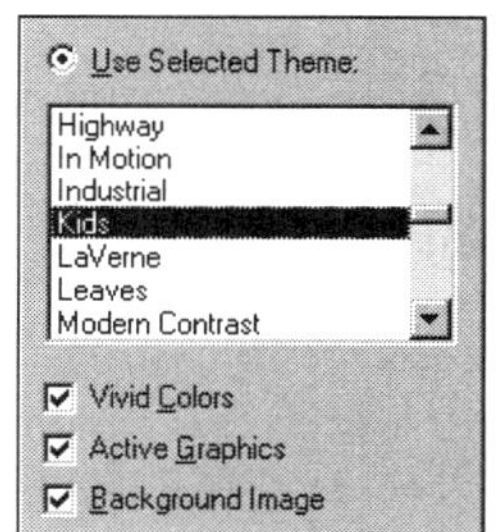

Figure 22. *Click the Use Selected Theme radio button, then choose a theme from the list box.*

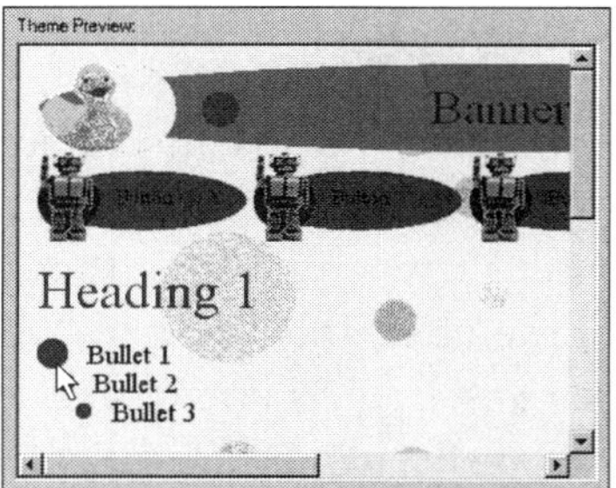

Figure 23. *A preview of the theme you've chosen appears in the Theme Preview pane.*

To apply a theme to an individual Web page:

1. In FrontPage Editor, open the Web page to which you want to apply the theme.
2. Choose Theme from the Format menu (**Figure 20**). The Choose Theme dialog box will open (**Figure 21**). Notice that this dialog box looks a lot like Themes view in Explorer (**Figure 16**).
3. Make sure the Use Selected Theme radio button is chosen, then use the list box to choose a theme (**Figure 22**). A preview of the theme will appear in the Theme Preview pane (**Figure 23**).
4. Click OK to apply the theme to the current Web page and close the dialog box.

Tips:

- If you select the Use Theme from Current Web radio button, the theme from the open Web site will be applied to the open page. You might want to do this, for example, if you applied a different theme to a page and then decided you wanted that page to match the other pages in the Web site after all.
- To remove a theme from a Web page, select the This Page Does Not Use Themes radio button.

Graphic File Formats and the Web

Graphic file formats for the Web come in two flavors, .gif (CompuServe bitmap) and .jpg (Joint Photographic Experts Group (JPEG)) bitmap. The JPEG file format is ideal for photographs and images with depth and small color changes such as lighting effects. The GIF file format is typically used for black and white art, line drawings, and images that are less than 256 colors.

There are two GIF Formats, 87a and 89a. 87a Format was developed in 1987 and is the standard GIF format. A special feature of this format is *interlacing*. An interlaced GIF file appears in the browser in chunks, starting at a low resolution, and progressing after several seconds to its final form.

89a Format, developed in 1989, is a descendant of the 87a Format. As with its predecessor, 89a Format offers interlaced images. The special feature of this format is *transparency*. Transparent images contain sections (usually in the background) that are invisible. This is handy when a Web page has a special background pattern. You don't have to try to match the graphic's background to the background on the Web page (an impossible task!); instead, the image's invisible background lets the Web page background shine through.

A new file format, .png (pronounced "ping"), has been created as an alternative to the .gif file format. At this time, you can add .png files to your FrontPage Web pages, but FrontPage will automatically reformat the file as a .gif.

FrontPage Editor will import many kinds of image file formats, including .bmp, .tif, .wpg, .eps, .pcx, and .wmf, and automatically convert them for you to either the .gif or .jpg format.

How to View File Extensions in Windows

To see all file extensions, open any Windows window—for instance, double click on My Computer to open that window—and select Options from the View menu. In the Options dialog box, click the View tab to bring that tab page to the front. For Windows 95, make sure the check box next to "Hide MS-DOS file extensions for file types that are registered" is unchecked. For Windows NT, make sure the check box next to "Hide file extensions for known file types" is unchecked.

Figure 24. *Click the Insert Image button on the Standard toolbar.*

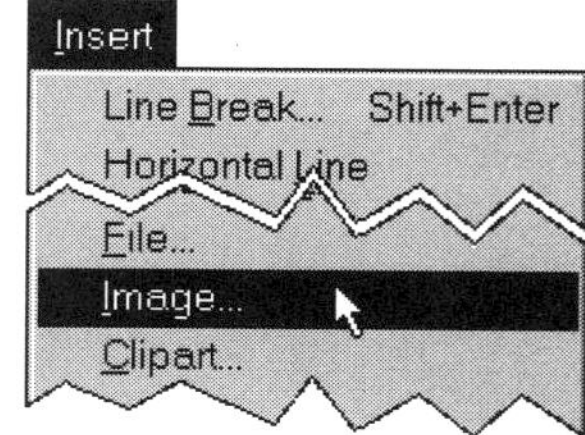

Figure 25. *Choose Image from the Insert menu.*

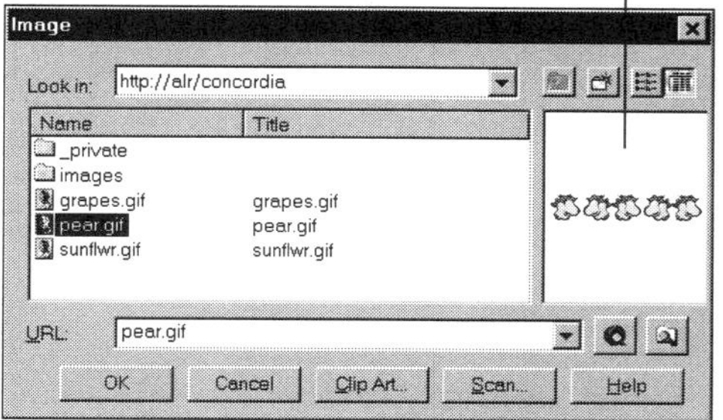

Figure 26. *Select an image from the list box in the Image dialog box.*

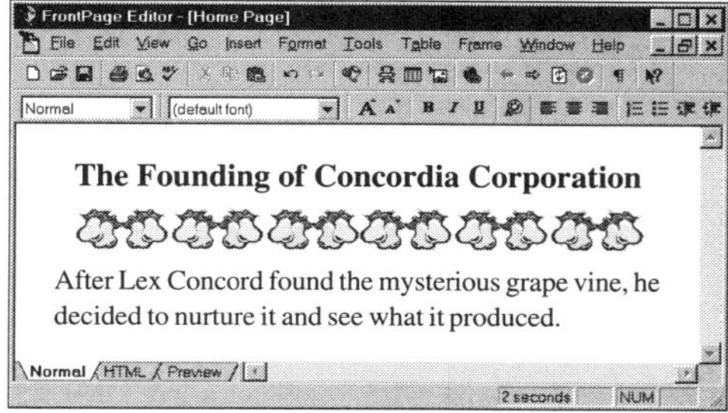

Figure 27. *The image appears on your Web page.*

There are several sources you can use to add an image to your Web page. You can select an image from the current Web site, from a location on your computer, from the World Wide Web itself, and from the FrontPage clip art collection. FrontPage 98 ships with an interesting library of clip art images, animations, and background textures that you can use in your Web pages.

To insert an image from the current Web site:

1. In the Editor, place the insertion marker where you would like to insert the image.
2. Click the Insert Image button on the Standard toolbar (**Figure 24**) or choose Image from the Insert menu (**Figure 25**). The Image dialog box will open displaying the open site's images and file folders (**Figure 26**). If you don't see any image files, double-click on the images folder.
3. Select the image you want to insert. A preview of the image will appear in the Preview pane on the right side of the dialog box.
4. Click OK. The dialog box will close and the image will appear in your Web page (**Figure 27**).

To insert an image from a location on your computer:

1. In the Editor, place the insertion marker where you would like to insert the image.
2. Click the Insert Image button on the Standard toolbar (**Figure 24**) or choose Image from the Insert menu (**Figure 25**). The Image dialog box will open (**Figure 28**).
3. If you know the exact location of the file, type the path and file name in the URL text box, and then click OK. The image will be added to the Web page (**Figure 29**).

   or

   If you don't know the exact location of the file, click the "Select a file on your computer" button (**Figure 30**). The Select File dialog box will open (**Figure 31**). Use the dialog box to locate the graphic file. When you have found it, select it, and then click Open. Both dialog boxes will close and the image will be added to the Web page (**Figure 29**).

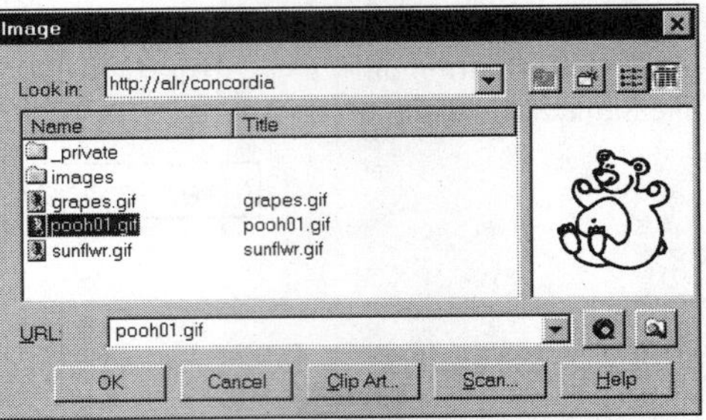

Figure 28. *Select the file using the Image dialog box.*

Figure 29. *After you enter the file name and click OK, the graphic appears on the Web page.*

Figure 30. *Click the "Select a file on your computer" button.*

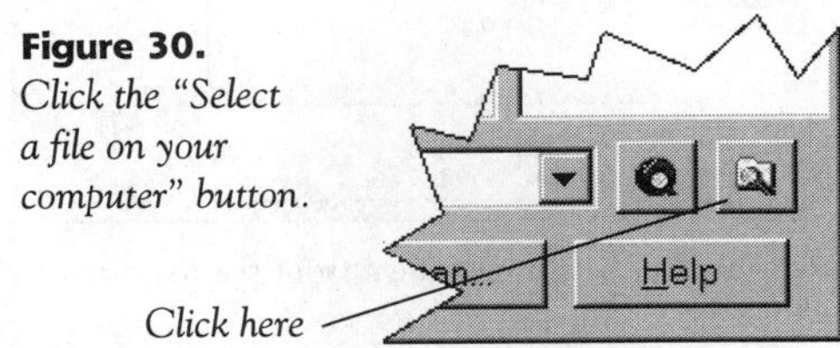

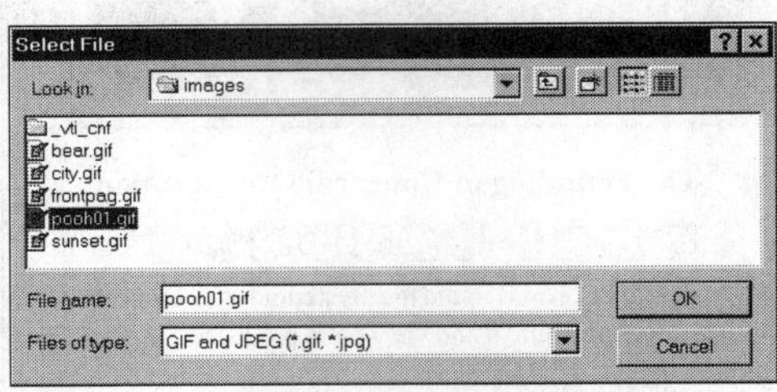

Figure 31. *Use the Select File dialog box to find the file you want to insert.*

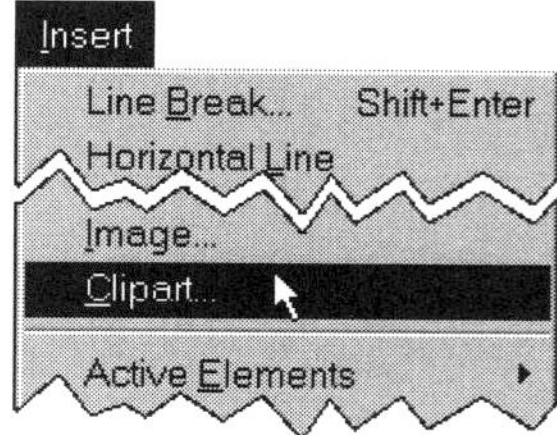

Figure 32. *Choose Clipart from the Insert menu.*

To insert an image from the FrontPage clip art collection:

1. In the Editor, place the insertion marker where you would like to insert the image.
2. Choose Clipart from the Insert menu (**Figure 32**). The Microsoft Clip Gallery 3.0 dialog box will open with the Clip Art tab page in front (**Figure 33**).
3. Use the list box at the left of the dialog box to select a group of clip art. Clip art images that are ready for the Web are listed in the categories that use the word "Web," found at the bottom of the list.
4. Select the image you want to insert by clicking on it in the preview area on the right.
5. Click Insert. The dialog box will close and the image will appear in your Web page (**Figure 34**).

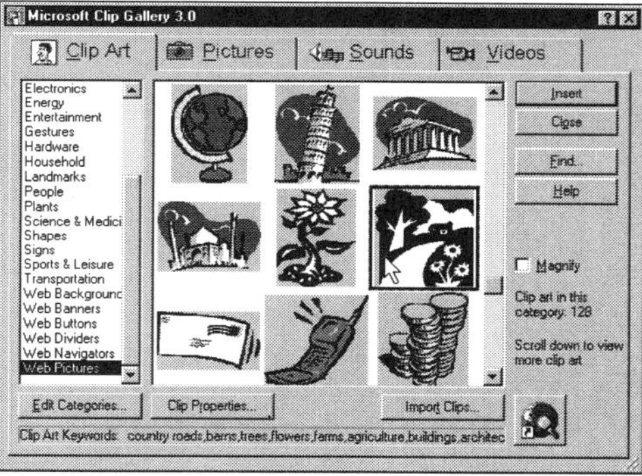

Figure 33. *Select an image using the Microsoft Clip Gallery 3.0 dialog box.*

Figure 34. *The FrontPage clip art appears in your Web page.*

Permission to use Images

Before you can use images from the World Wide Web, such as the BearHome welcome screen shown in Figure 36, you must get permission to use the image from the owner.

To insert an image from the World Wide Web:

1. Make sure you are connected to the Web via modem.
2. In the Editor, place the insertion marker where you would like to insert the image.
3. Click the Insert Image button on the Standard toolbar (**Figure 24**) or choose Image from the Insert menu (**Figure 25**). The Image dialog box will open (**Figure 26**).
4. Click the "Use your Web Browser to select a page or file" button (**Figure 35**). Your favorite browser will launch.
5. Use the browser to move to the Web page containing the graphic.
6. If you're using Netscape Navigator:
   - **a.** Right click on the graphic and choose Copy Image Location from the pop-up menu (**Figure 36**). Don't disconnect from the Web.
   - **b.** Return to FrontPage Editor and the Image dialog box.

   If you're using Microsoft Internet Explorer:

   - **a.** Right click on the graphic and choose Properties from the pop-up menu (**Figure 37**).

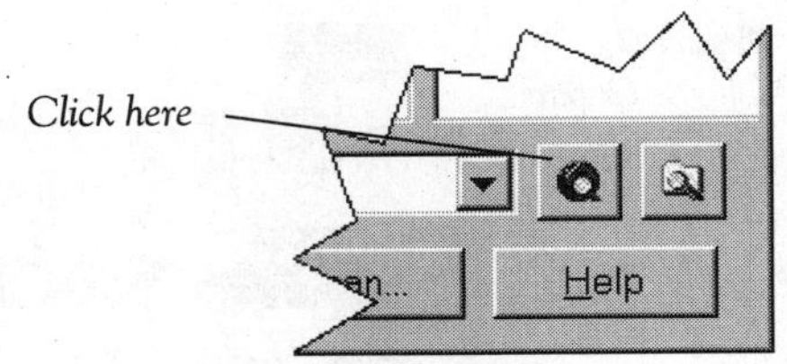

Figure 35. *Click the "Use your Web Browser to select a page or file" button.*

Figure 36. *In Netscape Navigator, right click on the image and select Copy Image Location from the pop-up menu.*

Figure 37. *In Microsoft Internet Explorer, right mouse click on the graphic and choose Properties from the pop-up menu.*

Figure 38. *Use the mouse to select the complete URL, then press Ctrl+C on the keyboard.*

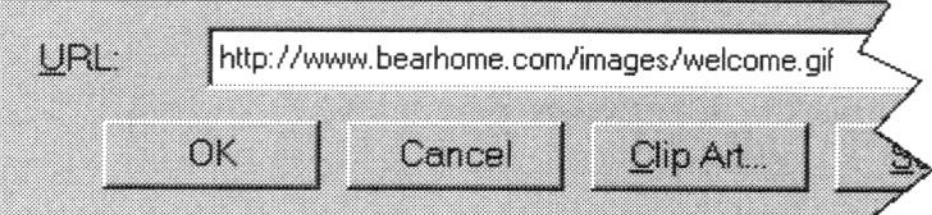

Figure 39. *Place the insertion marker in the URL text box, then press Ctrl+V on the keyboard.*

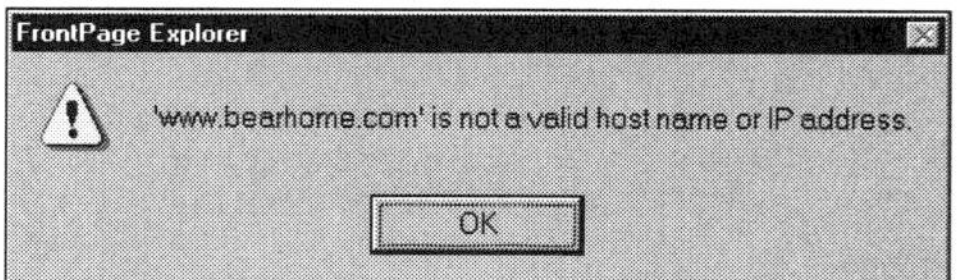

Figure 40. *If you are not connected to the Web, this dialog box will appear.*

Figure 41. *The broken image icon will appear where the graphic would be.*

b. Position the mouse at the beginning of the Address, press the left mouse button and drag to select the entire address (**Figure 38**).

c. Press Ctrl+C on the keyboard to copy the Address. Don't disconnect from the Web.

d. Return to FrontPage Editor and the Image dialog box.

7. Make sure the URL text box is empty.

8. Place the insertion marker in the text box and press Ctrl+V on the keyboard. The exact URL of the graphic will appear in the text box (**Figure 39**).

9. Click OK. It will take a few seconds before the image appears in your Web page.

Tip:

- If you are not connected to the Web, a warning dialog box will appear (**Figure 40**) and a broken image icon will appear where the graphic should be (**Figure 41**).

When you include an image from another Web site in your Web page, remember that the folks running that Web site may remove the image from their site or change its location. If this happens, the broken image icon will appear in your page.

When you first save your Web page after adding images, a Save Embedded Files dialog box will appear (**Figure 42**). This dialog box lets you rename a graphic and save it in a location you specify. In most cases, you will want to click Yes. This will make the graphics available for loading onto the Web page when you publish your Web site to a server. If you are saving a Web page for the first time, the Save As dialog box will open instead.

With FrontPage Editor, you can add interlacing and transparency to your .gif images and convert .jpg files to the .gif format and vice versa. (For details about these image formats, take a look at the "Graphic File Formats and the Web" sidebar on page 150.)

To convert a JPEG file to a GIF (and vice versa):

1. Right click on the image you want to convert and choose Image Properties from the pop-up menu (**Figure 43**) or select the image and choose Image Properties from the Edit menu (**Figure 44**) or press Alt+Enter on the keyboard. The Image Properties dialog box will open with the General tab page in front (**Figure 45**). In the Type area, if the image is a .jpg file, the JPEG radio button will be selected. If the image is a .gif file, the GIF radio button will be selected (**Figure 46**).

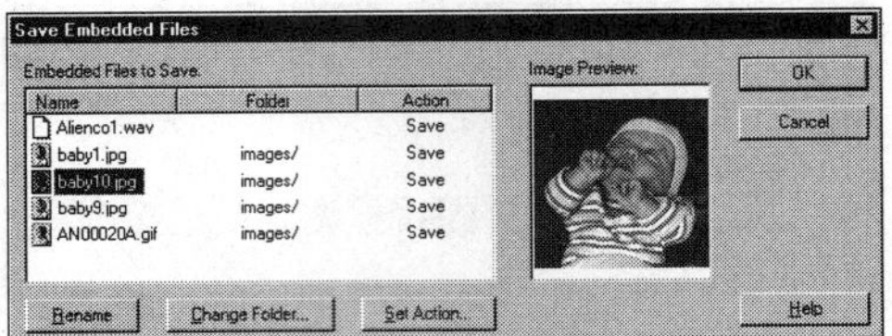

Figure 42. *The Save Embedded Files dialog box.*

Figure 43. *Choose Image Properties from the pop-up menu.*

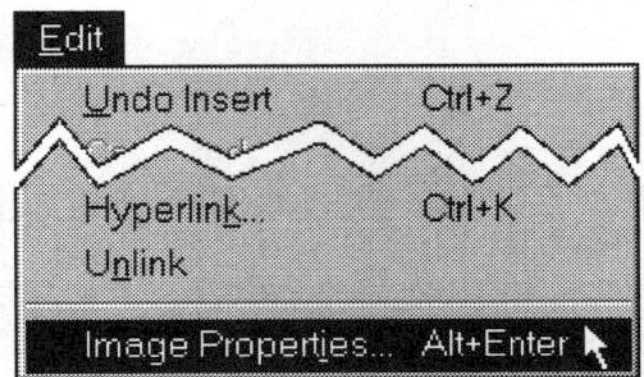

Figure 44. *Choose Image Properties from the Edit menu.*

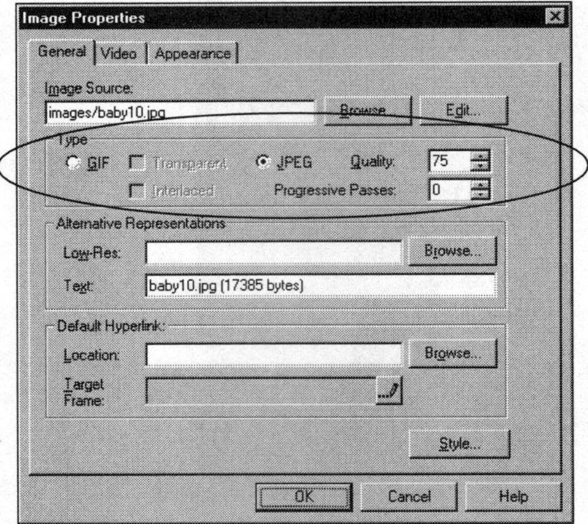

Figure 45. *Use the Type area of the Image Properties dialog box.*

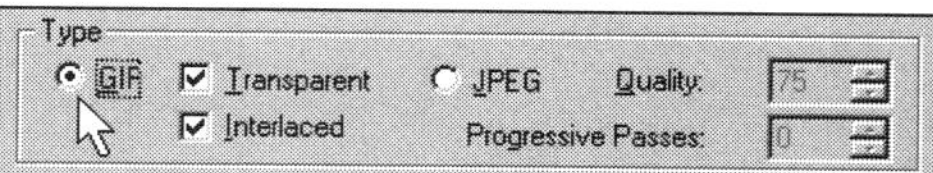

Figure 46. *In the Type area, select the GIF or JPEG radio button to convert the image to that file format.*

Figure 47. *Select the image with the mouse pointer.*

Figure 48.
Click the Make Transparent button on the Image toolbar.

Figure 49. *When you click on a color with the eraser pointer (in this case the gray background seen in Figure 47) the color disappears.*

2. Select the radio button for the type of file you want to convert the graphic to. If you choose JPEG, the Quality text box will become available. The number in this box controls the *file compression*. File compression removes tiny details from an image, squashing the size of the file down. The higher the number in the Quality text box, the lower the amount of compression will be. Hence, the image quality will be better, though, the file size will be larger. If you would like to, type a new number in the Quality text box, but keep in mind that smaller file sizes are best. You can always adjust the Quality again later if the image size is so large that it slows down load time.
3. Click OK. FrontPage will convert the graphic.

To make a GIF transparent:

1. Select the Image with the mouse (**Figure 47**). The Image toolbar will appear.
2. On the Image toolbar, click the Make Transparent button (**Figure 48**). As you pass the mouse over the image, the pointer will change to a pencil eraser with a little arrow attached to it.
3. Position the pointer over the color you want to make transparent.
4. Click the mouse. The color will disappear (**Figure 49**).

To create an interlaced GIF:

1. Right click on the graphic and choose Image Properties from the pop-up menu (**Figure 50**). The Image Properties dialog box will appear (**Figure 51**).
2. In the Type area on the General tab page, put a check mark in the Interlaced check box near the GIF radio button.
3. Click OK. The dialog will close. Next time you view your Web page in a browser, the image will load in chunks as it appears.

Figure 50. *Choose Image Properties from the pop-up menu.*

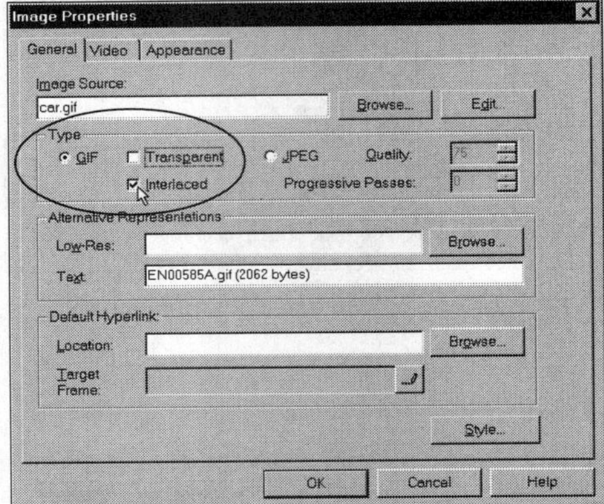

Figure 51. *Put a check mark in the Interlaced check box.*

Once you've added an image to your Web page, you can set its alignment in relation to surrounding text, the amount of empty space surrounding the graphic, and the size of the image.

To align an image with the surrounding text:

1. Open the Image Properties dialog box by right clicking on the image and selecting Image Properties from the pop-up menu (**Figure 50**) or selecting the image and choosing Image Properties from the Edit menu.
2. Click the Appearance tab to bring that tab page to the front (**Figure 52**).

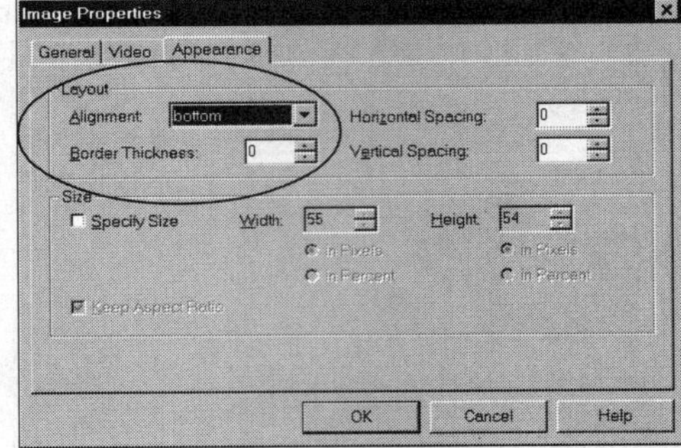

Figure 52. *On the Appearance tab page of the Image Properties dialog box, use the Alignment drop-down list in the Layout area to select an alignment.*

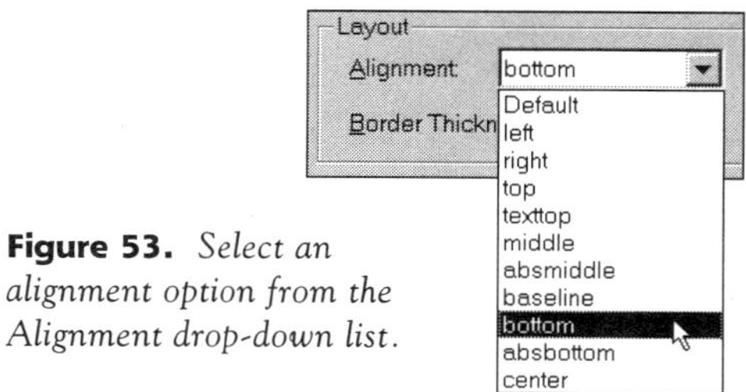

Figure 53. *Select an alignment option from the Alignment drop-down list.*

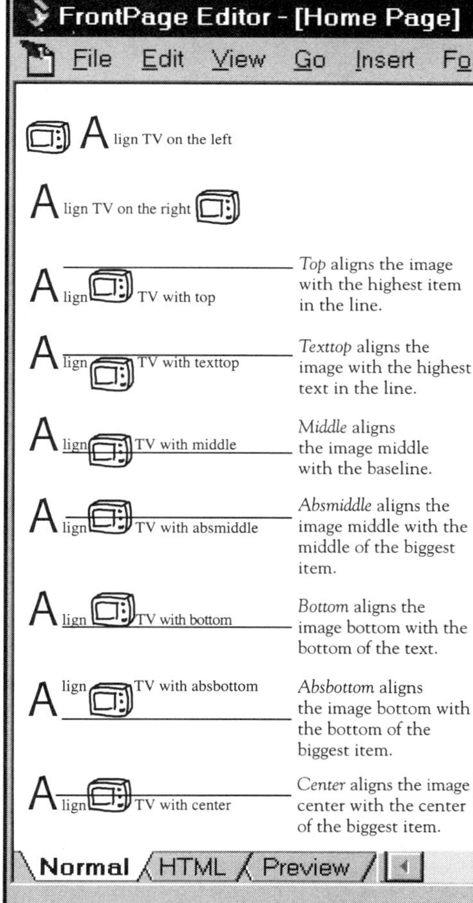

Figure 54. *There are 4 items on each line: a graphic of the letter A, some text, a graphic of a TV, and more text. The alignment positions are illustrated in relation to the TV.*

3. In the Layout area, use the Alignment drop-down list to select an option (**Figure 53**). Here are the alignments you can choose from (**Figure 54**):

- *Left* places the image in the left margin and wraps the text around the right side of the image.
- *Right* places the image in the right margin and wraps the text around the left side of the image.
- *Top* aligns the image with the highest element in the line.
- *Texttop* aligns the image with the highest text in the line.
- *Middle* aligns the middle of the image with the baseline of the text.
- *Absmiddle* aligns the middle of the image with the middle of the largest item.
- *Baseline* works the same as bottom.
- *Bottom* aligns the bottom of the image with the bottom of the text.
- *Absbottom* aligns the bottom of the image with the bottom of the largest item.
- *Center* aligns the center of the image with the surrounding text.

4. Click OK. The image's alignment changes to what you selected.

To set an empty space around the image:

1. Open the Image Properties dialog box by right clicking on the image and selecting Image Properties from the pop-up menu or selecting the image and choosing Image Properties from the Edit menu.
2. Click the Appearance tab to bring that tab page to the front (**Figure 55**).
3. In the Layout area, use the Horizontal Spacing text box to set the number of pixels of blank space between the image and what is to the right or left of the image (**Figure 56**).
4. Use the Vertical Spacing text box to set the number of pixels of blank space you want between the image and what is above and below it.
5. Click OK. The spacing around the image will change to the new settings (**Figure 57**).

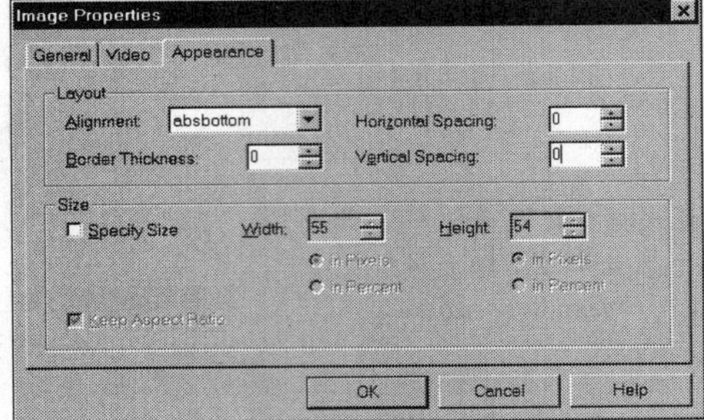

Figure 55. *Use the Appearance tab page to set the empty space around an image.*

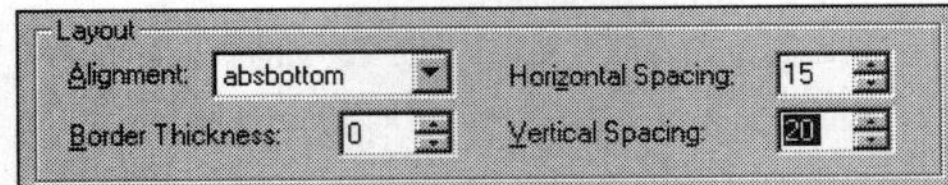

Figure 56. *In the Layout area, set the alignment and horizontal and vertical spacing.*

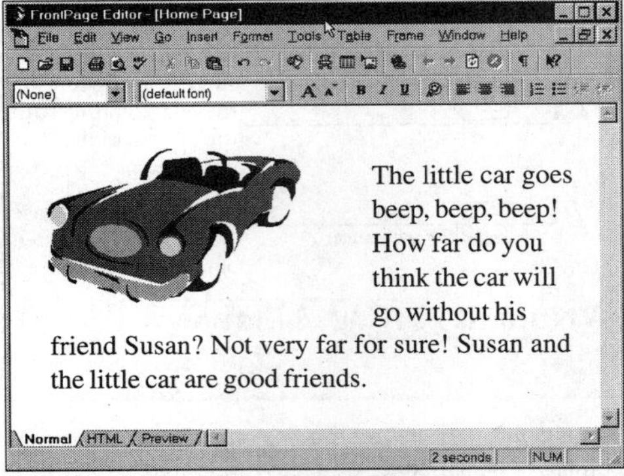

Figure 57. *When you click OK, the empty spacing appears around the image.*

To change the size of

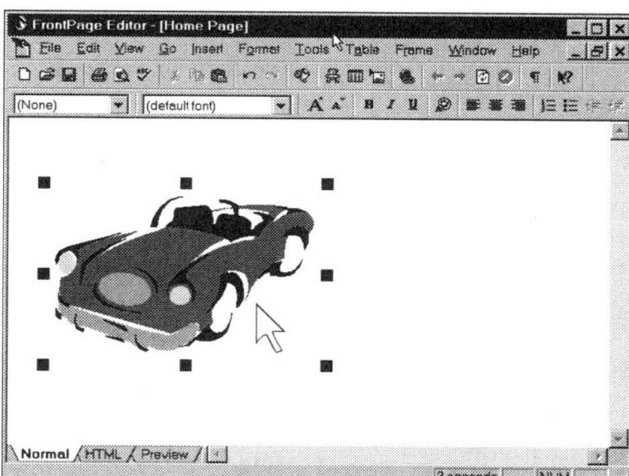

Figure 58. *When you select the image, eight handles appear around it.*

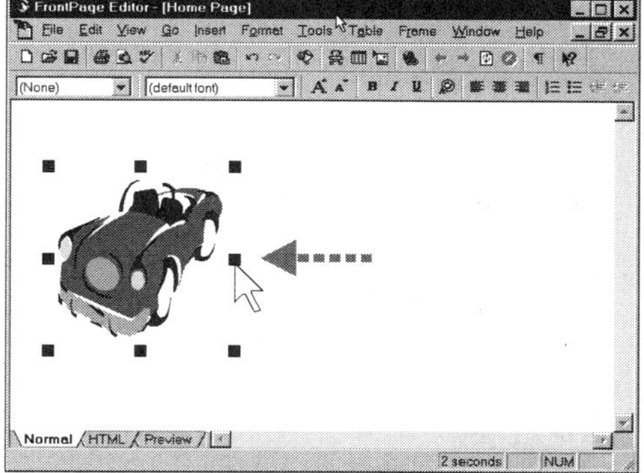

Figure 59. *Drag the handle to resize the image.*

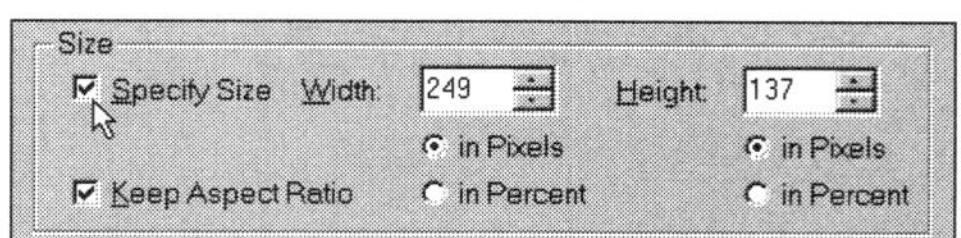

Figure 60. *In the Size area, put a check in the Specify Size check box, then use the Width and Height text boxes to set the new size for the image.*

an image:

1. Select the image. Eight black *handles* appear around it (**Figure 58**).
2. Position the mouse pointer over a handle, press the mouse button and drag. The image will resize (**Figure 59**).

or

1. Open the Image Properties dialog box by right clicking on the image and selecting Image Properties from the pop-up menu or selecting the image and choosing Image Properties from the Edit menu.
2. Click the Appearance tab to bring that tab page to the front (**Figure 55**).
3. In the Size area, put a check in the Specify Size check box (**Figure 60**).
4. Use the Width and Height text boxes to specify a number of pixels or a percentage of the original size.
5. Click OK. The image will resize (**Figure 59**).

Tip:

- Before you use the Width and Height text boxes the first time, the image's size is shown in pixels.

With FrontPage 98, it's easy to do nifty things to images right in the Editor, including cropping, adjusting contrast and brightness, rotating, and adding bevels.

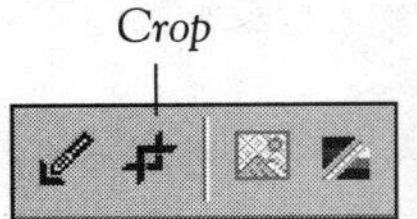

Figure 61. *Click the Crop button on the Image toolbar to crop an image.*

To crop an image:

1. Select the image you want to crop.
2. Click the Crop button on the Image toolbar (**Figure 61**). A cropping rectangle will appear around the selected image (**Figure 62**).
3. Position the mouse over a cropping handle.
4. Press the left mouse button and drag the handle to indicate which part of the image will be removed from view (**Figure 63**).
5. Press Enter on the keyboard or click the Crop button again to crop the image (**Figure 64**).

Figure 62. *When you click the Crop button, a cropping rectangle with handles appears around the image.*

Figure 63. *Press the left mouse button and drag the cropping rectangle to indicate how the image will be cropped.*

Figure 64. *When you press Enter or click the Crop button again, the image is cropped.*

To change the brightness or contrast of an image:

1. Select the image you want to change the brightness or contrast of (**Figure 65**).
2. Click the More Contrast, Less Contrast, More Brightness, or Less Brightness buttons (**Figure 66**) on the Image toolbar depending upon the effect you want to apply (**Figures 67a–d**).

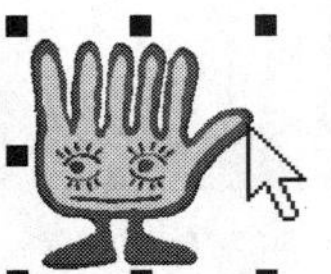

Figure 65. *Select the image you want to change.*

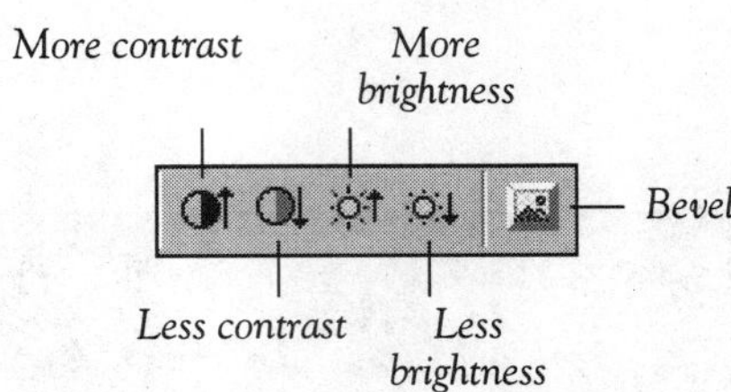

Figure 66. *Click the appropriate button on the Image toolbar, depending on the effect you want to apply.*

Figure 67a. *More brightness.*

Figure 67b. *Less brightness.*

Figure 67c. *More contrast.*

Figure 67d. *Less contrast.*

Figure 68. *Select the image you want to rotate reverse, or flip.*

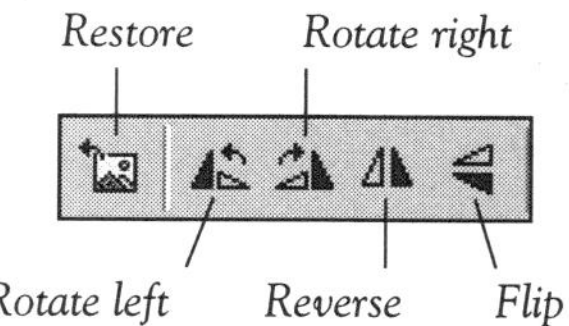

Figure 69. *Click the appropriate button on the toolbar depending on the effect you want to apply.*

Figure 70a. *Rotate right.*

Figure 70b. *Rotate left.*

Figure 70c. *Reverse.*

Figure 70d. *Flip.*

To flip and rotate images:

1. Select the image you want to rotate or flip (**Figure 68**).
2. Click the Rotate Left, Rotate Right, Reverse, or Flip buttons (**Figure 69**), depending on the effect you want to apply (**Figures 70a–d**).

To add a bevel effect to an image:

1. Select the image.
2. Click the Bevel button on the Image toolbar (**Figure 66**). A beveled border will appear around the image, giving it a three-dimensional look (**Figure 71**).

To restore an image to its original look:

1. Select the image.
2. Click the Restore button on the Image toolbar (**Figure 69**). All the effects you have applied since you last saved the image file, or since you inserted it into your Web page, will be reversed.

Figure 71. *When you click the Bevel button, a bevel is added around the edge of the image.*

As you add images to your Web pages, it's a good idea to give them *alternate text*. When someone is browsing your Web site, alternate text appears inside the placeholder where your graphic will appear once it loads. If the person is using a text-only browser, alternate text will give them an idea of what they are not seeing.

To set alternate text for an image:

1. Open the Image Properties dialog box (**Figure 72**) by right clicking on the image and selecting Image Properties from the pop-up menu or selecting the image and choosing Image Properties from the Edit menu.
2. On the General tab page in the Alternative Representations area, type the alternate text in the Text text box. (**Figure 73**).
3. Click OK. The next time you view your Web page in a browser, you will see the alternate text in the image placeholder while it loads (**Figure 74**).

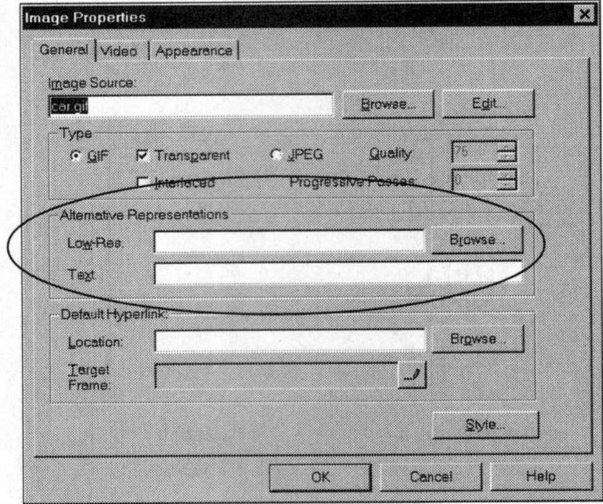

Figure 72. *To set the alternate text, use the Alternative Representations area of the Image Properties dialog box.*

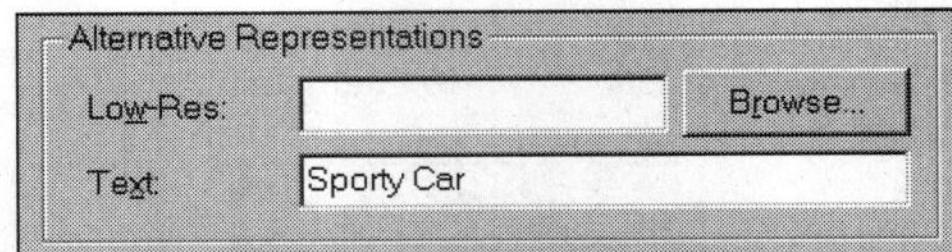

Figure 73. *Type the alternate text in the Text text box.*

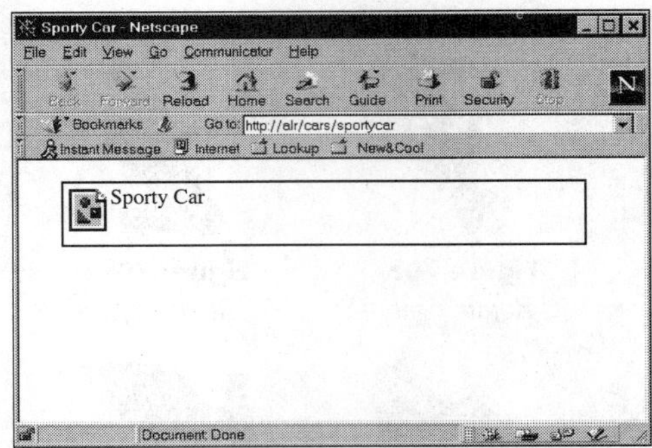

Figure 74. *As the Web page loads in a browser, the alternate text tells the user what's coming.*

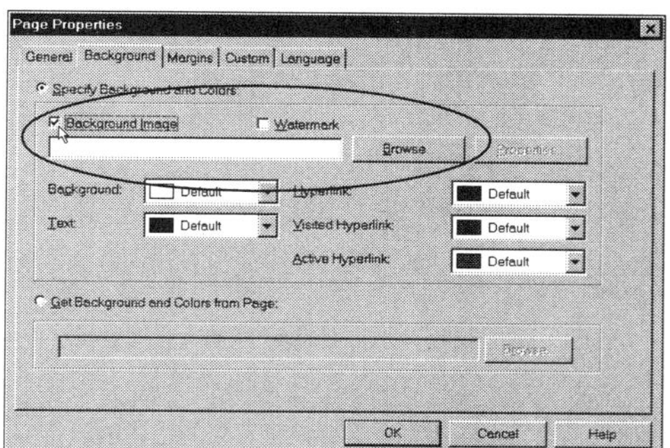

Figure 75. *Use the Background tab page to set a background image.*

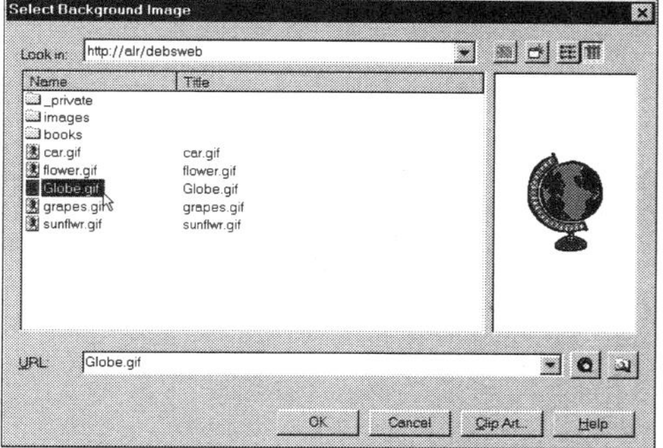

Figure 76. *Use the Select Background Image dialog box to select a graphic.*

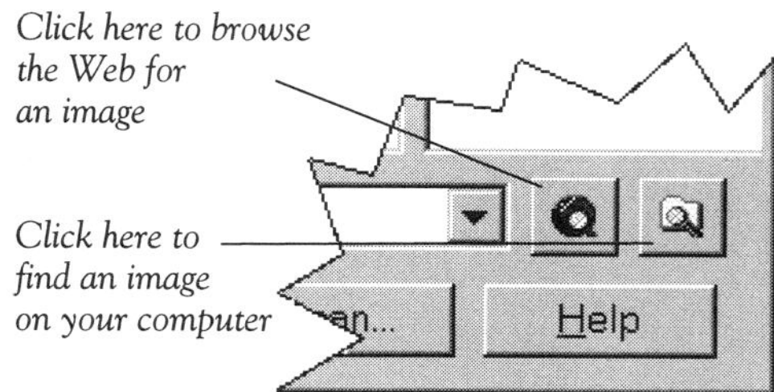

Figure 77. *Click the appropriate button to locate an image on the Web or on your computer.*

When you add a graphic as a background image, most browsers will *tile* the image automatically. This means that the image will be duplicated across and down, completely filling the background with the image.

To add an image as the page background:

1. Open the Web page to which you want to add the background.
2. Open the Page Properties dialog box by selecting Page Properties from the File menu or right clicking on the page area and selecting Page Properties from the pop-up menu.
3. Click the Background tab to move to that tab page (**Figure 75**).
4. Put a check mark in the Background Image check box, then click the Browse button. The Select Background Image dialog box will open (**Figure 76**).
5. There are several ways to choose a background:
   - Use the Select Background Image dialog box to select a graphic currently saved with the Web site (**Figure 76**).
   - Click the "Select a file from your computer" button to locate a file on your computer (**Figure 77**).

- Click the "Use your Web Browser to select a page or file" button to find an image on the Web (**Figure 77**).
- Click the Clip Art button to select a background from the Microsoft Clip Gallery 3.0 dialog box (**Figure 78**).

6. Click OK. The Select Background Image dialog box will close.
7. Click OK again to close the Page Properties dialog box. The background will appear on your Web page.

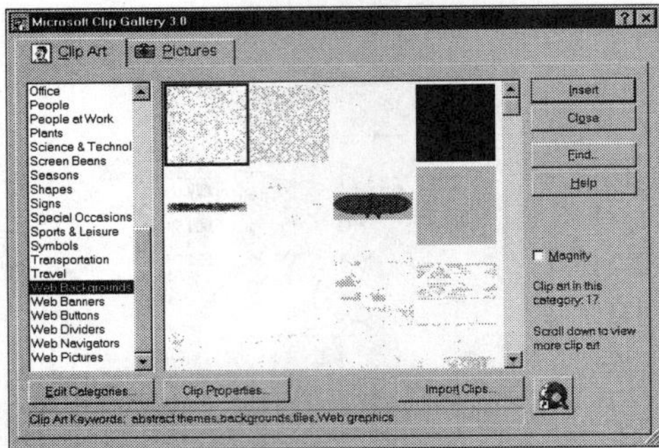

Figure 78. *Use the Microsoft Clip Gallery 3.0 dialog box to select a background.*

Graphics for Downloading from the Web

There are thousands of images to choose from on the Web, but not all of them are appropriate as background images. If an image is very dark or has a lot of "motion," most likely any text on this kind of background will be very hard to read. High contrast between your background image and text is good.

Yahoo contains an extensive list of sites that you can browse for images, animations, and backgrounds for your Web pages. Visit:

http://www.yahoo.com/computers_and_internet/internet/world_wide_web/page_design_and_layout/graphics/

Summary

In this chapter you learned how to:

- Insert a horizontal line
- Change background color
- Apply themes
- Insert graphics
- Convert a JPEG to a GIF
- Align images
- Crop and resize images
- Change brightness and contrast
- Set alternate text
- Add images as backgrounds

Add a Background Image

11 Multimedia

Now that you know how to add attention-getting images to your Web pages, it's time to add the multimedia elements—sounds, videos, and animation effects—that will make your site really snappy and interesting. Music, movies, animations, and words can be combined to create an impressive Web-page presentation for your viewers. FrontPage supports several different sound file formats, including Wave files (.wav), Midi sequences (.mid), AIFF files (.aif, .aifc, .aiff), and AU files (.au, .snd). FrontPage only supports one kind of video file—the Windows-based Audio-Visual file.

FrontPage 98 includes all sorts of fun animation effects that are easy to apply. You can add page transition effects that display when users switch from one page to the next, animation effects that cause words or images to move about the page, and banner ads that show a series of images one after another. If you want to get fancy, check out the GIF Animator that comes packaged with the Image Composer. This program lets you create animated GIFs composed of different images displayed one after another to give the illusion of movement.

Sounds, Videos, and Browsers

When you use sounds and videos in your Web pages, the folks browsing your Web site must have computers equipped with sound cards and speakers. Microsoft Internet Explorer includes the ability to play sounds, but Netscape Navigator needs a special plug-in. To check out and download the plug-ins, visit: *http://home.netscape.com/navigator/index.html;* click Plug-ins & Extras in the left-hand column.

Yahoo contains an extensive list of sites that you can browse for sounds and videos for your Web pages. To search for sounds, visit: *http://www.yahoo.com/computers_and_internet/multimedia/sound*

To search for videos, visit: *http://www.yahoo.com/computers_and_internet/multimedia/video*

Background sounds and music add another dimension to your Web site, creating a mood and giving it a sophisticated multimedia feel.

To add a background sound to a Web page:

1. In the Editor, choose Page Properties from the File menu (**Figure 1**) or right click in the page area and choose Page Properties from the pop-up menu (**Figure 2**). The Page Properties dialog box will open with the General tab page in front (**Figure 3**).
2. In the Background Sound area (**Figure 4**), type the exact path and file name of the sound file or click the Browse button to open the Background Sound dialog box (**Figure 5**).
3. To select a sound file, use any of the following techniques:

> **SOUNDS AND YOUR USERS**
>
> If you do choose to add sounds to your Web sites, remember that a sound playing over and over *can* get annoying. Usually a few iterations of a sound is enough. In other words, avoid leaving the Forever check box selected unless you have a *really good* reason to do so.

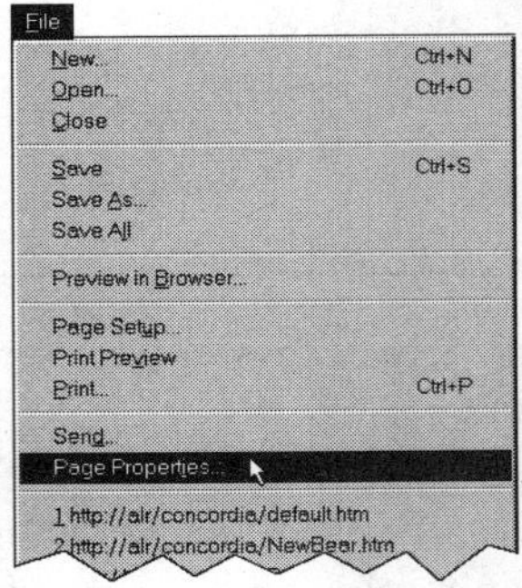

Figure 1. *Choose Page Properties from the File menu.*

Figure 2. *Choose Page Properties from the pop-up menu.*

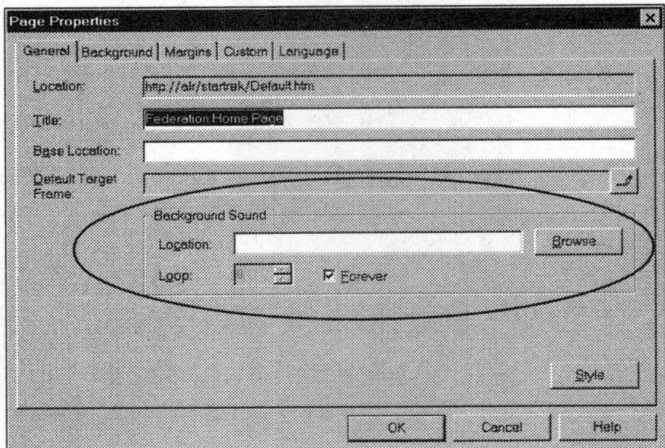

Figure 3. *Use the General tab page of the Page Properties dialog box to set a background sound for your Web page.*

Figure 4. *In the Background Sound area, type the name and path of the sound file or click the Browse button to locate the file.*

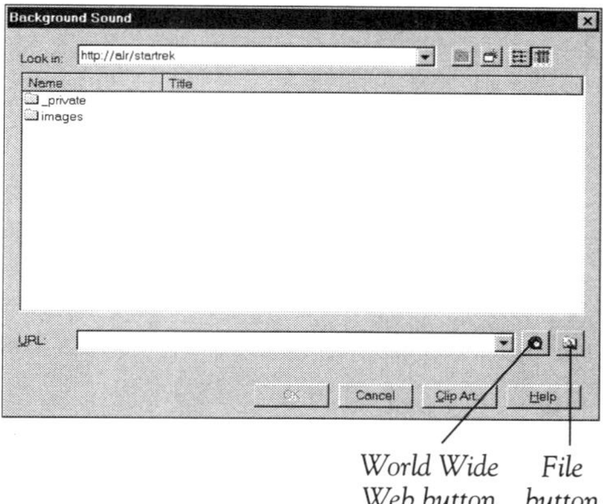

Figure 5. *Use the Background Sound dialog box to select a sound from the current Web site, in your file system, or on the World Wide Web.*

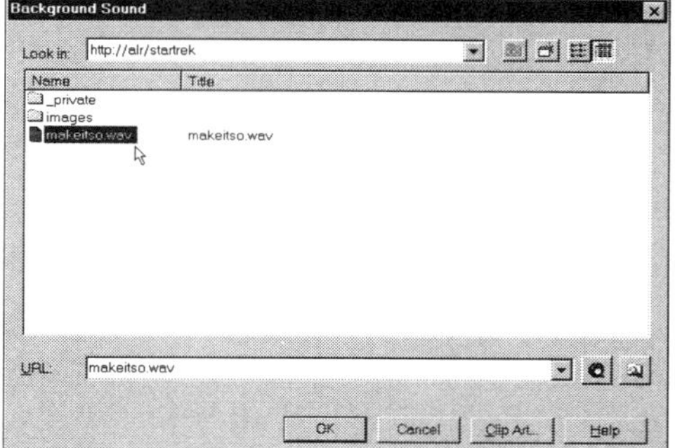

Figure 6. *Use the Select File dialog box to select a sound in your file system.*

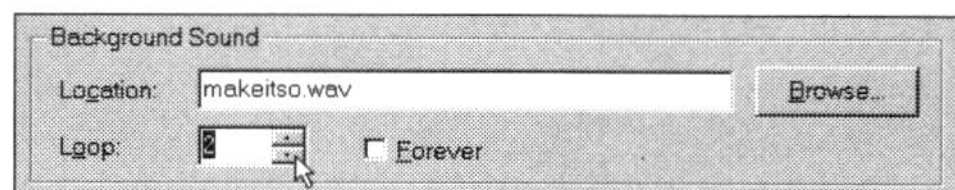

Figure 7. *In the Background Sound area of the Page Properties dialog box, use the Loop text box to set how many times the sound will play or put a check in the Forever check box.*

- Select a sound file from the open Web site (**Figure 5**) by choosing from the list displayed in the Background Sound dialog box.
- Click the File button to display the Select File dialog box (**Figure 6**), from which you can select a sound file on your computer.
- Click the World Wide Web button to look for a file on the World Wide Web.

4. When you have located the sound file, click OK to close the dialog box and return to the Page Properties dialog box.
5. Put a check in the Forever check box to make the sound repeat forever or uncheck the Forever check box and use the Loop text box to set how many times the sound will loop (**Figure 7**).
6. Click OK. When you view the Web page in the Preview tab or in a browser, the sound will play.

Tips:

- Sounds can take a long time to download. Think twice (or more than that!) before adding one or more hefty sound files to your site.
- To delete a sound file, just open the Page Properties dialog box to the General tab page, and clear the Location text box.

Yet another way to make your Web site really hot is to add a video. Video files are usually large, so transferring a video file to someone browsing your site can take a long time.

To add a video to your Web page:

1. Position the insertion marker where you want to place the video.
2. Choose Active Elements from the Insert menu and choose Video from the fly-out (**Figure 8**). The Video dialog box will open (**Figure 9**).
3. Use this dialog box to load a video file from the existing Web site, another location on your computer, or from the World Wide Web.
4. Click OK. The opening frame of the video file will appear on your Web page as a placeholder (**Figure 10**).
5. Right-click the video file placeholder and choose Image Properties from the pop-up menu (**Figure 11**). The Image Properties dialog box will open with the Video tab page in the front (**Figure 12**).
6. If you want a set of controls, Play and Stop, to appear on your Web page when the video plays, put a check in the Show Controls in Browser check box.

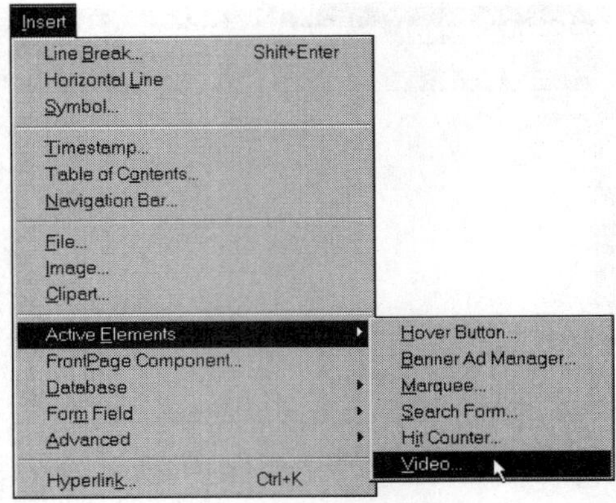

Figure 8. *Choose Active Elements from the Insert menu and choose Video from the fly-out.*

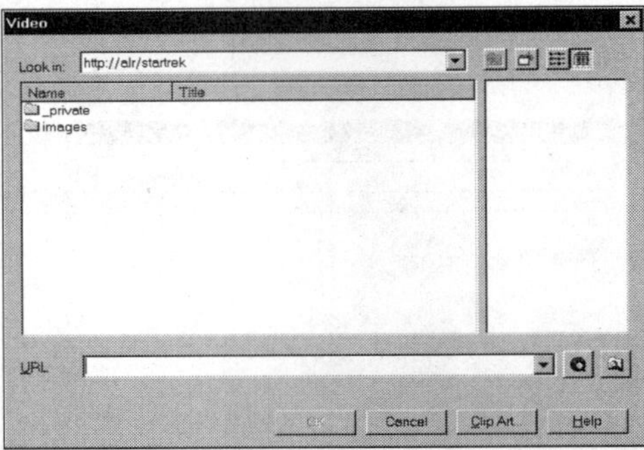

Figure 9. *Use the Video dialog box to select a video saved with the Web site, on your computer, or from the World Wide Web.*

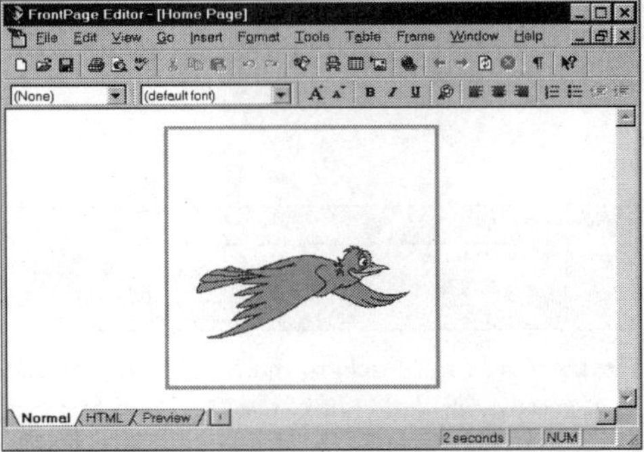

Figure 10. *The opening frame of the video appears as a placeholder.*

Figure 11. *Choose Image Properties from the pop-up menu.*

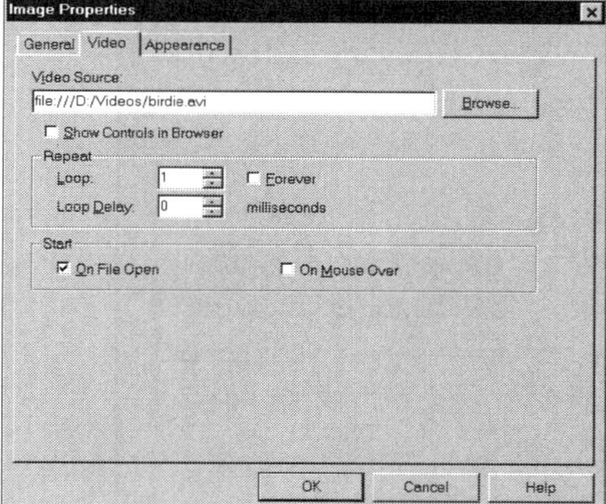

Figure 12. *Use the Video tab page of the Image Properties dialog box to set how many times the video will play.*

Figure 13. *When you view the Web page in a browser, the video plays.*

7. Use the Repeat area to set how many times the video will play, and the delay (in milliseconds) between each time it plays. For instance, if you wanted to set a 1 second delay, you would type 1000 in the Loop Delay text box.
8. Use the Start area to set whether the Video will play immediately when the page opens or when the user passes the mouse over the video placeholder.
9. Click OK. View your Web page in the Preview tab on a browser to watch the video play (**Figure 13**).

VIDEO FILE SIZE

Video files can be *huge*. Before you decide to add a video to a Web page, consider who will be using your Web site. If your site will be used over the Internet, you may want to reconsider, because it can take several minutes to download a video. (Some folks won't wait that long!) If you are working with a corporate site on an intranet, download times will be much quicker.

How Long Will My Page Take to Load?

When you have browsed the World Wide Web, you have probably come across Web pages that have many images with large file sizes that take forever to load.

If you aren't careful when you design your Web pages, graphic, sound, and video file sizes can add up, making for a long load time. Try to keep the size of your Web pages under 30k. It will take users with 14.4 kbps modems about 30 seconds to load a 30k Web page.

FrontPage includes a handy loading time counter at the bottom of the Editor window. In the Status Bar is the estimated number of seconds it will take your Web page to load in a user's browser with a computer equipped with a 28.8 kbps modem (**Figure 14**). As you add elements to your Web page, the estimated download time will automatically update.

Figure 14. *The bottom of the FrontPage Editor window shows the estimated number of seconds it will take your Web page to load.*

Choose Multimedia Effects Carefully

Besides adding to load times, many multimedia effects at one time can become overwhelming to visitors to your site. Pick the effects that you want and use them sparingly. Multimedia should enhance your site, helping to get your message across, not create distractions.

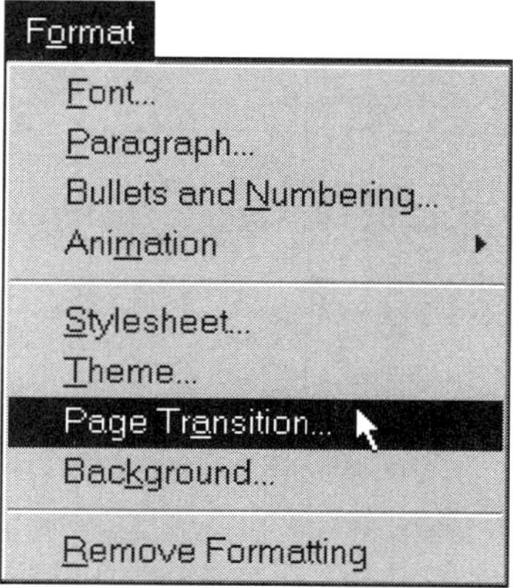

Figure 15. *Choose Page Transition from the Format menu.*

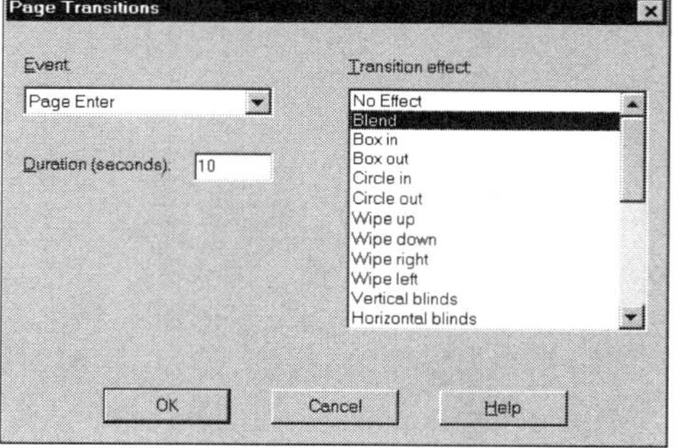

Figure 16. *You can choose from over a dozen transition effects in the Page Transitions dialog box.*

To bring pizzazz to your Web site, you can add page transitions—special visual effects that occur as visitors travel from one page to the next in your site. These transitions are much like the slide transitions in presentation programs such as PowerPoint: You can have one page blend into another, dissolve into another, and much more. Page transitions are a DHTML feature that is currently supported by Internet Explorer but not Netscape Navigator.

To add page transitions:

1. Open the page to which you want to add the transition effect.
2. Choose Page Transition from the Format menu (**Figure 15**). The Page Transitions dialog box will open (**Figure 16**).
3. Choose a transition effect from the list, and enter an amount of time in the Duration text box.
4. Under Event, choose whether the effect will occur when the user enters the page, exits the page, enters the Web site through the current page, or exits the Web site via the current page (**Figure 17**).
5. Click OK.

6. To view the transition effect, preview the page by clicking the Preview tab or choosing Preview in Browser from the File menu.

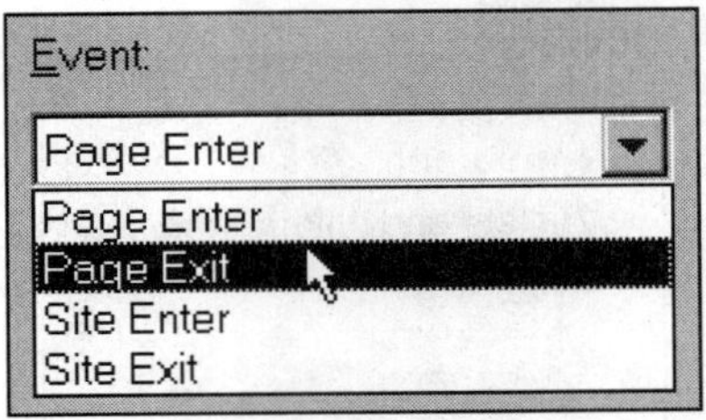

Figure 17. *The Event drop-down list lets you determine when the transition effect occurs.*

Tips:

- You need Internet Explorer 4.0 installed for your page transitions to show up in Preview view in the Editor.
- To remove transition effects, open the page to which the effect is applied, choose Page Transition from the Format menu, and choose No Effect from the list of transition effects.

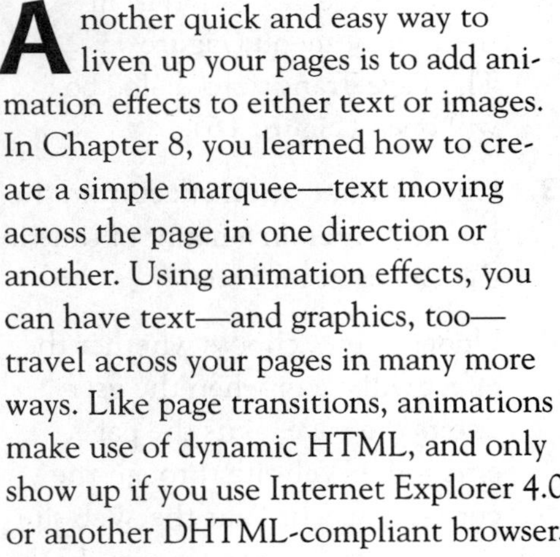

Another quick and easy way to liven up your pages is to add animation effects to either text or images. In Chapter 8, you learned how to create a simple marquee—text moving across the page in one direction or another. Using animation effects, you can have text—and graphics, too—travel across your pages in many more ways. Like page transitions, animations make use of dynamic HTML, and only show up if you use Internet Explorer 4.0 or another DHTML-compliant browser.

USING THE GIF ANIMATOR

The animation effects described don't really animate anything: The text or images don't actually change; they simply move across the page in a variety of ways. You can also use FrontPage to create genuine animations, in the form of animated GIFs. The Image Composer packaged with FrontPage 98 includes the Microsoft GIF Animator. You can use this feature to create animated GIFs that contain a series of different images, each of which is displayed for a designated amount of time—creating the illusion of movement.

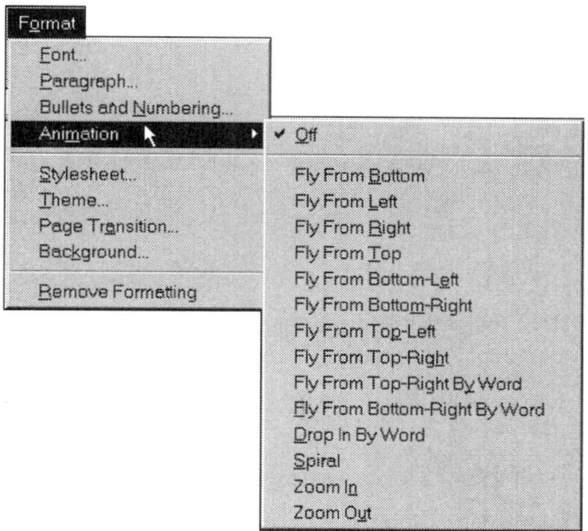

Figure 18. *Choose Animation from the Format menu to display this fly-out menu of animation effects.*

> **USE ANIMATIONS SPARINGLY!**
>
> After trying out the animation effects and finding the ones you like, use them sparingly! Too many effects may get your viewers a bit dizzy, or worse yet, seasick and annoyed.

To add animation effects:

1. Select the text or graphic to animate.
2. Choose Animation from the Format menu. You'll see a fly-out menu with a whole slew of animation effects (**Figure 18**).
3. Choose an effect from the fly-out menu.
4. To see the effect in action, click the Preview tab or choose Preview in Browser from the File menu.

Tips:

- Choose Off from the Animation fly-out to turn off the animation effect for the selected text or graphic.
- Some of the animation effects work only for text and not for graphics: This includes all the "By Word" effects as well as the Zoom In and Zoom Out effects.
- There are over a dozen animation effects to choose from. It's a good idea to experiment with them to get a sense of how they work and which ones might be useful to you.

Banner ads display a series of images one after another, often with spiffy transition effects in between. They can also provide a link to another site (presumably to the sponsor's page.) You can use this technique to create ads, and also to generate eye-catching visual effects for your Web page. FrontPage 98 comes equipped with a Banner Ad Manager that makes it simple to create banner ads.

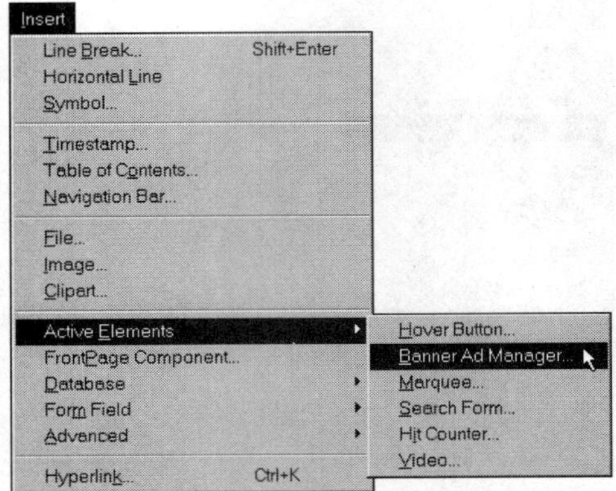

Figure 19. *Choose Active Elements from the Insert menu and choose Banner Ad Manager from the fly-out menu.*

To create a banner ad:

1. Open your Web page and place the insertion marker where you want the banner ad to go.
2. Choose Active Elements from the Insert menu and choose Banner Ad Manager from the fly-out (**Figure 19**). The Banner Ad Manager dialog box will appear (**Figure 20**).
3. Enter the width and height of your images in pixels in the Width & Height text boxes. It's best to use images of the same size. But, if your images are of slightly different sizes, enter the largest width and height in these text boxes.
4. In the Transition area, choose a transition effect from the Effect drop-down menu (**Figure 21**).
5. Set how long you want each image to appear by entering a value in the Show each image for text box.

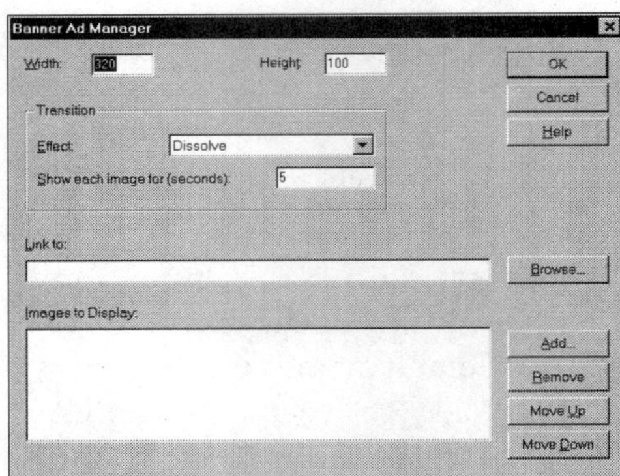

Figure 20. *The Banner Ad Manager dialog box is where you set which images to display, their duration, and any transition effects.*

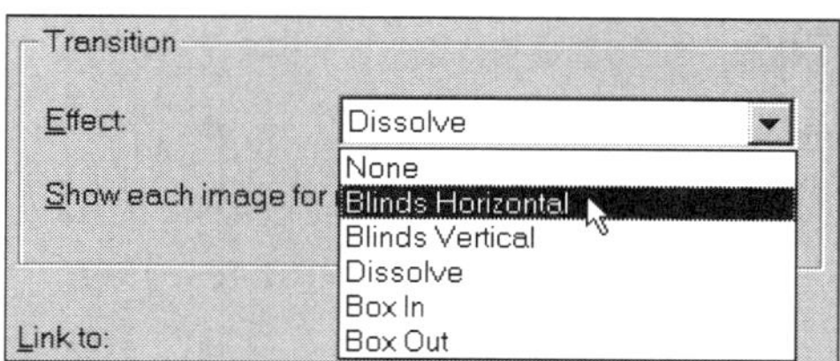

Figure 21. *You can choose from among these transition effects.*

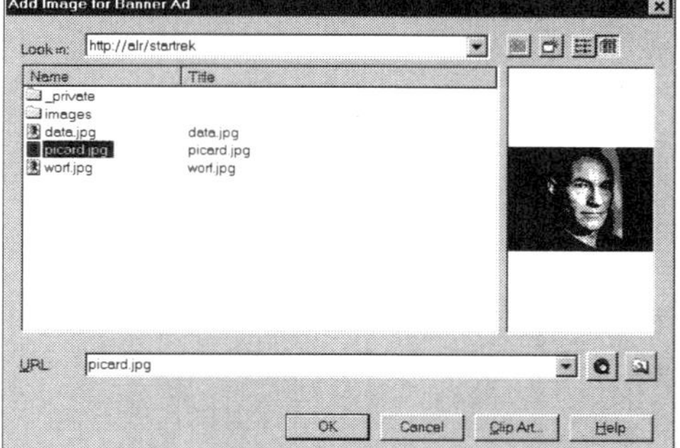

Figure 22. *You use the Add Image for Banner Ad dialog box to choose which images your banner ad will include.*

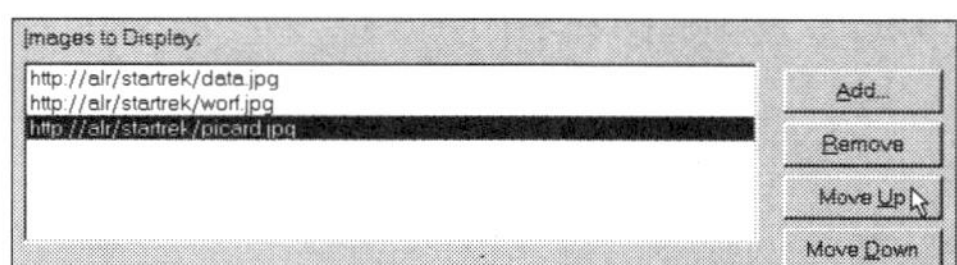

Figure 23. *Change the order of images with the Move Up and Move Down buttons, and delete images with the Remove button.*

6. In the Link to text box, enter the URL of the Web page the viewer will land on if she clicks the banner ad. You can type in a URL directly, or you can use the Browse button to track down the URL you need.

7. Click the Add button to choose the images for your banner ad. The Add Image for Banner Ad dialog box will appear (**Figure 22**). Using this dialog box, you can choose images from your hard drive or network drive, from the Microsoft Clip Gallery, or from the World Wide Web. Click OK when you find the image you want. Repeat this process for each image you want to include. Each time you click OK, the Add Image for Banner Ad dialog box will close and the selected image will appear in the Images to Display list box at the bottom of the Banner Ad Manager dialog box.

8. If you decide to change the order of the images, click the Move Up or Move Down button in the Banner Ad Manager dialog box; if you decide to remove an image from the ad, click the Remove button (**Figure 23**).

9. When you're done preparing your banner ad, click OK. The first image in the ad will appear in your Web page.

10. Save your page by choosing Save from the File menu. Type a URL and a page title in the Save As dialog box. In the Save Embedded Files dialog box, click OK to save all the image files with the current Web.
11. Preview your ad by clicking the Preview tab or choosing Preview in Browser from the File menu.
12. To edit your banner ad, double-click the image that appears on the Web page. This will display the Banner Ad Manager dialog box; from here you can make any changes you like to the banner ad.

Tips:

- Don't confuse banner ads with page banners. Banner ads display a series of rotating images. Page banners, in contrast, most often display the page title at the top of the page, although they can also display an image if the page has a theme applied to it.
- Images for banner ads must be stored with the current Web for the banner ad to work.

SUMMARY

In this chapter you learned how to:

- Add a background sound from the open Web site
- Add a background sound from your computer or the World Wide Web
- Add a video from the open Web site
- Add a video from your computer or the World Wide Web
- Add page transitions
- Add animation effects
- Create a banner ad

12 Tables Made Easy

Creating tables directly with HTML code is not much fun! FrontPage takes the drudgery out of creating tables. All that is left for you to do is add the table content you need. FrontPage 98 makes it even easier than before to create tables: You can draw them right on the Editor screen.

Tables are used to present information in an organized way. Tables let you position information accurately within *cells*. This means that you won't have to manually format text and image placement in an attempt to get it to line up. Tables do this for you.

Tables are made up of columns and rows of cells. These cells can contain text, images, forms, background images, and even another table. If you create a table and discover that you need to add or delete cells or change cell size, FrontPage Editor makes it easy to customize an existing table. **Figure 1** shows a Web page organized using an invisible table.

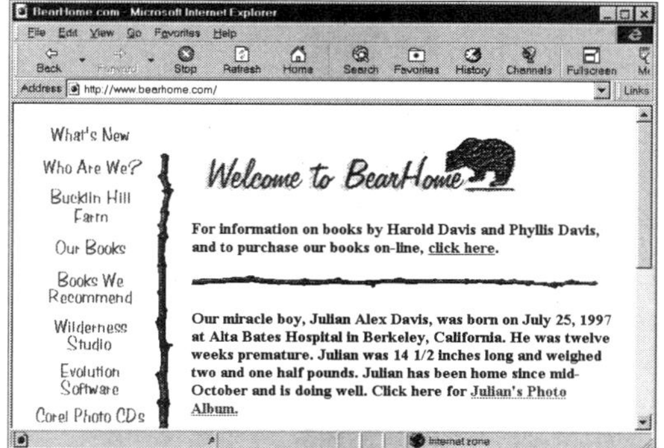

Figure 1. *The elements on this Web page are arranged with an invisible table. Invisible tables are often used as a way to precisely place Web page elements.*

In FrontPage 98, you can now draw tables directly on the desktop and can make modifications to them—changing their dimensions, the number of rows, and so on—by choosing from buttons on the Table toolbar. The approach is quick and intuitive, and you can see your results right away; it's perfect for those of us addicted to instant gratification. If you want more precision, you may still want to use the tried and true method of creating tables through a dialog box.

To draw a table:

1. Choose Draw Table from the Table menu (**Figure 2**). (If the Table toolbar is already visible, you can click the Draw Table button.) The Table toolbar will appear and the mouse pointer will turn into a little pencil (**Figure 3**).
2. Using the pencil pointer, drag across the Editor window to create a rectangle the size you want your table to be. You'll see a dashed rectangle indicating the size the table will be if you release the mouse button (**Figure 4**).
3. Release the mouse button. You'll see a table outline (**Figure 5**).
4. To add rows to your table, drag from the left to the right edge of the table, or vice versa. As you drag, a dashed line indicates where the row will be inserted (**Figure 6**). When you release the mouse button, the row border will appear.

Figure 2. *Choose Draw Table from the Table menu.*

Draw Table button

Pencil pointer for drawing tables

Figure 3. *When you draw tables, the Table toolbar appears and the mouse pointer turns into a pencil.*

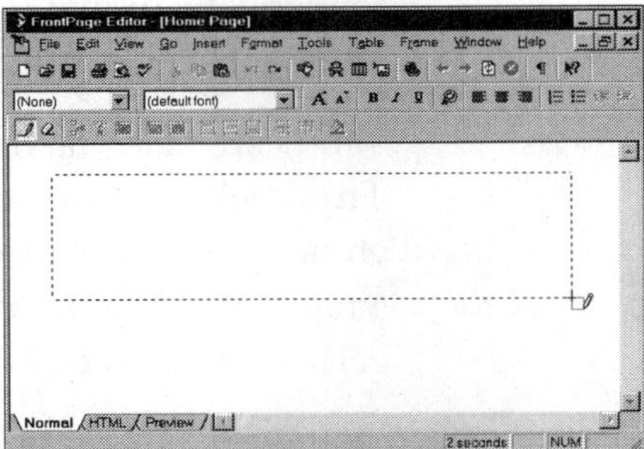

Figure 4. *The dashed rectangle tells you how big the table will be.*

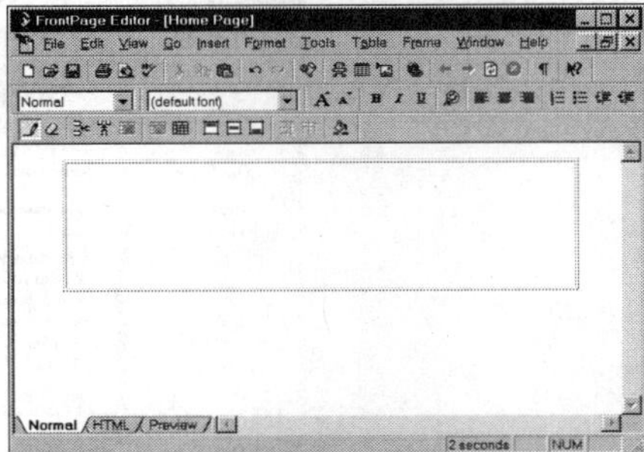

Figure 5. *Once you generate a table outline, you can add columns and rows to it.*

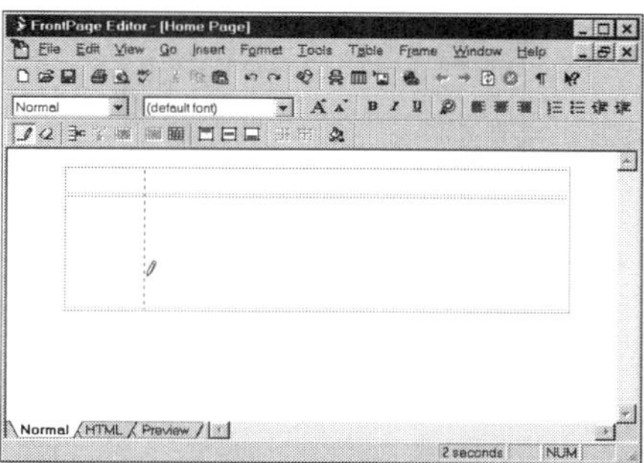

Figure 6. *Dragging from left to right creates a new row within the table.*

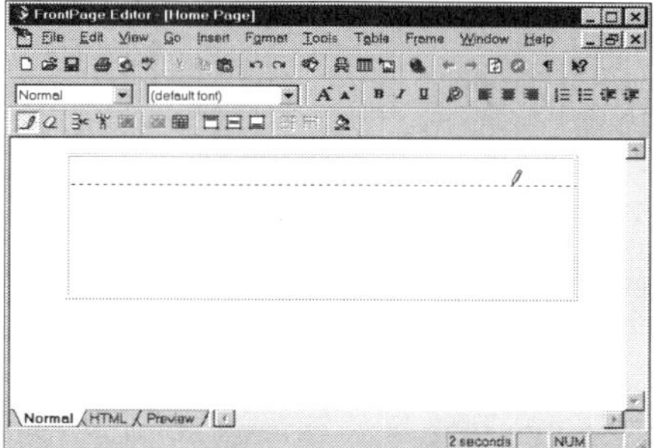

Figure 7. *Dragging from top to bottom creates a new column within the table.*

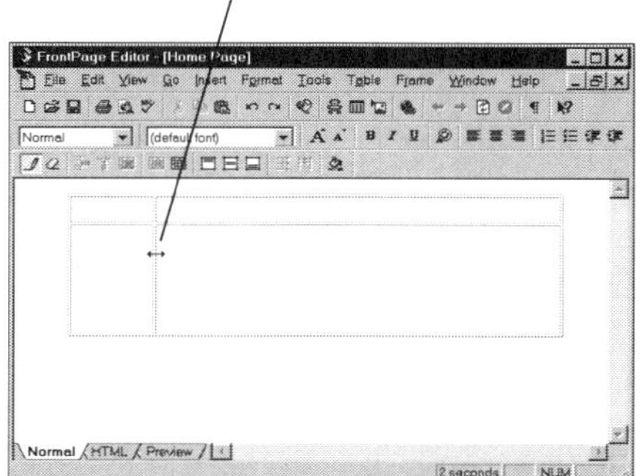

Figure 8. *You can drag a column or row border to change the size of the column or row.*

5. To add columns to your table, drag from the top to the bottom of the table, or vice versa. As you drag, you'll see a dashed line indicating where the column will be inserted (**Figure 7**). When you release the mouse button, the column border will appear. Continue drawing to add as many columns and rows as you need.
6. If you decide to change the size of a column or row, put the mouse pointer over the cell border. It should change into a double-headed arrow (**Figure 8**). Then drag to enlarge or shrink the size of the column or row.
7. When you're done working on the table, click the Draw Table toolbar button to turn this feature off.

Tips:

- You don't have to get everything perfect the first time when you draw tables, since it's simple enough to change them after the fact, as you'll learn throughout much of this chapter. But, if you want more precise control when creating tables, you can use the Insert Table dialog box, as described on page 182.
- When you draw a table, FrontPage guesses whether you want it aligned on the left, right, or center. It's a cinch to change the alignment after the fact if FrontPage guesses wrong, as described on page 193.

To create a table:

1. In the Editor, position the insertion marker on your Web page where you would like the table to begin.
2. Choose Insert Table from the Table menu (**Figure 9**). The Insert Table dialog box will appear (**Figure 10**).
3. In the Size area, enter the number of rows and columns that you will need in your table. (If you find you need to, you can add and delete rows and columns later.)
4. In the Layout area, use the Alignment drop-down list to set whether the table will appear on the left side of the page, in the center, or on the right side of the page (**Figure 11**).
5. If you would like a border around the table, enter the border's width in pixels in the Border Size text box.
6. Use the Cell Padding text box to enter the number of pixels you would like between a cell's contents and each of its borders.
7. In the Cell Spacing text box, enter the number of pixels you would like between each cell in the table. The default setting is 2.
8. You can use the Width area to specify the exact width of the table. (This setting is optional. If you don't specify an exact width, FrontPage will automatically create a table that spans the entire width of the Web page.) To set an exact Width, put a check in the

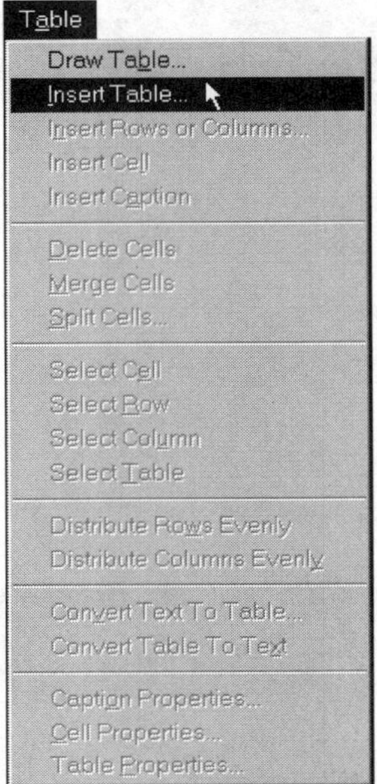

Figure 9. *Choose Insert Table from the Table menu.*

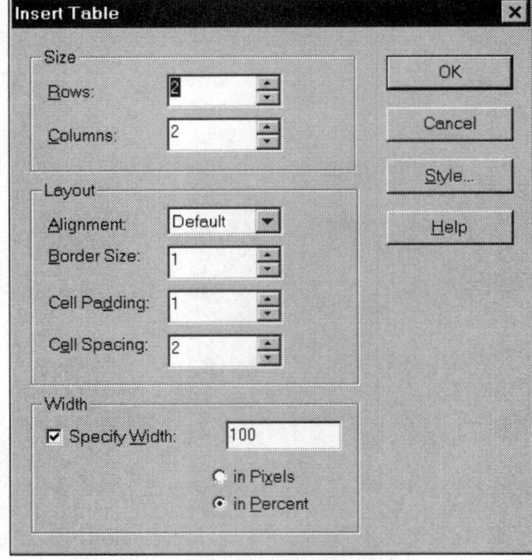

Figure 10. *Use the Insert Table dialog box to set up a table.*

Specify Width check box, then either enter the number of pixels or a percentage of the Web page's width. For instance, a table width of 50 percent will span half the width of the page.

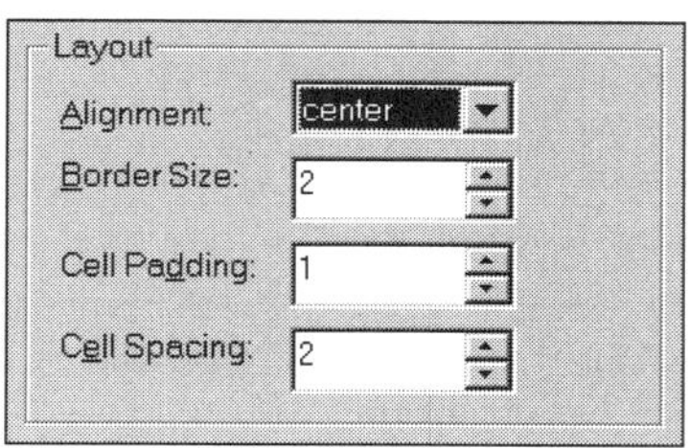

Figure 11. *Use the Layout area to set the table's alignment, border size, and cell padding and spacing.*

9. Click OK. The table will appear in the Web page (**Figure 12**).

or

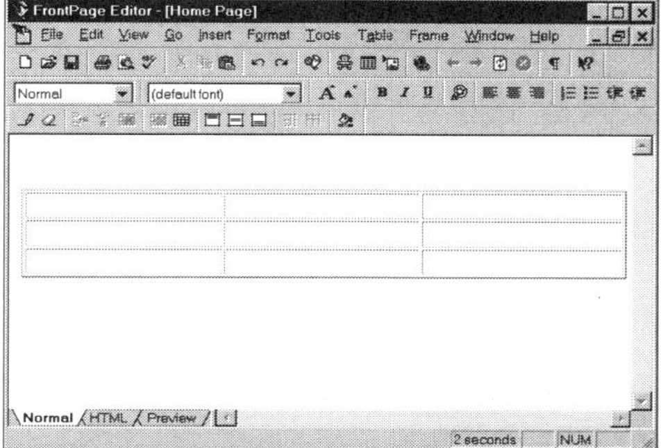

Figure 12. *The table appears in the Editor.*

1. Position the insertion marker where you would like the table to appear.
2. Click and hold down the left mouse button on the Insert Table button on the Standard toolbar (**Figure 13**). An empty grid appears below the button and your mouse.
3. Drag the mouse down and to the right to select the number of rows and columns that you want the table to contain (**Figure 14**). As you highlight grid boxes, table dimensions appear at the bottom of the grid. If you drag past the last grid box in a column or row, the grid will expand.
4. Release the mouse button. The table will appear on the page (**Figure 12**).

Figure 13. *Position the mouse pointer over the Insert Table button, then press the left button. A table grid appears.*

Figure 14. *Drag the mouse to select the number of rows and columns.*

Tip:

- When you use the Insert Table toolbar button, the table is created with the settings last used in the Insert Table dialog box.

To add text to a table:

1. Make sure the mouse pointer looks like an I-beam (I). If it looks like a pencil, click the Draw Table button on the Table toolbar to turn that feature off.
2. Place the insertion marker within a cell (**Figure 15**).
3. Type your text. The cell will automatically expand to accommodate the text.

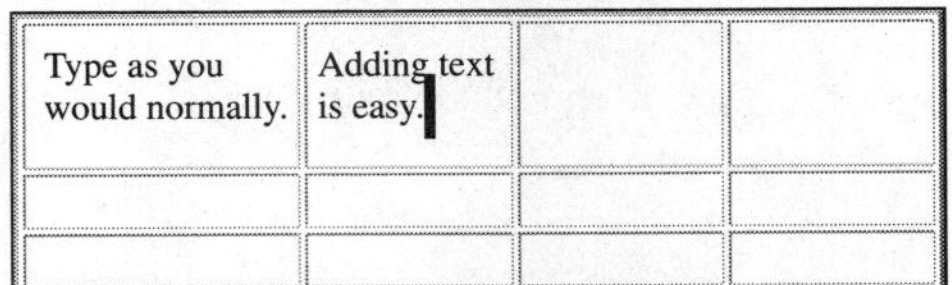

Figure 15. *Place the insertion marker in the cell, then type your text.*

Tips:

- You can quickly move from one cell to the next in a table by pressing the Tab key. You can move in the opposite direction by pressing Shift + Tab.
- To quickly add another row to a table, position the insertion marker in the lower-right cell and press the Tab key.

To add an image to a table:

1. Place the insertion marker in the cell where you want the image to appear.
2. Click the Insert Image button on the Standard toolbar (**Figure 16**).
3. Select an image using the Image dialog box (**Figure 17**), then click OK. The image will appear in the cell (**Figure 18**).

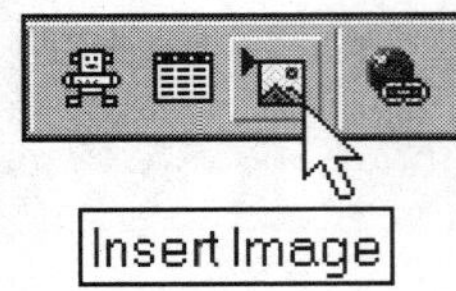

Figure 16. *Click the Insert Image button on the Standard toolbar.*

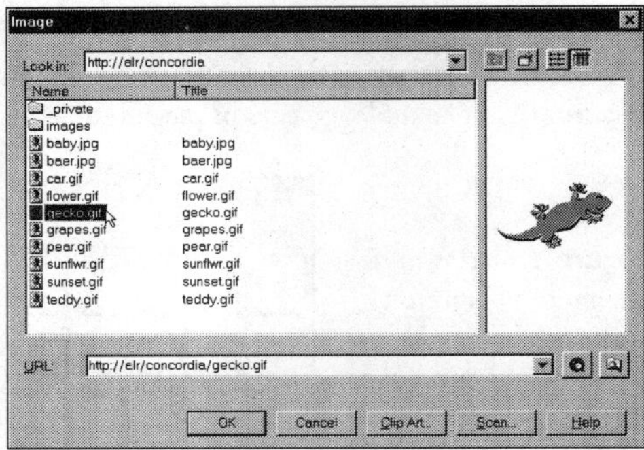

Figure 17. *Use the Image dialog box to select a graphic.*

Tip:

- Inserting images into Web pages is discussed in detail in Chapter 10.

Figure 18. *When you click OK, the image appears in the cell.*

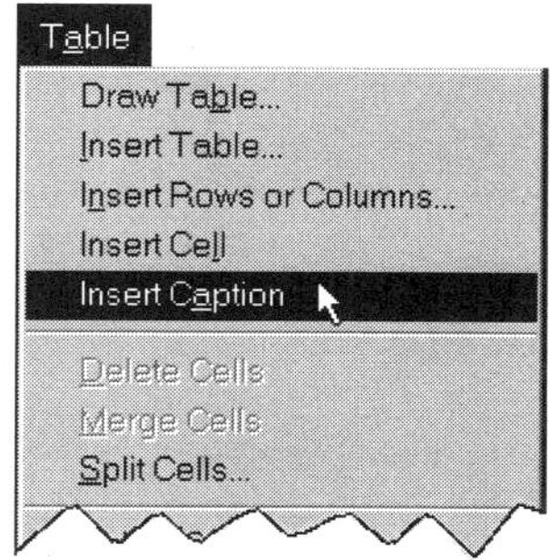

Figure 19. *Choose Insert Caption from the Table menu.*

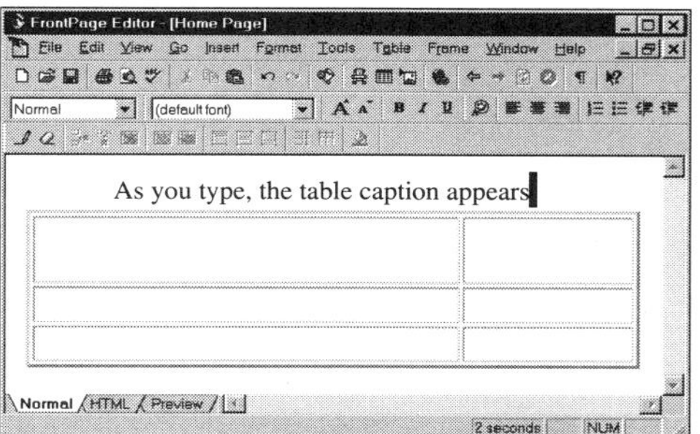

Figure 20. *When the insertion marker appears above the table, type the caption.*

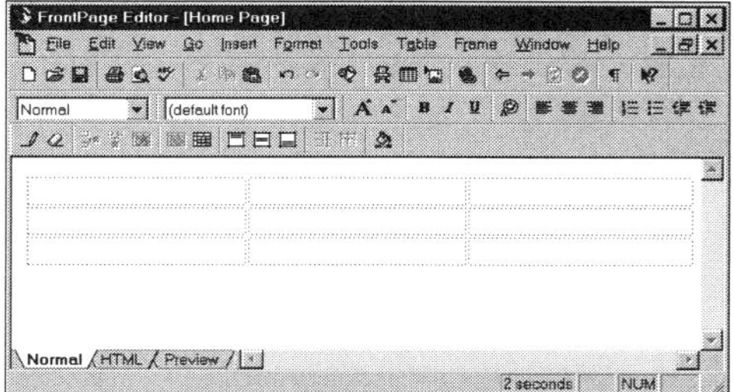

Figure 21. *A table with no borders is displayed with dashed lines so you can see it in the Editor.*

A table caption can help describe the information presented in a table. A caption can be placed above or below a table.

To add a table caption:

1. Place the insertion marker anywhere within the table.
2. Choose Insert Caption from the Table menu (**Figure 19**). The table will move down one line and the insertion marker will automatically appear centered above the table (**Figure 20**).
3. Type in the caption. You can now format the caption like any other Web page text, making it larger, smaller, bold, left aligned, etc.

Tables without Borders

If you create a table with no borders, FrontPage Editor automatically shows dashed lines surrounding each table cell (**Figure 21**). These dashed lines will not appear on the page when it is viewed in a browser or in the Preview tab.

To move a table caption below the table:

1. Place the insertion marker anywhere within the table caption text.
2. Choose Caption Properties from the Table menu **(Figure 22)** or right-click the caption and choose Caption Properties from the pop-up menu **(Figure 23)**. The Caption Properties dialog box will open **(Figure 24)**.
3. Select the Bottom of Table radio button, then click OK. The caption will move below the table **(Figure 25)**.

Tip:

- To move a caption from below to above a table, follow steps 1 and 2, then select the Top of Table radio button in the Caption Properties dialog box.

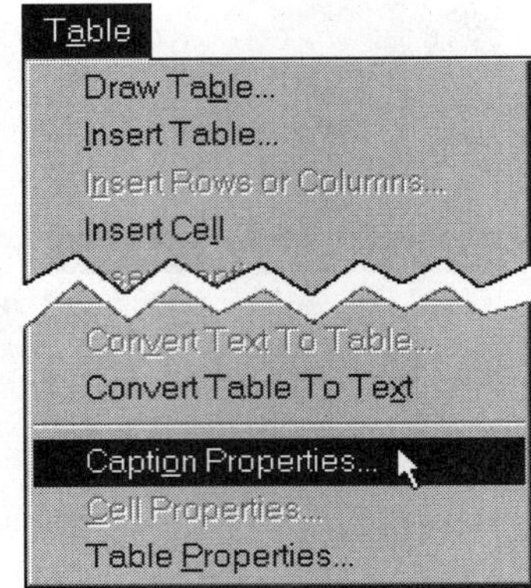

Figure 22. *Choose Caption Properties from the Table menu.*

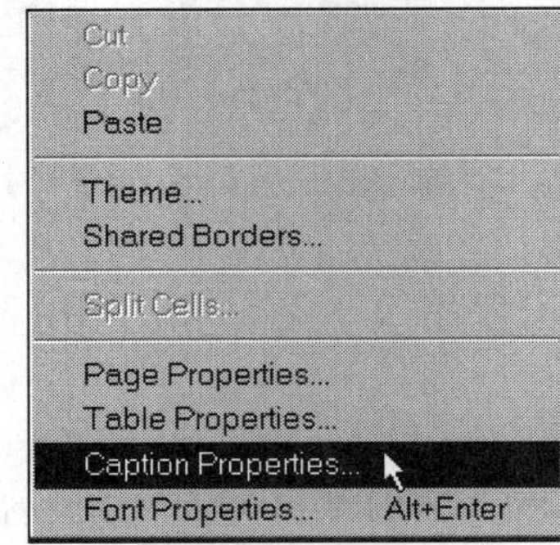

Figure 23. *Choose Caption Properties from the pop-up menu.*

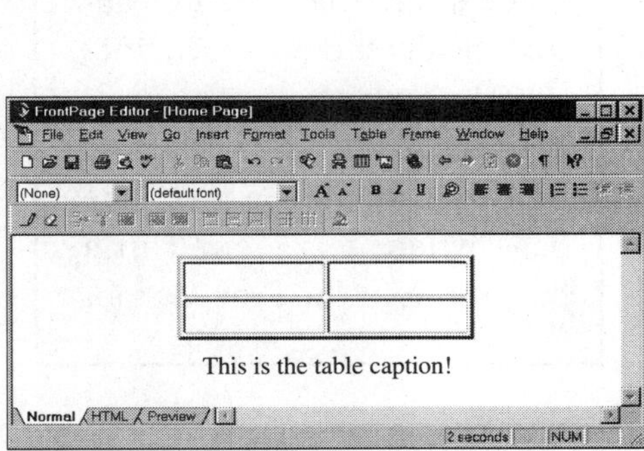

Figure 25. *The table caption moves below the table.*

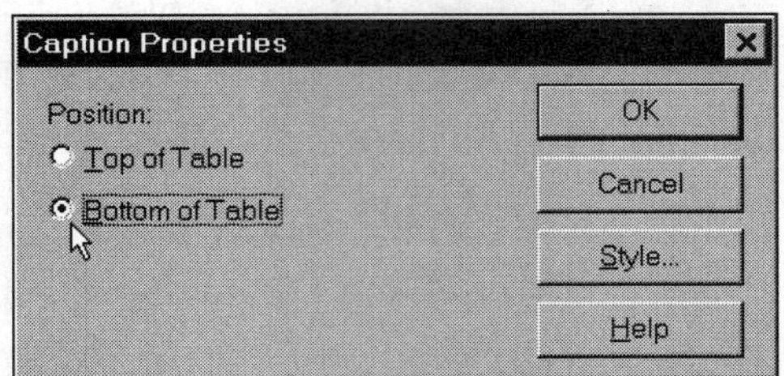

Figure 24. *Select the Bottom of Table radio button, then click OK.*

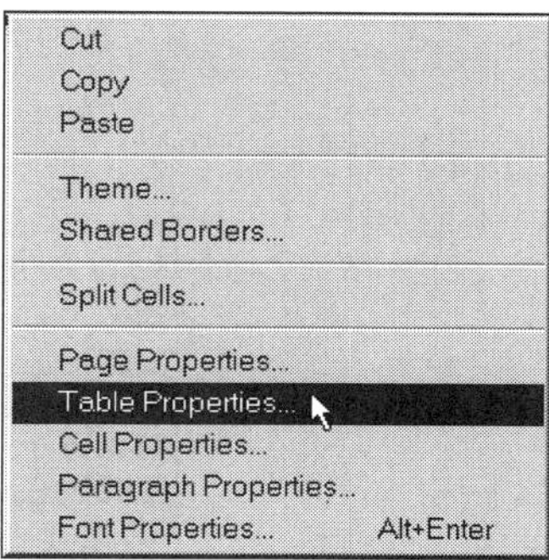

Figure 26. *Choose Table Properties from the pop-up menu.*

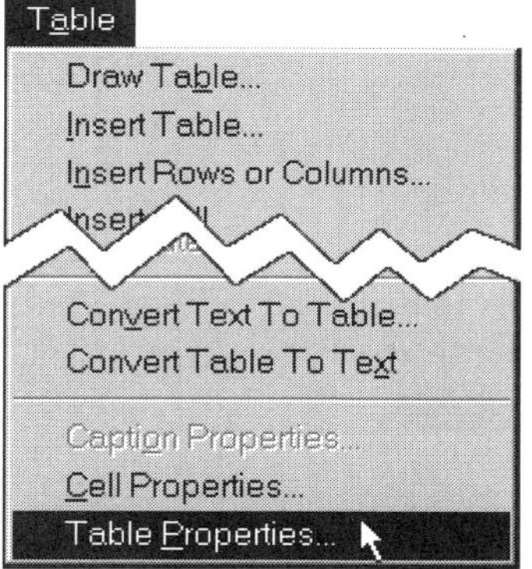

Figure 27. *Choose Table Properties from the Table menu.*

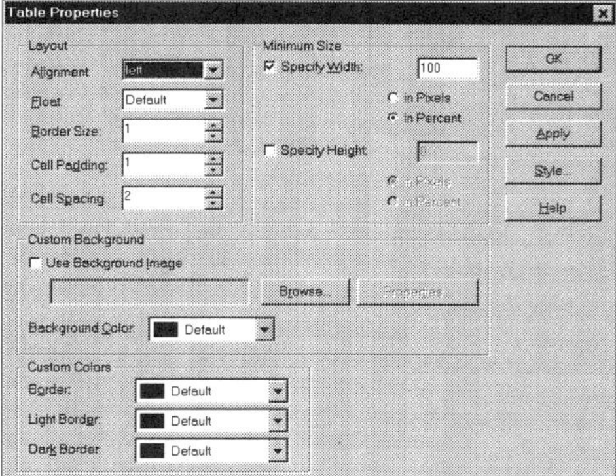

Figure 28. *Use the Table Properties dialog box to change the settings for your table.*

You can change the settings for a table at any time by using the Table Properties command. In addition, you can add a background image or color, and if your table has borders, use custom colors to create a three-dimensional look.

To change table settings:

1. Place the insertion marker anywhere in the table.
2. Right-click and select Table Properties from the pop-up menu (**Figure 26**) or choose Table Properties from the Table menu (**Figure 27**). The Table Properties dialog box will open (**Figure 28**).
3. Use the Layout area to select table alignment, choose how text will flow around the table (the Float option), set the border width in pixels, and add cell padding and cell spacing.
4. If you want to specify a minimum width for the table, make sure there is a check mark in the Specify Width check box in the Minimum Size area. Then set the table width in pixels or percent of the screen width.
5. If you want to specify a minimum height for the table, put a check mark in the Specify Height check box and set the table height in pixels or percent of screen height.

6. While you are working with this dialog box, you can click Apply to add the changes you have made to the table. The Table Properties dialog box will remain open so you can continue to select new settings.
7. When you are finished changing the settings, click OK. The table will assume the new settings.

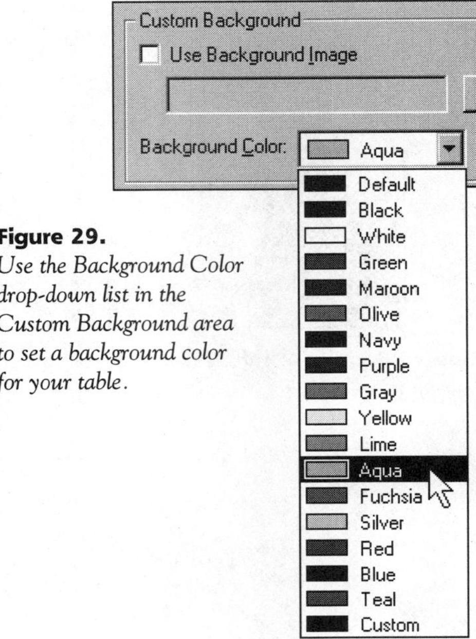

Figure 29. *Use the Background Color drop-down list in the Custom Background area to set a background color for your table.*

To add a background color or image to a table:

1. Place the insertion marker anywhere in the table.
2. Right-click and select Table Properties from the pop-up menu or choose Table Properties from the Table menu. The Table Properties dialog box will open (**Figure 28**).
3. In the Custom Background area, use the Background Color drop-down list to select a background color for the table (**Figure 29**).

   or

   In the Custom Background area, put a check in the Use Background Image check box, then click the Browse button (**Figure 30**). Use the Select Background Image dialog box to choose an image already saved with the Web site, from your computer, from the World Wide Web, or from the Microsoft Clip Gallery (**Figure 31**). (Using the Select Background Image dialog box is discussed in detail in Chapter 10.)

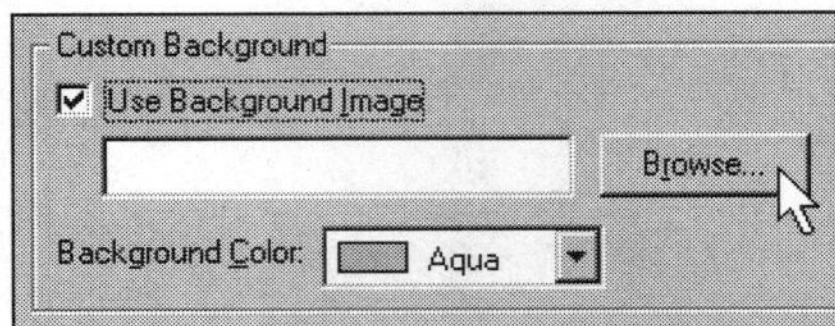

Figure 30. *Put a check in the Use Background Image check box, then click the Browse button.*

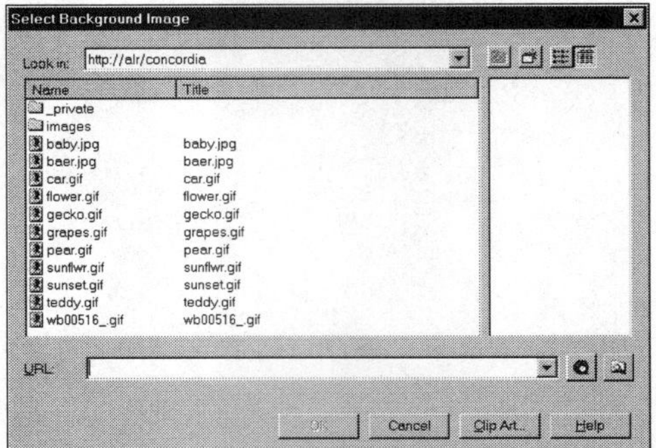

Figure 31. *Use the Select Background Image dialog box to choose an image from the current Web site, your computer, the World Wide Web, or the Microsoft Clip Gallery.*

Add a Custom Background to a Table

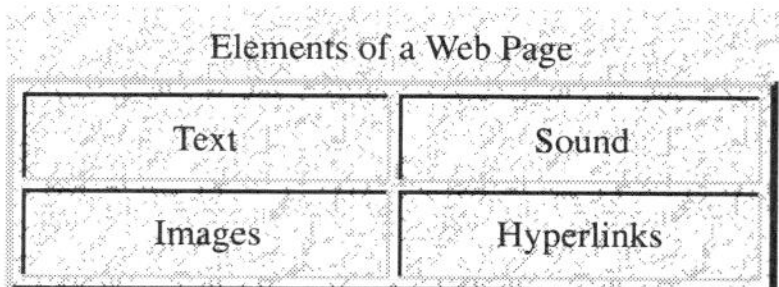

Elements of a Web Page	
Text	Sound
Images	Hyperlinks

Figure 32. *When you click OK, the background image appears in the table.*

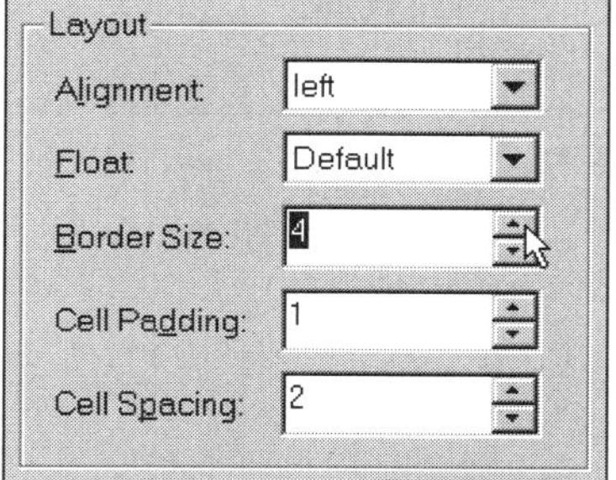

Figure 33. *Make sure the Border Size is set to at least 1.*

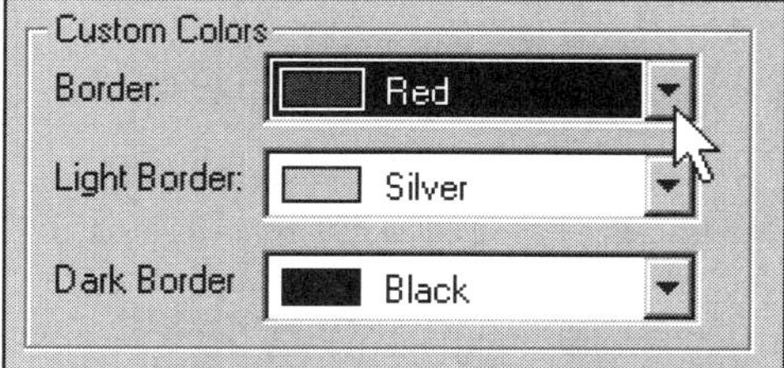

Figure 34. *Use the Custom Colors area to set the border color, highlight, and shadow.*

4. Click OK. The background image will appear in the table (**Figure 32**).

Tips:

- If the table has a caption, the background image will extend up (or down) to include the caption.
- As usual, if you add a background, make sure it's subtle enough that it doesn't obscure the text.

To give table borders a 3D look:

1. Place the insertion marker anywhere in the table.
2. Right-click and select Table Properties from the pop-up menu or choose Table Properties from the Table menu. The Table Properties dialog box will open (**Figure 28**).
3. In the Layout area, make sure the Border Size is set to at least 1 (**Figure 33**). (This means that the table has a 1-pixel width border.)
4. In the Custom Colors area, use the Light Border drop-down list to select the highlight color and the Dark Border drop-down list to select the shadow color (**Figure 34**).
5. Click OK. The table's border will assume the custom colors you have chosen.

Cells also have special properties of their own, such as text alignment within a cell, background color or image, the number of rows or columns a cell spans, and the minimum width. To change any of these properties you first need to know how to select a cell, row, column, or the entire table.

To select a cell:

1. Position the insertion marker in the cell you want to select.
2. Choose Select Cell from the Table menu (**Figure 35**). The cell will be highlighted (**Figure 36**).

Tips:

- To select more than one cell, you can also hold down the Shift key while clicking in the cells you want to select or you can drag across the cells you want to select.
- To select nonadjacent cells, select the first cell or cells, and then hold down the Ctrl key while clicking in the additional cells you want to select.

To select a row:

1. Position the insertion marker in one of the cells in the row you want to select.
2. Choose Select Row from the Table menu (**Figure 37**). The row will be highlighted (**Figure 38**).

   or

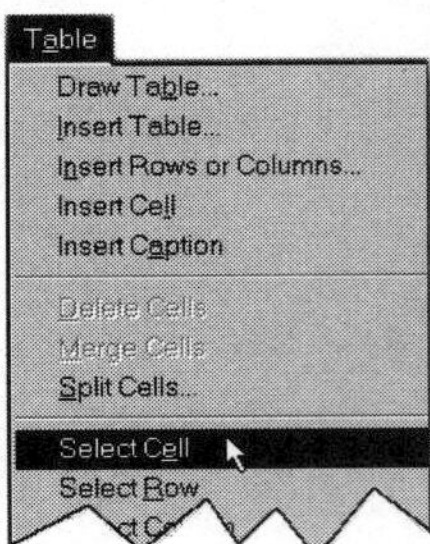

Figure 35. *Choose Select Cell from the Table menu.*

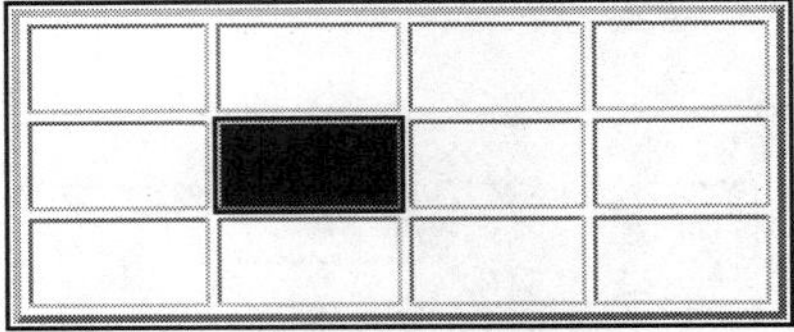

Figure 36. *When the cell is selected, it is highlighted.*

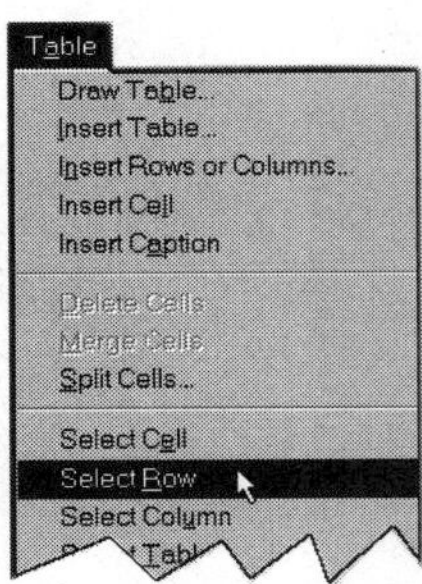

Figure 37. *Choose Select Row from the Table menu.*

Figure 38. *The selected row is highlighted.*

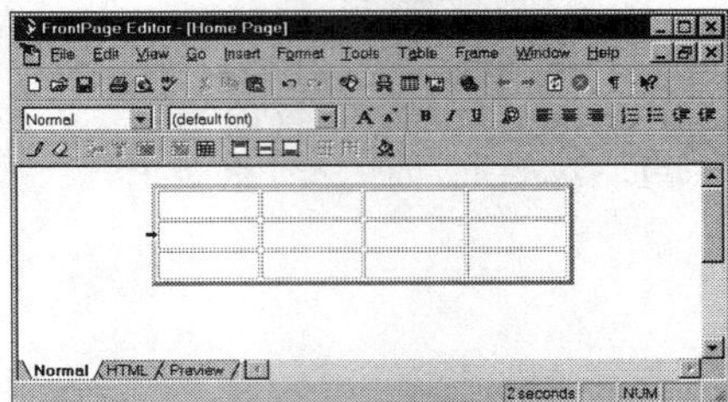

Figure 39. *When the mouse pointer changes into a black, right-pointing arrow, you can click to select the row.*

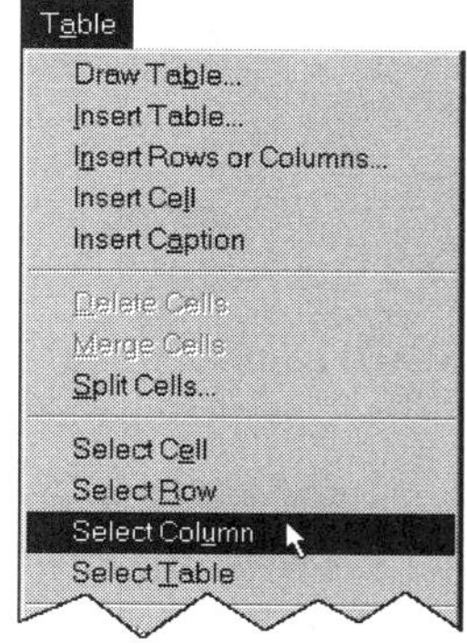

Figure 40. *Choose Select Column from the Table menu.*

Figure 41. *The selected column is highlighted.*

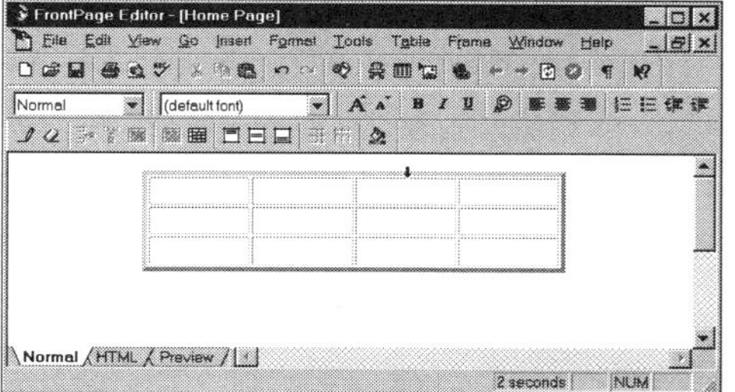

Figure 42. *When the mouse pointer changes into a black, downward-pointing arrow, you can click to select the column.*

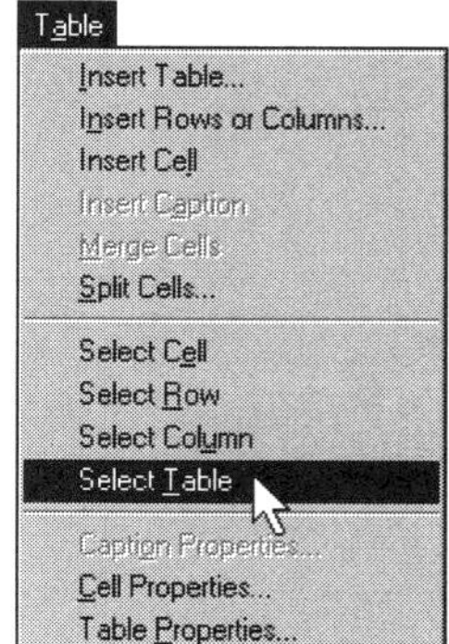

Figure 43. *Choose Select Table from the Table menu.*

1. Place the mouse pointer over the row's left border. You'll see a black right-pointing arrow (**Figure 39**).
2. Click to select the row, or drag up or down to select multiple rows.

To select a column:

1. Position the insertion marker in one of the cells in the column you want to select.
2. Choose Select Column from the Table menu (**Figure 40**). The column will be highlighted (**Figure 41**).

or

1. Place the mouse pointer over the column's top border. You'll see a black, downward-pointing arrow (**Figure 42**).
2. Click to select the column, or drag to the right or left to select multiple columns.

To select the entire table:

1. Place the insertion marker anywhere in the table.
2. Choose Select Table from the Table menu (**Figure 43**). The table will be highlighted (**Figure 44**).

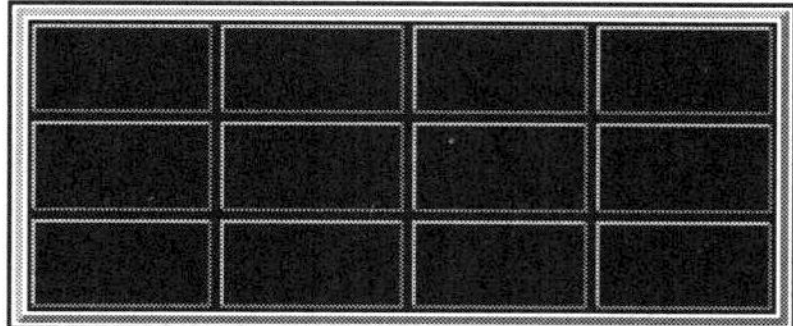

Figure 44. *The entire table is highlighted.*

To change cell settings:

1. Select the cells whose settings you want to change.
2. Right-click the selected cells and choose Cell Properties from the pop-up menu (**Figure 45**) or choose Cell Properties from the Table menu (**Figure 46**). The Cell Properties dialog box will appear (**Figure 47**).
3. In the Layout area, use the Horizontal Alignment and Vertical Alignment drop-down lists to set the alignment for the contents of a cell (**Figure 48**). For instance, if you want to align text in the center of the cell, select Center from the Horizontal Alignment drop-down list and Middle from the Vertical Alignment drop-down list.
4. Use the Minimum Size area to specify a width and height for the selected cells (**Figure 49**). Put a check in the Specify Width and/or Specify Height check boxes, then either enter the number of pixels or a percentage of the table's width or height. For instance, a cell width of 50 percent will span half the width of the table.

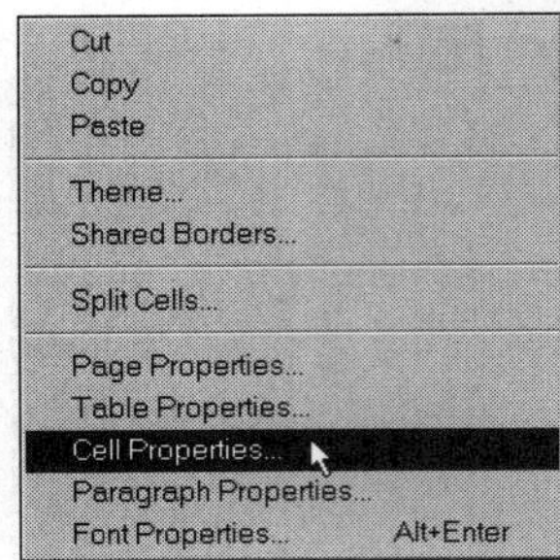

Figure 45. *Choose Cell Properties from the pop-up menu.*

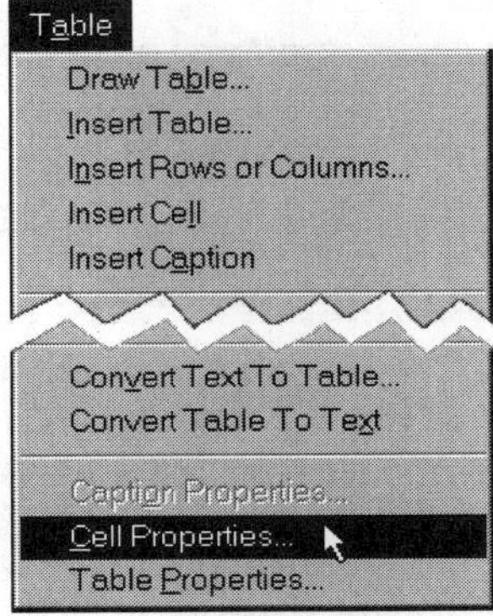

Figure 46. *Choose Cell Properties from the Table menu.*

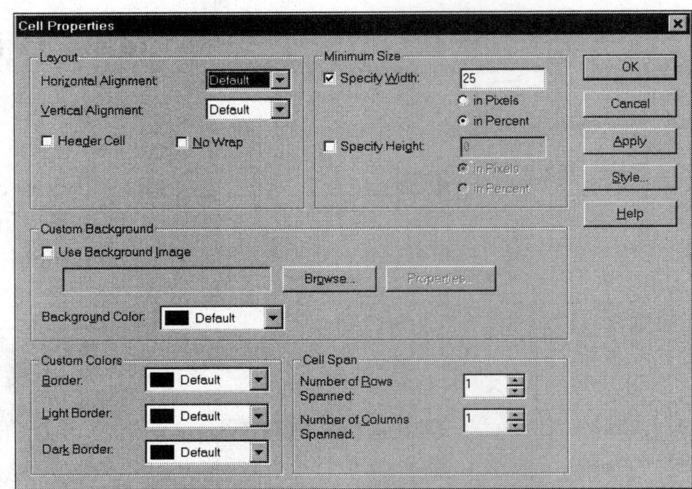

Figure 47. *The Cell Properties dialog box.*

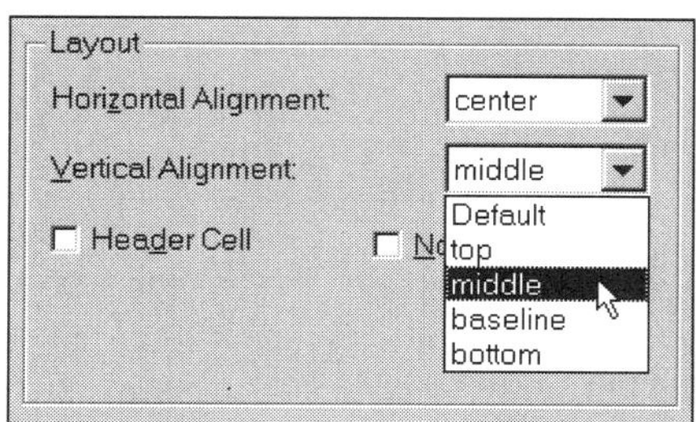

Figure 48. *Use the Layout area to set the horizontal and vertical alignment for the cell's contents.*

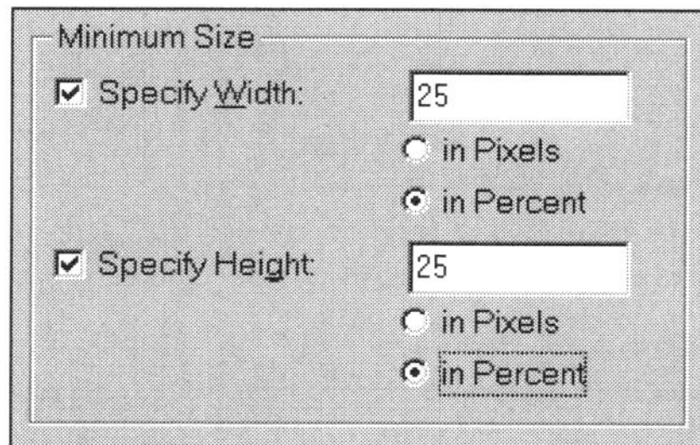

Figure 49. *You can use the Minimum Size area to set the minimum width and height for a cell.*

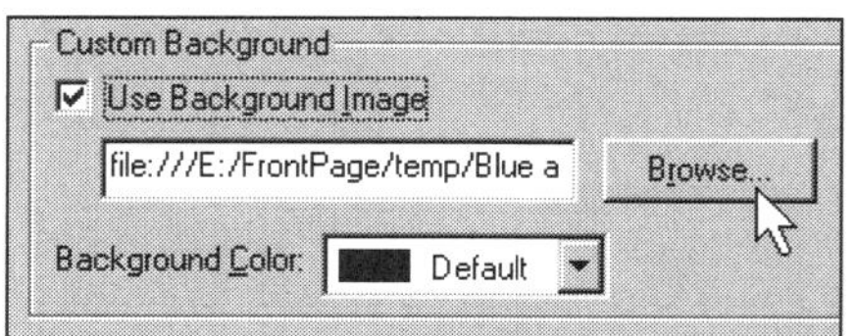

Figure 50. *Use the Custom Background area to set a background color or image for the cell.*

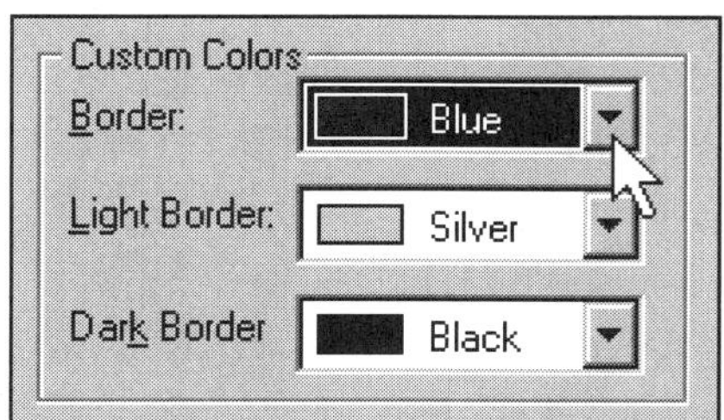

Figure 51. *To set a special 3D look for the cell's borders, use the Border, Light Border, and Dark Border drop-down lists.*

5. Use the Custom Background area to set a special background image or color for the selected cells (**Figure 50**). You can also use the Background Color button on the Table toolbar.
6. Use the Custom Colors area to set a special 3D border for the selected cells (**Figure 51**). This process is the same as applying 3D borders to table borders, as described on page 189.
7. When you are happy with your selections, click OK. The cells you selected will assume the changes you picked.

ALIGNING TABLE CONTENTS

Here are some quick ways to align the contents of your tables. To set the horizontal alignment, select the cells to align and click the Align Left, Center, or Align Right buttons on the Format toolbar.

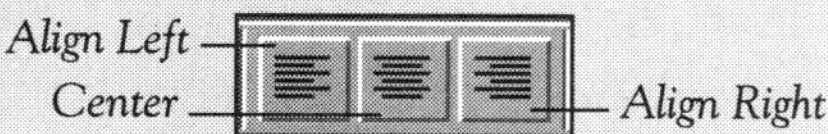

You can also set the vertical alignment of the selected cells by clicking the Align Top, Center Vertically, or Align Bottom buttons on the Table toolbar.

Aligning the contents of your table is not the same as aligning the table itself, which you do with the Table Properties dialog box.

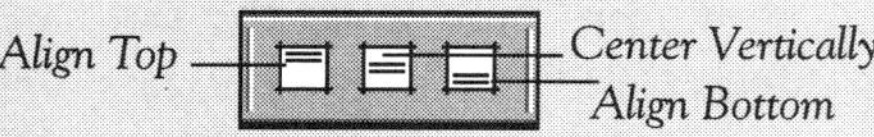

Change Cell Settings

Many times, a table will have a descriptive title in bold at the head of a column or to the left of a row. Also, any cell whose contents should be prominent could also be emphasized using bold text. To quickly create these special cells, change a regular cell into a *header cell.*

To change a cell into a header cell:

1. Place the insertion marker in the cell you want to change or select multiple cells if you want to change them all (**Figure 52**).
2. Choose Cell Properties from the Table menu or right-click the cell and choose Cell Properties from the pop-up menu. The Cell Properties dialog box will open (**Figure 47**).
3. In the Layout area, put a check mark in the Header Cell check box (**Figure 53**).
4. If you don't want the text to automatically wrap in the cell into two or more lines, put a check mark in the No Wrap check box.
5. Click OK. The cell will become a header cell and the text will become bold and centered within the cell (**Figure 54**).

Tip:

- You can also format text in individual cells using the Bold, Italic, and Underline buttons on the Format toolbar.

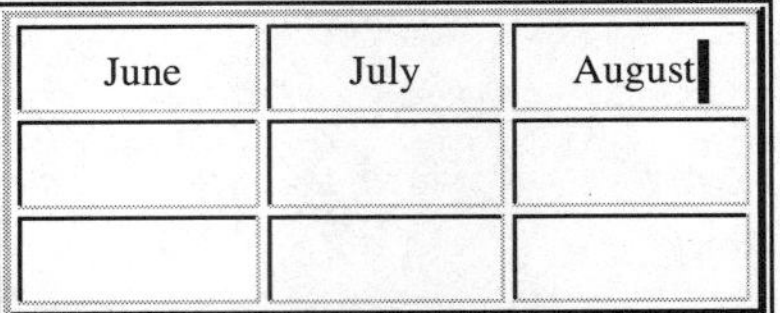

Figure 52. *Place the insertion marker in the cell you want to change to a header cell.*

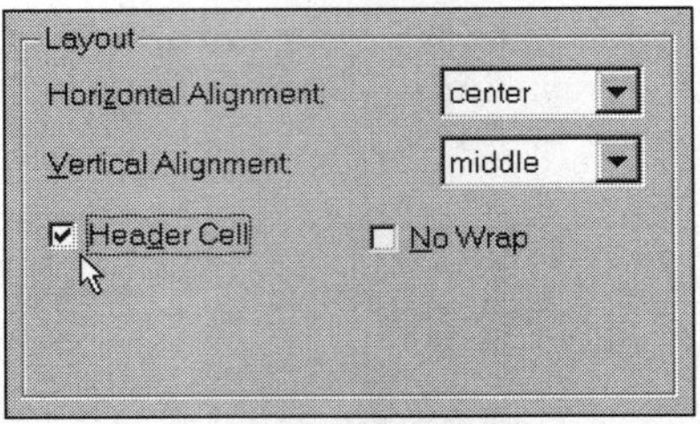

Figure 53. *In the Layout area of the Cell Properties dialog box, put a check in the Header Cell check box, then click OK.*

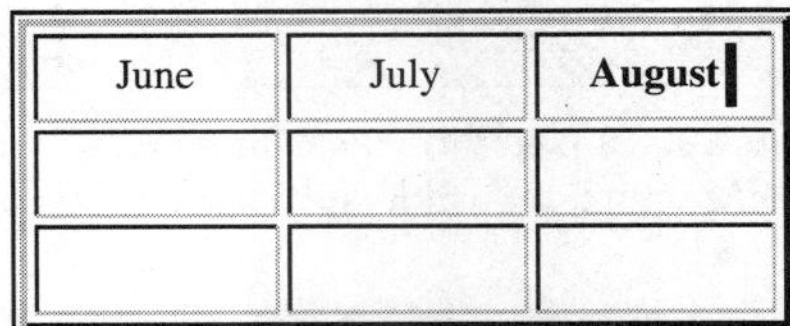

Figure 54. *The text in the header cell becomes bold.*

1	2	3	4
5	6	7	8
9	10	11	12

Figure 55. *Place the insertion marker in the cell whose span you want to change.*

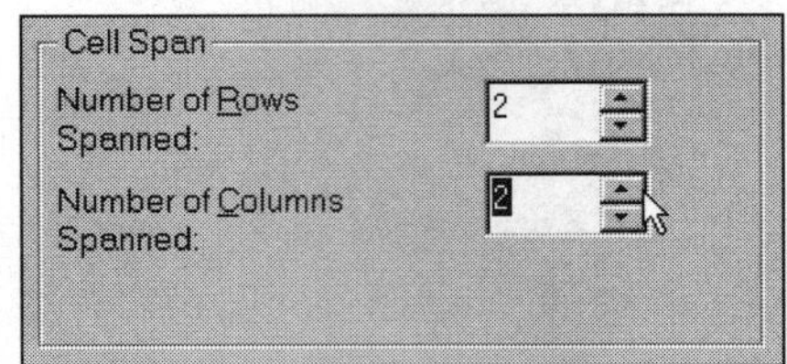

Figure 56. *Use the Cell Span area of the Cell Properties dialog box to set how many rows and columns the cell will span.*

Create a Header Cell

I WANT A SYMMETRICAL TABLE!

If you change the cell span of a cell and the table becomes irregularly shaped, you may want to make the table symmetrical again. To do so, select the empty cells creating the irregular shape (for instance, the cells numbered 8, 11, and 12 in Figure 57) and delete them. (Deleting cells is described on page 197.) If some of the cells contain data that you want to keep, add new cells to even out the irregular rows (for instance, two cells could be added next to cell 4 and one cell could be added next to cell 8 in Figure 57).

Instead of changing the span of a single cell, you can merge several cells together to create one larger cell, as you'll learn on page 200. (This way your table doesn't take on an irregular shape.)

If you wind up with rows or columns of different sizes, but you want everything to line up just so, you can use the Distribute Rows Evenly and Distribute Columns Evenly commands on the Table menu to make the selected rows or columns the exact same size. Or, click the Distribute Rows Evenly or Distri-bute Columns Evenly buttons on the Table toolbar.

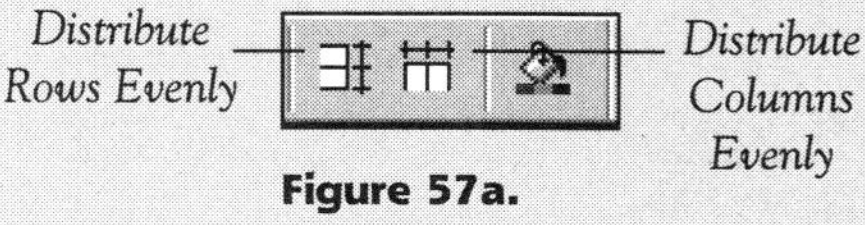

Figure 57a.

Using FrontPage Editor, you can easily set a cell to span more than one row or column. One reason you would want to do this is to include a large image in a cell below two cells of text.

To change the cell span:

1. Place the insertion marker in the cell whose span you want to change (**Figure 55**).
2. Open the Cell Properties dialog box (**Figure 47**) by choosing Cell Properties from the Table menu or right-clicking the cell and choosing Cell Properties from the pop-up menu.
3. In the Cell Span area, use the Number of Rows Spanned and the Number of Columns Spanned text boxes to set the cell's vertical and horizontal span (**Figure 56**).
4. Click OK. The cell span will change to the setting you chose (**Figure 57**).

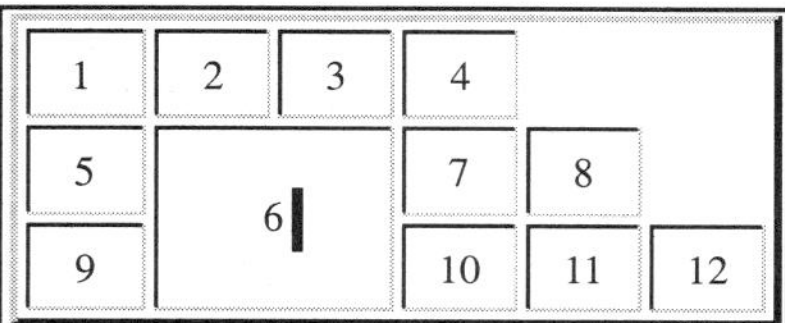

Figure 57. *Depending on the columns and rows the cell is spanning, the shape of the table can change and become irregular.*

Change the Cell Span

What if you decide your table is not large enough? Don't worry—it's easy to add cells, rows, and columns. And if you end up with too many columns, rows, or cells, it's just as easy to delete them.

To add a cell:

1. Place the insertion marker in the cell to the left of where you want the new cell to appear.
2. Choose Insert Cell from the Table menu (**Figure 58**). The new cell will appear in the table and the existing cells in that row will all be pushed right one column.

To add new rows:

1. Place the insertion marker in a cell below or above where you want the new row to appear.
2. Choose Insert Rows or Columns from the Table menu (**Figure 59**). The Insert Rows or Columns dialog box will appear (**Figure 60**).
3. Select the Rows radio button.
4. Type in how many rows you want to add in the Number of Rows text box, then select whether the rows will appear above or below the insertion marker.
5. Click OK. The number of rows you entered will appear in the table.

or

1. Select the row above which you want to insert a row (select several rows to insert that many new rows).
2. Click the Insert Rows button on the Table toolbar (**Figure 61**).

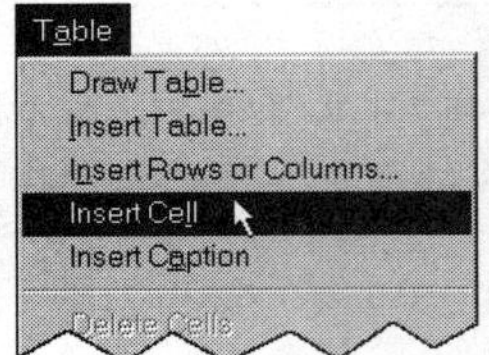

Figure 58. *Choose Insert Cell from the Table menu.*

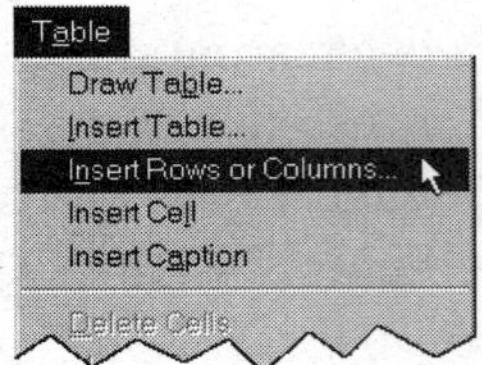

Figure 59. *Choose Insert Rows or Columns from the Table menu.*

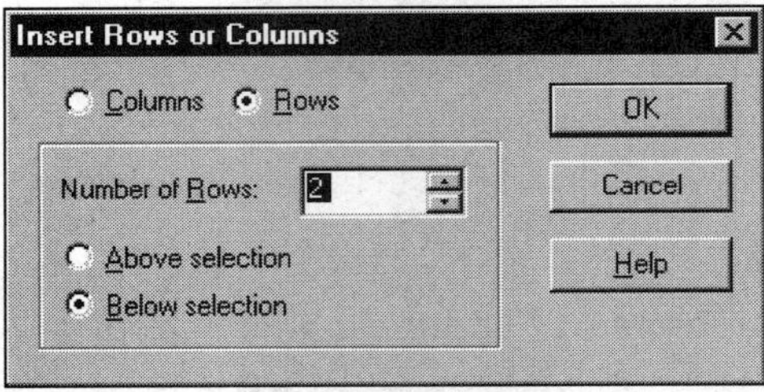

Figure 60. *Select the Rows radio button, then set the number of rows to be added and whether they will appear above or below the insertion marker.*

Figure 61. *The Insert Rows button automatically inserts a row above the selected row, and the Insert Columns button automatically inserts a column to the left of the selected column.*

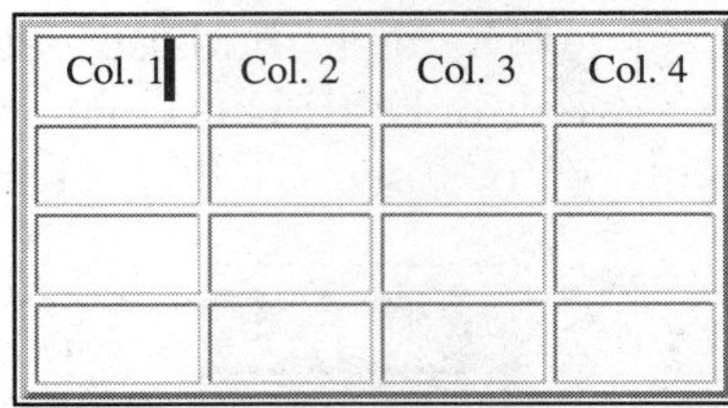

Figure 62. *Place the insertion marker in a cell next to where you want the new column to appear.*

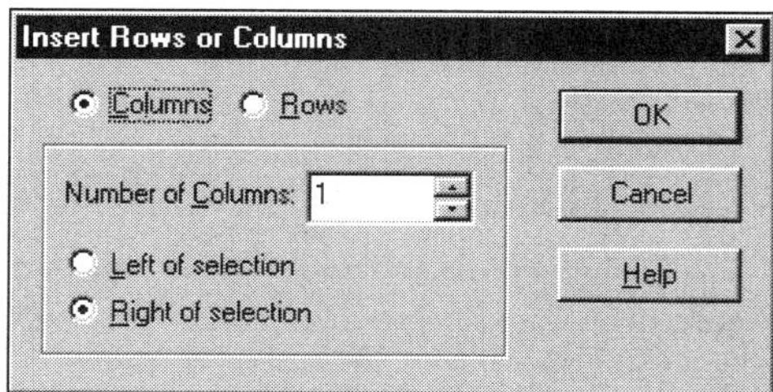

Figure 63. *Select the Columns radio button, then set how many columns will be added to the table and whether they will appear to the right or left of the insertion marker.*

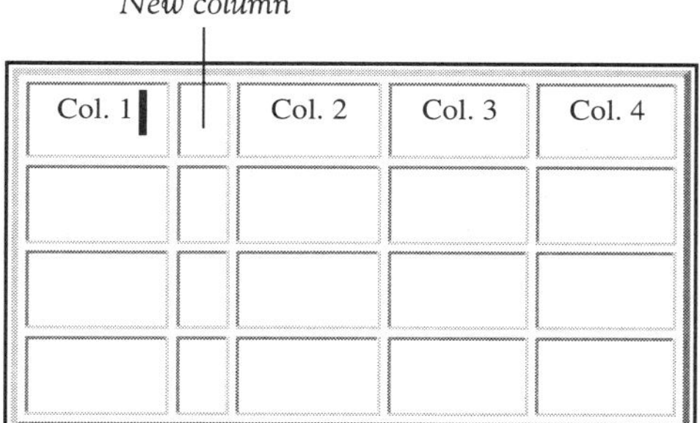

Figure 64. *When you click OK, the new column appears in the table.*

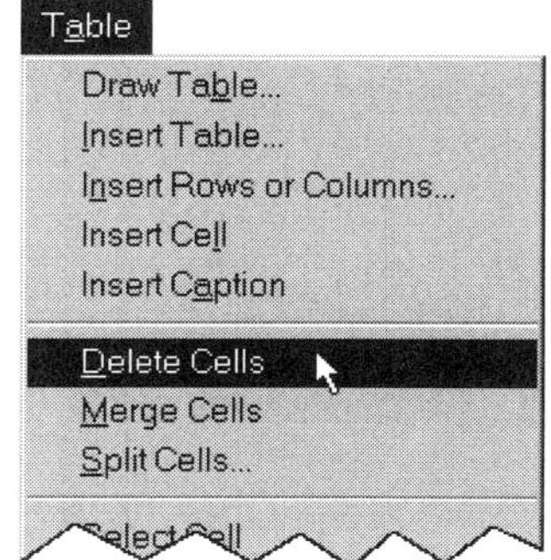

Figure 65. *Choose Delete Cells from the Table menu.*

To add new columns:

1. Position the insertion marker to the right or left of where you want the new column to appear (**Figure 62**).
2. Choose Insert Rows or Columns from the Table menu (**Figure 59**). The Insert Rows or Columns dialog box will appear (**Figure 63**).
3. Select the Columns radio button.
4. Type in how many columns you want to add in the Number of Columns text box, then select whether the columns will appear to the left or the right of the insertion marker.
5. Click OK. The number of columns you entered will appear in the table (**Figure 64**). You can now enter text or images in the new cells or change the new cells' settings using the Cell Properties dialog box.

or

1. Select the column to the left of which you want to insert a column (select several columns to insert that many new columns).
2. Click the Insert Columns button on the Table toolbar (**Figure 61**).

To delete a cell, row, or column:

Select the cell, row or column you want to delete, then choose Delete Cells from the Table menu (**Figure 65**) or click the Delete Cells button on the Table toolbar (**Figure 61**).

Sometimes information in a cell can be quite complex and is more easily explained if it is in table format. With FrontPage, it's simple to insert a table into an individual cell. Some folks refer to this as "a table in a table."

Figure 66. *Place the insertion marker in the cell where you would like to add the new table.*

To insert a table in a table:

1. Position the insertion marker in the cell where you want to add the new table (**Figure 66**).
2. Use the Insert Table button on the Standard toolbar (**Figure 13**) to add the table or choose Insert Table from the Table menu (**Figure 9**) and use the Insert Table dialog box (**Figure 10**) to set up the new table. The new table will appear in the cell (**Figure 67**).

Figure 67. *The table within the cell can be used like any other table.*

1	2	3	4
5	6	7	8
9	10	11	12

Figure 68. *Place the insertion marker in the cell you want to split.*

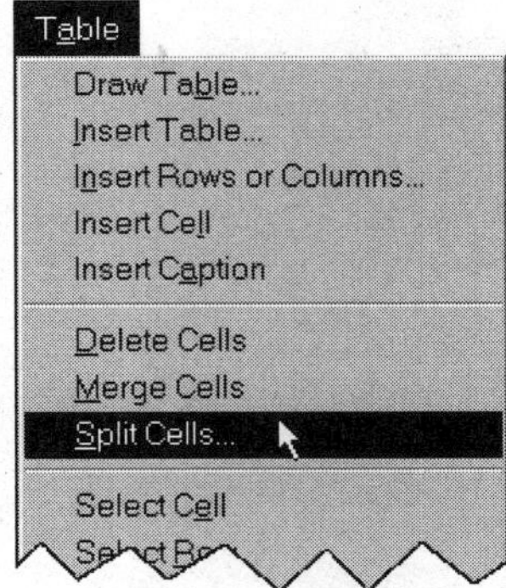

Figure 69. *Choose Split Cells from the Table menu.*

INSERTING EXCEL SPREADSHEETS INTO YOUR WEB PAGES

When you insert an Excel spreadsheet into the Editor, it's automatically converted into table format. To add an Excel spreadsheet to your Web page, choose File from the Insert menu. In the Select a File dialog box that opens, use the Files of Type drop-down list to find Microsoft Excel Worksheet (*.xls, *.xlw), then move to the folder where the spreadsheet is saved. Select the spreadsheet file, then click Open. The spreadsheet will appear in your Web page.

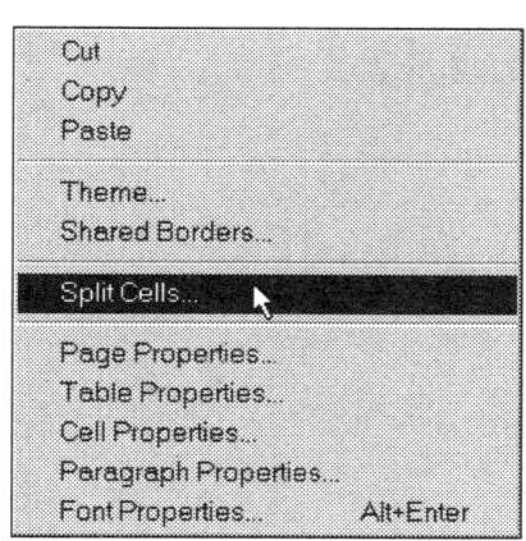

Figure 70. *Choose Split Cells from the pop-up menu.*

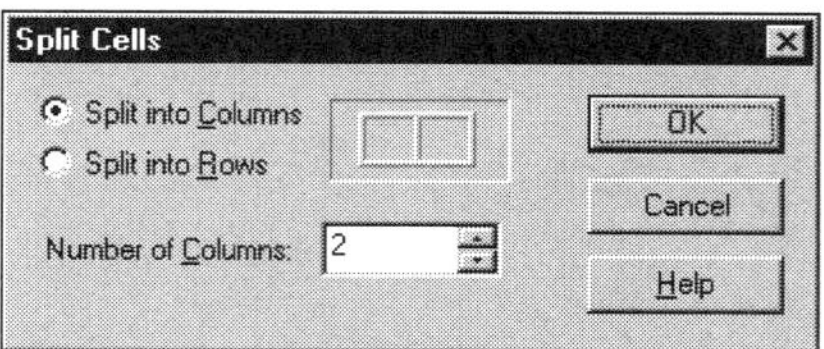

Figure 71. *Select whether you want to split the cell into columns or rows.*

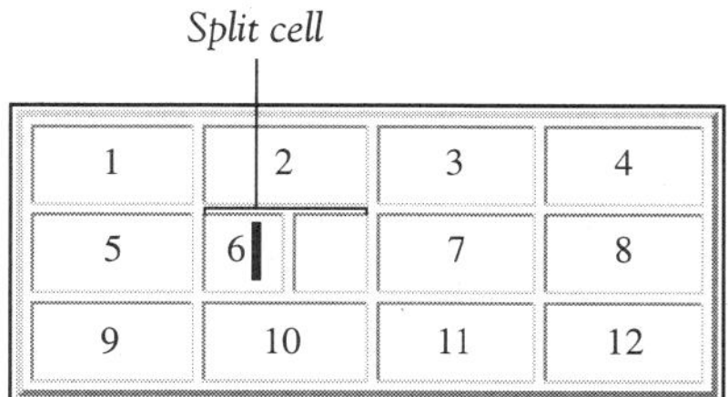

Figure 72. *When you click OK, the cell splits as you specified.*

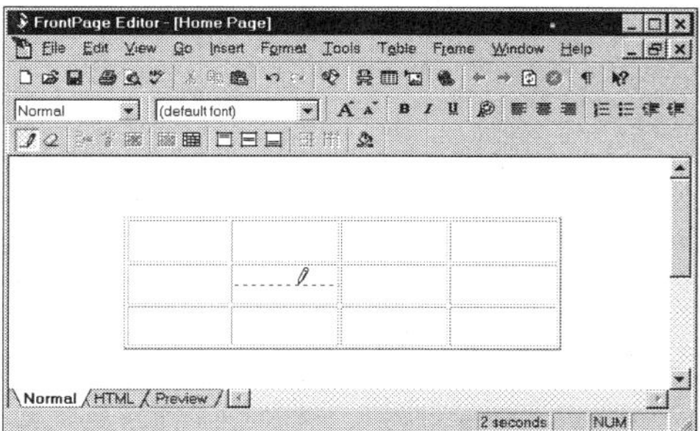

Figure 73. *You can also split cells by dragging within them when the Draw Table toolbar button is selected.*

Besides adding cells and changing the span of a cell to adjust how a table presents information, you can also split and merge cells. Splitting cells can let you give more detailed information or, if you're using an invisible table to line up the contents of a page, help clean up formatting. Merging cells is handy when you want to combine the contents of several adjoining cells into one cell.

To split a cell:

1. Place the insertion marker in the cell you want to split (**Figure 68**).
2. Choose Split Cells from the Table menu (**Figure 69**) or right-click the cell and choose Split Cells from the pop-up menu (**Figure 70**). The Split Cells dialog box will appear (**Figure 71**).
3. Select either the Split into Columns radio button or the Split into Rows radio button, then enter the number of new columns or rows you want to appear in that cell.
4. Click OK. The cell will split as you specified (**Figure 72**).

or

1. Click the Draw Table tool in the Table toolbar.
2. Drag within a cell to split it into rows or columns (**Figure 73**).
3. Click the Draw Table button again to deselect it.

Merging cells combines several neighboring cells into one cell. While it may look similar to changing the cell span, cell span does not join cells together, it spreads one cell across any number of rows and/or columns. In addition, changing cell span will alter the size and shape of a table, whereas merging cells will not.

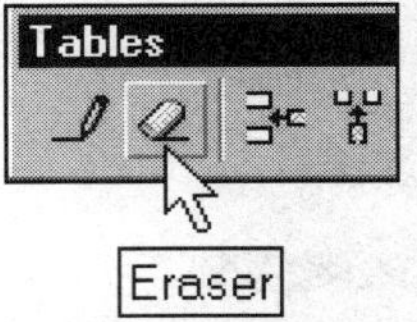

Figure 74. *Click the Eraser button on the Table toolbar.*

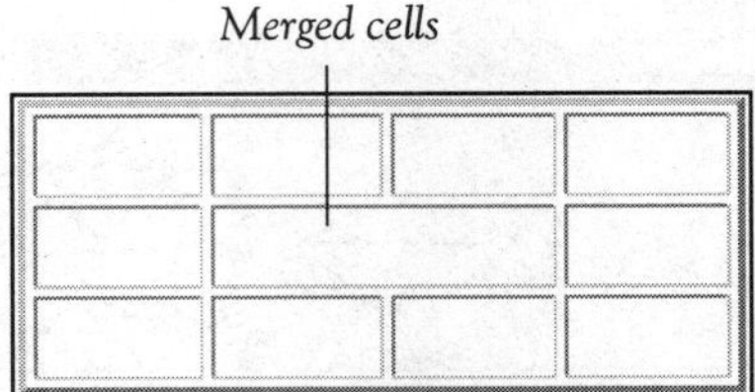

Figure 75. *The cells that you selected merge together.*

To merge cells:

1. Click the Eraser button on the Table toolbar (**Figure 74**).
2. Drag with the Eraser to erase the borders between any cells you want to merge.
3. Release the mouse button to merge the cells (**Figure 75**).
4. Click the Eraser button again to turn it off.

Merge Cells

SUMMARY

In this chapter you learned how to:

- Draw tables
- Add text, images, and backgrounds to tables
- Add a table caption
- Create a header cell
- Select cells, rows, and columns
- Add cells, rows, and columns
- Insert a table in a table
- Split a cell
- Merge cells together

13 Using Tasks View

Keeping track of tasks can be hard to do. When building a Web site, by yourself or as part of a team, there are many small details that need to get done. Unfortunately, sometimes things fall through the cracks. Luckily, FrontPage Explorer creates a Tasks view every time a new Web site is created. This list of tasks is shared across a Web site by all the folks helping to build it. (In case you're wondering, Tasks view used to be called the To Do List.)

Tasks view displays a roster of tasks that need to be completed for a particular site. It lists each task with a status, description, and priority, also listing to whom the task is assigned. You can completely customize the list of tasks by adding, deleting, changing, and reassigning tasks. **Figure 1** shows Tasks view.

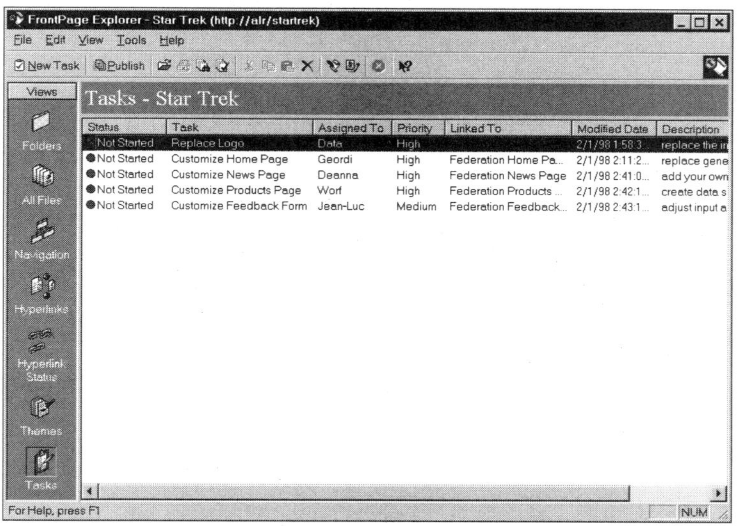

Figure 1. *Tasks view is used to assign tasks, show what needs to be done, and help you stay organized while you create your Web site.*

You open Tasks view from the Explorer. If you are in the Editor, you must first switch over to the Explorer.

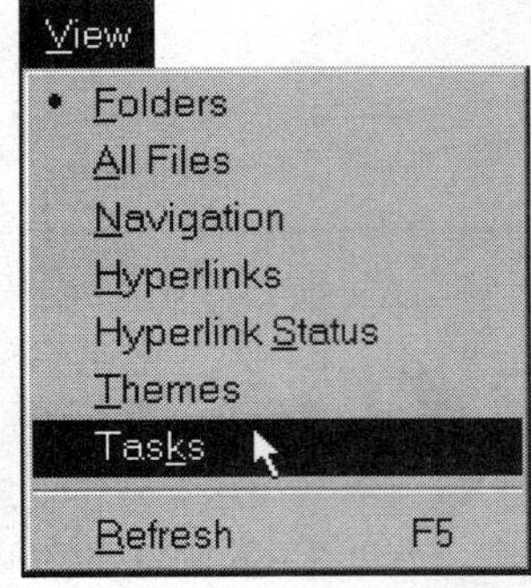

Figure 2. *Choose Tasks from the View menu.*

To open Tasks view:

In the Explorer, choose Tasks from the View menu (**Figure 2**) or click the Tasks button on the Views bar (**Figure 3**). The Tasks view window will open (**Figure 1**).

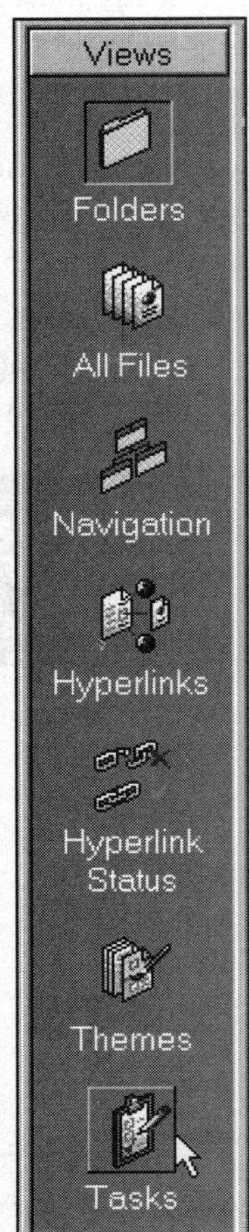

Figure 3. *Click the Tasks button in the Views bar.*

Tip:

- You can add tasks from within the Editor, even though you can't open Tasks view from there.

Tasks View Features

If you take a look at the Tasks view window shown in **Figure 4**, you will see that the task status is listed in the left-most column, followed by the task name. The next column, Assigned To, lists who is responsible for completing a particular task. Next to that, the Priority column shows a low, medium, or high priority for each task. The Linked To column displays the page (if any) that needs to be edited in order for the task to be completed. The right-most column, Description, gives a brief summary of what needs to be done.

Before you use the Tasks view, there are some other features you should know about.

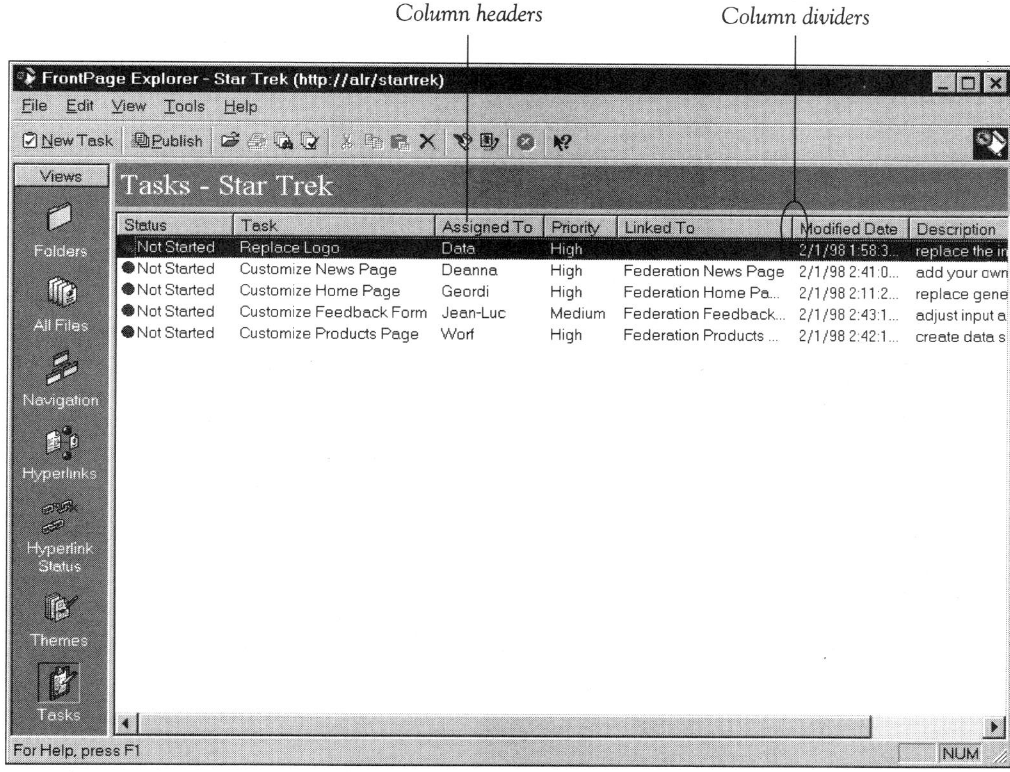

Figure 4. *In Tasks view, you can sort the tasks by column type and resize the columns themselves.*

Column headers

Column headers are handy because you can use them to sort your list. To sort by a particular column type, click that column header. For instance, if you want to find all the tasks assigned to you, click the Assigned To column header. The list will sort alphabetically by name.

Column dividers

You can use the column dividers to make any column wider or narrower. Position the mouse pointer on a column divider. The pointer will change to a double-headed black arrow. Press the left mouse button and drag the column divider to resize the column.

When you create a new task, you can decide to associate the task with a particular Web page or not. Tasks don't have to be linked to a particular page. For instance, you could add a task reminding yourself to create a certain graphic.

To add a new task linked to a particular Web page:

1. Select the page in the Explorer; you can be in Folders, All Files, Navigation, or Hyperlinks view. Choose New from the File menu and choose Task from the fly-out menu (**Figure 5**). You can also right-click the desired page and choose Add Task from the pop-up menu (**Figure 6**).

   or

   Open the page in the Editor and choose Add Task from the Edit menu (**Figure 7**). The New Task dialog box will open (**Figure 8**).
2. In the Task Name text box, type in a name for the task (**Figure 9**). (This item will appear in the Task column in Tasks view.)
3. Use the Assign To text box to assign the task to a particular person.
4. Use the Priority area to select a High, Medium, or Low priority for the task (**Figure 10**).
5. Add a brief description for the task in the Description text box (**Figure 11**).
6. Click OK. The task will be added to the list.

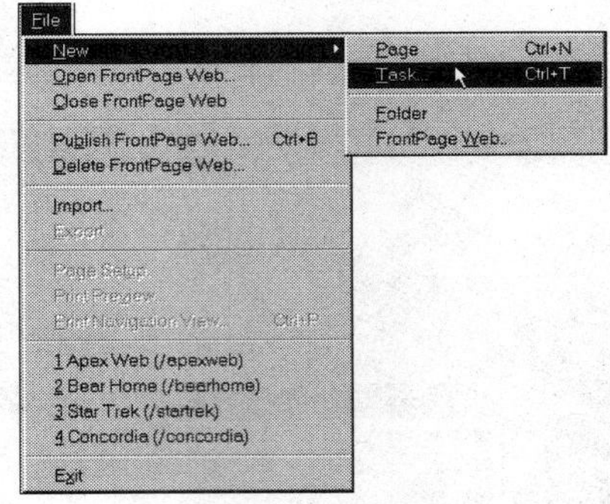

Figure 5. *Choose New from the File menu and then choose Task from the fly-out.*

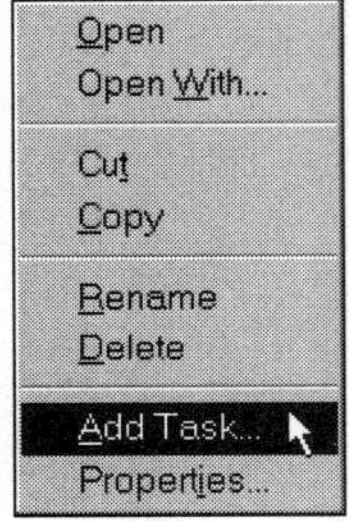

Figure 6. *Choose Add Task from the pop-up menu.*

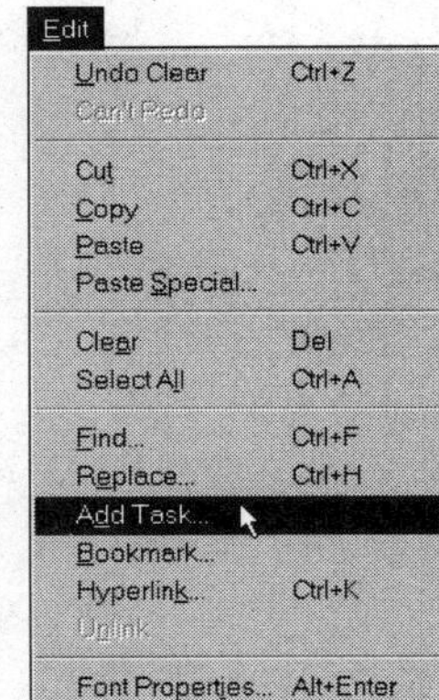

Figure 7. *In the Editor, choose Add Task from the Edit menu.*

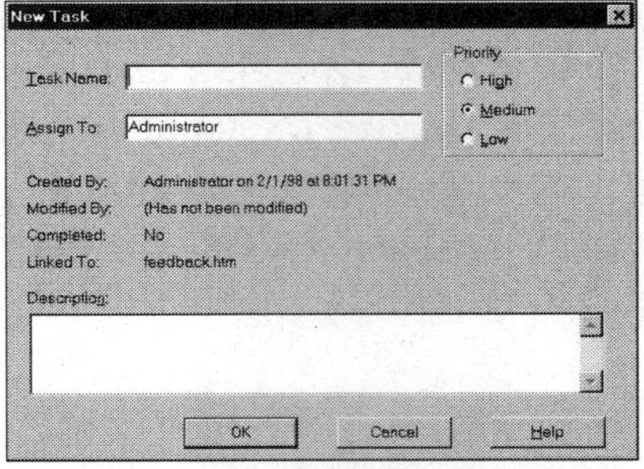

Figure 8. *The New Task dialog box is used to set a task name and priority, assign the task, and give it a description.*

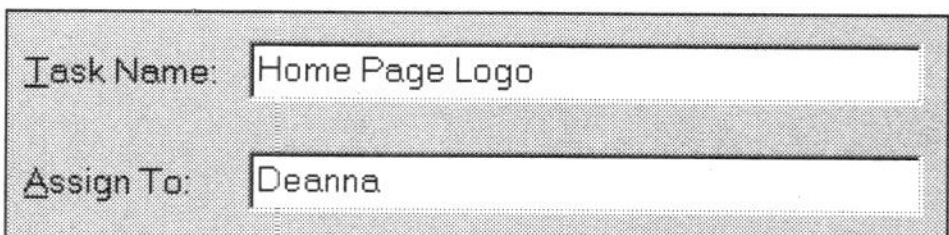

Figure 9. *Use the Task Name and Assign To text boxes to give the task a name and assign it to a particular person.*

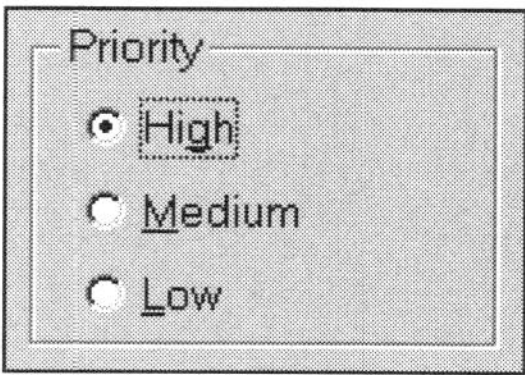

Figure 10. *Use the Priority area to select a High, Medium, or Low priority for the task.*

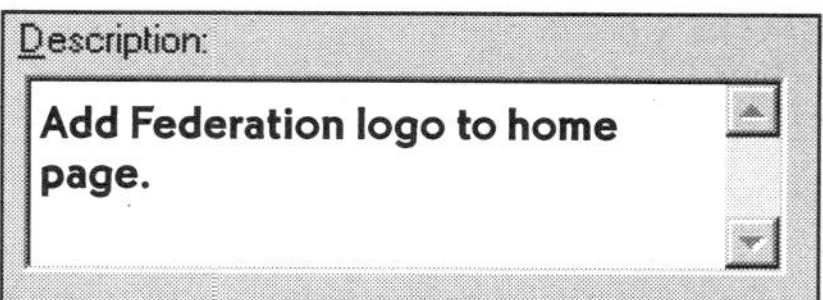

Figure 11. *Type a brief description of the task in the Description text box.*

Figure 12. *Click the New Task button in the Explorer toolbar.*

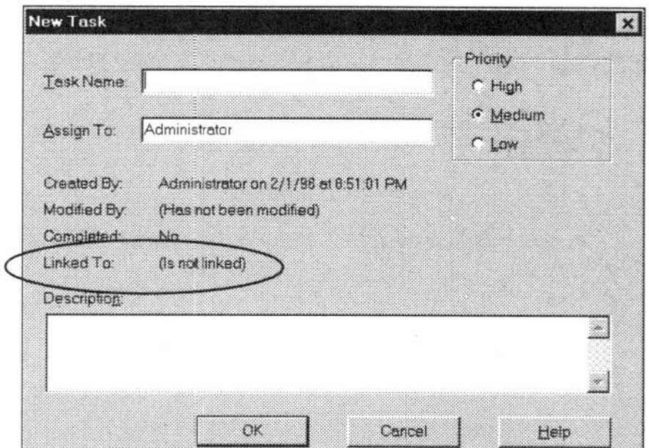

Figure 13. *When you add a task that is not linked to a specific page, the Linked To area will state just that.*

To add a new task not linked to a specific page:

1. Open Tasks view by clicking the Tasks button on the Views bar or choosing Tasks from the View menu.
2. Click the New Task button (**Figure 12**). The New Task dialog box will appear (**Figure 13**).
3. Use the dialog box as described from steps 2 through 6 on the previous page.

Tips:

- Notice that there is no page listed after Linked To in the New Task dialog box in Figure 13.
- You can also add tasks not linked to specific pages from Folders, All Files, and Navigation view, if you first make sure no file is selected.

Which Web Pages Need the Most Work?

To see which pages have the most tasks assigned to them, click the Linked To column header to sort the tasks by page.

When you work on a Web site, the information in Tasks view will need to be kept up-to-date. For instance, you can change the description of a task if it changes. And once a task is finished, you can mark it as completed, or you can delete it altogether.

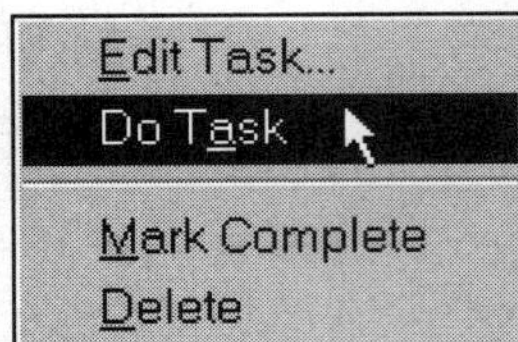

Figure 14. *Choose Do Task from the pop-up menu.*

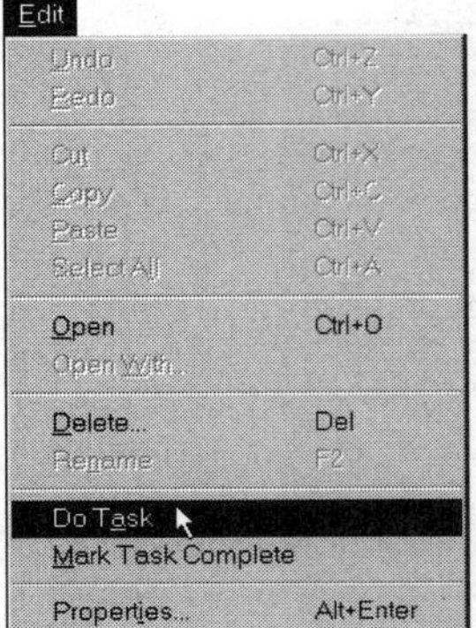

Figure 15. *Choose Do Task from the Edit menu.*

To work on a task:

1. Right-click a task and choose Do Task from the pop-up menu (**Figure 14**) or choose Do Task from the Edit menu (**Figure 15**). The Editor will open to the page where the task needs to be done.
2. Work on the task until it's finished or until you have to stop.
3. Save the page containing the task. FrontPage will ask you whether you want to mark the task as completed (**Figure 16**).
4. If you finished the task, click Yes. The task will be marked as completed and removed from the list. (If you want to see what items have been completed, display the Task history, as described on page 210.) If you left the task unfinished, click No. The task will not be marked as completed and you can continue working in the Editor later.

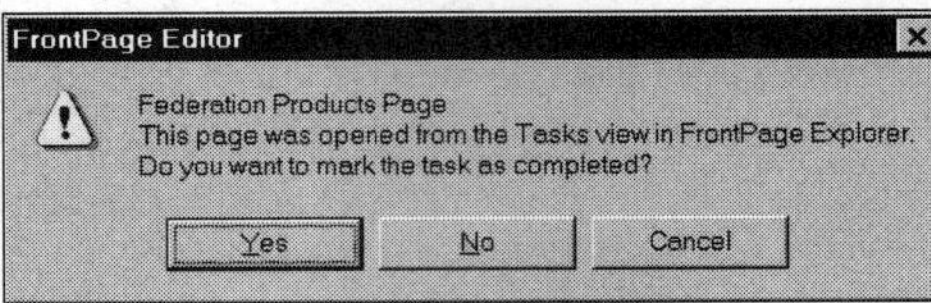

Figure 16. *When you save the page you've been working on, FrontPage Editor asks whether you want to mark the task as completed.*

Tip:

- If a task is not associated with a specific Web page, the Do Task option will be grayed out.

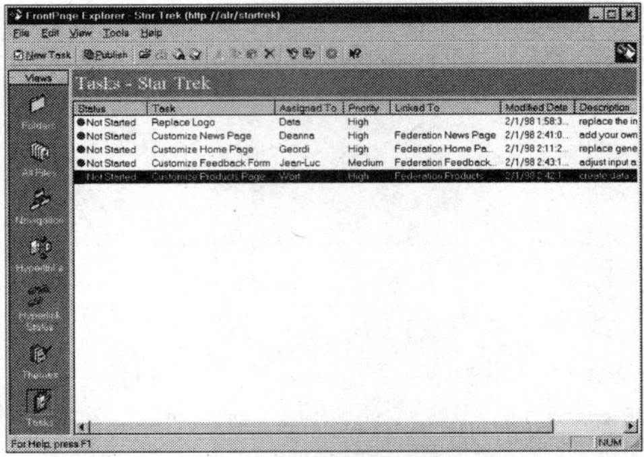

Figure 17. *First select the task you want to change.*

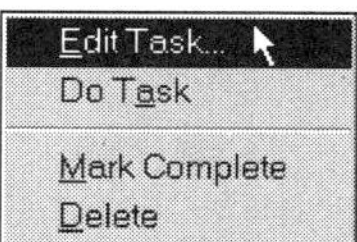

Figure 18. *Choose Edit Task from the pop-up menu.*

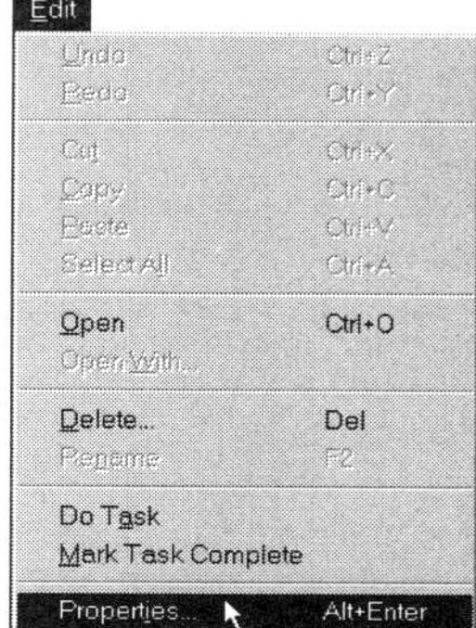

Figure 19. *Choose Properties from the Edit menu.*

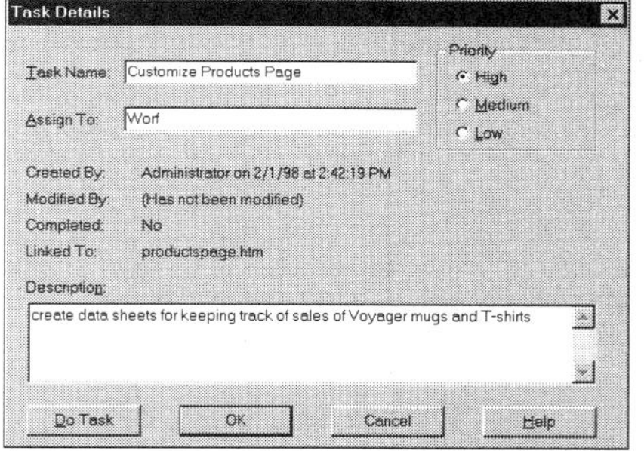

Figure 20. *Use the Task Details dialog box to make any changes you need.*

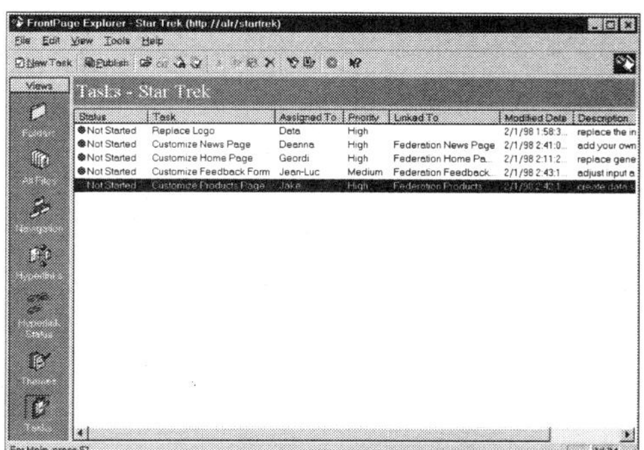

Figure 21. *When you click OK, the task's details change. In Figure 17, the Customize Products Page task was assigned to Worf. Here it has been reassigned to Jake.*

You may find that you need to change the details for a particular task, assign the task to a different person, or give it a different priority.

To change task details:

1. In Tasks view, select the task whose details you want to change (**Figure 17**).
2. Right-click the task and choose Edit Task from the pop-up menu (**Figure 18**), or choose Properites from the Edit menu (**Figure 19**). The Task Details dialog box will open (**Figure 20**).
3. Use the Task Name text box to change the task name if necessary.
4. Use the Assign To text box to reassign the task to another person.
5. Use the Priority area to change the task's priority by selecting the High, Medium, or Low radio buttons.
6. Change the task's description using the Description text box.
7. Click OK. The task's details will change in the Task List (**Figure 21**).

Change Task Details

Tips:

- Does the Task Details dialog box shown in Figure 20 look familiar? That's because it is much the same as the New Task dialog box shown in Figure 8.
- Click the Do Task button in the Task Details dialog box to open the web page and make needed changes.

To mark a task as completed:

1. In Tasks view, select the task you want to mark as completed.
2. Right-click the task and choose Mark Complete from the pop-up menu (**Figure 22**), or choose Mark Task Complete from the Edit menu (**Figure 23**). The task will be marked as completed (**Figure 24**). The next time you switch to Tasks view, that task will not be visible, unless you display the task history, as described on page 210.

Tip:

- If you will never need to refer back to a task, you can delete it rather than marking it as completed, as described next.

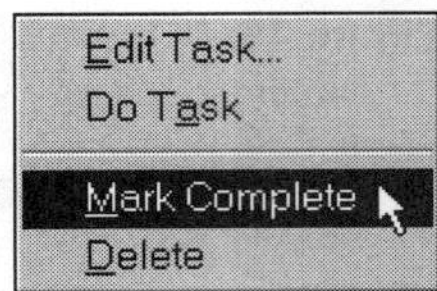

Figure 22. *Choose Mark Complete from the pop-up menu.*

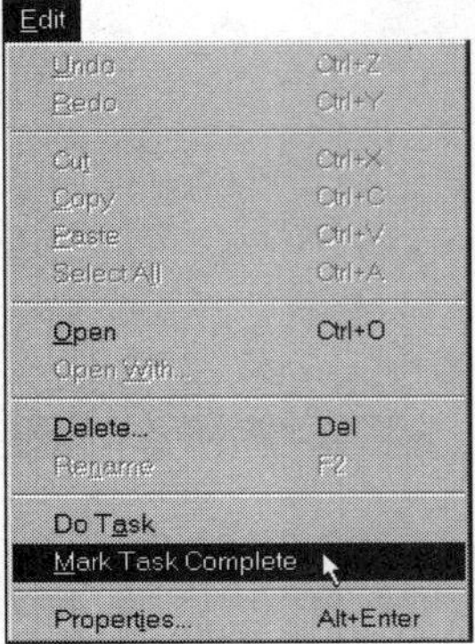

Figure 23. *Choose Mark Task Complete from the Edit menu.*

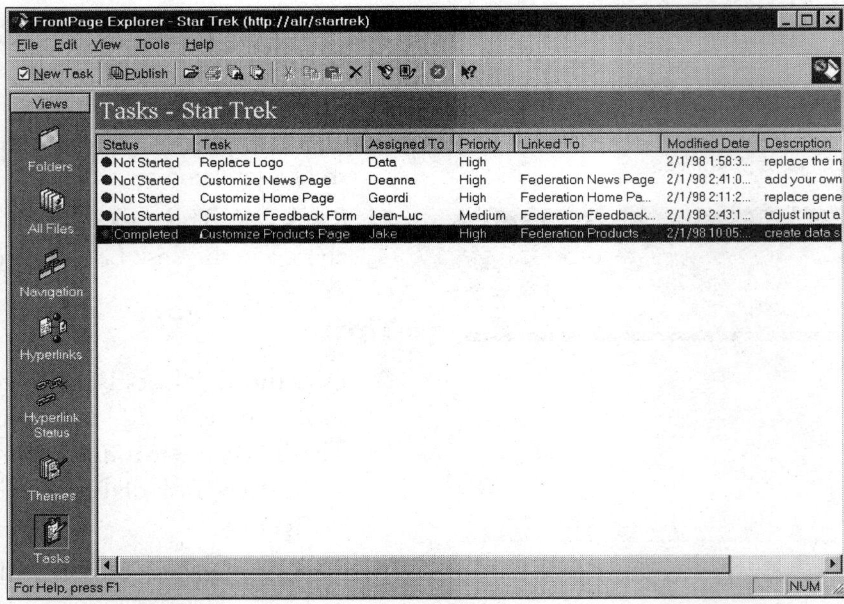

Figure 24. *When you mark a task as completed, its status changes from "Not Started" to "Completed" and the red mark to its left changes to green.*

Figure 25. *Click the Delete toolbar button.*

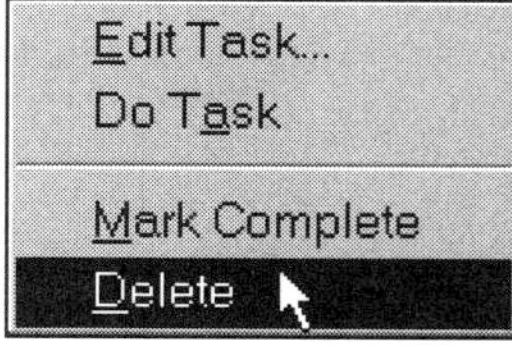

Figure 26. *Choose Delete from the pop-up menu.*

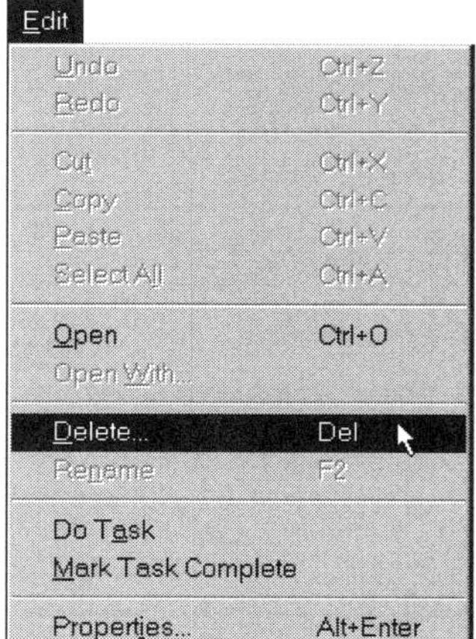

Figure 27. *Choose Delete from the Edit menu.*

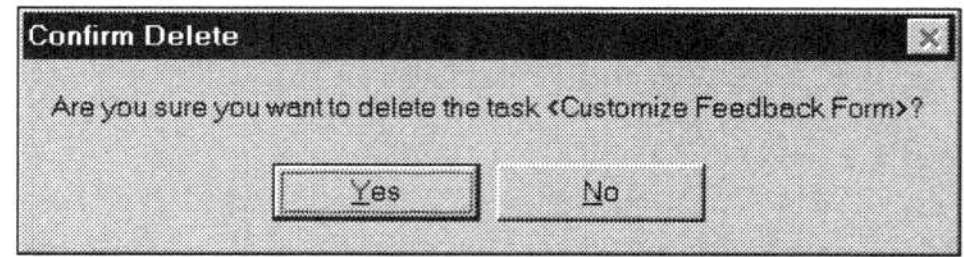

Figure 28. *Choose whether or not to delete the task.*

To delete a task:

1. In Tasks view, select the task you want to delete.
2. Click the Delete button on the toolbar (**Figure 25**), or right-click the task and choose Delete from the pop-up menu (**Figure 26**), or choose Delete from the Edit menu (**Figure 27**). You'll see a dialog box confirming that you want to delete the task (**Figure 28**).
3. Click Yes to go ahead and delete the task, and click No if you change your mind. If you click Yes, the task is removed from the list.

Tip:

- Think twice before deleting a task, since you can't get it back afterward. (Notice that there's no Undo button in Tasks view.) If you think you may want to keep a record of your tasks, consider just marking them as completed so you can view them in the task history, as described next.

When you delete tasks, they're gone forever. When you mark them as completed, however, they simply disappear from view, unless you display the task history. This is a great way to remove clutter from Tasks view, but still maintain a record of tasks that have been carried out.

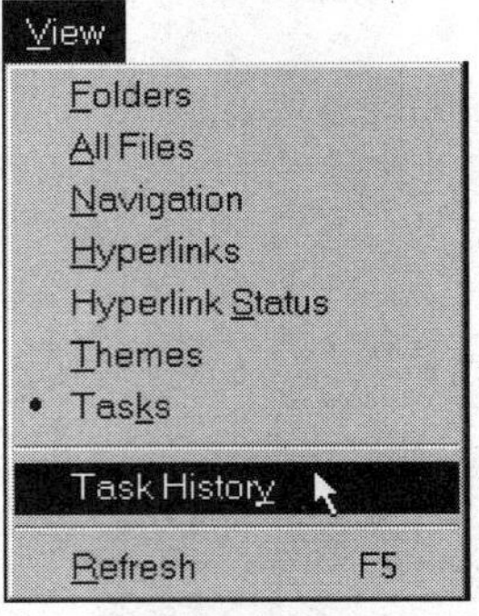

Figure 29. *Choose Task History from the View menu.*

To show the task history:

1. Switch to Tasks view, if you're not there already.
2. Choose Task History from the View menu (**Figure 29**). Tasks you had marked as completed will reappear in Tasks view.

TASKS VIEW AND YOUR TEAM'S WORK LOAD

If you are heading up a team working on a Web site, check Tasks view periodically to see if your team's workload is evenly distributed. If there's one person with much more work than the rest of the team, even up the workload by reassigning some of that person's tasks.

SUMMARY

In this chapter you learned how to:

- Switch to Tasks view
- Add tasks
- Work on tasks
- Change task details
- Mark a task as completed
- Delete a task
- Display the Task history

14 Navigating Your Web Pages

This chapter describes several different ways of setting up a navigation system on your Web. If you've surfed the Web, you've undoubtedly moved from one page to another within a site or from one Web site to another. FrontPage provides various ways of setting up these connections between Web pages, including hyperlinks, hotspots, hover buttons, and navigation bars.

Hyperlinks, also called *links*, are the underlined text and bordered images that a user can click to jump to another location. Links work by including the URL of the destination Web page within the HTML codes associated with the text or image clicked by the user. The text or image is usually descriptive of where the hyperlink will take the user. For instance, a text link that says "Home" will take the user to the site's home page. A comparable image could be one of a little house.

Another type of hyperlink, a *bookmark* or *anchor*, moves the user around a Web page. When the user clicks a bookmark, the Web page moves to a specific location in the browser. For instance, suppose you had a Web page with a large article divided into sections. You could have a mini table of contents at the top of the article with bookmark links that would jump the user to the various sections.

Hotspots are specific areas of an image that a user clicks to jump to another location. Hotspots are contained within an *image map*. An image map is automatically created by FrontPage when you add hot spots to an image. The image map tells a Web browser the precise location of each hotspot, using coordinates in pixels.

Figure 1. *When you select a graphic, eight black handles appear around the image.*

Hover buttons are text buttons or images that can change color or shape when the mouse pointer "hovers" over them. Clicking a hover button takes you to the associated Web page or site.

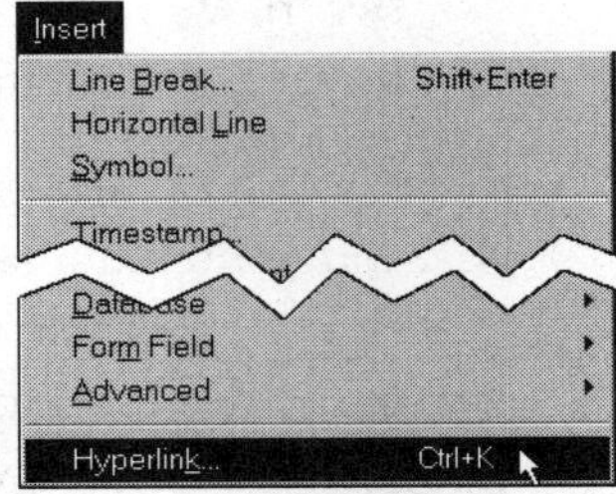

Figure 2. *Choose Hyperlink from the Insert menu.*

Navigation bars are sets of links that make it easy for users to travel between the pages in your site. If you set up your site structure in Navigation View, FrontPage will generate navigation bars for you, and, better yet, will update the navigation bars if the structure of your site changes.

When you create a hyperlink, there are several places you can link to: any Web page on your system, a site or page on the World Wide Web, or a new Web page that will be added to the open Web site. You can even create a link that sends e-mail.

Figure 3. *Click the Create or Edit Hyperlink button on the Standard toolbar.*

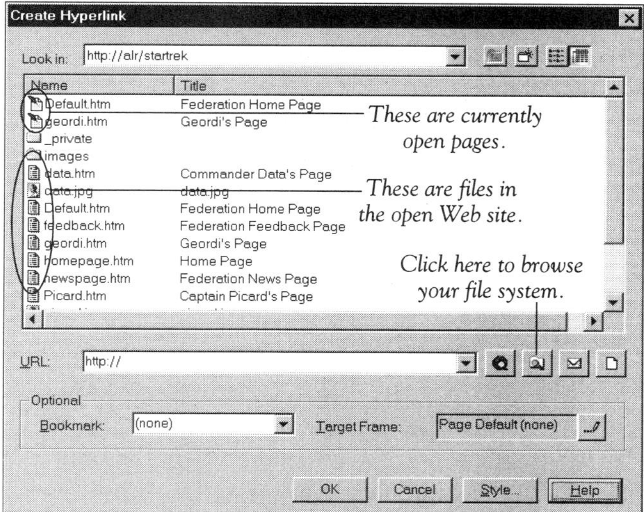

Figure 4. *You can create links to open pages from the Create Hyperlink dialog box.*

Figure 5. *A border appears around the hyperlinked image.*

To create a hyperlink to a page on your system:

1. In the Editor, select the text or image that will become the link to another place (**Figure 1**). If you are using an image, click on it to select it. Eight black handles will appear around the image.
2. Choose Hyperlink from the Insert menu (**Figure 2**) or click the Create or Edit Hyperlink button on the Standard toolbar (**Figure 3**) or press Ctrl+K on the keyboard. The Create Hyperlink dialog box will open (**Figure 4**).
3. Under Name, select the name of a Web page. Open Web pages have a page icon with a red quill. The other listed files are in the open Web. To search for a file elsewhere on your hard drive or network drive, click the File button. Then you can hunt for the file you want using the Select File dialog box.
4. Click OK. The link will be embedded in the HTML code underlying the Web page. If you selected text for the hyperlink, it will be underlined. If you selected an image, a blue border will appear around it (**Figure 5**).

Once you've added a hyperlink to your Web page, you'll want to test it to make sure it doesn't lead readers down the wrong path, or, worse yet, lead nowhere at all. (You can use these strategies to test any kind of hyperlink.)

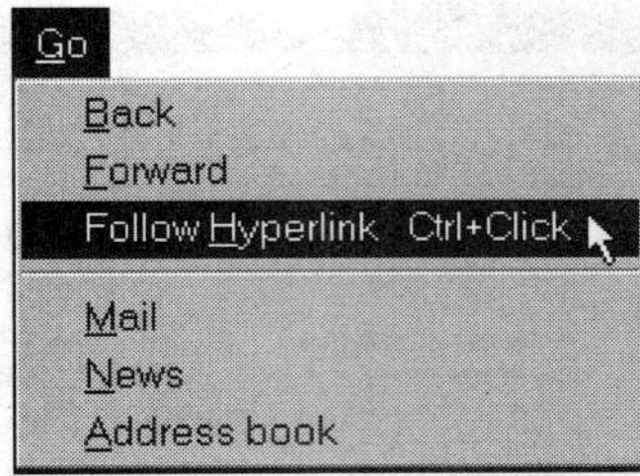

Figure 6. *Choose Follow Hyperlink from the Go menu.*

To test a hyperlink:

1. Click the link and choose Follow Hyperlink from the Go menu (**Figure 6**), or hold down the Ctrl key and click on the hyperlink. The destination page should appear in the Editor.

   or

   Click the Preview tab and click the hyperlink to follow it.

Tip:

- If you want to check where your hyperlink goes without actually travelling to that page, simply hold the mouse pointer over the link. You'll see the text "Use Ctrl+Click to follow a hyperlink" and the name of the linked page will appear in the lower-left corner of the status bar.

To create a hyperlink to a World Wide Web site:

1. In the Editor, select the text or image that will become the link to the World Wide Web site.
2. Choose Hyperlink from the Insert menu or click the Create or Edit Hyperlink button on the Standard toolbar. The Create Hyperlink dialog box will open (**Figure 4**).
3. In the URL text box, enter the URL of the Web page or site you want to link to (**Figure 7**) or click the World Wide Web button to browse to the desired Web site.

Figure 7. *Type the address for the Web site or page in the URL text box.*

Tip:

- You may have noticed that FrontPage entered the protocol http:// automatically in the URL text box so you don't have to type it yourself. If you need to use a different protocol, such as ftp, just delete http:// and type the protocol you need.

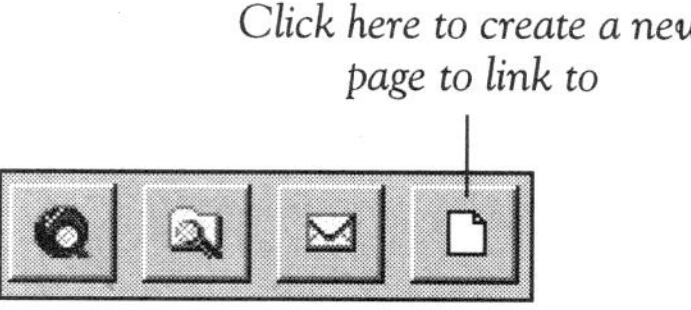

Figure 8. *Click the button on the right that looks like a page to create a new page and also create a link to it.*

4. Click OK. The link will be embedded in the HTML code underlying the Web page. If you selected text for the hyperlink, it will be underlined. If you selected an image, a blue border will appear around it.

To create a hyperlink to a Web page that has not been created yet:

1. In the Editor, select the text or image that will become the link to the page not yet created.
2. Choose Hyperlink from the Insert menu or click the Create or Edit Hyperlink button on the Standard toolbar. The Create Hyperlink dialog box will open.
3. Click the New Page button to the right of the URL text box (**Figure 8**). This opens the New dialog box (**Figure 9**).
4. Choose a template for the new Web page and click OK. FrontPage creates the new page and deposits you in the Editor. Build and save the page as usual.

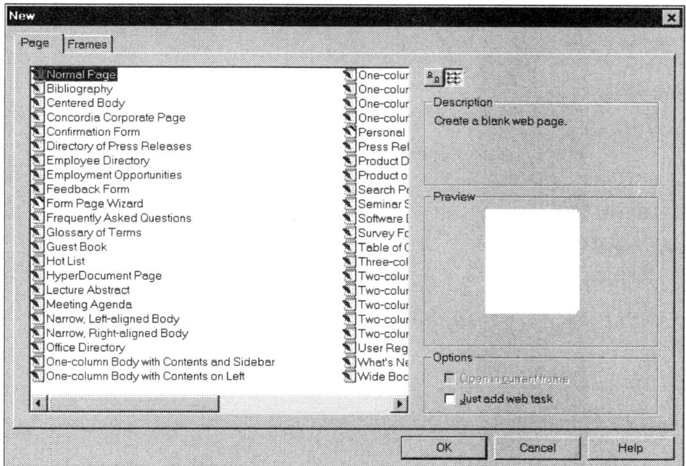

Figure 9. *Choose a template for the new page and click OK.*

To create a link that sends e-mail:

1. In the Editor, select the text or image that will become the link that will send e-mail.
2. Choose Hyperlink from the Insert menu or click the Create or Edit Hyperlink button on the Standard toolbar. The Create Hyperlink dialog box will open.
3. Click the E-mail button to the right of the URL text box—it looks like a little envelope (**Figure 10**). You'll see the Create E-mail Hyperlink dialog box (**Figure 11**).
4. Enter an e-mail address and click OK to return to the Create Hyperlink dialog box. In the URL text box, you'll see the e-mail address you entered preceded by the mailto: protocol (**Figure 12**).
5. Click OK. The e-mail link will be embedded in the HTML code underlying the Web page.
6. When you click the link in the Preview tab or when previewing the page in a browser, your e-mail program opens and automatically addresses mail to the designated recipient.

Click here to create a hyperlink that sends e-mail

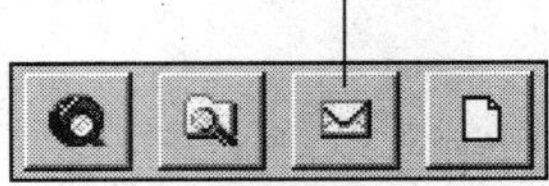

Figure 10. *Click the button that looks like an envelope to create a hyperlink that sends e-mail.*

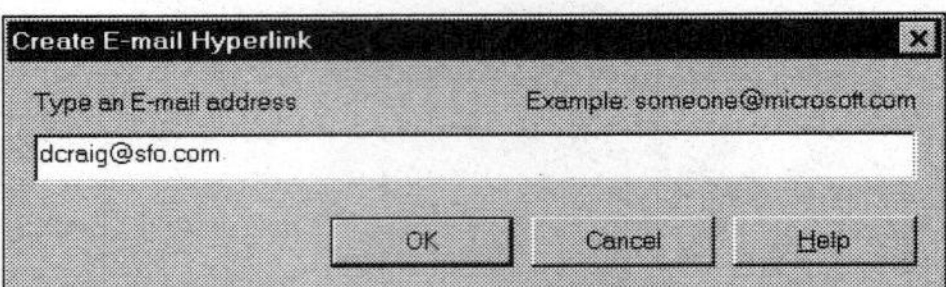

Figure 11. *Type the e-mail address and click OK.*

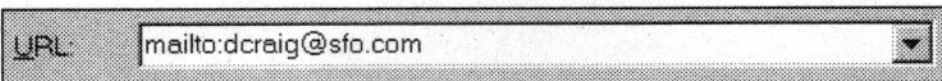

Figure 12. *The e-mail address you typed will be preceded by the mailto: protocol.*

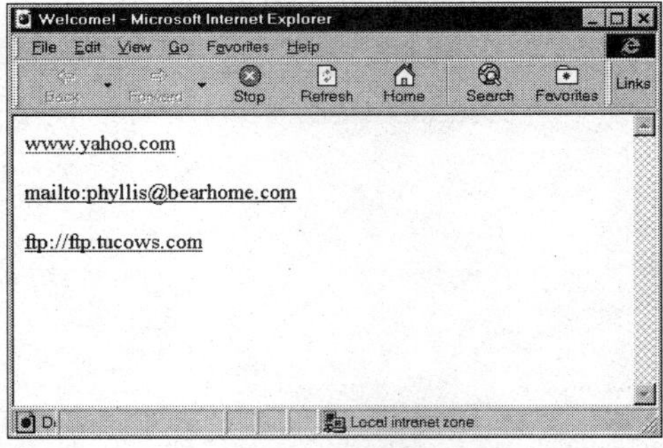

Figure 13. *These hyperlinks were created automatically.*

Creating Hyperlinks Automatically

The FrontPage Editor will automatically create hyperlinks for you if you type in a specific protocol or Web address. For instance, if you type mailto:info@bearhome.com, the Editor will create an e-mail hyperlink, underlining that text. The hyperlinks shown in **Figure 13** were all created automatically just by typing them in the Editor window. The Create Hyperlink dialog box didn't even open!

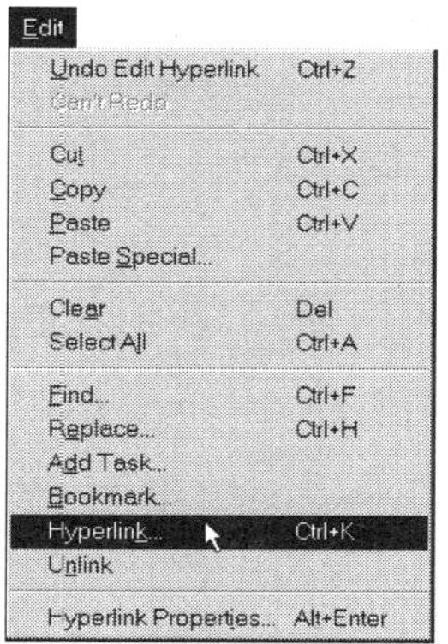

Figure 14. *Choose Hyperlink from the Edit menu.*

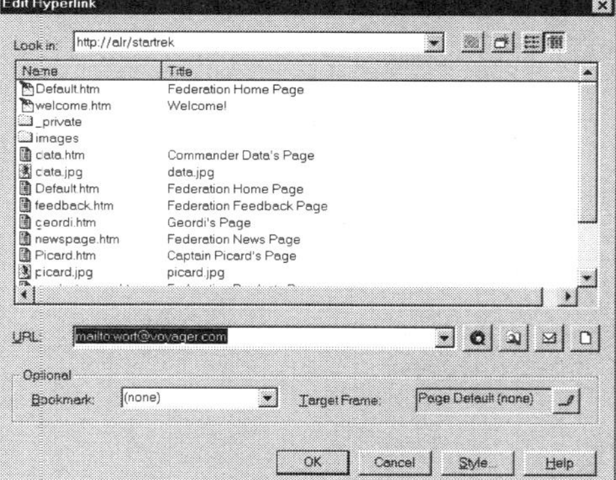

Figure 15. *The Edit Hyperlink dialog box is almost exactly like the Create Hyperlink dialog box, but it lets you make changes to an existing link.*

Suppose you create a hyperlink and the URL changes, or you decide to link to a different page, site, or e-mail address? Happily, editing hyperlinks is just as easy as creating them in the first place.

To edit a hyperlink:

1. Select the link you want to change. (If it's a text link, you can just place the insertion marker anywhere within it.)
2. Choose Hyperlink from the Edit menu (**Figure 14**), or press Ctrl+K, or click the Create or Edit Hyperlink button on the Standard toolbar. You'll see the Edit Hyperlink dialog box (**Figure 15**).
3. Make any needed changes to the hyperlink and click OK when you're done.

Dragging to Create Hyperlinks

One last way of creating hyperlinks is to drag pages or other files from the FrontPage Explorer to the Editor window. You need to have both windows displayed at once; in the Explorer, you can be in Folders, All Files, Navigation, or Hyperlinks view. Once you drag the mouse pointer over the Editor window, it will turn into an arrow with the shortcut icon attached (the shortcut icon is a little curved arrow). When you release the mouse button, the hyperlink will be inserted into the currently open page in the Editor.

Bookmarks, also known as *anchors*, are a set of text characters that you select in the Editor window. These characters become the target of a hyperlink. Using hyperlinks to bookmarks lets the user jump to any point within a Web page.

To create a bookmark:

1. Select the text that will become the bookmark. This is the text that you want the user to jump to when she clicks a hyperlink (**Figure 16**).
2. Choose Bookmark from the Edit menu (**Figure 17**). The Bookmark dialog box will open (**Figure 18**).
3. The text you selected appears in the Bookmark Name text box. You can also type a new book-mark name if you want. This name should be something distinctive because later you will have to select it from a list when you create the hyperlink to the bookmark.
4. Click OK. The text that you selected will become underlined with a blue-dashed line indicating that it is a bookmark (**Figure 19**).

Figure 16. *Select the text that the user will jump to when a hyperlink is clicked.*

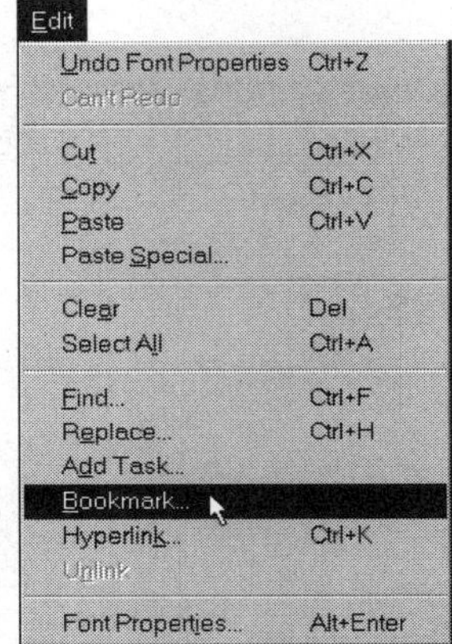

Figure 17. *Choose Bookmark from the Edit menu.*

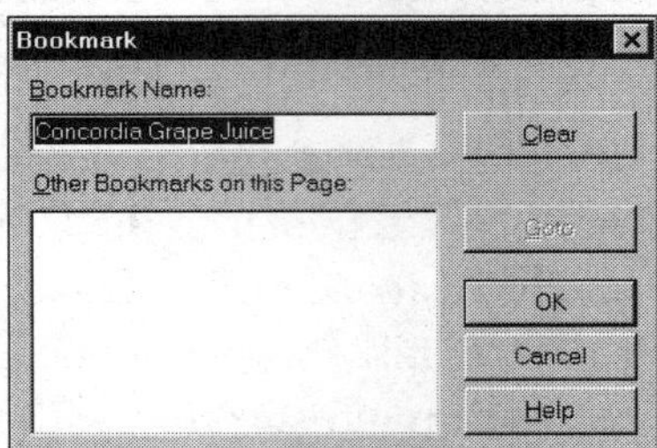

Figure 18. *The selected text is entered as the bookmark name, but you can enter a new name if you like.*

Figure 19. *A dashed line appears under the text that was selected as a bookmark.*

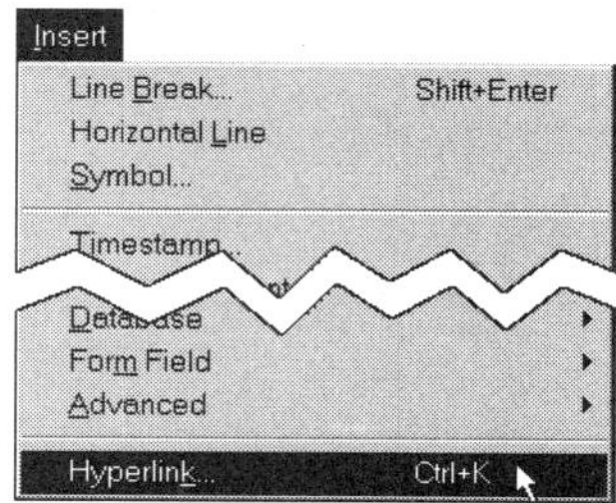

Figure 20. *Choose Hyperlink from the Insert menu.*

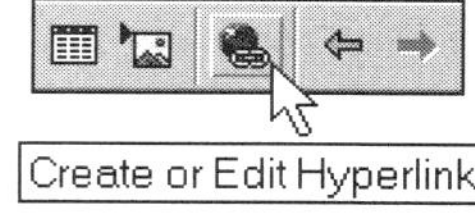

Figure 21. *Click the Create or Edit Hyperlink button on the Standard toolbar.*

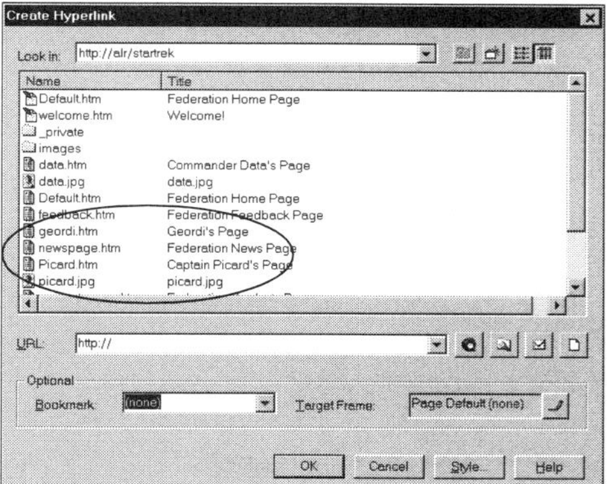

Figure 22. *Use the Bookmark drop-down list to select a bookmark to link to.*

To create a hyperlink using a bookmark:

1. Select the text or image that will become the link to the bookmark. If you are using an image, click on it to select it. Eight black handles will appear around the image.
2. Choose Hyperlink from the Insert menu (**Figure 20**) or click the Create or Edit Hyperlink button on the Standard toolbar (**Figure 21**) or press Ctrl+K on the keyboard. The Create Hyperlink dialog box will open (**Figure 22**).
3. In the Bookmark drop-down list, select the name of the bookmark (**Figure 23**).
4. Click OK. Then save your changes. The hyperlink will be set up. The next time you preview the page in the Preview tab or in a browser, you'll be able to use the hyperlink to jump to the bookmark.

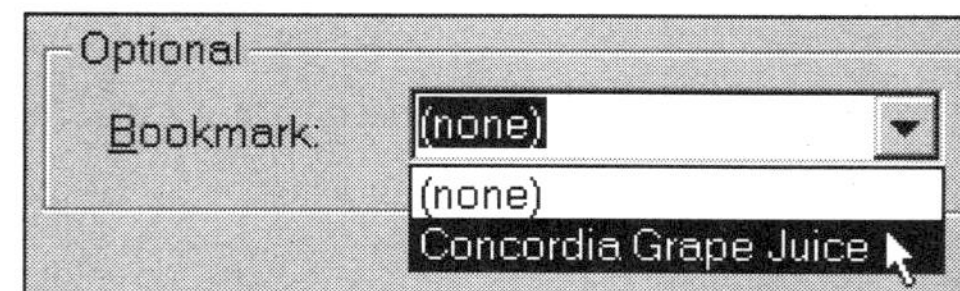

Figure 23. *Choose your bookmark from the Bookmark drop-down list.*

You can use bookmarks to easily move around a Web page. Or if you forget where a bookmark is, the Bookmark dialog box will take you right to it.

To go to a bookmark:

1. Choose Bookmark from the Edit menu (**Figure 17**). The Bookmark dialog box will open (**Figure 24**).
2. Select the bookmark you want to go to from the Other Bookmarks on this Page list box.
3. Click Goto. The Web page will move to the bookmark location and the bookmark will be selected (**Figure 25**). Click OK to close the Bookmark dialog box.

To delete a bookmark:

1. Choose Bookmark from the Edit menu (**Figure 17**). The Bookmark dialog box will appear (**Figure 24**).
2. Select the bookmark you want to delete.
3. Click the Goto button. This will move you to the bookmark and select it. Its name will appear under Bookmark Name.
4. Click the Clear button (**Figure 26**). The text will remain and the bookmark will be removed.

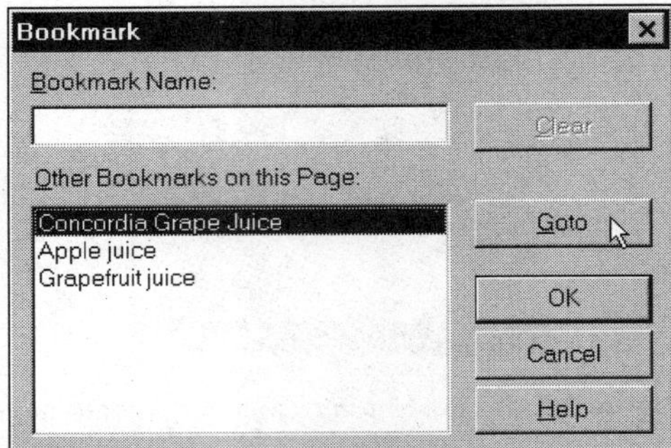

Figure 24. *Select the bookmark, then click the Goto button.*

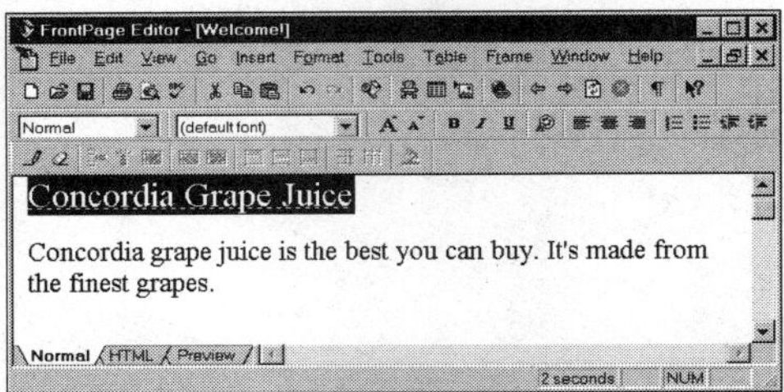

Figure 25. *FrontPage Editor will scroll to the bookmark and select it.*

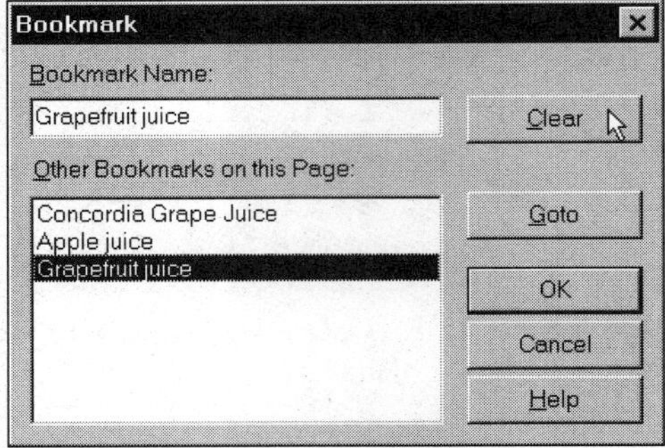

Figure 26. *Click the Clear button to delete the bookmark.*

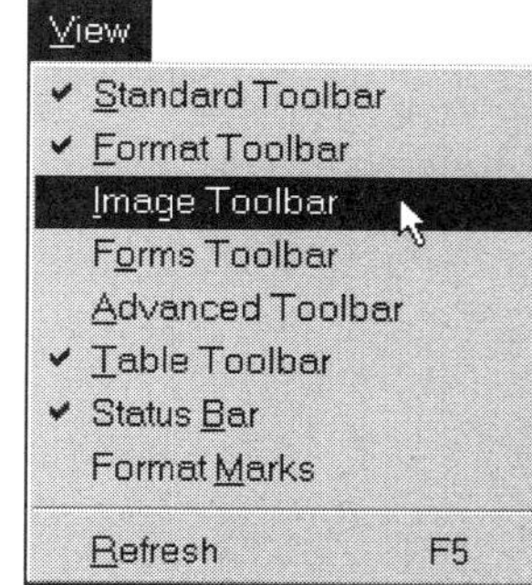

Figure 27. *Choose Image Toolbar from the View menu.*

In order to create hotspots on an image, you will need to use the Image toolbar. Usually, when you select an image with the mouse, the Image toolbar will appear on the Editor screen. If it doesn't appear, it's easy to open.

To view the Image toolbar:

Choose Image Toolbar from the View menu (**Figure 27**). The Image toolbar will appear (**Figure 28**). If an image is not selected, the Image toolbar will be grayed out and unusable.

Tip:

- To remove the Image toolbar from view, just choose Image Toolbar from the View menu.

FLOATING THE IMAGE TOOLBAR

The Image toolbar will probably be "docked" on the edge of the screen by default. To make it float, drag it onto the Editor screen. (You can't drag on any of the buttons; it's easiest to drag on the far left side of the toolbar.) Floating toolbars can be moved around the screen and placed where they won't be in the way. To move a floating toolbar, position the mouse pointer over the toolbar's title bar, press the left mouse button, and drag it to its new position. If you want to dock the toolbar, just drag it to the top of the Editor window or double-click its title bar.

You can make all or part of an image into a hotspot that links to other locations. For instance, suppose you were creating a Web page for Concordia Corp., a maker of fine fruit juices. You could use an image of different kinds of fruits as the link to other juice pages. You could add a hotspot on an apple that would link to an apple juice page, a hotspot on a pear that would link to a pear juice page, and a hotspot on some cherries for a link to a cherry juice page.

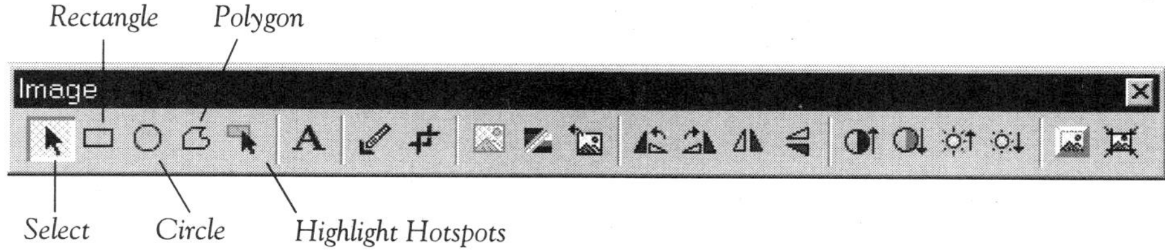

Figure 28. *You can use the Image toolbar to create and view hotspots.*

View the Image Toolbar

To create a hotspot:

1. Select the image to which you'll be adding the hotspot (**Figure 29**). The Image toolbar will appear, if it is not already visible, and it will become enabled with the Select button depressed.
2. Figure out what shape you want the hotspot to be. Will it be square, round, or irregularly shaped?
3. Click the Rectangle, Circle, or Polygon toolbar button, depending upon the shape of the area you want to define as the hotspot (**Figure 28**). The Rectangle button will create a rectangular hotspot, the Circle button a circular hotspot, and the Polygon button an irregularly shaped hotspot.
4. Draw the hotspot around the part of the image you want to become the link to another location.
   - If you are using the Rectangle toolbar button to create a hotspot, position the mouse pointer at the upper-left corner of the area you want to select as the hotspot. Press the left mouse button and drag diagonally towards the lower-right corner to create the hotspot (**Figure 30**).
   - If you are using the Circle toolbar button, place the mouse pointer in the middle of the area you want to select as a hotspot, and then drag outward to create the hotspot (**Figure 31**).

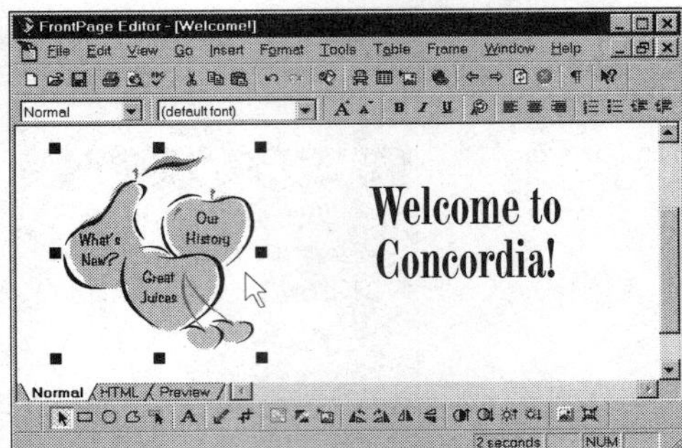

Figure 29. *Select the image you want to add the hotspot to.*

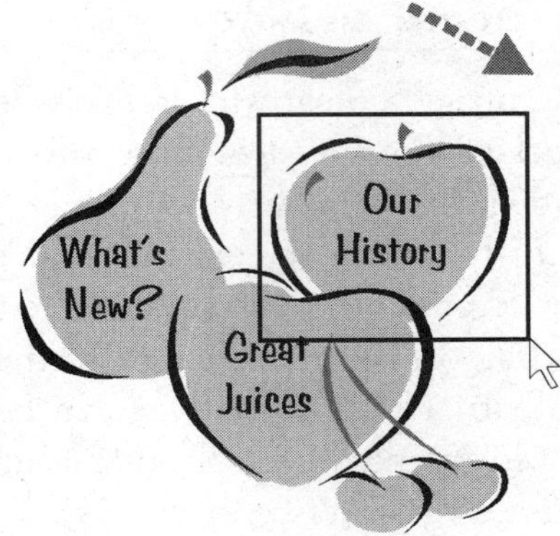

Figure 30. *After you select the Rectangle button, press the left mouse button and drag diagonally to create the hotspot.*

Figure 31. *After you select the Circle button, press the left mouse button and drag outward to create the hotspot.*

Figure 32. *After you click the Polygon button, position the mouse pointer where you want to start the polygonal hotspot and click. Continue moving the mouse and clicking until the desired shape of the hotspot is complete.*

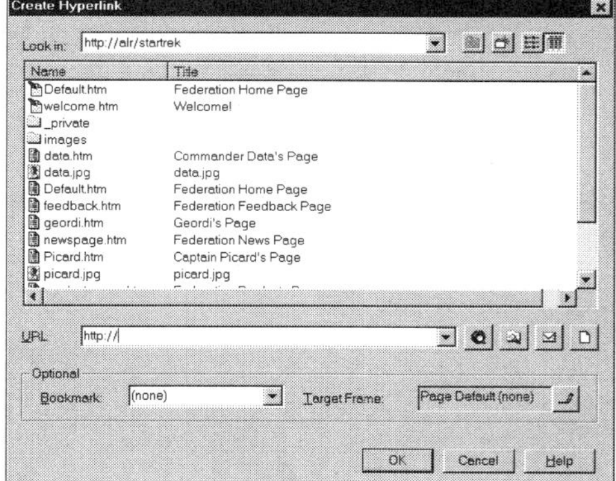

Figure 33. *Use the Create Hyperlink dialog box to add the link that the hotspot will jump the user to.*

- If you are using the Polygon toolbar button to create an irregularly shaped hotspot, position the mouse pointer where you want the hotspot to start and click the left mouse button. The first point of the polygon will appear. Move the mouse to the next place where you want to insert a point of the polygon and click the mouse. Continue moving the mouse and clicking until you have encompassed the entire irregularly shaped area. To complete the hotspot, click on the original place where you created the first point of the polygon (**Figure 32**). (If you have trouble clicking the right spot, you can double-click to complete the polygon.)

5. When you have completed drawing the hotspot on the image, the Create Hyperlink dialog box will appear (**Figure 33**). Use this dialog box to set the target for your hyperlink. You can link to Web pages on your system, Web pages on the World Wide Web, or a new page that hasn't been created yet. Click OK when you're done.

Tip:

- If your hotspot is not in the exact location you intended, don't worry! You can move and resize it.

To move or resize a hotspot:

1. Select the image containing the hotspot you want to move or resize. The different hotspots will become apparent (**Figure 34**) and the Image toolbar will appear enabled.
2. Select the hotspot you want to move or resize.
3. To move a hotspot:
   - **a.** Position the mouse pointer within the hotspot.
   - **b.** Press the left mouse button and drag the hotspot to its new location (**Figure 35**). (You can also use the arrow keys on the keyboard to nudge the hotspot around.)

   To resize a hotspot:
   - **a.** Position the mouse pointer over the hotspot point you want to move to change the size.
   - **b.** Press the left mouse button and drag the point to its new position (**Figure 36**).

Tip:

- What if you move or resize a hotspot and decide you don't like the change you have made? *Before you release the left mouse button you've been dragging* press the Esc key on the keyboard. This will return the hotspot to its original position and/or shape. You can undo changes to a hotspot with the regular Undo command.

Figure 34. *Select the image containing the hotspot you want to move or resize.*

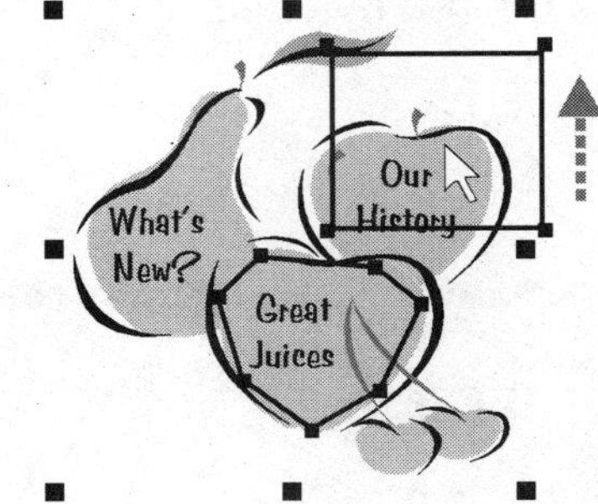

Figure 35. *Press the left mouse button and drag the hotspot to its new position.*

Figure 36. *Position the mouse over one of the hotspot points and drag it to its new location.*

Move or Resize a Hotspot

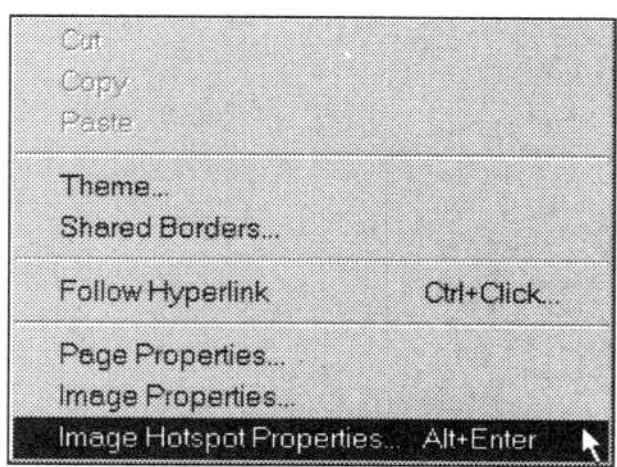

Figure 37. *Choose Image Hotspot Properties from the pop-up menu.*

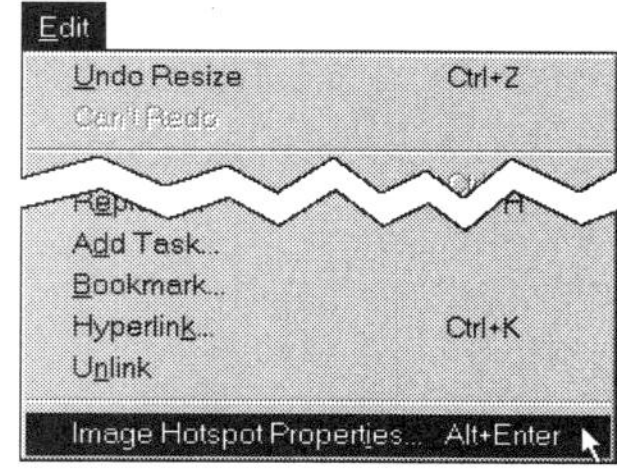

Figure 38. *Choose Image Hotspot Properties from the Edit menu.*

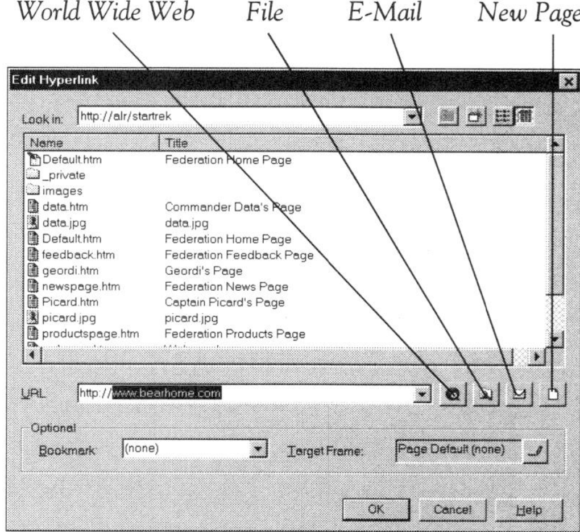

Figure 39. *Use the Edit Hyperlink dialog box to change your hotspot link.*

To edit a hotspot link:

1. Select the image containing the hotspot.
2. Open the Edit Hyperlink dialog box, and then:

   Right-click the hotspot and choose Image Hotspot Properties from the pop-up menu (**Figure 37**).

   or

   Choose Image Hotspot Properties from the bottom of the Edit menu (**Figure 38**).

   or

   Press Alt+Enter on the keyboard.

   The Edit Hyperlink dialog box will appear (**Figure 39**).
3. In the Edit Hyperlink dialog box change the target for your hyperlink:
   - Click the World Wide Web button to create links to sites or pages on the World Wide Web.
   - Click the File button to create links to Web pages on your system.
   - Click the E-mail button to create a link to an e-mail address.
   - Click the New Page button to create links to a new page that hasn't been created yet.
4. When you are finished editing the hyperlink, click OK to close the Edit Hyperlink dialog box.

Sometimes it can be hard to see all the hotspots you've added to an image, especially if the image is complex.

Figure 40. *Select the image containing the hotspots you want to see.*

To show all hotspots on an image:

1. Select the image (**Figure 40**). The Image toolbar will appear.
2. Click the Highlight Hotspots button on the Image toolbar (**Figure 41**). The image will become invisible and the hotspot borders will appear in aqua (**Figure 42**).

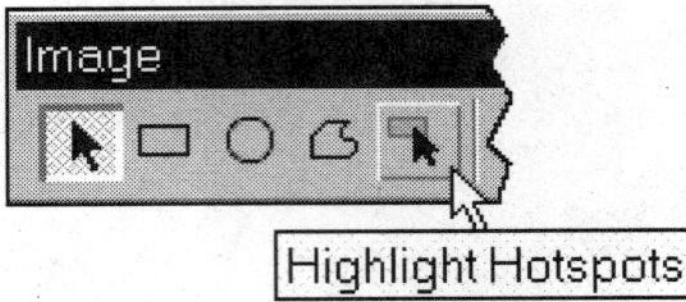

Figure 41. *Click the Highlight Hotspots button on the Image toolbar.*

Tip:

- To make the image visible, click the Highlight Hotspots button again.

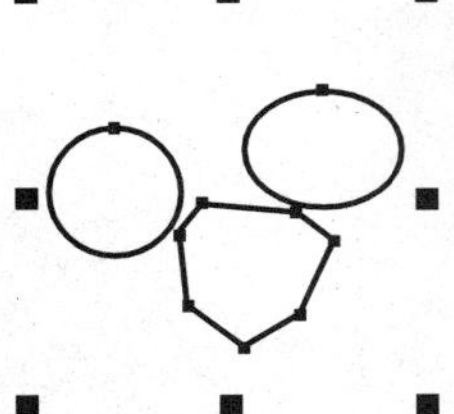

Figure 42. *When the image becomes invisible, the hotspots are easy to see.*

To delete a hotspot:

1. Select the image containing the hotspot you want to delete.
2. Select the hotspot, then press the Delete or Backspace key on the keyboard.

The Target Frame Text Box

You've probably noticed the Target Frame text box in the Edit Hyperlink and Create Hyperlink dialog boxes. This text box is used to create hyperlinks to Web pages that contain *frames*. Frames will be discussed in detail in Chapter 15.

Show Hotspots; Delete a Hotspot

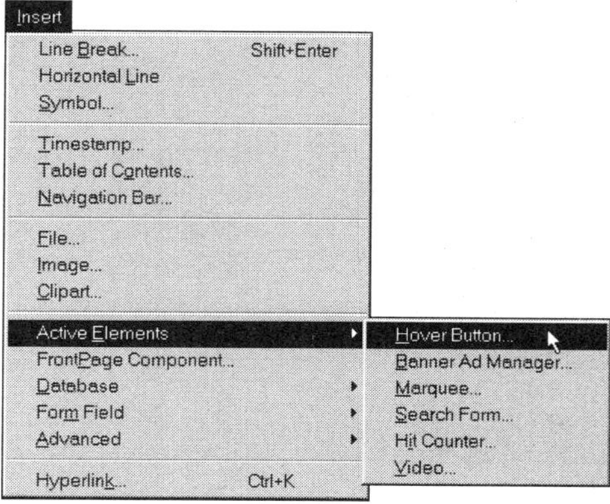

Figure 43. *Choose Active Elements from the Insert menu and choose Hover Button from the fly-out.*

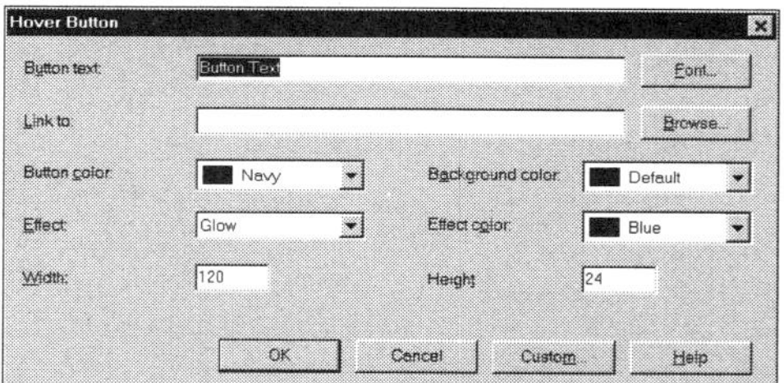

Figure 44. *The Hover Button dialog box is where you set up all the attributes of your hover button.*

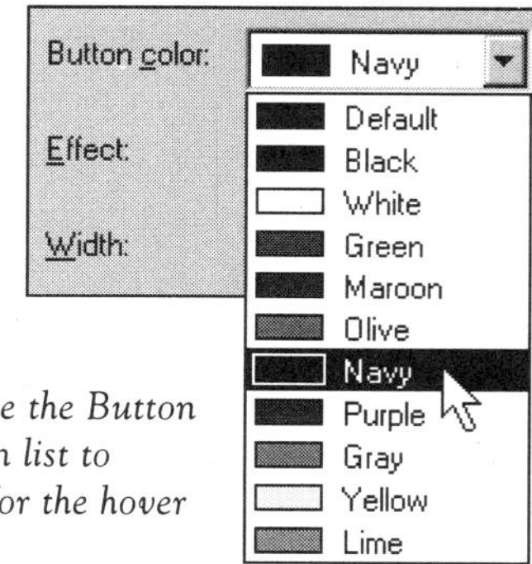

Figure 45. *Use the Button color drop-down list to choose a color for the hover button.*

FrontPage 98 includes several great new navigation features, including hover buttons. These buttons change shape and/or color when the mouse pointer passes (hovers) over them. You can associate links with hover buttons, so clicking the button jumps the user to a different spot on the same page, a different Web page, or a new Web site.

To insert a hover button:

1. Place the insertion marker where you want the hover button to go.
2. Choose Active Elements from the Insert menu and choose Hover Button from the fly-out (**Figure 43**). You'll see the Hover Button dialog box (**Figure 44**).
3. In the Button text box, enter the text for the hover button. If you want to customize the text for your hover button, click the Font button. This brings up a Font dialog box, from which you can choose a new font, font style and size, and text color.
4. In the Link to text box, type the URL for the location you want the user to travel to when she clicks the hover button. You can also click the Browse button and use the Select Hover Button Hyperlink dialog box that appears to go to the page you want to create a link to.
5. Use the Button color drop-down list to choose a color for the hover button (**Figure 45**).

6. Choose a background color from the Background color drop-down list. You should pick a color that is similar to the background color of your Web page. (This option is relevant primarily if you're using a custom image for your hover button.)
7. From the Effect drop-down list, choose an effect that will occur when the mouse pointer "hovers" over the button (**Figure 46**). For example, if you choose the option Bevel out, the hover button looks raised (beveled) when the mouse pointer rests over it.
8. Use the Button color drop-down list to choose a color that will determine the button's appearance when the mouse pointer hovers over it. (This color does not affect the Light glow, Bevel out, or Bevel in effects.)
9. In the Width and Height text boxes, enter the width and height of the button, in pixels (**Figure 47**). If you're using an image, make sure the sizes you enter here match the size of your image.
10. If you want to customize your hover button by using an image or associating a sound with it, click the Custom button. You'll see the Custom dialog box (**Figure 48**).
11. Under Play Sound, in the On click text box, enter the sound to play when the user clicks the hover button (**Figure 49**). In the On hover text box, enter the sound to play when the user rests the mouse

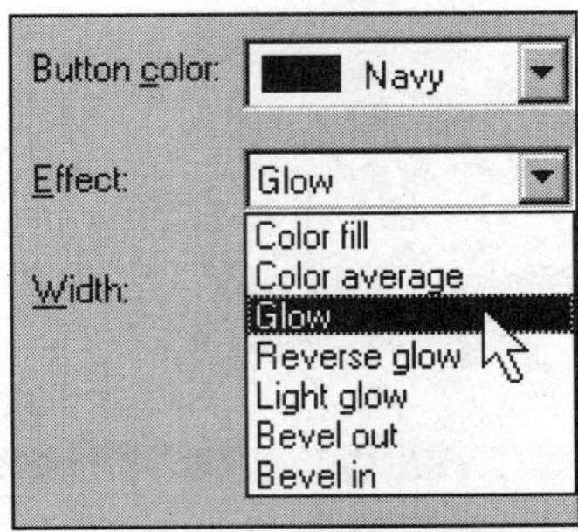

Figure 46. *Choose an effect from the Effect drop-down list that will occur when the mouse pointer "hovers" over the button.*

Figure 47. *In the Width and Height text boxes, enter the width and height of the button.*

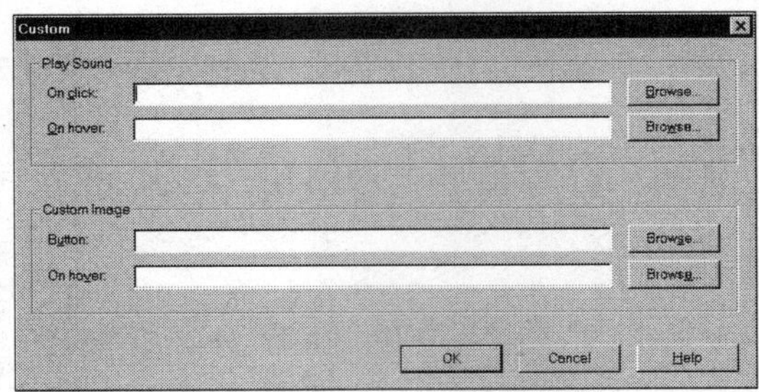

Figure 48. *The Custom dialog box lets you choose sounds and images to use with your hover button.*

Insert a Hover Button

pointer over the hover button. You can click the appropriate Browse button to find the sound file you need.

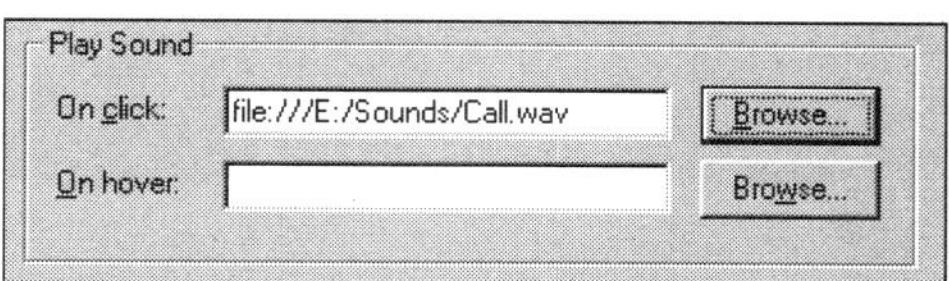

Figure 49. *Under Play Sound, in the On click text box, enter the sound to play when the user clicks the hover button.*

12. Under Custom Image, in the Button text box, enter the image to use as the hover button. In the On hover text box, enter the image to use when the mouse pointer hovers over the button. Again, you can click the Browse button to find the image file you want to use.
13. Click OK to return to the Hover Button dialog box, check that all your settings look right, and then click OK again.
14. Save the revised Web page; you'll be prompted to save the images with the Web site (you'll see the Save Embedded Files dialog box), and then preview it by clicking the Preview tab or choosing Preview in Browser from the File menu.

To edit a hover button:

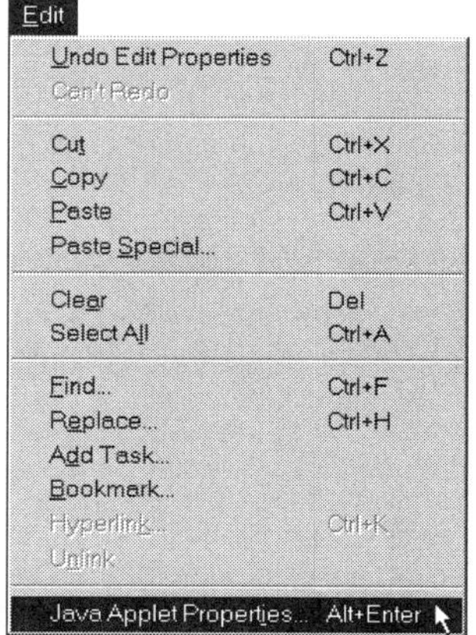

Figure 50. *Choose Java Applet Properties from the Edit menu.*

1. Select the hover button and choose Java Applet Properties from the Edit menu (**Figure 50**) or press Alt+Enter.

   or

   Right-click the hover button and choose Java Applet Properties from the pop-up menu (**Figure 51**).
2. You'll see the Hover Button dialog box. Now you can change any properties of your hover button.

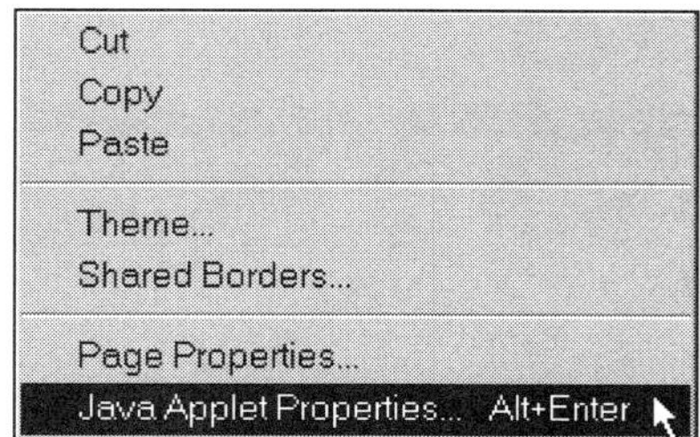

Figure 51. *Choose Java Applet Properties from the pop-up menu.*

Another new way to make your site easier to maneuver in is to use navigation bars. Navigation bars are areas of the page—typically in the top and left shared borders—that include a set of links to other pages in your Web. When you set up your Web structure in Navigation view, FrontPage turns on shared borders and creates navigation bars for you based on the site structure. (Navigation bars are also generated automatically if you base your Web on one of the templates or wizards, except for the discussion wizard.) Best of all, FrontPage updates navigation bars automatically when you change the structure of your Web site. Even if you didn't build your Web structure in Navigation view, you can still create navigation bars. Plus, you may want to make changes to existing navigation bars. All of these things are simple enough to do.

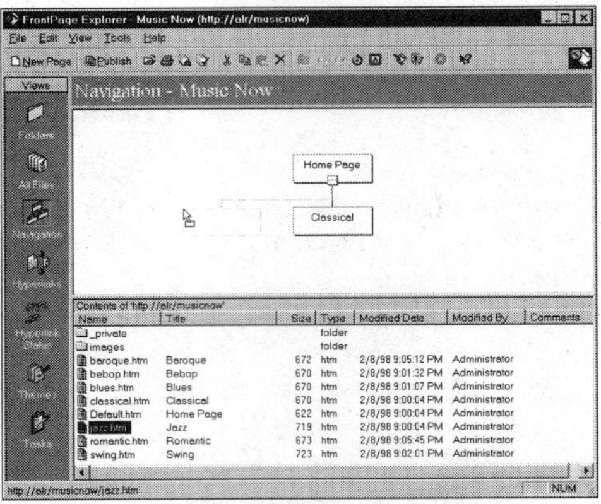

Figure 52. *You can drag a file from the Files pane up to the Navigation pane to add it to the structure of your Web site.*

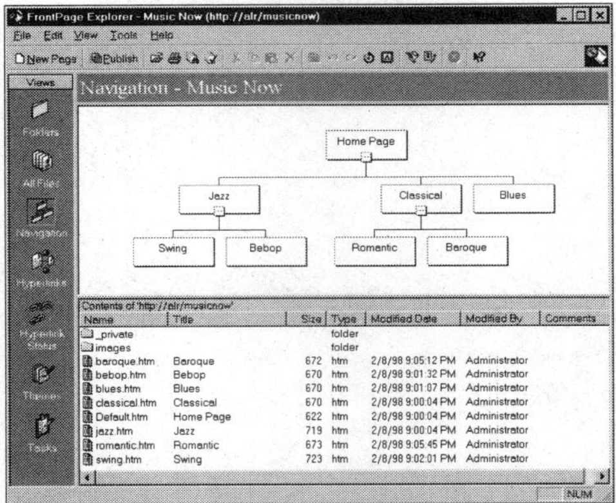

Figure 53. *Once you add more files to your site hierarchy, it might look something like this.*

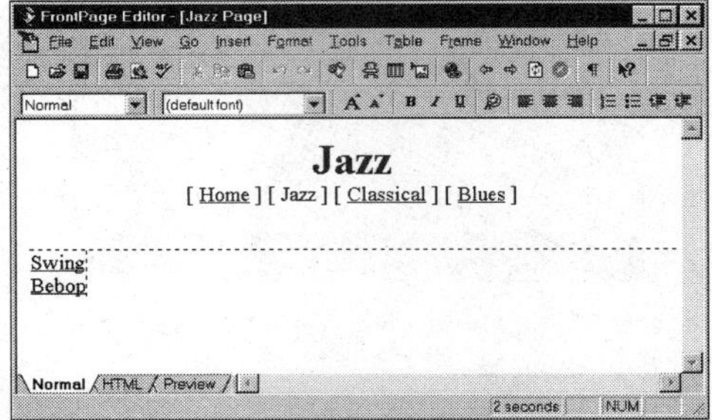

Figure 54. *By default, FrontPage adds navigation bars to the top and left shared borders if you set up your site structure in Navigation view.*

To set up your Web structure in Navigation view:

1. Open the Explorer, open the Web site whose structure you want to set up or modify, and click the Navigation button in the Views bar to switch to Navigation view.
2. Drag a file from the Files pane up to the Navigation pane to add it to the diagram illustrating the structure of your site. As you drag, you'll see the outline of a box indicating the file, plus a line indicating which page it will be located under

Tips:

- If you see the text [Button] instead of a link to a specific page, don't think you did something wrong. These are just placeholders; they appear when there are no relevant links on this particular page. (They show up in Normal and Preview view, but don't appear when you use the Preview in Browser command. Don't try to delete them, or you'll delete all your navigation bars!) For example, if you're on a page at the bottom of the hierarchy, there will be no links in the left border, since the page has no child page. The [Button] placeholders will also appear if you haven't set up your Web site structure in Navigation view.
- It's not recommended to use navigation bars together with frames. These are essentially two mutually exclusive ways of providing a navigation system for your Web site. You'll learn all about frames in the next chapter.
- If your Web has no theme applied to it, navigation bars will appear as text links. If there's a theme applied, the links in the navigation bars may instead look like graphical buttons.

in the site structure. For example, here the file jazz.htm will fall directly underneath the home page in the hierarchy (**Figure 52**).

3. When the file is in the right place in the hierarchy, release the mouse button. Repeat this process to add other files to the site hierarchy, making pages into child pages of either the home page or the pages beneath it (**Figure 53**).
4. Switch to the Editor. Notice the navigation bars in the left and top shared border (**Figure 54**). By default, the top navigation bar contains links to the home page, to the parent page of the current page if it's different from the home page (this link will be marked [Up]), and to other pages in the same level of the site hierarchy as the current page. (The top border also contains the page banner—it's just the page title.) The navigation bar in the left border contains links to child pages of the current page. You can also change these defaults, as you'll learn in a moment.
5. You can try out the links by Ctrl+clicking them, by switching to the Preview tab, or by choosing the Preview in Browser command from the File menu. Using the Preview in Browser command will give you the most accurate preview of what the navigation bars will actually look like.

When you create your site structure in Navigation view, FrontPage turns on shared borders automatically. But you can also turn on shared borders for a site that doesn't already have them, or change which shared borders are turned on.

To turn on or off shared borders for an entire Web site:

1. Open the Web in the FrontPage Explorer.
2. Choose Shared Borders from the Tools menu (**Figure 55**). You'll see the Shared Borders dialog box (**Figure 56**).
3. Click Top, Left, Right, or Bottom to turn on the borders you want. If any of these options are already checked, you can click them again to turn them off. When you turn on an option, a dark line appears in the dialog box to indicate which borders are turned on (**Figure 57**).
4. Click OK.

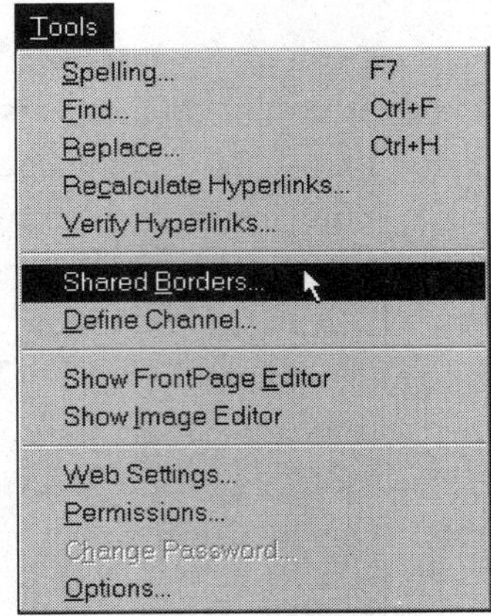

Figure 55. *Choose Shared Borders from the Tools menu.*

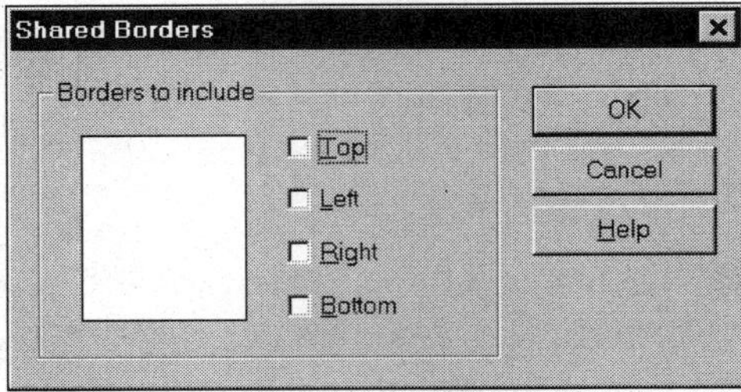

Figure 56. *You can choose which borders to turn on in the Shared Borders dialog box.*

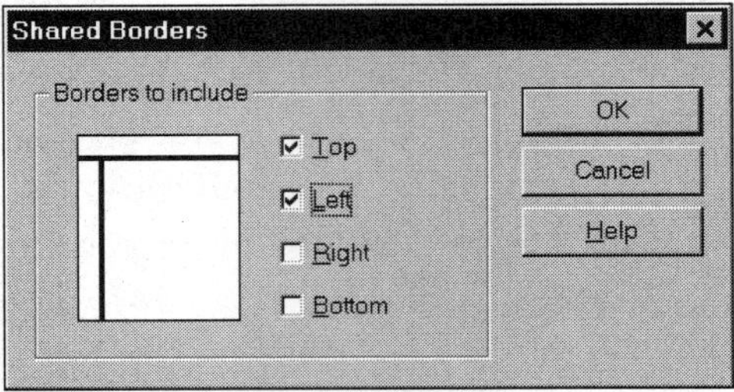

Figure 57. *Here the top and left borders have been selected.*

Tip:

- Don't confuse turning on shared borders with creating navigation bars. Turning on and off shared borders just shows existing navigation bars that reflect the site structure in Navigation view.

Turn On or Off Shared Borders

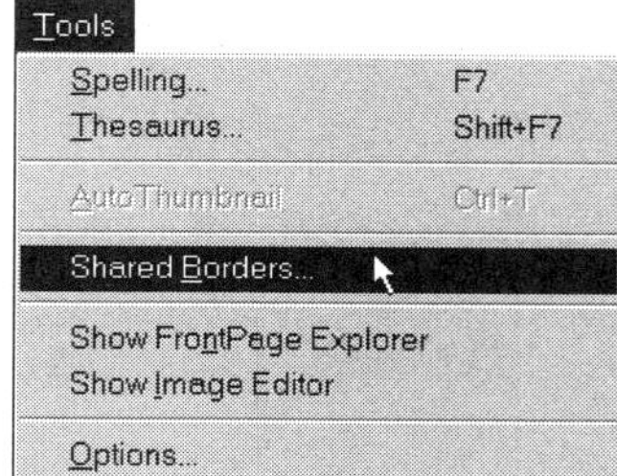

Figure 58. *Choose Shared Borders from the Tools menu.*

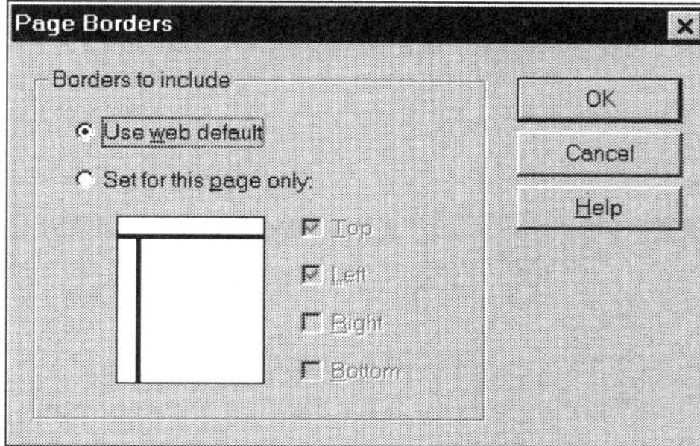

Figure 59. *You can use the Page Borders dialog box to set the shared borders for an individual Web page.*

To turn on or off shared borders for a single Web page:

1. In the Editor, open the page you want to affect.
2. Choose Shared Borders from the Tools menu (**Figure 58**). You'll see the Page Borders dialog box (**Figure 59**).
3. To use the borders already in use for the entire Web site, click the radio button Use web default. To use borders set up specifically for this page, click the radio button Set for this page only. Then check or uncheck the Top, Left, Right, and Bottom check boxes, as needed.
4. Click OK when you're done.

WHAT ARE SHARED BORDERS?

You need to know a bit about shared borders to understand how navigation bars work. Shared borders are just what their name implies: borders that are shared by several Web pages. Usually, you'll turn on shared borders for every page in a FrontPage Web, although you can also turn borders on and off for individual pages. When you alter a shared border, those changes are automatically applied to all pages in the site for which shared borders are turned on. This is a great way to maintain consistency in your Web site, as well as to create repeating elements, such as page footers, without having to enter them over and over. The reason you need to know all this is that navigation bars live within shared borders. This arrangement lets you create navigation bars for your entire site in one operation, instead of having to create a navigation bar for each page individually.

The Page Borders dialog box lets you display or hide borders on a particular page, but it doesn't actually let you set up different borders for individual pages. The borders on all pages are still shared, which means that changes to them affect all other pages with those shared borders. If you want individualized navigation bars on different pages, you can create navigation bars on single pages, outside of the Web's shared borders.

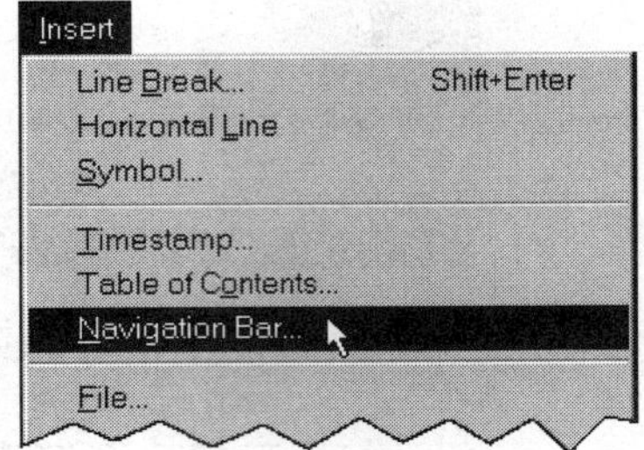

Figure 60. *Choose Navigation Bar from the Insert menu.*

To create navigation bars on a single Web page:

1. In the Editor, open the Web page you want to add a navigation bar to and put the insertion marker where the navigation bar will go.
2. Choose Navigation Bar from the Insert menu (**Figure 60**). You'll see the Navigation Bar Properties dialog box (**Figure 61**).
3. Under Hyperlinks to include, choose which pages the current page will include hyperlinks to (**Figure 62**). Choose Parent level to show pages one level up in the site hierarchy; choose Same level to show all pages at the same level in the site hierarchy (in computer lingo these are sometimes referred to as *peer pages*); choose Back and Next to show links to the peer pages before and after the current page; choose Child level to show pages one level down in the hierarchy; and choose Top level to show all pages other than the home page that are at the same level as the home page.

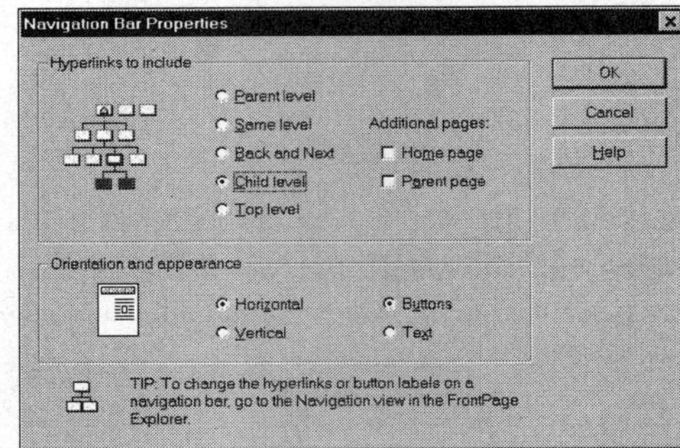

Figure 61. *The Navigation Bar Properties dialog box lets you set the characteristics of the navigation bar you're inserting.*

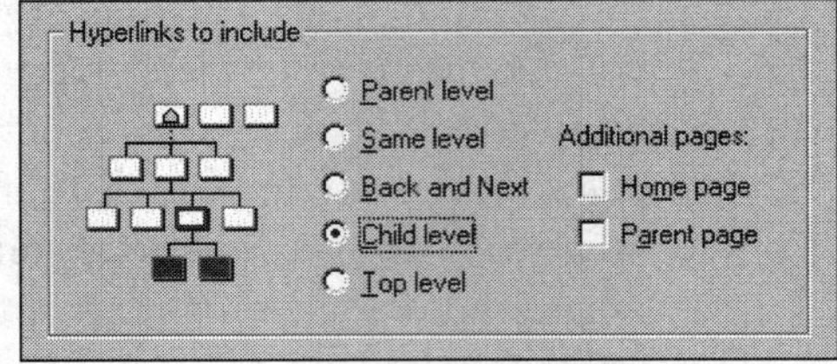

Figure 62. *Under Hyperlinks to include, choose which pages the current page will include hyperlinks to.*

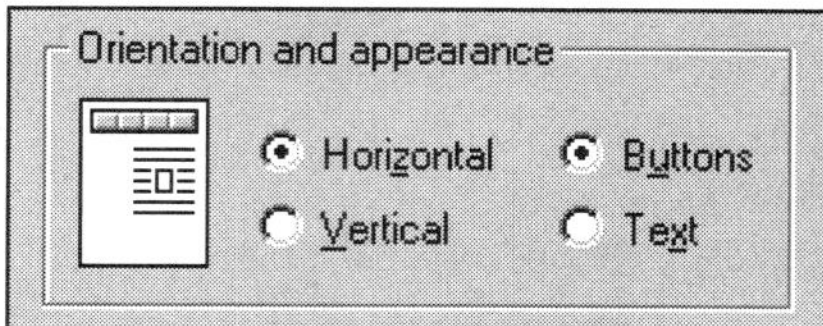

Figure 63. *Under Orientation and appearance, choose whether the links will appear in a horizontal or vertical list, and choose whether they'll show up as text or as buttons.*

Figure 64. *The robot icon indicates that you're pointing to a FrontPage component.*

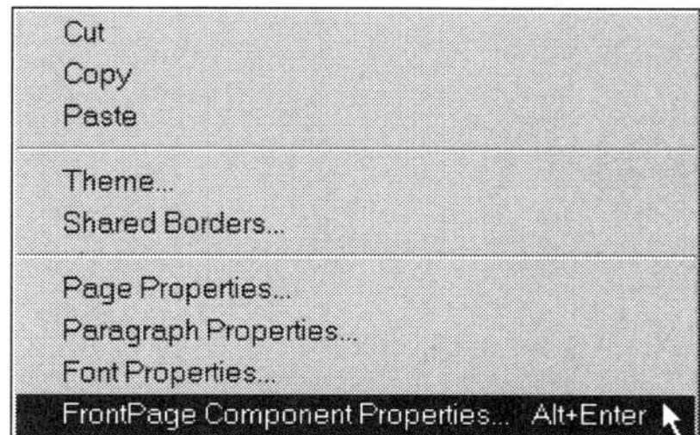

Figure 65. *Choose FrontPage Component Properties from the pop-up menu.*

4. Under Additional pages, choose whether to include hyperlinks to the home page and/or the parent page of the current page.
5. Under Orientation and appearance, choose whether the links will appear in a horizontal or vertical list, and choose whether they'll show up as text or as buttons (**Figure 63**). (When there's no theme applied to the page, the links will always appear as text.)
6. Click OK when you're done.

To edit navigation bars:

1. Click the navigation bar to select it. Now when you hold the mouse pointer over it you'll see a little robot pointer (**Figure 64**), which tells you that this is a FrontPage component; navigation bars are a type of FrontPage component. (See Chapter 17 for the lowdown on FrontPage components.)
2. Right-click the navigation bar and choose FrontPage Component Properties from the pop-up menu (**Figure 65**) or press Alt+Enter. You'll see the Navigation Bar Properties dialog box (**Figure 61**). This is exactly the same dialog box you used to set up an individual navigation bar just a moment ago.
3. Under Hyperlinks to include, choose which pages the current page will include hyperlinks to.

4. Under Additional pages, choose whether to include hyperlinks to the home page and/or the parent page (**Figure 66**).
5. Under Orientation and appearance, choose whether the links will appear in a horizontal or vertical list, and whether they'll appear as text or as buttons.
6. Click OK.

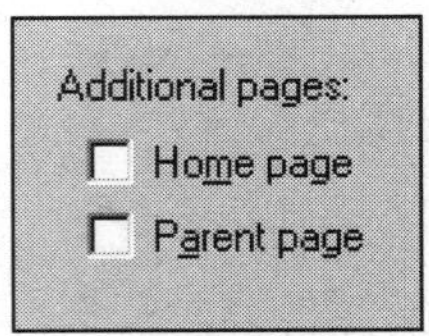

Figure 66. *Under Additional pages, choose whether to include hyperlinks to the home page and/or the parent page.*

To delete navigation bars:

1. Open the page whose navigation bar you want to delete.
2. Click the navigation bar to select it.
3. Press the Delete key or choose Clear from the Edit menu to remove the navigation bar (**Figure 67**).

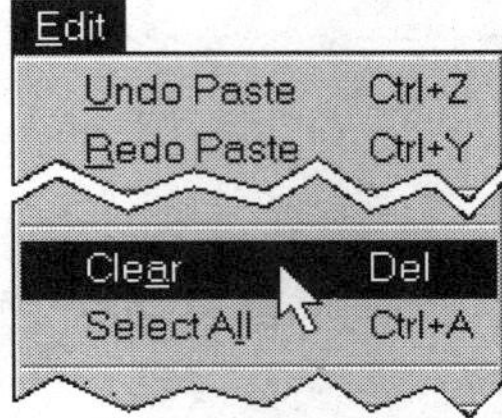

Figure 67. *Choose Clear from the Edit menu to remove the navigation bar.*

SUMMARY

In this chapter you learned how to:

- Create hyperlinks
- Test hyperlinks
- Make an e-mail hyperlink
- Edit hyperlinks
- Create bookmarks and link them to target locations
- Go to bookmarks
- Delete bookmarks
- View the Image toolbar
- Create hotspots
- Move and resize hotspots
- Delete a hotspot
- Add and edit hover buttons
- Set up your Web structure
- Turn shared borders and navigation bars on and off
- Create navigation bars on a single page
- Edit and delete navigation bars

Using Frames

Frames split the browser window into separate rectangular regions. Each region can display a Web page. You can have as many frames on a page as you want. A *frames page* is a special kind of Web page that doesn't contain any content but just divides the window into separate frames. (Frames pages used to be called framesets.)

When someone is browsing a page made up of frames, the content of one frame can change while the others remain the same or hyperlinks in one frame can make the page shown in another page change. A typical use for frames is to have a Web page divided into three frames. A frame across the top of the Web page displays a company name or topic. A left frame displays a table of contents page that contains hyperlinks to every page on the site. When the user clicks one of these hyperlinks, the right frame displays the Web page. The Web page shown in the right frame depends on what the user clicks in the left frame (**Figure 1**). **Figure 2** shows a Web page using this table of contents plan.

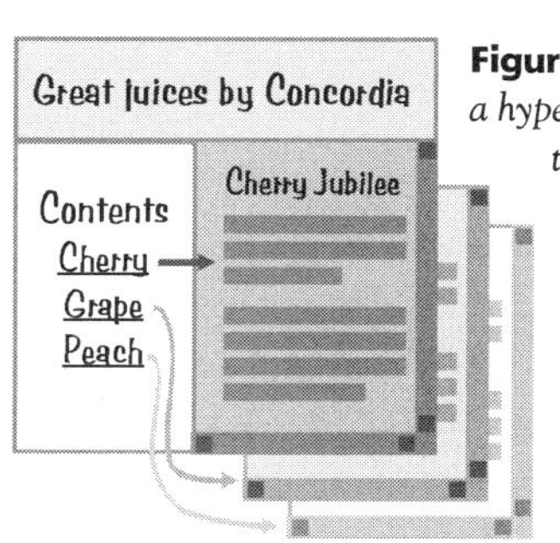

Figure 1. *When a user clicks a hyperlink in the left frame, the right page displays the Web page that it links to.*

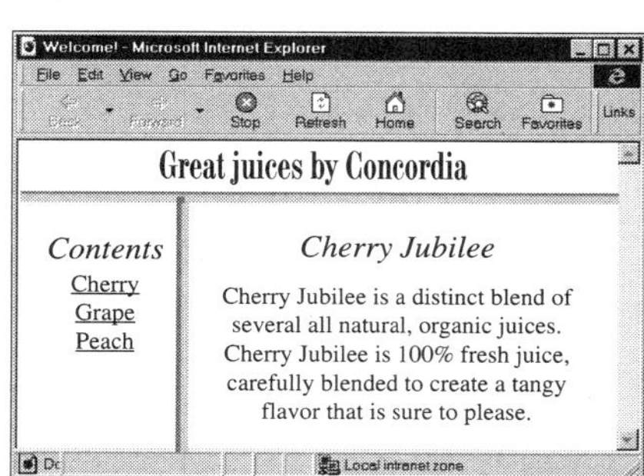

Figure 2. *A Web page displaying a table of contents frame on the left with hyperlinks to pages that display in the right frame.*

How Frames Work

The Web page displayed in Figure 2 actually shows four Web pages. Each of the three frames shows a Web page—the upper frame shows a page that says "Great juices by Concordia," the left frame shows a page that contains the table of contents with hyperlinks, and the right frame shows a page that tells about Cherry Jubilee juice. The fourth Web page contains the frames that display the three Web pages.

This chapter will take you through creating a Web page with frames set up in this arrangement.

To get started, launch FrontPage Explorer and create a one-page Web site. (Choose New from the File menu and choose FrontPage Web from the fly-out. Click the One Page Web radio button, provide a Web title, and click OK.)

Use the Editor to create the Web pages that will become the frame contents. For this example, the Web page that says "Great juices by Concordia" will be named concordia.htm (**Figure 3**),

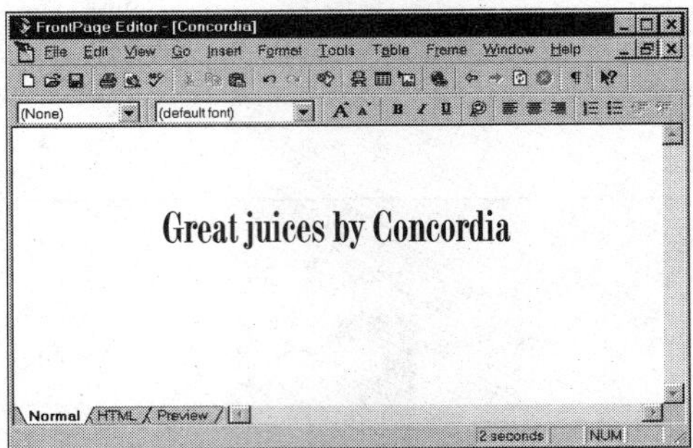

Figure 3. *The concordia.htm Web page will eventually become the banner across the frames page.*

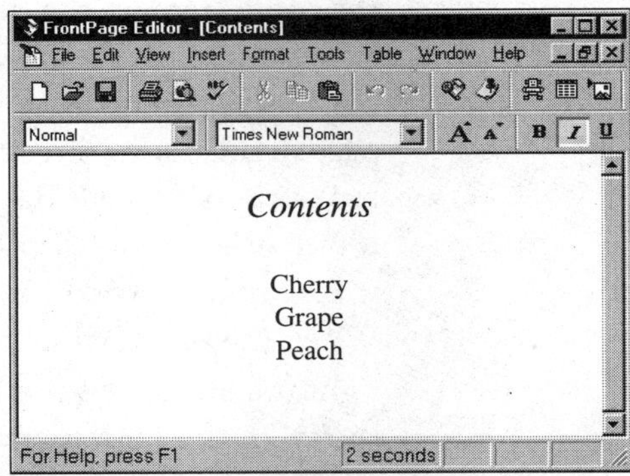

Figure 4. *The contents.htm Web page will eventually fill the left table of contents frame on the frames page.*

LEARNING MORE ABOUT FRAMES ON THE WEB

If you want to learn more about what frames can do for your Web site, visit:

http://www.microsoft.com/workshop/design/

http://www.netscape.com/comprod/products/navigator/version_3.0/layout/

DON'T USE FRAMES WITH NAVIGATION BARS/SHARED BORDERS

It's not a wise idea to use shared borders and/or navigation bars in pages that contain frames. These are two different ways of providing navigation systems for your sites and they don't work well together.

In fact, before you continue with the example in this chapter, you should turn off shared borders for your Web site. To do this, get into the Explorer, choose Shared Borders from the Tools menu, deselect all the check boxes, and then click OK. Turn back to Chapter 14 if you want more information about working with shared borders and navigation bars.

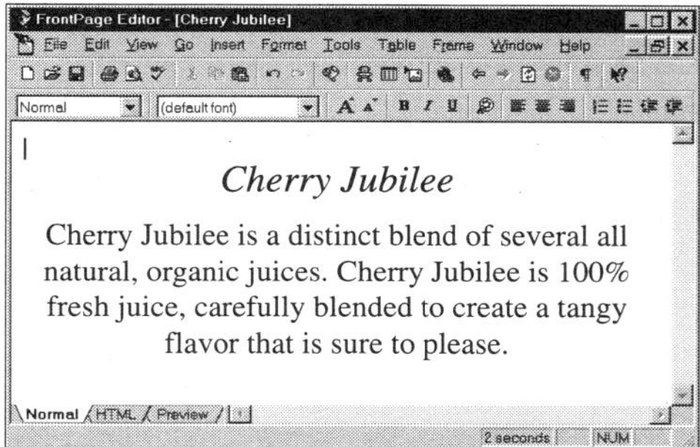

Figure 5. *The cherry.htm Web page will become the default Web page filling the right frame in the frames page. In addition, a hyperlink in the table of contents frame will link to this page.*

and the page containing the table of contents and hyperlinks will be named contents.htm (**Figure 4**). The Web pages that appear in the right frame when a hyperlink is clicked in the left table of contents frame will be named cherry.htm (**Figure 5**), grape.htm, and peach.htm.

Although more and more Web browsers can handle frames, some users will still have browsers that cannot. Just to be on the safe side, FrontPage automatically supplies a simple Web page that is displayed if the user's browser does not support frames. You can easily customize this alternate contents page, as you'll learn on pages 253–254.

DON'T OVERUSE FRAMES

As a Web design element, frames tend to be overused. If more than three or four frames are used on a Web page, the page can have a crowded feeling. In addition, frames can be a cause of browser crashes. Frames are a powerful design tool, but they should be used sparingly in Web sites.

Once you've created the Web pages that will become the contents for the frames, it's time to create the frames page that will contain the frames.

To create a frames page:

1. Launch the FrontPage Explorer and open the Web site containing the Web pages that will become the frame contents.
2. Start the Editor by double-clicking on a Web page in the Explorer or clicking the Show FrontPage Editor button on the toolbar.
3. In the Editor, choose New Frames Page from the Frame menu (**Figure 6**). You'll see the New dialog box with just the Frames tab displayed (**Figure 7**).

   or

   Choose New from the File menu and click the Frames tab in the New dialog box.

   In the Frames tab page of the New dialog box, you can choose from among several frames page templates. Notice that the Banner and Contents frames page is selected (click it to select it if necessary), and look over the description and preview on the right-hand side of the dialog box.

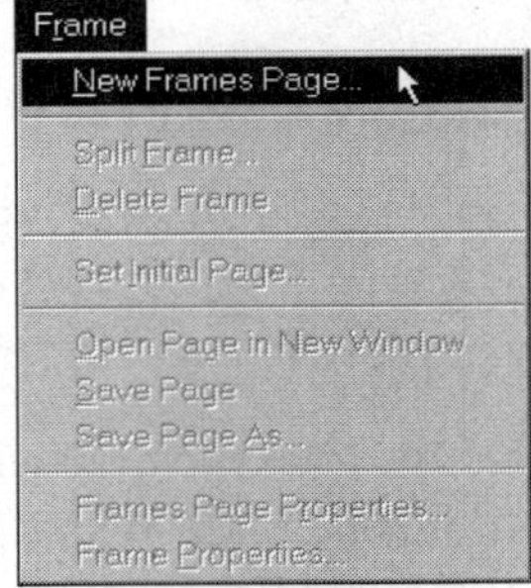

Figure 6. *Choose New Frames Page from the Frame menu.*

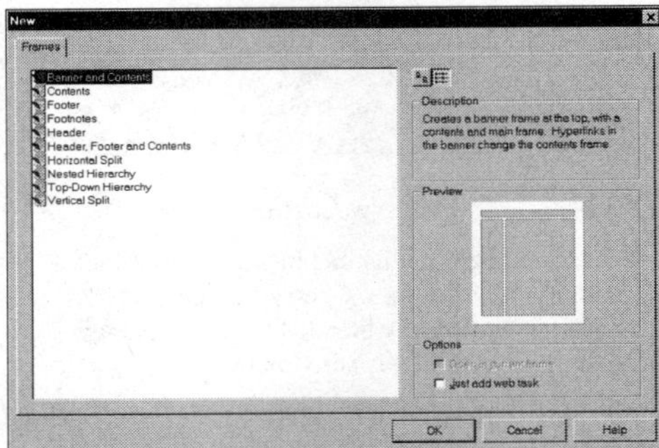

Figure 7. *In the New dialog box, you can choose from among several frames page templates.*

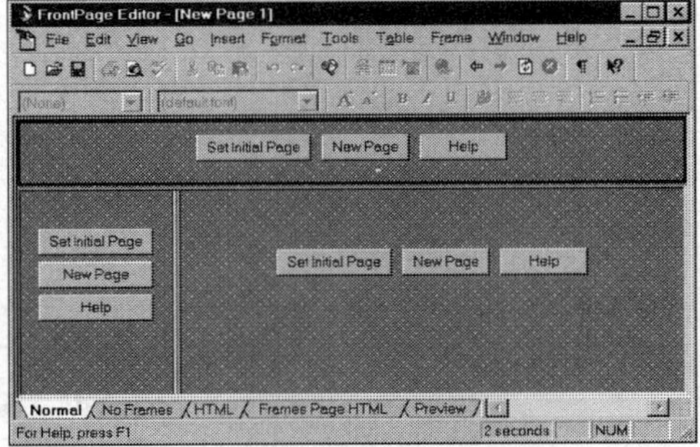

Figure 8. *Choosing a frames page template from the New dialog box places you in the WYSIWYG ("what you see is what you get") frame environment, where you can choose which Web page to associate with which frame, resize frames, add frames, and more.*

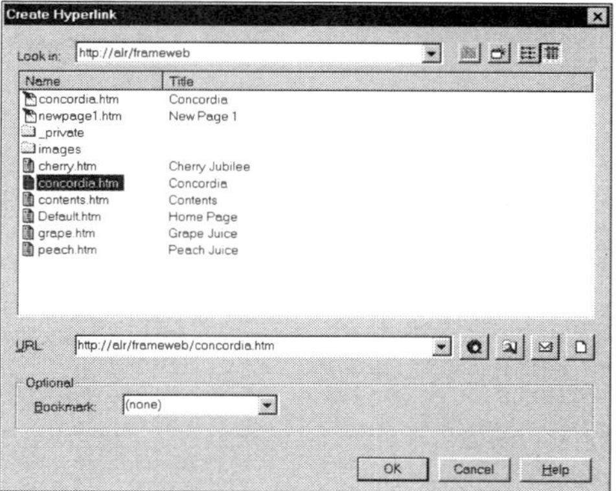

Figure 9. *In the Create Hyperlink dialog box, choose the page you want to display initially in the current frame.*

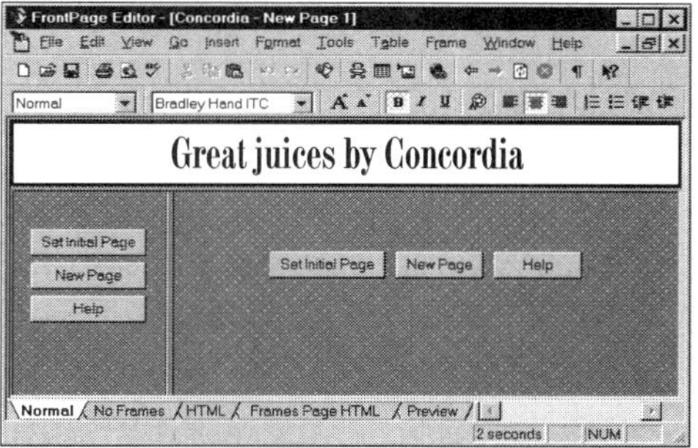

Figure 10. *The page you selected will appear in the top frame.*

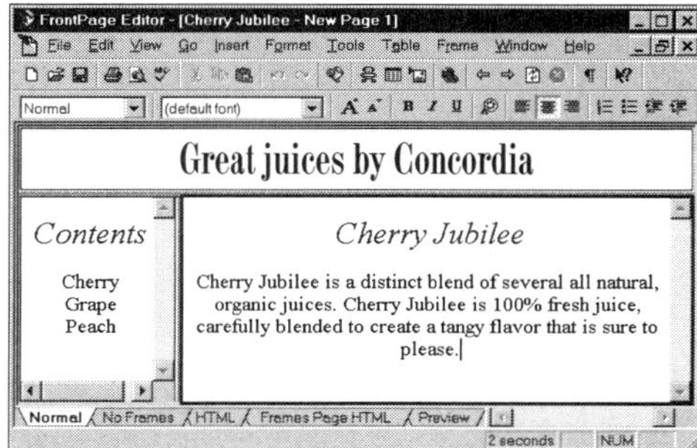

Figure 11. *When you're done associating Web pages with frames, your frames page will look something like this.*

4. Click OK to select the Banner and Contents frames page. FrontPage displays the WYSIWYG ("what you see is what you get") environment for working with frames (**Figure 8**). You can see the three frames in your frames page. In each frame, you can click the Set Initial Page button to choose a page to display when the frames page is first displayed. You can also click the New Page button to create a new page to display in the frame, and you can click the Help button to get online help about frames.

5. Click the Set Initial Page button in the top frame. FrontPage displays the Create Hyperlink dialog box (**Figure 9**).

6. Click the page that you want to appear as the banner in the frames page (concordia.htm in this case), and then click OK. You may see a message that FrontPage is retrieving the file. Then the file will appear in the frame (**Figure 10**).

7. Click the Set Initial Page button in the left-hand frame and choose the contents.htm file from the Create Hyperlink dialog box.

8. Do the same thing for the right frame: Click its Set Initial Page button and choose the cherry.htm file. Now all three Web pages should appear in the appropriate frame (**Figure 11**).

9. Choose Save from the File menu. You'll see the Save As dialog box (**Figure 12**). The diagram on the right tells you that you're saving the entire frames page, rather than any individual frames.
10. Enter a name and title for your frames page, and click OK.

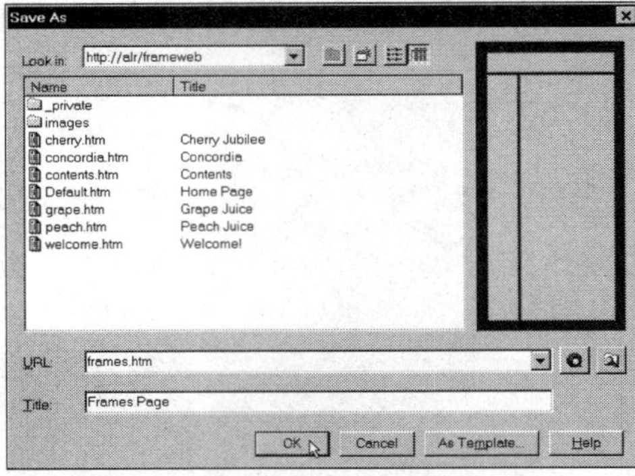

Figure 12. *You should save your frames page when you're done setting it up.*

Tips:

- This example assumes that you've generated all your individual Web pages before creating your frames page. But if you weren't that organized, you can create a Web page for a particular frame after the fact by clicking the New Page button in the WYSIWYG frames environment (**Figure 8**).
- If you want to work on a frame individually, first click within it to select it. You'll see a dark border around it telling you that it's the active frame.
- When you open a frames page, there are several tabs at the bottom of the FrontPage Editor, including: No Frames and Frames Page HTML. Use the No Frames tab to modify the Web page that appears when your Web site is viewed with a browser that doesn't support frames. The Frames Page HTML tab displays the HTML code for the frames page, as opposed to the HTML for individual Web pages that appears when you click the HTML tab.

CREATING FRAMES VISUALLY

In the previous version of FrontPage, setting up a frames page (then called a frameset) was a fairly elaborate process that involved using a Frames Wizard and stepping through many dialog boxes. Now it's easy to create frames visually, in the WYSIWYG frames environment that you saw in Figure 8. You can set up a ready-made frames page in just a few steps using one of the templates supplied in the New dialog box. What's more, it's simple to modify your frames page after the fact—adding and removing frames, resizing frames, and more. You'll learn how to do all of these things in the sections that follow.

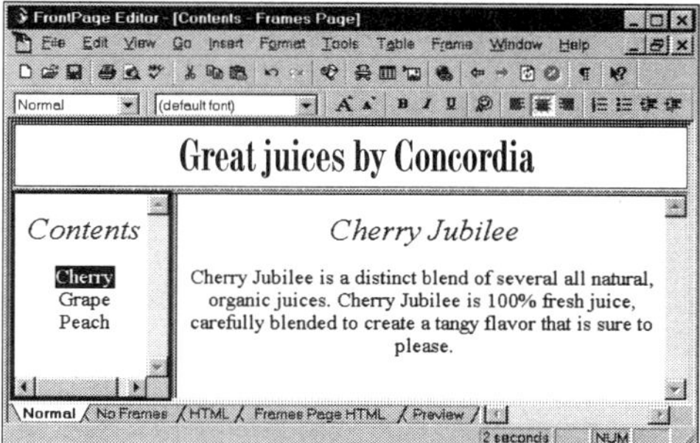

Figure 13. *Open the Web page or frames page that will contain the hyperlinks the user will click.*

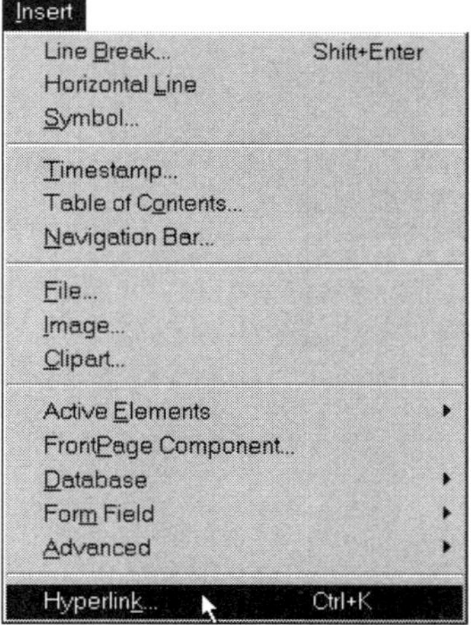

Figure 14. *Choose Hyperlink from the Insert menu.*

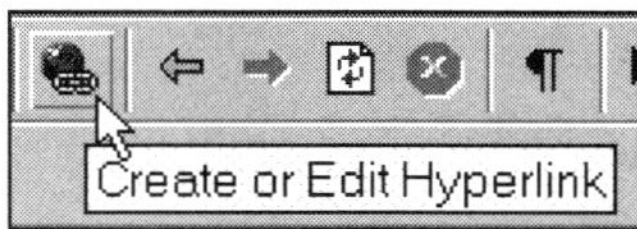

Figure 15. *Click the Create or Edit Hyperlink button in the Standard tolbar.*

The next thing you need to do is create the hyperlinks in the table of contents that will make the juice descriptions appear in the right frame.

To create a hyperlink to a frame:

1. In the Editor, open the frames page or the Web page that will contain the hyperlinks the user will click. In this example, frames.htm is open (**Figure 13**).
2. Select the text or image that will become the hyperlink. "Cherry" is selected in Figure 13.
3. Choose Hyperlink from the Insert menu (**Figure 14**) or click the Create or Edit Hyperlink button on the Standard toolbar (**Figure 15**). The Create Hyperlink dialog box will open (**Figure 16**).
4. Select the Web page that will appear when the hyperlink is clicked by the user. In Figure 16, cherry.htm is selected.
5. Make sure the Target Frame text box contains the name of the frame that you want the Web page to appear in when the hyperlink is clicked (**Figure 17**). In this case, the target frame is the right frame. It's the default target for all links in the current frame (Page Default). The name of the frame is main—the name FrontPage automatically assigns to the right-hand frame in the Banner and Contents frames page template.

6. Click OK to close the dialog box. The hyperlink will be created and the text underlined. If you selected an image, a border will appear around the image.

7. Create any additional hyperlinks you need by following steps 2 through 6. For this example, you would create the hyperlinks to the Grape Juice page and the Peach Juice page.

8. When you are finished creating hyperlinks, save the Web page by choosing Save from the File menu, pressing Ctrl+S, or clicking the Save toolbar button. If you're working with a single frame in an open frames page, you can also choose Save Page from the Frame menu.

9. Now you can check that your frames page is working as planned. Click the Preview tab in the Editor, or choose Preview in Browser from the File menu to get a glimpse of your new frames page (**Figure 18**).

10. Try clicking some of the links in the Contents frame to make sure that they display the correct linked pages in the right-hand frame.

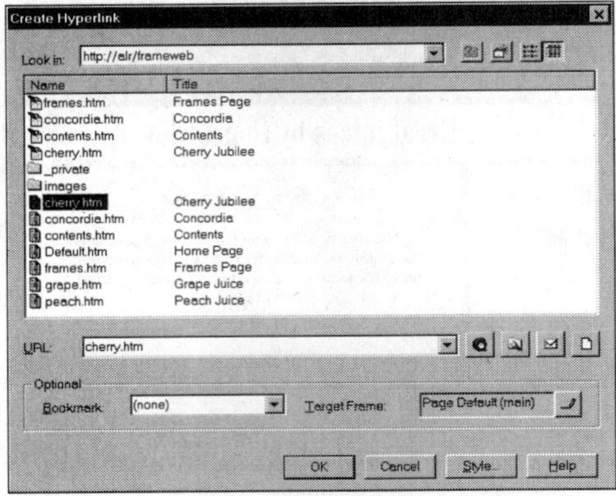

Figure 16. *Use the Create Hyperlink dialog box to link a Web page to a frame.*

Figure 17. *In the Target Frame text box, check that the name of the frame that the hyperlinked Web page will appear in is correct.*

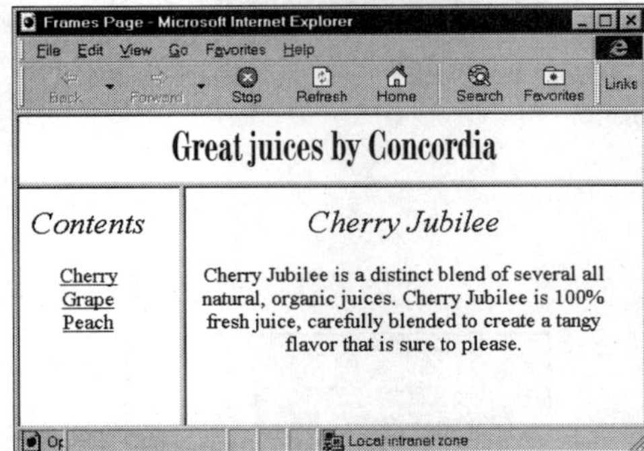

Figure 18. *When you check out the frames page you created, you'll discover a sophisticated, professional looking Web page.*

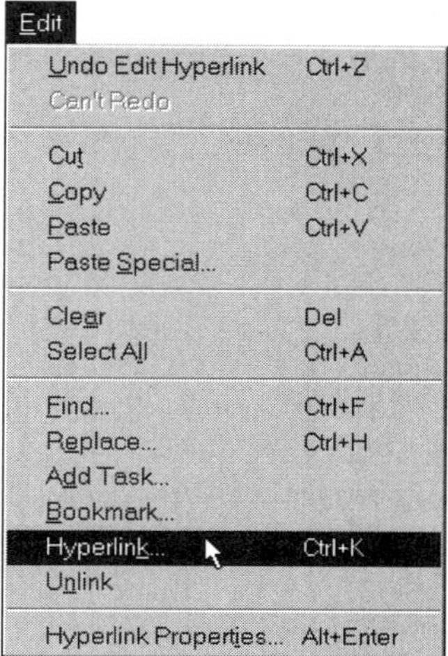

Figure 19. *Choose Hyperlink from the Edit menu.*

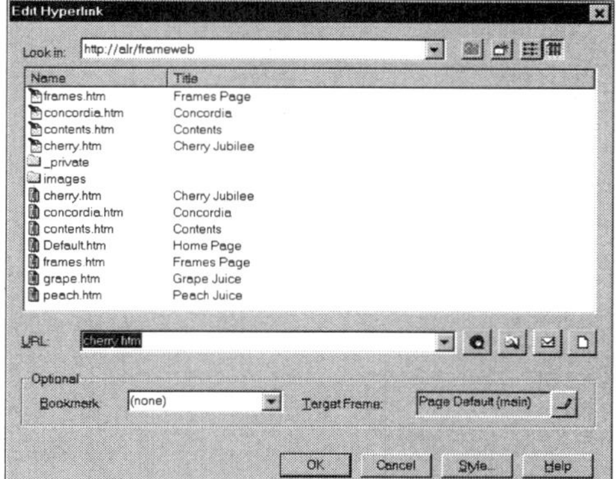

Figure 20. *The Edit Hyperlink dialog box lets you modify existing links.*

Figure 21. *Clicking the Change Target Frame button opens the Target Frame dialog box.*

When you set up links in your frames page in the previous section, you didn't need to change the target frame—that is, the frame in which FrontPage will open the linked page. That's because FrontPage did a good job of guessing which frame should be the target. But sometimes you'll need to change the target frame, either for individual hyperlinks or for an entire frame.

To change the target frame for an individual link:

1. Select the link and then choose Hyperlink from the Edit menu (**Figure 19**) or click the Create or Edit Hyperlink toolbar button (**Figure 15**). You'll see the Edit Hyperlink dialog box (**Figure 20**), which is the same as the Create Hyperlink dialog box except for the name.

   or

   To set a new target frame while creating a new link, select the text or image to be the link and choose Hyperlink from the Insert menu (**Figure 14**) or click the Create or Edit Hyperlink toolbar button. You'll see the Create Hyperlink dialog box (**Figure 16**).

2. Click the Change Target Frame button to the right of the Target Frame text box (**Figure 21**). This opens the Target Frame dialog box (**Figure 22**).

3. Under Current Frames Page, there's a little "map" illustrating the frames within the current frames page. Click the area representing the frame you want to turn into the target frame; the frame will become selected (it will darken) and its name will appear in the Target Setting text box (**Figure 23**).

4. If you don't want a frame within the current frames page to be the target page, you can choose from the options under Common Targets.

   - Page Default sets the target frame to the default for the page. (See the next section for more about default target pages.) In this case, the default target is main, but with other frames pages it may be something else.
   - Same Frame sets the current frame, the one the hyperlink is in, as the target frame. Use this option if you want a linked Web page to replace the Web page containing the hyperlink. (This displays the text _self in the Target Setting text box.)
   - Whole Page removes the frames page and displays the target page in a new browser window that fills the whole screen. (This displays the text _top in the Target Setting text box.) You might want to use this option for a link to a Web page on the World Wide Web (as opposed to within your Web site).

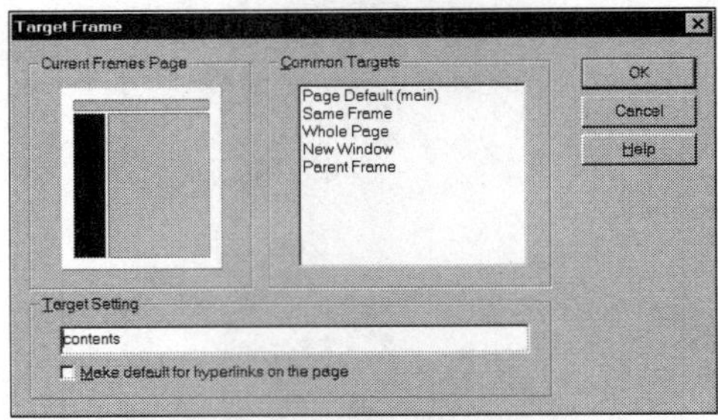

Figure 22. *The Target Frame dialog box is where you change which frame the linked page will appear in. Click a frame under Current Frames Page to choose a target frame from within the current frames page.*

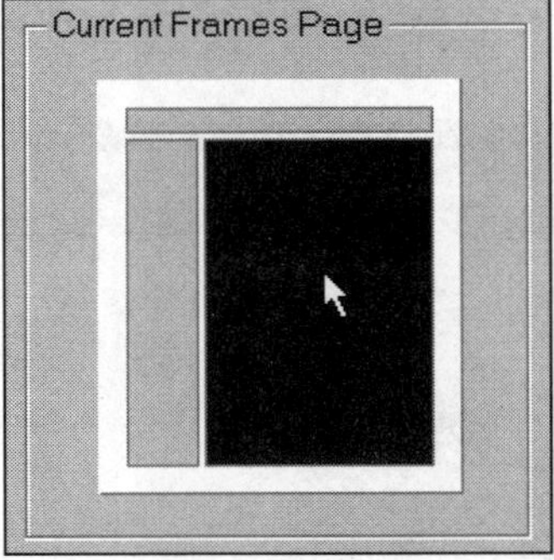

Figure 23. *When you click an area under Current Frames Page, that frame becomes the target frame.*

Change the Target Frame

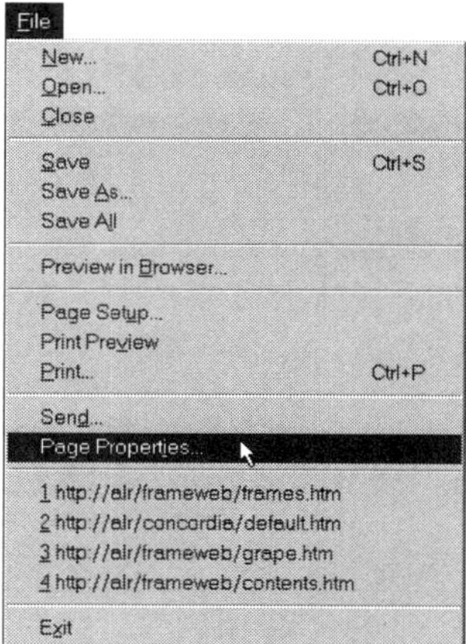

Figure 24. *Choose Page Properties from the File menu.*

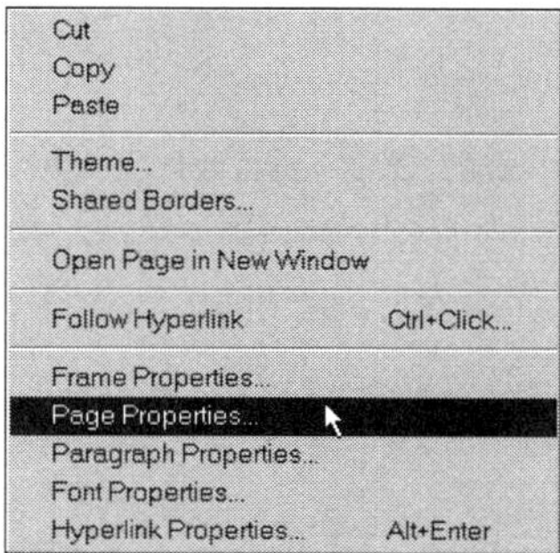

Figure 25. *Choose Page Properties from the pop-up menu.*

- New Window loads the linked page in a new browser window, leaving the frames page undisturbed in its own browser window. (Choosing this option displays the text _blank in the Target Setting text box.)
- Parent Frame is an advanced feature.

5. Click OK.
6. Test out the revised hyperlink by switching to the Preview tab or by choosing Preview in Browser from the File menu. The linked page should open in the new target frame.

Tips:

- When you create links within nonframe pages, you don't need to tinker with target frames. Clicking the link fills the entire screen with the linked page.
- When you open the Target Frame dialog box from the Create Hyperlink or Edit Hyperlink dialog box, it includes the check box "Make default for hyperlinks on the page." You can select this check box to change the target frame for all hyperlinks within the current frame. You'll learn another way to do this in the following section.

To change the default target frame:

1. Open the frames page if it's not already open, and select the frame whose default target you want to change.
2. Choose Page Properties from the File menu (**Figure 24**) or right-click the frame and choose Page Properties from the pop-up menu (**Figure 25**). The Page Properties dialog box will appear (**Figure 26**).
3. Click the Change Target Frame button to the right of the Default Target Frame text box. You'll see the Target Frame dialog box (**Figure 27**); it's almost exactly the same as the Target Frame dialog box you saw in Figure 22.
4. Under Current Frames Page, choose which frame you want to be the target frame. Or, use one of the options under Common Targets. (See pages 246–247 for the lowdown on these options.)
5. Click OK.

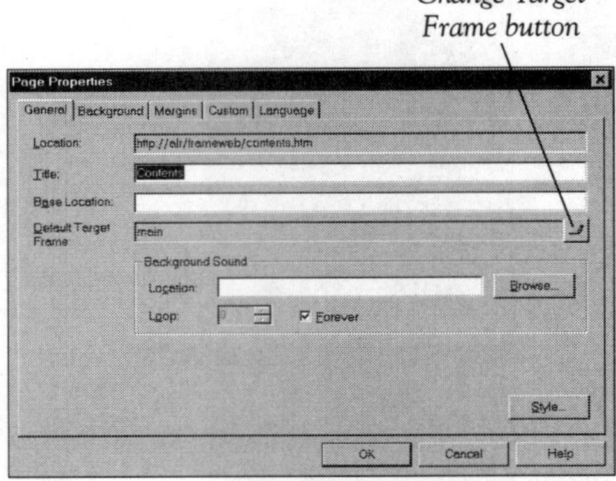

Figure 26. *You can set the default target frame by clicking the Change Target Frame button in the Page Properties dialog box.*

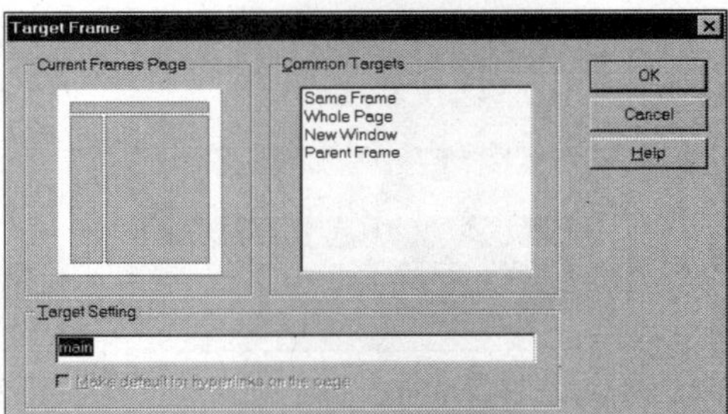

Figure 27. *Use the Target Frame dialog box to set the default target frame for the current Web page.*

You can drag frame borders to resize frames

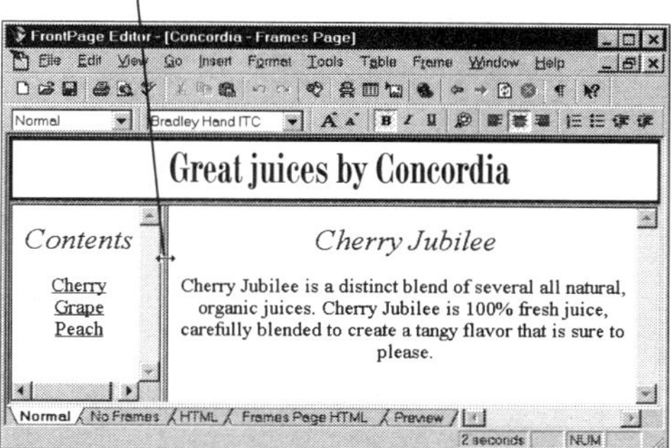

Figure 28. *When the mouse pointer is shaped like a double-headed arrow, you can drag to resize the frame.*

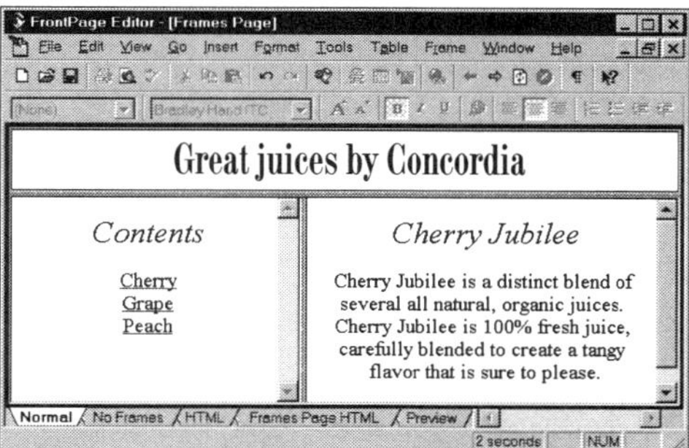

Figure 29. *Enlarging one frame shrinks the adjacent frame.*

The Frames page tab in the New dialog box might include a frames page template that suits your needs exactly. But if not, the WYSIWYG frames environment makes it simple to tweak frames pages until they're just the way you want them. Among other things, you can resize, add, and delete frames.

To resize a frame:

1. Open the frames page containing the frame you want to resize.
2. Place the mouse pointer over the border of the frame to resize. The pointer should change into a double-headed arrow (**Figure 28**).
3. Drag the frame border to resize the frame, and release the mouse button when you're done (**Figure 29**).

Tip:

- Dragging a frame border that is between two frames enlarges one frame and shrinks the other (**Figures 28** and **29**). But dragging an outside frame border (for example, the right-hand border of the frame containing the Cherry Jubilee description in Figure 29) actually splits the frame, dividing it in two and creating a new frame. You'll learn how to split frames next.

Resize a Frame

If you want to add new frames to your frames page, you can split existing pages. You do this by using the menus, or by dragging with the mouse.

To split frames:

1. Click in the frame you want to split.
2. Choose Split Frame from the Frame menu (**Figure 30**). You'll see the Split Frame dialog box (**Figure 31**).
3. Choose the radio button Split into Columns to split the frame vertically. Choose the radio button Split into Rows to split the frame horizontally.
4. Click OK to split the frame into two equal portions (**Figure 32**). The new frame has Set Initial Page and New Page buttons that you can use to set the page that first appears in the frame.

Tips:

- A fast way to split frames is to drag on a frame border while holding down the Ctrl key; using this method you can make the frames any size.
- Using the menus to split frames creates two equal sized frames, but you can easily resize them to any size you want by dragging on the frame borders.

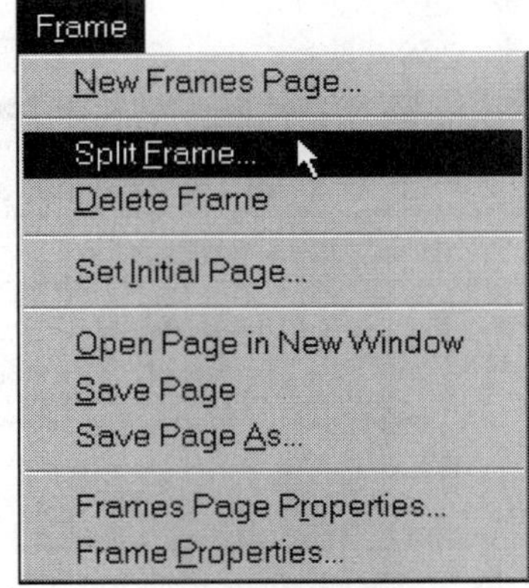

Figure 30. *Choose Split Frame from the Frame menu.*

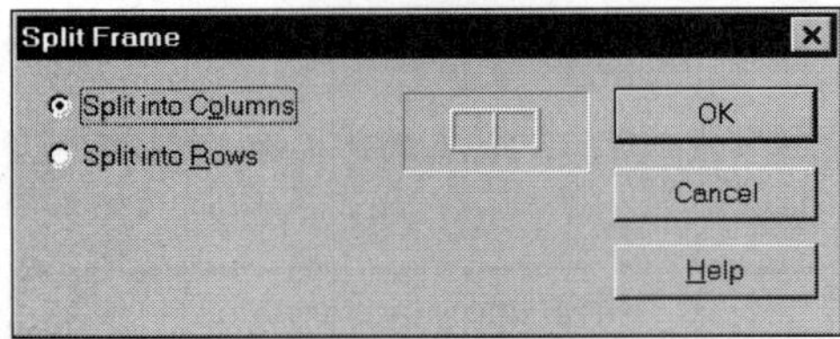

Figure 31. *You can use the Split Frame dialog box to split a frame vertically or horizontally.*

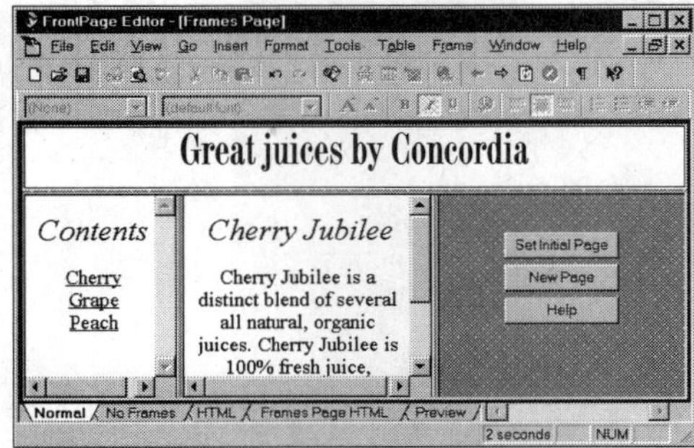

Figure 32. *Splitting a frame using the menus divides it into two equal portions.*

Split a Frame

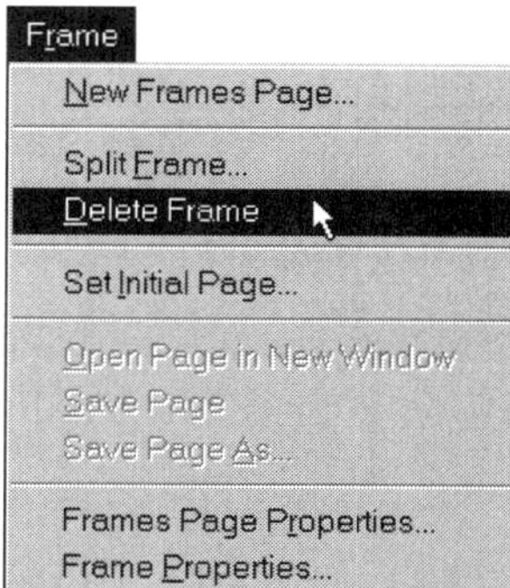

Figure 33. *Choose Delete Frame from the Frame menu.*

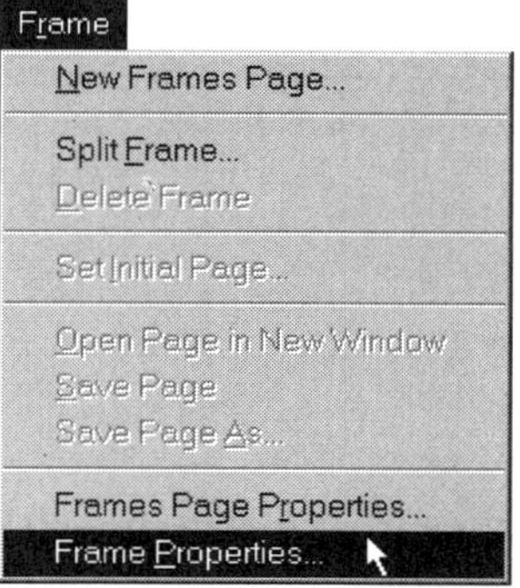

Figure 34. *Choose Frame Properties from the Frame menu.*

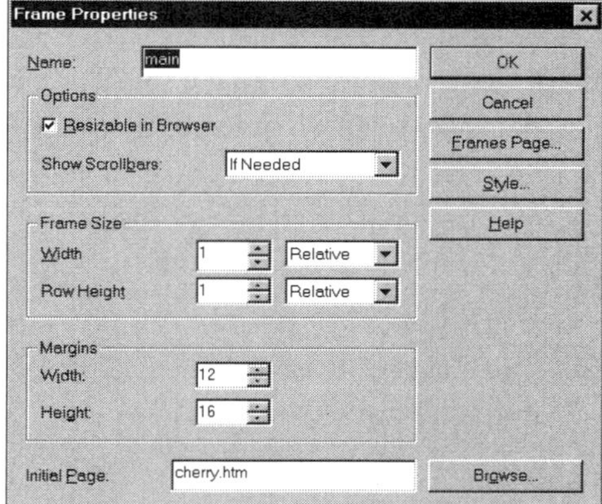

Figure 35. *The Frame Properties dialog box is where you modify the properties of individual frames.*

To delete a frame:

1. Click within the frame you want to delete to make it the active frame; it will acquire a dark border.
2. Choose Delete Frame from the Frame menu (**Figure 33**). The selected frame is deleted and the other frames are enlarged to fill the space it occupied.

There are a number of other changes you can make to frames, most of which you make using several different dialog boxes. You can modify individual frames, and you can edit the properties of the frames page itself.

To edit an individual frame:

1. Click within the frame you want to modify.
2. Choose Frame Properties from the Frame menu (**Figure 34**). (You can also right-click in the frame and choose Frame Properties from the pop-up menu.) The Frame Properties dialog box will appear (**Figure 35**).
3. If you like, you can set a new name for the frame in the Name text box. This is not the same as the file name of the Web page that is displayed; instead, it's the frame name used to specify which is the target frame.
4. Leave the Resizable in Browser check box selected if you want users to be able to adjust the size of the frame. If you want to make sure the frame size can't be changed, uncheck this check box.

5. Choose an option from the Show Scrollbars drop-down list to determine scroll bar behavior (**Figure 36**). When you select If Needed, scroll bars appear if there's too much material to fit in the frame all at once. If you select Never, scroll bars won't appear. And if you choose Always, scroll bars are always there, whether they're needed or not. Unless you have a good reason to change this setting, it's probably best to leave it at If Needed.

Figure 36. *You can choose to never show scroll bars, always show them, or show them only when they're needed.*

6. Under Frame Size, you can set the precise width and height of the frame. You can set these values as relative values, as pixels, or as percentages (**Figure 37**).

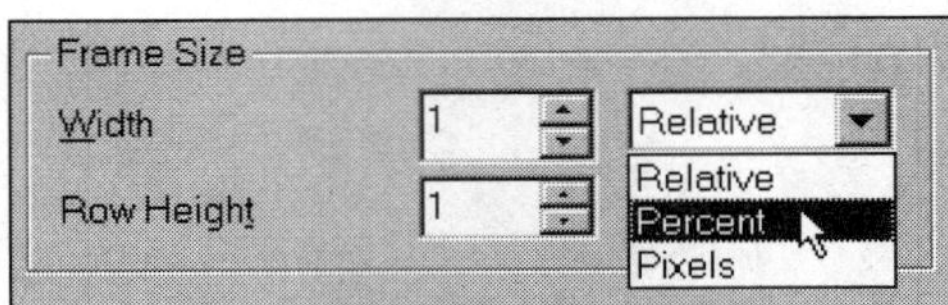

Figure 37. *You can set the height and width of the frame as a relative size, as a percentage, or as pixels.*

7. Under Margins, you can set the Width and Height of the margins between frame borders (**Figure 38**).

8. In the Initial Page text box, you can enter a new page to be loaded when the frames page is first open (**Figure 39**). If you need to, you can click the Browse button to hunt for the page via the Edit Hyperlink dialog box. (You can also change the initial page by choosing Set Initial Page from the Frame menu and choosing a new page in the Create Hyperlink dialog box.)

9. Click OK when you're done.

Tips:

- Under Frame Size, use the Pixels setting if you want the frame to always be the specified size (you might do this for navigation buttons).
- Choose Percent to make the frame width or height a percentage of the browser window (you could have one frame take up 33% of the width and the adjacent frame take up the remaining 67%).
- Use Relative to determine the size of frames relative to one another.

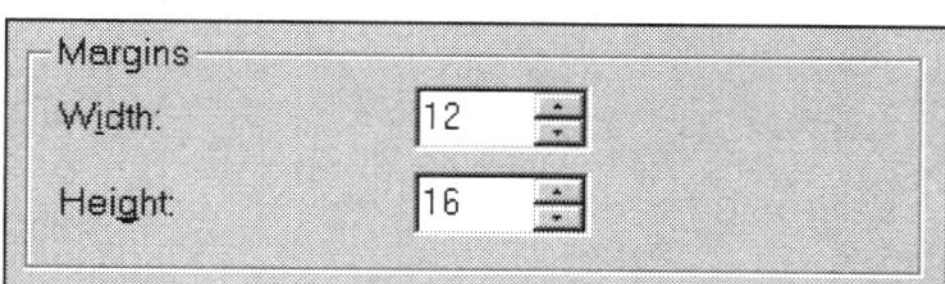

Figure 38. *The Width and Height boxes under Margins let you set the margins within the current frame.*

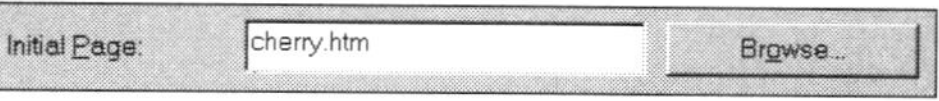

Figure 39. *The Initial Page text box lets you specify a new page to be loaded when the frames page first opens.*

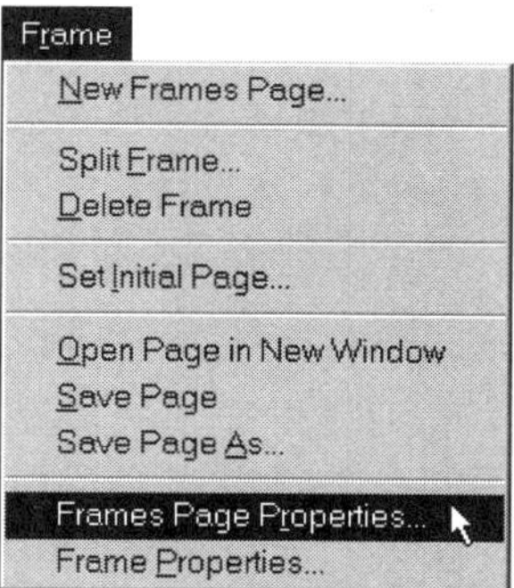

Figure 40. *Choose Frames Page Properties from the Frame menu.*

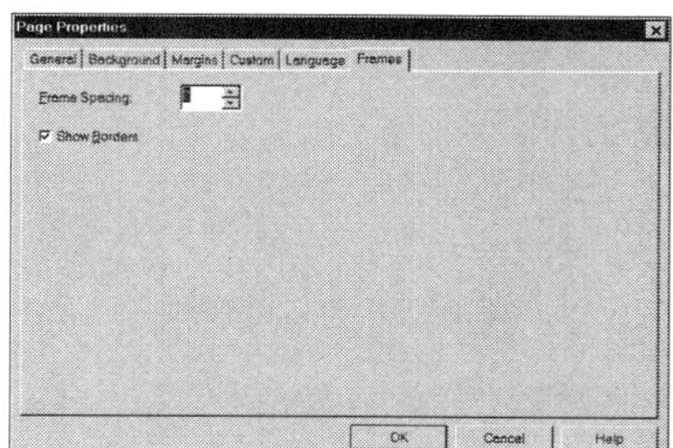

Figure 41. *The Frames tab of the Page Properties dialog box lets you set the spacing between frames and determine whether the frames will have borders.*

To edit a frames page:

1. Choose Frames Page Properties from the Frame menu (**Figure 40**). You'll see the Page Properties dialog box, with the Frames tab displayed (**Figure 41**).
2. Enter a value in the Frame Spacing box to set the set the spacing, in pixels, between frames in the frames page.
3. The Show Borders check box is selected by default. Deselect it if you don't want to display borders between frames.
4. Click OK.

FrontPage provides a simple alternate content page that displays for users who don't have a frames-capable browser. If you want to provide something more helpful than this page—which just displays a brief nformational message—you can create your own alternate content page, with text and maybe even some helpful links and other spiffy items.

To modify the alternate contents frame:

1. Open the frames page and click the No Frames tab at the bottom of the screen. You'll see a message, which will be displayed in browsers that don't support frames (**Figure 42**).
2. Modify the page as needed. You can simply add more friendly and helpful text. Or, you can add links and other elements that will help users travel through your site, even though they can't view frames.
3. Choose Save from the File menu (**Figure 43**), click the Save toolbar button, or press Ctrl+S to save your changes to the alternate contents page.

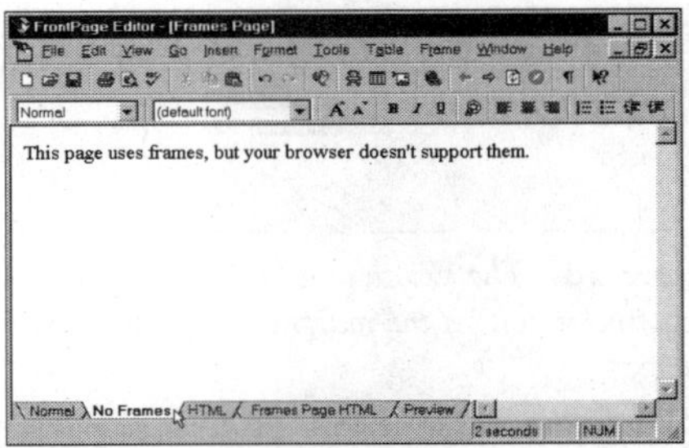

Figure 42. *Clicking the No Frames tab displays this Web page, with a short message to users whose browsers don't support frames.*

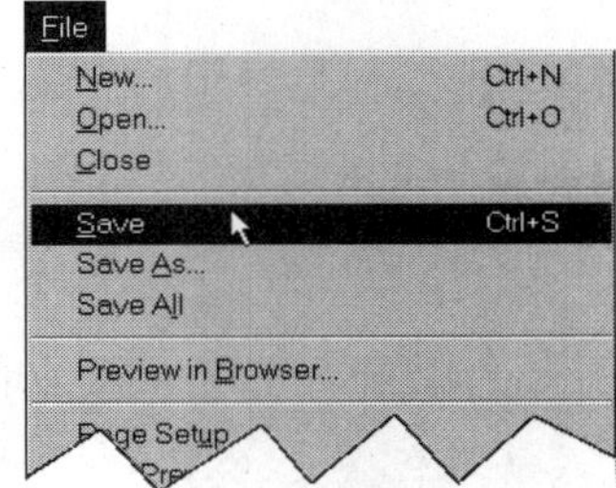

Figure 43. *Choose Save from the File menu.*

Summary

In this chapter you learned how to:

- Create a frames page
- Create hyperlinks to a frame
- Change the target frame for individual hyperlinks
- Change the default target frame
- Resize frames
- Split frames
- Delete frames
- Edit individual frames
- Edit the frames page
- Modify the alternate contents Web page

Web Site Administration

16

Many Web sites are built by one person, others by a team. Even if you are "flying solo," you may want to know about administration. If you are working with a team, it's important to understand Web site administration.

Members of a Web site design team have different jobs. One person might write the text for a page while another might lay it out. These people would need different types of access to the Web site—one person would only be able to look at a site while another would be able to create, edit, and delete pages.

If you are the administrator for a Web site team, it's your job to decide what kind of access each person on your team should have. FrontPage 98 calls these different levels of Web site access *permissions*.

There are three permissions levels that can be designated:

- *Administrator*—an administrator can set who has access to a Web site, and can also create and delete Web sites, and create, edit, and delete Web pages.
- *Author*—an author can create, edit, and delete Web pages but cannot add or delete Web sites.
- *Browse*—someone with browse access can only look at the Web page in a browser.

Every Web site must have at least one administrator. Using FrontPage Explorer, an administrator can designate other administrators for a Web site, as well as authors and browsers.

FrontPage Root Webs

The default Web page that will show up in a browser when a FrontPage Web site is posted to a server is located in the Web server's *Root Web*. The Root Web contains the main Web site. You can create other Web sites that are sub-sites of this Root Web. These sub-Web sites can link to the main Web site or be separate, unconnected sites. **Figure 1** shows a diagram of this structure. All the Webs that you've created in FrontPage so far have actually been sub-webs of the Root Web.

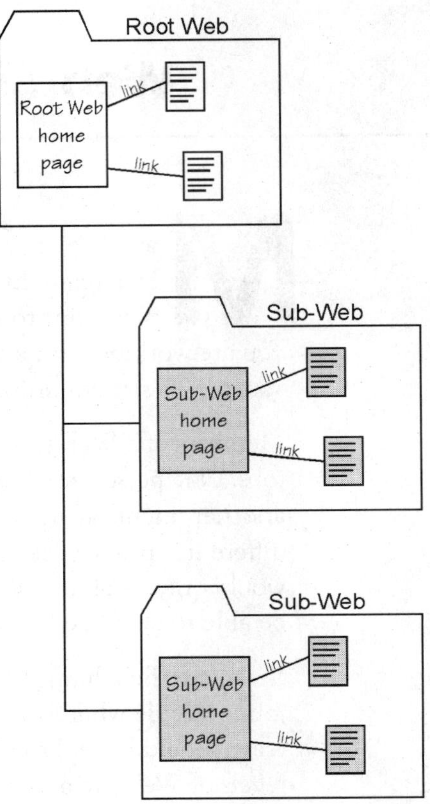

Figure 1. *A Root Web contains the main Web site and can have as many sub-Web sites as you want.*

Permissions can be set using the Root Web, meaning that all Web sites contained within the Root Web, the main site and the sub-Web sites, will use the same permissions. Or, permissions can be set on a site-by-site basis. In addition, you can set up access rights for individual users, using separate passwords, or groups of users.

WHAT THIS CHAPTER COVERS

This chapter assumes you are using the Microsoft Personal Web Server. If you try to set permissions for any other server using FrontPage, the Permissions feature may behave differently than described here. To set access rights for other servers, see the documentation that came with the software.

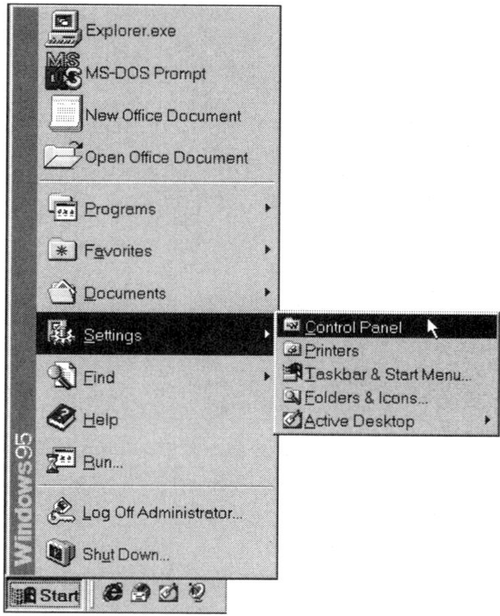

Figure 2. *Choose Settings from the Windows Start menu and choose Control Panel from the fly-out.*

Figure 3. *You can choose the Personal Web Server from the Control Panel window.*

If you're using Microsoft Personal Web Server, you may need to add users and groups (sets of users) from outside of FrontPage before you set permissions for them from within FrontPage.

To add users:

1. Choose Settings from the Windows Start menu and choose Control Panel from the fly-out (**Figure 2**). You'll see the Control Panel window (**Figure 3**).
2. Double-click Personal Web Server in the Control Panel. (You can single-click if you have Windows set up to behave like a browser.) You'll see the Personal Web Server Properties dialog box (**Figure 4**).

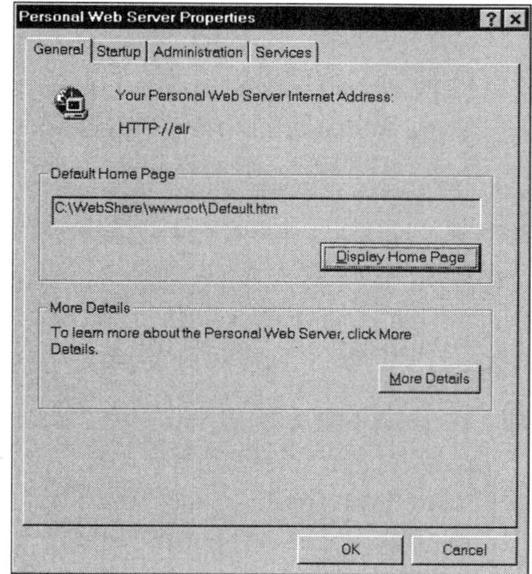

Figure 4. *The Personal Web Server Properties dialog box lets you change various settings having to do with your Web server.*

3. Click the Administration tab (**Figure 5**), and then click the Administration button. Your default browser will open, displaying the Internet Services Administrator Web page (**Figure 6**).
4. Click the Local User Administration option. The Internet Local User Administrator page appears (**Figure 7**).
5. In the Users tab, click the New User button to display the Add New User to Web Server Database screen. Enter a user name and password (**Figure 8**), and enter the password a second time in the Confirm Password text box to make sure you got it right.
6. Click the Add button. The user you added will show up in the User List (**Figure 9**).
7. Repeat the process outlined in steps 5 and 6 to add additional users as needed.
8. When you're done, you can close your browser.

Tip:

- You can edit a user's name and password by selecting the user's name from the User List and clicking the Proper-ties button, and you can remove a user by selecting the user name and clicking the Remove button.

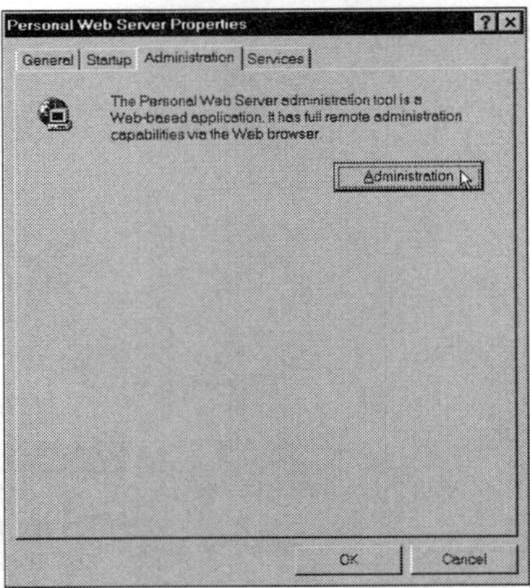

Figure 5. *Click the Administration button in the Administration tab of the Personal Web Server Properties dialog box.*

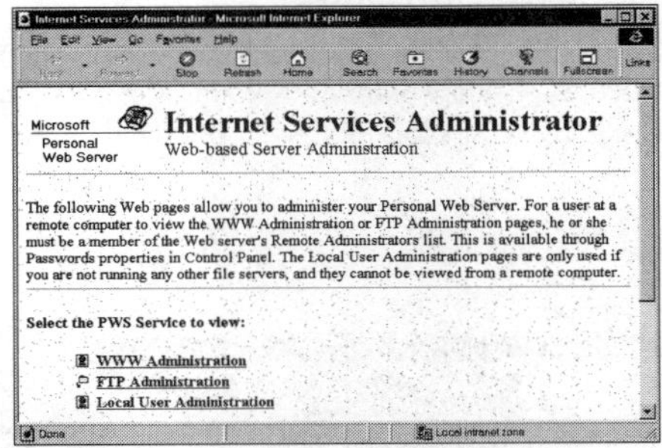

Figure 6. *The Internet Services Administrator screen lets you administer your Web in various ways.*

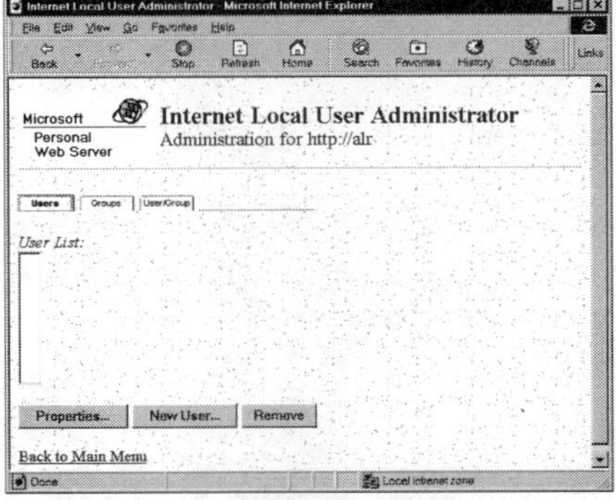

Figure 7. *The Local User Administrator screen lets you choose whether to add or edit groups or users.*

Add Users

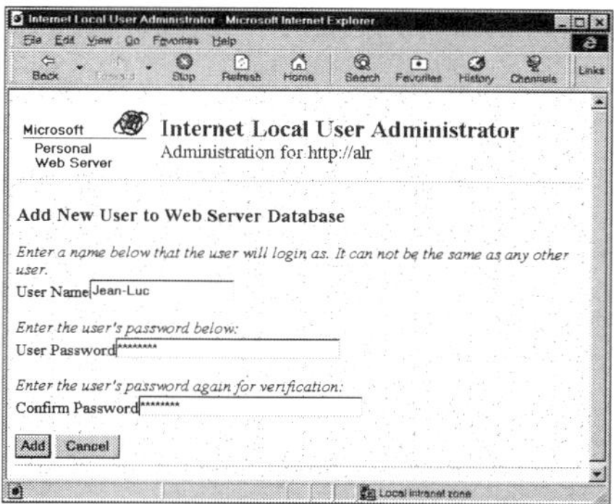

Figure 8. *Enter a user name and password in the screen Add New User to Web Server Database.*

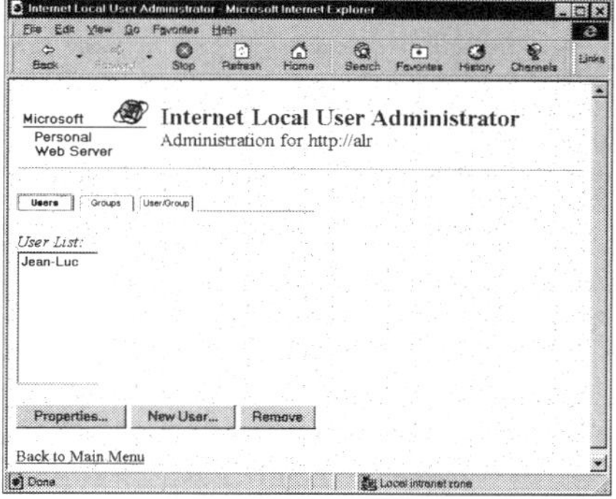

Figure 9. *Users you add appear in the User List.*

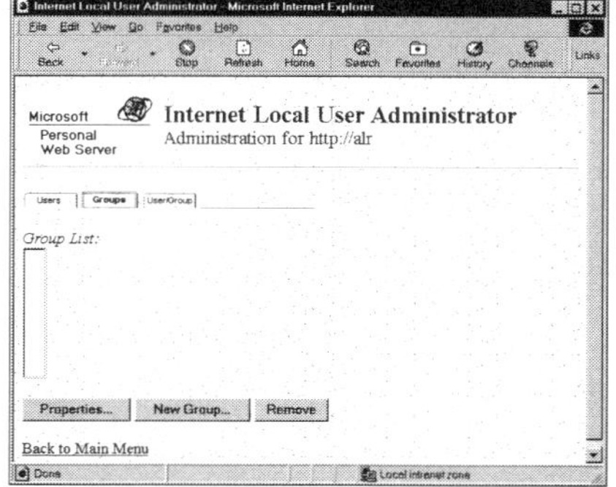

Figure 10. *The Groups tab of the Internet Local User Administrator lets you add and edit groups.*

To add groups:

1. Choose Settings from the Windows Start menu and choose Control Panel from the fly-out (**Figure 2**).
2. Double-click Personal Web Server in the Control Panel. You'll see the Personal Web Server Properties dialog box (**Figure 4**).
3. Click the Administration tab and then click the Administration button. Your default browser will open, displaying the Internet Services Administrator Web page (**Figure 6**).
4. Click the Local User Administration option. The Internet Local User Administrator page appears (**Figure 7**).
5. Click the Groups tab. You'll see a screen for adding groups that looks similar to the screen for adding users (**Figure 10**).
6. Click the New Group button. You'll see the Add New Group to Web Server Database screen (**Figure 11**).
7. Enter a group name in the Group Name text box and click the Add button. The group you added will appear in the Group List (**Figure 12**).
8. Close your browser when you're done.

Add Groups

To add users to groups:

1. Choose Settings from the Windows Start menu and choose Control Panel from the fly-out (**Figure 2**).
2. Double-click Personal Web Server in the Control Panel. You'll see the Personal Web Server Properties dialog box (**Figure 4**).
3. Click the Administration tab and then click the Administration button. Your default browser will open, displaying the Internet Services Administrator Web page (**Figure 6**).
4. Click the Local User Administration option. The Internet Local User Administrator page appears (**Figure 7**).
5. Click the User/Group tab to select it (**Figure 13**).
6. Highlight a user you want to add to a group in the User List and highlight a group you want to add that user to in the Group List.
7. Click the Add user to group button.
8. When you're done, close your browser.

Tip:

- To remove a user from a group, select the user, select the group, and click the Remove user from group button.

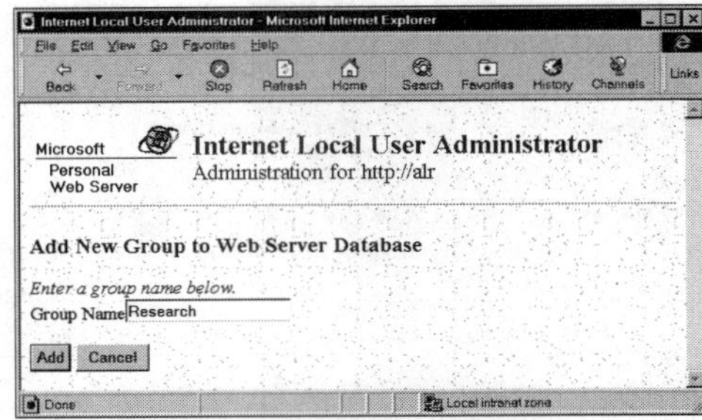

Figure 11. *Enter a group name in the screen Add New Group to Web Server Database.*

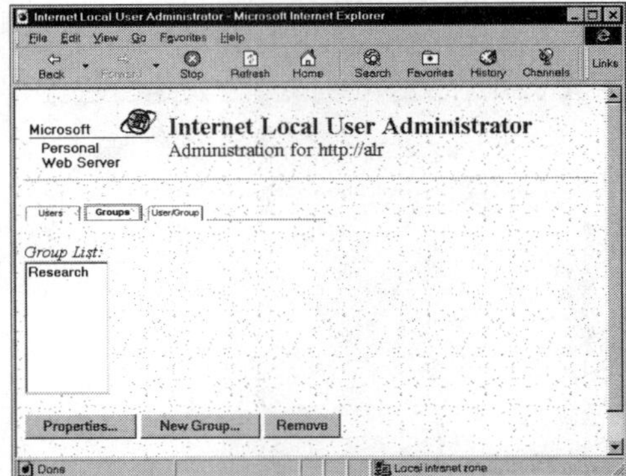

Figure 12. *Groups you add appear in the Group List.*

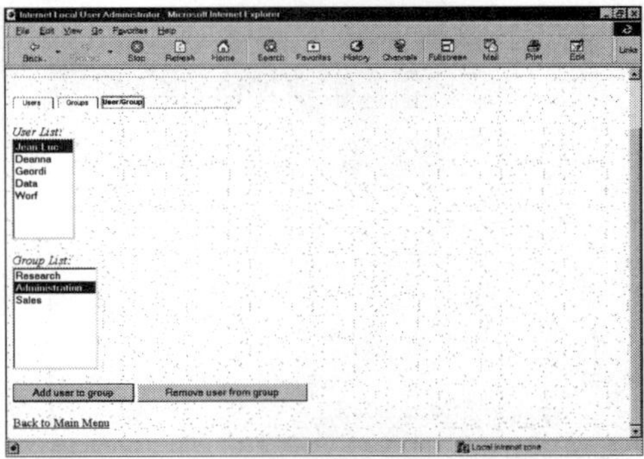

Figure 13. *The User/Group tab of the Internet Local User Administrator lets you assign users to groups.*

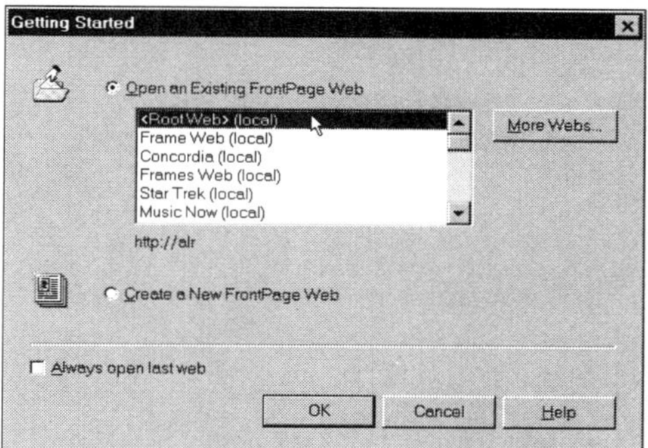

Figure 14. *You may be able to open the Root Web directly from the Getting Started dialog box.*

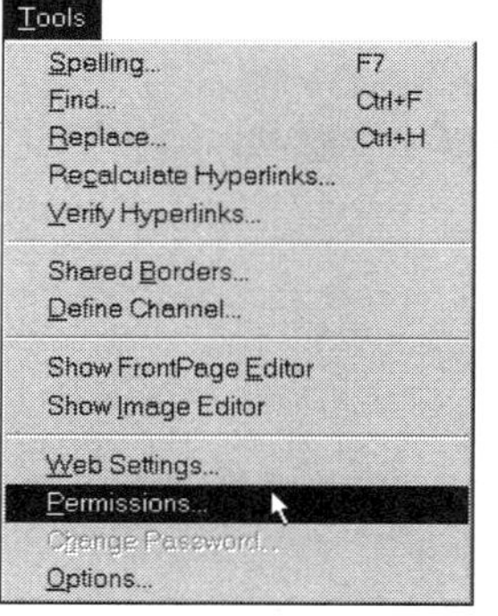

Figure 15. *Choose Permissions from the Explorer's Tools menu.*

To set permissions for an individual user with the Root Web:

1. Launch FrontPage Explorer. The Getting Started dialog box will appear (**Figure 14**).
2. In the Getting Started dialog box, check that the Open an Existing FrontPage Web radio button is selected, select <Root Web>, and click OK. (If you don't see the <Root Web> option, click the More Webs button, click the List Webs button in the Open FrontPage dialog box that appears, select <Root Web>, and click OK.) The Root Web will open in Explorer.
3. Choose Permissions from the Tools menu (**Figure 15**). The Permissions dialog box will appear with the Users tab page in front (**Figure 16**). With this tab page, you can add new users, edit user's access rights, and remove users.

To add a new user:

a. Click the Add button. The Add Users dialog box will open (**Figure 17**).

b. In the Obtain list from drop-down list, choose where you'll obtain the list of users from.

c. Select the name of the new user in the Names text box. (If no names appear here, you need to add them, as described on pages 257–258.)

d. Click the Add button to add the user to the Add Names list.

e. In the Users Can area, select the radio button for the access you want to give the person: Browse this web, Author and browse this web, or Administer, author, and browse this web.

f. Click OK to close the Add Users dialog box and return to the Permissions dialog box. The new user's name will appear in the Name list box.

g. Repeat steps **c** through **f** for as many users as you want to add. (If you want to add multiple users with the same permissions, you can select users in the Add Users dialog box and click the Add button repeatedly.)

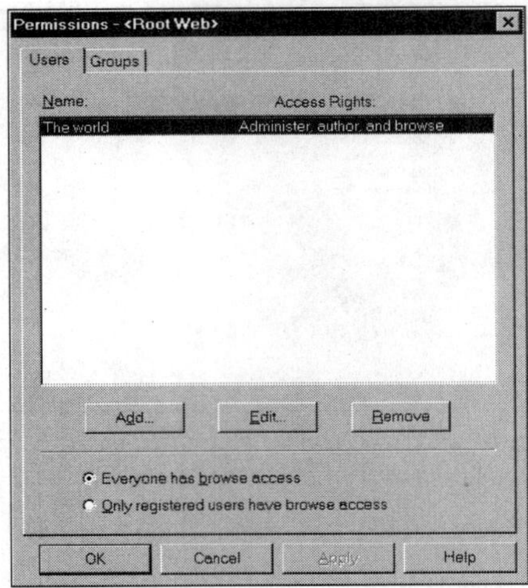

Figure 16. *The Permissions dialog box is used to add users, edit their rights, and remove users.*

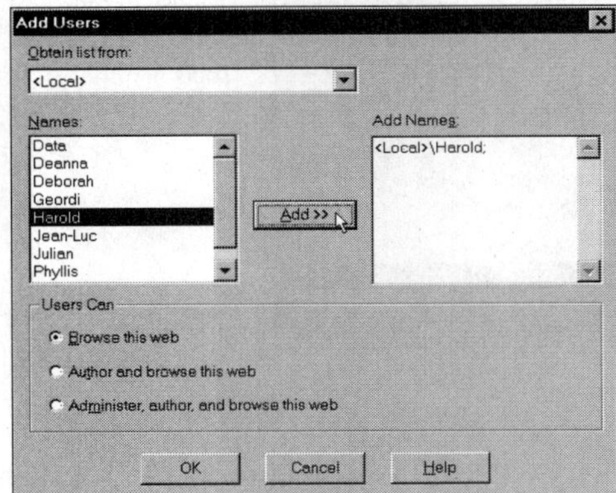

Figure 17. *In the Add Users dialog box, add the user's name to the Add Names list. Then select the type of access for the user.*

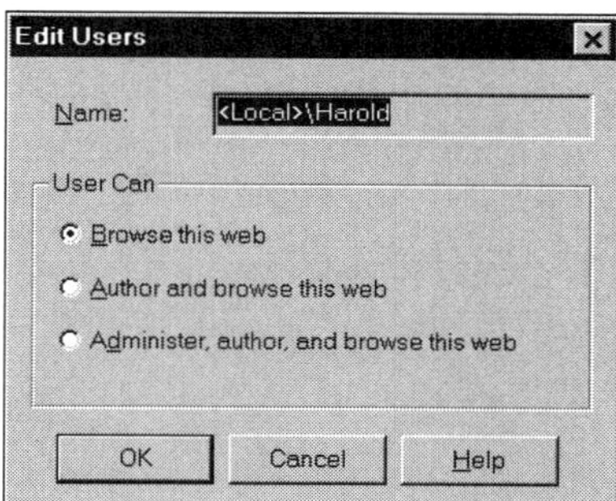

Figure 18. *In the Edit Users dialog box, select the new access rights for the user.*

Permissions and FrontPage

FrontPage permissions only work if you are working on a Web site located on a Web Server. If your Web site is saved in a folder on a computer, for instance C:\MyWeb, the Permissions item on the Tools menu will be grayed out and unavailable.

To edit a user's access rights:

a. Select the user whose access rights you want to change.

b. Click the Edit button in the Permissions dialog box. The Edit Users dialog box will appear (**Figure 18**).

c. In the User Can area, select the radio button for the access you want to give the person: Browse this web, Author and browse this web, or Administer, author, and browse this web.

d. Click OK to close the Edit Users dialog box and return to the Permissions dialog box. The user's changed access rights will appear in the Access Rights column.

To remove a user:

a. Select the user's name in the list box on the Users tab page of the Permissions dialog box.

b. Click the Remove button. The user will disappear from the list.

4. When you are finished adding users, editing their access rights, and removing users, click OK to close the Permissions dialog box and return to Explorer.

A *group* is a collection of users that have the same access privileges. For example, you could make a group of all users in a particular department or job category. You learned how to create a group using the Internet Local User Administrator page on page 259. From within FrontPage, you can establish which groups have access—to all Webs or to individual Webs.

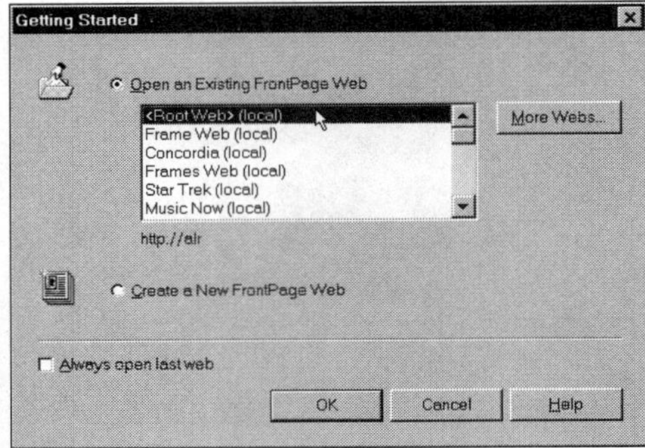

Figure 19. *You may be able to open the Root Web from directly within the Getting Started dialog box.*

To set permissions for a group with the Root Web:

1. Launch FrontPage Explorer. The Getting Started dialog box will appear (**Figure 19**).
2. Make sure the Open an Existing FrontPage Web radio button is selected, select <Root Web>, and click OK. The Root Web will open in Explorer. (If you don't see the <Root Web> option, click the More Webs button and click the List Webs button in the Open FrontPage Web dialog box that appears. Select <Root Web> and click OK.)
3. Choose Permissions from the Tools menu (**Figure 20**). The Permissions dialog box will appear (**Figure 21**).
4. Click the Groups tab to bring that tab page into view (**Figure 22**). With this tab page, you can add new groups, edit groups' access rights, and remove groups.

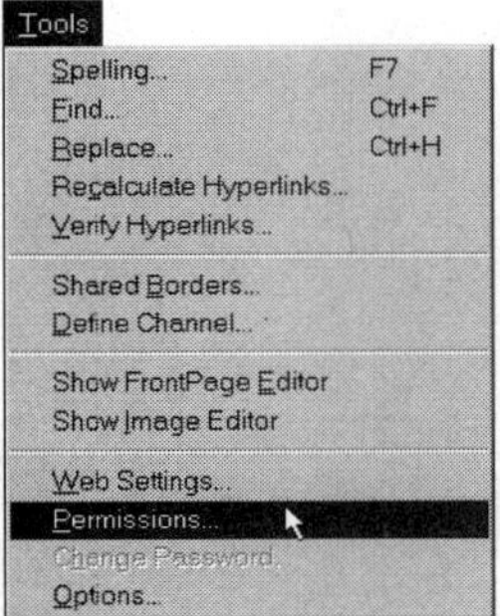

Figure 20. *Choose Permissions from the Tools menu.*

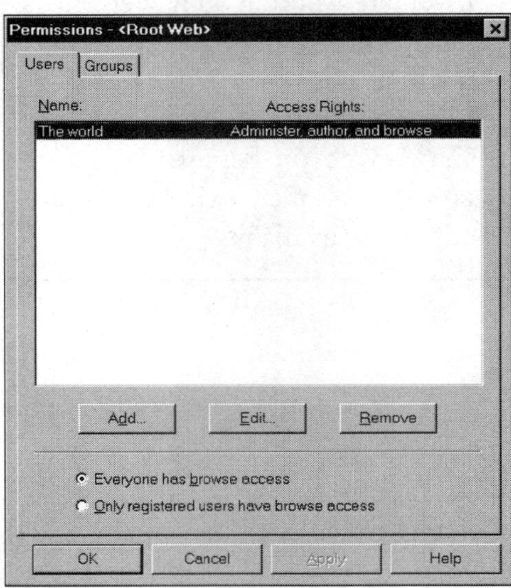

Figure 21. *The Permissions dialog box lets you add users, edit their rights, and remove users.*

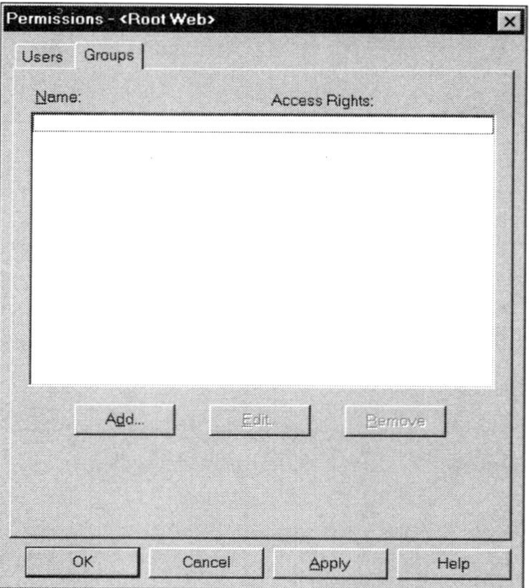

Figure 22. *The Groups tab of the Permissions dialog box lets you add and remove groups and edit their access rights.*

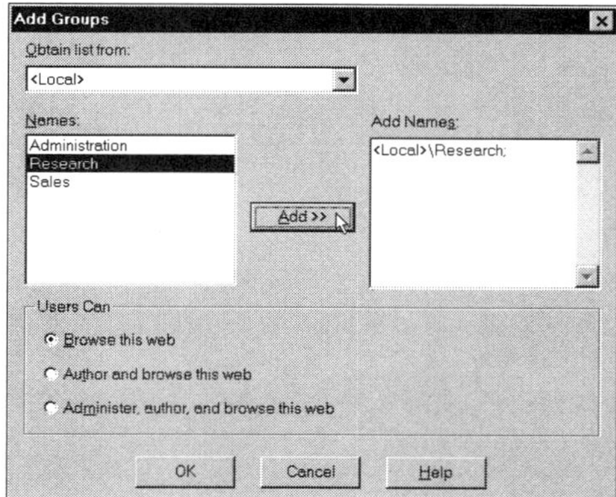

Figure 23. *In the Add Groups dialog box, add the group name to the Add Names list. Then, under Users Can, select the type of access for the group.*

To add a new group:

a. Click the Add button. The Add Groups dialog box will open (**Figure 23**).

b. In the drop-down list Obtain list from, choose where you will obtain the list of groups from.

c. Select the name of the new group in the Names text box. (If there are no group names here, you need to add them as described on page 259.)

d. Click the Add button to add groups to the Add Names list.

e. In the Users Can area, select the radio button for the access you want to give the group: Browse this web; Author and browse this web; or Administer, author, and browse this web.

f. Click OK to close the Add Groups dialog box and return to the Permissions dialog box. The new group name will appear in the Name list box.

g. Repeat steps **c** through **f** for as many groups as you want to add. (If you want to add multiple groups with the same level of permissions, you can keep choosing group names and clicking the Add button in the Add Groups dialog box.)

Edit Access Rights; Remove a Group

To edit a groups' access rights:

a. Select the group you want to edit.

b. Click the Edit button in the Permissions dialog box. The Edit Groups dialog box will appear (**Figure 24**).

c. In the User Can area, select the radio button for the access you want to give the group: Browse this web; Author and browse this web; or Administer, author, and browse this web.

d. Click OK to close the Edit Groups dialog box and return to the Permissions dialog box. The group's changed access rights will appear in the Access Rights column.

To remove a group:

a. Select the group's name in the list box on the Groups tab page of the Permissions dialog box.

b. Click the Remove button. The group will be removed from the list.

5. When you are finished adding groups, editing their access rights, and removing groups, click OK to close the Permissions dialog box and return to Explorer.

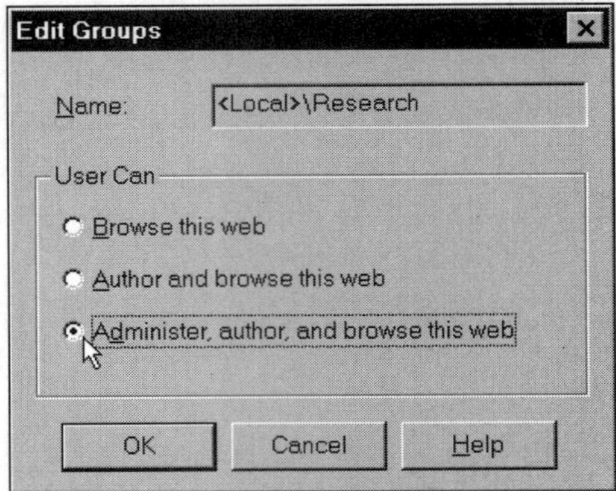

Figure 24. *In the Edit Groups dialog box, select the new access rights for the group.*

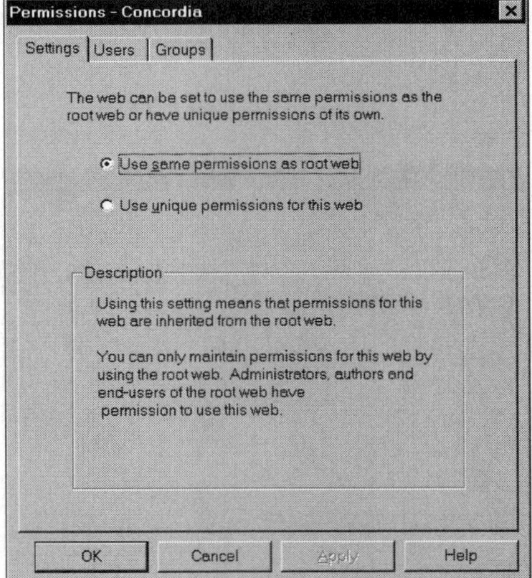

Figure 25. *With the Settings tab page, you can set whether an individual site uses the same permissions as the Root Web or has unique permissions.*

Setting Access Rights by Computer

Although Microsoft Personal Web Server doesn't support this feature, some types of server software, such as FrontPage Personal Web Server, let you control access based on which computer is being used. (There will be a Computers tab in the Permissions dialog box.) You do this by specifying an IP address for the computer. An IP address consists of four sets of numbers separated by periods, such as 207.71.18.55. You can even set permissions for several computers, if they have similar IP addresses, by using what's called an IP address mask. (If you've ever used wildcards to stand in for multiple characters in Windows or DOS, you'll feel right at home with these address masks.) An IP address mask is made up of a combination of these numbers and asterisks. This mask is then used to check whether a computer has access to a particular location on the Internet, such as a FrontPage Web site. For example, the IP address mask 207.*.*.* would allow connection to the above IP address, as well as to any other IP address beginning with the numbers 207.

To set permissions for a single Web site:

1. Open the Web site you want to set access rights for in Explorer.
2. Choose Permissions from the Tools menu (**Figure 20**). The Permissions dialog box will open with the Settings tab page in front (**Figure 25**).
3. Select the Use unique permissions for this web radio button (**Figure 26**).
4. Click Apply. The new setting will take affect.
5. You can now set individual access rights with the Users tab page (see step 3 on page 261) or access rights for an entire group with the Groups tab page (page 264).
6. When you are finished setting permissions for the Web site, click OK to close the Permissions dialog box and return to Explorer.

Use same permissions as root web

Use unique permissions for this web

Figure 26. *Select the Use unique permissions for this web radio button, then click Apply.*

Whether you are a Web site administrator or a designated user, you may want to change your password from time-to-time for security reasons.

To change your password:

1. Choose Settings from the Windows Start menu and choose Control Panel from the fly-out (**Figure 27**).
2. Double-click Personal Web Server in the Control Panel. You'll see the Personal Web Server Properties dialog box (**Figure 28**).
3. Click the Administration tab, and then click the Administration button. Your default browser will open, displaying the Internet Services Administrator page (**Figure 29**).
4. Click the Local User Administration option. The Internet Local User Administrator page appears (**Figure 30**).

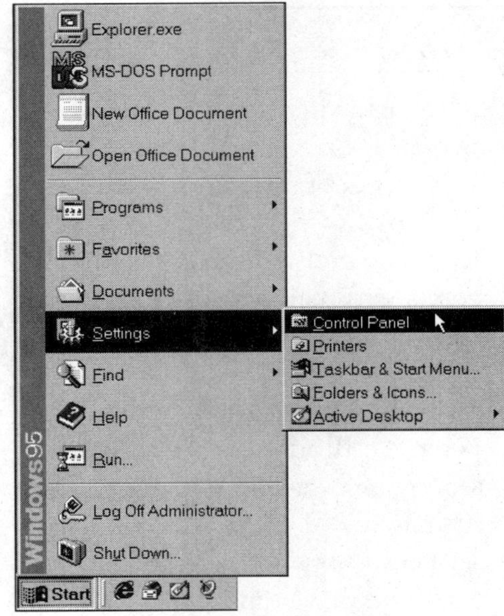

Figure 27. *Choose Settings from the Windows Start menu and choose Control Panel from the fly-out.*

CHANGING PASSWORDS FROM WITHIN FRONTPAGE

With FrontPage Personal Web Server installed, you could conveniently change passwords from right within FrontPage. (You just choose Change Password from the Tools menu in Explorer.) But if you're running Microsoft Personal Web Server, you don't have it so easy. In fact, the Change Password option on the Tools menu will be grayed out.

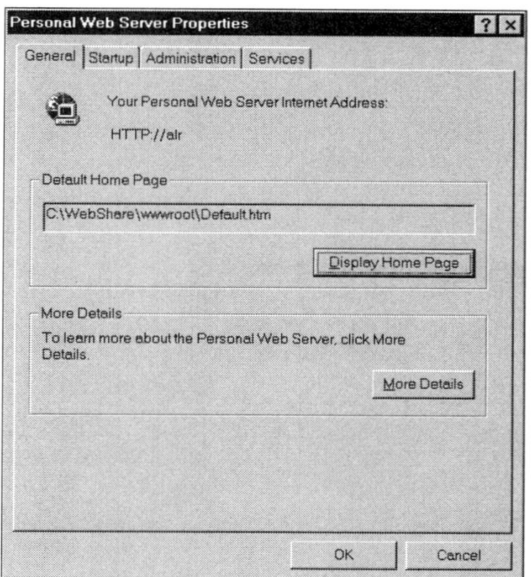

Figure 28. *The Personal Web Server Properties dialog box leads to the Internet Services Administrator, where you can change passwords, among other things.*

5. In the Users tab, select the user whose password you want to change and click the Properties button. You'll see a screen that lets you enter a new user password (**Figure 31**).
6. Enter the new password in the User Password text box, and then enter it a second time in the Confirm Password text box.
7. Click the Change Password button.
8. Repeat the process outlined in steps 5 through 7 to change any additional passwords.
9. Close your browser when you finish changing passwords.

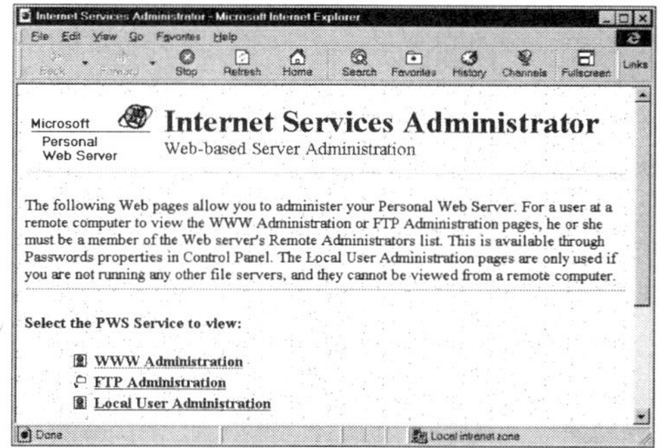

Figure 29. *From the Internet Services Administrator, click Local User Administration.*

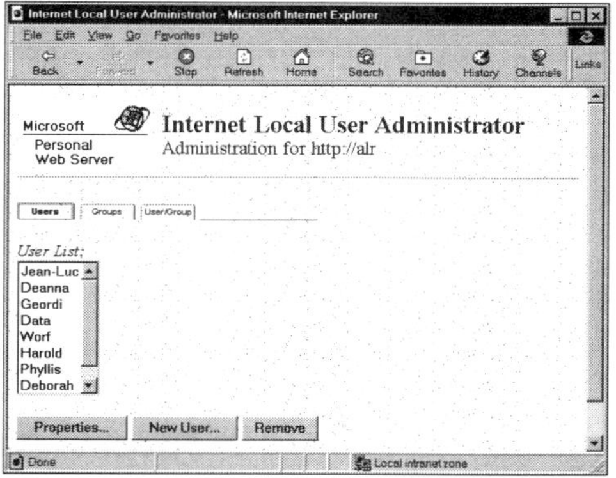

Figure 30. *The Internet Local User Administrator page lets you change users' passwords.*

Tip:

- Passwords are case sensitive, so be sure you type yours the same every time!

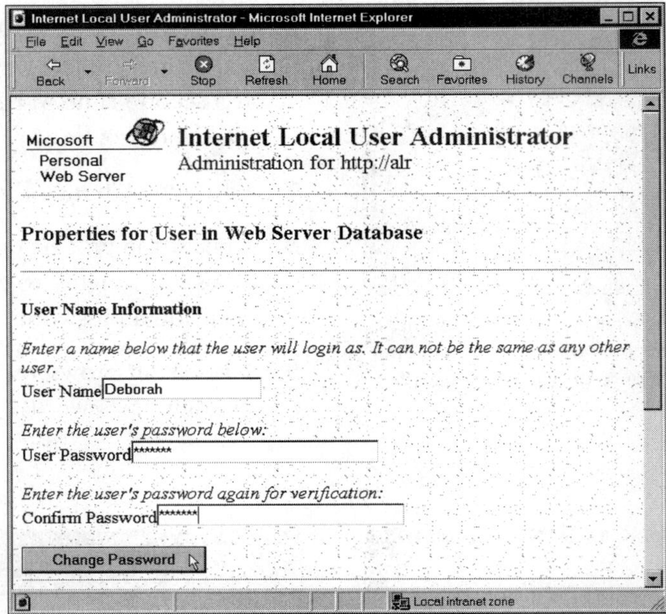

Figure 31. *Enter the new password, and then enter it again in the Confirm Password text box to make sure you have it right.*

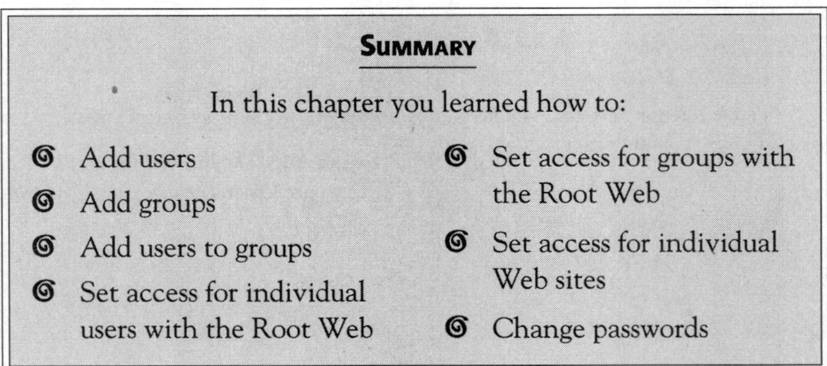

SUMMARY

In this chapter you learned how to:

- Add users
- Add groups
- Add users to groups
- Set access for individual users with the Root Web
- Set access for groups with the Root Web
- Set access for individual Web sites
- Change passwords

17 FrontPage Components

FrontPage components are programs you can add to Web pages using the FrontPage Editor. FrontPage components work with the FrontPage Server Extensions and the Microsoft Personal Web Server (for more about the Server Extensions, see page 46). When a FrontPage component is inserted into a Web page, it is actually creating a reference that tells the FrontPage-enabled servers to activate the FrontPage component program.

Many FrontPage components ship with FrontPage. Some of them, such as the Confirmation Field and Substitution components, are meant to work with forms and will be discussed in Chapter 18. The following FrontPage components are covered in this chapter:

- *Include Page* FrontPage component lets you quickly insert the same information from one Web page, such as copyright notices and logos, onto as many pages as you want in your Web site.
- *Scheduled Include Page* FrontPage component works like the Include Page component, but inserts its information during a specified time period.
- *Scheduled Image* FrontPage component also works like the Include Page component, but inserts a graphic during a specified time period.
- *Table of Contents* FrontPage component creates a table of contents for a Web site with hyperlinks to each Web page.
- *Timestamp* FrontPage component shows the time and date a Web page was last updated.
- *Hit Counter* FrontPage component tells you how many people have visited your site.

The Include Page FrontPage component

The Include Page FrontPage component works in a similar fashion to the *master pages* of a page layout program. Whatever you place on the master pages appears on the regular pages of a document.

The Include Page component uses a Web page as the master page. The FrontPage component itself is placed on the page where you want the text and/or images to appear. For instance, if you want a copyright notice to appear on all your Web pages, create a master page with the copyright notice on it, then insert the Include Page FrontPage component on all the pages where you want the copyright to appear, referencing the master page. If you want to update the copyright notice, all you need to do is change the master page. The Web pages with the Include Page component on them will update automatically.

> **WHAT ARE WEBBOTS?**
>
> You might see FrontPage components referred to as "WebBots," their former—and far more colorful—name. This gives you a hint why the Insert FrontPage Component toolbar button, and the FrontPage component mouse pointer, are shaped like cute little robots.

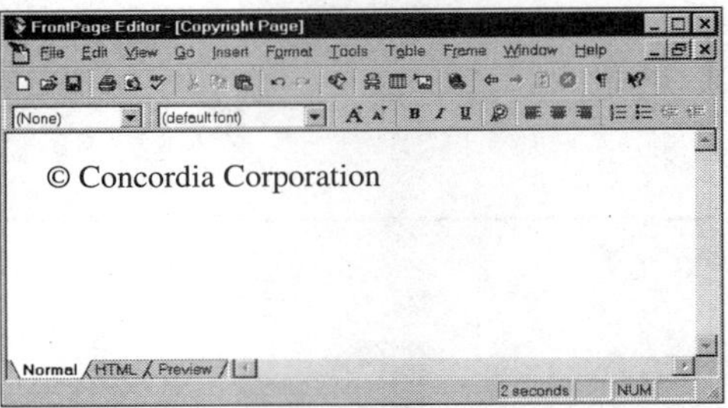

Figure 1. *Create a master Web page that contains the information you want to add to other Web pages.*

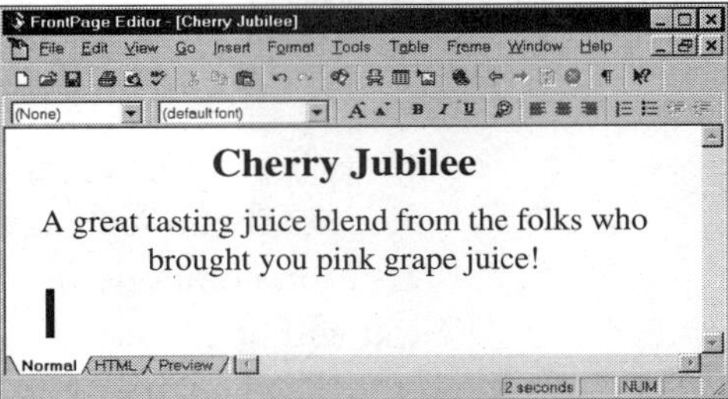

Figure 2. *Position the insertion marker where you want the FrontPage component inserted.*

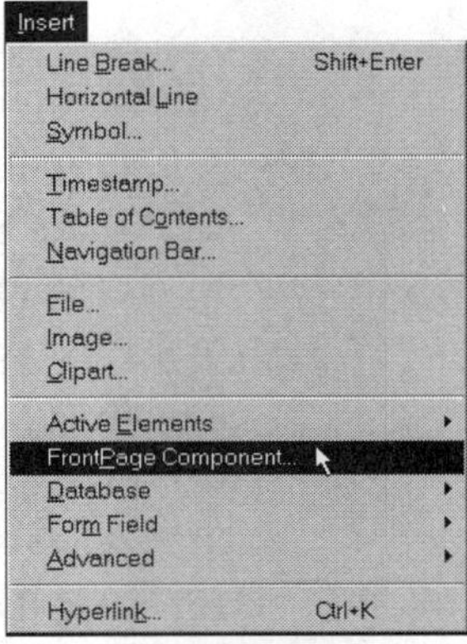

Figure 3. *Choose FrontPage Component from the Insert menu.*

Figure 4. *Click the Insert FrontPage Component button on the Standard toolbar.*

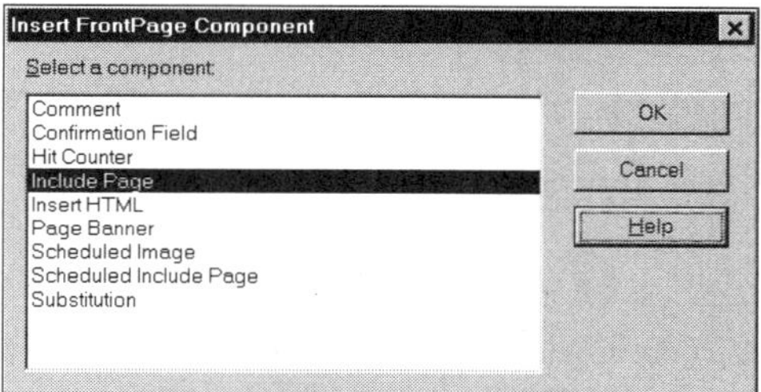

Figure 5. *In the Insert FrontPage Component dialog box, select Include Page, then click OK.*

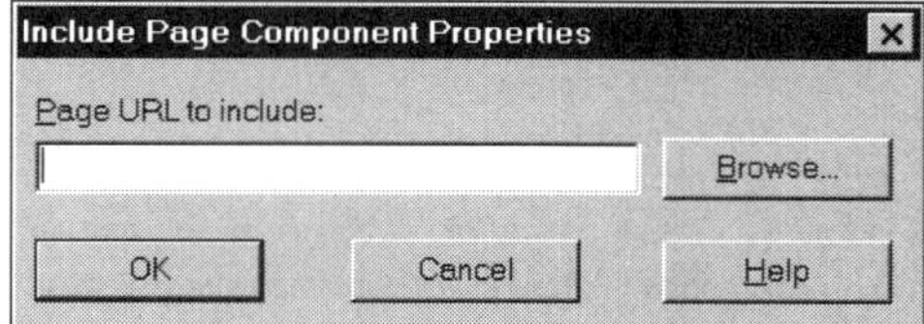

Figure 6. *Click the Browse button in the Include Page Component Properties dialog box.*

To insert the Include Page FrontPage component on a Web page:

1. In the Editor, create the master page with the information you want to include on other pages (**Figure 1**).
2. Open a Web page to which you want to add the contents of the master page.
3. Position the insertion marker on the Web page where you want the FrontPage component to appear (**Figure 2**).
4. Choose FrontPage Component from the Insert menu (**Figure 3**) or click the Insert FrontPage Component button on the Standard toolbar (**Figure 4**). The Insert FrontPage Component dialog box will appear (**Figure 5**).
5. Select Include Page from the Select a component list box, then click OK. The Insert FrontPage Component dialog box will close and the Include Page Component Properties dialog box will appear (**Figure 6**).
6. Click the Browse button. The Current Web dialog box will appear (**Figure 7**). Select the master page from the list box.

7. Click OK. The Current Web dialog box will close and the Web page's filename will appear in the Page URL to include text box in the Include Page Component Properties dialog box (**Figure 8**).

8. Click OK to close the Include Page Component Properties dialog box. The text from the master Web page will appear where the insertion marker was positioned (**Figure 9**).

Tips:

- You can use text and images in the master Web page, but be sure to save the images in the same place as the master Web page. Otherwise, a broken image icon will appear when the page loads.

- When you pass the mouse over an inserted FrontPage component, a little robot appears next to the pointer. This robot is there to remind you that the text or image you're seeing on the Web page is there because of a FrontPage component. (Remember, FrontPage components used to be called WebBots!)

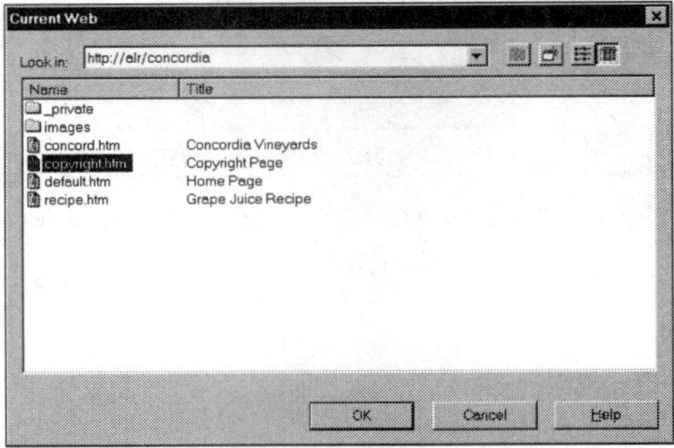

Figure 7. *Select the master Web page from the list box in the Current Web dialog box, then click OK.*

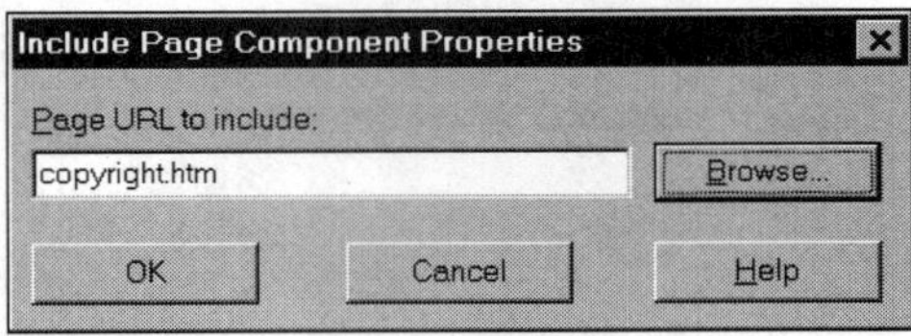

Figure 8. *The filename for the master Web page appears in the Page URL to include text box.*

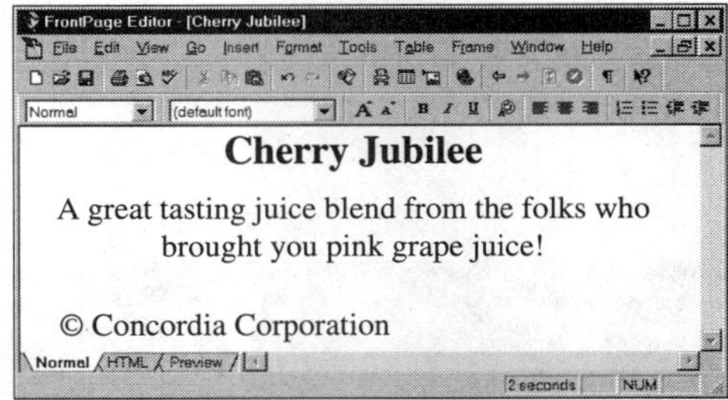

Figure 9. *The text and/or images from the master Web page appear where you positioned the insertion marker.*

Figure 10. *Create the master page containing the information that will appear during a specific time frame.*

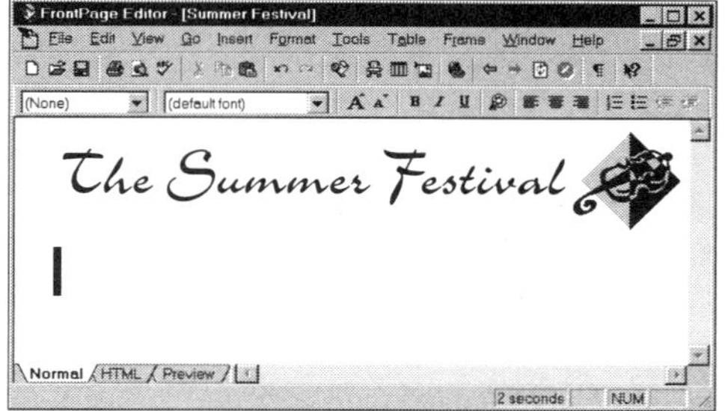

Figure 11. *Position the insertion marker where you want the FrontPage component to appear.*

The Scheduled Include Page FrontPage component

The Scheduled Include Page component works just like the Include Page component except that the information that appears on the Web pages happens only during a specific period of time.

This FrontPage component is handy if you need to announce upcoming events. Instead of having to manually update a Web page to make sure the next event is shown, you can get the Scheduled Include Page component to do it for you automatically. To have a schedule change, you would need to create a master Web page for each schedule change, then insert several Scheduled Include Page components onto the target Web page, one for each change of schedule.

To insert the Scheduled Include Page FrontPage component:

1. In the Editor, create the master page with the information you want to include on other pages (**Figure 10**).
2. Open a Web page to which you want to add the contents of the master page.
3. Position the insertion marker on the Web page where you want the FrontPage component to appear (**Figure 11**).

4. Choose FrontPage Component from the Insert menu (**Figure 3**) or click the Insert FrontPage Component button on the Standard toolbar (**Figure 4**). The Insert FrontPage Component dialog box will appear (**Figure 12**).

5. Select Scheduled Include from the Select a component list box, then click OK. The Insert FrontPage Component dialog box will close and the Scheduled Include Page Component Properties dialog box will appear (**Figure 13**).

6. Click the Browse button next to the Page URL to include text box near the top of the dialog box. The Current Web dialog box will appear (**Figure 14**).

7. Select the master Web page from the list box. This is the information that will appear on the Web page during the scheduled period.

8. Click OK to close the dialog box and return to the Scheduled Include Page Component Properties dialog box.

9. In the Starting date and time area, use the drop-down list boxes to select the year, month, day, and time that the information from the master Web page will appear (**Figure 15**).

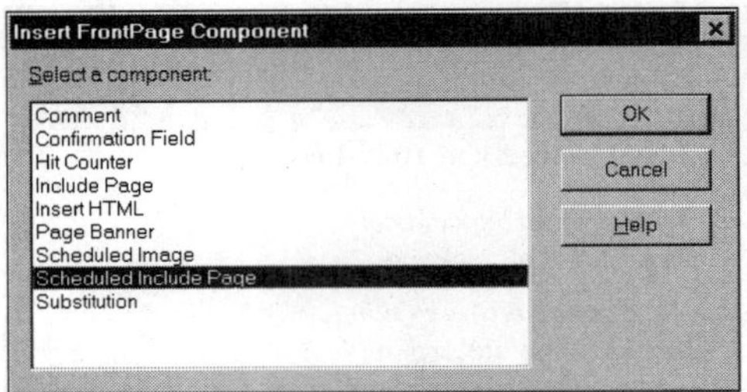

Figure 12. *Select Scheduled Include Page from the list box, then click OK.*

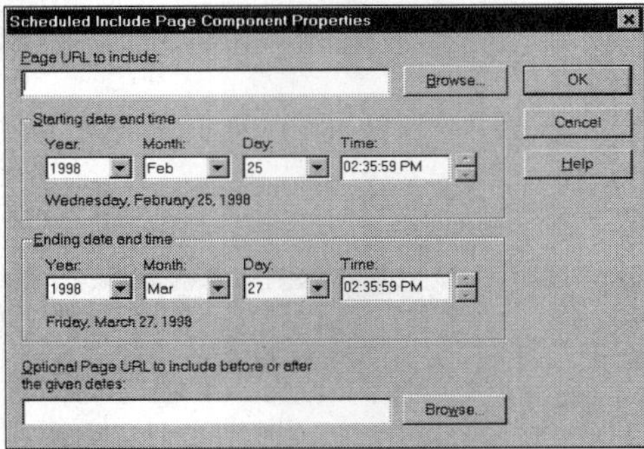

Figure 13. *Click the Browse button near the top of the dialog box.*

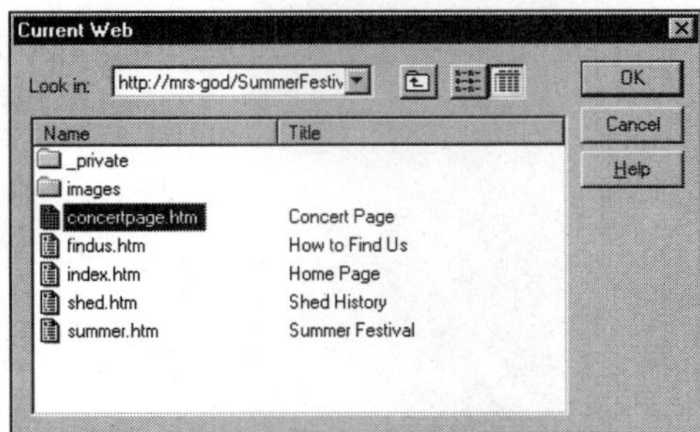

Figure 14. *Select the master Web page from the list box, then click OK.*

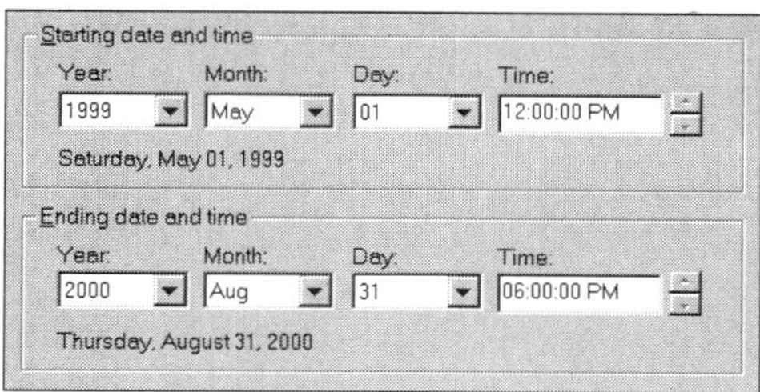

Figure 15. *Use the Starting and Ending date and time areas to set when the information will appear and disappear.*

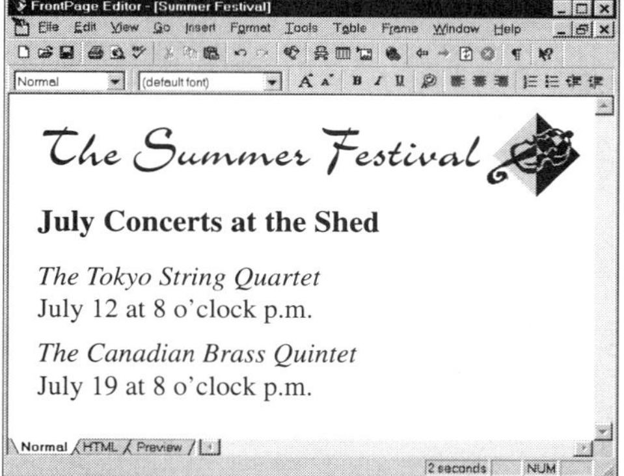

Figure 16. *If the scheduled date and time has not arrived or has gone by, a message appears in the Editor. Otherwise, the information appears in the Web page.*

Images and the Scheduled Include Page FrontPage component

You can use text and images in the master Web page, but be sure to save the images in the same place as the master Web page. Otherwise, a broken image icon will appear when the page loads.

10. In the Ending date and time area, use the drop-down list boxes to select the year, month, day, and time that the information from the master Web page will no longer be valid and will disappear (**Figure 15**).
11. As an optional item, you can add another master page that will be shown before and after the scheduled one, by clicking the Browse button next to the Optional Page URL to include before or after the given dates text box. If you do click the Browse button, the Current Web dialog box will appear (**Figure 14**). Select the master page from the list box, then click OK.
12. When you are finished setting the properties for the Scheduled Include Page component, click OK to close the dialog box. The message *[Expired Scheduled Include Page]* will appear in the Web page if the date and time you scheduled has not arrived yet or has gone by (**Figure 16**). If you added the optional master page, the information from that page will appear instead of the message.

Tip:

- Even though the *[Expired Scheduled Include Page]* message appears on your Web page in the FrontPage Editor, this message will be invisible to anyone browsing your site.

The Scheduled Image FrontPage component

The Scheduled Image FrontPage component works the same as the Scheduled Include Page FrontPage component, but instead of inserting the contents of a master Web page onto a Web page, the Scheduled Image component inserts an image for a specified period of time.

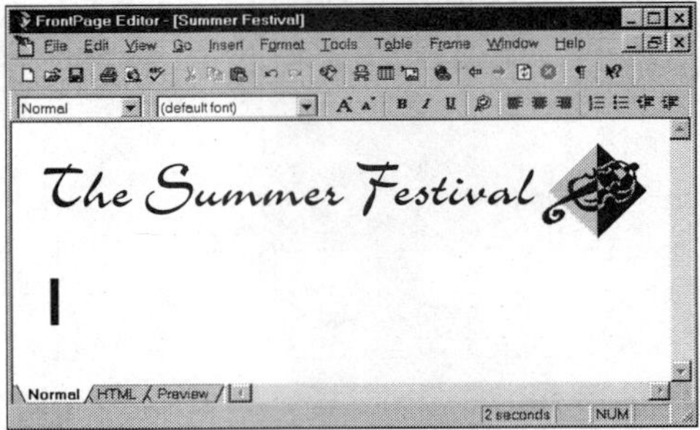

Figure 17. *Position the insertion marker where you want the FrontPage component to appear.*

To insert a Scheduled Image FrontPage component:

1. Create the image you want to appear at the scheduled time and save it in the Web site where you want it to appear.
2. Position the insertion marker on the Web page where you want the FrontPage component to appear (**Figure 17**).
3. Choose FrontPage Component from the Insert menu (**Figure 3**) or click the Insert FrontPage Component button on the Standard toolbar (**Figure 4**). The Insert FrontPage Component dialog box will appear (**Figure 18**).
4. Select Scheduled Image from the Select a component list box, then click OK. The Insert FrontPage Component dialog box will close and the Scheduled Image Properties dialog box will appear (**Figure 19**).

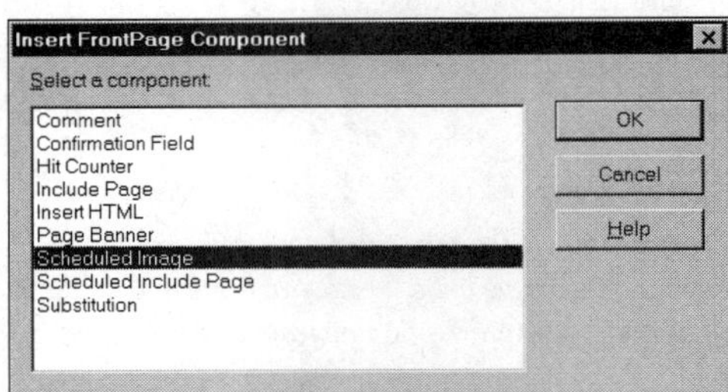

Figure 18. *In the Insert FrontPage Component dialog box, select Scheduled Image, then click OK.*

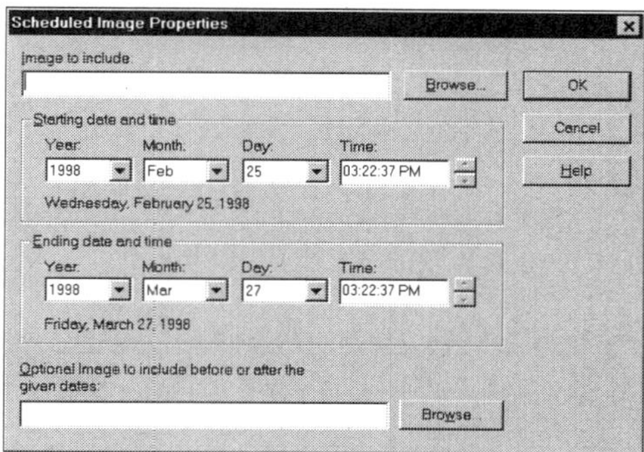

Figure 19. *Click the Browse button near the top of the dialog box.*

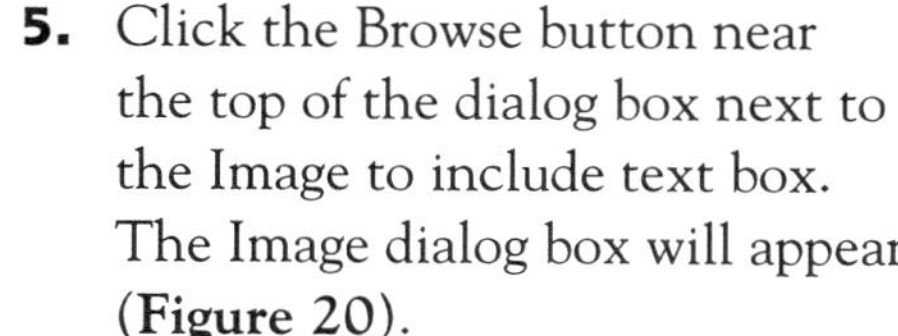

5. Click the Browse button near the top of the dialog box next to the Image to include text box. The Image dialog box will appear (**Figure 20**).

6. Select the image from the list box. (If you don't see the image, you may have saved it in the Images folder. To open the Images folder, double-click on it).

7. Click OK to close the dialog box and return to the Scheduled Image Properties dialog box.

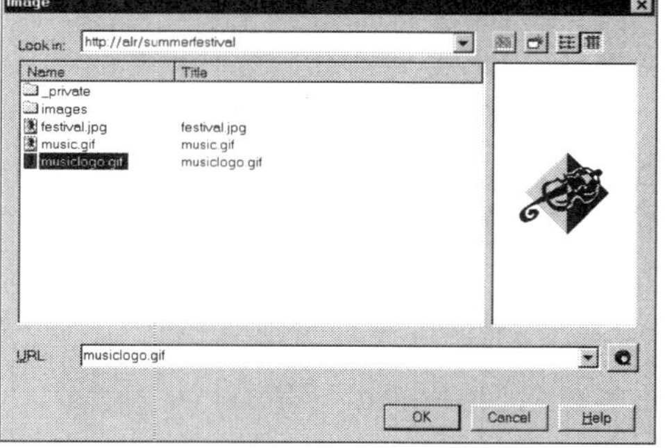

Figure 20. *Select the image using the Image dialog box, then click OK.*

8. In the Starting date and time area, use the drop-down list boxes to select the year, month, day, and time that the image will appear (**Figure 21**).

9. In the Ending date and time area, use the drop-down list boxes to select the year, month, day, and time that the image will no longer be valid and will disappear (**Figure 22**).

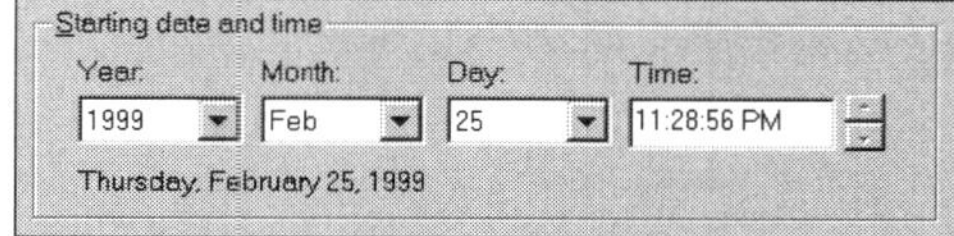

Figure 21. *In the Starting date and time area, use the drop-down list boxes to set the year, month, day, and time.*

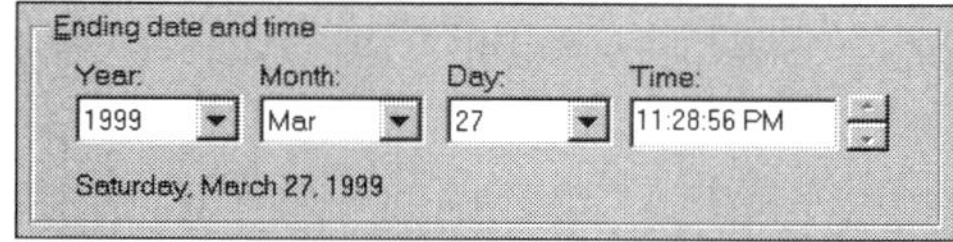

Figure 22. *In the Ending date and time area, use the drop-down list boxes to set the year, month, day, and time.*

10. As an optional item, you can add another image that will be shown before and after the scheduled one, by clicking the Browse button next to the Optional Image to include before or after the given dates text box. If you do click the Browse button, the Image dialog box will appear (**Figure 23**). Select the image from the list box, then click OK.

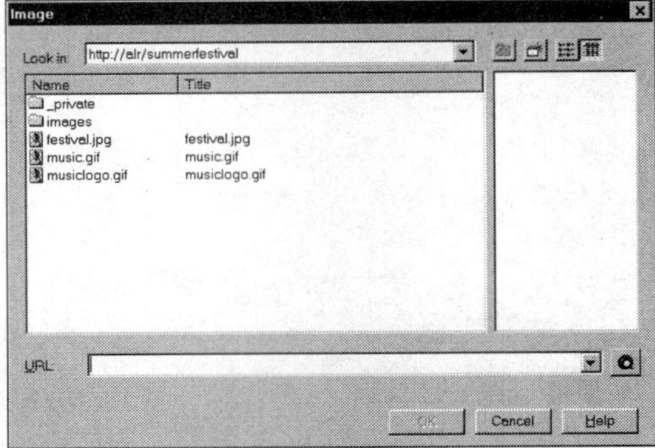

Figure 23. *Use the Image dialog box to select an alternate image.*

11. When you are finished setting the properties for the Scheduled Image FrontPage component, click OK to close the dialog box. The message *[Expired Scheduled Image]* will appear in the Web page if the date and time you scheduled has not arrived yet or has gone by (**Figure 24**). If you added the optional image, that image will appear instead of the *[Expired Scheduled Image]* message.

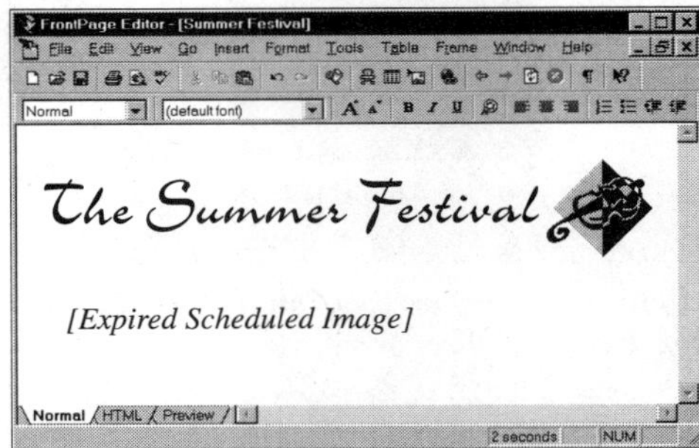

Figure 24. *If the scheduled date and time has not arrived yet or has passed by, the message [Expired Scheduled Image] appears in the Editor. Otherwise, the image appears in the Web page.*

Tip:

- Even though the *[Expired Scheduled Image]* message appears on your Web page in the FrontPage Editor, this message will be invisible to anyone browsing your site.

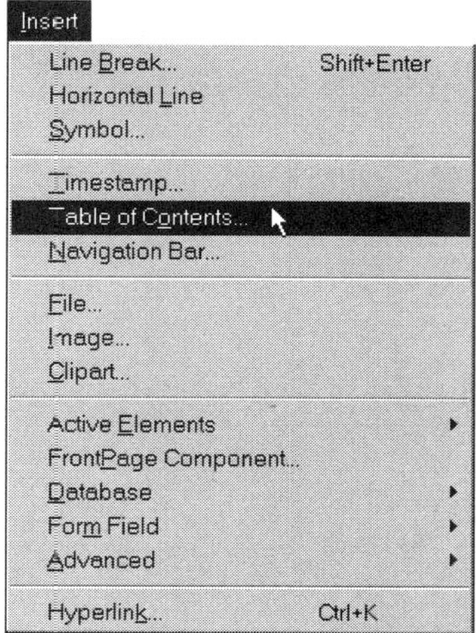

Figure 25. *Choose Table of Contents from the Insert Menu.*

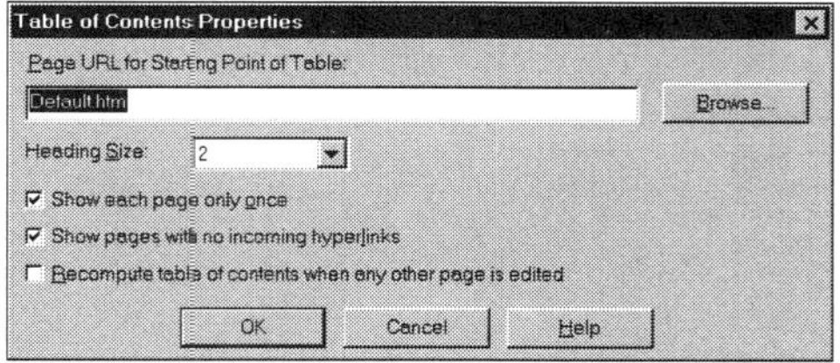

Figure 26. *Use the Table of Contents Properties dialog box to set which page to use as a starting point for the table of contents, set heading size, and set Web page options.*

The Table of Contents FrontPage component

A great way to help folks browsing your site find their way around is to include a table of contents. A good table of contents shows the titles for the entire site's Web pages with links to each page. If you have a large site, the enormity of this task can be overwhelming. This is where the Table of Contents FrontPage component comes in. This component will create a full hierarchical table of contents with links *and* it will automatically update the table of contents if any pages change.

To insert a Table of Contents FrontPage component:

1. Position the insertion marker on the Web page where you would like the table of contents to appear.
2. Choose Table of Contents from the Insert menu (**Figure 25**).The Table of Contents Properties dialog box will appear (**Figure 26**).
3. The Page URL for Starting Point of Table text box automatically displays the home page for the Web site. This is the page that will appear at the top of the Table of Contents. If you want a different page to appear in this position in the Table of Contents:

a. Click the Browse button next to the text box. The Current Web dialog box will appear (**Figure 27**).

b. Select a Web page from the list box, then click OK to return to the Table of Contents Properties dialog box.

4. Use the Heading Size drop-down list to select the type size for the first item in the table of contents (**Figure 28**). By default, the heading will be the title of the page the Table of Contents Component is on. (Heading sizes are discussed in detail on page 128). If you don't want a heading, select none.

5. Put a check mark in the Show each page only once check box, if you want each page to appear only once in the table of contents (**Figure 29**). If you don't select this option, Web pages with links to more than one page in the Web site will appear more than once in the table of contents.

6. Put a check mark in the Show pages with no incoming hyperlinks check box, if you want pages without any hyperlinks to appear in the table of contents. If you select this option, the only access the user will have to these pages will be through the table of contents.

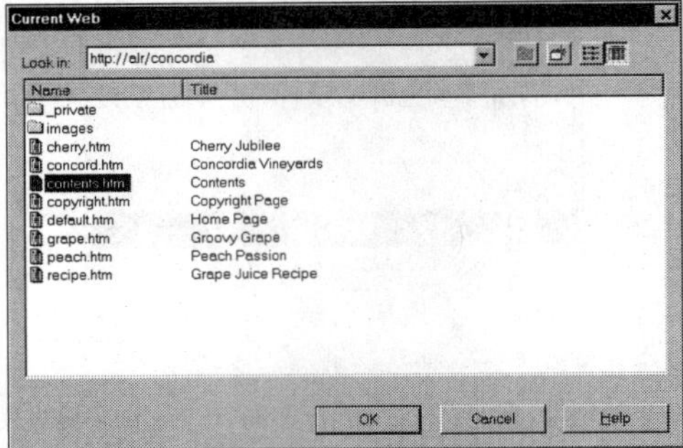

Figure 27. *If you want to select a different starting point for the table of contents, use the list box in the Current Web dialog box to select a Web page.*

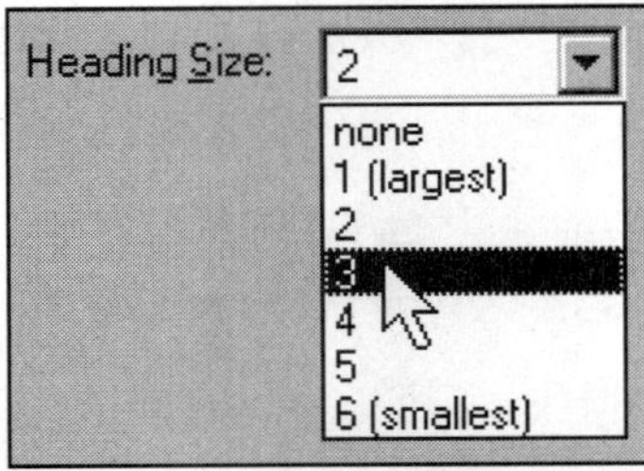

Figure 28. *Use the Heading Size drop-down list to select the type size of the first item in the table of contents.*

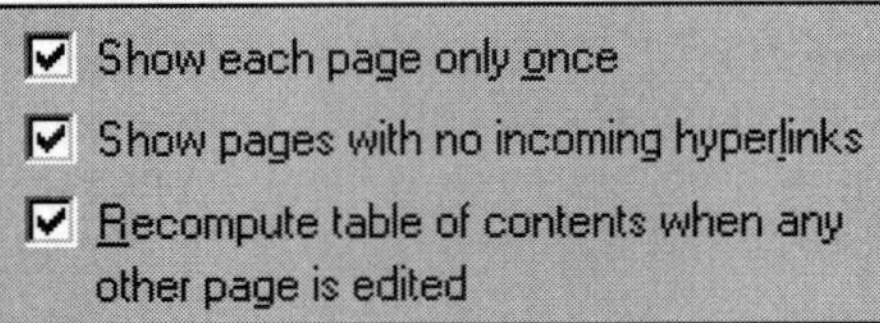

Figure 29. *Use the check boxes to set how many times a page is shown, to show pages with no links to them, and to automatically update if any Web pages change.*

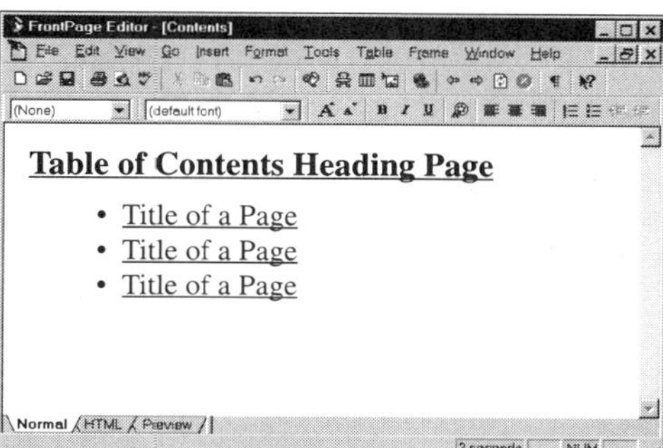

Figure 30. *No matter how large the table of contents will actually be, a four-line placeholder appears in the Web page in the Editor.*

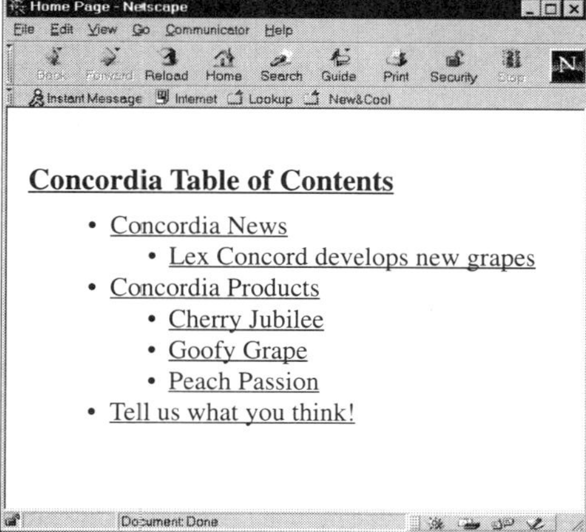

Figure 31. *To see the actual table of contents, view the Web page in a browser.*

7. Put a check mark in the Recompute table of contents when any other page is edited check box, if you want the FrontPage component to automatically update the table of contents when a Web page changes. If you don't select this option and a Web page changes, you will have to recalculate the site's hyperlinks manually. (Recalculating hyperlinks is discussed in Chapter 19 on page 321).

8. When you are finished setting options, click OK. A table of contents placeholder appears in the Editor (**Figure 30**). To see the actual table of contents with all its topics, view the Web page in a browser (**Figure 31**).

Tip:

- You can't see the actual table of contents in the Preview tab; you need to view it in your browser.

The Timestamp FrontPage component

The Timestamp FrontPage component is used to insert the time and/or date a Web page was last modified. This can be a handy way to help you keep track of updated pages on your Web site. It can also let users who browse your site frequently know that there's something new on a particular Web page.

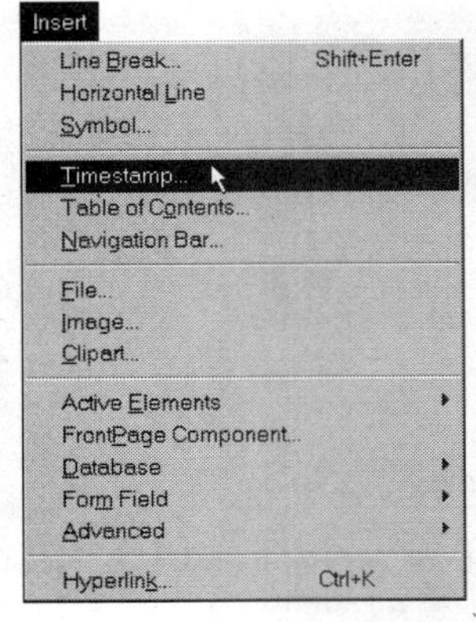

Figure 32. *Choose Timestamp from the Insert Menu.*

To insert a Timestamp FrontPage component:

1. Position the insertion marker on the Web page where you would like the timestamp to appear.
2. Choose Timestamp from the Insert menu (**Figure 32**). The Timestamp Properties dialog box will appear (**Figure 33**).
3. Depending on what you want displayed, select either the Date this page was last edited radio button or the Date this page was last automatically updated radio button.
4. Use the Date Format drop-down list to select the way the date will be displayed (**Figure 34**). If you don't want to display the date, select (none).

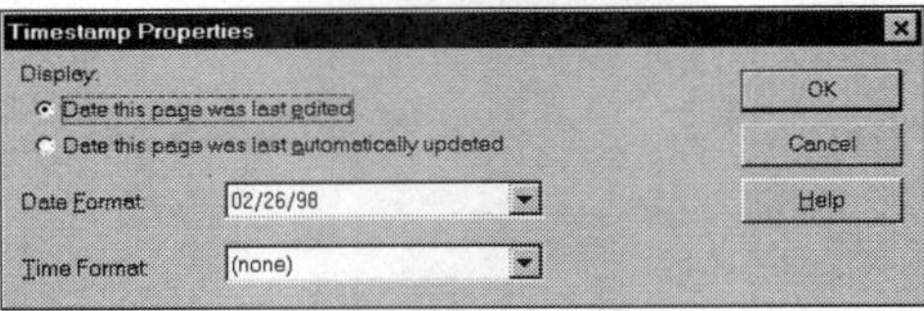

Figure 33. *Use the Timestamp Properties dialog box to set when the timestamp updates and whether it displays the date and/or time.*

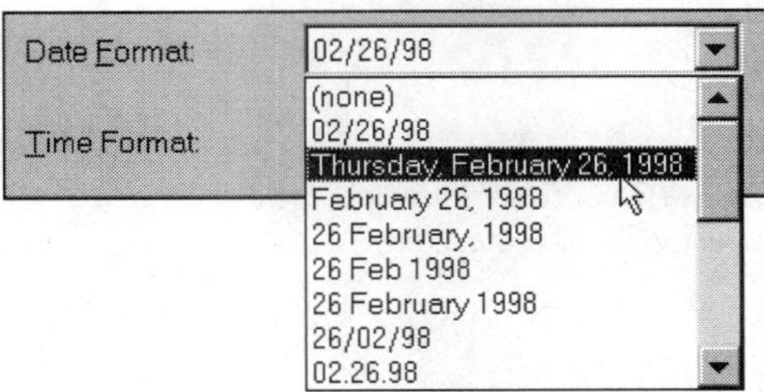

Figure 34. *Use the Date Format drop-down list to select the way the date is displayed.*

Figure 35. *Use the Time Format drop-down list to select how the time will be displayed.*

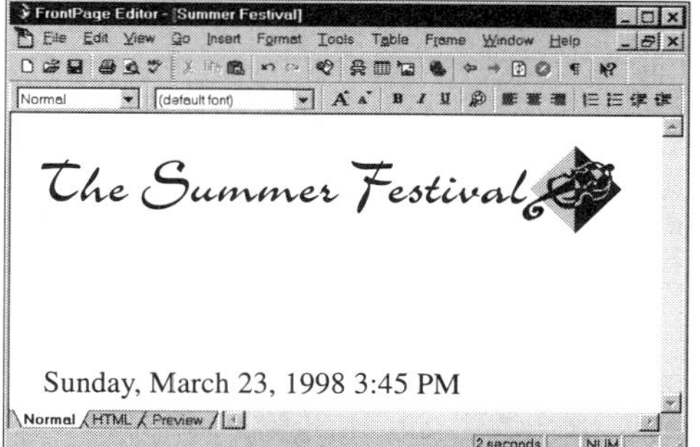

Figure 36. *The timestamp appears where the insertion marker was placed.*

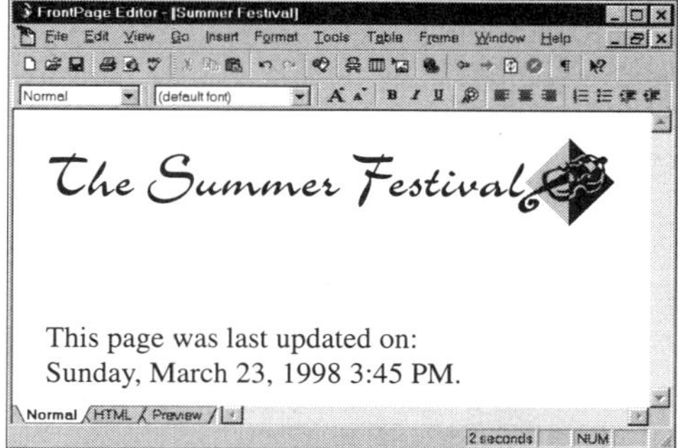

Figure 37. *You can add text before and after a timestamp to indicate the purpose of the timestamp.*

5. Use the Time Format drop-down list to select the way the time will be displayed (**Figure 35**). If you don't want to display the time, select (none).

6. When you are finished selecting date and time options, click OK. The date and/or time the Web page was last modified will appear where you positioned the insertion marker (**Figure 36**).

Tip:

- You can add text before and after the Timestamp FrontPage component, indicating what the timestamp is for (**Figure 37**).

What's My Time Zone?

If you want to set a timestamp showing your time zone after the time, select one of the time formats with the letters "TZ" after it from the Time Format dialog box.

A hit counter tells you the number of people who have visited your site. This is an excellent device for tracking how many (or few!) visitors you've had.

To insert a Hit Counter FrontPage component:

1. Open the Web page into which you want to insert a hit counter, and place the insertion point where you want the hit counter to go.
2. Choose FrontPage Component from the Insert menu (**Figure 3**) or click the Insert FrontPage Component button on the Standard toolbar (**Figure 4**). You'll see the Insert FrontPage Component dialog box (**Figure 38**).
3. Choose Hit Counter and click OK. You'll see the Hit Counter Properties dialog box (**Figure 39**).
4. Under Counter Style, choose a look for your counter (**Figure 40**).
5. If you want to reset your counter, select the Reset counter to check box and enter a starting value in the accompanying text box (**Figure 41**).
6. If you want the hit counter to be a fixed number of digits, instead of however many digits it takes to accommodate the number of visitors, click the Fixed number of digits check box and enter the number of digits in the accompanying text box (**Figure 42**).

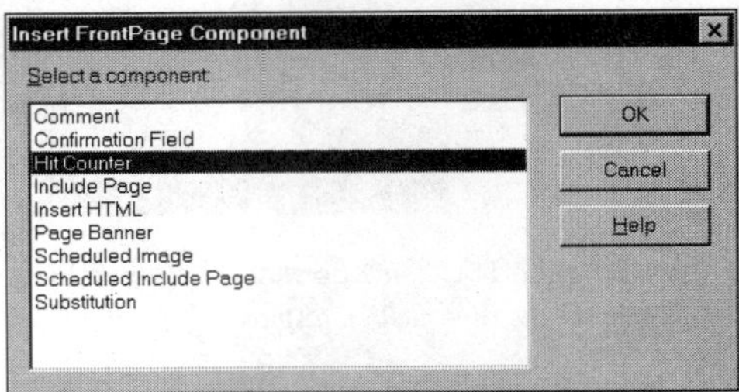

Figure 38. *In the Insert FrontPage Component dialog box, select Hit Counter, then click OK.*

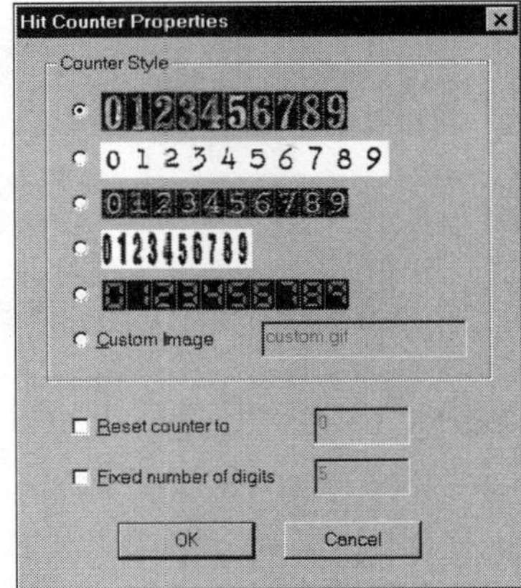

Figure 39. *In the Hit Counter Properties dialog box, you can choose the counter style, the starting number, and the number of digits to use in the counter.*

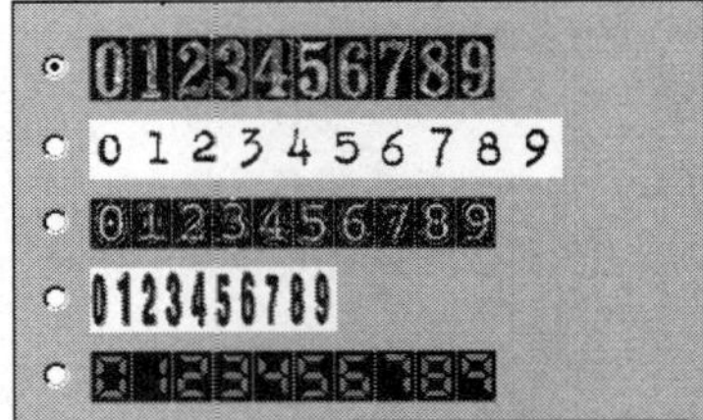

Figure 40. *You can choose from among five preset counter styles.*

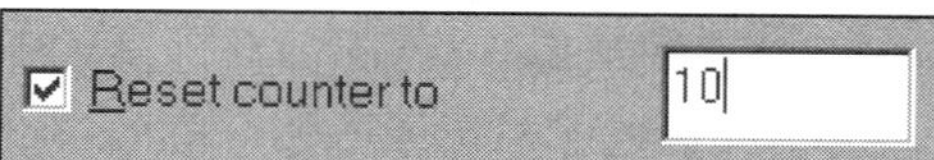

Figure 41. *Select the Reset counter to check box and enter a starting value for your counter.*

Figure 42. *Select the Fixed number of digits check box and choose a number of digits for the counter.*

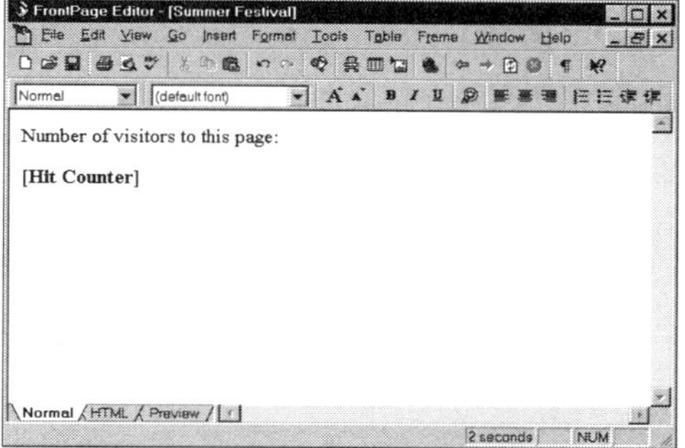

Figure 43. *When you insert a hit counter, you'll just see this placeholder in your page. To see the hit counter itself, you need to preview the page in a browser.*

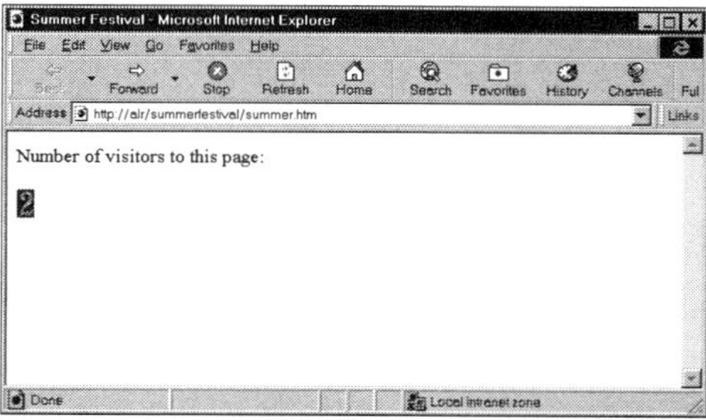

Figure 44. *When you preview the page containing the hit counter in a browser, you should see a counter showing how many visitors your site has had.*

7. When you've chosen the settings you want in the Hit Counter Properties dialog box, click OK. You'll see the text [Hit Counter] (**Figure 43**).

8. To see how many visitors you've had, save the page and preview it in your browser (**Figure 44**).

Tips:

- If you want to use a customized GIF to give the hit counter a specialized look, you can click the Custom Image check box. Enter the URL for the GIF file in the text box to the right. The file should contain the digits 0 through 9, from left to right, as is shown in the Counter Style area of Figure 39. FrontPage 98 needs the 10 digits that would be used to make up a number.

- You can put text before and or after a hit counter to make its purpose extra clear. For example, you could have the text "Number of visitors to this page:" before the hit counter.

After you've inserted a FrontPage component, you may need to edit its properties. This is easy to do.

To edit a FrontPage component's properties:

1. Select the FrontPage component whose properties you want to edit.
2. Right-click the component and choose FrontPage Component Properties from the pop-up menu (**Figure 45**). The appropriate properties dialog box for that FrontPage component will appear. (If you need help with the properties dialog box for a FrontPage component, take a look at the directions for inserting that particular FrontPage component in this chapter.)
3. Edit the component's properties, then click OK to return to the Editor.

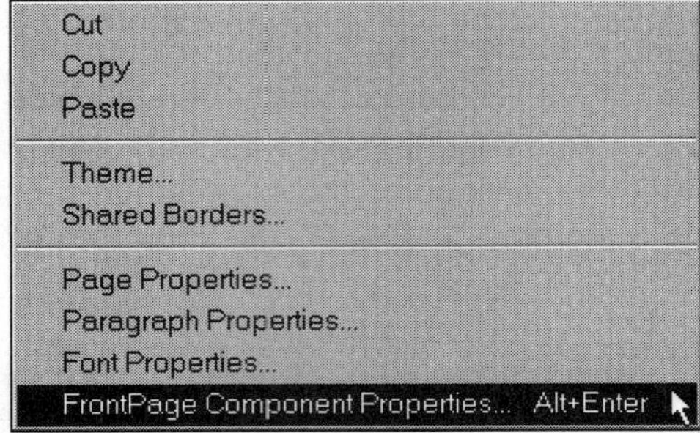

Figure 45. *Choose FrontPage Component Properties from the pop-up menu.*

ANOTHER WAY TO ACCESS A FRONTPAGE COMPONENT'S PROPERTIES

Select the FrontPage component with the mouse pointer, then press Alt+Enter on the keyboard. The appropriate properties dialog box for that FrontPage component will open.

SUMMARY

In this chapter you learned how to:

- Add an Include Page FrontPage component
- Insert a Scheduled Include Page FrontPage component
- Insert a Scheduled Image FrontPage component
- Add a Table of Contents FrontPage component
- Add a Timestamp FrontPage component
- Add a Hit Counter FrontPage component
- Edit the properties of a FrontPage component

Edit a FrontPage Component's Properties

18 Forms and User Input

Forms add user interactivity to Web pages. Instead of just browsing a page, a user can input information, letting her search your Web site, register for events, complete surveys, order items, and so on.

Forms work by collecting information from users who enter it into text boxes or select specific items using radio buttons and drop-down lists. These places, where users enter information, are called *form fields*. After entering information into the form fields, users click a button, submitting the information.

When submitted, this information is organized into *name* and *value* pairs. A name is a unique label assigned to a field. This field name is invisible to users; it only appears in the HTML code. A value is the information submitted by the users in a particular field.

After the information is submitted, a *form handler* (a program on a Web server) takes the form data and processes it, responding to the user by displaying a confirmation page, while saving the information or formatting the results as a Web page and sending it back to the browser.

FrontPage forms use special form FrontPage components (see Chapter 17). In order for these components to work, your Web site must be loaded on a server that supports the FrontPage Server Extensions. (For more about finding Internet Service Providers who support the FrontPage Server Extensions, see page 26.)

Form Templates Make Life Incredibly Easy

FrontPage ships with a number of page templates and wizards that quickly create forms. You can get started with a template or wizard and, if you need to, modify it to suit your needs.

- Confirmation Form: this form helps you generate a confirmation page to acknowledge that you have received information from a form a user submitted.
- Feedback Form: this form is used to collect comments and suggestions from folks using your site.
- Form Page Wizard: this wizard lets you design a custom form.
- Guest Book: this form collects a person's information, and saves the submissions on a public Web page.
- Product or Event Registration: this form lets customers register products or register for events.
- Search Page: this form uses the Search FrontPage component to create an index of your Web pages, letting users perform word searches of your site.
- Survey Form: this form is great for collecting customer information about popular opinions, marketing, and specific products.
- User Registration: this form lets users create a Web site log on name and password for access to a members-only Web site.

Figure 1. *Click the Show FrontPage Editor button on the Explorer's toolbar.*

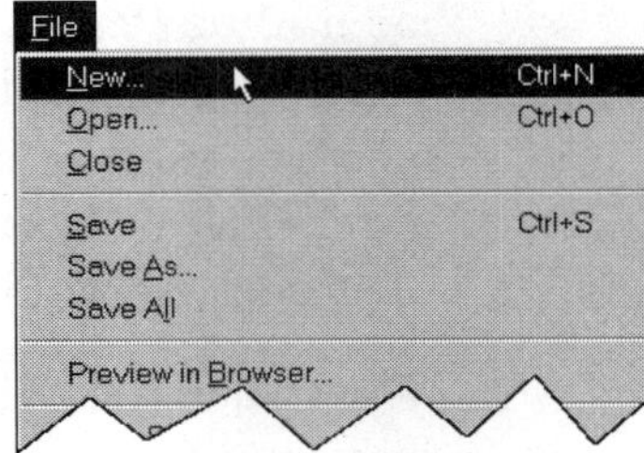

Figure 2. *Choose New from the Editor's File menu.*

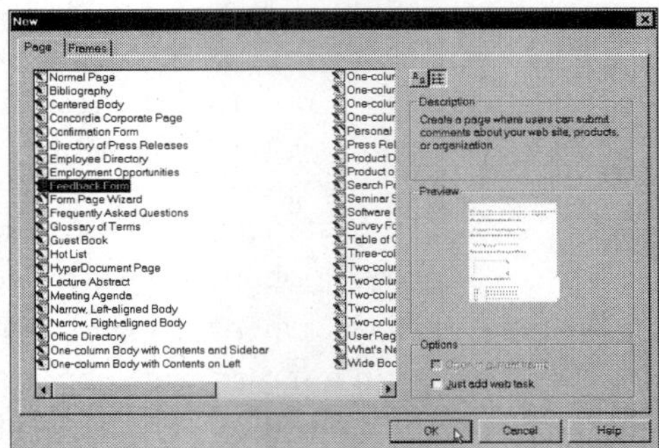

Figure 3. *In the New dialog box, select a form template or wizard from the list box, then click OK.*

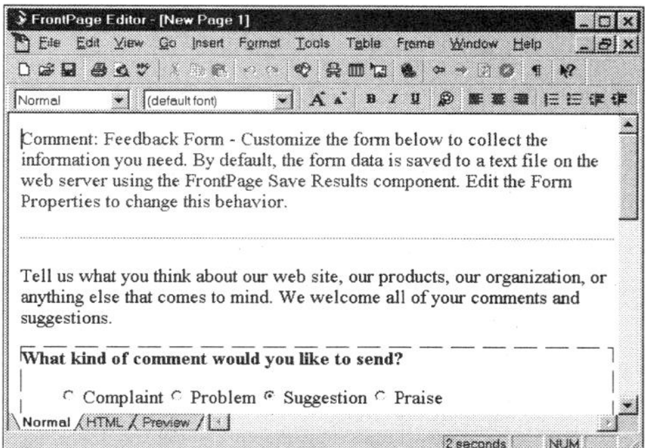

Figure 4. *The new form Web page appears in the Editor.*

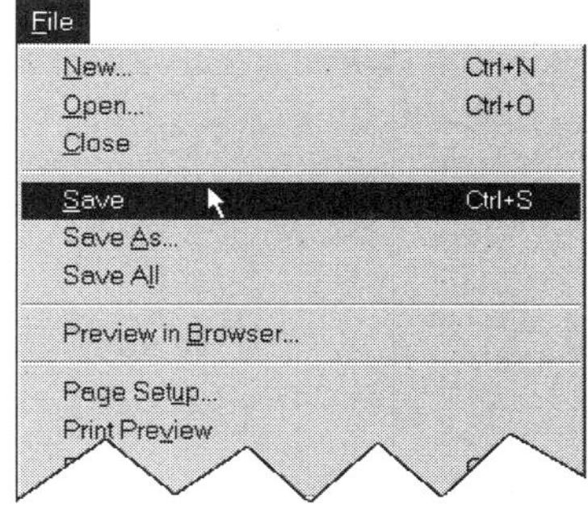

Figure 5. *Choose Save from the File menu.*

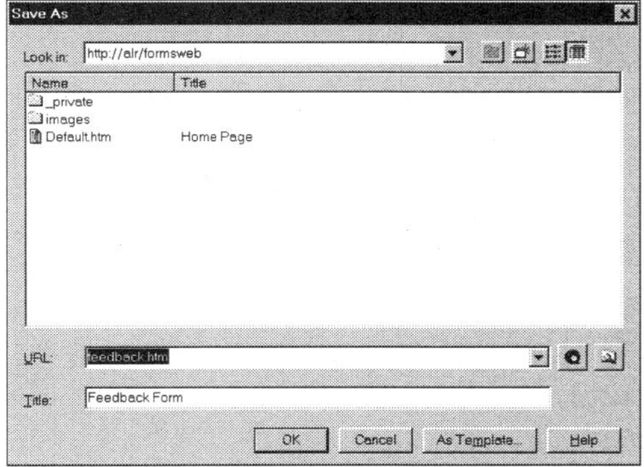

Figure 6. *Use the Save As dialog box to give the page a file name and title.*

To create a Web page using one of the form templates:

1. Using the Explorer, open the Web site to which you want to add the page.
2. Launch the Editor by double-clicking one of the Web pages in the Explorer or clicking the Show FrontPage Editor button on the toolbar (**Figure 1**).
3. In the Editor, choose New from the File menu (**Figure 2**). The New dialog box will appear (**Figure 3**).
4. Select one of the form templates from the list box, then click OK. The new Web page will appear in the Editor (**Figure 4**). (For this example, the Feedback Form has been selected.)
5. Customize the form as needed. (You'll learn how to modify form field properties throughout this chapter.)
6. Save the new page by choosing Save from the File menu (**Figure 5**). The Save As dialog box will appear (**Figure 6**).
7. Use the text boxes to set the page's title and its file name. (For the example feedback form, the title is set as Feedback Form and the file name as feedback.htm.)
8. Click OK to save the Web page and close the Save As dialog box.

Form Field Types

If you take a look at the feedback form just created in the previous section, you'll see that it includes several kinds of form fields. Actually, the Feedback Form contains at least one of every form field type, including two push buttons.

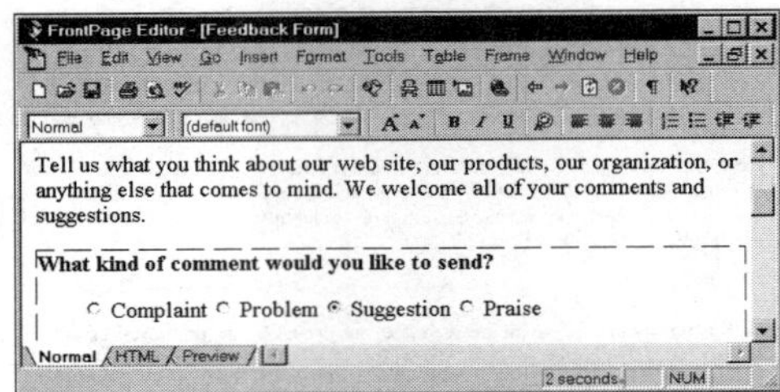

Figure 7. *Radio buttons are used in groups, letting the user select an item from a number of options.*

- *Radio buttons*—Beneath the line, "What kind of comment would you like to send?" you'll see a group of radio buttons (**Figure 7**). Radio buttons work together as a group. They are used when you want the user to select a specific option from a group of options.
- *Drop-down menu*—Beneath the line, "What about us do you want to comment on?" is what FrontPage calls a drop-down menu (**Figure 8**). (Some folks call this form field a drop-down list.) The choices on the menu can be customized when you set the form field's properties.

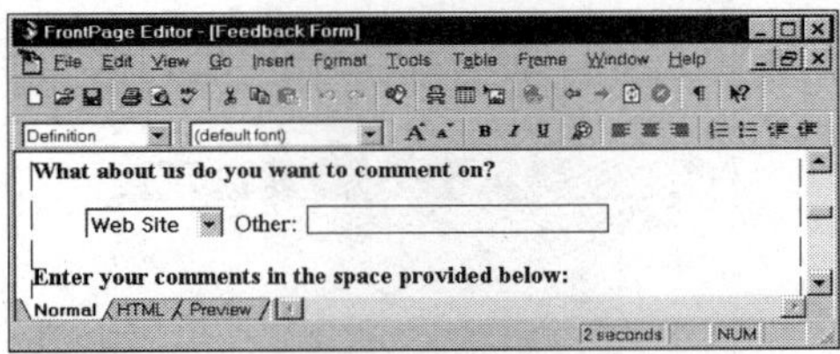

Figure 8. *Drop-down menus let the user select from a list or menu of items.*

- *One-line text box*—Right next to the drop-down list (to the right of the word "Other") is what FrontPage calls a one-line text box (**Figure 9**). Users of your site can type text into this form field.
- *Scrolling text box*—Below "Enter your comments in the space provided below" is a scrolling text box (**Figure 10**). (This is sometimes called a multiline text box.) This text box lets users enter long descriptions or comments.

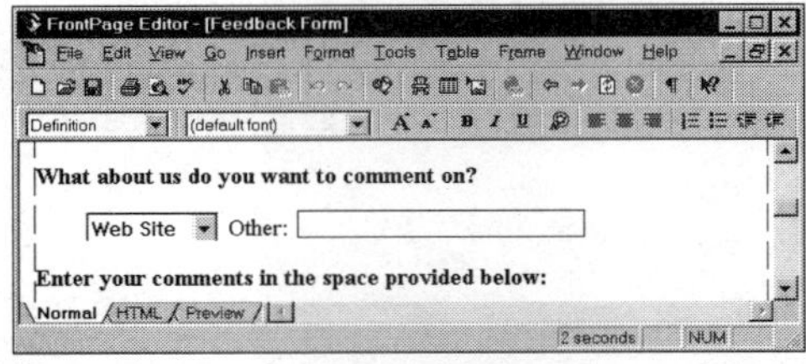

Figure 9. *One-line text boxes let users enter a line of text.*

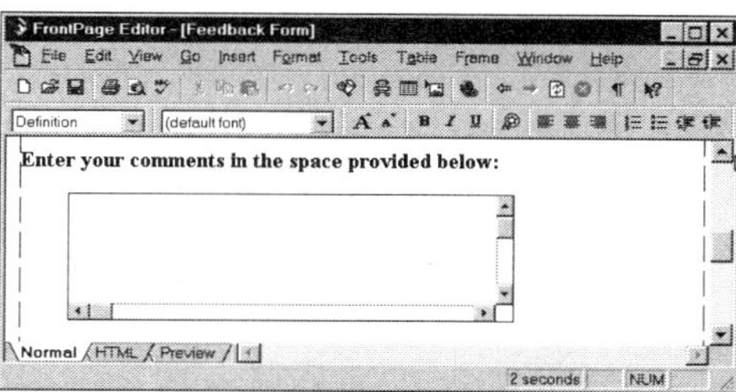

Figure 10. *A scrolling text box lets users enter several lines of text.*

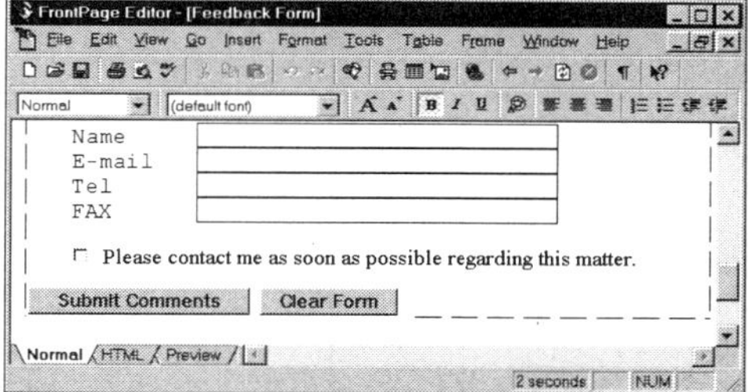

Figure 11. *A check box lets a user decide between a yes or no choice. Push buttons make something happen when the user clicks them.*

- *Check box*—Near the bottom of the form, next to "Please contact me as soon as possible regarding this matter" is a check box (**Figure 11**). Check boxes let users decide between a yes or no choice.
- *Push button*—Below the check box are two push buttons (**Figure 11**). This type of button usually has a few words on it, describing what will happen if users click it. (There are also Image form fields, which are similar to push buttons but have an image on them instead of text.) There are three types of push buttons to choose from: Submit, Reset, and Normal. Submit buttons pass the form data to the selected form handler; Reset buttons reset the form to its original state. You have to assign a script (like a program) to Normal buttons for them to do anything.

CREATING FORMS USING TABLES

If you decide to design your own form or modify an existing one, you can use tables to line up the form fields. (Create the form first, then create the table within it, and then add form fields within the table.) To make the table invisible, use the Table Properties dialog box to set the border width to 0 (see page 187).

Inserting form fields

The next sections show you how to add each of the form fields described on pages 292–293 and how to set their properties.

To make adding form fields easy, you should use the Form Fields toolbar (**Figure 12**).

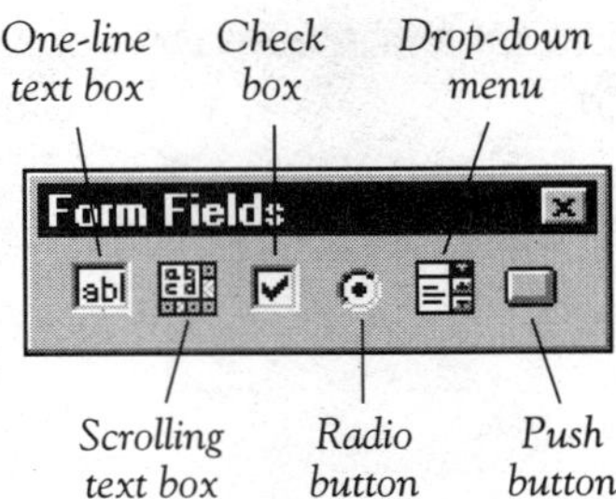

Figure 12. *The Form Fields toolbar lets you quickly add fields to a form.*

To view the Form Fields toolbar:

Choose Forms Toolbar from the View menu (**Figure 13**). The Form Fields toolbar will appear.

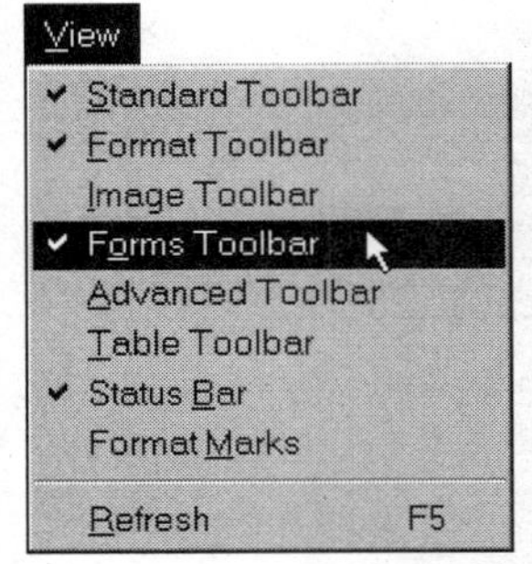

Figure 13. *Choose Forms Toolbar from the View menu.*

Radio Buttons

Radio buttons work as a group. They present a group of options that you must decide between, picking only one. Each radio button needs a *Group Name* and a *Value*. The Group Name must be the same for all the radio buttons in the group and the Value is what that particular button represents. For instance, suppose you wanted to find out someone's favorite ice cream flavor. You could set up a group of radio buttons. The Group Name for the entire group of radio buttons could be FavoriteFlavor and the Value for one radio button could be Vanilla while the Value for another radio button could be Chocolate.

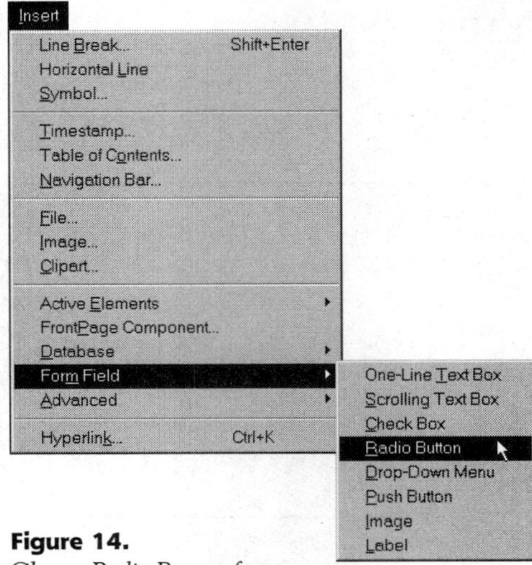

Figure 14. *Choose Radio Button from the Form Field fly-out found on the Insert menu.*

View the Form Fields Toolbar

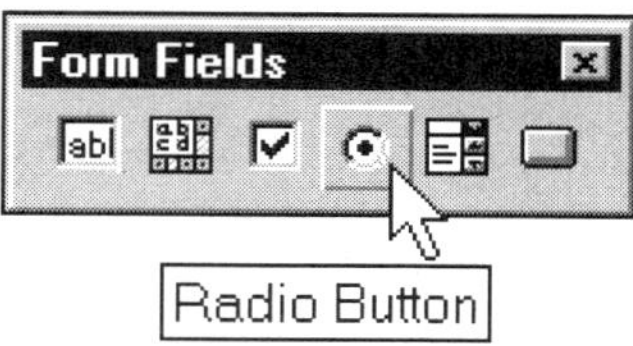

Figure 15. *Click Radio Button on the Form Fields toolbar.*

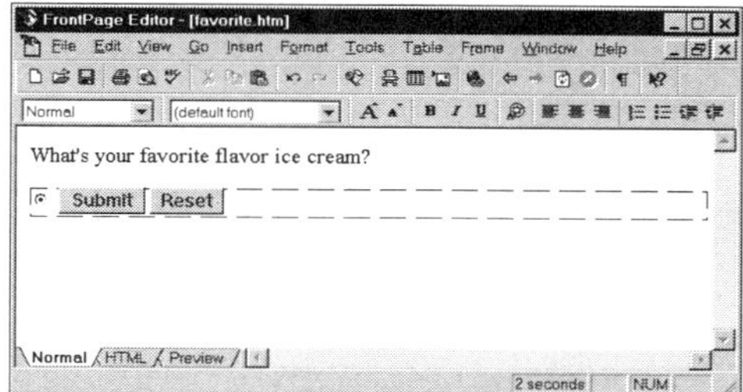

Figure 16. *The radio button appears where the insertion marker was positioned and a dashed rectangle appears around the form area.*

Figure 17. *Choose Form Field Properties from the pop-up menu.*

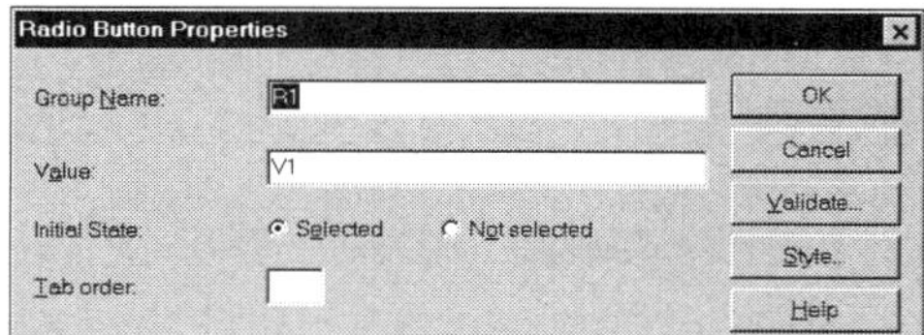

Figure 18. *The Radio Button Properties dialog box opens with default values in the Group Name and Value text boxes.*

To insert a group of radio buttons:

1. Position the insertion marker where you want to add the radio button group.
2. Choose Radio Button from the Form Field fly-out on the Insert menu (**Figure 14**) or click Radio Button on the Form Fields toolbar (**Figure 15**). A radio button will appear on the Web page (**Figure 16**). You'll also see two push buttons, labeled Submit and Reset.
3. Right-click the radio button and select Form Field Properties from the pop-up menu (**Figure 17**) or double-click the radio button. The Radio Button Properties dialog box will appear (**Figure 18**).
4. Enter the name for the group of radio buttons in the Group Name text box (**Figure 19**). For the ice cream flavor example, the Group Name is FavoriteFlavor. (Note that you can't use spaces in the names.)
5. Type in the value for the radio button in the Value text box. For the ice cream flavor example, this radio button's Value is Vanilla.
6. Use the Initial State radio buttons to set whether this radio button will be the one that is selected when the Web page first opens. (Selecting any button deselects any previously selected button.)

7. In the Tab order text box, enter a number that will determine how users move between form fields when they press the Tab key. (Only Internet Explorer 4.0 and later browsers support this feature.)
8. Click OK to close the Radio Button Properties dialog box and return to the Editor window.
9. Click the mouse to the right of the radio button. The insertion marker will appear there, blinking. Type in the value for that radio button (**Figure 20**). Even though you gave the button a value in the Radio Button Properties dialog box, you still need to give the button a descriptive label in the Web page itself. For the ice cream flavor example, you would type Vanilla.
10. Position the insertion marker where you want to add the next radio button for the group. This may be to the right of the first radio button or below it.
11. Create a second radio button and set its Group Name and Value properties by repeating steps 2 through 9. For the ice cream flavor example, the Group Name would be FavoriteFlavor (just like the first radio button) and the Value would be Chocolate.
12. Click the mouse to the right of the second radio button and type in the value for that radio button (**Figure 21**). For the ice cream flavor example, you would type Chocolate.

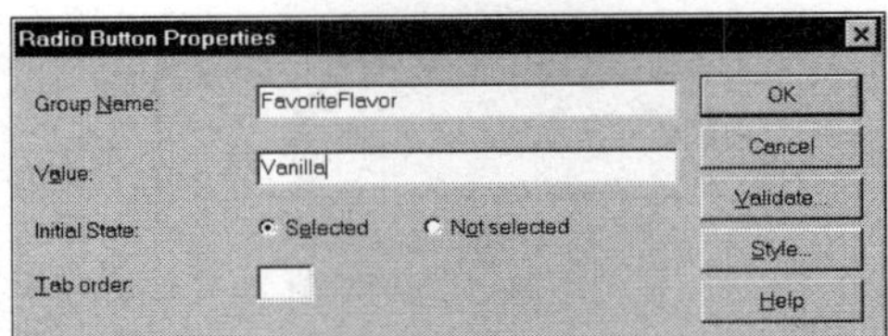

Figure 19. *Use the text boxes to enter a group name and value for the radio button.*

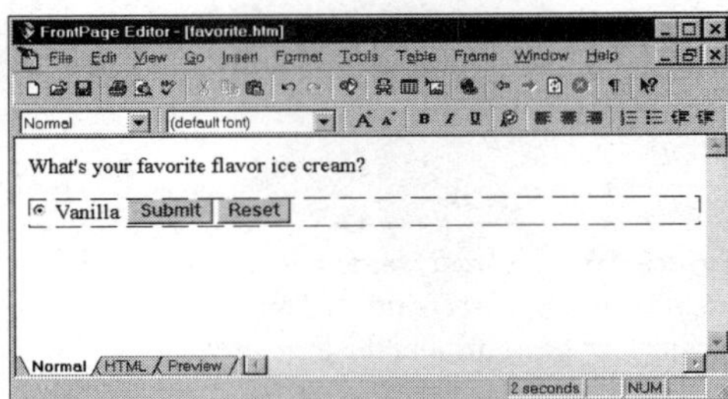

Figure 20. *Type a descriptive label next to the radio button, indicating what the choice is to the user.*

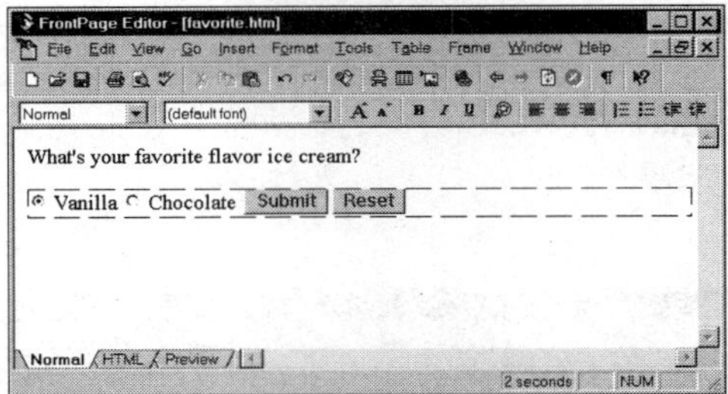

Figure 21. *Add a second radio button to give the user something to choose between.*

13. Continue following steps 2 through 10 until you have created all the options you want the user to choose from (**Figure 22**).

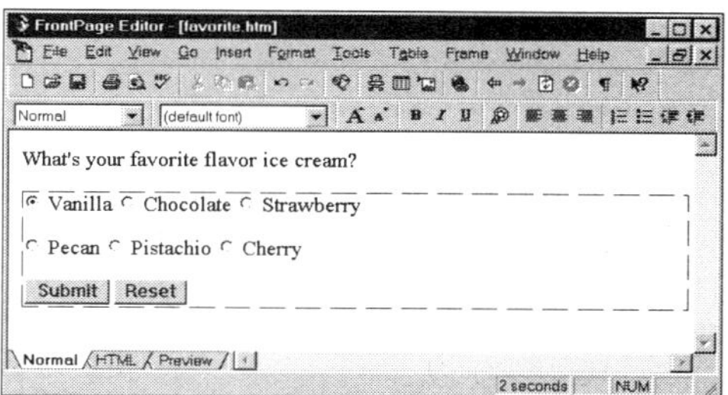

Figure 22. *Continue adding radio buttons to the group until you have added all the items you want the user to choose from.*

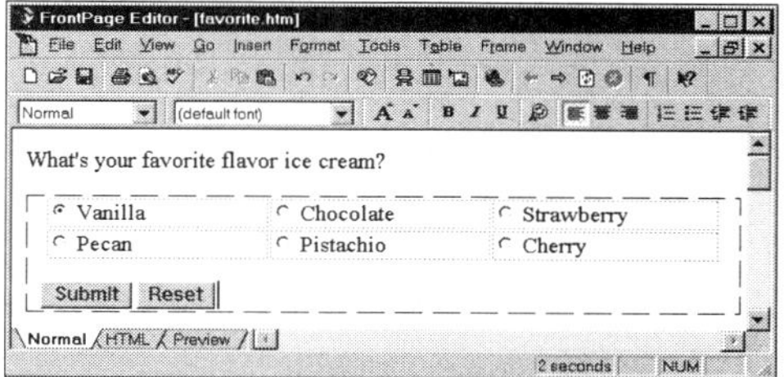

Figure 23. *You can use a table with invisible borders to line up the radio buttons.*

Tips:

- When you insert your first form field, FrontPage automatically creates a form—indicated by a dashed rectangle—and adds Submit and Reset buttons to it. Adding additional form fields within the form doesn't generate new push buttons, but adding more form fields outside the form does.
- An easy way to get radio buttons to line up is to use an invisible table (**Figure 23**).
- Don't forget to type a line of text above the radio buttons, telling the user what they are selecting. For instance, "What's your favorite flavor ice cream?"
- If you want both the text and the radio button to be "clickable," select the text, select the radio button (hold down Shift while clicking it), choose From Field from the Insert menu, and choose Label from the fly-out menu. The technique works for other form fields as well.

Where's My Form?

A form on a FrontPage Web page is shown in the Editor contained within a dashed rectangle that surrounds the form fields. This rectangle is not visible to the user in a browser.

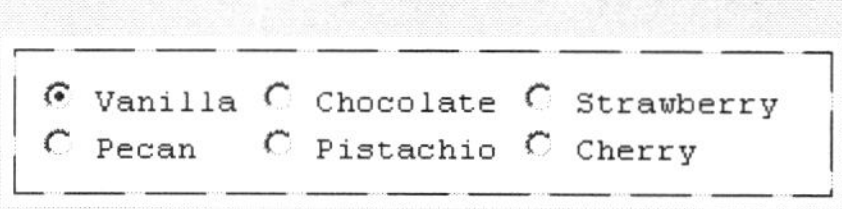

Drop-Down Menus

Another way to have users select one item from a group of choices is to use a drop-down menu. To continue the ice cream flavor example, you could have someone choose their favorite flavor from a drop-down menu.

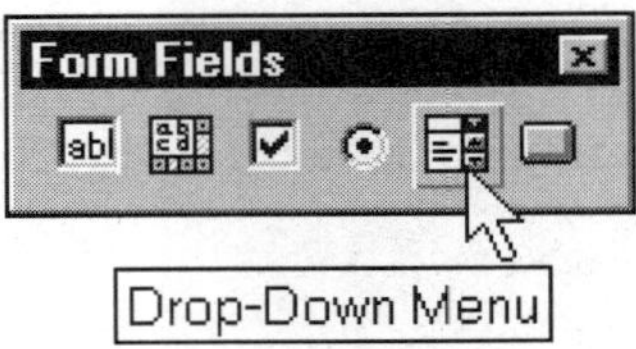

Figure 24. *Click the Drop-Down Menu button on the Form Fields toolbar.*

To insert a drop-down menu:

1. Position the insertion marker where you would like the drop-down menu to appear.
2. Click the Drop-Down Menu button on the Form Fields toolbar (**Figure 24**) or choose Drop-Down Menu from the Form Field fly-out on the Insert menu (**Figure 25**). A drop-down menu will appear where the insertion marker was positioned (**Figure 26**).
3. Right-click the drop-down menu and choose Form Field Properties from the pop-up menu (**Figure 27**). The Drop-Down Menu Properties dialog box will open (**Figure 28**).
4. Type in a name to identify the drop-down menu in the Name text box. For the ice cream example, type in FavoriteFlavor.
5. From this point there are several things you can do. You can add items that will appear in the drop-down menu, modify the properties of an item in the list, remove an item, and change the order of the menu by moving items up or down.

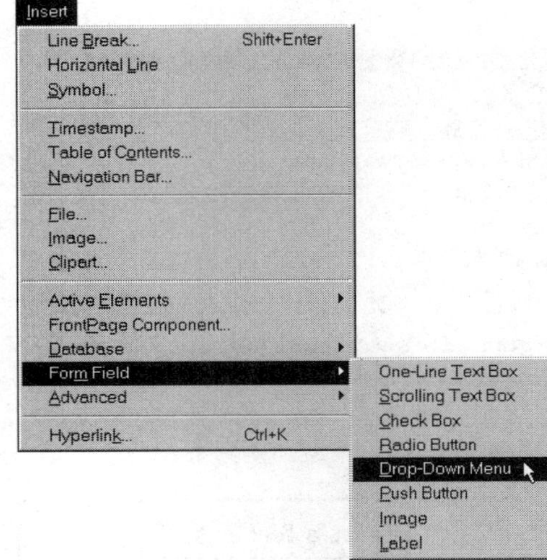

Figure 25. *Choose Drop-Down Menu from the Form Field fly-out on the Insert menu.*

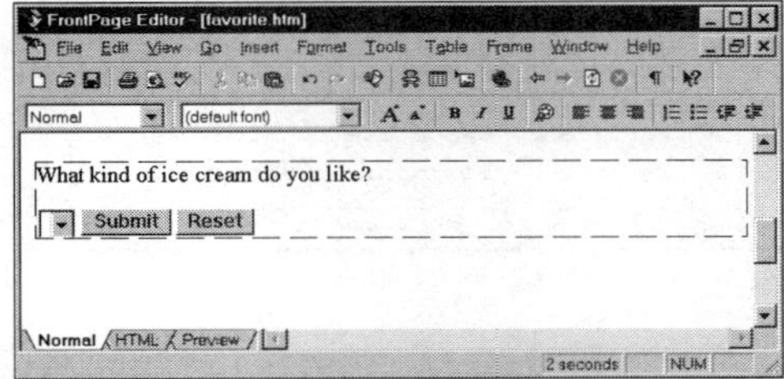

Figure 26. *An empty drop-down menu appears where the insertion marker was positioned.*

Insert a Drop-Down Menu

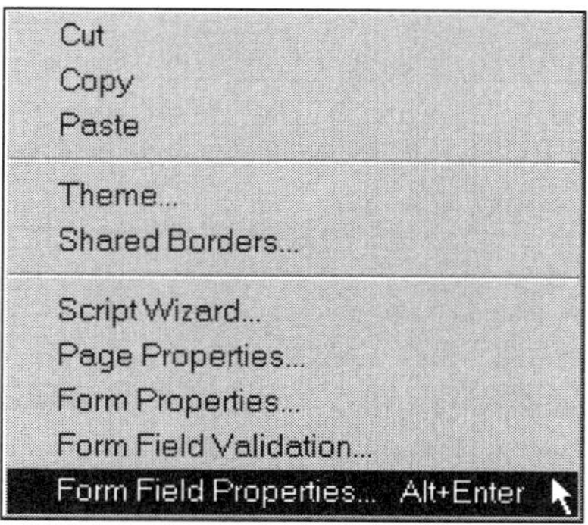

Figure 27. *Choose Form Field Properties from the pop-up menu.*

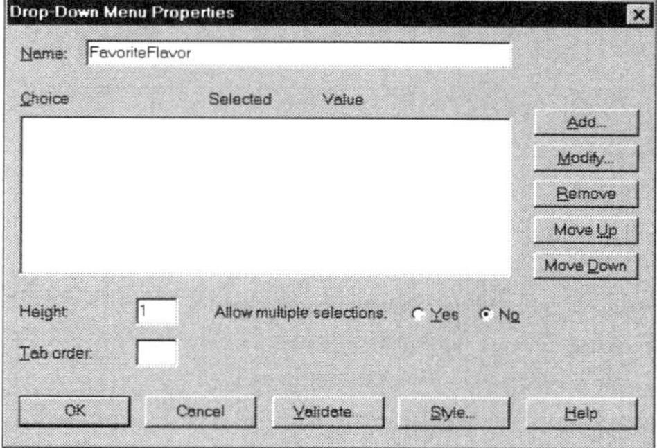

Figure 28. *The Drop-Down Menu Properties dialog box is used to add, modify, remove, and position the items on the portion of the form field that drops down.*

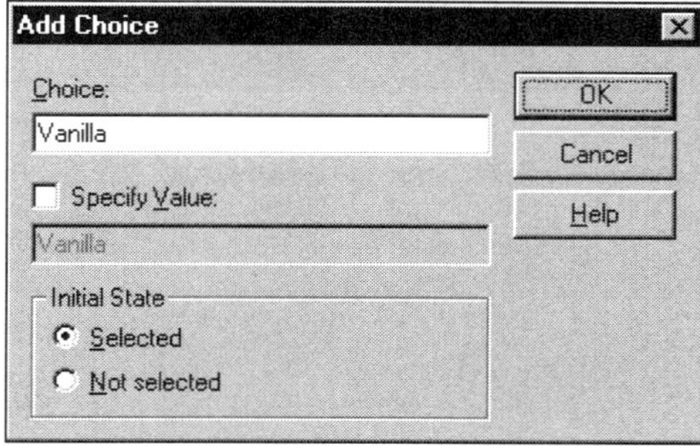

Figure 29. *Use the Add Choice dialog box to add items to the list.*

To add an item to the drop-down menu:

a. Click the Add button. The Add Choice dialog box will appear (**Figure 29**). This dialog box is used to add the choices that will appear on the drop-down portion of the form field that the user can select from.

b. Type one item that the user could select in the Choice text box (**Figure 30**). For the ice cream example, you could type Vanilla.

c. The value of the item is the same as its Choice name by default. If you want the value to be different than the name (for instance, the flavor Vanilla could be equated to 1), put a check in the Specify Value check box, then type the value in the text box.

d. Use the radio buttons in the Initial State area to set whether the item will be the one that appears selected in the drop-down menu when the Web page first opens (**Figure 31**).

e. Click OK to close the Add Choice dialog box and return to the Drop-Down Menu Properties dialog box. You can continue adding items using these five steps.

To modify the properties of an item:

a. Select the item from the list box in the Drop-Down Menu Properties dialog box (**Figure 32**).

b. Click the Modify button. The Modify Choice dialog box will open (**Figure 33**). Using this dialog box you can: change the choice the user will see in the drop-down menu by typing a new name in the Choice text box; use the Specify Value check box to set a value for the item that is different than the choice name; and set whether the item is selected or not using the radio buttons in the Initial State area.

c. When you are finished making changes, click OK to return to the Drop-Down Menu Properties dialog box.

To remove an item:

a. Select the item from the list box in the Drop-Down Menu Properties dialog box.

b. Click the Remove button.

To rearrange the order of items on the drop-down menu:

a. To move an item up the list, select it, then click the Move Up button.

b. To move an item down the list, select it, then click the Move Down button.

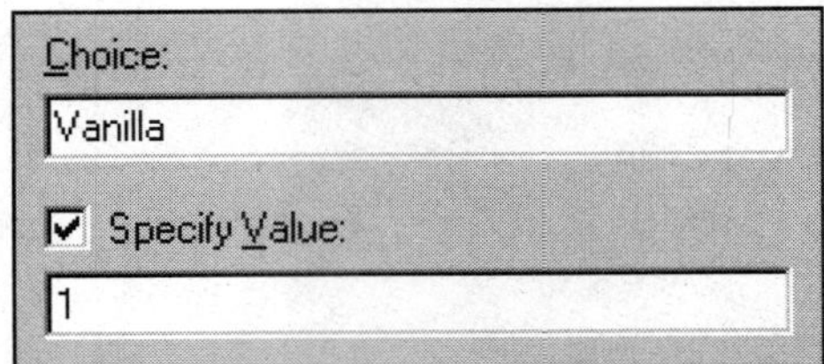

Figure 30. *In the Choice text box, enter an item that the user could select. If you want to use a value that is different than the Choice name, put a check in the Specify Value check box and enter a value in the text box.*

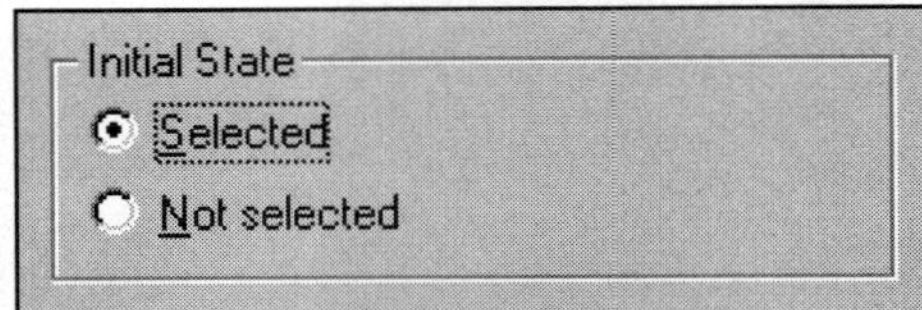

Figure 31. *Use the radio buttons in the Initial State area to set whether the item will be selected when the Web page first loads in a browser.*

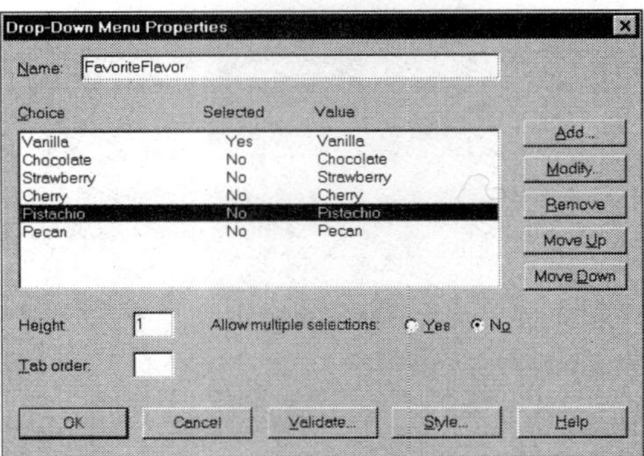

Figure 32. *Select the item that you want to modify in the list box, then click the Modify button.*

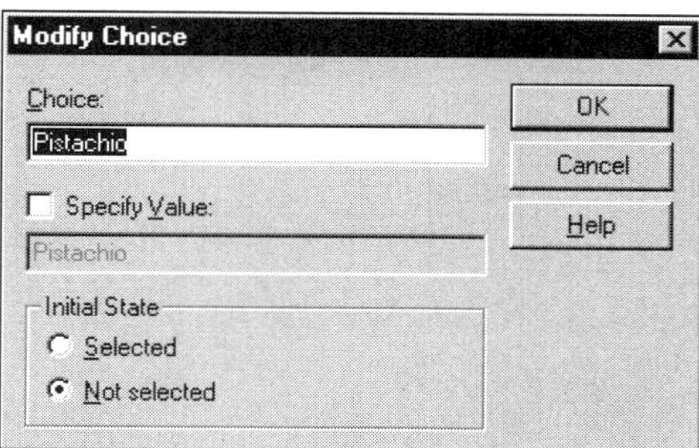

Figure 33. *Use the Modify Choice dialog box to change the item's Choice name, specify a value for the item, and change its initial state.*

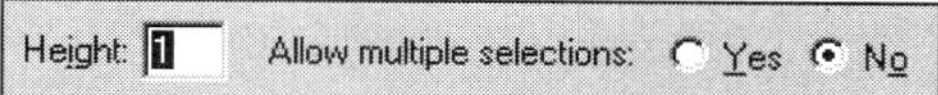

Figure 34. *Use the Height text box to set how many lines show at once and select whether the user can choose more than one item at a time.*

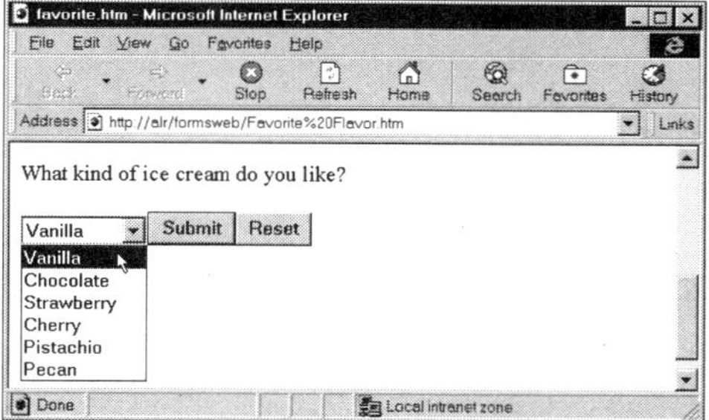

Figure 35a. *This drop-down list is set to a height of 1 and lets the user select from a list that drops down.*

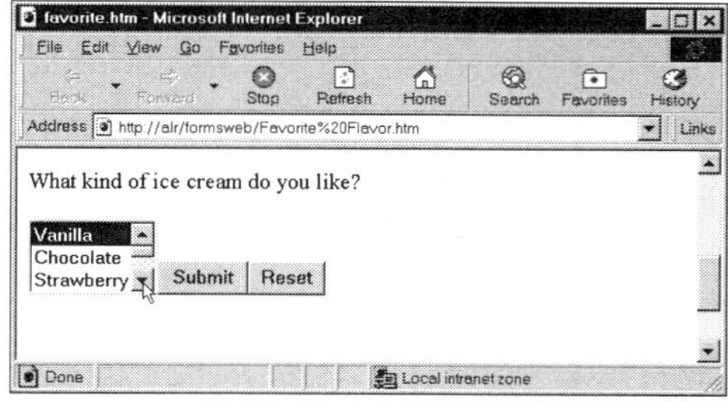

Figure 35b. *The drop-down list shown here is set to a height of 3 and lets the user choose from a scrolling list.*

6. Using the Height text box in the Drop-Down Menu Properties dialog box, you can set how many items the drop-down menu will show at one time (**Figure 34**). If this number is left at 1, the default, the drop-down menu will display one item and let the user access the rest by clicking a down arrow button (**Figure 35a**). If the number is set at 2 or more, the drop-down menu will appear with a scroll bar on the right side (**Figure 35b**).
7. If you want the user to be able to select more than one item at a time, click the Yes radio button next to Allow multiple selections near the bottom of the Drop-Down Menu Properties dialog box (**Figure 34**).
8. If you like, enter a value in the Tab order text box to determine how users move from field to field when they press the Tab key.
9. Click OK to close the dialog box. If you view the Web page in the Preview tab or in a browser, you'll see that the drop-down menu is ready to go (**Figures 35a–b**).

Tip:

- The drop-down menu resizes its width automatically, stretching to fit the longest menu item.

One-Line Text Boxes

One-line text boxes let users enter a line of text. This text could be a name, address, comment, telephone number, e-mail address, and so on.

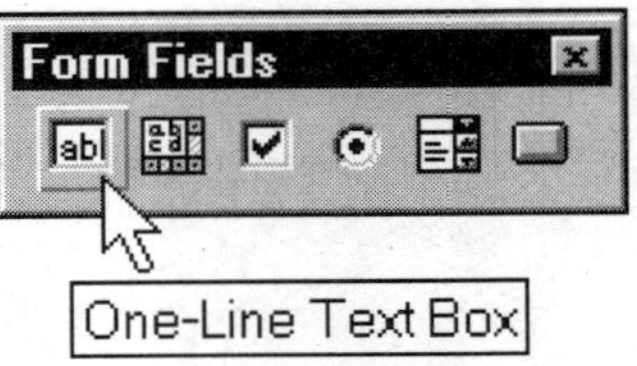

Figure 36. *Click the One-Line Text Box button on the Form Fields toolbar.*

To insert a one-line text box:

1. Position the insertion marker where you would like the one-line text box to appear. This could be next to some descriptive text that lets the user know what type of information should be entered in the text box.
2. Click the One-Line Text Box button on the Form Fields toolbar (**Figure 36**) or choose One-Line Text Box from the Form Field fly-out on the Insert menu (**Figure 37**). A one-line text box will appear where the insertion marker was positioned (**Figure 38**).
3. Right-click the one-line text box and choose Form Field Properties from the pop-up menu (**Figure 27**) or double-click the text box. The Text Box Properties dialog box will open (**Figure 39**).
4. In the Name text box, type in a name that will identify the text box.
5. If you want some text to appear in the text box when the Web page first opens, enter that text in the Initial value text box.

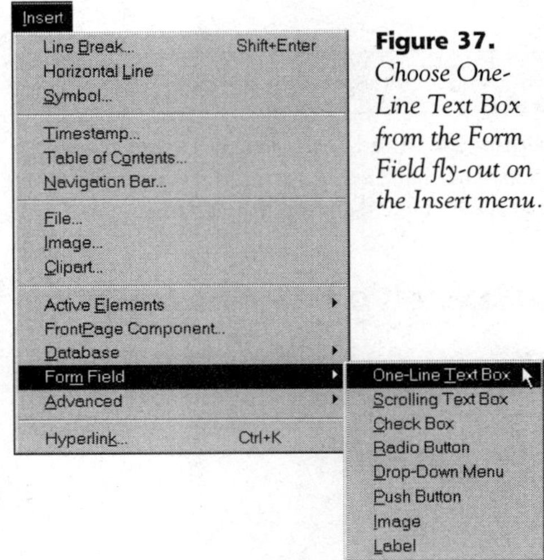

Figure 37. *Choose One-Line Text Box from the Form Field fly-out on the Insert menu.*

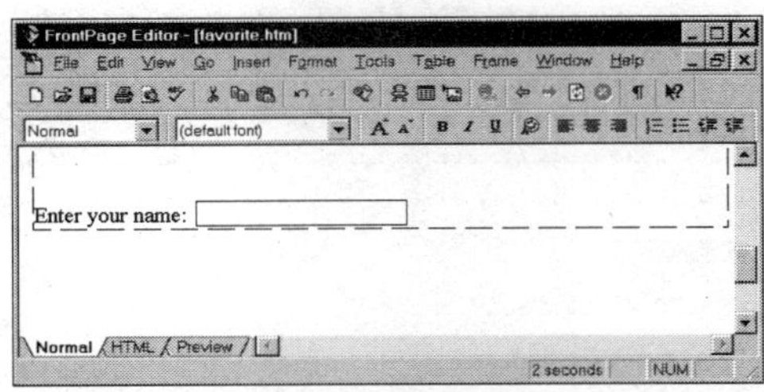

Figure 38. *The one-line text box appears where the insertion marker was positioned.*

Insert a One-Line Text Box

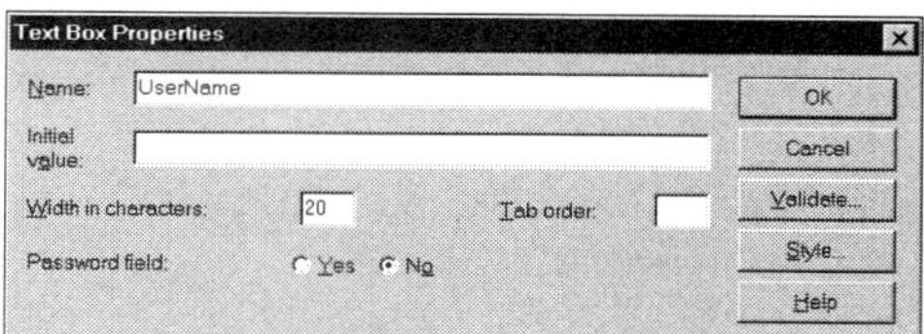

Figure 39. *Use the Text Box Properties dialog box to set a name for the one-line text box and whether there will be text in the box when it opens in a browser.*

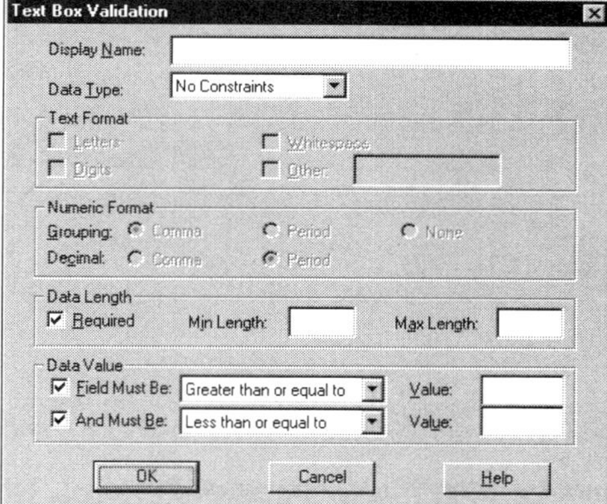

Figure 40. *Use the Text Box Validation dialog box to set what the user can enter in the one-line text box. This can come in handy if you want the user to enter a date in numeric form, for instance. If the user tries to enter text, the one-line text box won't let her.*

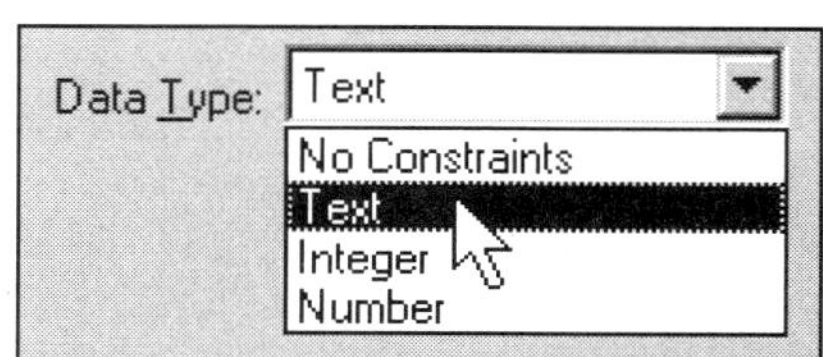

Figure 41. *Use the Data Type drop-down list to select the kind of information the user can type in the one-line text box.*

6. Use the text box next to Width in characters to set how wide the text box will be. If you're not sure how wide you want it to be, leave it at the default of 20. You can always resize the text box later by dragging its handles.

7. If you want to set the tab order, enter a value in the Tab order text box.

8. If this text box is going to be used for entering a password, select the Yes radio button next to Password field. Otherwise, leave the No radio button selected.

9. To set restrictions as to what can be entered in the text box, click Validate. The Text Box Validation dialog box will appear (**Figure 40**). Using the Data Type drop-down list, you can set whether the text box will accept any kind of entry, or text, integers, or numbers only (**Figure 41**). Depending on what is selected in the Data Type drop-down list, a portion of the dialog box becomes active so you can select more specific items. When you are finished with this dialog box, click OK to close it.

10. When you are finished using the Text Box Properties dialog box, click OK to close it. Your one-line text box is ready to be used.

Scrolling Text Boxes

A scrolling text box is similar to a one-line text box in that the user enters text in it. The difference is that users can enter more than one line of text and use the scroll bars to see what they've typed.

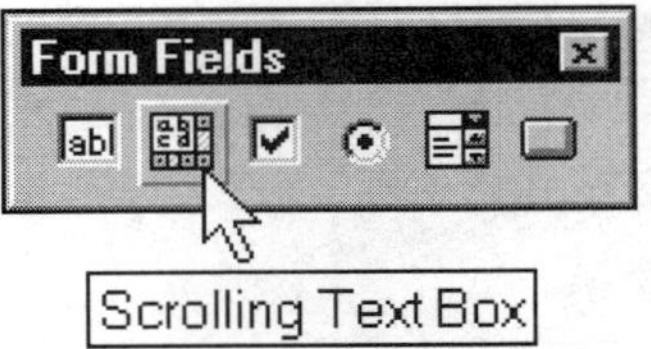

Figure 42. *Click the Scrolling Text Box button on the Form Fields toolbar.*

To insert a scrolling text box:

1. Position the insertion marker where you want the scrolling text box to appear. This could be next to or below some text describing what the user is supposed to enter in the text box.

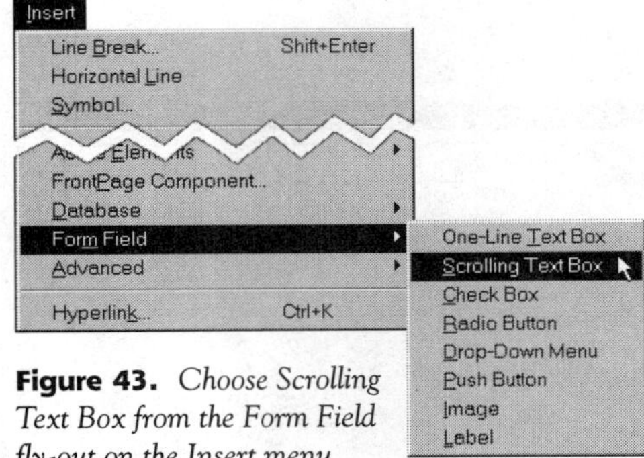

Figure 43. *Choose Scrolling Text Box from the Form Field fly-out on the Insert menu.*

2. Click the Scrolling Text Box button on the Form Fields toolbar (**Figure 42**) or choose Scrolling Text Box from the Form Field fly-out found on the Insert menu (**Figure 43**). The scrolling text box will appear where the insertion marker was positioned (**Figure 44**).

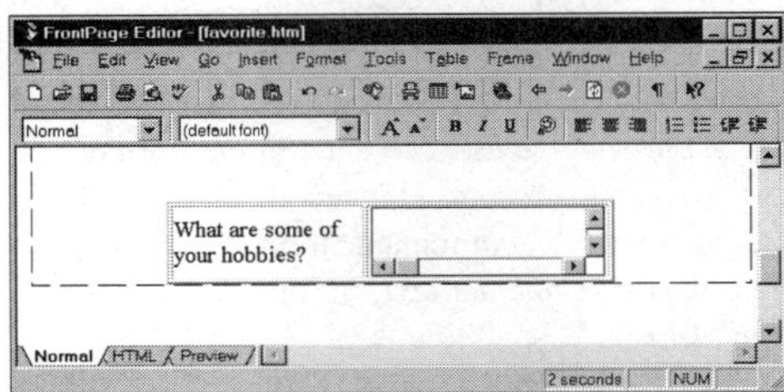

Figure 44. *The scrolling text box appears where the insertion marker was positioned. In this figure, the text box is located in a table.*

3. Right-click the text box and choose Form Field Properties from the pop-up menu (**Figure 45**) or double-click on the text box. The Scrolling Text Box Properties dialog box will open (**Figure 46**).
4. Enter a name to identify the scrolling text box in the Name text box (**Figure 47**).
5. If you want some text to appear in the scrolling text box when the page loads in a browser, enter that text in the Initial value text box.

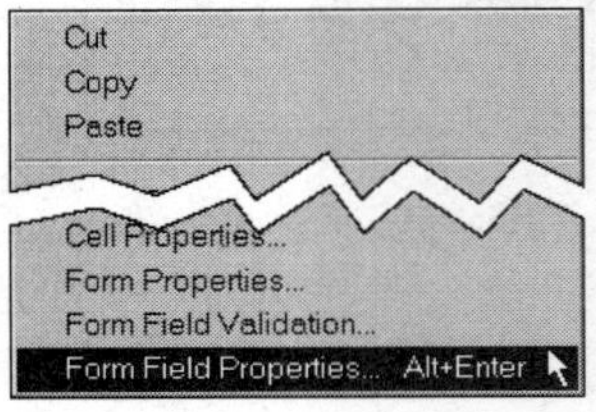

Figure 45. *Right-click the scrolling text box and choose Form Field Properties from the pop-up menu.*

Insert a Scrolling Text Box

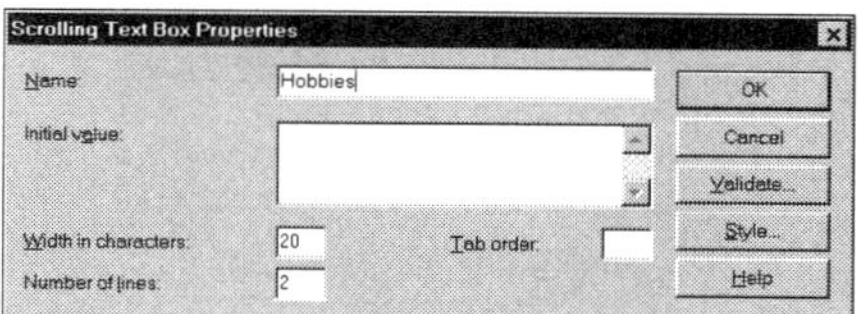

Figure 46. *Use the Scrolling Text Box Properties dialog box to set a name for the text box, whether there will already be text in it when the Web page loads in a browser, and its width and height.*

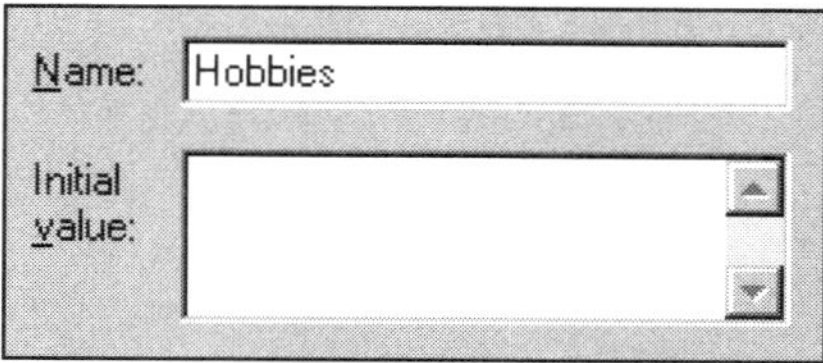

Figure 47. *Use the Name text box to enter a descriptive label for the text box.*

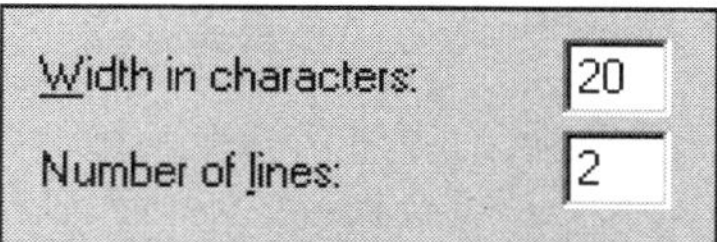

Figure 48. *Enter the width of the scrolling text box in the Width in characters text box and the height of the scrolling text box in the Number of lines text box.*

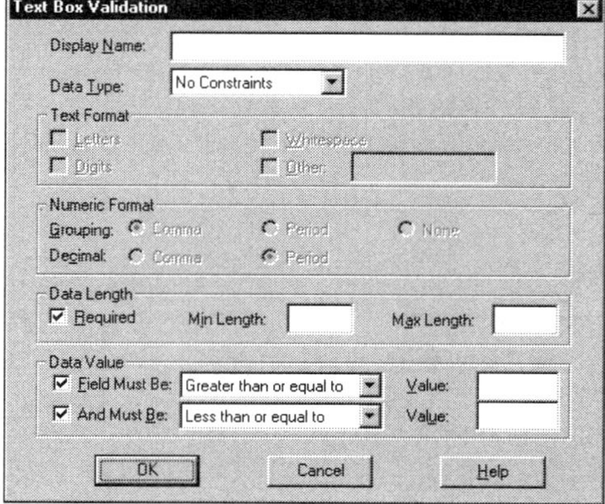

Figure 49. *If you want to restrict the type of information that can be entered in the scrolling text box, use the Text Box Validation dialog box.*

6. Use the text box next to Width in characters to set how wide the text box will be (**Figure 48**).

7. Use the Number of lines text box to set the length of the scrolling text box. (If you aren't sure how big the text box should be, you can always resize it later by selecting it and dragging its handles.)

8. If you want to set the tab order, enter a value in the Tab order text box.

9. To set restrictions as to what can be entered in the text box, click Validate. The Text Box Validation dialog box will appear (**Figure 49**). Using the Data Type drop-down list, you can set whether the text box will accept any kind of entry, or text, integers, or numbers only (**Figure 41**). Depending on what is selected in the Data Type drop-down list, a portion of the dialog box becomes active so you can select more specific items. When you are finished with this dialog box, click OK to close it.

10. When you are finished setting the properties for the scrolling text box, click OK. The Scrolling Text Box properties dialog box will close. To see the scrolling text box work, you will need to view the Web page in a browser.

Check Boxes

Check boxes can be used to let users choose between "Yes" (checked) or "No" (unchecked) and also to let them select many items from a predefined list. To use the favorite ice cream flavor example again, you could ask the user to put checks in the check boxes next to the various flavors she likes. With radio buttons, she could only select a single favorite; with check boxes, she can select as many flavors as she wants!

To insert a check box:

1. Position the insertion marker where you want the check box to appear. (This could be next to or below a description of what the user is supposed to be selecting.)
2. Click Check Box on the Form Fields toolbar (**Figure 50**) or choose Check Box from the Form Field fly-out on the Insert menu (**Figure 51**). The check box will appear where the insertion marker was positioned (**Figure 52**).

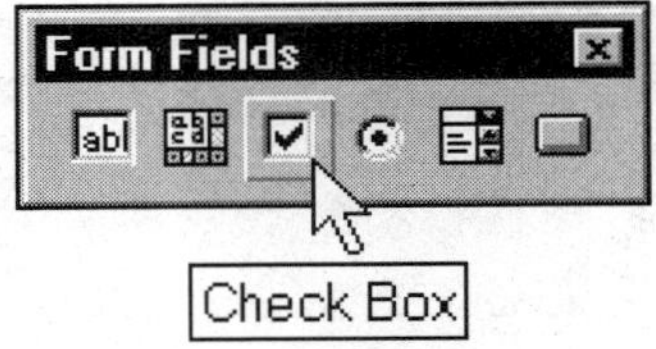

Figure 50. *Click Check Box on the Form Fields toolbar.*

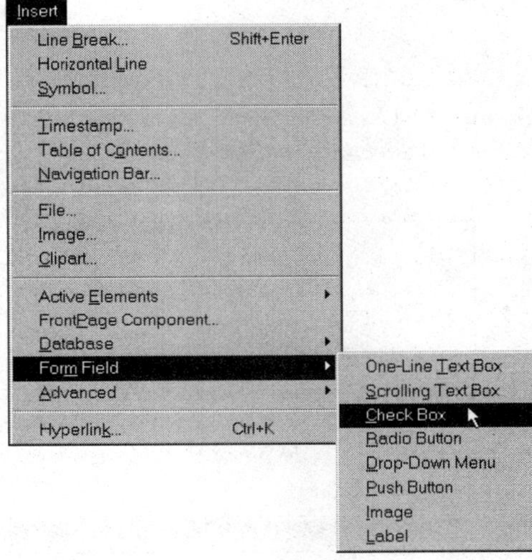

Figure 51. *Choose Check Box from the Form Field fly-out on the Insert menu.*

> **ADDING INITIAL TEXT TO YOUR TEXT BOXES**
>
> Setting initial text in some text boxes can be helpful to your users. For instance, if your form collects a country name as part of an address and most of your users are from the United States, you could set the text box's initial text to USA.

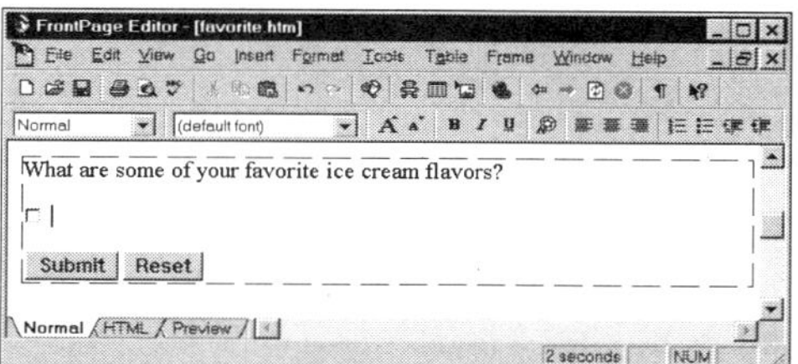

Figure 52. *A check box appears where the insertion marker was positioned.*

Figure 53. *Use the Check Box Properties dialog box to set a name and value for the check box and to set whether it is initially selected when the Web page loads in a browser.*

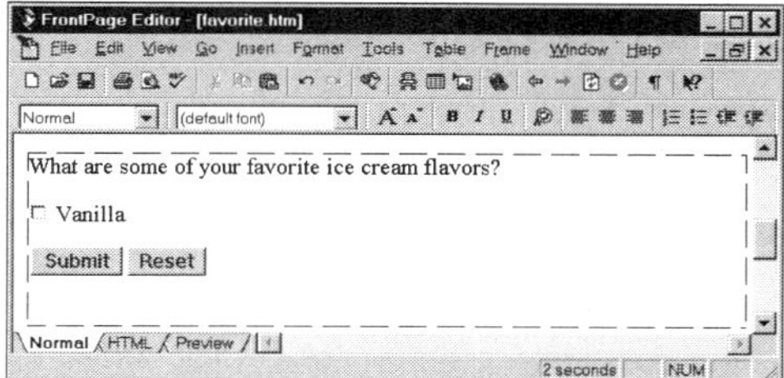

Figure 54. *Type a descriptive label next to the check box to let the user know what the box means.*

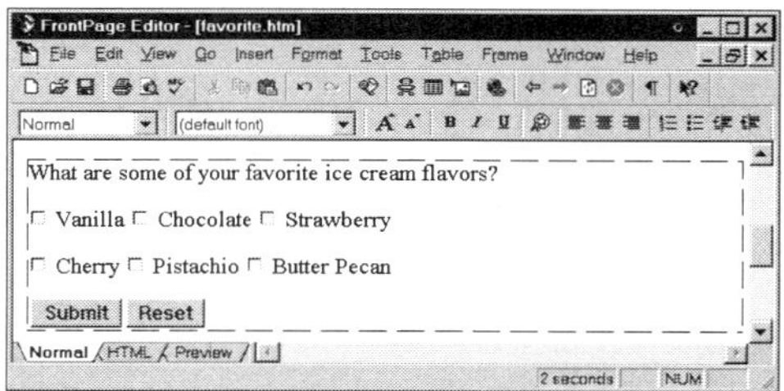

Figure 55. *Insert as many check boxes as you need to display all the items the user can choose.*

3. Right-click the check box and select Form Field Properties from the pop-up menu (**Figure 45**) or double-click the check box. The Check Box Properties dialog box will open (**Figure 53**).
4. Use the Name text box to enter a name that will identify the check box. For the favorite ice cream flavor example, you could enter Vanilla.
5. In the text box next to Value, enter a word showing the value of the box if it is checked. You could use, for instance, On, Selected, or Checked.
6. Use the radio buttons next to Initial State to set whether the check box will have a check mark in it when the page loads in a browser.
7. Use the Tab order text box to set the tab order for the check box.
8. When you are finished setting the properties for the check box, click OK to close the dialog box.
9. If necessary, click the mouse to the right of the check box and type the description of what this check box means if the user checks it (**Figure 54**).

Tip:

- You can continue adding as many check boxes as you need using the steps outlined above (**Figure 55**).

Push Buttons

The user clicks a push button when she wants a specific action to occur, such as submitting a form, resetting a form so she can start again, or playing a sound. Push buttons come in three flavors: Normal, Submit, and Reset. As you've seen, FrontPage automatically generates Submit and Reset buttons when you create a form. If you want to modify those buttons, or add new ones, you can follow the steps outlined here.

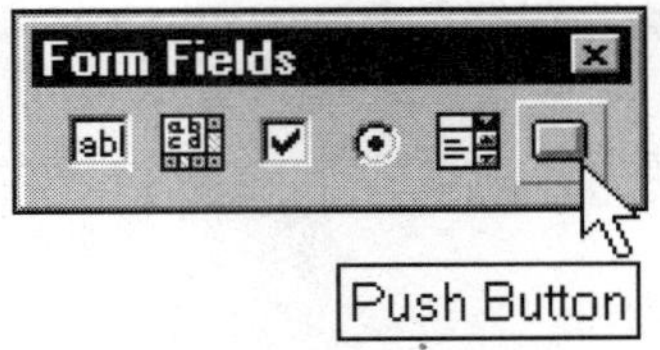

Figure 56. *Click Push Button on the Form Fields toolbar.*

To insert a push button:

1. Position the insertion marker where you want the push button to appear.
2. Click Push Button on the Form Fields toolbar (**Figure 56**) or choose Push Button from the Form Field fly-out on the Insert menu (**Figure 57**). The push button will appear where the insertion marker was positioned (**Figure 58**). By default, this is a Normal push button (labeled "Button"). You can change this in a minute if you want to.
3. Right-click the push button and choose Form Field Properties from the pop-up menu (**Figure 45**) or double-click the push button. The Push Button Properties dialog box will appear (**Figure 59**).

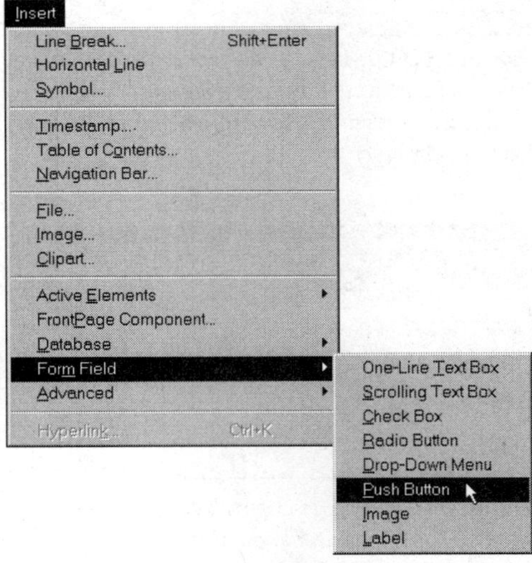

Figure 57. *Choose Push Button from the Form Field fly-out on the Insert menu.*

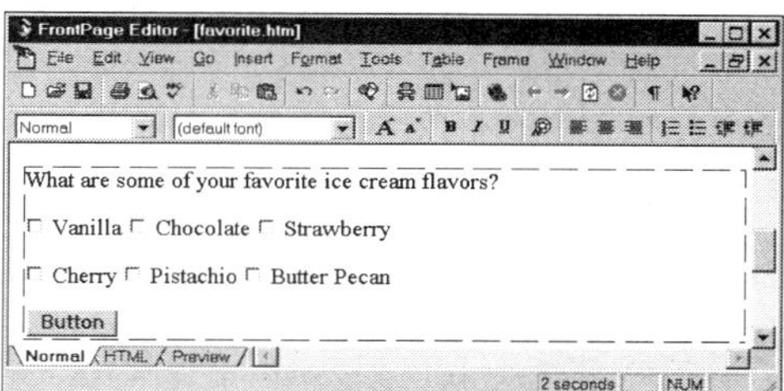

Figure 58. *A push button appears where the insertion marker was positioned. By default, the push button is a Normal button. You can change this using the Push Button Properties dialog box.*

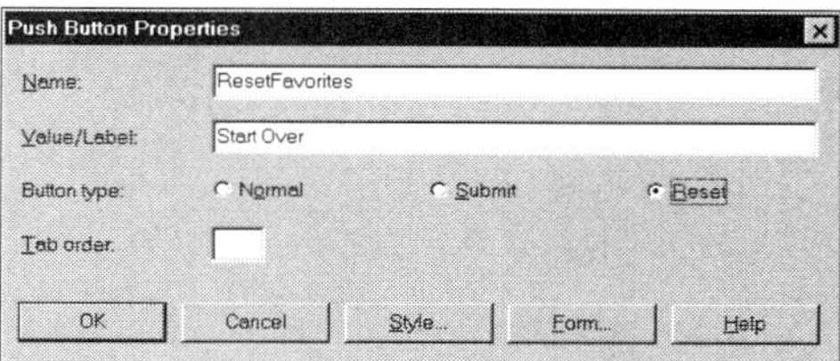

Figure 59. *Use the Push Button Properties dialog box to set a Name for the button (this is optional), to enter the words that will appear on the button (Value/Label), and to choose the type of button it is: Submit, Reset, or Normal.*

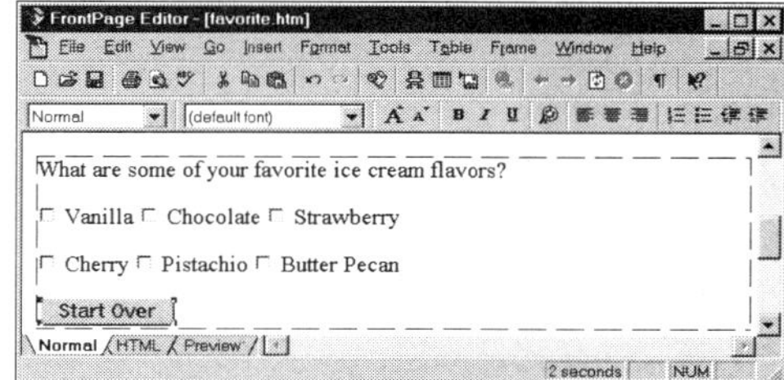

Figure 60. *When you close the Push Button Properties dialog box, the words you entered in the Value/Label text box appear on the push button.*

4. Use the Name text box to set a name identifying the push button. This is optional.
5. In the Value/Label text box, enter the words that will appear on the push button, letting the user know what the button's for.
6. Use the radio buttons next to Button type to set the type of button. The default setting is Normal.
7. If you like, enter a value in the Tab order text box to set the tab order of the button.
8. When you are finished setting the push button's properties, click OK. The push button will appear with the text you entered in the Value/Label text box (**Figure 60**).

Tip:

- You'll probably just use Submit and Reset buttons. Normal buttons don't do anything until you assign a script (like a program) to them.

To edit a form field's properties:

Double-click the form field or right-click the form field and choose Form Field Properties from the pop-up menu (**Figure 61**). The properties dialog box for that particular form field will appear. If you need help with this dialog box, take a look at the individual sections in this chapter for inserting that type of form field. The properties dialog box will be discussed there.

Figure 61. *Right-click the form field and choose Form Field Properties from the pop-up menu.*

Selecting a Form Handler

The form handler is used to process form results. The form handlers in FrontPage use FrontPage components to work. This means that your Web site must be published on a server that supports the FrontPage server extensions.

FrontPage supplies three form handlers: the default form handler (also called the Save Results Component), the Discussion Form Handler, and the Registration Form Handler. Advanced users can also create their own form handlers. If you created a Web page using one of the FrontPage form templates discussed on page 290, then a form handler has already been selected and partially configured. If you created a form of your own just by adding form fields to a Web page, the default form handler has been applied.

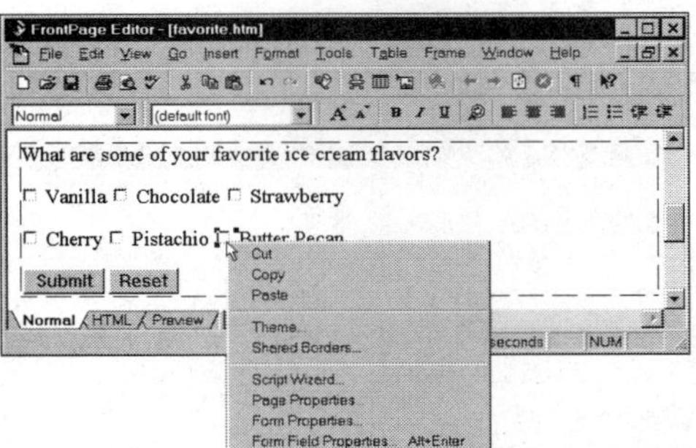

Figure 62. *Right-click anywhere in the form area defined by the dashed rectangle to access the pop-up.*

Select a Form Handler

Figure 63. *Choose Form Properties from the pop-up menu.*

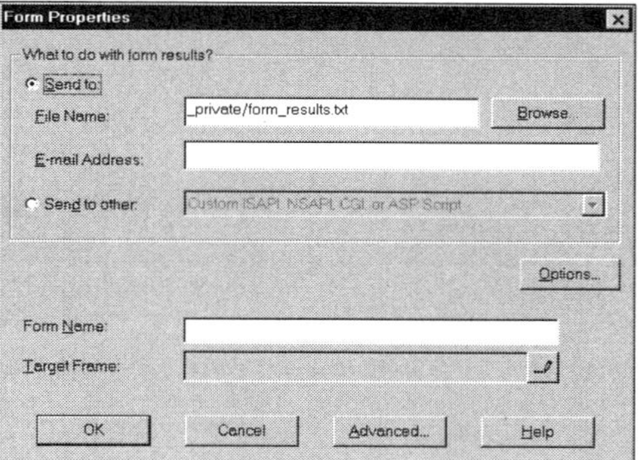

Figure 64. *Use the Form Properties dialog box to select a form handler, set up the form handler, and define the file the submitted information will be sent to.*

Figure 65. *If you want the form results sent to an e-mail address instead of a file, enter that address in the E-mail Address text box.*

To select a form handler:

1. Position the mouse pointer over the dashed form area and right-click (**Figure 62**). Choose Form Properties from the pop-up menu (**Figure 63**). The Form Properties dialog box will appear (**Figure 64**).

2. To use the Save Results Component form handler, leave the Send to radio button selected. This form handler saves the form results in the file designated in the File Name text box.

3. To save the form results to a file, enter the file name in the File Name text box. You can enter the URL for a Web page or you can enter the complete path if you want to save the file to a location on your hard drive or network drive. You can also click the Browse button and select a new location from the Current Web dialog box. When you use any of these methods, all the form results are saved in a single file.

4. To have the form results sent as e-mail instead of appended to a results file, type the e-mail address in the E-mail Address text box (**Figure 65**). When you use this approach, each submission is sent as a separate e-mail.

5. Click the Send to other radio button to use a form handler other than the default. Use the drop-down list to select a form handler (**Figure 66**). You can choose from:

   - Custom ISAPI, NSAPI, CGI, or ASP Script: lets you create a custom form handler.
   - Discussion Form Handler: lets users partake in an online discussion group. The form handler collects the information from a form, makes it into an HTML page, and saves the page on a Web server. Configuring this form handler is quite complicated. If you want to create a discussion Web site, use the Discussion Web Wizard. The wizard will set up the discussion Web site for you and configure the Discussion Form Handler.
   - Registration Form Handler: lets users register for something offered in your Web site. For example, if you use the User Registration form template to create a Web page (see page 290), this handler will be selected and configured for you automatically.

Figure 66. *In the Send to other drop-down list, you can select the type of form handler you want to use.*

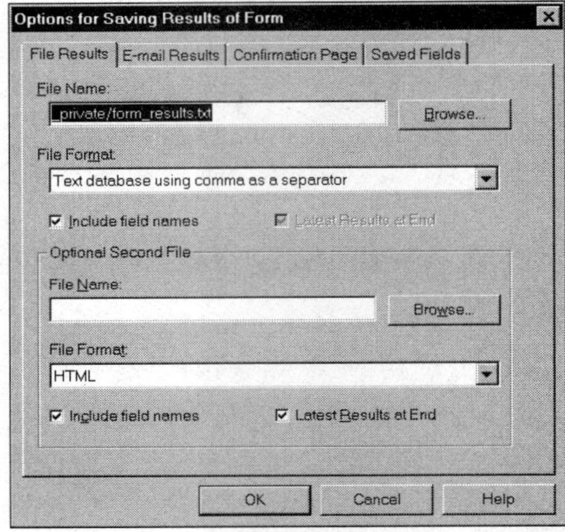

Figure 67. *Use Options for Saving Results of Form dialog box to configure the form handler.*

Figure 68. *Enter the name of the file where the submitted information will be saved in the File Name text box.*

Select a Form Handler

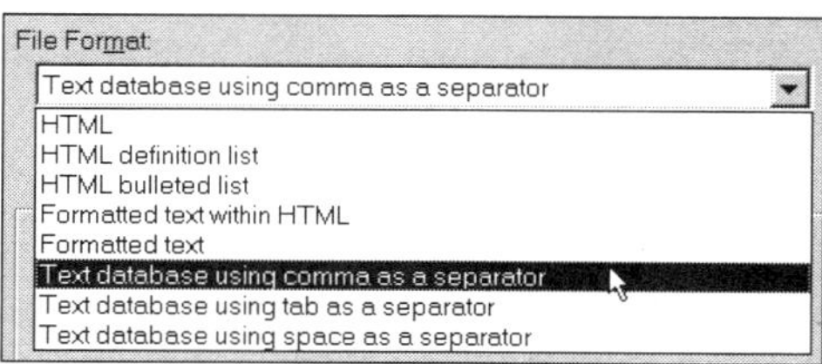

Figure 69. *Select a file format from the File Format drop-down list.*

Figure 70. *If you want the names of the form fields included with the value data, put a check in the Include field names check box. If you selected an HTML file format, you can also choose to append the latest form results to the end of the results file.*

> **View Your Form Web Page in a Browser**
>
> After you have finished designing a form, you will need to view the Web page in a browser to see how the form will look and work when you publish your FrontPage Web site.

To configure a form handler:

1. Click the Options button in the Form Properties dialog box. You'll see the Options for Saving Results of Form dialog box with the File Results tab page in front (**Figure 67**).
2. In the File Name text box, type the name and folder location of the file where you want the results saved (**Figure 68**). (You may have already specified the location in the Form Properties dialog box.) This folder location can be within the Web site or in another location on the server. If the file does not exist when FrontPage goes to save the first results, it will automatically create the file. If necessary, you can click the Browse button to search for the results file in the Current Web dialog box.
3. In the File Format drop-down list, select how the submitted results will be formatted (**Figure 69**). You can choose from:
   - HTML: this will format the file in HTML using Normal text style.
   - HTML definition list: this will format the file in HTML using the Definition text style.
   - HTML bulleted list: this will format the file in HTML using the Formatted text style.

- Formatted text within HTML: this will format the file in HTML using the Formatted text style.
- Formatted text: this will format the file in a text format (readable in a text editing program such as Notepad).
- Text database using comma as a separator: this will format the file in a text format with a comma separating each element.
- Text database using tab as a separator: this will format the file in a text format with a tab separating each element.
- Text database using space as a separator: this will format the file in a text format with a space separating each element.

4. To include field names with the values in the results file, put a check in the Include field names check box (**Figure 70**). (A field name is the name assigned to a form field using its properties dialog box.)
5. If you chose an HTML file format, you can select the Latest Results at End check box to place the most recent form results at the end of the results file (**Figure 70**).

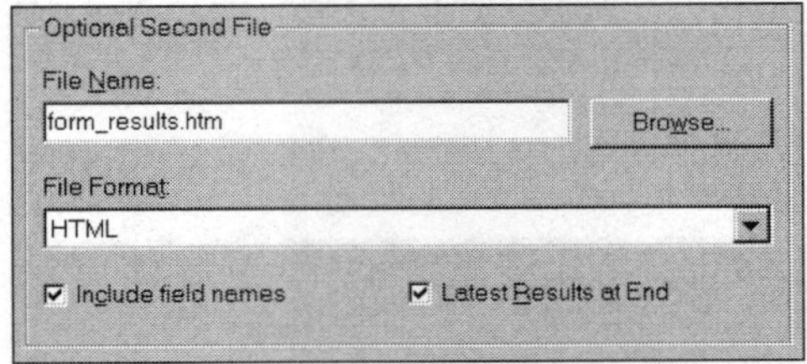

Figure 71. *In the Optional Second File area, you can enter a name and choose a file format for an optional second file in which to store the form results.*

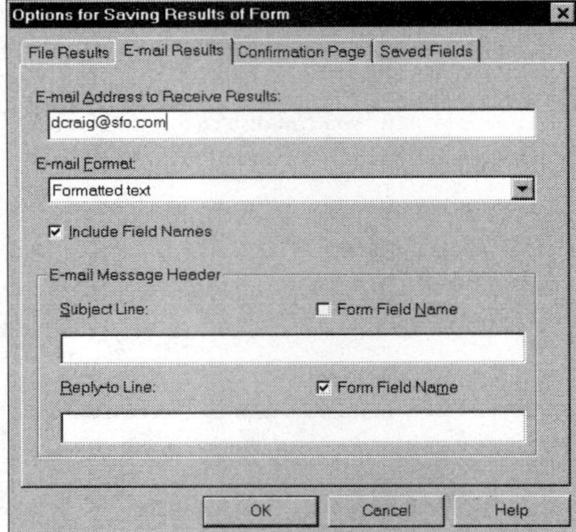

Figure 72. *In the E-mail Results tab page, you can choose several settings that affect where and how the form results are e-mailed.*

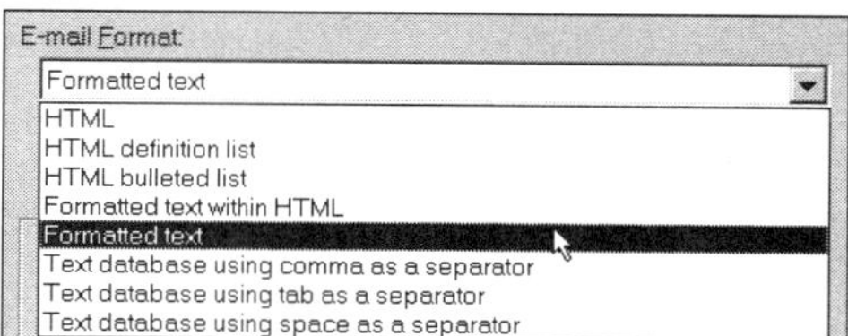

Figure 73. *In the E-mail Format drop-down list, you can select a format for the form results being e-mailed.*

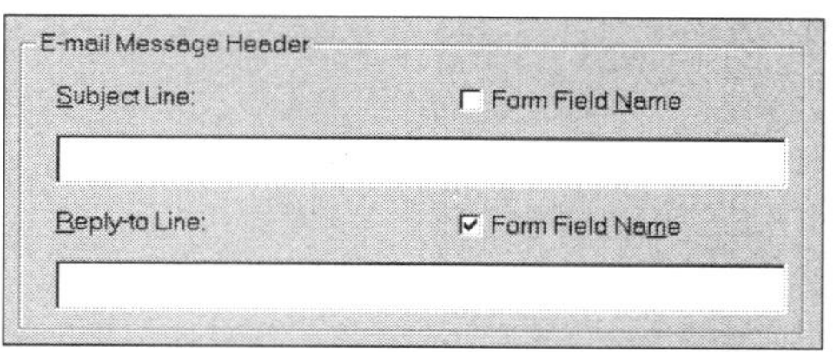

Figure 74. *In the E-mail Message Header area, you can enter text that will appear by default in the subject and reply-to lines of the e-mail message.*

6. In the Optional Second File area (**Figure 71**), choose a name and format for an optional second file in which to save the form results. This is handy if you want to store two different versions of the file—maybe one that's easier for humans to read and another that machines will be happier with.
7. Click the E-mail Results tab to bring that tab page to the front (**Figure 72**).
8. In the E-mail Address to Receive Results text box, you can specify the e-mail address to which form results are mailed. (This is the same as the E-mail Address text box in the Form Properties dialog box).
9. In the E-mail Format drop-down list box (**Figure 73**), you can select the format for the e-mail. The formatting options are the same as those for files that were described in step 3 above.
10. Select the Include Field Names check box if you want to include field names with the values.

11. In the E-mail Message Header area, you can specify text that will automatically appear in the subject line and reply-to line of the e-mail message (**Figure 74**). The subject line text can help you see at a glance which form the results are from. If you want the subject line to contain the contents of a particular form field (such as the user's name), click the Form Field Name check box and enter the name of the form field in the Subject Line text box.

12. In the Reply-to Line text box (**Figure 74**), enter the name of the form field whose results should appear in the reply-to line of the e-mail message. If the Form Field Name check box is not selected, enter any other text that you want to appear in the e-mail message's reply-to line.

13. Click the Confirmation Page tab to bring that tab page to the front (**Figure 75**). Using this tab page, you can set an optional confirmation Web page informing users that their information was received. (If you leave the URL of confirmation page text box blank, FrontPage creates a standard confirmation page showing the information the user entered into the form.) You can also set an optional page that will show a validation error. (The URL of validation failure page

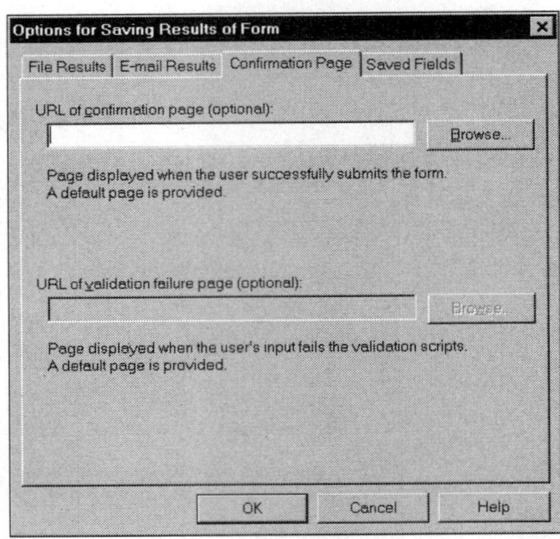

Figure 75. *Use the Confirmation Page tab page of the Options for Saving Results of Form dialog box to set a confirmation Web page and a validation error Web page. Setting both of these pages is optional.*

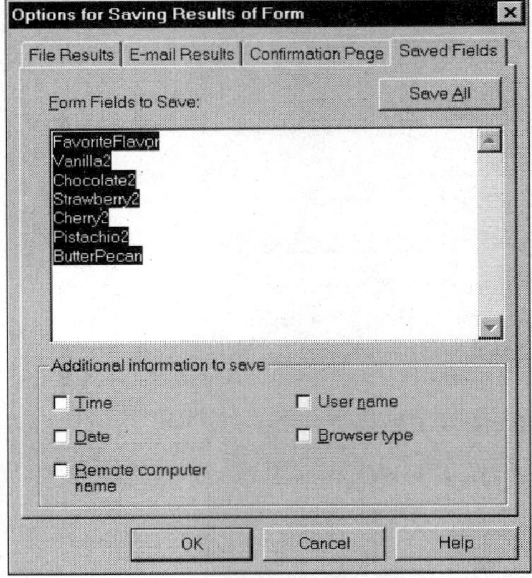

Figure 76. *Use the Saved Fields tab page of the Options for Saving Results of Form dialog box to select which form fields are saved in the results file.*

Configure a Form Handler

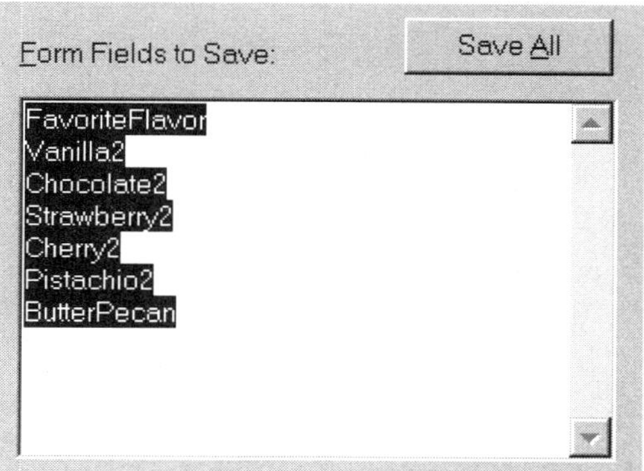

Figure 77. *FrontPage lists all fields in the Form Fields to Save list box and places the information in the results file.*

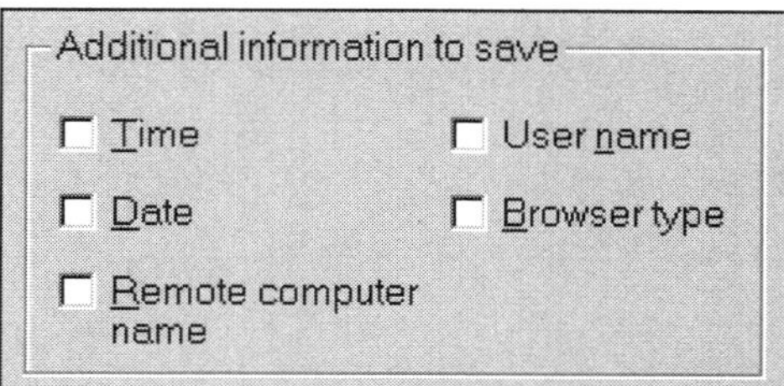

Figure 78. *In the Additional information to save area, put checks in the check boxes next to the type of information you would like saved with the submission.*

text box is only available if you've established validation rules for your form.) A validation error occurs when the user has not entered information in a particular field.

14. Click the Saved Fields tab to bring that tab page to the front (**Figure 76**). Using this tab page, you can specify which form fields appear in your results file and the order in which they appear. By default, FrontPage lists all fields in the Form Fields to Save list box (**Figure 77**), and places the information from all fields in the results file. You can delete fields if you don't want them listed in the results, and you can rearrange the fields to have the results appear in a different order. If you delete all the fields from the Form Fields to Save list, FrontPage places all the form fields in the results file in the order in which they appear.
15. In the Additional information to save area (**Figure 78**), you can put checks in the check boxes next to the type of information you would like saved with the submission.
16. Click OK to close the Options for Saving Results of Form dialog box and return to the Form Properties dialog box.
17. Click OK to close the Form Properties dialog box. The form handler is all set up.

CREATING YOUR OWN CONFIRMATION FORM

Creating a custom confirmation form is not difficult, but it does involve several steps. Here's what you do: Make sure you know the names of the form fields whose contents you want to appear in the confirmation form. (You can do this by double-clicking each form field and jotting down its name.) Create a new Web page that will become the confirmation page. (You can start with a blank page or you can start with the Confirmation Form template, described on page 290.) In that Web page, each place you want the confirmation data to appear, choose FrontPage Component from the Insert menu, choose Confirmation Field from the Insert FrontPage Component dialog box, and click OK. In the Confirmation Field Properties dialog box, enter the name of the form field whose contents you want to display, and then click OK. (You may want some explanatory text, such as "Your zip code is:," to precede the confirmation field.) Repeat this process until you've created as many confirmation fields as you need, and then save the confirmation Web page. Finally, open the form for which you just created a confirmation page, right-click within the form, and choose Form Properties from the pop-up menu. In the Form Properties dialog box, click the Options button. Select the Confirmation Page tab page, enter the URL for the confirmation page you just created in the URL of confirmation page text box, and click OK.

SUMMARY

In this chapter you learned how to:

- Use a form template to create a form Web page
- View the Form Fields toolbar
- Add radio buttons
- Insert drop-down menus
- Add one-line and scrolling text boxes
- Insert check boxes and push buttons
- Edit a form field's properties
- Select a form handler
- Configure a form handler

Publishing and Testing Your Site

19

Ready, set, go! Once you've finished creating your Web site, it's time to let the world see it. FrontPage calls this *publishing* your Web site. In order for your site to always be accessible to folks browsing the World Wide Web, you will need to store the site on a *dedicated* Web server—a server that is connected to the Internet 24 hours a day. For information on finding an Internet Service Provider that will be able to handle your FrontPage Web site, see page 26.

There are two stages to testing your Web site. The first comes when you've completed the site. You should use the Preview in Browser command found on the Editor's File menu or the Preview tab to check your pages and all the hyperlinks on your pages. You can also use the Editor to move from hyperlink to hyperlink. In addition, you can use FrontPage Explorer to verify hyperlinks and fix broken links to images or URL addresses. The second stage of testing comes when you publish your site. You should run through the pages and links again, making sure everything works, all the images load correctly, and everything looks fine.

In addition to testing your site after you've published it to a dedicated Web server, you should check to see how long it takes for each Web page to load. If a page takes a long time, you might want to rework the page, using different graphics and/or multimedia files that are smaller in file size.

To follow hyperlinks using the Editor:

1. Open the Web site you want to check in Explorer.
2. Double-click on a Web page in the Explorer window to launch the Editor.

   or

   Click the Show FrontPage Editor button on the toolbar (**Figure 1**).
3. In the Editor, open the Web page you want to test (if it's not open already).
4. Hold down the Ctrl key and click on the linked image or text.

   or

   Select the linked image or position the insertion marker within the linked text and choose Follow Hyperlink from the Go menu (**Figure 2**).

   The page that the text or image links to will open in the Editor.

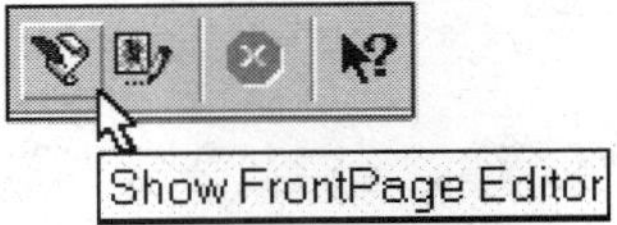

Figure 1. *Click the Show FrontPage Editor button on the Explorer's toolbar.*

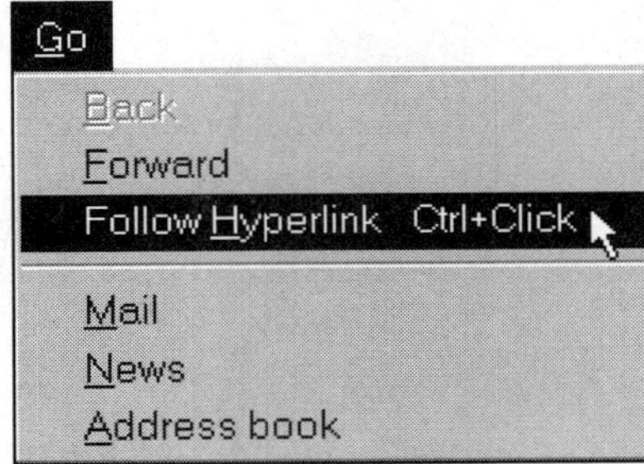

Figure 2. *Choose Follow Hyperlink from the Go menu.*

Tips:

- If you want to test a link to a site on the Web, make sure you are connected to the Web first, otherwise a message will appear, telling you that FrontPage cannot open the site (**Figure 3**). Click OK.
- You can also test links by clicking on them in the Preview tab.

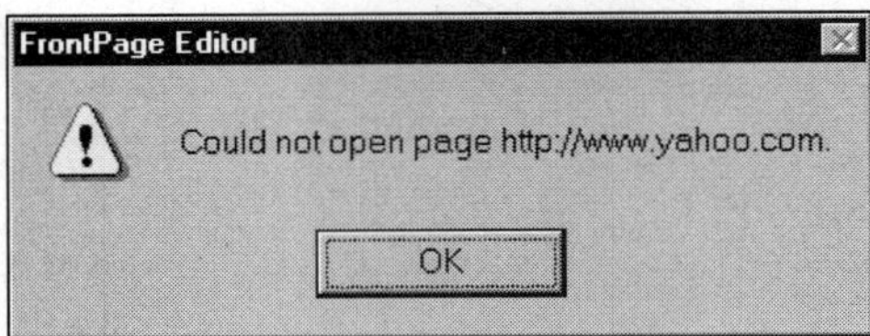

Figure 3. *If you are not connected to the Web and try to verify a Web URL, FrontPage will not be able to open the page.*

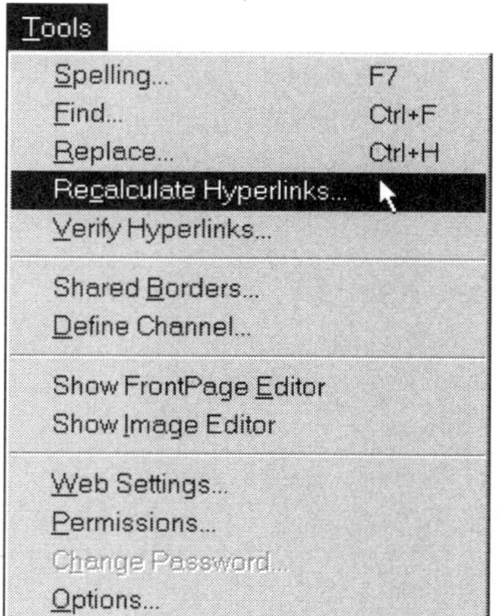

Figure 4. *Choose Recalculate Hyperlinks from the Tools menu.*

If you have added new pages, hyperlinks, or FrontPage components to your site, you should recalculate the hyperlinks for the entire site. It's a good idea to do this before verifying the links on your site. Recalculating hyperlinks will update your site and also update the table of contents FrontPage component if you've used one, as well as any include components.

To recalculate hyperlinks using Explorer:

1. Open the Web site you want to recalculate in Explorer.
2. Choose Recalculate Hyperlinks from the Tools menu (**Figure 4**).
3. FrontPage will ask you whether you want to proceed (**Figure 5**). Click Yes. Depending on the size of your site, Explorer will work for a while resetting the hyperlinks.

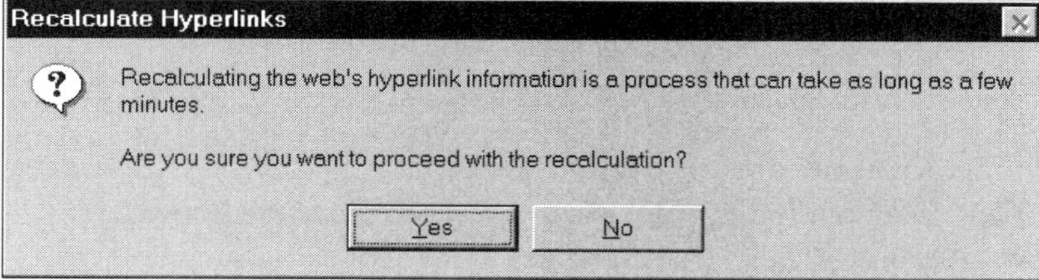

Figure 5. *FrontPage will ask you if you really want to recalculate hyperlinks. Click Yes.*

If you want to verify the validity of both the internal and external links on your site, you can use the Verify Hyperlinks command available in the Explorer.

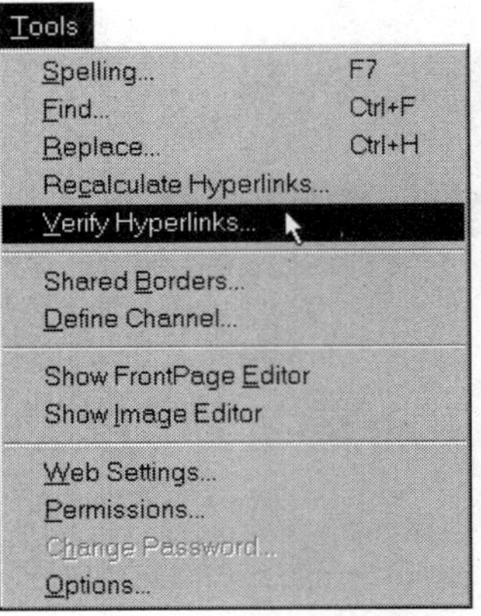

Figure 6. *Choose Verify Hyperlinks from the Explorer's Tools menu.*

To verify links using Explorer:

1. Make sure you're connected to the Web. (If you're not, you won't be able to check external links.)
2. Open the Web site you want to check in Explorer. (If the site's already open, save any changes you've made so FrontPage checks the latest version.)
3. Choose Verify Hyperlinks from the Tools menu (**Figure 6**). FrontPage will switch to Hyperlinks Status view (if you weren't already in that view) and display the Verify Hyperlinks dialog box (**Figure 7**). Before each displayed link will be a colored circle (**Figure 8**):
   - ●Broken A red circle with the word "Broken" next to it indicates a broken link.
   - ○Unknown A yellow circle with the word "Unknown" next to it indicates an external hyperlink that hasn't been checked yet. (FrontPage automatically checks all internal links, but doesn't check external links automatically because this process can take quite some time, especially if you have a large site with many external links.)

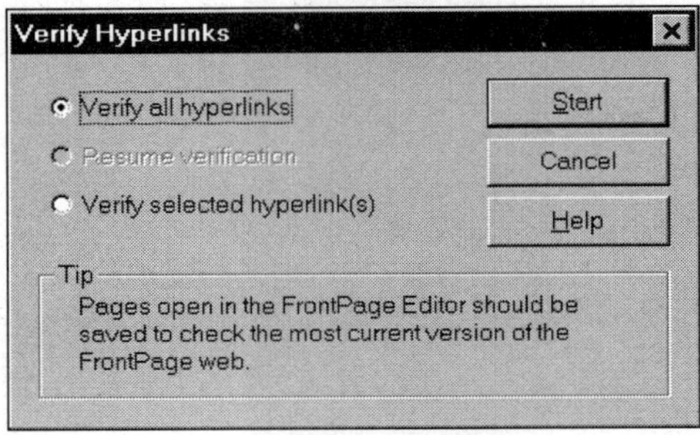

Figure 7. *The Verify Hyperlinks dialog box lets you choose whether to verify all hyperlinks or only selected hyperlinks.*

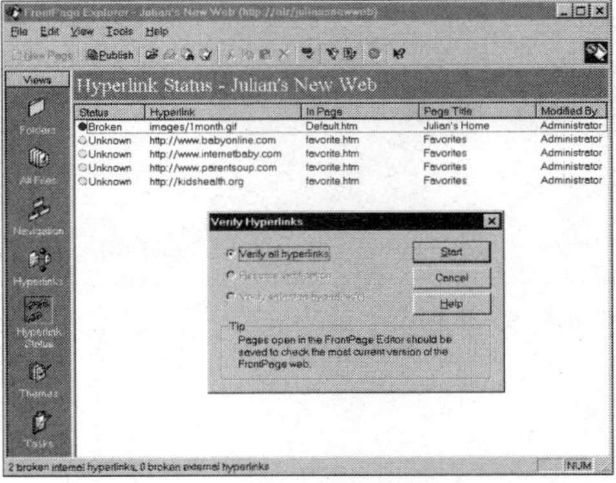

Figure 8. *Hyperlink Status view will display a list of hyperlinks that you can check and fix if needed.*

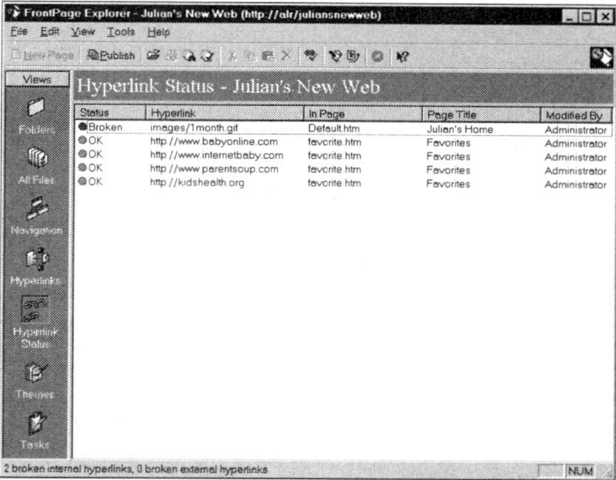

Figure 9. *After you click the Start button, the status of unknown links may change to OK. Other links which are truly broken will remain so until you fix them.*

- After all the links are checked and fixed, the red and yellow circles will change to green ones with the word "OK" next to them, indicating that the links are good. (Internal links that check out OK are not listed by default; if you want to see them, choose Show All Hyperlinks from the View menu.) If no links are listed, your site has no broken or unverified links.

4. To continue the verification process, make sure the radio button Verify all hyperlinks is selected and click the Start button in the Verify Hyperlinks dialog box. FrontPage will verify all the links, then adjust the colored circles in the Status column as necessary (**Figure 9**). In Figure 9, the URL addresses checked out and the yellow circles labeled "Unknown" changed to green ones labeled "OK," but the broken link, indicated by the red circle labeled "Broken," remained red.

5. To repair a broken link, right-click the link and choose Edit Hyperlink from the pop-up menu that appears (**Figure 10**). You'll see the Edit Hyperlink dialog box (**Figure 11**).

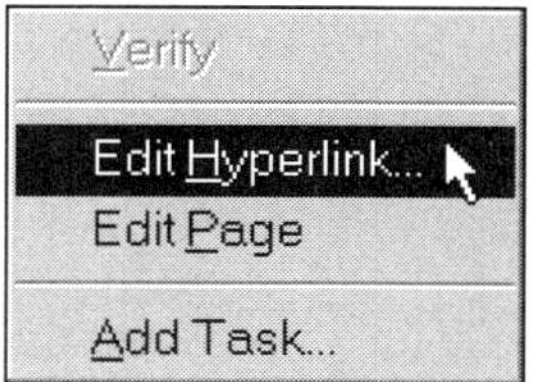

Figure 10. *Choose Edit Hyperlink from the pop-up menu.*

6. Fix the link by typing the correct URL in the Replace hyperlink with text box. If you're not sure of the exact URL, click the Browse button, navigate to the desired location (you'll be asked to connect if you're not already online), and then return to FrontPage Explorer. The correct URL will appear in the Edit Hyperlink dialog box. (For more about hyperlinks, turn to Chapter 14.)

7. To fix the link in all pages containing the broken link, make sure the radio button Change in all pages is selected. To fix the link in selected pages only, select the radio button Change in selected pages and choose the pages to change from the list below (**Figure 12**).

8. Click the Replace button to fix the hyperlink. Next to the link you just edited, the red circle will have changed to a yellow circle with the word "Unknown" next to it for external links. Internal links that check out OK will either disappear from view (if Show All Hyperlinks is not selected from the View menu), or will appear with a green circle next to them (**Figure 13**).

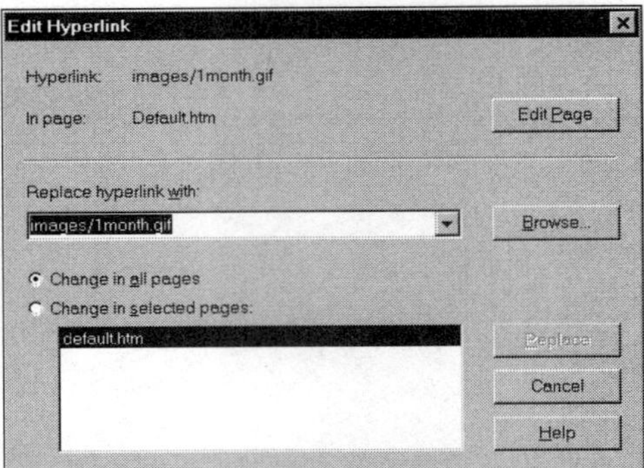

Figure 11. *In the Edit Hyperlink dialog box, you can fix broken links by typing in the correct URL or clicking the Browse button and navigating to the desired location.*

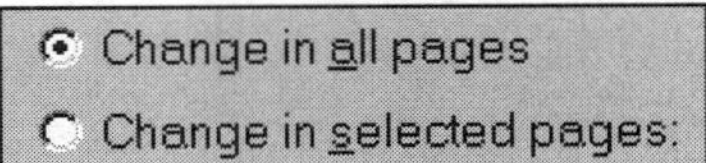

Figure 12. *You can instruct FrontPage to change the broken link in all pages in the Web, or only in selected pages.*

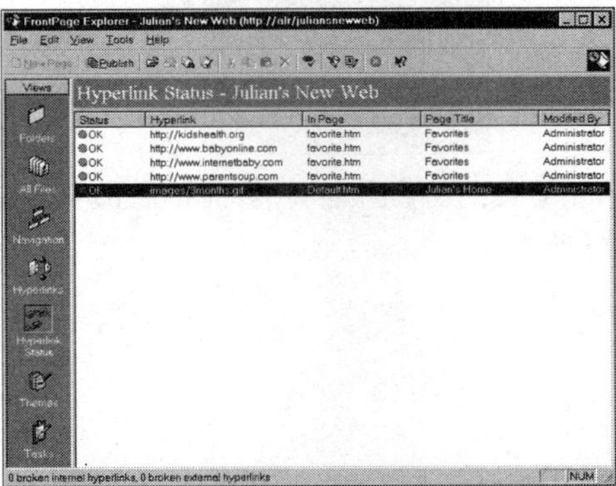

Figure 13. *If Show All Hyperlinks is selected from the View menu, corrected links that check out OK will appear with a green circle next to them.*

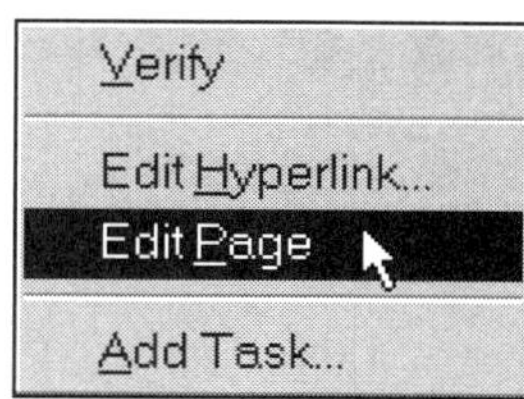

Figure 14. *Choose Edit Page from the pop-up menu.*

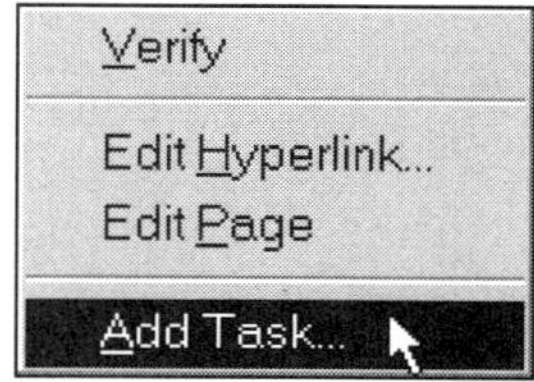

Figure 15. *Choose Add Task from the pop-up menu.*

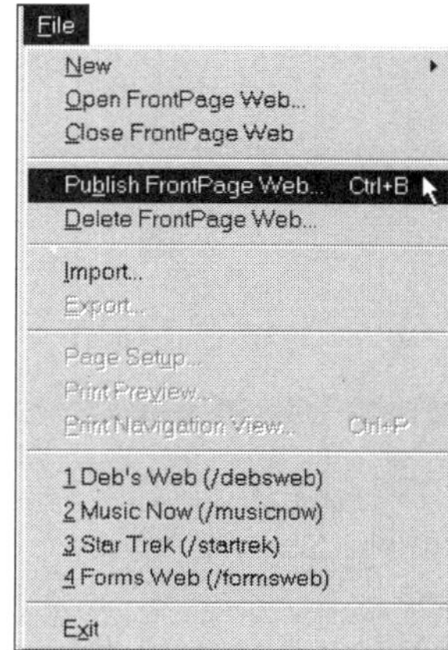

Figure 16. *Choose Publish FrontPage Web from the Explorer's File menu.*

9. Continue editing any broken links, following steps 5 through 8.
10. When all the circles are yellow or green, choose Verify Hyperlinks from the Tools menu again (**Figure 6**).
11. Double-check that you're online, and click the Start button in the Verify Hyperlinks dialog box. FrontPage will verify all the links and, if you've fixed them correctly, all circles will change to green.

Tips:

- If you want to edit the actual Web page containing a broken hyperlink, right-click the hyperlink in Hyperlink Status view and choose Edit Page from the pop-up menu (**Figure 14**).
- If you have broken hyperlinks that you don't want to fix right away, you can add them to the Task List by right-clicking them and choosing Add Task from the pop-up menu (**Figure 15**). Fill in the New Task dialog box to assign the task to a person and give it a priority.

Before you publish your Web site, contact the Internet Service Provider you are going to use to get their directions about specific publishing procedures. If you are publishing your site to an intranet, talk with your system administrator.

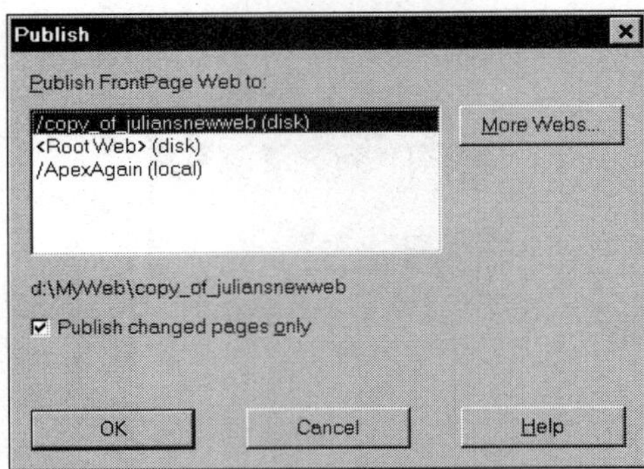

Figure 17. *Use the Publish dialog box to select a location to which to publish your Web site. If you don't see the site you want, click the More Webs button.*

To publish your Web site:

1. In the Explorer, open the Web site you want to publish.
2. If you are publishing your site to an Internet Service Provider on the Web, use your dial-up connection to connect to the Web.
3. Choose Publish FrontPage Web from the File menu (**Figure 16**). The Publish dialog box will open (**Figure 17**).
4. If you see the desired Web site in the Publish FrontPage Web to list box, click it to select it.
5. *Uncheck* the Publish changed pages only check box if this is the first time you are publishing your Web site (**Figure 18**). If you are updating your Web site and want to only publish the pages that have changed, put a check in this check box.
6. If you don't see the Web site you want in the Publish FrontPage Web to list box, click the More Webs button. You'll see the Publish FrontPage Web dialog box (**Figure 19**).
7. If you don't already have an Internet Service Provider, you can click the button "Click here to find an

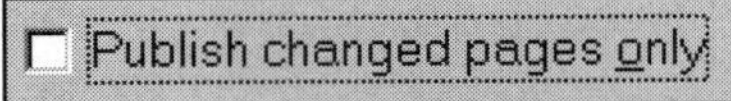

Figure 18. *If this is the first time you are publishing your Web site, make sure the Publish changed pages only check box is unchecked. If you are updating a site that is already published, put a check in the check box so only those files that have changed will be published.*

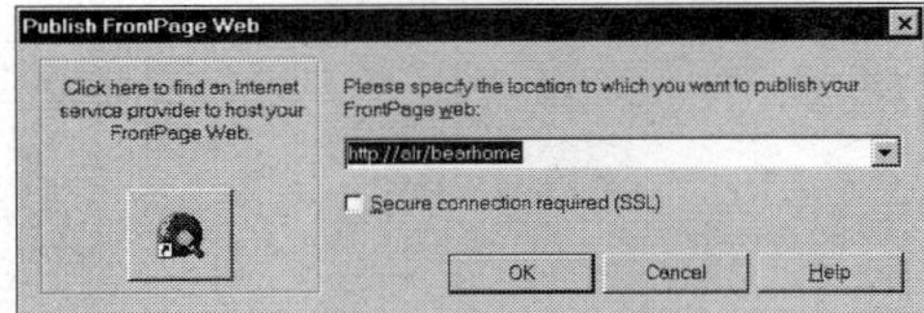

Figure 19. *The Publish FrontPage Web dialog box lets you enter the URL of the site to which you want to publish. From here, you can also hunt for a suitable service provider to host your Web.*

Publish Your Web Site

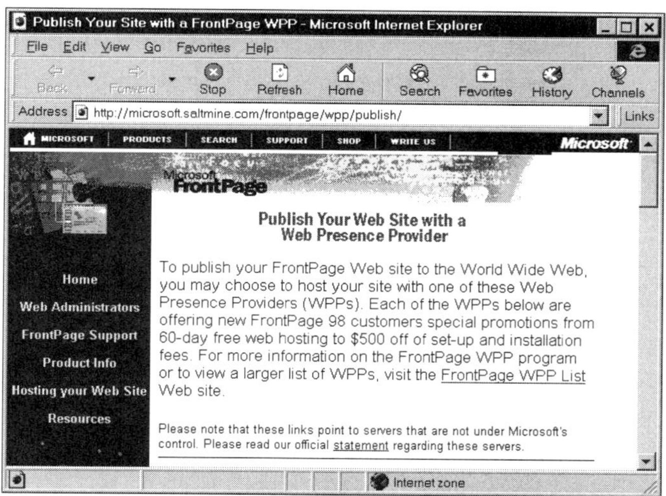

Figure 20. *If you don't already have an Internet Service Provider, this page can help you find one that can host your FrontPage Web.*

Internet service provider to host your FrontPage Web" in the Publish FrontPage Web dialog box. This launches your default browser and displays a Web site listing Web Presence Providers (service providers who will host your Web site) who already have the FrontPage Server Extensions installed (**Figure 20**).

8. If you're already set up with a service provider, simply enter the URL of the Web site to which you want to publish your Web and click OK.

9. FrontPage will start copying the pages of your Web site, displaying an indication of your progress at the left end of the status bar. When the Web site is done loading on the server, you'll see a message that it has been published (**Figure 21**). *Your site is now published. Congratulations!*

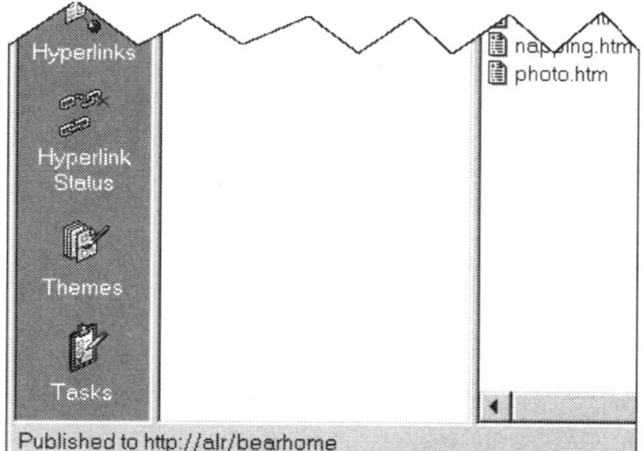

Figure 21. *When your FrontPage Web is transferred to the server, you'll see a message to that effect on the left side of the status bar.*

Tip:

- Once your Web site is published to the dedicated Web server, the Internet Service Provider or your system administrator will need to manually restart the Web server in order for your site to be recognized. Contact your ISP or system administrator for help with this.

From here, you should start stage two of the testing procedure and make sure that everything on your site looks right to you and loads correctly using a browser. You might want to look at your site using several different browsers, because the Web pages may appear different in each one.

In addition, if you have included hyperlinks on your site to other sites on the World Wide Web, you should test these links periodically. Web sites change and Web pages are removed. So a page you've set up a link to may disappear.

You've come a long way from the first time you launched FrontPage Explorer and started a Web site. You've created a fully functional, professional Web site that is available to folks browsing the Web or an intranet. Congratulations!

SUMMARY

In this chapter you learned how to:

- Follow hyperlinks in the Editor
- Recalculate hyperlinks in Explorer
- Verify links using Explorer
- Publish your Web site and go "live"

Good Books

Listed below are a few good books to get you started and help you along with any special Web-related interests you may have.

For those who want to learn more about HTML code and tags:

- *HTML 4 for the World Wide Web: Visual QuickStart Guide*, by Elizabeth Castro (Peachpit Press)
- *HTML: The Definitive Guide* by Chuck Musciano and Bill Kennedy (O'Reilly & Associates)
- *Creative HTML Design* by Lynda Weinman and William E. Weinman (New Riders)

To find out more about creating Web graphics:

- *Designing Web Graphics 2* by Lynda Weinman (New Riders)
- *Web Graphics Tools and Techniques* by Peter Kentie (Peachpit Press)

For learning how to create amazing graphical effects using Photoshop:

- *The Photoshop Wow! Book* by Linnea Dayton and Jack Davis (Peachpit Press)

A few books with interesting and provocative ideas about Web site and page design:

- *Creating Killer Web Sites* by David Siegel (Hayden Books)
- *Creating Web Pages for Dummies* by Bud Smith and Arthur Bebak (IDG Books)
- *Elements of Web Design* by Darcy DiNucci, Maria Giudice, and Lynne Stiles (Peachpit Press)
- *The Non-Designer's Web Book* by Robin Williams and John Tollett (Peachpit Press)

For hints on how to promote your Web site:

- *Getting Hits* by Don Sellers (Peachpit Press)

To find Web sites with topics that interest you, take a look at:

- *Search Engines for the World Wide Web: Visual QuickStart Guide*, by Alfred and Emily Glossbrenner (Peachpit Press)

A useful guide of computer terms:

- *Jargon* by Robin Williams with Steve Cummings (Peachpit Press)

For those of you who are interested in advanced topics, such as working with the FrontPage Software Developer's Kit, Java applets, and ActiveX controls:

- *Web Developer's Secrets* by Harold Davis (IDG Books)

Index

G

Index

Index

L

M

N

O

P

R

S

T